THE
CATHOLIC CHURCH
IN DETROIT

THE
CATHOLIC CHURCH
IN DETROIT,
1701–1888

George Paré

Published for the Archdiocese of Detroit by
Wayne State University Press, Detroit

Library of Congress Cataloging in Publication Data
Paré, George.
  The Catholic Church in Detroit, 1701-1888.
  Reprint. Originally published: Detroit: Gabriel
Richard Press, 1951.
  Includes bibliographical references and index.
  1. Catholic Church—Michigan—Detroit—History.
2. Detroit (Mich.)—Church history. I. Title.
BX1418.D6P3 1983   282'.77434   83-6742
ISBN 0-8143-1758-8

THE CATHOLIC CHURCH *is the oldest organization in the United States and the only one that has retained the same life and polity and forms through each succeeding age. Her history is interwoven in the whole fabric of the country's annals. Guiding the explorers, she left her stamp in the names given to the natural features of the land. She announced Christ to almost every tribe from one ocean-washed shore to the other, and first to raise altars to worship the living God, her ministers edified in a remarkable degree by blameless lives and often by heroic deaths alike the early settlers, the converted Indians, and those who refused to enter her fold. At this day she is the moral guide, the spiritual mother of millions of the inhabitants of the republic, people of all races and kindreds, all tongues and all countries, blended in one vast brotherhood of faith. In this she has no parallel. No other institution in the land can trace back an origin in all the nationalities that once controlled the portions of North America now subject to the laws of the republic. All others are recent, local, and variable. She alone can everywhere claim to rank as the oldest.*

—JOHN GILMARY SHEA, Introduction to
The Catholic Church in Colonial Days.

Foreword

When *The Catholic Church in Detroit, 1701–1888* was published in 1951, the City of Detroit was celebrating its 250th anniversary. Frank R. Woodford, author of a biography of General Lewis Cass of Michigan, offered the following tribute in the *Detroit Free Press* on August 13, 1951: "When Detroit begins to count the solid achievements resulting from its 250th birthday festival, its people ought to find, high on the list [Father Paré's] splendid book. . . . He has done a tremendous service to this community in thus recording its past." Father Paré's achievement also brought national acclaim as "a volume which will have enduring value" and earned him the John Gilmary Shea Prize of the National Catholic Historical Association for 1951.

After thirty-two years, Father Paré's "splendid book" is once again making a contribution to an anniversary celebration. As the Archdiocese of Detroit celebrates its 150th anniversary in 1983, we are pleased to be able to reissue this volume in collaboration with Wayne State University Press. We hope that the interest it aroused in 1951 both locally and nationally will be again awakened among a new generation of people who are curious about the roots of Detroit and Michigan, as well as the origins of the Catholic Church in the United States. The rich history of both communities is interwoven in a very striking way in southeastern Michigan, from the earliest contacts of seventeenth-century missionaries to the establishment of Fort Pontchartrain and on to the Detroit of modern times.

The solid scholarship of Father Paré will also serve as a foundation for further research. As part of our anniversary celebration, the Archdiocese of Detroit has commissioned a new history, which we hope will respond to the questions and interests of our own day with as much success as Father Paré achieved in 1951. This new volume, which is intended as a work of social as well as institutional history, will begin with the establishment of the Archdiocese in 1833, building on the latter part of Father Paré's research from a new perspective and in light of later developments. It will complete the history of the Archdiocese to the death of its first Cardinal, Edward Mooney, in 1958, with an epilogue on the momentous changes that followed in the last twenty-five years. We are confident that this new volume will be of the greatest interest not only to church historians but to the larger community of historians as well as the general reader.

Finally, I want to express my special thanks to the members of the Archdiocesan Archives Advisory Committee who are responsible for both the reprinting of this volume and for the supervision of the new history: Father Leonard P. Blair; Dr. Francis X. Blouin, Director of the Bentley Historical Library, University of Michigan; Monsignor Francis X. Canfield; and Sister Claudia Carlen, I.H.M.

Most Reverend Edmund C. Szoka, J.C.L., D.D.
Archbishop of Detroit

March 8, 1983

Preface

SOME twenty-five years ago the Most Reverend Michael James Gallagher, looking forward to the 100th anniversary of the Diocese of Detroit to be observed in 1933, commissioned the writer to undertake the production of a diocesan history. In the wake of 1929, that fateful year, this and other projects planned for the centenary were held in abeyance, and a very condensed summary of the history was published in a special edition of the diocesan weekly, the *Michigan Catholic*, in December, 1933. The death of Bishop Gallagher in 1937, and the ensuing war years during which the writer was engaged in arduous parish duties precluded anything more than desultory contacts with a work whose future was somewhat indefinite. As 1951 approached and the City of Detroit began planning to celebrate the 250th anniversary of its founding, His Eminence, Edward Cardinal Mooney, was quick to decide that no occasion could more appropriately call for a record of the Catholic life and activity so inseparably bound up with the history of the city and the state.

The diocesan history naturally fell into two well defined divisions. There was first what might be called the pioneer stage, to which was necessarily linked a long, anterior French period, and which was definitely over with the retirement of Bishop Caspar Henry Borgess in 1887. The second stage paralleled the amazing transformation of Detroit into one of the world's great industrial centers. The process began during the closing years of Bishop John Samuel Foley's long episcopate ending in 1918. On Bishop Gallagher was laid the burden of providing priests and parishes for the Catholic portion of the thousands who streamed into Detroit to make it the automobile capital of the world. Seven months after his death Detroit became a metropolitan see, a gesture from the Roman Pontiff which, quite apart from its purely ecclesiastical significance, might be interpreted as a recognition of the city's importance in the affairs of the world, and of its particular impact upon the habits and lives of men in every corner of the earth.

The evidences of this remarkable progress in Catholic growth and activities are all around us, and could be recorded without much difficulty. However, there are always developments, events, and trends which can be better appraised from a vantage point somewhat removed from the actualities of the present. The writer hesitates to delve into modern complexities and is content in an anniversary year, when our thoughts turn instinctively to the past, to record as best he can the trials and the heroisms of the forgotten men who laid the foundations on which the contemporary achievements rest. Accordingly, this volume confines itself to the history of the Catholic Church in Detroit, and to some extent in Michigan, during the pioneer stage from 1701 to the beginning of Bishop Foley's episcopate in 1888.

The treatment of such a theme, if it is to be kept within reasonable limits, must be to a large extent selective. It presupposes a fairly comprehensive knowledge of the history of New France, and of Michigan and Detroit, and does not have to repeat what can be found in any number of well known works which are available to everyone. Therefore, of set purpose no more secular history has been introduced here than is necessary to explain a situation or a course of action.

The span of years from 1701 down to the American occupation of Detroit in 1796, which for convenience may be called the French period, offers a fascinating field for research. Little had been written concerning its strictly Catholic history save the occasional papers contributed by Richard R. Elliott to the periodicals of the early Catholic historical societies in the East. It was hoped that our knowledge of the Recollects who served in Detroit could be expanded, but long investigation has failed to pierce the obscurity that covers all of them excepting Father Bocquet.

Because Father Richard was such an important figure, bridging as he did the transition between the French period and the erection of the diocese, he was given a great deal of attention, although much was omitted that would find place in a formal biography. His activities in the field of education and printing were passed over rather lightly since they had already been detailed in monographs.

For the diocesan period there was a distressing lack of documentary material, especially in the case of Bishop Rese. Not too much remains from the episcopate of Bishop Lefevere, and a known deposit of Bishop Borgess' papers has vanished. This dearth of documentation necessarily affected the contents of the three chapters dealing with the respective bishops, and must be taken into account if any judgement is to be passed on their adequacy.

The form in which the diocesan history has been presented may call for a word of explanation. It was planned as a narrative whose continuity should be preserved as much as possible by excluding a certain amount of material which could later be placed conveniently in

well defined categories. Consequently, the last four chapters deal with
Indian Missions, Education, Charity, and the Press. The first of these
could be fairly completed, but it was unavoidable that the time limi-
tation imposed by the narrative should cut off the other three precisely at the moment when the activities they dealt with were beginning to assume important proportions. The reader may consider
them somewhat unsatisfactory, but the convenient grouping of related facts affords some compensation.

The writer gratefully acknowledges the help that he has received
from every quarter in the preparation of this volume. It could not
have appeared without the impetus given by His Eminence, Edward
Cardinal Mooney, who has followed its final stage with deep interest,
has offered valuable suggestions and corrections, and has provided
both the necessary leisure time and financial assistance. The Right
Reverend Monsignor Edward J. Hickey has been a constant source
of help and encouragement. Himself a deep student of American
ecclesiastical history, and the author of an indispensable monograph
on the Society for the Propagation of the Faith, he has made available
important manuscript material collected during his studies in Europe as well as unlimited use of his extensive private library.

There were two important archival sources to be consulted in Quebec. The Quebec Seminary besides offering gracious hospitality allowed access to its archives under the wise guidance of Monsignor
Amédée Gosselin. From this source a photostat copy of the St. Joseph
Mission register was procured. The Quebec Chancery archives yielded
much material of value, especially the letters of Father Bocquet and
Marchand. Here the genial secretary, Monsignor P. Benoît Garneau,
unfailingly set aside his arduous duties to answer every request.

In this country Archbishop Michael Curley permitted full use of
the precious Baltimore Chancery archives. The Dominican convent
in Washington was a haven, where kindly Father Vincent O'Daniel,
O.P., gave freely out of his accumulated fund of information. The
Notre Dame University archives were of the greatest value since
many important items from the Detroit Chancery archives had been
deposited there by Bishop Borgess. The officials of the University
generously offered every facility for long periods of research through
their extensive collection of documents, and the writer gratefully
acknowledges the interest and counsel of the archivist, the Rev.
Thomas T. McAvoy, C.S.C. Through the kindness of the Very Rev.
Charles Souvay, C.M., of Kenrick Seminary, copies of many valuable
letters in the St. Louis Chancery archives were secured.

Next in importance to these strictly ecclesiastical sources was the
Burton Historical Collection, that unique treasury of books and

manuscripts bearing on the history of Detroit and Michigan to whose assembling Clarence M. Burton devoted his life and fortune, and which.is housed in the Detroit Public Library. The writer was privileged to receive the most cordial cooperation from this distinguished citizen of Detroit, and to accept from him, rather timorously it must be confessed, the accolade he was always ready to bestow on anyone seriously engaged in the study of the city's history. No one influenced the composition of this volume more than Milo M. Quaife, for many years Secretary-Editor of the Burton Historical Collection, and a nationally known scholar in the field of American history. His criticisms and suggestions were always valuable, and it was a fortunate experience to have been directed and overseen by so competent a guide. The staff working in the Collection has given constant assistance, and the writer owes a debt of gratitude to Miss Gracie B. Krum, Mrs. Elleine H. Stones, and Miss Louise Rau, all of whom have cheerfully responded to every demand made either on their time or their store of knowledge.

Nor can the writer forget the many profitable hours spent in conferences with the kindly, beloved George B. Catlin of the *Detroit News* staff. The author of *The Story of Detroit* had an inexhaustible fund of information on the *minutiae* of Detroit history, and took an unusual interest in the figure and career of Father Martin Kundig. The writer is particularly grateful to Walter Romig, both for counsel and advice on many points, and for having applied his expert knowledge of bookmaking and publishing to the task of seeing the manuscript through the press. Finally, acknowledgement must be made to the editor of the *Mississippi Valley Historical Review* for his kind permission to reprint here the contents of Chapter V which first appeared in the *Review* for June, 1930.

GEORGE PARÉ

Table of Contents

List of Illustrations

CHAPTER I

Origins

THE Faith came to America by three distinct advances. From the West Indies as a base Spanish explorers and missionaries gradually extended their influence along our southern and western coasts from Florida to California. The English colonies were strung along the Atlantic seaboard. Here the Church gained entry through the efforts of persecuted English Catholics to find sanctuary in Maryland. They, as well as succeeding groups in other centers, could not escape the blight of the hatred and intolerance which surrounded them, and up to post-Revolutionary days the history of the Church in the Colonies is the record of a struggle to maintain her bare existence. France penetrated into the continent through the St. Lawrence River and its allied waterways, and unrolled her stirring pageant of political and religious history in the very heart of America.

Michigan once formed part of a vast colonial empire visioned as reaching from Hudson Bay to the delta of the Mississippi, and from the Appalachian to the Rocky Mountains. Hence the origins of its secular and religious history are deeply rooted in the history of New France. Every policy that emanated from Versailles or from the rock of Quebec worked out its measure of good or evil in the forests of Michigan. The same missionary zeal that from the days of Champlain had dared all things to make a new conquest for Christ drove its heroes to the Straits of Mackinac.

At the outset, and to understand subsequent developments, it must be borne in mind that the Church was more than a mere auxiliary in the foundation of the Canadian colonies. In the words of Bancroft: "It was neither the spirit of commercial enterprise nor royal ambition which carried the power of France into the heart of our continent; the motive was religion." [1] Nor could Parkman begrudge this tribute: "One great fact stands out conspicuous in Canadian history, —the Church of Rome. More even than the royal power, she shaped the character and destinies of the colony. She was its nurse and almost its mother; and, wayward and headstrong as it was, it never broke the ties of faith that held it to her." [2]

[1] *History of the United States* (New York, 1882), III, 299.
[2] *The Old Regime in Canada* (Boston, 1895), 450.

Had Parkman's sympathies been wider he might not have qualified even her motherhood. With all due consideration to the commercial and political factors that attended the origin of the Canadian colonies it can be fairly well established that the Christian missionary ideal, both as animating the Church and as represented by her, was the greatest single force that brought about the peopling of New France. The royal power was engaged in what to it were more important matters at home. The French holders of trading privileges had no strong desire to see the colonies self-supporting. Supplies would no longer be needed; furs would have to be purchased in an open market. Much less did they relish having missionaries interfering with their exploitation of the Indian. Champlain could make no headway against such conceptions. It was the Recollects and the Jesuits who by their writings and their personal crusades finally started the thin stream of colonists toward the wilderness that was Canada.

For instance, there is the letter of Father Denis Jamet, the first superior of the Recollects, written soon after his arrival in the Quebec colony. His analysis of the situation is typical.

. . . As for that which concerns us most, which is the conversion of these barbarians, it is a difficult matter according to human judgment; for the Montagnais and Algonquins are wanderers and live scattered about in various places, and only as long as they can find there game and fish. Hence, because we see them so seldom, and because it is impossible to live with them, we shall never learn their language and no one knows it. As for the Hurons, they are a people grouped in populous villages near a large lake whose extremity they have never seen. All around the lake there is an almost infinite number of divers nations; but access to them is difficult, for one must travel in the canoes of the Hurons, inasmuch as the river is beset with obstacles, in some places being very shallow, and in others full of rocks. . . .

These people live far inland, for they take a month to go there from the Sault which is sixty leagues from Quebec in their canoes which are swifter than any skiff in France. Despite all these difficulties, Father Joseph, and he is the one to whom you deigned to speak, went there with nothing else but faith and hope. In one year, God willing, we shall see him, and shall learn from him whether we can reap a harvest there.

The most assured means, Monseigneur, is to have colonists from France. The King can have greater possessions in this country with less cost than he can anywhere else at great expense and with the shedding of blood, for, thanks be to God, there are no enemies to combat. The Indians wish it for their own welfare. The Hurons promise to leave their country, although it is cleared and fertile in corn, and dwell here near the French, inasmuch as moose, deer and other animals are plentiful. I counsel parents no longer to compel their children to become monks in order not to divide their lands, but to send them to this country where there is plenty of good land, and to defray their expenses for this purpose. The nobility that consumes its lands in extravagance would do better to retrench somewhat, and send, each one, a colony of fifteen men.

This is also a business for the King. . . . There is in France every year a good number of persons guilty of one or two lawless deeds, but who are otherwise honest folk. If they were sent here I deem that both mercy and justice would be served; mercy by granting them their lives, and justice by banishing them from their country. Thus in a few years we could build up a second France. I can promise fine lands and fair streams, good hunting and better fishing to whosoever knows how to profit from them.

If we had colonists we could live somewhat apart from them in humble houses. The Indians, even the wanderers, seeing the results of our labors, would be tamed little by little.

Those who are in the hinterland would come down, and the French would advance as they pleased toward the interior, and thus we could instruct them all as widely as we could reach. . . .[3]

Later on, Father Le Jeune, the Jesuit superior, piled up his arguments on the same theme.

. . . Shall the French be the only people among the nations of the earth deprived of the honor of expanding and spreading itself over this New World? More thickly populated than any other kingdom, has France inhabitants only for itself? Or do its children, when they leave her, go here and there, losing the name of Frenchmen among strangers?

The Geographers, the Historians, and experience show us that every year a great many persons leave France to establish themselves elsewhere, for even though the soil of our country is most fecund, the women of France have this blessing, that they are all the more so. For this reason the Gauls of old went to divers parts of the earth in search of the land which they lacked. . . . Today our Frenchmen are no less numerous than the ancient Gauls, but they no longer go out in bands. Singly, one here, one there, they seek their fortunes among strangers. Instead of peopling foreign countries, is it not better to pour Ancient France into the new by the colonies that can be sent? . . . I enlarge upon a point which seems remote from my subject, although it is closely related thereto; for if I could see here a number of towns or villages gathering enough of the fruits of the earth for their needs, our wandering savages would soon settle down under their protection; having been made sedentary by our example and our help, they could easily be instructed in the Faith. As for the stationary tribes farther back in the interior, we could go in greater numbers to succor them,

[3] The entire letter is quoted in Odoric-Marie Jouve, O.F.M., *Les Franciscains et Le Canada* (Quebec, 1915), 58–68.

and would have much more authority and less fear if we felt we had the support of those Towns and Villages. The more imposing the power of our French people is made in these countries, the more easily they can make their belief received by these Barbarians, who are influenced even more through the senses than by reason.[4]

In his admirable work on the religious origins of Canada, Goyau, although not making the point explicitly, brings out that the missionary viewpoint, as exemplified in the foregoing passages, meant nothing less than a revolution in national psychology. The Frenchman had no natural disposition toward colonization. He might search the world over for adventure or fortune, but he had no desire to take root save in his native soil. In this he was abetted by a tradition current in the French literature of the sixteenth and seventeenth centuries which derided any Frenchman foolish enough to seek happiness outside his own fair land.[5] Here was a double barrier to their program which the missionaries set out deliberately to break down. The Frenchman must begin to feel a willingness for colonization, not from political or economic reasons but precisely because he will thereby make possible the fulfillment of the divine command to preach the Gospel to every creature.

To Lescarbot, the pious lawyer of Vervins, caught up by the missionary ideal, the issue is plain and cannot be shirked.

Many weaklings affrighted at the sight of ocean waves scare off the simple people saying (as does the poet Horace) that the fury of Neptune is better contemplated from afar, and that in New France there is no pleasure. It is true that there are no orchestras, masquerades, dances,

[4] The Relation of Father Paul Le Jeune for 1635, Chap. III. The passage is translated from the edition of the *Jesuit Relations* published by the Dominion Government (Quebec, 1858). The Jesuit missionaries in North America sent every year to their Canadian superior an account of their activities. These letters were combined into a long narrative called a Relation, which was sent to the superior in Paris where they were printed by Sebastian Cramoisy. The *Relations* proper begin in 1632 and continue to 1673. From 1896 to 1901 Reuben Gold Thwaites, secretary of the State Historical Society of Wisconsin, edited a page for page translation of the Relations, to which was added a mass of related documentary material. This imposing publication comprising seventy-three volumes is known as the *Jesuit Relations and Allied Documents* (Cleveland, 1896–1901). A one-volume selection was edited by Edna Kenton (New York, 1925). In her foreword the editor thus describes the Relations. ". . . From 1611 to 1768 their reports—their Relations—of their life in North America were sent to the superior . . . and these reports . . . are travel, exploration and adventure narrations of high dramatic calibre, as well as rare source material for the historian, the geographer, the philologist, and the ethnologist. . . . Yet, in the *Jesuit Relations*, the folk-lore, the religion, the mythology, the manners and morals, even the speech and detailed daily living of these vanished peoples, what they did and what they were, are set down minutely, keenly, zestfully by men than whom no men of the 17th and 18th centuries were more shrewdly trained in the subtle arts of rhetoric, diplomacy, observation, psychology, and humanity. . . .

[5] Georges Goyau, *Les Origines Religieuses Du Canada* (2d ed.; Paris, 1939), 24–26.

palaces, cities, and beautiful buildings such as are found in France. To these people I have spoken in many passages of my history. And I now tell them further that not to them belongs the glory of establishing the name of God among wandering tribes deprived of a knowledge of Him, nor of founding French and Christian Republics in a new world, nor of doing anything worth while that can help and give courage to posterity. Cravens like these, judging others by themselves, not knowing how to make the earth bear fruit, and having no zeal for God, consider all great projects impossible. If we were disposed to believe them we would never do anything.

Tacitus speaking of Germany said the same as these do of New France: 'What man braving a frightful and unknown sea would quit Italy, Asia, or Africa for Germany unless he were born in that rugged dreary land where the climate is rigorous, and the earth gives only scanty yields?' He spoke as a Pagan, and as a man whose hope lay in the enjoyment of the things of this world. But the Christian bethinks himself otherwise, and has for aim that which pertains to the glory of God, and for this all exile is sweet, all travail delights, all perils no more than sportings. . . .[6]

For although kings are often only too ambitious to rule over the whole earth, and over new worlds if it were possible . . . yet must they be encouraged and kindled to a worthy design, one especially which redounds to the glory of God, and does no harm to men. In this our century is meaner than preceding ones, even though by the grace of God we enjoy a pleasant peace, the King is feared, and has more resources than any of his predecessors wherewith to establish a Christian and French Kingdom in the Western regions beyond the sea. . . . Nevertheless, scarcely any one (I mean of those who have standing at court) favors this design, certainly not much in his own mind, and less in his counsels to His Majesty. They like to hear it spoken of, but they are not disposed to further it. They would find the treasures of Atabalippa without trials and labors, but they come too late, and to find one must search and spend, a thing that the great care not for. These are the usual questions that one hears: Do treasures lie there? Are there Mines of gold and silver? Nobody asks: Is that people disposed to listen to Christian doctrine? As for mines there are some in truth, but they must be dug with industry, labor and patience. The best mine that I know of is wheat, and wine, and fodder for domestic animals. He who has these has money. . . .[7]

The power of this holy propaganda carried on over a period of years, and calculated to reach everyone affiliated in any way with the Catholic life of France, must not be underestimated. It was to bear fruit sooner or later. First came Louis Hebert, the druggist, with his wife and three children. His name deserves to be remembered for, as

[6] Marc Lescarbot, *Histoire de la Nouvelle-France* (Tross ed.; Paris, 1866), I, xiv–xv.
[7] *Ibid.*, 15–16.

Le Clerq quaintly observes, "He was the Abraham of the colony, the father of all the living and faithful." Twenty men came out in 1626 but were obliged to return the next year because the trading company would not feed them while they were getting established. But the leaven was working. On April 29, 1627, Cardinal de Richelieu signed the charter erecting the Company of the Hundred Associates. Beyond a doubt he was persuaded thereto by the Jesuits.

Here are some of the provisions of that famous charter: Only French Catholics, no Huguenots nor Calvinists, are to be sent to Canada. From two to three thousand are to be transported every year until at least four thousand are across. For three years they are to be supplied and cared for. The expenses of the Church are to be defrayed for fifteen years, and three missionaries are to be supported in every mission post. Agriculture is to be fostered. The Indians are to be converted. Finally, the most remarkable provision of all, mere baptism is to confer absolute equality, and any baptized Indian may come to France and enjoy without further formality the plenitude of French citizenship. There is no denying that these provisions were violated; enthusiasm was smothered by reality. But this much was accomplished, that Frenchmen began to look on Canada as a place to live in as well as a place to trade.

Barely had the Company begun its work when disaster overtook the colony. There were about a hundred souls all told who surrendered to the Kirkes on July 20, 1629. Piloted by the French traitor Michel, a Huguenot, six English ships had anchored before Quebec, knowing that it had to fall because its supplies had failed to arrive the previous year. Champlain and the missionaries were restored to France unharmed, and thus closed the first phase of the colony.[8]

Should France attempt to regain Canada? Opinion at court was divided. One side maintained that New France was nothing but a barren wilderness. Why run the risk of depopulating France by efforts to colonize a worthless waste of ice and snow that had brought disaster to everyone connected with it? On the other hand it was argued that Canada could become the granary of France, that it was rich in timber for shipbuilding, in fisheries, and in furs.

This sterile debate between ministers was ended by a force that was neither economic nor political, but religious. Champlain would not let go. In person at the English court he remonstrated that he had been obliged to surrender Quebec three months after peace had been signed with Richelieu, victorious at La Rochelle.[9] And Champlain's interest in Canada, shining clearly in his writings, was primarily and

[8] Parkman, *Pioneers of France in the New World*, Chap. XVI.
[9] The Treaty of Suze was signed April 24, 1629.

above all religious, the conversion of the Indian. While he was negotiating in London, Catholic France was praying. "The Jesuits had remained fully equipped to resume their labors. These years of exile seemed to them like a night under arms. Every day in their province of Paris a Mass was said with this express intention that God would set them back on the banks of the St. Lawrence." [10] In every religious house prayer went up night and day that the missionaries might be returned to their labors. It was the prayer of a multitude awakened to the missionary ideal that decided the issue. Canada was restored to France in 1632.

Now began in earnest the work of colonization and of conversion. Giffard, the physician, with his thirty followers settled down at Beauport. A whole contingent of Normans took up the shore along Ste. Anne de Beaupré. Holy women like Marie de l'Incarnation and Madame de la Peltrie, Mlle. Mance and Marguerite Bourgeoys began their schools and hospitals. Maisonneuve and the "Gentlemen of Montreal" founded their island colony, be it remembered, not as a trading post but as a veritable City of God from which should stream the light of the Faith.

The Church therefore was truly the mother of New France. Without her it might never have survived the crushing blow of 1629. Through her it was reborn as the embodiment of a great religious adventure to widen the kingdom of Christ. It is the glory of the Church in Michigan that she is linked with at least the latest heroes of that great missionary enterprise. We must now begin to trace the reaches of that enterprise in our direction.

The earliest known contact of the Church with Canada was made through the voyages of Jacques Cartier. On his first expedition in 1534 he did nothing more than reconnoiter the Gulf of St. Lawrence. He was accompanied by an unnamed priest who said Mass for the first time on July 11 after a landing at what is now known as l'Anse du Vieux-Fort on the Labrador coast.[11] In the following year Cartier returned to push his explorations up the St. Lawrence River as far as Montreal. This time he had with him two secular priests, Dom Antoine and Dom Guillaume Le Breton, who shared the horrors of that terrible winter of 1535–36 at Stadaconé, the ancient name for the site of Quebec.[12] The remnant of the party returned to France in the spring, and sixty-seven years elapsed before Canada again became the scene of priestly ministrations.

In 1604 De Monts sailed from Le Havre to seek his fortune in

[10] Goyau, *op. cit.*, 105.
[11] *Bulletin des Recherches Historiques* (Quebec), XXX, 171.
[12] Parkman, *Pioneers of France* . . . , 215–18.

that indeterminate Acadia that had just been granted to him by Henry IV. Although himself a Calvinist he lay under the royal injunction to make provisions for the instruction of the Indians in the Catholic faith. The expedition was a curious medley of Catholics and Huguenots, and of honest men and criminals pressed into service. There were priests and ministers abroad; how many of each is not known. One priest is named, Nicolas Aubry, a secular from Paris.[13] Champlain, who was associated with De Monts, was sorely grieved by the inevitable religious dissensions that followed.

> . . . There is something blameworthy in this enterprise, and it is this: two contrary religions can never bring forth much fruit for the glory of God among the Infidels who are to be converted. I have seen the minister and our Curé coming to blows over religious differences. I do not know who was the more doughty, or who could strike the harder blow; but I do know that the Minister sometimes complained to the Sieur de Mons that he had been beaten. . . . I leave you to judge whether this was a pleasing sight; the Savages were sometimes on one side, and sometimes on the other, and the French in confusion by reason of their religious beliefs reviled one religion and then the other. . . .[14]

De Monts first planted his colony on the island of St. Croix at the mouth of the river now bearing the same name which forms a portion of the boundary between Maine and New Brunswick. In the spring of 1605 another site was chosen at the mouth of the Annapolis River in Nova Scotia, and called Port-Royal. However, the exclusive trading privileges accorded to De Monts had aroused resentment at home, and as a consequence he was dislodged from the royal favor, and the colony was abandoned in 1607.

The Baron de Poutrincourt, who had been De Monts' associate, and to whom the leader of the expedition had transferred his rights to Port-Royal, was determined to continue the enterprise. Successful in his representations to Henry IV the baron was empowered to return to Port-Royal; but one stipulation in his charter called for the introduction of Jesuit missionaries to labor among the Indians. Poutrincourt although a Catholic shared the prejudices of his day,

---

[13] l'Abbe C. Tanguay, *Répertoire Général du Clergé Canadien* (Quebec, 1868), 20.

[14] *Works of Champlain*, ed. Laverdiere (Quebec, 1870), V, Part I, 709. The priest who was Father Aubry's unnamed companion and the minister died at the same time, and were buried in the same grave. See also Camille de Rochemonteix, S.J., *Les Jesuites et la Nouvelle-France au XVII Siècle* (Paris, 1895), I, 10. This indispensable work for the study of the Church in New France will be often quoted. It consists of two series. The first, dealing with the Jesuits of the seventeenth century, comprises three volumes published in 1895–96. The second series dealing with the Jesuits of the eighteenth century has two volumes issued in 1906. For the sake of convenience the work will be here quoted as a continuous series of five volumes.

and when he sailed in 1610 he had evaded the royal order and taken along Father Jessé Flèche, a secular priest of the diocese of Langres. To prove that Jesuits were unnecessary he immediately set one of his sons to the task of instructing a number of friendly Indians at Port-Royal—the priest could not have known a word of the Indian language—and on June 24, 1610, Membertou, the hundred-year-old chief, was baptized by Father Flèche together with twenty of his kinsfolk.[15]

The baron's son, Biencourt, was shortly ordered to France for supplies, and he hoped at the same time to prove his competence as a missionary by presenting the list of his converts to his sovereign, Henry IV. It was not the King who read his memorial, for Henry had lately died at the hands of Ravaillac, but Marie de Médicis, the queen regent. She was not impressed, and she insisted that Jesuit missionaries be installed at Port-Royal. To obtain his supplies Biencourt was obliged to enter into partnership with two Protestant merchants of Dieppe. Probably with his connivance they doggedly refused to outfit his ship if any Jesuit should be allowed to sail in her. They were neatly circumvented by a spirited Catholic laywoman.

The Marquise de Guercheville, a woman of beauty and verve and the staunch friend at court of the Jesuits, was not to be balked by such a subterfuge. She circulated a subscription list and raised a sum sufficient to buy out the two merchants. When Biencourt finally set sail for Port-Royal he had two Jesuits on board, and they were not passengers but supercargoes.[16]

On May 22, 1611, the *Grace of God* dropped anchor at Port-Royal bearing the first Jesuits to exercise their ministry in Canada. They were Fathers Pierre Biard and Ennemond Massé. Diligently they began the task of mastering Micmac, the language of the Indians who surrounded them. Massé went out to live with them at a distance from Port-Royal, while Biard remained in the colony studying with an intelligent Indian youth who understood some French. At the end of a year they had compiled a catechism intelligible to their prospective converts.[17]

Meanwhile, Poutrincourt had gone to France in the interests of his colony. Finding everywhere a deaf ear to his pleas for help he was at last obliged to turn to Madame de Guercheville. She was willing enough provided she could share in his trading profits and in his land holdings. He would not yield to the second condition, and his refusal proved to be his undoing.

[15] Lescarbot, *op. cit.*, III, 612–14.
[16] Rochemonteix, *op. cit.*, I, 32–35.
[17] *Ibid.*, I, 45–48.

The marquise discovered that De Monts was still the owner of Acadia by royal patents that had not been revoked, and that Poutrincourt held Port-Royal only by virtue of a grant from him. She prevailed on De Monts to cede to her that sterile region from which he had abandoned hope of ever profiting, and thus a woman, had she been able to enforce her rights, would have become mistress of a fifth of North America, from Florida to the St. Lawrence.[18]

Madame de Guercheville now determined to establish on her own account a colony wherein the Jesuits might be free from all interference. She outfitted a ship which sailed from France in March, 1613, carrying Father Jacques Quentin and Brother Gilbert du Thet. At Port-Royal the two Jesuit confreres, who by now were in serious difficulties with Biencourt, were taken aboard and the company coasted along the Maine shore until Mt. Desert Island was reached. Here it was decided to establish the colony. But preparations had hardly been set on foot when the brutal and unscrupulous Argall from Virginia fell upon the unsuspecting Frenchmen. After many strange adventures the missionaries were returned to France, Port-Royal was destroyed, and thus ended for a time the mission of Acadia.[19]

We must now turn from these abortive attempts at settlement and missionary work to the one attempt that did succeed. Despite his failure in Acadia, De Monts still had hopes of rebuilding his shattered fortune somewhere in the New World. He was able to obtain trading privileges for one year, and he confided his enterprise to that faithful comrade who had served him so well on former occasions, leaving to him the choice of a site for the establishment. On July 3, 1608, Samuel de Champlain landed at Quebec to begin what was destined to be the definite colonization of New France. Jacques Cartier had been there before him unable to gain a foothold, and Roberval had tried to plant a colony near Montreal, but without success. This time, in spite of distress and famine the indomitable will and energy of Champlain prevailed. Through all his travails for his little company clinging tenaciously to the rock of Quebec shine his deep piety and zeal for the conversion of souls.

At the head of his treatise on the duties of a good navigator he laid down this indispensable requisite:

> . . . Above all he must be a man of righteousness, and one fearing God; he must not allow the holy Name to be blasphemed in his ship for fear that in his many perils he may be chastised by the divine Majesty. He must see to it that prayers be said night and morning before every other duty, and if it be possible for him to do so I counsel

[18] *Ibid.,* I, 55–56.
[19] *Ibid.,* 62–84. See also Parkman, *Pioneers of New France . . . ,* 307–30.

the navigator to bring with him a churchman or a Religious qualified
and capable, who should preach to the soldiers and mariners from time
to time in order to keep them ever in the fear of God. . . .[20]

If his employers and associates were interested in Canada for the
wealth they could draw out of it no mercenary motive ever tainted
Champlain. He faithfully executed their commissions, which to him
meant only further opportunities for knowledge, and if the glory of
France was concerned it was only the glory coming out of the fact
that it was preparing the way for the reign of Christ in a hitherto unknown portion of the earth.

> I have always desired to see in New France the lily bloom in union
> with the Catholic, Apostolic, and Roman church. . . . I hope that God
> will grant the grace to his Majesty of one day doing this much for the
> service of God, his own grandeur, and the good of his subjects, that he
> bring many poor peoples to the knowledge of the Faith so that they
> may enjoy some day the heavenly kingdom. . . .[21]

In 1614 Champlain was in France making a determined effort to
procure missionaries to accompany him back to the colony. Himself
too poor to finance their establishment he had hitherto been unsuccessful in his attempts to induce any one to make the necessary outlay. This time he was more fortunate. Canada was now in the hands
of a trading company headed by Henri de Bourbon, Prince de
Condé, and one article of the company's charter inserted through the
pleadings of Champlain called for the sending of missionaries to New
France. On the recommendation of his friend Houel, secretary to the
King, Champlain offered the Canadian mission field to the Recollects
of the Province of St. Denis, who joyfully accepted it.[22] The States
General was in session at Paris, and after the Clergy had listened to
Champlain it voted him fifteen hundred livres wherewith to pur-

---

[20] Laverdiere, *op. cit.,* .V, Part 2, 1333.

[21] *Ibid.,* III, 137–47.

[22] "Recollection-houses are, strictly speaking, those monasteries to which friars
desirous of devoting themselves to prayer and penance can withdraw. . . . The foundation of "recollection houses" in France, where they were badly needed even by the
Observants, was perhaps due to Spanish influence. . . . In 1595 Bonaventure of
Caltagirone, as general of the order, published special statutes for these French houses,
but with the assistance of the Government which favored the reforming party, the
houses obtained in 1601, the appointment of a special commissary Apostolic. The
members were called the Récollets, since Réformés was the name given by the French
to the Calvinists. . . . From 1606 the Récollets had their own provinces, amongst them
being that of St. Denis, a very important province which undertook the missions in
Canada and Mozambique." From the *Catholic Encyclopedia*, Friars Minor, subheading,
Recollects. The Recollects as a branch of the Franciscan order disappeared in the
general reorganization completed under Leo XIII in 1897. See also Heribert Holzapfel,
Handbuch der Geschicte des Franziskanerordens (Freiburg im Breisgau, 1909), 333–38:
348–52.

chase vestments and other necessities for divine worship. The associates in the trading company offered free supplies and transportation. On the 24th of April, 1615, the *St. Etienne* of 350 tons stood out to sea from the crooked streets of Honfleur. She carried four gray-clad sons of St. Francis, the vanguard of the future church of Quebec. They were: Father Denys Jamet, the Superior; Fathers Jean Dolbeau and Joseph Le Caron, and Brother Pacifique Duplessis.[23]

Probably the first important document in the story of the Canadian Church is the letter sent to France by Father Dolbeau soon after his arrival.

> The affection which you have for the salvation of souls of this country of New France, which has made us desire and even seek in person the means of assisting them, obliges me to give you news of our mission. We sailed from Honfleur on the 24th of April, and arrived May 25 at a port where vessels sailing here stop. This port is called Tadoussac; it is full eighty leagues up the great river of Canada. Thirty-five leagues above is the French settlement, which I reached on the second of June, unaccompanied by our other religious, who came after us as they found opportunity. The reverend father-commissary and Father Joseph did not stop here, but sailed forty or fifty leagues along the river, in order to see the goodness of the country and to see the Indians, who arrive there in great numbers to trade with the French. On the 25th of June, in the absence of the reverend Father-commissary, I celebrated holy Mass, the first that has been said in this country, whose inhabitants are truly savage in name and fact.[24] They have no fixed abode, but cabin here and there as they can find game and fish, their ordinary food. Both men and women are dressed in skins and always go bareheaded, wear their hair long, paint their faces black and red, are generally of good stature. As to mind I cannot speak positively, having thus far conferred only with a few individuals. Thus far the temperature of the air has seemed to me like that of France. The land appears good, but we must winter here to judge. . . .
>
> Friar Jean Dolbeau
>
> Quebec, In New France, July 20, 1615.[25]

The Fathers held many conferences with Champlain and the men of the colony to decide on the best method of approach to the tremendous task that lay before them. Finally, this disposition of their

---

[23] The names of these first religious have been variously spelled, but are here given as in the authoritative work of Father Jouve already quoted.

[24] Father Dolbeau was here in error. He had remained in Quebec to supervise the erection of a chapel, and when it was sufficiently advanced he said Mass on the date noted. Meanwhile the other two priests had continued up the St. Lawrence, and one of them celebrated Mass on the Island of Montreal just one day earlier than Father Dolbeau. See Jouve, *op. cit.*, 45–54.

[25] Father Christian Le Clercq, *First Establishment of the Faith in New France*, translated and edited by John Gilmary Shea (New York, 1881), I, 89–90.

forces was agreed upon. Father Dolbeau was to take his post at Tadoussac and from that point evangelize the Indians along the Saguenay River. To Father Le Caron fell the lot of penetrating far into the interior to evangelize the Huron. It is he whom we must follow, for he is the first priest to reach the country of the Great Lakes.

However, for the proper understanding of the Huron mission under Le Caron and his successors some notion of the Indians and their distribution is necessary. The region of the Great Lakes together with a broad belt north and south of the St. Lawrence was occupied by two great Indian stocks, the Algonquian and the Iroquoian, separated by fundamental linguistic and cultural differences. Within each stock further differentiations in dialect and customs resulted in tribal divisions. In Champlain's time the Algonquian stock was to be found mainly around the Great Lakes, along the northern shore of the St. Lawrence up to Hudson Bay, in New England, and in the Maritime Provinces. All the tribes whose names stud the pages of early Michigan history belonged to the Algonquian family. They were characterized not only by their proper dialects and customs but also by their loose tribal organization, and by their disinclination to form compact groups in any definite locality, a trait which made the task of the missionaries doubly difficult.

A striking contrast was presented by the Iroquoian family. Its stronghold was in central New York from the Hudson River to the Genesee. It had a closely knit tribal organization and lived in fortified towns. The Iroquois proper were a confederacy comprising the following tribes: the Mohawk, Oneida, Onondaga, Seneca, Cayuga, and later the Tuscarora. For ruthless cruelty and ferocity they had no equals, and their forays terrified alike the settlements and the neighboring tribes. Belonging to the same family, but for some obscure reason always an object of bitter hatred, were the Huron or Wyandot who lived in Ontario between Lake Simcoe and Georgian Bay. Southwest of them lay the kindred Tionnontates or Tobacco Nation, and along the banks of the Niagara River and the northern shore of Lake Erie the Attiwandaron or Neutral Nation.

Because the confederacy was so powerful and so feared by the other tribes it is plain that its friendship or enmity would profoundly influence the future of the colony. Had Champlain been sufficiently informed and given time to appraise the Iroquois as potential friends or enemies he doubtless would have planned his first contact with them as a friendly one. Unfortunately, in his eagerness to begin his westward explorations when he had been in Canada barely a year he became the unwitting abettor of a serious blow to their pride.

In the summer of 1609 Champlain was invited to accompany a

band of Ottawa and their Huron allies on a foray into the Iroquois country. Since he knew little then about the redoubtable foes into whose territory he was trespassing he supposed them to resemble the half-starved Indians whom he saw around Quebec. Near the southern end of the lake which bears his name, Champlain and his Indian party surprised a band of Iroquois. Frightened by the sight of his armor and the roar of his blunderbuss they fled in consternation. A few were killed, and others taken prisoners and tortured.

The Iroquois never forgot. On account of their proximity to the English and the Dutch they were exposed to the full tide of anti-French propaganda, and hence it is no wonder that once their hate and resentment had been kindled by Champlain's hostile act they became the scourge of the French and their Indian allies, and played a large part in the events that led to the final defeat on the Plains of Abraham.[26]

The geographical position of the Iroquois coupled with their enmity was bound to modify and affect the direction both of French expansion and of missionary activity. On the southeast they were in contact with the English who supplied them with arms and ammunition. To the west and southwest the Great Lakes country was open to them. Hence the only safe route for the French to follow on their way to the west was not the St. Lawrence into Lake Ontario but the Ottawa River into Lake Huron. Mackinac lies directly west of Montreal by this route, and its early importance is thus explained. As we shall see, the various Algonquin tribes flying before their hereditary foes found safety only along the northern shores of Lakes Huron and Michigan, and the southern shore of Lake Superior. There were no Indians in the southern peninsula of Michigan when the missionaries first came to Mackinac. It was too close to the Iroquois. The shores of Lake Erie were the last of the lake shores to be explored.

We left Father Le Caron planning his journey to the Huron country. About July 1, 1615, he set out from Montreal accompanied by a few Frenchmen and a flotilla of canoes manned by the Ottawa and Huron braves who had come down to Three Rivers to the trading post. His route lay through the Ottawa River into Lake Nipissing, thence by the French River into Georgian Bay. He then coasted along the eastern shore of the bay to its extreme southern end, crossed Matchedash Bay, and landed in an inlet somewhere in the neighborhood of Penetanguishene. A few miles to the south lay the first of the Huron villages. The hardships that the missionary endured can easily be imagined. His enumeration of them is only the prelude to the epic story of the French missions in North America.

[26] Parkman, *Pioneers of New France* . . . , Chap. X.

. . . It would be difficult to tell you the fatigue I have suffered, having been obliged to have my paddle in hand all day long and row with all my strength with the Indians. I have more than a hundred times walked in the rivers over the sharp rocks which cut my feet, in the mud, in the woods, where I carried the canoe and my little baggage, in order to avoid the rapids and the frightful waterfalls; I say nothing of the painful fast which beset us, having only a little sagamity, which is a kind of pulmentum composed of water and the meal of Indian corn, a small quantity of which is dealt out to us morning and evening. Yet I must avow that amid my pains I felt much consolation. For alas! when we see such a great number of infidels and nothing but a drop of water is needed to make them children of God, one feels an ardor which I cannot express to labor for their conversion and to sacrifice for it one's repose and life. . . .[27]

The Huron received him with signs of friendship. When he complained that he could hardly exercise his ministry to the best advantage in their long houses they built him a separate lodge. In it, on August 12, 1615, he said Mass for the first time, and in the presence of Champlain who had followed after him with a few soldiers. After Mass a tall cross was erected while muskets volleyed and rough soldier voices chanted the Ambrosian hymn.

Champlain went on to continue his explorations and Father Joseph set to work to learn the language of his hosts. During the long winter months he compiled a dictionary which was to be of great service to the later missionaries. On the return of Champlain in January he explored the outlying Indian groups, the villages of the Tobacco Nation, and of another unnamed tribe farther west. For all his toil there was not much to console him: a number of children and a few dying old men had been baptized. In May, 1616, the missionary set out by the same way he had come on the long journey back to Quebec.[28]

Seven years elapsed before the Huron mission was resumed.[29] Meanwhile the initial band of Recollects had been reinforced by new arrivals. On July 16, 1623, three missionaries, all with imperishable names, left Quebec to begin anew the evangelization of the Huron. Father Le Caron was accompanied by Father Nicolas Viel, the first

[27] Le Clercq, *op. cit.*, 95–96.
[28] *Ibid.*, 98–106.
[29] Shea states that the Huron were visited by Father William Poulain in 1622. See his *History of the Catholic Missions Among the Indian Tribes of the United States* (New York, 1854), 167. He is most likely mistaken. Father Guillaume Poulain arrived in Canada in 1619, and was stationed at Three Rivers. In 1622 he set out on a missionary tour to the West, but was taken prisoner by the Iroquois near Montreal, and had already begun to undergo the usual tortures when he was exchanged. As a result of his experience he died in France the following year. See Jouve, *op. cit.*, 195–97.

of the Canadian martyrs, and Brother Gabriel Sagard, the first historian of the Canadian Church. At Montreal they parted company to continue with separate Indian bands and thus lost sight of one another during most of the arduous journey to the Huron country. Brother Sagard, who has described it at length, thus pictures himself as they started.

> There were five men in my canoe, and I made the sixth. One who acted as steersman sat so close behind my back that he occasionally struck the top of my head with the end of his long oar, as I crouched as low as possible to avoid the blows. . . . I was rolled up almost like a ball alongside a paddler. Two more sat side by side in front of me, and the fifth barbarian was in front. . . . In this style we were conducted to their country without ever seeing our Brothers on the way, save for the first two evenings when we happened to make camp for the night with Father Joseph. As for Father Nicolas I found him for the first time two hundred leagues from Quebec in a nation that we call the Ebicerinys or Sorcerors. . . .[30]

At last the Recollects came together in the Huron village called Caragouha, where Father Le Caron had lived before, and which he had renamed St. Joseph. Here they decided to build their monastery. On poles stuck in the ground and tied together at the top they fastened long strips of bark until they had constructed a shelter about twenty-five feet long, and fifteen feet wide. The interior was divided into three rooms. Nearest the exit lay the combined kitchen, sleeping chamber, and reception room for their prospective converts. Behind it a small room gave the missionaries space in which to store their effects. Then came the chapel in which the Holy Sacrifice was daily offered on an altar stone resting upon stakes driven into the earth.

We must skip lightly over Sagard's absorbing story of life in the Huron village. He shows us the missionaries working in their tiny palisaded garden with no other implements than a hatchet and a crooked stick. Occasionally they made altar wine by straining the juice of wild grapes through a piece of altar linen into a tub made of bark. Every day they spent hours in the study of the Huron language. In the mornings the children thronged the chapel for a catechism lesson—and for what they could pilfer. Their elders came to make interminable visits, and to touch and handle everything. When the friars went into the chapel for their devotions they were usually surrounded by their guests, who imitated every movement. Despite all this friendliness the missionaries were compelled to move warily; savage passions could flare up in an instant. On one occasion an Indian, angered at the request for quiet in the chapel, almost brained Father Le Caron with his war club. Apologies were later made, and with

[30] Sagard quoted in Jouve, *op. cit.,* 242.

them came presents of pumpkins and corn. As for conversions the missionaries were in no great hurry to make them; they were not disposed to confer baptism until they had assurance that their converts were well enough instructed. When the chief of Caraghoua asked Brother Sagard for baptism the answer was this:

> ‹You are not fit for it yet, my uncle. You must wait awhile until you have corrected yourself. God will not have him for his child who does not renounce his superstitions, and who is not contented with one wife. If you do that we will baptize you, and after your death your soul will go to be happy with God in paradise.[31]

At the end of the year it was decided that Father Le Caron and Brother Gabriel should return to Quebec to replenish the supplies needed for the continuance of the mission. Father Viel was to remain alone in the Huron country until reinforcements came. The two missionaries reached the colony in the middle of July, 1624, just in time to participate in a momentous discussion that was agitating the minds of their brethren.

The magnitude of the task confronting them was just beginning to dawn upon the Recollects. Although nine priests in all had come to the colony there had never been more than four or five working in the missions at one time. The field of apostolate was so vast that the Recollects began to realize that neither their number nor their resources could cope with the tremendous undertaking involved in the evangelization of the Indian. There was only one thing to do, and that was to call in auxiliaries. But whom should they invite? The decision had just about been reached when the two missionaries came in from the Huron country. On August 15 two Recollects sailed from Quebec bound for France: one, Brother Gabriel, because he had been recalled, the other, Father Irénée Piat, entrusted with the delicate business of inviting the Jesuits to share the Canadian mission field with their Franciscan brethren.[32]

From the time of the disaster in Acadia the Jesuits had never given up hope of some day returning to the Canadian missions. Father Massé after his return to France had been assigned as minister to the great Jesuit college at La Flèche. Year after year the young candidates for the Society listened with breathless interest to his adventures, and to his observations on the opportunities for widening the Kingdom that lay in New France. The provincial of the Paris province, the famous Father Coton, had promoted with all his influence the Acadian enterprise, and after its failure had retained a keen interest in Champlain's experiment. However, the latter's engagement with the Recol-

---

[31] *Ibid.,* 261.
[32] *Ibid.,* Chap. XXV; Rochemonteix, *op. cit.,* I, 134-40.

lects and the hostility of the trading companies apparently barred the Jesuits from realizing their desires.

The second obstacle was the first to be overcome, and that in a manner reminiscent of Madame de Guercheville's adroitness. Henri de Montmorency had, in 1619, purchased trading rights in Canada from the Prince de Condé and having held them for five years was now looking for a buyer on whom to unload his unprofitable investment. A nephew, Henri de Levis, Duc de Ventadour, unlike his uncle was a man of piety, who had withdrawn from the frivolities of the Court to devote himself to a life of asceticism under the direction of Jesuit monitors.[33] Through them he learned of his uncle's intention, and he was urged for the good that could result to take over Montmorency's interests. He was only too willing, and by a stroke of good fortune found himself proof against antagonism when he was named viceroy of New France in January, 1625.[34] The appointment had scarcely been announced when Father Piat appeared before him with his request for Jesuit auxiliaries. Needless to say it was immediately granted. The long wait was over.

On June 15, 1625, there landed at Quebec the forerunners of that long line of valiant missionaries whose names and lives are inseparably linked with the history of the Church in Michigan: Fathers Charles Lalemant, Ennemond Massé, and Jean de Brébeuf. With them came a Recollect, Father Joseph de la Roche d'Aillon.[35] The newcomers found hospitality in the convent of the Recollects until they should have a house of their own, and thus united the missionaries began to plan their future course of action.

The most promising field for immediate results seemed to be the Huron mission whence Father Viel, living there alone, had sent encouraging reports from time to time. He was now on his way to Quebec to make a retreat, and to procure supplies. Accordingly it was decided that Fathers Brébeuf and Roche d'Aillon should return with him to the Huron country. Fired with zeal to acquaint themselves with their work as soon as possible the two priests went up the St. Lawrence to meet Father Viel at Three Rivers, the great mart for Indian trade. They could not know that his body was thrashing against a cluster of jagged rocks in the rapids above Montreal. What happened is told us by Le Clercq.

> . . . This good religious who had gone up to the Hurons two years before with Father Joseph Le Caron and Brother Gabriel Sagar, who had remained there all that time with some Frenchmen who took turns

[33] Rochemonteix, op. cit., I, 144.
[34] Ibid., 149.
[35]Ibid., 152–53.

going and returning to Quebec, had been solicited by the Hurons to go down with them to trade. He seized the opportunity to come and make his retreat at our convent of Our Lady of the Angels, and even took one of his disciples, little Ahautsic, whom he had instructed in the Faith and baptized.

There were in the party many pretty good Hurons, among whom were some brutal men, enemies of religion, yet pretending to love and respect the good Father. A storm scattered the canoes, and unfortunately this religious was left in his with three wicked and impious Indians, who hurled him into the water with his little disciple, Ahautsic, at the last Sault descending to Mont-royal, the deep and rapid waters of which engulfed them in a moment. They saved only his chapel and some writings which he had drawn up in books of bark paper, comprising a kind of mission journal; he had left his dictionary and other memoirs among the Hurons in the hands of the French. The place where this good religious was drowned is still called 'Sault au Recollect.'

If we may acknowledge as martyrs those who die in apostolic labors either by the cruelty of the Indians of these countries, who have little or no light of any divinity, true or false, we might justly acknowledge Father Nicholas and his little disciple as the two first martyrs of Canada. He was, moreover, a very great religious, who, after having lived in the odor of sanctity, came to Canada only from his burning zeal for martyrdom. The pains and toils he had to undergo in his mission, as reported by Frenchmen worthy of credit, cannot be described. He had produced much fruit; and, finally, we learned from the Hurons themselves assembled at the trade the cruel manner in which he and his neophyte had been put to death, whom God had received into his glory as the first fruits of the Huron mission. The Hurons had scattered his vestments, except the chalice; strips of them were gathered, of which they had made trimmings in their style. . . .[36]

When Fathers Brébeuf and Roche d'Aillon on their arrival at Three Rivers heard of Father Viel's death they were harassed by misgivings. Should they attempt to go on under the circumstances, or should they return to Quebec? Well disposed Indians advised them to turn back, and the French traders knowing the uncertain temper of the Huron convinced the missionaries that this was no time to trust themselves to savage guides for hundreds of miles through the wilderness. Their counsel prevailed, and the missionaries turned back.

In the summer of 1626 the same two priests and Father Anne de

---

[36] Father Viel's death occurred on June 25, 1625. In 1903 a monument was erected to Canada's first martyr at Sault-au-Récollet, so named because the site of his death, near Montreal. See Jouve, op. cit., Chap. XXVII. The Montreal suburb, Ahuntsic, preserves the name of the priest's child companion.

Noüe, a confrere of Father Brébeuf, succeeded in reaching the Huron country. Discouraged by the difficulties of the language Father de Noüe remained only a year. Father Roche d'Aillon prolonged his stay until 1628. Through him the torch of the Faith was carried a little farther into the wilderness, for he spent some months among the Tobacco Indians and in the Neutral Nation. He may thus have been the first missionary to gaze upon the waters of Lakes Ontario and Erie. The following extract is taken from the rather lengthy account of his excursion.

. . . I received a letter from our reverend Father Joseph Le Caron, by which he encouraged me to pass on to a nation we call Neutral, of which the interpreter (Bruslé) told wonders. Encouraged, then, by so good a Father and the grand account given me of these people, I started for their country, setting out from the Hurons with his design October 18, 1626, with a man called Grenolle and Lavallée, Frenchmen by birth.

Passing to the Petun nation, I made acquaintance and friendship with an Indian chief who is in great credit, who promised to guide me to this Neutral Nation and supply Indians to carry our baggage and what little provisions we had; for to think to live in these countries as mendicants is self-deceit; these people giving only as far as you oblige them, so that you must often make long stages and often spend many nights with no shelter but the stars. He fulfilled what he had promised to our satisfaction, and we slept only five nights in the woods, and on the sixth day we arrived at the first village, where we were very well received, thanks to our Lord, and then at four other villages, which envied each other in bringing us food. . . . All were astonished to see me dressed as I was, and to see that I desired nothing of theirs except that I invited them (by signs) to lift their eyes to heaven, make the sign of the cross, and receive the Faith of Jesus Christ. What filled them with wonder was to see me retire at certain hours in the day to pray to God and attend to my spiritual affairs (for they had never seen religious, except towards the Petuneux and Hurons, their neighbors). At last we arrived at the sixth village where I have been advised to remain. . . .

I did my best to learn their manners and way of living. During my stay I visited them in their cabins to know and instruct them. I found them tractable enough, and I often made the little children, who are very bright, naked, and dishevelled, make the sign of the (holy) cross. I remarked that in all this country I met no humpback, one-eyed or deformed persons.

During three months I had every reason in the world to be satisfied with my people; but the Hurons, having discovered that I talked of leading them to the trade, spread in all the villages where we passed very bad reports about me: that I was a great magician; that I had tainted the air of their country and poisoned many; that if they did not kill me soon I would set fire to their villages and kill all their children. . . .[37]

At last ten men of the last village, called Ouaroronon, one day's journey from the Iroquois, their relatives and friends, came to trade at our village and to visit me and invited me to come and visit them in their village. I promised to do so without fail when the snows ceased, and to give them all some little presents, with which they seemed satisfied. Thereupon they left the cabin where I was living, always concealing their evil designs against me. Seeing that it was growing late, they came back after me, and abruptly began a quarrel without provocation. One knocked me down with a blow of his fist, another took an axe and tried to split my head. God averted his hand; the blow fell on a bar near me. I also received much other ill treatment; but that is what we come to seek in this country. . . .

We hope heaven from God's goodness (by the favor of our good God) and for it most willingly serve in the salvation of these blinded nations; we risk our lives, in order that it may please Him, if he accepts our efforts, to make Christianity bud forth in these countries. . . .

Father Brébeuf continued on alone for another year, but no record of his labors has survived. When the Indians went down to trade in 1629 he accompanied them. He arrived in Quebec just in time to find himself caught in the surrender of the colony to the Kirkes.

No matter what play of diplomatic interest lay behind the restoration of Canada to France in 1632 there is no doubt but that it was as much due to the love of Champlain for the spot where he had planted his colony, and to the zeal of the missionaries, only whetted by seeming failure, for the souls of a savage people who roamed the fastnesses of a yet unexplored country. When the Jesuits returned to the missions they had been forced to abandon they threw themselves into the field with an ardor and a heroism which has hardly been paralleled in the Church since Apostolic times. The next chapter will see them in Michigan. It may be added that up to the end of the period that has been dealt with there is no evidence thus far available to show that any priest saw or touched upon the territory now comprised within the actual boundaries of the state.

---

[37] The territory inhabited by the Neutral Nation is thus described. "The country of this Neutral Nation is incomparably larger, more beautiful, and better than any other of all these countries. There is an incomparable number of stags, a great abundance of moose or elk, beaver, wild cats, and black squirrel larger than the French (variety); a great quantity of wild geese, turkeys, cranes, and other animals, which are there all winter, which is not long and rigorous as in Canada. . . . A stay there is quite recreating and convenient; the rivers furnish much excellent fish; the earth gives good grain, more than is needed. They have squashes, beans, and other vegetables in abundance, and a very good oil, which they call Atouronton (à Touronton)." Le Clercq, *op. cit.*, I, 263–72. Shea ventures the opinion that this is the earliest allusion to petroleum.

CHAPTER II

The Jesuits

CANADA was restored to France by the treaty of St. Germain-en-Laye, signed March 29, 1632. The Hundred Associates headed by Cardinal Richelieu, and organized by him at the instance of the Jesuits, were again in control of the destiny of New France.[1] While preparations were being made to resume the missionary labors so rudely interrupted the personnel itself of the priests came up for review. The Cardinal was not unaware that there were latent possibilities of friction in the arrangement that had existed in Canada before the fall of Quebec, and "he judged that it would better serve the interests of the new colonies if each had only religious of the same Institute so that among the missionaries there would be better understanding, more accord and mutual dependence."[2] This was a valid enough reason, and there may have been others, for the introduction of a yet untried mission band, and the Canadian mission was accordingly offered to the Capuchins. They respectfully declined the honor, and ventured the suggestion that the field belonged rightfully to those who had been expelled from it.[3] The Cardinal judged the point well taken, but with an eye to economy he ruled that only the Jesuits should return to the colony since they could possess property and incomes and would therefore be less of a charge on the Company of the Hundred Associates. Accordingly, when Emery de Caen entrusted with the formal taking over of the French possessions arrived before Quebec on July 5, 1632, he was accompanied by Paul Le Jeune and Anne de Noüe. Within five years there were twenty-three priests laboring in Canada. Indian missions were established at Sillery, Tadoussac, and Three Rivers. Provision was made for divine worship in all the scattered posts. A college was begun at Quebec, the second on the American continent.[4] But there was one project which

---

[1] Rochemonteix, *op. cit.*, I, 161–62.

[2] *Ibid.*, 182.

[3] Etienne-Michel Faillon, *Histoire de la Colonie Francaise en Canada* (Villemarie, 1865), I, 279.

[4] Rochemonteix, *op. cit.*, I, 205–25. The first college on the North American continent was founded at Santa Cruz, Mexico, in 1534 by the Franciscan bishop Zumarraga; the Jesuits began theirs at Quebec in 1635. Harvard, the third oldest, dates from 1636.

loomed up above all the others and that was the resumption of the Huron mission.

It has already been mentioned that the missionaries looked to the conversion of some fixed Indian population for the groundwork of their evangelistic endeavor. Here every resource could be brought to bear, and the conversion of an entire tribe was calculated to have a profound effect on the others. Moreover, the peculiar geographical location of the Huron nation, pointing like a wedge into the heart of an undiscovered country, was a vantage ground from which the Faith could sally forth to outlying tribes yet unknown.

Father Brébeuf, who had arrived from France in 1633, strained with a holy impatience against the circumstances which held him back from his former mission. In July of the next year his desires were fulfilled. Setting out from Three Rivers accompanied by Father Antoine Daniel, and soon followed by Father Ambroise Davost, he succeeded in reaching the Huron country after undergoing unusual hardships. The Cross was again on its conquering march to the West. The locale of the Huron mission has thus been described.

> The home of the Hurons during the first half of the XVII century was of very limited extent. From northwest to southeast it comprised a tract of country at most forty miles in length with a width from southwest to northeast of less than twenty. Its western shore was washed by the waters of Nottawasaga Bay, a name given to the southernmost part of Georgian Bay, itself but a landlocked extension of Lake Huron towards the east. To the north, Huronia was separated from what is now the Muskoka District by Matchedash Bay, another inlet of Georgian Bay, into which flows the river Severn. This river in a circuitous course west, northwest, and southeast receives the outflow of Lakes Couchiching and Simcoe, the latter of which bounds Huronia to the southeast. Two lines, the one drawn across the map from the mouth of the Coldwater to a point on Couchiching Lake, a couple of miles north of the present town of Orillia, the other a mile or so east of Barrie, would with the shore lines of Nottawasaga and Matchedash Bays compass about the whole region in which lie scattered the towns and villages of "Old Huronia." [5]

Near the northwestern shore of Penetanguishene Bay, Father Brébeuf and his companions established a residence at an Indian village called Ihonatiria, which they renamed St. Joseph. In the next two years five more priests arrived and a second mission post was begun at Ossossané.[6] In consequence of a smallpox epidemic in 1637 Ihona-

[5] Arthur E. Jones, S.J., *Huronia, Fifth Report of the Bureau of Archives for the Province of Ontario* (Toronto, 1909), 5.

[6] Near the present Point Varwood on Nottawasaga Bay.

tiria was abandoned and a new center organized at Teanaustaye, which was now called St. Joseph II.[7] In 1639 Father Jérôme Lalement, who had just been made superior of the mission, decided that all the Fathers should work out of one well located headquarters. Accordingly, the mission of Sainte Marie was founded on the right bank of the river Wye between Mud Lake and Matchedash Bay. From this central point the missionaries visited the scattered Indian villages, and to it they returned for rest and spiritual exercises. A census of Huronia found in the *Relation* of 1640 shows about 12,000 souls dispersed among thirty-two villages.

Any detailed account of the growth and development of the Huron mission belongs properly to the history of the Church in Canada. Our interest in it lies chiefly in this that it brought the Church nearer to Michigan, and that from it came the first priests to set foot on the soil of this state. To explain their coming it must be remembered that the Jesuit missionaries were not only apostles in the truest sense but at the same time men of superior education and interested in the scientific knowledge of their times. Indeed, the *Relations* are a mine of exact data for several sciences. During the period with which we are dealing the French were still in search of a passage to the Western Sea. They were confident that from the Great Lakes there was an all-water route to China and Japan. Jolliet and Marquette were looking for it on their momentous voyage down the Mississippi. Hence, we can understand how eagerly the priests in Huronia, the farthest outpost, were waiting for whatever chance of further exploration the Indians might offer them.

The occasion presented itself in the fall of 1641. The Nipissing, the Chippewa, and other tribes living along the northern shore of Lake Huron came that year to the southern end of Georgian Bay to celebrate the Feast of the Dead.[8] Some of the Fathers had witnessed the Huron version of the ceremonial, and were interested in comparing it with the variant Algonquin customs. The *Relation* of 1642 describes the arrival of the Indians, the war dance, the pantomimes, the councils, the feastings, the "soft, sad" chanting of the women seated before the bones of their dead in the smoky gloom of the longhouse. The priests distributed presents to the Indians to win their good will, and were repaid by an invitation from the Chippewa to visit them in their villages far to the north. Father Charles Raymbaut, having some knowledge of the language, was immediately

---

[7] In the vicinity of Hillsdale in Medonte Township, Simcoe County.

[8] See the description of the Huron Feast of the Dead in Parkman, *The Jesuits in North America,* Chap. VII.

chosen by his superior to make the journey, and because a few Huron were to be in the party Father Isaac Jogues went along.[9] This first missionary excursion to Michigan was duly chronicled as follows.

. . . They left our House of Sainte Marie at the end of September, and after seventeen days of navigation on the great Lake, or freshwater sea which bathes the lands of the Hurons, they came ashore at the Sault. They found there about two thousand souls, and confirmed the reports of a great number of other sedentary Peoples, who have no knowledge of Europeans, and have never heard speak of God, among others of a certain Nadouëssis Nation situated Northwest or West of the Sault, eighteen days farther on. The first nine days are passed in crossing another great Lake which begins above the Sault; for the last nine days one must go up a River which penetrates far inland. These Peoples cultivate the land in the fashion of our Hurons, and raise crops of Indian corn and Tobacco. Their Towns are larger and better defended, by reason of the continual wars they wage against the Kiristinons, Irinions, and other great Nations which inhabit the same Countries. Their Language differs from the Algonquin and the Huron.

The Chiefs of this Nation of the Sault invited our Fathers to begin a residence among them. We gave them to understand that this was not impossible provided they were disposed to heed our instructions. After holding a council they answered that they greatly desired this happiness; that they embraced us as their Brothers, and that they would profit by our words. But we must have laborers for this work; we must first strive to gain the Peoples who are nearest to us, and meanwhile we must pray Heaven to hasten the time of their conversion.[10]

There is nothing to indicate that the Fathers exercised any sort of religious ministrations at the Sault. They had received orders to

[9] The names of the Jesuit missionaries have been variously spelled. Here the spelling will follow the latest and authoritative list of the missionaries in North America compiled, and published in 1929, by Arthur Melançon, S.J., of the College Sainte-Marie in Montreal. Father Charles Raymbaut was born April 6, 1602, and came to Canada in 1637. Immediately on his return from the Sault he was sent to evangelize the Nipissing living around the lake of the same name. His health broke down under the hardships suffered in this mission and he was compelled to return to Quebec, where he died, October 22, 1642. He was the first Jesuit to die in Canada.

Father Isaac Jogues was born at Orleans, June 10, 1607. He came to Canada in 1636 and was sent to the Huron mission. Returning to it from a visit in Montreal he was captured by the Mohawk in August, 1642, and tortured. Kept prisoner for a year he finally escaped through the good offices of the Dutch at Fort Orange, and returned to France. He came again to Canada in 1644, and was sent to the Iroquois, who had sued for peace with the French, in 1646. On October 1 he was treacherously tomahawked in the Mohawk village of Ossernenon, the present Auriesville, New York. He was canonized June 29, 1930, along with Fathers Jean de Brébeuf, Gabriel Lalement, Antoine Daniel, Charles Garnier, Noël Chabanel, René Goupil, the lay brother, and Jean de la Lande, the "donné" or lay servant.

[10] The Relation of 1642. Chap. XII.

make an exploratory journey only, and immediately after the Indian council they returned to Sainte Marie in the Huron mission.

As far as known records go, this visit to what is today Sault Ste. Marie marks the first appearance of Jesuit missionaries in the territory now comprised within the boundaries of Michigan. However, there is a bare possibility that the shore in the neighborhood of Detroit may have been at least seen by two other missionaries engaged in the extension of the Huron mission to the Tobacco and Neutral tribes. The first contact of the Jesuits with the Tobacco Indians was made by Fathers Garnier and Jogues in 1639. The nearest of the nine villages which the tribe occupied lay two days journey west of the last Huron settlement. In November, 1640, Fathers Brébeuf and Chaumonot found their way to the Neutral Indians living along the Niagara River and the northern shore of Lake Erie.[11] During a stay of four months the missionaries visited eighteen villages. The *Relation* of 1641 which describes the beginning of the mission states that no one had gone there to preach the gospel from the time of Father de la Roche d'Aillon. In the village of Khioetoa, the farthest one they reached, and which they renamed St. Michel, they were well received and conferred the first adult baptism.

From the *Relation* of 1642 we learn that the missionaries were withdrawn from these outlying missions, and Father Lalemant's policy of concentrating all efforts upon the Hurons until the entire tribe should be converted went into effect. This course was adhered to until 1647, when, unable to resist the pleadings of some scattered Christians, the Fathers went back to the Tobacco tribe and were with them until the end. No new missions were undertaken among the Neutral Indians.

How far to the west did the Neutral tribe extend? Where lay the village of Khioetoa? An attentive study of the *Relations* gives no satisfactory answer. It is known that Father Chaumonot drew up a map of his missionary tour, but there is no existing copy of it. In 1656, Sanson, geographer to the King, published the first map showing the full extent of Lake Erie and its connection with Lake Huron through the Detroit River, Lake St. Clair, and the St. Clair River. It is most likely that he derived his knowledge of the region from the Jesuits, for on his map he marks the location of their missions. Du Creux, the Jesuit historian, issued a map of the Lake region in 1664

[11] "Their path lay, so far as I can make out from researches, through the towns of Bedton, Orangeville, Georgetown, the north-western ends of the city of Hamilton and the city of St. Catherines. Thirty-six villages of the Neutrals were in Canadian territory, and the last of the four or five towns on the American side was where the city of Lockport now stands." Very Rev. W. R. Harris, *History of the Early Missions in Western Canada* (Toronto, 1893), 120.

which differs only slightly from Sanson's.[12] In both maps the mission of St. Michel, or Khioetoa, is located on the Canadian side of Lake St. Clair near the entrance to the Detroit River. From these particulars it has been alleged that the mission lay somewhere in the neighborhood of Windsor.[13]

The two maps are admittedly imperfect and seriously defective in their details even of the Huron country, which, on the supposition that the Jesuit missionaries furnished the information, should have been reliably drawn. Unless one has the will to believe they are scarcely conclusive. However, the possibility they present cannot be absolutely excluded, and there is a bare chance that either Father Brébeuf or Father Chaumonot came as far as Lake St. Clair during the mission to the Neutral Indians in the winter of 1640–41, and may have set foot in Michigan a few months preceeding the visit of Fathers Jogues and Raymbaut to the Sault.

There remains to be told the sad fate of the Huron mission. Although the Iroquois had made inroads into the Huron country as early as 1643, the full fury of their attacks came in 1648. On July 4, the mission of St. Joseph on the Iroquois frontier was destroyed and Father Antoine Daniel murdered. There was some respite until the spring of the next year. This time the missions of St. Ignace and St. Louis were laid waste. Father Brébeuf was martyred on March 16, and Father Gabriel Lalement on the following day. In December of the same year the Iroquois went as far as the Tobacco tribe, destroyed the mission of St. Jean, and killed Father Garnier. An apostate Huron struck down Father Noël Chabanel in a neighboring mission. Some of the Huron together with the priests who were left took refuge for a while on Charity Island a few miles off from the Huron peninsula. Everyone now realized that the Huron mission was doomed. On June 10, 1650, the Fathers accompanied by some three hundred converts made the long arduous journey back to Quebec.

The destruction of the Huron mission brought to an end the first phase of missionary endeavor in the region of the Great Lakes. Although the Indians had at first proved quite intractable to the efforts of the missionaries there had been a remarkable change of heart beginning with 1647. The dream of the conversion of a whole tribe was in a fair way to be realized. By the middle of 1649 more than twenty-seven hundred persons had been baptized. In many of the villages religious life went on with all the regularity of a well organized parish. When this infant church was battered down in a welter

[12] For these early maps of the Great Lakes region see Louis C. Karpinski, *Bibliography of the Printed Maps of Michigan* (Lansing, 1931).
[13] Jones, *op. cit.,* 323.

of blood after such unparalleled efforts to build it up, the problem of converting the Indians of New France assumed almost insurmountable proportions. Yet it lay perhaps in the design of Divine Providence that the dispersal of the Huron was to scatter the seeds of the Gospel in fields that were still untouched.

The Huron, demoralized and panic-stricken, fled in every direction, homeless wanderers. The descendants of the group that accompanied the Fathers back to Quebec 'are still to be found at La Jeune Lorette some ten miles outside the city. Other hundreds made their way to Manitoulin Island and to the northern shores of Lakes Huron and Michigan, and even into Wisconsin. Those who hoped to find sanctuary among the Neutral Indians were involved in the general destruction that overtook their hosts. Another band fled to the Tobacco Indians, and after being shunted back and forth from the Mississippi to Mackinac finally built their lodges near the infant settlement of Detroit, and were henceforth known as Wyandots. The remainder begged the mercy of their savage foes and, strange to say, were incorporated among them, retained what they had learned, and were the nucleus of what later became the flourishing Iroquois mission. Wherever succeeding missionaries encountered a Huron they were almost certain to find, if not a Christian, at least a friend.

To complete the picture of the disaster brought about by the Iroquois the following passage is quoted from an authority on Indian history.

> In 1660 there was not an Indian on the shores of Lake Huron, or on any of its islands. The whole peninsula of Upper Canada was a solitude. Lower Michigan too was a desert. A voyageur from the island of Montreal, paddling his canoe up the Ottawa and descending through Lake Nipissing and the French River, the accustomed thoroughfare to Lake Huron, would not on the whole route meet a single Algonquin hunter; nor was the smoke of a wigwam likely to greet him until he came to the neighborhood of the broad Menomonee, that now forms the boundary between Upper Michigan and Wisconsin. Or, if the term of his journey lay to the north, and he entered the bay of Keweenaw, ninety leagues beyond the Rapids of St. Mary's, even at this great rendezvous of Algonquin fishermen, no less than in the straits of Mackinac, "the true home of the trout and the whitefish," he would only have found the gull and the eagle left to feed on the dainties of the red man. But perchance our traveller, while skimming the waves of Lake Huron or Michigan, might have fallen in with half a thousand warriors from the neighborhood of the Dutch settlements on the Mohawk. . . . To such an extent the daring and resoluteness of a few thousand savages had prevailed over an enemy more than tenfold their number.[14]

[14] Rev. Edward Jacker, "Catholic Indians in Michigan and Wisconsin," *American Catholic Quarterly Review* (1876), I, 407–08.

There can be no better epilogue to the drama of the Huron mission than the story of a strange meeting told by Charlevoix. Father Adrien Grelon was stationed in the Huron mission when the Iroquois overran it. He was living with Father Léonard Garreau in an Indian village not far from St. Jean when it was destroyed, and Father Garnier killed, and together the two priests buried the blackened remains of the martyr. On the close of the Huron mission Father Grelon returned to France, and in 1654 he was sent to the Jesuit missions in China. One day while on the road to one of his villages he was amazed to encounter a Huron woman whom he had known in his former mission. She fell at his feet overjoyed to find a friend who could speak her native tongue. According to her own story she had been handed on from tribe to tribe, through channels of communication that can only be conjectured, from Ontario to the interior of China.[15]

THE OTTAWA MISSION

For ten years following the destruction of the Huron mission there was not a priest in the western solitude. Then appeared the pathetic yet heroic figure of Father René Ménard, the third priest to reach the shores of Michigan. He had been sent to Huronia in 1641. In him abilities of a high order and a burning zeal for souls were united to a remarkable facility for reaching the heart of the Indian.[16] His personal austerities and mode of life soon gained for him a reputation for sanctity both among his converts and his confreres. Together with Father Claude Pijart he went to the Nipissing Indians in April, 1642, and labored among them for eighteen months. He most likely went back to the Huron mission field, for he was among the Fathers who returned to Quebec in 1650.

Six years later Father Ménard was assigned to the Iroquois mission, where with two French laymen he took up his station in the principal town of the Cayugas. Here, as he wrote in the *Relation* of 1657, he lived in the ever present danger of violent death: "We walk with our heads uplifted in the midst of dangers, through insults, hootings and calumnies, through hatchets and knives with which they frequently follow us to put us to death. Almost daily we are on the point of being massacred." In the spring of the following year a plot to murder all the missionaries in the Iroquois mission was discovered. Aided, however, by the ingenuity of a young Frenchman who had been

[15] Pierre Francois Xavier De Charlevoix, *Journal of a Voyage to North America*, Louise Phelps Kellogg ed. (Chicago, 1923), I, 45. Father Grelon told the story himself in his *Histoire de la Chine sous la domination des Tartars* (Paris, 1671). Charlevoix was also edited by John Gilmary Shea, *History of New France* (New York, 1866–72).

[16] Rochemonteix, *op. cit.*, I, 428.

adopted by a Cayuga chief the priests were enabled to escape and to reach Quebec. Father Ménard was then made superior of the Jesuit residence at Three Rivers.[17]

These were dark days in the history of the Canadian missions. The reverses experienced in Huronia and among the Iroquois had dampened enthusiasm and almost paralyzed activity. Many of the Fathers had returned to France. Those who remained carried on at Quebec, Three Rivers, Sillery, and Tadoussac. To add to their discouragement differences had arisen between them and the Abbé Gabriel de Queylus, lately come to Canada as vicar-general of the archbishop of Rouen who claimed jurisdiction over New France.

It would lead us too far afield to study the clash of interests which attended the beginnings of ecclesiastical jurisdiction in the colony, and the barest outline must suffice.[18] The Jesuits had been exercising their ministry in New France by virtue of faculties granted directly by the Holy See in 1629. In the course of time the need of a resident bishop became more and more apparent; but, although the General Assembly of the French clergy took up the matter in 1646, nothing was decided. The next year the Jesuits were notified that the Primate of Normandy, the archbishop of Rouen, claimed the Canadian colony as part of his diocese. They had never thought it necessary to hold faculties from him, and this pretension, if true, would have invalidated many of their official acts.

The source of the Primate's claim seems to have been nothing more than this, that most of the departures for New France were made from seaports, Le Havre and Dieppe for instance, which belonged to his diocese. The few secular priests who had come to Canada had received their faculties from him, and even the Jesuits were accustomed to make this gesture of dependence, but only for the oversea voyage. Little by little the pretension was built up without any definite authorization to substantiate it, and was finally deflated in 1659, when the Congregation of the Propaganda notified the archbishop that he had never been given any jurisdiction over the Canadian colony.

Meanwhile, the agitation went on in France for the erection of a Canadian see until a candidate was finally chosen in the person of Francois de Montmorency-Laval. Named bishop of the titular see of Petrée and Vicar Apostolic of Canada he was consecrated at Paris, December 8, 1658, and arrived in Quebec, June 16, 1659. The arch-

[17] For the interesting story of their escape see Shea, *Hist. of Cath. Miss.*, 288 ff.
[18] The reader interested in the rather tortuous diplomacy involved will find the question treated at length by the Church historians of Canada. See especially Rochemonteix, *op. cit.*, II, 189 ff; Faillon, *op. cit.*, II, Chap. XII; l'Abbé Auguste Gosselin, *Vie de Mgr De Laval* (Quebec, 1890), I, 93–137.

bishop of Rouen was not to be so easily overridden. He inveigled Louis XIV into supporting him, and, as we have seen, sent the Abbé Queylus to Canada as his vicar-general with residence at Montreal. The firmness of Bishop Laval triumphed over this deplorable situation. Recognizing his error the King summoned the Abbé back to France, and ordered him to stay there. Instead, he went on to Rome and in some manner procured authorization for the erection of an independent parish in Montreal to which the archbishop should have the right of nomination. In defiance of the royal prohibition he again appeared in the colony, and respectfully presented to Bishop Laval a document ordering him to install the bearer as pastor of Montreal. However, his flagrant disobedience had overshot its mark, and this time the King testily ordered the Governor to deport the Abbé. Two months after his arrival he was on his way back to France, the victim of a lost cause.[19]

With the coming of Bishop Laval the Church in the colony took on new life; for the Jesuits the dark period of doubt and discouragement was over. One of the early acts of his administration was the turning over to the Jesuits the entire Indian mission field. The Sulpicians and the diocesan clergy were to do parish work exclusively. The Jesuits joyfully accepted their renewed commission, and decided to strike out westward to the shores of Lake Superior. This territory had long been known to the French as the Ottawa country because the Indians so named controlled the river which led to it. From now on all missionary labors in Michigan and Wisconsin were comprised under the general term, the Ottawa mission.

In the month of August, 1660, Bishop Laval was returning to Quebec from a visitation in Montreal. Not far from Three Rivers his party encountered a band of Ottawa three hundred strong manning a flotilla of sixty canoes, in one of which the bishop was astonished to perceive the bent and prematurely aged figure of Father Ménard. While the Indians rested on their paddles the bishop asked for and received an explanation. Two Frenchmen, Pierre Esprit and Medard Chouart, better known as Sieur de Radisson and Sieur des Grosseilliers, had just returned from a journey to the interior which had taken them along the entire south shore of Lake Superior. They brought knowledge of many unknown tribes who lived in the northern lake region and beyond. There were new conquests to be made for Christ, and he had been chosen by his superior to break ground

<hr />

[19] That the archbishop of Rouen established jurisdiction over New France seems to have been accepted by John Gilmary Shea in his *Catholic Church in Colonial Days* (New York, 1886), 246 ff. The facts hardly justify such an opinion. The Abbé Queylus returned to Canada in 1668 as Superior of the Sulpicians with residence at Montreal. He died in Paris in 1677. Faillon, *op. cit.*, III, 186.

for a new mission.[20] He saw surprise and anxiety in the bishop's face. "What should I do my Lord?"

"Father, there is every reason why you should remain here; but God who is stronger than all must want you there." [21]

The priest bowed to receive the episcopal blessing, the Indians bent to their task and were soon lost in the distance. It was the memory of this meeting which supported him through almost unbelievable hardships. On the frozen shore of Lake Superior he wrote in his journal: "How often have I revolved those words in my mind amid the roar of torrents and in the solitude of our great forests."

The Indians had promised the missionary that he would be taken along as a passenger, and that he would be spared any unusual labor. He was, nevertheless, obliged to swing his paddle from morning till night, and to carry heavy loads at all the portages. His food was mostly wild berries and a moss growing on the rocks from which a sort of broth was made. Somewhere on the Lake Superior shore his canoe was broken by a falling tree, and he was left behind with three Indians while the others pressed on. He was stranded for six days subsisting on the offal around a deserted lodge, and a stew made from the decaying bones that lay scattered about. Finally, with the help of some passing Indians he was able to catch up with the main party.

On October 15, the feast of St. Theresa, Father Ménard landed at the head of a wide bay, which he named in honor of the saint. He proceeded to say Mass, thus to pay himself back with interest, as he wrote, for all the privations he had suffered. The Indians decided to camp there for the winter, and the missionary began his work of instruction. He had landed in what is now called Keweenaw Bay, and his mission was probably a few miles north of the present city of L'Anse.

For all his zeal and sacrifices Father Ménard could make but little impression on the savages hardened by brutality and licentiousness. A few adults and a number of dying children were all that he could glean. Early in the spring he accompanied some French traders to the head of Chequamegon Bay, where a large band of Ottawa had assembled. Here he was visited by delegates from a Huron group, which had fled from the Iroquois as far as the headwaters of the Black River in Wisconsin. Many of them had been baptized, and they urged

[20] An attempt had been made four years before. Fathers Léonard Garreau and Gabriel Druilletes were descending the Ottawa River on their way to the northern lake region with a party of Ottawa and Frenchmen, when they were ambushed by an Iroquois war party on August 30, 1656. Father Garreau fell mortally wounded and died a few days later at Montreal. Father Druilletes escaped.

[21] The *Relation* of 1664, Chap. I.

the missionary to make his residence in their village. This was an invitation that he could not resist. At last he had caught up with the refugees from Huronia. Accordingly, on July 13, 1661, he set out with high hopes on the journey that was to be his last.

Taking with him a few Indians and a French blacksmith, and carrying a provision of smoked meat and a bag of dried sturgeon, the missionary made his way by land to Lake Court Oreilles. The Indians soon went off by themselves, and the priest waited fifteen days in vain at the lake for them to appear. His French companion finally discovered a canoe, in which the two men followed the shore of the lake until they reached the outlet of the Chippewa River. About five days' journey up the river they encountered a stretch of treacherous water.[22] The Frenchman decided to run the rapids, but Father Ménard left the canoe and started to walk through the woods intending to get aboard in the still water below. When the Frenchman had passed safely through, he sat down to wait for the priest and then becoming alarmed he searched for him through the woods, shouting and repeatedly discharging his gun; but all to no avail. The missionary had disappeared, and although the Indians arrived later to help in the search no trace of him was ever found. Whether he lost his way to die later on of hunger and thirst, or whether he was set upon by some lurking savage will never be known. Years later, his breviary and cassock were seen by Nicolas Perrot among the Sioux.[23] Thus perished Michigan's first apostle in a manner so unlike the martyrdom he had for long desired. He had walked with death on the Iroquois mission, and had smiled into the faces of the brutal Indians who for a mere whim would have sent their axes crashing into his head. A worthy companion he to Jogues, and Brébeuf, and Lalement.[24]

Four years went by without any attempt to reopen the Ottawa mission. The story begins again on the morning of August 8, 1665, at Three Rivers. The hundreds of Indians who had come down from the lake region to barter their furs were in a hurry to return to their haunts three hundred leagues to the west. As they went up the river, their paddles glittering in the morning sunshine, they were followed by six Frenchmen manning a canoe in which sat a priest.[25] Perhaps his mind was filled with the thoughts he was later on to pen as the portrait of a true missionary.

[22] Father Ménard's route has been traced by Louise Phelps Kellogg in a sketch of the missionary for the *Wisconsin Magazine of History*, IV, 417–45.

[23] Rochemonteix, *op. cit.*, II, 350.

[24] Father René Ménard was born at Paris, September 7, 1605, and entered the Society in 1624. He arrived in Canada, July 8, 1640. Rochemonteix, *op. cit.*, I, 429.

[25] The *Relation* of 1667, Chap. II.

The religious of the Society of Jesus who pass from Old France to the New should be called there by a special and a strong vocation. They must be persons dead to the world and to themselves; apostolic men and holy, who seek only God and the salvation of souls. They must love the Cross and mortification; they must not spare themselves; they must desire the conversion of one Indian above an empire. They must be in the forests of Canada as so many precursors of Jesus Christ; as so many lesser John the Baptists they must be as so many voices of God crying in the deserts to call the savage races to the knowledge of the Savior. Finally, they must put all their support, all their contentment, all their treasure in God alone to whom alone belongs the choosing of what He will for Canada.[26]

The man who thought and wrote thus was Father Claude Allouez, the "Francis Xavier" of the western missions. Born June 6, 1622, at St. Didier in the Velay, he had entered the Society at seventeen. Professed in 1657, he arrived at Quebec the following year. Of medium height and stockily built, a mountaineer bred and inured to hardships, prudent, learned, forceful, and enterprising, Allouez presents the picture of the ideal missionary.[27]

He needed all his courage and power of endurance. The Indians, having vainly tried to make him turn back, took him into one of their canoes where he had to paddle all day, and often half the night. When food ran out he learned to dine on bitter roots, and a broth made of lichens. One morning his party stumbled on the carcass of a deer that had been dead for some time. Hunger compelled him to eat his share, but, as he candidly observes, there was a bad taste in his mouth until the next day. When portages had to be made the Indians roared with laughter as he fell under the loads that they piled on him.

The flotilla passed out of the St. Mary's River into Lake Superior on September 2, and the remainder of the month was spent in coasting along the south shore. In the bay where Ménard had wintered Father Allouez found two Indian women, who still remembered the instructions given them five years before. A few days later the long voyage ended at the head of Chequamegon Bay. Here, most likely near the present city of Ashland, Wisconsin, Allouez began a mission post which he dedicated to the Holy Ghost. He erected a small bark chapel, and adorned its sides with pictures of the infernal regions and of the General Judgment which, as he states, furnished him with matter well suited to his hearers.

The Ottawa mission thus begun by Father Allouez bore little re-

[26] Pierre Margry, *Découvertes et Établissements des Francais* (Paris, 1876), I, 71–72.
[27] Rochemonteix, *op. cit.*, II, 353–54.

semblance to the Huron mission. The northern lake region was the refuge of all the Algonquin tribes who had been harried by the Iroquois on one side, and by the Sioux on the other. On Lake Superior and the northern shore of Lake Huron the various clans of the Ottawa and Chippewa predominated.[28] Green Bay on the western shore of Lake Michigan was perhaps a greater magnet for Indian migration on account of the wild rice found there in abundance. Its shores were inhabited by a mixed population of Menominee, Winnebago, and Potawatomi. Later additions were the Sauk, driven out of the Saginaw valley in Michigan, and the Fox from northern Wisconsin. Behind the bay there were Prairie Indians, Miami, and various Illinois tribes. All together there were perhaps some twelve thousand souls within four or five days' journey from its shores. Into this babel of tongues and tribes, driven here and there by the exigencies of war, came Allouez and his successors.[29]

After laboring for two years along the Lake Superior shore, Allouez went down to Quebec to make a report on his missions. It must have been this visit which prompted the issuing of what is "probably the first ecclesiastical act applying directly and exclusively to the Church in the West." [30]

Francis, by the Grace of God and of the Holy See, Bishop of Petraea, Vicar-Apostolic in New France, and nominated by the King first Bishop of said country: To our well-beloved Father Claude Allouez, Superior of the Mission of the Society of Jesus among the Ottawas, Health.

On the report which we have received of the disorder prevailing in your missions in regard to the French who go thither to trade, and who do not hesitate to take part in all the profane feasts held there by the pagans, sometimes with great scandals to their souls, and to the edification which they ought to give to the Christian converts, we enjoin you to take in hand that they shall never be present when these feasts are manifestly idolatrous, and in case they do the contrary of what you decide ought to be done or not done on this point, to threaten them with censures if they do not return to their duty, and in case of contumacy, to proceed according to your prudence and discretion, as also towards those who are given in an extraordinary degree to scandalous impurity, to act in like manner. Given at Quebec this 6th of August, one thousand six hundred and sixty-seven.

Francis, Bishop of Petraea.

Two years later the missionary again visited Quebec, and on his return was met at the Sault by a number of Potawatomi who com-

---

[28] The Chippewa were also called the Ojibwa. The latter name is perhaps more familiar to Michigan readers.
[29] Jacker, "Catholic Indians . . . ," 410.
[30] Shea, *The Catholic Church . . . Days*, 270.

plained about the conduct of some French traders at Green Bay. He had long been eager to establish a mission there as he had come in contact with many of its tribes through the emissaries who had made the long trip to the Lake Superior mission, curious to see the man who could speak six languages. He therefore gladly availed himself of the opportunity given him by the Potawatomi to visit their villages.

It took no little courage to start out from the Sault in the month of November on a canoe trip to Green Bay.[31] Nevertheless, the intrepid missionary and two companions left on the third, and one month later they reached their destination. The day after their arrival being the feast of St. Francis Xavier, Allouez said Mass and chose the saint as patron of the new mission.[32]

From this time on Father Allouez labored almost exclusively in Wisconsin, and Illinois; but, as will be seen later, Michigan also can in all likelihood claim a place in the missionary orbit of this most famous apostle of the Ottawa mission. For length of service, for indefatigable zeal, for results accomplished, he is not overshadowed by any of the saintly men who were his confreres.[33]

In order to follow the development of the Ottawa mission based on the labors of Father Allouez we must come now to those historic sites in our own state, Sault Ste. Marie and Mackinac. From 1660 there had been intermittent peace between the French and the Iroquois so that the Algonquin tribes had more freedom of movement. In 1666 the expedition of De Tracy and De Courcelles, which destroyed the Mohawk strongholds, effectually tamed the Iroquois spirit; they were no longer dreaded as they had been in the past. The Indians began to reoccupy their old haunts along the St. Mary's River and the northern shores of Lake Huron lured by the abundance of their favorite food, the savory whitefish.

It is not surprising that, as soon as practicable, the missionaries should station themselves in a locality having such strategic value. They were certain to meet along the St. Mary's River representatives from every Algonquin tribe. It was the natural gateway for travel from the north to the French settlements. Of more importance still because of the greater volume of traffic going through them were the Straits of Mackinac. We need only recall the military value attached

---

[31] The *Relation* of 1670, Chap. XII.

[32] The mission was founded near the present town of De Pere, Wisconsin. A monument to Father Allouez was erected there and dedicated September 6, 1899. See Thwaites, *Jesuit Relations* . . . , LVI, 303.

[33] More detailed accounts of Father Allouez's activities will be found in Shea, *Hist. of the Cath. Miss.*, 358 ff.; Rev. T. J. Campbell, S.J., *Pioneer Priests of North America* (New York, 1916), III, 147–64.

to the island of Mackinac as France, England, and America struggled for the possession of the Northwest.

When returning from his first visit to Quebec Allouez had brought with him Father Louis Nicolas to help in the Holy Ghost mission. In the early fall of 1668 Father James Marquette and Brother Louis de Boêsme were sent to the Ottawa mission, and took up their station at the Sault, most likely in the same locality that had been visited by Jogues and Raymbaut in 1641.[34] Here a rudimentary mission building was erected wherein Marquette exercised his ministry for a year until he was transferred to Chequamegon Bay.[35] He was replaced by Father Claude Dablon, whose appointment as superior over the Fathers laboring in the lake region reflected the growing importance of the Ottawa mission. We catch a glimpse of the post as Gallinée, the Sulpician, saw it in 1670.

> ". . . Since last year they (the Jesuits) have had two men in their service who have built them a fairly good fort, that is to say, an enclosure of cedar posts twelve feet high within which there is a chapel and a house. They have a very large clearing, well sown, from which they should harvest some of their provisions; they even hope to be able to have bread to eat before two years. . . ."[36]

During the winter of 1670–71 Father Dablon spent much of his time at the Straits establishing relations with the Indians who were drifting back, and as is plain from the report of his work in the *Relation* of 1671 he saw the necessity of establishing there another mission post, and actually did begin one, which he named St. Ignace. The precise location of this mission, whether on the island of Mackinac, or on the mainland at St. Ignace, has occasioned much discussion, which stems from the fact that the French applied the word Missillimackinac, or Michilimackinac indiscriminately to the island, the straits, and the territory about the straits. It does seem, however, that the site of the mission can be determined by its proximity to a fort, whose location has never been questioned, built by the Huron in the following circumstances.

In the summer of 1670 the Indians of Father Marquette's mission treacherously killed a Sioux chieftain and his four companions whom they were entertaining in apparent friendship. When the excitement of the bloody orgy had subsided they realized that the Sioux would

---

[34] The *Relation* of 1668, Chap. VI.
[35] The *Relation* of 1669, Chap. VI.
[36] It has been conjectured that the mission stood at the foot of Bingham Avenue in the present Sault Ste. Marie on the American side of the river. See Stanley Newton, *The Story of Sault Ste. Marie and the Chippewa Country* (Sault Ste. Marie, 1923).

retaliate in abundant measure. The more timorous Indians hastily sought refuge in the islands of Lake Huron, and in the early spring of the following year the last of the Ottawa and Huron, accompanied by Marquette, made their way through the floating ice of Lake Superior to the Straits of Mackinac and to Manitoulin Island. The site of the mission was abandoned for one hundred and sixty-four years, and Marquette had no successor in it until a priest of the diocese of Detroit, Frederic Baraga, began his heroic labors there in 1835.

This forced exodus brought Marquette to what was destined to be the most important of all the stations in the Ottawa mission, St. Ignace of Michilimackinac. In the *Relation* of 1672 he reports to Dablon, who had meantime gone down to Quebec to become superior over all the Jesuit missions in New France, that "the Hurons called Tionnontateronnons, or the Tobacco nation, who compose the mission of Saint Ignace at Michilimakinang, began last summer a fort near the Chapel in which their Cabins were enclosed." The same *Relation* gives some interesting details of his work at St. Ignace. The Huron thronged his chapel, and came to pray and to sing their favorite hymns even in his absence. He was generally successful in prevailing upon his converts to give up their indecent dances; he permitted the more decorous varieties. However, he noticed the inconstancy of the Indian character, for some of the women were loath to avoid temptation declaring—with quite modern casuistry—that this was the only time they had for diversion, and that he had not explicitly forbidden dancing. Through the cold of winter the Indians kept coming to the chapel twice a day. He began to prepare them for general confession, and notes that some of them spent more than a fortnight in examining their consciences. The influence of the gentle and affable missionary left an indelible impression on the Indians, and his successors in the mission found an orderly and Christian people.

The subsequent events of Marquette's life are too well known to need more than a mention here. Together with Louis Jolliet and five Frenchmen he left St. Ignace on May 17, 1673, on that ever memorable journey of exploration down the Mississippi to its junction with the Arkansas River. After his return in September, somewhat impaired in health, he remained at the Jesuit mission in Green Bay until October of the following year, when he set out to begin a mission among the Illinois Indians at Kaskaskia, near the present Utica, La Salle County.[37] However, he was obliged to winter at the Chicago portage, and did not reach the Indian villages until April 10. Only a few days of ministry so exhausted him that he reluctantly consented

[37] *Illinois Catholic Historical Review*, I, 414.

to return to St. Ignace, where he could receive medical attention. As two faithful companions, bringing him back, were paddling silently along the west shore of Michigan Marquette knew that he could go no farther. He asked to be put ashore at the mouth of a river which opened to them, and there he died, May 18, 1675.[38]

While Marquette was thus spending his last years in laying the foundation of what was later to become the flourishing Illinois Mission reinforcements were coming to St. Ignace and to the Sault. For the next twenty years there travelled back and forth through the Straits of Mackinac men of exalted virtue and heroic zeal, the romance of whose lives runs through the tangled skein of Canadian history.

There was Father Gabriel Druilletes. Coming to Canada in 1643, he experienced all the hardships of missionary work along the St. Lawrence from Quebec to the Gulf, and then became the apostle of the Abnaki in Maine. Later, he was sent to the New England colonies as envoy from Quebec to conclude a defensive alliance against the Iroquois.[39] At Plymouth, Governor Bradford welcomed him on a Friday, and with nice courtesy was his host at a fish dinner. He met Governor Dudley at Roxbury, and Endicott at Salem. There, too, he conversed far into the night with the kindly Eliot, the first Protestant missionary to the Indians. Then came years of labor deep in the Saguenay region. In 1670, "the oldest and most esteemed of our missionaries" came to the Sault to give the last years of a long and arduous life to the service of God before going down to Quebec to die.[40]

A worthy co-laborer was Father Charles Albanel. For twenty years after his coming to Canada in 1649 he had ministered to the Indians around Tadoussac through sickness and famine. Then came rumors that the English were trading with the northern Indians at Hudson Bay. As yet the French knew no overland route to this inland sea, and Albanel was commissioned to discover one. While Marquette was still planning his exploration of the great river Albanel was on his way, and his journal tells how he and Denys de Saint-Simon became the first accredited white men to reach Hudson Bay by land.[41] He

---

[38] Father Marquette died at the mouth of the Marquette River near the present city of Ludington. For a study of the actual spot of the burial see the *Ill. Cath. Hist. Rev.*, IX, 348–62. In the preceding volumes of the *Review* many phases of the Missionary's life are dealt with. For thorough accounts of the Mississippi journey see Francis Borgia Steck, O.F.M., *The Jolliet-Marquette Expedition* (Quincy, 1928); Jean Delanglez, S.J., *Life and Voyages of Louis Jolliet* (Chicago, 1948).

[39] For an account of his journey to New England see Parkman, *The Jesuits in North America*.

[40] See Campbell, *op. cit.*, III, 70–108; 109–46.

[41] The *Relation* of 1672, Chap. VI.

went back later only to fall into the hands of officials of the Hudson Bay Company, who resented his presence, charged him with intrusion on their preserve, and sent him to England a prisoner. Released in 1676, he returned to Canada and was assigned to the Ottawa mission. For the next twenty years he was stationed either at Green Bay or at the Sault, where he died in January, 1696.

Along with these veterans there were at one time or another in the northern lake region many priests no less worthy of notice. Pierre Bailloquet, exhausted from ceaseless missionary journeys, died at Green Bay in 1692, at the age of seventy-nine. At his lowly chapel on Manitoulin Island labored Louis André, sometimes stewing the leather covers of his books to keep from starving, and when all was well playing his flute to teach hymn tunes to the admiring Indians who crowded around him.[42] Phillippe Pierson was with the sorrowing Indians who paddled silently out of St. Ignace to bring the body of Marquette from its grave on the lake shore to its final resting place under the mission church. Living too at St. Ignace were André Bonnault, Jean Enjalran, and Henri Nouvel.[43] The last named priest deserves a special place in the Catholic history of Michigan.

Strangely enough, during all this period of intense activity in the Mackinac region there is no record of missionary work undertaken anywhere in the southern peninsula save in the extreme southwestern corner, and at a relatively later date. The origin and history of this mission will be given in another chapter. Apart from this instance there is no evidence to show even the presence of a missionary in the southern peninsula except on two occasions, one the passage of Father Enjalran through the Detroit River, to be mentioned later, and the other the journey of Father Nouvel which we must now take up. Father Jacker, the well known authority on the Indians of Michigan, gave this explanation.

> . . . The puzzle, however, is easily solved by pointing to the one great fact which plays such an important part in most other questions bearing on the fate of Canada and its dependencies under French rule—the implacable hostility of the Iroquois against the Algonkin allies of France; for two of its consequences were the insecurity of the southern lake route and the complete depopulation of Lower Michigan. No resident tribe, roving through its woods and to be reclaimed from paganism, invited the missionary; no prospect of gain attracted the trader; and the advantage of the lower lakes as an easy thoroughfare to the West was far outweighed by the dangers of the passage. . . .[44]

[42] The *Relation* of 1671, Chap. II, gives his own account of his labors.
[43] We shall have occasion to refer to Father Enjalran later.
[44] *United States Cath. Hist. Mag.* (1887), I, 261-62.

Father Dablon first made the statement, which has since been many times repeated, that Nouvel wintered with some Indians near Lake Erie. Fortunately, we have Nouvel's own account of his journey, which seems to have been generally overlooked, and we can follow him with a fair degree of accuracy.[45] Nouvel, after his arrival in Canada in 1662 was engaged in the missions at Sillery and Three Rivers. Succeeding Dablon as superior of the Ottawa mission in 1671, he was stationed first at the Sault, and later at St. Ignace. While there, late in the fall of 1675, he was visited by a party of Chippewa, who requested a missionary to accompany them on their winter hunt in the direction of Lake Erie. He promised to follow them later himself, and drew up a map according to the directions given by the Indians. On November 8 he set out from St. Ignace with two Frenchmen, and for ten days he travelled along the northeastern shore of the lower peninsula. On the southern side of Thunder Bay he had the unexpected pleasure of meeting some Indian women who had been converted at Tadoussac, and whom he had known there. We take up his narrative at this point.

After ten day's navigation I met a lodge of certain Indians called Oupenengous, married with Algonkin women, whom I had before seen at Tadoussac and Sillery. These women being Christians and their children baptized, they expressed great joy at thus unexpectedly meeting with a missionary, whom they had once seen at a distance of more than 400 leagues thence; nor did I feel less happy rendering them all the services of my ministry.

We started all together on the following day, and, going south, we found quite a different country; an abundance of large oaks, maples, and other excellent timber, even fine apple trees, where the Hurons and the Algonkin women did not neglect to gather a good provision.

On the twelfth day of the journey, having changed our course to the southwest, we came to marshy grounds, where we had much difficulty finding a proper place for camping.[46] We fared so badly there, that, pressed as we were at the same time by bad weather, we broke up camp on the following morning to throw ourselves into the recess of a bay, where we were none the better. I had, however, the consolation to find here another cabin of Oupenengous married with Nipissing women, whom I was thus enabled to instruct.

On the following morning, having started in very foggy weather, we threw ourselves into a bay, where rain and thunder held us fast the whole day; [47] but in the succeeding night a northwest wind chilled the air to such a degree, that the whole bay having frozen over, we re-

[45] The journal was edited with critical notes in the publication mentioned in the preceding note, pp. 266–80. The same notes will here be used.
[46] This spot was about ten miles south of Tawas City.
[47] A cove near the mouth of the Au Gres River.

mained, as it were, in prison for six days, without any hope of being able to proceed, until, having addressed ourselves to the Holy Virgin Immaculate, through the mediation of St. Ignatius and St. Francis Xavier, she inspired us with the thought of transporting our canoes and all our baggage to a little island, which was quite near, and there, breaking the ice before us, we happily embarked.

On the following day, which was the first of December, we left the lake in order to enter a fine river, where traveling is much more pleasant.[48] The winter, which was fast approaching, compelled us to make haste, and pushing on with all our might, we missed a branch of the river which we should have entered in order to pursue our journey; [49] this obliged us to retrace our steps and pass the night in the camp we had started from. But it happened thus by a stroke of divine providence, in order that we might be able to celebrate the feast of St. Francis Xavier in goodly company, for we met at that spot several Christian Hurons, who assisted at the holy sacrifice of mass.[50]

On the following day I came to the camp, which the Indians whom I sought, and with whom I was to spend the winter, had left not long before. There I saw the traces of their good hunting, the skins and offal of the bears, deer and wild turkeys they had killed; of the pike and other fish they had caught. This gave joy to our folks; but I felt very sad upon seeing a large dog suspended at the top of a painted pole—a sacrifice they had offered to the sun. We turned the whole thing over, broke the pole, and threw the dog into the river, together with the skin of an uncommonly large and hideous bear's head, which had also been offered up. After that, we went on our knees to ask pardon of God, and to pray for those poor Indians, who not as yet being Christians, consider the sun as a divine being to whom they address themselves in their necessities.

On the 4th of December we came to a place where the river divides into two branches.[51] This is properly the country of the Sacs, very advantageous for the chase. There are all sorts of beasts there—stags, deer, bears, raccoons and other game. Wild fowl abound. You see there large groves of wild apple trees, and very tall walnut trees, whose fruits are larger than those of France. They are of a longish shape, and like middle-size oranges.

On the shore of this river we saw certain trees of uncommon beauty. They are taller and larger than oaks, quite bushy, and have a scaly

[48] "This fine river which, first of all streams in Lower Michigan, bore on its water an envoy of the Savior, is the Saginaw, beyond the shadow of a doubt."

[49] This branch was undoubtedly the Tittabawassee.

[50] "There, then, or at any event, somewhere between Saginaw City and the junction of the Flint and Shiawassee, the holy sacrifice was offered up for the first time in the interior of Lower Michigan, December 3rd, 1675."

[51] "The Tittabawassee is the only tributary, or head stream, of the Saginaw that divides into what may properly be called branches (i.e., streams of about equal size), at a sufficient distance from the mouth of the Cass to account for the length of the journey, as described in the journal."

bark.[52] As the leaves were all fallen, we have seen only the fruit they bear. These are quite round, and hang to the branches by slender stems of a finger's length.

Pursuing our journey on one of the branches of the river,[53] without meeting either falls or rapids, we arrived at last, on the 7th of December, the eve of the Immaculate Conception of the Blessed Virgin, at the place where we were to spend the winter.[54] There I found the Indians who, having waited for me with impatience, now welcomed me with great joy.

Our cabin was soon built, and the chapel likewise. Three logs of a large oak formed the foundation on which the latter was raised in the form of a bower.[55] The floor, the walls, and the vault were only of bark; but within it Our Lord was pleased to be honored throughout the winter, perhaps more than in the sumptuous edifices of Europe. On the very evening of my arrival, I went into every cabin to prepare the Indians for the feast of the following day, and to begin our mission under the favorable auspices of the Glorious Virgin.

I am unable to describe the consolation I felt on the morrow in celebrating our adorable mysteries in our chapel, on a spot so far off, in the midst of these great woods, and there administering the Sacraments to such as were worthy of them. O, vocation for these dear missions, how precious thou art! Among thy pains and fatigues, what treasures dost thou conceal! Oh, what a good reason had the late Father Marquette, of blessed memory, who died quite near this spot, for binding himself by a vow never to abandon these rude but amiable missions, unless holy obedience should recall him! God granted him the grace to die in them. Oh! what a happiness.

Since that time I was able every day to say Mass, whereat all the Indians presented themselves, according as their hunts enabled them; and to give instructions more conveniently than in the cabins.

God has been pleased to use this chapel for the working of some extraordinary cures. Besides the healing of two children, who, upon some

[52] The shagbark hickory.
[53] The branch on which the party pursued their journey was the Chippewa River.
[54] "Three or four days' travel (from the forenoon of Dec. 4th to the afternoon of Dec. 7th) may have brought the party well-nigh up into the western part of Isabella County (the neighborhood of Bloomfield or Sherman City), if not still nearer to the headwaters of the river in the northwest corner of Mecosta County.

There, then, in the centre of the peninsula, the first humble edifice was raised for the worship of God, and consecrated by the preaching of the Gospel and by the holy sacrifice; being most befittingly built by the owners of the soil, and occupied by a member of that society which was first, in time and zeal, to carry the tidings of salvation to the Indians in the northern part of our country."
[55] "The chapel was built in the usual bower shape, like an inverted cradle, on three sills, the fourth being dispensed with for the sake of easier access; the whole front probably serving as door, and being covered, after the Indian fashion, with the skins of bear or other large animals. The light entered through an opening in the roof, which also served for the escape of the smoke, if the commodity of a fire was considered necessary."

prayers, were delivered from dysentery, I here note two cures by which Our Lord has shown how much He approves of our addressing ourselves to the Holy Virgin and His Saints, in order to obtain what we are praying for. A little boy of 10 or 11 years, called Francis, being very low with a violent headache and strong fever, was brought by his grandmother to our chapel. This good woman, full of faith, thus spoke to me: "I bring thee my sick grandchild. I have recourse, for his cure, to nothing but the prayer. He has already once been cured by this means; I hope he thus shall be again." Her prayer was granted; for, when after Mass I recited a Gospel over him, he was perfectly restored, and on the following day, I saw him free from every ailment.

A similar boon has been accorded to a pagan woman, whom her husband, of the Missisagué tribe, brought hither from the grounds where his clansmen were. She was very sick, as I could see on the day of her arrival when I visited her. I gave her a little treacle, and began to instruct her with a view to prepare her for baptism. I continued my instruction for three days, and seeing that her illness would not abate, I felt strongly incited to recommend to her a supernatural remedy, that is, to take in water, on three days, a little of the dust I had from the grotto of Manresa, where St. Ignatius performed his penance; and upon her having five times invoked the Holy Name of Jesus, and five times the name of His Holy Mother, and begged of that great saint to obtain for her the restoration of her health and the grace of being baptized, her prayer was heard, and she felt perfectly restored. Three days later she came to our chapel to thank Our Lord, and there to receive holy baptism.

We celebrated Christmas in a very devout manner. Having constructed a little crib at the side of our altar, our Christians went thither at midnight and during the day to make these forests resound with their hymns in honor of the new-born Jesus. What a joy for us, both at the midnight Mass and at that of the day to see the Infant Jesus recognized by the Indians in this land, where the demon has held sway for so long a time!

My mission was not confined to the Indians who wintered on the same grounds with me, but I extended it by making excursions to those who hunted in the neighborhood. For this purpose I started on the 29th of December for the quarters of the Nipissing Indians, nine or ten leagues further in the woods, in order to pray with them and instruct them.

On that journey I saw the great destruction of timber caused by the beaver in those regions where they are not hunted. I found a great number of lodges with several stories, and constructed in a manner that made us admire the skill and strength of these animals in cutting great trees with their teeth and dragging and adjusting them so adroitly that they are very comfortably lodged therein.

I made a second excursion as far as the Missisagués, at several days' journey from our quarters. The cold was very severe then. It was about the month (the middle?) of January. The nights, especially, being bitingly cold, afforded us precious opportunities to earn something for heaven. At last, I reached the Indians, and without delay visited their lodges to see what could be done for religion. I found a sick person to instruct, and three new-born children to baptize. I spent some days in catechizing, teaching from lodge to lodge, and preparing some catechumens for baptism.

I made some other journeys yet, after which, returning to my quarters, I learned that a sick catechumen had had recourse to the sun, by the sacrifice of a dog offered to him by hanging it on the top of a long pole. I reprimanded him as he deserved, and also those who had co-operated in this impiety. I commanded them, in order to repair their fault, to construct a large cross, and plant it on the shore of the river, opposite the chapel, which they did; and after I had blessed it, the guilty parties came to make amends to Jesus Christ, and to ask pardon of God, recognizing Him as the absolute Master and sovereign Lord of all creatures, and especially of the sun, whom He had created but for our use. After this, all the Christians saluted the cross by singing in their own language, *O crux ave.*

I continued in my functions till the middle of March, teaching the pagans, preparing the catechumens for baptism, and baptizing the children and such adults as I found worthy of that sacrament.

Finally, the season proper for our return coming on, I concluded this winter mission by a solemn act of thanksgiving, which I made all our Indians offer up to God for having passed the winter so devoutly, and with that abundance of game which God had granted them. They easily recognized the greatness of this benefit by comparing it with what had happened to those that did not belong to our band, for we learned that among the Missisagué Indians, who had parted with us to hunt at a distance of several days' journey from where we were, sixty-five had died of hunger. My consolation in this disaster was that there were many children and adults among them who had been baptized.

Such, Reverend Father, has been the result of my wintering in the woods. If I had, during that time, something to suffer for the salvation of these poor savages, it was not without experiencing much joy and consolation in seeing Our Lord so greatly honored in a country where he had never before been glorified by a creature endowed with reason.

There are few pages in missionary literature to compare with this idyl of priestly zeal and ministration. It leads to speculation as to what might have been accomplished had the missionaries been left unhampered in their efforts to civilize and christianize the Indian. This episode marks the golden age of the Ottawa mission, a period lasting about twenty years. During it, in the comparative isolation of the northern lake region, the missionaries had no other obstacles to overcome but the ignorance and the innate savagery of a primitive people. In this they might have been successful as the narrative just quoted abundantly proves. But the missionaries were doomed to failure, and that because of the sins of their own countrymen. The increasing number of French traders who combed the West for furs demoralized the Indian by the liquor traffic with all its attendant debauchery and corruption. The missionaries gradually lost their influence over the Indian, and were unsupported by those in power in the government, who brooked no interference with their profits.

When Cadillac came to Mackinac as commandant in 1694, the breaking point had been reached. Some time between that date and 1700 the mission at the Sault was abandoned. There was open hostility between Cadillac and the Jesuits; but that will be dealt with in another chapter. The labors of the valiant men from Ménard onward were swept away in a flood of greed and licentiousness. To remain became impossible. In 1705 the Fathers set fire to the mission buildings at St. Ignace to prevent their profanation, and returned to Quebec.[56]

The Ottawa mission has been dealt with summarily but sufficiently for the purpose in view, that of tracing the genesis of Catholic life in the State of Michigan. We must now leave the northern area for a while to follow the course of events in the southern peninsula which preceded the actual founding of Detroit.[57]

[56] *The Michigan Historical Collections,* XXXIII, 275–76

[57] It is to be regretted that there has been thus far no adequate treatment in English of the Ottawa Mission. Even Rochemonteix, considering the vast field he covered, could not give it too much attention.

CHAPTER III

The Sulpicians

WHILE the Jesuits were establishing and developing their missions in northern Michigan important events were taking place along the lower waterways. To narrate them an entirely new cast of characters must be introduced.

In 1637 there lived in Paris a young priest, born a few months after Champlain had founded Quebec, and who owed his vocation to the encouragement and prayers of St. Francis de Sales. He had received his classical training from the Jesuits at Lyons, and had afterwards come to Paris to study theology at the Sorbonne. For a while he had endangered the career which the saint had pointed out to him by leading a worldly life, and by the pride which he took in the display of his brilliant talents. An attack of partial blindness had chastened him. The vainglorious student had been transformed into Jean-Jacques Olier, the priest. In centuries to come his name would be known throughout the world for the system of seminary training he was to institute in his parish of St. Sulpice. Just now his imagination was fired by the missionary reports coming in from Canada, and he felt himself strongly called to take an active part in the conversion of the Indians in New France.

At this juncture there came to Paris Jérôme le Royer de la Dauversière, tax collector at La Flèche in the Sarthe. For two or three years he had been mulling over the beginning of a distinctively religious colony in Canada, to whose establishment he believed he had been divinely called. A pious layman in ordinary circumstances, and the father of six children, he could see no way to carry out this mission that had been entrusted to him. In the hope that Providence would somehow enlighten him he had decided to seek counsel in Paris. He happened to meet Father Olier, and, as their biographers tell us, the instant their eyes met the two were miraculously aware of their mutual interest. Dauversière's project was precisely the outlet for his zeal which Olier had been seeking, and he threw himself whole-heartedly into the enterprise. Without much difficulty a few wealthy patrons were induced to finance the missionary venture, and thus was founded the Society of Notre Dame de Montreal.

It would be difficult to find in all missionary history anything to parallel the aim and spirit of the Gentlemen of Montreal, as the members of the Society were called. It was proposed to establish in the very heart of the Canadian wilderness, as then known, a colony whose sole purpose should be the glory of God and the conversion of the Indian. There was to be no trade nor commerce of any sort. On virgin soil was to arise a new Christian community whose members were to revive in their lives the spirit of the primitive church. Three religious congregations were to be founded: one of priests to evangelize the Indian, another of teaching sisters to instruct the children of both the natives and the colonists, and a third of hospital nuns to care for the afflicted. In fact, Dauversière, even before his meeting with Olier, and in anticipation of some day realizing his project, had already begun at La Flèche an association of pious women to nurse the sick. The colonists were to till the soil and teach the art of agriculture to the Indian converts. A body of soldiers was to protect and police the settlement.

The site of this establishment was to be on the Island of Montreal. From the early days of the Canadian colony it had been considered as a possible and advantageous location for settlement; but the inroads of the Iroquois, from which even Quebec itself was not safe, made any venture at Montreal too hazardous. It lay on the confines of the Indian country and had no natural means of defense. Now, the Gentlemen of Montreal would make the venture. Aided by the Jesuits they obtained the island from de Lauson, the former president of the Hundred Associates, and the grant was confirmed by the King.

The founders of the Society realized that the man chosen to act as military leader and civil governor of the settlement would have to be endowed with unusual qualities and abilities. While they were deliberating on whom to approach, Paul de Chomedy, Sieur de Maisonneuve, was discovering the *Relations* of the Jesuits. An able soldier who had seen much warfare, he was at the same time a pious man untouched by the contagion of his surroundings. The soldier, who in his spare time practiced on the lute to escape the temptations of idleness, was now inspired to use his talents for God as well as for his king. Through a Jesuit who had returned from Canada he was introduced to Dauversière. When the aims of the Gentlemen of Montreal were broached to him there was no hesitation on his part, or on the part of the Society.

Provided with ample funds the Society now proceeded to carry out its project. In July, 1641, Maisonneuve was ready to sail. But the personnel of the expedition was not yet complete. There was need of a woman of uncommon ability to act both as housekeeper for the colonists, and as nurse in time of sickness. To Rochelle had lately come, moved by interior promptings to undertake some work as yet unknown to her, Mademoiselle Jeanne Mance. Once she had been brought to the notice of the Society her fitness was as evident as the inspiration by which she had been led. She was thirty-four when she left with Maisonneuve for Montreal, and she served until her death where her name is even now held in benediction.

The expedition arrived so late in the fall that the colonists were obliged to spend the winter in Quebec. There, every effort was made to deter the leader from carrying out his enterprise. Montmagny, the governor, invited him to an assembly of leading citizens, who pointed out the dangers that would confront him at Montreal, and contrasted them with the attractive features of the location they were ready to offer him on the Island of Orleans just below Quebec. But Maisonneuve was resolute. "I have not come to deliberate but to act. If every tree on the island of Montreal were changed into an Iroquois I would still be in duty and in honor bound to establish my colony there."

Early in May, Maisonneuve and his company, together with the governor and a little band of Jesuits, set out for their promised land. On the seventeenth they caught their first glimpse of the island with its somber forests and its flower-spangled shores. The next morning they landed, and Maisonneuve followed by the rest fell to his knees in joyful thanksgiving. Some one broke out into a hymn, and in an instant the whole company was singing in a burst of religious fervor. Mass was offered, and after it the Blessed Sacrament was exposed to the daylong devotion of the colonists. Thus passed the first day at Villemarie, and when the fires had died down and everyone was asleep, a score of fireflies, captives in a jar of glass, gleamed before the first tabernacle in Montreal.[1]

We cannot linger over the fascinating story of Villemarie. But some reference to its founding was necessary to explain the origin of another current of missionary endeavor that touched, if ever so lightly, the shores of Michigan. The project of the Gentlemen of Montreal was never fully realized, and many years elapsed before it reached some semblance of the original conception. Dauversière went back to La Flèche to strengthen his little community; but it was not until 1659 that some of them left France to begin their work in

---

[1] The foregoing résumé is taken from Faillon, op. cit., I, 379–440. The same story, but marred by his dour prejudice, will be found in Parkman, The Jesuits in North America, Chap. XV.

Montreal. With them came the first teaching sisters, led by Marguerite Bourgeoys, to establish the famous Congregation of Notre Dame. Father Olier, despite his early enthusiasm for the Canadian missions, had been diverted into the work of establishing seminaries, and the priests whom he had gathered around him were thus employed. The Jesuits, who had said the first Mass for the colonists, generously continued their ministrations in Villemarie.

Maisonneuve, however, was not satisfied with this temporary arrangement, and in 1665 he undertook a journey to France with the express purpose of forcing Father Olier to abide by the original plans of the Society.[2] In this he was successful, and in 1657 four Sulpicians, three priests and a deacon, arrived in Canada led by Father Gabriel de Queylus as superior. They were the pioneers of that long line of priests, molded in the spirit of Olier, who have rendered such distinctive service to the Church in Canada.

The record of the missionary work among the Indians accomplished by the Sulpicians is not a long one. As we have seen, Bishop Laval had confided the Indian missions to the Jesuits as their special field. Nevertheless in 1668 he sent two Sulpicians, Fathers Trouvé and de Fénelon, to begin a mission among the Iroquois who had moved out of New York to the northern shore of Lake Ontario in the neighborhood of Kingston. This mission was maintained for about ten years, and many of the Indians were subsequently removed to the Island of Montreal.[3] Almost a century later the Abbé Picquet began the famous Presentation mission on the site of the present Ogdensburg, New York.[4] But there is no telling how extensive the Sulpician beginnings might have become had everything gone according to plan on the memorable journey undertaken by François Dollier de Casson.

The Sulpician just named was one of the most striking figures among the early Canadian clergy. After a brilliant college course he had entered the army, where he had served with distinction under the great Turenne. Later he had abandoned all worldly prospects to embrace the priesthood in the community of St. Sulpice. Coming to Canada in 1666 he immediately became an outstanding personage in the Colony. A giant in stature and in strength, who could hold up two men in his outstretched hands, he was no less remarkable for his warm and engaging personality.[5]

[2] Faillon, *op. cit.*, II, 268–70.
[3] Shea, *Hist. of the Ind. Miss* . . . , 308–11; Harris, *op. cit.*, 297 ff.
[4] Shea, *The Cath. Church in Col. Days*, 614–18.
[5] For an interesting description of Dollier de Casson see Parkman, *The Old Regime in Canada*, Chap. XIV.

While his confreres were beginning their mission near the Bay of Quinte Dollier de Casson was sent to spend the winter among a band of Nipissing Indians. The chief with whom he lodged had an Indian slave from the unknown region far to the southwest. Sent on an errand to Montreal the slave met the Abbé de Queylus.[6] The latter was so impressed by what he heard concerning unknown tribes and unexplored country that he made the slave the bearer of a letter to the missionary, wherein he pointed out the opportunity of opening a new mission field if the slave could be persuaded to lead the way to his own people. The missionary welcomed the suggestion, made every effort to learn the Indian's language, and finally exacted the desired promise. In the spring the priest returned to Montreal to begin preparations for his journey to the West.

Dollier de Casson's project happened to coincide with a new and enlightened policy which was beginning to direct the destinies of New France. In 1663 the charter of the Hundred Associates had been surrendered to the Crown, which from that time on had assumed direct control of the Canadian colonies. Under the great Colbert, minister to Louis XIV, the value of Canada as a French possession began to be appreciated. The home government became acutely conscious of the English on the Atlantic seaboard, and of the Spaniards to the south and west, and determined to forestall their expansion. The idea of a French empire in the western world began to take hold.

The results of this new policy of consolidation were soon apparent. The military and civil administration of the Colony was reorganized. Stringent regulations regarding trade were passed with the object of building up important centers of commerce. The great river known to exist somewhere in the interior was to be explored to determine whether it opened a new route to China, or whether it connected with the Gulf of Mexico. Missionary enterprise was stimulated by admitting new groups to labor alongside the Jesuits. New settlements were organized, and troops were sent at the King's expense to protect them. The copper mines known to exist along the shores of Lake Superior were to be developed, and some easy route for bringing the ore to Montreal had to be found.

Into this ambitious program Dollier's venture was to be fitted. He went to Quebec to seek the approval of Bishop Laval and to obtain faculties, which were granted to him on May 15, 1669. On his formal visit to Courcelles, the Governor, he found his project warmly endorsed. He was urged, however, to accompany another expedition

---

[6] The Abbé de Queylus was back again in Montreal, but now as Superior of the Sulpicians. The old troubles were forgotten.

which was just then preparing for the exploration of the southwest under the leadership of La Salle.[7]

> It was at this place that M. de Courcelles requested him to unite with M. de la Salle, a brother of M. Cavelier, in order that they might together make the journey M. de la Salle had been long premeditating towards a great river, which he had understood (by what he thought he had learned from the Indian) had its course towards the west, and at the end of which, after seven or eight months' traveling, these Indians said the land was "cut," that is to say, according to their manner of speaking, the river fell into the sea. The river is called in the language of the Iroquois, "Ohio." On it are settled a multitude of tribes, from which as yet no one has been seen here, but so numerous are they that, according to the Indians' report, a single nation will include 15 or 20 villages. The hope of beaver, but especially of finding by this route the passage into the Vermillion Sea, into which M. de la Salle believed the river Ohio emptied, induced him to undertake this expedition, so as not to leave to another the honor of discovering the passage to the South Sea, and thereby the way to China.
>
> M. de Courcelles, the Governor of this country, was willing to support the project, in which M. de la Salle showed him some probability by a great number of fine speeches, of which he has no lack. But in short, this expedition tended to a discovery that could not be otherwise than glorious to the person under whose government it was made, and, moreover, it was costing him nothing.[8]

From the foregoing it can be inferred that the Sulpician superior had already discerned the disagreeable qualities which marred the character of the great adventurer, and he distrusted him. While conforming to the governor's wishes the Abbé de Queylus was determined that his missionaries should not find themselves stranded in the wilderness by some whim of La Salle's. He had chosen Father Michel Barthelmy to accompany Dollier; but at this turn of events he replaced him with a deacon, René Bréhant de Galinée. The reason for the substitution is evident from the latter's statement: "I had already some smattering of mathematics, enough to construct a map in a sort of fashion, but still sufficiently accurate to enable me to find my way back again from any place I might go to in the woods and streams of this country." [9]

The sagacity of the Superior was justified for, as we shall see, La Salle and the missionaries did go their separate ways. Fortunately for us Galinée was a keen and careful observer, and the record of the itinerary of the two Sulpicians is one of the most interesting journals

---

[7] La Salle will be dealt with at greater length in the following chapter.

[8] Quoted from Galinée's narrative to be mentioned presently, p. 5.

[9] *Ibid.*, 7.

of exploration that have come down to us.[10] To him belongs the distinction of having made the first map of the southern shore of Lake Ontario and the northern shore of Lake Erie from personal observation.[11]

On July 5, 1669, the combined parties left Montreal. In all there were seven canoes, piled high with baggage and holding twenty-one men. Ahead of them went two canoes manned by Seneca Indians. They had been visiting in Montreal, and it was their stories which had fired La Salle to begin his search for the Ohio. Thirty-seven days later, having followed along the south shore of Lake Ontario, the canoes came to Irondequoit Bay in the neighborhood of which lay a Seneca village. Here it was hoped that guides could be obtained; but the Indians tried to dissuade the Frenchmen from going any farther. After a month of futile effort the Frenchmen went on, guided by an Iroquois from the western end of the lake, who agreed to direct them by the easiest route to the Ohio.

They passed the mouth of the Niagara River, where they heard the roar of the cataract, and proceeded to the head of Burlington Bay. A few miles inland, near the present village of Westover, there was an Indian settlement called Tinawatawa. Here the travelers were well received and found an Indian guide who promised to take them to the Ohio in a few weeks. They were about to continue their journey when, to their amazement, they learned that there were two Frenchmen in a neighboring village. A meeting soon followed, and according to the narrative the Sulpicians had a long conference with "Monsieur Jolliet." The identity of the Frenchman is not without interest. It has generally been assumed that he was Louis Jolliet, who was later to explore the Mississippi with Marquette. However, in the light of recent investigation it is much more probable that it was Adrien, a brother of Louis, with whom the missionaries conferred.[12]

Jolliet was returning to Quebec from Lake Superior whither he had been sent by the government to make a study of the copper deposits. An Iroquois prisoner whom he had saved from torture at the hands of the Ottawa had offered to show him a hitherto unknown passage to the St. Lawrence. It proved to be the straits connecting Lake Huron with Lake Erie. Jolliet is therefore the first white man known to have paddled down the Detroit River. After entering Lake Erie he had followed the northern shore for a considerable distance

10 The journal of the expedition at present preserved in the Bibliothèque Nationale in Paris was translated and edited by James H. Coyne in *Papers and Records of the Ontario Historical Society* (Toronto, 1903), Vol. IV. The account given in the text and the quotations are taken from this edition.

11 Galinée is careful to state that his map details only his own observations.

12 See Jean Delanglez, S.J., "Louis Jolliet—Early Years," in *Mid-America*, XXVII, 3–29.

and then, in fear of roving Indians, had hidden his canoe and made his way overland to the western end of Lake Ontario.

When Jolliet had heard what the Sulpicians were planning he drew for them a rough sketch of the route he had followed. But he had more interesting news for Dollier de Casson. While in the north he had heard of a numerous tribe living to the southwest called the Potawatomi. No missionary had as yet visited them although they were said to be well disposed to listen to the new teaching. Here at last was a definite objective for the missionary; he would find the Potawatomi and begin his missions among them.

At this point La Salle balked. The missionaries could search for the Potawatomi and the Mississippi if they wished; he had started out to find the Ohio. Moreover, he had contracted some sort of fever while hunting and was uncertain about continuing his explorations. The narrative gives as the cause of the fever the sight of a few rattlesnakes which he had encountered, a statement palpably untrue but showing that to the Sulpicians La Salle was not too heroic a figure. In short, the expedition broke up, La Salle going his way, and the missionaries deciding to follow Jolliet's directions.[13]

> The last day of September, M. Dollier said Holy Mass for the second time in this village, when most of us, as well on M. de la Salle's side as on ours, received the Sacrament in order to unite in our Lord at a time when we saw ourselves on the point of separating. Hitherto we had never failed to hear Holy Mass three times a week, which M. Dollier said for us on a little altar prepared with paddles on forked sticks and surrounded with sails from our canoes.[14]

Including the priest and the deacon the party now comprised about nine men. With three canoes they left the village of Tinawatawa and made their way to the Grand River, which they descended to its outlet in Lake Erie. Toward the end of October, as they were coasting along the northern shore of the lake, they realized that winter would soon be upon them making travel impossible. Coming to the mouth of a little stream they ascended it for some distance and there built their winter quarters.[15] Against a hill they constructed a small granary and stored it with bushels of walnuts and chestnuts, apples and berries. From an abundance of wild grapes they made wine for Mass. Galinée gives us a charming glimpse of their snug retreat.

[13] No one knows with certainty just where La Salle went after parting from the Sulpicians.

[14] Galinée narrative, 49.

[15] They wintered just above the forks where Black Creek joins the River Lynn, otherwise known as Patterson's Creek, at Port Dover, Ontario. The exact spot was identified in August, 1900, when the outlines of the buildings were still evident. Editor's note to the narrative, xxv.

We erected a pretty altar at the end of our cabin, where we had the happiness to hear Holy Mass three times a week without missing, with the consolation you may imagine of finding ourselves with our good God in the midst of the woods where no European had ever been. Monsieur Dollier often told us that that winter ought to be worth to us, as regards our eternal welfare, more than the best ten years of our life. We confessed often, received holy communion as well. In short, we had our parochial mass, holydays and Sundays, with the necessary instructions; prayer evening and morning, and every other Christian exercise. Orison was offered with tranquility in the midst of this solitude, where we saw no stranger for three months. . . .[16]

They remained about five months in their winter quarters until the ice in the lake had melted sufficiently to allow them to proceed. On Passion Sunday, March 23, 1670, the whole party went down to the lake shore to erect a cross in memory of their safe sojourn in the wilderness, and to offer their prayers of thanksgiving. To the cross they affixed the royal coat of arms, and a formal declaration that they thereby took possession of all the surrounding country in the name of the King.

We, the undersigned, certify that we have seen, on the lands of the lake named Erie, the arms of the King of France attached (to the foot of a Cross) with this inscription: "The year of Salvation 1669, Clement IX seated in the chair of St. Peter, Louis XIV reigning in France, Monsieur de Courcelles being Governor of New France, and Monsieur Talon being intendant therein for the King, there arrived in this place two Missionaries (of the Seminary) of Montreal, accompanied by seven other Frenchmen, who the first of all European people have wintered on the lake, of which they have taken possession in the name of their King, as of unoccupied territory, by affixing his arms which they have attached here to the foot of this Cross." In testimony whereof we have signed the present certificate.
    Francois Dollier, Priest of the Diocese of Nantes, in Brittany.
    De Galinée, Deacon of the Diocese of Rennes, in Brittany.[17]

Three days later they resumed their journey meeting unexpected hardships until they finally camped on the sands of Point Pelee. Here occurred a most serious mishap which upset all the plans of the missionaries. We let Galinée tell the story in his own words.

We landed there on a beautiful sand beach on the east side of the point. We had made that day nearly twenty leagues, so we were all very much tired. That was the reason why we did not carry all our packs up on the high ground, but left them on the sand and carried our canoes up on the high ground.

[16] Narrative, 55.
[17] Ibid., 76.

Night came on, and we slept so soundly that a great north-east wind rising had time to agitate the lake with so much violence that the water rose six feet where we were, and carried away the packs of M. Dollier's canoe that were nearest the water, and would have carried away all the rest if one of us had not awoke. Astonished to hear the lake roaring so furiously, he went to the beach to see if the baggage was safe, and seeing that the water already came as far as the packs that were placed the highest, cried out that all was lost. At this cry we rose and rescued the baggage of my canoe, and of one of M. Dollier's. Pieces of bark were lighted to search along the water, but all that could be saved was a keg of powder that floated; the rest was carried away. . . . But the worst of all was that the entire service was lost. We waited for the wind to go down and the waters to retire, in order to go and search along the water, whether some debris of the wreck could not be found. But all that was found was a musketoon and a small bag of clothes belonging to one of the men; the rest was lost beyond recall. . . .

This accident put it out of our power to have the aid of the sacraments or to administer them to the rest. So we took counsel together to know whether we ought to stop with some tribe to carry on our mission there, or should return to Montreal for another altar service, and other goods necessary to obtain provisions, with a view to returning afterwards and establishing ourselves in some spot, and this suggestion seemed to us the best. As the route to the Ottawas seemed to us almost as short from the place where we were as the way we had come, and as we proposed to reach Sainte-Marie of the Sault, where the Ottawas assemble in order to descend in company, before they should leave, we thought we should descend with them more easily. Add to this, moreover, that we were better pleased to see a new country than to turn back.[18]

We cannot help musing over what the course of history in the lake region might have been had this accident not occurred. If the Potawatomi had been reached it is quite possible that the Sulpicians might have been the first explorers on the Mississippi, for they would soon have been aware of its nearness to them, Moreover, had they been successful in establishing a mission among the Potawatomi their brethren in Montreal might have gone to great lengths to maintain and extend it. Thus there might have arisen a chain of missions to a great extent immune from the influences that wrecked the Jesuit posts.

We pursued our journey accordingly toward the west, and after making about 100 leagues on Lake Erie arrived at the place where the Lake of the Hurons, otherwise called the *Fresh Water Sea* of the Hurons, or Michigan, discharges into this Lake. This outlet is perhaps half a league in width and turns sharp to the north-east, so that we were almost re-

18 *Ibid.,* 65–67.

tracing our path. At the end of six leagues we discovered a place that is very remarkable, and held in veneration by all the Indians of these countries, because of a stone idol that nature has formed there. To it they say they owe their good luck in sailing on Lake Erie, when they cross it without accident, and they propitiate it by sacrifices, presents of skins, provisions, etc., when they wish to embark upon it. The place was full of camps of those who had come to pay their homage to this stone, which had no other resemblance to the figure of a man than what the imagination was pleased to give it. However, it was all painted, and a sort of face had been formed for it with vermillion. I leave you to imagine whether we avenged upon this idol, which the Iroquois had strongly recommended us to honor, the loss of our chapel. We attributed to it even the dearth of provisions from which we had hitherto suffered. In short, there was nobody whose hatred it had not incurred. I consecrated one of my axes to break this god of stone, and then having yoked our canoes together we carried the largest pieces to the middle of the river, and threw all the rest also into the water, in order that it might never be heard of again.[19]

In this interesting episode we have, as far as we know, the record of the first time that a priest set foot within the territory of the present diocese of Detroit.[20] On his map Galinée locates the position of the idol on the American side of the river. Six leagues from Lake Erie would bring the party somewhere between the mouth of the Rouge River and the army post at Fort Wayne.[21]

That very same day the travelers killed a bear and a roebuck, and went on rejoicing into Lake St. Clair, or the Salt Water Lake, as it had been called in Sanson's map. They passed up through the river into Lake Huron, coasted along its eastern shore, and finally landed at Saint Ignace. After a short visit with the Jesuits they hired some experienced canoe men, and returning by the Ottawa River route reached Montreal on June 18, 1670.

Although Father Dollier fully intended to make another attempt to reach the Potawatomi he was caught up in the current of affairs at Villemarie. He became Superior of the seminary, vicar-general of the diocese, and died at Montreal in 1701. Galinée returned to France,

---

[19] In the *Relation* of 1671, Part III, Chap. V, Allouez notes the presence of another such idol near Green Bay. "We found a sort of idol that the Indians honor there never failing, when passing it, to offer it some kind of sacrifice either of tobacco, or of arrows, or of paints. . . . It is a rock whose natural formation resembles the torso of a man, and from a distance one apparently distinguishes a head, shoulders, breast, and especially the face that the passers-by ordinarily paint with their brightest colors. To do away with this occasion of idolatry, we had it dragged away by main strength and thrown to the bottom of the river nevermore to reappear."

[20] The episode marks as well the first recorded advent of white men to the site of Detroit.

[21] Clarence M. Burton, *The City of Detroit* (Detroit, 1922), I, 61–63.

where he died in 1678. The Indian missions in the western lake region remained the exclusive tenure of the Jesuits.

The missionary journey just described was the last *élan* of the zeal that had inspired the foundation of the Society of Notre Dame de Montreal. Only five of the original incorporators were left in 1663. Seeing itself faced with extinction the Society decided to transfer all its rights and privileges in the Island of Montreal to the spiritual sons of Father Olier. Accordingly, an act of donation was executed by which the Seminary of St. Sulpice in Paris became the sole owner of the colony at Villemarie and its appurtenances. After the Treaty of Paris, in 1763, the Seminary ceded its possessions in Canada to the Sulpicians of Montreal, who have held them in major part to this day.

CHAPTER IV

La Salle and the Recollects

THE tourist who goes down from the Great Lakes to Montreal by water knows the thrill of shooting the Lachine Rapids that swirl and foam past the town of the same name about eight miles above the city. But he may not know just how the name La Chine, or China, came to be applied to the locality. When the expedition described in the last chapter broke up at Tinawatawa, the majority of La Salle's men straggled back to Montreal while he pushed on into the wilderness. The stay-at-homes had no end of poking fun at the crestfallen voyageurs. What tidings of new lands did they bring? Had Monsieur La Salle, inflamed by his wild schemes of western discovery, taken them as far as China? The word caught the popular fancy; henceforth La Salle's men were "Chinamen," and his extensive domain above Montreal was "China." Dollier de Casson, who was not lacking a sense of humor, puts down the origin of the name in his *History of Montreal*, and Lachine it is to this day.[1]

It is perhaps ungracious to the memory of Canada's greatest explorer to recall the gibings of his neighbors and contemporaries, but at least they point to an estimate of him that reflects the strange blending of conflicting elements which interweave in the pattern of his life-story. In La Salle were dauntless courage and determination, integrity and nobility of purpose; but in him were arrogance and harshness, a feverish desire for continued movement, and, most significant of all, the delusion of persecution by the Jesuits to whose Society he had once belonged.[2] With this enigmatic personality we must deal at some length because of his connection with our local history, and of some details of his early life not usually adverted to.

René-Robert Cavelier, the descendant of a rich and honorable family, and in later life known as the Sieur de La Salle, was born at Rouen, November 22, 1643. At the age of fifteen he entered the Society of Jesus, and after two years' novitiate pronounced his vows

[1] *Bulletin des Recherches Historiques*, XIX, 378–81.
[2] For conflicting views on La Salle's character compare Parkman's *La Salle . . . Discovery of the Great West* with Rev. Edward Jacker's estimate in the *Amer. Cath. Quat. Rev.*, III, 404 ff.

on October 10, 1660.[3] Because of his ardent devotion to the founder of the Society, the novice asked to be given his name, and was henceforth known to his confreres as Robert Ignatius Cavelier.

The next few years were spent in study and in teaching. Little by little the flaws which his novice master had discovered in La Salle, and endeavored to correct, grew more pronounced. He showed himself opinionated and stubborn, and lacked prudence in his dealings with his pupils. When reporting on the candidate's fitness to begin theology, in 1666, his Superior made the following notation: *Ingenium bonum, judicium tenue, prudentia parva.*[4]

Meanwhile, it was evident that in the daily round of duties prescribed by his rule the mind of La Salle found no peace. To allay his discontent frequent changes of occupation were accorded him, but his restlessness grew to such a point that he felt it necessary to sever himself completely from the scene of his scholastic life. Accordingly, on April 5, 1666, he wrote to the General asking to be sent to the foreign missions. To his request he received the only reply possible.

> I heartily approve the zeal that you are showing, and I urge you to maintain it courageously and to hold yourself as you are doing in the most perfect indifference. However, the time is not ripe for putting your design into execution, and you must not think of it at present. While you are waiting, strive to make yourself useful for the work of foreign missions which you ask; acquire the knowledge necessary for such a ministry.[5]

This letter with its mild rebuke could not have been very acceptable to La Salle. Following his entry into theology at La Flèche there were again outbursts of temper and unruliness. Against his own will, and despite honest efforts to conquer himself, the life became so distasteful to him that he determined upon a change at any cost. Twice he applied to the General for permission to prosecute his studies in Portugal, and when that was denied him he made formal application to be released from his vows, honorably exposing all the character defects which made it impossible to conform either to the spirit or to the duties of the Society.

On March 28, 1667, La Salle was definitely released from his religious vows, and returned to the world.[6] From that time on he displayed a growing antipathy to his former confreres somewhat difficult

---

[3] Rochemonteix, *op. cit.,* III, 42.

[4] "Of ordinarily good talent, judgment not too good, notably lacking in prudence."

[5] Rochemonteix, *op. cit.,* III, 45.

[6] "After a serious examination of the information you have sent us, we order you to dismiss from the Society Robert Ignace Cavelier . . ." Letter of the General to the Paris Provincial, January 28, 1667. Rochemonteix, *op. cit.,* III, 48.

to explain. Certainly he had no reason to complain of the treatment he had received while a member of the Society, nor is there any evidence that he openly did so. He had been shown extreme consideration and kindness, and every exception had been made in his favor. Perhaps his pride may have been deeply wounded by the consciousness of his unfitness to remain in the Society. He may have felt, if not shame, at least constraint in associating with men to whom he had once been bound in the closest fellowship, but from whom he had been obliged to sever his relations on account of what he himself termed his "moral infirmities." His is no isolated case of the corrosive effects of such thoughts and the revulsion of feeling which accompanies them.

The young man of twenty-four now put this crisis definitely behind him, and prepared to begin life anew. His brother, Jean Cavelier, a Sulpician, had gone to Canada the preceding year and was now stationed in Montreal. In the hope of getting a land grant through the good offices of his brother La Salle determined to follow him.

Arriving in the colony in 1667, he was not disappointed in his expectations. The Sulpicians gave him a large tract of virgin land, the one already mentioned, whose resources La Salle worked energetically to develop. He rented out his acres to the settlers who joined him, and built a palisade for protection against Indian attack. A supply of merchandise was laid in to attract the swarthy hunters who passed by with their furs on the way to the great mart at Montreal.[7]

The Indians fascinated him. He beheld them issuing out of an unknown hinterland which he tried vainly to imagine. Forgetful of his agricultural interests he spent much of his time questioning the individuals that chance brought to his door, and trying to master their languages. Gradually, to the exclusion of everything else, the lure of discovery took possession of him. When, in the fall of 1668, he heard from the lips of some passing Iroquois the description of a great river called the Ohio that emptied into the southern sea, his mind was made up. The petty details of his estate's administration could hold him no more than could the daily grind of teaching in the past. To a man of his temperament the call to honor and wealth must have proved irresistible.

His first venture, with Dollier de Casson, has already been described. The funds necessary for his outfitting were secured from the Sulpicians, who generously purchased from him the major portion of the lands they had given him two years before. But, as we have seen, they were far from putting implicit trust in either the ability or the

[7] For a description of La Salle's domain see Parkman's *La Salle,* Chap. I.

design of La Salle. When the break came, as was to be expected, at Tinawatawa between such strong characters as the explorer and the missionary the Sulpicians felt that their mistrust was justified. From now on their relations were not entirely cordial.[8] The strange fate that marred La Salle's efforts was already at work. With the Jesuits he would have no dealings, and he had now alienated the Sulpicians. Still, in a colony where Church and State were so closely associated, he needed the support of at least some churchmen to carry out his ambitious designs.

Fortunately for La Salle there was now another community to which he could ally himself, the Recollects. We have seen that when Canada was restored to France in 1632, only the Jesuits were permitted to return to the mission field. The Recollects never seemed to get over feeling that they had been unfairly excluded, and continued to watch for a favorable opportunity to return. That they finally did so resulted from a situation which can here only be outlined.

When the Company of the Hundred Associates gave up its charter to the King, in 1663, Louis XIV was obliged to create a new governing body for New France. This took the form of a Sovereign Council composed of the following members: a Governor and an Intendant, both named by the King; the Bishop, having equal authority with the Governor; five Councillors, an Attorney-General, and a Secretary, all to be chosen by the Bishop in concert with the Governor.[9]

For a while the new government functioned smoothly, and there was perfect accord between Bishop Laval and Saffray de Mésy, whom the King had appointed at the Bishop's request. But a clash of interests was inevitable. It came first over the question of tithes for the support of the Church, and then over that momentous problem which underlies so much of the history of New France, the liquor traffic with the Indian. The measures taken by the Bishop and the Jesuits in the name of decency and morality were looked upon as attempts to take the government into their own hands. The governor, resenting any diminution of his authority, acted in such arbitrary fashion that the King decided to remove him. Although de Mésy died before his successor arrived in Quebec, he had done enough complaining to set afoot a new policy. The life of the Jesuits was none too placid in the mother country as they were in the heat of their controversy against Jansenism. When Talon, the Intendant, arrived in Canada accompanied by de Courcelles, the new Governor, a portion of the instructions transmitted to him by Colbert read as follows:

[8] Rochemonteix, *op. cit.*, III, 61.
[9] For further details see Parkman's *The Old Regime in Canada,* Chap. X.

It is absolutely necessary to hold a just balance between the temporal authority which resides in the person of the King and his representatives, and the spiritual authority which resides in the person of the Bishop and the Jesuits, but in such a way that the latter remain inferior to the former.[10]

Talon, who had declared shortly after his arrival that he saw no reason for the hue and cry against the Jesuits and the Bishop, wrote to the minister only two years later, in 1667, repeating many of the old calumnies and suggesting that some of the Jesuits be recalled to France and be replaced by seculars, or by priests of another order. These fresh accessions to the ministry in Canada were to be authorized to administer the sacraments independently of the Bishop's jurisdiction.[11] The reason for this unusual provision, proposed as necessary to bring comfort to many consciences, was simply this, that the Bishop had pronounced sentence of excommunication against those who sold liquor to the Indians, and was, of course, upheld by all the clergy who received their faculties from him. In the minds of the Intendant and the Minister this stern morality had to be toned down if the commerce of Canada were not to suffer an irreparable loss. When Talon, after a year spent in France, returned to Canada in 1670 he brought with him three Recollect priests and two lay brothers.[12]

The motive which prompted the coming of the Recollects to Canada was plainly a motive hostile to Bishop Laval and the Jesuits. They came on the invitation, not of the Bishop, but of the civil authorities. We can assert that their coming was against his desire and his wishes; he had a thousand reasons to fear that they came to sow division in the Canadian church.[13]

Happily, the misgivings of the Bishop were not justified. It is true that some unpleasant incidents occurred, that the Recollects manifested more or less hostility to the Jesuits, and that they were always closer to the ruling powers than the rest of the clergy. It is likewise true that they may have erred by lending themselves to a policy which to some extent was directed against the authority of the

[10] Rochemonteix, op. cit., II, 341.
[11] Ibid., III, 86.
[12] Le Clercq, op. cit., II, 71–72. "The fleet being ready to sail weighed anchor in the latter part of May (1670) in company with Monsieur Talon, the intendant, and, after a pretty long and dangerous voyage of three months, arrived at last at Quebec, where our Fathers were received by Monsieur de Petraea, Monsieur de Courcelles, the Governor, by the reverend Jesuit Fathers, and a great crowd of settlers, with every mark of joy which could be expected in a country where our Fathers were desired with eagerness for so many years."
[13] Auguste Gosselin, op. cit., II, 81.

Church, but whose effects they most likely did not foresee. Nevertheless, the sons of St. Francis took up with zeal and enthusiasm the posts assigned them by the Bishop, and as they grew in number their devotion and simplicity won them a lasting place in the affections of the Canadian people.

In September, 1672, there landed at Quebec to begin his term of office the most distinguished governor in the history of New France, Louis de Buade, Count of Palluau and Frontenac. At the age of fifty, covered with military glory but penniless, he had accepted the new post offered him, "resolved to live and die in Quebec rather than starve to death in France." [14] Endowed with many qualities of a good administrator, and sincerely interested in the welfare and expansion of New France he might have brought peace to its troubled existence had not his new dignity gone to his head. His predecessors had signed themselves, "Governor and Lieutenant-General for the King"; he preceded the title by the words, "High and Puissant Lord." His first months were characterized by a series of reckless and arbitrary acts beyond the limits of his authority. For example, all priests were obliged to show a passport to travel from one village to another, and their mail to and from France was subject to his scrutiny. [15] Intensely jealous of his authority and prerogatives, he could brook no interference with his policies. [16]

It can readily be seen that the old difficulties would not be ironed out by a man of his stamp. As soon as the bishop and his clergy, resting on their legal rights, refused to conform to Frontenac's arbitrary display of power they were of course in his eyes resisting the government or seeking to control it. The Recollects, however, were the objects of his particular affection. He proclaimed himself their "Spiritual Father," and strove to increase their number and influence.

Given the basis of the quarrel between the religious and civil power, the astute governor realized how much his success depended upon attaching to his interests the prominent business men and fur traders of the Colony. The number of trading permits was fixed by law, but his favorites could obtain any number of them without difficulty. To the inner circle many restrictions could be done away with, especially if his complaisance were rewarded with a share of the profits. There is evidence that Frontenac was not above accepting such gratuities, and positive evidence that Fort Frontenac in addition to its military value was counted on to augment his personal fortune. [17]

[14] *Memoires de Saint-Simon* quoted by Rochemonteix, *op. cit.*, III, 96.
[15] Faillon, *op. cit.*, III, 493; Rochemonteix, *op. cit.*, III, 103.
[16] Charlevoix, (Shea ed.), III, 177.
[17] Parkman's *La Salle* . . . 101.

The foregoing rapid sketch of La Salle, the Recollects, and Frontenac, in which certain details have been stressed, shows how likely it was that they should be linked together in common enterprise. The governor and the explorer had many traits in common, and both were great enough to vision the scheme of empire which they strove to realize. They chafed against a restraint which they judged inimical to their interests; they both found willing helpers in a body of churchmen more pliant to their design, and who, unlike the Jesuits, had no definite policy to maintain at any cost.

In 1673, Frontenac held his important peace parley with the Iroquois at the mouth of the Cataraqui River. The English had been making heavy inroads into the fur trade. From Hudson Bay they were reaching out to all the tribes of the northern lake region, and the New England colonies and the Dutch, with the help of the Iroquois, were diverting trade that would otherwise have gone down the St. Lawrence. The necessity of a French outpost on Lake Ontario had already been seen by de Courcelles, and Frontenac decided to establish it. Not only would the English activities be cut at a vital point but, with the right man in charge, the governor might expect some increase in income to maintain the lavish style of living which he affected. The mission of sounding out the Indian chiefs and assuring their presence at the parley was confided to La Salle, who by his adroitness ensured the success of the governor's plans. Soon after the council fires had died down, the erection of Fort Frontenac was begun on the site of the present city of Kingston, Ontario.[18] La Salle remained as commander of the new post, and with him Father Gabriel de la Ribourde, a Recollect, was left as chaplain. The following year La Salle went to France, and with Frontenac's backing, succeeded in having the fort and the surrounding territory granted to him as the Seigneurie of Cataraqui.[19]

But, however advantageous his situation as Seigneur of Cataraqui, La Salle was not satisfied; the lure of western exploration beckoned him on. In 1677 he sailed for France to present to the King a memorial asking for an extension of his privileges, and for the authority to explore the unknown country to the west to find possible means of entry into Mexico. His petition was acceded to on May 12, 1678, and by September he was back in Canada beginning preparations for the great enterprise.

La Salle's plan included a daring innovation, a sailing vessel that would expedite travel over the inland seas, and would serve as a base

---

[18] *Ibid.*, Chap. VI for a description of the Council and the beginning of Fort Frontenac.

[19] Margry, *op. cit.*, I, 281-86.

for further land explorations. An advance party was sent out from Fort Frontenac to find a suitable location for a shipyard above the falls of Niagara. At the mouth of Cayuga Creek the ship carpenters set to work despite the evident displeasure of the Indians, who were determined to destroy whatever the workmen had it in mind to build.

On the 22th of the said Month (January 22, 1679) we went two Leagues above the great Fall of *Niagara,* where we made a Dock for Building the Ship we wanted for our Voyage. This was the most convenient place we could pitch upon, being upon a River which falls into the Streight between the Lake *Erie* and the great Fall of *Niagara.* The 26th, the Keel of the Ship and some other Pieces being ready, M. *de la Salle* sent the Master-Carpenter to desire me to drive in the first Pin; but my Profession obliging me to decline that Honour, he did it himself, and promised Ten *Louis d'Or's,* to encourage the Carpenter and further the Work. The Winter being not half so hard in the Country as in *Canada,* we employ'd one of the two Savages of the Nation call'd the *Wolf,* whom we kept for Hunting, in building some Cabins made of the Rinds of Trees; and I had one made on purpose to perform Divine Service therein on *Sundays,* and other occasions. . . .

When I return'd to our Dock, I understood that most of the *Iroquese* were gone to wage War with a Nation on the other side of Lake *Erie.* In the meantime, our Men continu'd with great Application to build our Ship; for the *Iroquese* who were left behind, being but a small number, were not so insolent as before, though they came now and then to our Dock, and expressed some Discontent at what we were doing. One of them in particular, feigning himself drunk, attempted to kill our Smith, but was vigorously repuls'd by him with a red-hot Iron-barr, which, together with the Reprimand he received from me, oblig'd him to be gone. Some few Days after, a Savage Woman gave us notice, that the Tsonnontouans had resolv'd to burn our Ship in the Dock, and had certainly done it, had we not been always upon our Guard.

The Ship was call'd the *Griffin,* alluding to the Arms of Count Frontenec which had two *Griffins* for *Supporters*; and besides, M. de la Salle us'd to say of this Ship, while yet upon the Stocks, That he would make the *Griffin* fly above the *Ravens.* We fir'd three Guns, and sung *Te Deum,* which was attended with loud Acclamations of Joy; of which those of the *Iroquese* who were accidentally present at this Ceremony, were also Partakers; for we gave them some Brandy to drink, as well as to our Men, who immediately quitted their Cabins of Rinds of Trees, and hang'd their Hammocks under the Deck of the Ship, there to lie with more security than a-shore. We did the like, insomuch that the very same Day we were all on board and thereby out of the reach of the Insults of the Savages.

But before we start out on the bosom of Lake Erie aboard *Le Griffon* we must become acquainted with the historian of the expedition, the writer of the foregoing passage. We shall see the course of events through his eyes, and it is he and his two clerical companions, rather than La Salle and his crew, who make the journey of the *Griffon* so important for the Catholic history of Michigan.[20]

Friar Louis Hennepin was born about 1640 in the little town of Ath, in Belgium, about twenty miles southeast of Tournai. While yet at school he felt, as he says, "a strong Inclination to retire from the World, and regulate my Life according to the Rules of pure and severe Virtue; and in compliance with this Humour, I entered into the *Franciscan Order,* designing to confine myself to an austere Way of living. . . ." As he grew older the pursuit of austerity palled somewhat, and he became obsessed with the desire to travel, and that, of course, only that he might thereby instruct the "Ignorant and the Barbarous." He goes on detailing his various transfers and occupations until he was sent to Calais during the herring season.

Being there, I was passionately in love with hearing the Relations that Masters of Ships gave of their Voyages. Afterwards I return'd to our Convent at *Biez,* by the way of *Dunkirk*; But I us'd oft-times to sculk behind the Doors of Victualling-Houses, to hear the Sea-men give an Account of their Adventures. The Smoak of Tobacco was offensive to me, and created Pain in my Stomach, while I was thus intent upon giving ear to their Relations; But for all I was very attentive to the Accounts they gave of their Encounters by Sea, the Perils they had gone through, and all the Accidents which befell them in their long Voyages. This Occupation was so agreeable and engaging, that I have spent whole Days and Nights at it without eating; for thereby I always came to understand some new thing, concerning the Customs and Ways of Living in remote Places; and concerning the Pleasantness, Fertility, and Riches of the Countries where these Men had been.[21]

At last the friar's longing was fulfilled when he received orders from his superior to repair to Canada as a missionary. He sailed from

[20] The reader may be aware that among historians Hennepin's reputation for veracity, to say the least, is not of the best. He has suffered the usual fate of those who are not content to let well enough alone. He had the first best seller on the doings of the French in America, and he certainly made the best of it. His *Description de la Louisiane Nouvellement Découverte* was published at Paris in 1683. This work is considered to be generally truthful, for Hennepin. He revamped the entire narrative, and published it at Utrecht in 1697 as the *Nouvelle Decouverte d'un très grand Pays situé dans l'Amerique.* This volume not only embroiders the first narrative, but records Hennepin's descent of the Mississippi to its mouth, something which he certainly did not do, and which directly contradicts his first account. As far as his journal bears on our local history there is no reason for questioning its veracity. The references here are to Shea's edition of the *Description* . . . (New York, 1880), and to Thwaite's edition of the *Nouvelle Découverte* . . . (Chicago, 1903). A competent study of Hennepin will be found in l'Abbé H. A. Scott, *Nos Anciens Historiographes* (Quebec, 1930).
[21] *Nouvelle Découverte,* 28-29.

Rochelle in 1675 on the same ship with Bishop Laval and La Salle. He most likely served as chaplain, for he says, "I performed the divine office every calm day, and we then sang the Itinerary in French set to music, after we had said our evening prayers." The ship was nearly captured by Turkish pirates, but after that episode the voyage was uneventful. On board there was a number of young women coming to Canada in the hope of finding husbands.

> This charge one day obliged me, while we were at sea, to censure several girls who were on board. . . . They made a great noise by their dancing and thus prevented the sailors from getting their rest at night; so that I was obliged to reprimand them severely, in order to oblige them to stop, and to observe due modesty and tranquility.
>
> This afforded the Sieur Robert Cavalier de la Salle an occasion of anger against me, which he never forgot. He made a show of wishing to uphold these girls in their amusement. He could not refrain from telling me one day somewhat angrily, that I acted like a pedant towards him and all the officers and persons of quality who were on the vessel, and who enjoyed seeing these girls dance, since I criticized them for trifles; but Mgr Francis de Laval, created first Bishop of Quebec, who made the voyage with us, having given me the direction of the girls, I thought that I had a right to reply to the Sieur de la Salle, that I had never been a pedant, a term, which as all the world knows, signifies a man of foolish and impertinent turn of mind, and who affects to display on all occasions, an ill digested learning. I added, moreover, that these girls were under my direction, and that I thus had a right to rebuke them and censure them as they took upon themselves too much liberty.
>
> This answer which I made with no other view than to show the said Sieur de la Salle that I was doing my duty, made him livid with anger, and in fact he raged violently against me. I contented myself with telling him, seeing him thus disposed against me, that he took things ill, and that I had no intention of offending him, as in fact it was not my design.
>
> Monsieur de Barrois, who had formerly been secretary to the French ambassador in Turkey, and who at this time filled the same post under the Count de Frontenac, seeing this affair, drew me aside, and told me that I had inadvertently put the Sieur de la Salle in a great passion, when I told him that I had never been a pedant, because he had plied the trade for ten or eleven years while he was among the Jesuits and that he had really been regent or teacher of a class among these religious.
>
> I replied to the Sieur de Barrois that I had said this very innocently; that I had never known that the Sieur de la Salle had lived in that famous order; that had I been aware of it, I should doubtless have avoided that word *pedant* in addressing him; that I knew it to be an offensive term, that, in fact, men generally expressed by it an "ill polished savant" according to the French expression of the Gentlemen of

Port Royal; that thus I should have avoided using that term had I been better informed than I was in regard to the life of the said Sieur de la Salle.[22]

On his arrival in Canada Hennepin was for a while given charge of scattered missions along the St. Lawrence. He describes himself as traveling from place to place on snowshoes, his portable chapel service strapped to his back, and his few belongings carried along on a dog sled. Later, he was sent as missionary to Fort Frontenac, where he and Father Luke Buisset erected a mission house and conducted a school for the French and Indian children.[23] He was in Quebec when La Salle returned from France in 1678, and to his great joy the explorer brought him a letter from the Provincial asking him to accompany La Salle on his impending western explorations.

He was one of the advance party which went to Niagara to start the building of the *Griffon*. Here he could indeed gratify the cravings of his early years by gazing with astonishment upon the great falls of Niagara. Although the Jesuits had mentioned them before, and the Sulpicians had been close enough to hear the roar of the cataract, it is quite certain that none of the missionaries had actually seen them. Hennepin was the first European to describe the falls from actual view, and to publish a picture of them.

> Four Leagues from Lake Frontence there is an incredible Cataract or Waterfall, which has no equal. The Niagara river near this place is only the eighth of a league wide, but it is very deep in places, and so rapid above the great fall, that it hurries down all the animals which try to cross it, without a single one being able to withstand its current. They plunge down a height of more than five hundred feet, and its fall is composed of two sheets of water and a cascade, with an island sloping down. In the middle these waters foam and boil in a fearful manner. They thunder continually and when the wind blows in a southerly direction, the noise they make is heard for from more than fifteen leagues.[24]

About the end of June, 1679, Father Hennepin returned to Fort Frontenac to make final preparations for the momentous journey. There were at least three of his brethren at the mission house, and he hoped to induce some of them to make the voyage with him. This evidently fell in with La Salle's plans, for when the *Griffon* was ready to sail she carried Fathers Zenobius Membré and Gabriel de la Ribourde along with Father Hennepin.

[22] This is a passage from the Notice to the Reader in the original French edition of the *Nouvelle Découverte*, and quoted by Shea in his edition of the *Description*, 17.
[23] *Description*. . . . 59.
[24] *Ibid.*, 71–72.

Unfortunately, we know very little concerning the early history of Hennepin's companions. Father Membré was born in Bapaume, then in the Spanish Netherlands but now in France. He entered the Recollect house at Artois and came to Canada in 1675. He was pastor of St. Anne de Beaupré for a while before being sent to Fort Frontenac in 1678. Father de la Ribourde is said to have been the last scion of a noble family in Brie, and to have abandoned everything to become a son of St. Francis. He was one of the Recollects who came with Talon in 1670, was for a while superior of the missions around Quebec, and was then sent to Fort Frontenac. Although he was now sixty-nine years old, he entered upon this new enterprise with all the enthusiasm of youth.[25]

On the 7th of August the whole party to the number of thirty-two were assembled, the arms and the merchandise including seven small iron cannon were loaded on board, and the *Griffon* making way slowly against the stiff current of the river finally floated into Lake Erie.

> Our voyage was so fortunate that on the morning of the tenth day, the feast of St. Lawrence, we reached the entrance of the Detroit by which Lake Orleans empties into Lake Conty, and which is one hundred leagues distant from Niagara River.[26] This strait is thirty leagues long and almost everywhere a league wide, except in the middle where it expands and forms a lake of circular form, and ten leagues in diameter, which we called Lake St. Clare, on account of our passing through it on that Saint's day.[27]
>
> The country on both sides of this beautiful strait is adorned with fine open plains, and you can see numbers of stags, does, deer, bears, by no means fierce and very good to eat, poules d'inde and all kinds of game, swans in abundance. Our guys were loaded and decked with several wild animals cut up, which our Indian and our Frenchmen killed. The rest of the strait is covered with forests, fruit trees like walnuts, plum and apple trees, wild vines loaded with grapes, of which we made some little wine. There is timber fit for building. It is the place in which deer most delight.[28]

With some difficulty the ship made its way into Lake Huron, and coasted along the eastern shore. Later, a storm blew her across the

[25] There is a sketch of Father Membré in Shea's *Discovery and Exploration of the Mississippi Valley* (edit. 1852), 147.

[26] The word "detroit" means in French, a strait. The early French explorers considered the Detroit and St. Clair Rivers as forming a strait between Lakes Erie and Huron, and Lake St. Clair was only a bulge in the strait.

[27] The lake was named after St. Clare of Assisi, b. 1194, d. 1253. Her feast is kept on August 12. The French name is "Claire" and local historians can give no satisfactory explanation for the actual spelling.

[28] *Description . . . Louisiane*, 91–92.

lake to the vicinity of Saginaw Bay. Following the western shore she encountered days of heavy weather.

> At this crisis, the Sieur de la Salle entered the cabin, and quite disheartened told us that he commended his enterprise to God. We had been accustomed all the voyage to induce all to say morning and evening prayers together on their knees, all singing some hymns of the church, but as we could not stay on the deck of the vessel, on account of the storm, all contented themselves with making an act of contrition. There was no one but our pilot alone, whom we were never able to persuade.
>
> At this time the Sieur de la Salle adopted in union with us Saint Anthony of Padua as the protector of our enterprise and he promised God if He did us the grace to deliver us from the tempest, that the first chapel he should erect in Louisiana should be dedicated to that great Saint.

The *Griffon* finally reached St. Ignace on August 27. The entire ship's company attended Mass at the Jesuit chapel in the Ottawa village led by La Salle, "very well dressed in his scarlet cloak trimmed with gold lace." As they came out of the chapel they could see the bay where the *Griffon* lay at anchor, and the scores of Indian canoes going and coming from the fishing grounds. The Huron braves came out of their village to welcome the new arrivals with a triple round of musketry.

La Salle experienced a great deal of trouble from the desertion of his men. In anticipation of the *Griffon's* voyage advance parties had been sent out to the Straits of Mackinac and to the Illinois country to gather food supplies and furs. When La Salle arrived, quite a number of his men were missing as were the goods which were to be used in barter with the Indians. Some days were spent in rounding up the deserters before the *Griffon* again took off on the next lap of her journey. She sailed down into Lake Michigan until she reached one of the islands at the head of Green Bay.

> Contrary to our opinion, the Sieur de la Salle who never took any one's advice resolved to send back his bark from this place, and to continue his route by canoe, but as he had only four, he was obliged to leave considerable merchandise in the bark, a quantity of utensils and tools, he ordered the pilot to discharge everything at Missilimakinac, where he could take them again on his return. He also put all the peltries in the bark with a clerk and five good sailors. Their orders were to proceed to the great fall of Niagara, where they were to leave the furs, and take on board other goods which another bark from Fort Frontenac . . . was to bring them, and that as soon as possible thereafter, they should sail back to Missilimakinac, where they would find

instructions as to the place to which they should bring the bark to winter.[29]

On the 18th of September, with a light west wind blowing, the
Griffon fired a single cannon to say farewell, and started back. As she
receded in the distance she carried more than furs; she was freighted
with the hopes and anxieties of the man who had staked his fortune
on her building, and his chance to success on the supplies she would
bring him. His fears were justified, for the fate of the *Griffon* is the
first mystery of the Great Lakes; she was never seen again. There are
indications that her salt-water pilot held the inland seas in contempt.
They proved first to him what they have often since, that their fury
is not to be despised.

The day following the *Griffon's* departure, the fourteen persons
left behind started out for the southern end of Lake Michigan in four
heavily laden canoes. We need not go into the details of their struggle
against the elements, and of the sufferings from cold and hunger
which marked their progress. Occasionally, when the wind and the
waves died down after a stormy day which had kept them on shore,
the canoes glided along in the moonlight. Other times when the party
was forced to land to avoid disaster, Father Hennepin hoisted good
old Father Gabriel on his shoulders and waded into shore, while the
old man, all drenched as he was, "never failed to display an extraordinary cheerfulness." Several times Father Gabriel fainted from lack of
food and the hardships which he could scarcely bear; but Father
Hennepin brought him to "with a little confection of hyacinth, which
I had preserved preciously." [30] One day as they paddled along the
shore they saw several crows and eagles milling around together. This
could mean only one thing. "Plying our paddles with redoubled zeal
towards the carnivorous birds, we found there half a very fat deer
which the wolves had killed and half eaten. We recruited ourselves
on the flesh of this animal, blessing Providence which had sent us
such timely aid." All the while there were hostile Indians to be
watched out for, or to be fought, or to be placated.

On the morning of October 30, the party was attacked by a band
of Outagami determined to rescue a fellow tribesman whom La Salle
was holding as a hostage against the return of some stolen goods.

There were only seven or eight who had guns, the others had bows
and arrows only; and during all these manoeuvres on both sides we
three Recollects were there saying our office, and as I was the one of the

[29] *Ibid.*, 105–06.
[30] Father Allouez relates that once, when almost dying of hunger, he was much
strengthened by eating a clove which he found in his handkerchief.

three who had seen most in matter of war, having served as King's chaplain . . . I came out of our cabin to see what figure our men made under arms and to encourage two of the youngest whom I saw grow pale, and who nevertheless made for all that a show of being brave and haughty as much as their leader. I approached in the direction of the oldest Indians, and as they saw that I was unarmed, they readily inferred that I approached them with a view to part the combatants and to become the mediator of their differences. One of our men seeing a band of red stuff, which served as a head band to one of these Indians, went and tore it off his head, giving him to understand that he had stolen it from us. This bold act of eleven armed Frenchmen against a hundred and twenty-five Indians, so intimidated these savages that two of their old men . . . presented the peace calumet. . . .[31]

After a day spent in celebrating their new-found friendship, the Frenchmen started out to follow the bend in the lake which should bring them up along the Michigan shore. Before leaving Mackinac La Salle had given orders to his lieutenant, Henry de Tonty, to proceed with twenty men to the mouth of the river of the Miami and there await his commander. When La Salle and his party reached the rendezvous they found the solitude undisturbed; there was no sign of Tonty and his detachment. Although his men protested against any delay, and were all for getting down into the Illinois country as soon as possible, La Salle was inflexible in his determination to wait for his lieutenant.

The river of the Miami, named after the Indian tribe which lived along its banks, is today called the St. Joseph. Taking its rise in Hillsdale County it flows west and south until in the vicinity of South Bend, Indiana, it runs sharply to the northwest to empty into Lake Michigan at St. Joseph. "There was at the mouth of the river of the Miamis an eminence with a kind of platform on top and naturally fortified. It was high and steep, of triangular figure, formed on two sides by the river, and on the other by a deep ravine." Here, La Salle began the construction of a fort, not so much for defense as to keep his men occupied. It was forty feet long by eighty feet broad, made of squared beams lying one upon the other, and with inclined palisades facing the river side, and palisades twenty-five feet high on the land side.

The month of November was spent in these exertions. It needed all the watchfulness and dominance of La Salle to hold his men at work. The weather was cold and disagreeable. There was nothing to eat but fat bear meat, at which the men constantly rebelled. The days went by without sign of Tonty, and La Salle was visibly discouraged.

---

[31] *Description . . . Louisiane,* 124–25.

Perhaps the only thing that prevented a wholesale desertion was the the presence of the priests.

> We had made a Cabin, wherein we performed Divine Service every Sunday, and Father Gabriel and I, who preached alternatively, took care to take such texts as were suitable to our present Circumstances, and fit to inspire us with Courage, Concord and brotherly love. Our Exhortations produc'd a very good Effect and hinder'd our Men from deserting, as they design'd.[32]

For the history of the Church in Michigan this passage of Father Hennepin's narrative must always remain of the deepest interest. It records the erection of a second altar for divine worship in the lower peninsula, four years after Father Nouvel's encampment in Isabella County. The passing years and the march of commerce have long since obliterated all vestiges of the spot whereon the little bark chapel stood. Yet the locality must ever be hallowed by its association with the devoted sons of St. Francis, who were the first to break the Holy Bread in this hitherto untouched portion of the Michigan wilderness.

We would give much for further details of their stay; but they are lacking. To them their month on the St. Joseph was only an episode, a prelude to greater deeds. They pass on out of our history to further adventures, and for two of the priests, to tragic endings.

Tonty arrived with his men near the end of November. On December 3 the party, now numbering thirty men in eight canoes began the ascent of the St. Joseph looking for the portage which they knew would bring them to the headwaters of the Kankakee River. After various mishaps they were finally directed to it by an Indian hunter attached to the expedition. The portage was about two miles long, and ran from the St. Joseph in a line just west of the present city of South Bend to the marshes where the Kankakee took its rise.[33] From then on the travelers had little difficulty, and by the end of the month they had reached a large Illinois town near the present village of Utica, Illinois. The Frenchmen were soon on good terms with the Indians whom they had at first surprised.

> We made known by our interpreter that we, Recollects, had not come among them to gather beaver, but to give them a knowledge of the great Master of Life, and to instruct the children; that we had left our country which was beyond the sea to come and dwell among them, and to be of the number of their greatest friends.
>
> We heard a great chorus of voices, Tepatoui Nicka, which means: "See what is good, my brother, you have a mind well made to conceive

[32] *Nouvelle Découverte,* 139.

[33] For the location and description of the portage see George A. Baker, *The St. Joseph-Kankakee Portage* (South Bend, 1899).

this thought," and at the same time they rubbed our legs down to the sole of the feet near the fire with bear's oil and buffalo grease to relieve our fatigue. They put the first three morsels of meat in our mouths with extraordinary marks of friendship.[34]

At some distance from the Indian village, and near the present city of Peoria, Illinois, La Salle decided to build Fort Crevecoeur, and at the same time construct another vessel to take him down the Mississippi. He needed rigging and equipment, and to get them he set out, at the beginning of March, 1680, across country to Fort Frontenac, thus performing one of the most memorable feats in the history of American exploration. The day before he left, he witnessed the departure of Father Hennepin whom he had commissioned to explore the Illinois River to its mouth and to continue up the Mississippi.

We cannot follow the priest and his two companions through all their fascinating adventures.[35] Captured by the Sioux, the three men were forced to live for many months wandering about with their savage hosts. Hennepin named and was the first to describe the Falls of St. Anthony, along which is built the city of Minneapolis. Finally, in the fall, du Luth, who had been exploring along Lake Superior, heard of their plight and came down to rescue them. They all returned to St. Ignace, where Father Hennepin spent the winter at the Jesuit mission, often skating with Father Pierson, or fishing through the ice. He improved his opportunities by conferring the cord of St. Francis on forty-two Frenchmen who were there trading. In Easter week of 1681 he started back on the long journey to Montreal, where he spent twelve days recruiting his strength in the company of Frontenac, who could scarcely believe that the gaunt figure in tattered robe patched with pieces of buffalo skin was his beloved Father Hennepin. He soon returned to France to publish his first book, and then went on to Holland. The last we know of him is that he was living in the Ara Coeli convent in Rome in 1701 trying to induce Cardinal Spada to help him found a new mission in the Mississippi country.[36]

Now we must leave good Friar Hennepin satisfied that we have done something to make the words come true which he wrote when describing the country about the Detroit River: "Those who shall be so happy as to inhabit that Noble Country cannot but remember with Gratitude those who have discover'd the way by venturing to sail upon an unknown Lake for about one hundred Leagues." [37]

The lives of Father Hennepin's two priest companions ended in

---

[34] Description . . . Louisiane, 158.
[35] See Parkman's La Salle, Chap. XVII.
[36] Description . . . Louisiane, Introduction, 30.
[37] Nouvelle Découverte, 109.

tragedy. When La Salle left Fort Crevecoeur on his overland journey to Fort Frontenec, Tonty remained in command of the dozen men at the fort, not counting Fathers Membré and la Ribourde. During a temporary absence most of his men deserted, and Tonty found himself with only three companions and the two priests. In September, the Iroquois attacked the Illinois among whom the Frenchmen were living, and all five were forced to flee. One day as they were ascending the Illinois River, their canoe began to leak so badly that they were obliged to stop for repairs. Father de la Ribourde, breviary in hand, went into the woods along the bank to say his prayers. When the repairs were completed the old man had not yet returned. The party went in search of him firing their guns at frequent intervals, but to no avail. It was later learned that a band of roving Kickapoo had come upon the aged priest and murdered him. His body was thrown into a hole, and his scalp carried off in triumph to their encampment. His breviary later came into the hands of the Jesuits. "Thus died this holy man of God by the hands of some mad youths . . . His death, I doubt not, has been precious before God, and will some day have its effects in the vocation of these nations to the Faith, when it shall please God to use his great mercy." [38]

Father Membré with Tonty and the others reached St. Ignace, where they met La Salle, and then returned to Fort Frontenac. In the spring of 1681 the indefatigable explorer made another attempt to reach the mouth of the Mississippi, and this time was successful. Father Membré accompanied him, and was apparently the only priest to do so. On the 9th of April the party discovered the open sea.

> With all possible solemnity, we performed the ceremony of planting the cross and raising the arms of France. After we had chanted the hymn of the church "vexilla Regis," and the "Te Deum," the Sieur de la Salle, in the name of his majesty, took possession of that river, of all the rivers that enter into it, and of all the countries watered by them. An authentic act was drawn up, signed by all of us there, and, to the sound of a volley from all our muskets, a leaden plate, on which were engraved the arms of France and the names of all those who had just made the discovery, was deposited in the earth.[39]

This new empire thus added to the French crown was called Louisiana. Both Father Membré and La Salle returned to France, the one to retire to his convent at Bapaume, the other to lay before the King his ambitious schemes for the colonization of the new possessions. On July 24, 1684, La Salle sailed from Rochelle intending to enter the

---

[38] Le Clercq, op. cit., 147.

[39] Ibid., II, 177. Father Membré wrote a journal of this second attempt which has been edited by Shea in his Discovery and Exploration. . . . Valley, 165–84.

mouth of the Mississippi from the Gulf, and to establish his colony sixty miles inland. There were several priests with him, and of the number was Father Membré.

The story of that expedition is like a nightmare. The mouth of the great river could not be found, and La Salle tramped through the wilds of Texas in a frenzy of despair until he was shot down by one of his own men. At the head of Metagorda Bay he had built Fort St. Louis, where his colonists, wasted by famine and ravaged by disease, died off one by one. In the spring of 1689 the fort was surprised by a band of Indians, and when the Spaniards arrived some three months later they gazed upon a scene of utter desolation, marked here and there by half-buried bodies. Of these one was the body of Father Membré. His dust like his commander's lies in an unknown grave.

CHAPTER V

The Saint Joseph Mission

THE Indian migrations under pressure of the Iroquois during the last half of the seventeenth century have already been pointed to as determining the centers of missionary activity. The lower peninsula of Michigan was emptied of its native population which took refuge mainly to the north and the west of Lake Michigan. The two strategic mission stations became St. Ignace, and St. Francis Xavier for the Green Bay area. From the latter the missionaries worked southward, but always west of Lake Michigan, to develop what they called the Illinois mission field, which owed its beginnings to Marquette's journey down the Mississippi. In the course of time as the Iroquois menace abated, especially after De Tracy's campaign in 1660, the tribes that had been expelled from southwestern Michigan began to drift back to their original locations in sufficient numbers to warrant the establishing of the first Jesuit mission in the southern peninsula, the Saint Joseph Mission. A precise date for its founding cannot be assigned with certainty; the *Jesuit Relations* as a series were discontinued in 1672, and we must depend for information on scattered references in contemporary writings. For the later history of the mission we are fortunate in being able to draw upon the extant baptismal register.

Alongside the mission, as was usually the case, there arose a military emplacement called Fort St. Joseph. Although the fort, and its occupants at various intervals, enters to some extent into the history of Detroit proper, the same cannot be said of the mission. There seems to have been little or no connection between the activities of the priests in the mission and those at Detroit. For this reason, and, moreover, because the mission undoubtedly antedates Detroit, its history will here be dealt with in its entirety. The advantage of having all available information in one place will outweigh the rather undesirable anticipation of names and dates that will be necessary.

The founding of the mission resulted from the concern of the Jesuits for two Indian tribes, the Miami, and the Potawatomi. The former in its flight from the Iroquois had apparently gone as far west as Iowa before turning back to settle along the upper Fox River in

Wisconsin.[1] Here they were visited by Allouez, to whose preaching they listened with eager interest.[2] By 1679, a number of them had already been for some time in northern Indiana, and in Michigan along the St. Joseph River. La Salle encountered them there while searching for the portage to the Kankakee on his first journey to the Mississippi.[3]

The Potawatomi, we are told in the *Relation* of 1671, "had been driven by fear of the Iroquois from the lands which lay between the lake of the Hurons and that of the Illinois (Lake Michigan)." They had settled first on some islands at the entrance to Green Bay, and later on the Wisconsin mainland, where Allouez came in contact with them as early as 1667. About 1680 they began moving southward around the end of Lake Michigan and into the valley of the St. Joseph River.[4]

There is no reason to doubt that converts had been made among these two tribes during their stay in Wisconsin, and that the priests kept in touch with them after their migration. But the identity of the first missionary to visit them in Michigan is as much a matter for conjecture as is the time from which a permanent establishment can be dated. That a resident mission was contemplated as early as 1686 is disclosed from the following land grant on the St. Joseph River made to the Jesuits by the government in Quebec and confirmed by the King.

> The concession made to Father Dablon, and the other missionaries of the Society of Jesus established in the said region on October 1, 1686, by the Sieur Marquis de Denonville and of Champigny, of a stretch of land of twenty arpents fronting on the River St. Joseph, heretofore called the Miamis, which falls into the south of the lake of the Illinois and of the Outagamis, by twenty arpents in depth at the place they shall find the most suitable for the erection of a chapel and residence, and for the planting of grain and vegetables, to be held by Father Dablon and other missionaries above mentioned, their successors and assigns in perpetuity as their own property as is stated in the said concession.
>
> Versailles, May 24, 1689.[5]

Today the St. Joseph River winds through the fertile farms and orchards of Berrien County. The natural advantages which the early American settlers were quick to perceive had been no less apparent to the Indians, and to the missionaries. Some unknown French scout

---

[1] Louise Phelps Kellogg, *The French Regime in Wisconsin and the Northwest* (Madison, 1925), 99.
[2] The *Relation* of 1671.
[3] Margry, *op. cit.*, I, 463.
[4] Kellogg, *op. cit.*, 271.
[5] Margry, *op. cit.*, V, 35.

reporting to the Quebec officials in 1718, was enthusiastic in his praise of the lands watered by the river.

> 'Tis a spot the best adapted of any to be seen for purposes of living and as regards the soil. There are pheasants as in France; quail and perroquets; the finest vines in the world, which produce a vast quantity of very excellent grapes, both white and black, and the berry very large and juicy, and the bunch very long. It is the richest district in all that country.[6]

Somewhere in this earthly paradise the missionaries selected a spot for their house and chapel. There is no reason for believing that the location was other than the one visited by Father Charlevoix in 1721. According to his reckoning it was twenty leagues, about sixty miles, from the mouth of the St. Joseph to the mission. This must be understood as the actual distance traveled by his canoe in following the tortuous course of the river. Upon leaving the mission, he gives the distance to the portage by which the Kankakee River may be reached as six leagues, about eighteen miles. The portage, first used by La Salle, began about two and three-quarters miles northwest of the center of South Bend, Indiana.[7]

From these data we must conclude that the mission was situated on the river anywhere from one to three miles south of the present city of Niles, Michigan. Although the locality has been carefully gone over, the site of the mission has not yet been determined. From Charlevoix's account we gather that the Miami had a village on one side of the river, and on the other side lay the Potawatomi settlement in which stood the chapel and residence of the missionary. At the time of his visit Fort St. Joseph had been in existence for many years, and this too, he tells us, was on the Potawatomi side.[8] In Bellin's map of 1744, which accompanies the first edition of Charlevoix's work, the fort is located on the southern bank of the river.[9]

When did the Jesuits begin their establishment on the St. Joseph? Who was the first priest to labor in this new field? In the present state of our knowledge these questions find no satisfactory answer. Much has been written on the matter so fanciful and unreliable as to be use-

[6] E. B. O'Callaghan (ed.), *Documents Relative to the Colonial History of the State of New York* (Albany, 1855), IX, 890. In future references this work will be designated as the N. Y. Col. Docs.

[7] Baker, *op. cit.*

[8] For details regarding Fort St. Joseph see the *Mich. Hist. Colls.*, XXVIII, 179 ff.; XXXV, 545 ff.; XXXIX, 280 ff. The site of the fort is marked by a huge granite boulder unveiled July 4, 1913. It may be well to remind the reader that this fort must not be confused with the one built by La Salle at the mouth of the river. The latter was called the Fort of the Miami, and was destroyed a few months after its erection.

[9] The writings of Pierre Francois-Xavier Charlevoix, S.J., relating to New France were first published in 1744 at Paris.

less. It is commonly stated that Father Allouez was the founder of the mission, but the statement rests more on inference than evidence.

Allouez left Three Rivers in 1665 to begin his missionary career in the West. Four years were spent along the southern shore of Lake Superior, and his first visit to Green Bay occurred in December, 1669. Meanwhile, Dablon and Marquette had come into the field, and the next year saw the beginnings of the establishment at St. Ignace. Allouez was now definitely assigned to the Indians of Wisconsin, where he remained for six years with headquarters at a mission which he founded in the neighborhood of Lake Winnebago. In 1676, he was ordered to the promising field which had been opened by Marquette's exploration, but which had been untouched after his death. He spent a few months with the Kaskaskia and Illinois Indians, and then returned to Wisconsin. A second visit to the Illinois country, in 1678, was prolonged until 1680, when Allouez returned to the northern missions.[10] Here we lose sight of him until 1683.

In that year, the Jesuit superior in Quebec, Father Beschefer, forwarded to his French provincial a report upon the Jesuit missions. The Ottawa mission is thus described: "In the Outaouc missions we include not only the outaouacs or upper Algonquins. . . . We also include the hurons who reside at St. Ignace . . . the Pouteouatamis along the bay des Puants . . . the Mokoutens and the ouiamis; the Kischigamins along Lake Ilinois; and the Ilinois themselves, as we more nearly approach the south. We have houses with chapels at sault de ste Marie, at st. Ignace, at st. francois de Borgia, and at st. francois Xavier . . . The missionaries frequently go on journeys among the surrounding nations . . ."[11] Speaking of Father Allouez the report continues: ". . . his special mission is among the Miamis and Ilinois where he labors with as much ardor as if he were in the prime of life." He follows the Indians into the woods on their hunting trips, is deterred by no hardships, and has succeeded in erecting a chapel. But Father Allouez is soon to be withdrawn, for "we shall be obliged to discontinue that mission because the Iroquois have gone to continue the war with more ardor . . ."

The report, dated October 21, was written with evident knowledge of what was taking place in the West. La Salle and his faithful lieutenant, Tonty, having heard rumors of an Iroquois invasion, had begun in December, 1682, the building of Fort St. Louis near the present town of Utica, Illinois.[12] The fort was completed in March of the

---

[10] There is a sketch of Allouez in Shea, *Discovery*. . . . *Miss. Val.*, 67 ff.

[11] Thwaites, *Jesuit Relations* . . . , LXII, 193. The St. Francis Borgia mission was situated a few miles from St. Ignace.

[12] Parkman, *La Salle*. . . . *Great West*, appendix to Chap. XVI.

following year, and Tonty was left in command while La Salle returned to France. A year later the Iroquois advanced as Father
Beschefer had predicted, besieged the fort for six days, and then withdrew. From Tonty's report we gather that Father Allouez had meanwhile been recalled to St. Ignace.

> . . . The winter passed, and on March 20, 1684, being informed that
> the Iroquois were about to attack us, we prepared to receive them and
> dispatched a canoe to M. de la Durantaye, Governor of Missilimakinac
> for assistance in case the enemy should hold out against us a long
> time. . . . M. de la Durantaye, with Father Daloy, a Jesuit, arrived at
> the fort with about sixty Frenchmen whom they brought to our assist-
> ance, and to inform me of the orders of M. de La Barre to leave the
> place. . . .[13]

Another mention of Father Allouez comes three years later. After
the death of La Salle, a remnant of his followers succeeded in finding
the Mississippi and returned to Quebec. From March 19, 1687, the
date of the assassination, the little party slowly struggled northward,
and it was not until September that they reached Fort St. Louis.
Joutel, who wrote the journey of their wanderings, thus describes
their entry.

> . . . On Sunday, the 14th, having resumed our journey . . . about
> two in the afternoon we arrived at Fort St. Louis where we greatly sur-
> prised those who were there, since they were not expecting us. . . .
> After the usual greetings, we went up to the fort, where we found the
> Frenchmen under arms, and they fired several volleys on our arrival to
> show their delight. As soon as we entered the fort M. Cavalier asked the
> location of the chapel in order to render thanks to God for having so
> happily conducted us. . . .[14]

At the fort, and apparently serving as chaplain, Father Allouez lay
ill. Joutel describes him as being fearful of La Salle's return because
of some intrigue which he had set on foot against him. This passage
has been used to confirm the charge of Jesuit opposition to La Salle.
Joutel was strongly partisan, and the accusation is sufficiently refuted
by the fact that Tonty, commanding the fort, was no less devoted to
Father Allouez than to his chief.

The survivors, always pretending that La Salle was still alive and
would come on later, prepared to resume their journey towards Quebec at the end of February, 1668. Joutel writes:

[13] Pierre Margry, *Relations et Memoires Inédits* (Paris 1867), I, 36.
[14] Journal of Henri Joutel in Margry, *Découvertes* . . . , III, 91–535. For this passage
see pp. 477–79. The M. Cavalier referred to is the Sulpician brother of La Salle. The
other priest in the party was Father Anastasius Douay, a Recollect who left France with
La Salle on his ill-fated expedition.

I have before recounted that the Jesuit Father had been alarmed by our telling him that M. de La Salle might arrive at the fort according to what he had said when he left us. The Father was afraid of meeting him there, perhaps because something had occurred between the gentlemen, as I think I have stated, which was injurious to the Sieur de La Salle. . . . In fine, the good Father fearing to be found there, preferred to take precautions by starting first. . . . It troubles us to see that these gentlemen were to be left without a priest; but we had decided to keep our secret, and so there was no help for it. Although M. Cavelier told the priest that he could remain, he left seven or eight days ahead of us. . . .[15]

Here we have Father Allouez returning to St. Ignace early in 1688. Of his subsequent movements we know practically nothing. Shea thinks it likely that he was at Fort St. Louis in 1689.[16] What we do know is the date of the missionary's death, found in a letter of Father Dablon to his superior, and dated, Quebec, August 29, 1690. It is an admirable summary of the great missionary's activities. He had carried the Faith to more than eight nations. He had instructed more than one hundred thousand Indians, and had baptized more than ten thousand. He was in truth a second Francis Xavier. The letter goes on to describe his last moments.

One of our servants who was with his testifies that the stricken Father, having made frequent acts of contrition, tried to make a spiritual communion as his viaticum; that he next addressed himself to St. James to obtain through this Apostle the salutary effects of Extreme Unction; that finally having thrice pronounced the holy names of Jesus and Mary to obtain the indulgence of the Society he quietly expired the night of the 27 to the 28 of August, 1689. It is the seventy-sixth year of his age, the forty-seventh of his entry into religion, and the beginning of his thirty-ninth since his arrival in Canada.[17]

Unfortunately, the letter leaves the place of death unmentioned; it states simply that he died on the Ottawa mission. As we have seen, this term included all missionary activity in the western country; only later was the Illinois mission spoken of as a separate field. There is yet to be found a contemporary statement to the effect that Father Allouez died within sight of the St. Joseph River.

Another vague reference to the missionary's death is found in a letter of Father Gabriel Marest to Father Germon, dated November 9, 1712. Dealing with the beginning of the Illinois mission he writes: "It was Father Daloës who took it upon himself; he knew the lan-

15 Ibid., 499–500.
16 Shea, op. cit:, 70. "I am inclined to believe from a deed which fell into my hands that he (Allouez) was at Fort St. Louis in 1689."
17 Margry, Découvertes . . . , I, 63.

guage of the Oumiamis which somewhat resembles that of the Illinois; however he made a very short stay there because of the opinion that he would accomplish greater results in another district where indeed he ended his apostolic life." [18] One could read into this passage the supposition that Allouez died in his Wisconsin missions, for he had greater opportunities there than with the relatively insignificant number of Indians along the St. Joseph at the time.

Supplementing these unsatisfactory contemporary references to Father Allouez is the positive statement of Father Charlevoix that the great missionary died at the St. Joseph mission.[19] There is no denying the weight of his assertion. On the occasion of his visit to the mission in 1721 he must have become thoroughly acquainted with its history. Moreover, when writing the record of his travels, it is safe to assume that he had access to documents and sources which are now lost. It is true that there are blunders in his *History and General Description of New France* published more than twenty years after his return to France; but it seems improbable that he was mistaken in naming the place where died a member of his own Society whose greatness was apparent even to his contemporaries.

There is another bit of evidence in this matter which must not be ignored. The Indian had a tenacious memory. The first white settlers in the vicinity of Niles mention a large wooden cross standing on a bluff near the river. They were told by the Indians that it marked the grave of a missionary, and that it had been replaced as often as it had fallen from age and decay.[20] From contemporary records of the Society a definite place of death can be assigned to every Jesuit missionary who labored in the western missions, save to Allouez. There is, hence, the strongest presumption that if the cross guarded a missionary's grave, it was the grave of the "Francis Xavier" of the Ottawa mission.[21]

[18] *Lettres Édifiantes* (Toulouse, 1810), VI, 269-70. There have been several editions of this work which is virtually a continuation of the *Jesuit Relations*, but which deals mostly with the missions in the Far East. The master edition in 26 vols. was published at Paris, 1783.

[19] Shea (ed.), P.F.X. de Charlevoix, *History and General Description of New France* (New York, 1862-66), V, 132. See also p. 202, where referring to Father Aveneau, the writer states that this missionary's influence over the Indians was as great as that of his predecessor.

[20] *Mich. Hist. Colls.*, XXXV, 546; XXXIX, 289.

[21] A short distance south of Niles, on the Low Road, an imposing granite cross has been erected to replace the last wooden one. It bears the following inscription:

To the memory of Father Claude Jean Allouez, S.J., whose intrepid courage won the admiration of the Indians, and whose apostolic zeal earned for him the title of the Francis Xavier of the American missions. Father Allouez was born at St. Didier, France, in 1622, and died near this spot August 27, 1689.

Erected by the Women's Progressive League of Niles, Mich., 1918.

Beginning with the year 1690 we are on more solid ground. According to Ferland, Father Claude Aveneau was sent in that year to labor in the St. Joseph mission.[22] He gives no authority for his statement, but he doubtless relies on a letter of Vaudreuil to the home government, dated November 14, 1708. The Governor was annoyed by Cadillac's constant diatribes against the Jesuits, and by his high-handed attempts to remove the Jesuit missionary from the St. Joseph establishment. He complains to the Minister that "the Sieur de Lamothe, on his own authority and without any reason, has taken away from the Jesuits their mission among the Miamis; he has ordered the retirement of a missionary, who has been with these Indians for eighteen years, and who knows their language and customs, in order to replace him with a Recollect who knows neither." [23]

This letter would justify placing the coming of Father Aveneau in 1690. Yet, the question of his term of service is complicated by the obituary notice found in a letter of Father Germain, dated November 5, 1711.

> Two fathers also died in this college. (Quebec). . . . One was Father Claude Aveneau who labored for more than twenty-five years in instructing the miamis. . . . This year he was attacked by a complication of several diseases, which did not permit him to continue his apostolic labors; and our fathers among the Outaouats thought it advisable to send him down to Quebec in a canoe, hoping that he would find there more remedies to restore his health, for his mission was at the river St. Joseph, 300 leagues from here. . . .[24]

We know that Father Aveneau was sent to the West in 1685, and according to the preceding letter his service among the Miami must have begun in 1686. However it is not difficult to harmonize this account with Vaudreuil's statement if it be remembered that not all the Miami were at St. Joseph, but only one or two bands. There were many more in the Illinois country, and on the Maumee and Wabash Rivers.[25]

As for the mission itself there is nothing to indicate its location prior to 1693. In that year, Frontenac sent Courtemanche to build a military post on the St. Joseph to prevent the Iroquois from corrupting the loyalty of the Miami, and the English from trading with

---

22 J. B. A. Ferland, *Cours d'Histoire du Canada* (Quebec, 1865), II, 336.

23 Rochemonteix, *op. cit.*, III, 526.

24 Thwaites, *Jesuit Relations* . . . , LXVI, 213–15. The letter goes on to state that Father Aveneau died on the seventh day in the octave of the Nativity of the B.V.M., that is, on September 14, 1711.

25 For further details concerning Father Aveneau see Rochemonteix, *op. cit.*, III, 513, 526; IV, 67–70.

them.[26] Whether Courtemanche selected his own site for the fort, or located it where the missionary was already settled, cannot be determined. In all likelihood the spot visited by Charlevoix in 1721 had been, since 1693, the actual site of the mission.

Father Aveneau pursued his apostolic work alone until a helper was sent him in the person of Father Jean Mermet.[27] He came to Canada in 1698, and seems to have been sent directly to the Ottawa mission, arriving at St. Joseph probably some time in 1699. Along with Father Aveneau he became a target for Cadillac's strictures for having failed to induce the Miami to move to the new post on the Detroit River. To this circumstance we owe two letters from the missionaries explaining their stand in the matter.[28] Some time in the summer of 1702, Father Mermet went as chaplain to the post which Juchereau was trying to establish on the Ohio near the present city of Cairo, Illinois.[29] The post was abandoned in 1704, and Father Mermet seems to have been sent on to the Illinois mission where he died, September 15, 1716.[30]

Father Aveneau's next assistant was Father Jean Baptiste Chardon. Coming to Canada in 1699, he had been sent to the western missions in 1701.[31] He was probably stationed at St. Ignace for a while before being appointed to the St. Joseph mission where he appears for the first time in 1705.[32] The following year a projected raid on the Miami by the Ottawa from the north was foiled, but fears were felt for the safety of the missionaries. Their superior wrote to Vaudreuil:

> I asked the savages whether I could safely send a boat(load) of Frenchmen to St. Joseph('s) River; they replied that I could do so, and have even escorted me there, seeming to take an interest in the priests there; for while they are there, they do not think they are at liberty to make war on the Miamis as they would like to do. For this reason they would be pleased to see all the priests out of this post; but I do not think that

[26] Emma Helen Blair, *Indian Tribes of the Upper Mississippi Valley and Region of the Great Lakes* (Cleveland, 1911), II, 16.

[27] Rochemonteix *op. cit.*, III, 513, 548; Thwaites, *Jesuit Relations* . . . , LXVI, 339.

[28] See the *Mich. Hist. Colls.*, XXXIII, 123, for letter of Father Aveneau, dated June 4, 1702; *ibid.*, for letter of Father Mermet dated April 19, 1702.

[29] *Magazine of Western History*, XII, 578; Thwaites, *Jesuit Relations* . . . , LXVI, 39.

[30] Although Father Mermet is generally thought to have gone directly to the Illinois after the abandonment of Juchereau's post, he seems to have been for some time with the Ouiatanons, or Weas, a kindred tribe to the Miami. Their town was near the present site of Lafayette, Ind. See the *Mich. Hist. Colls.*, XXXIII, 234; Oscar J. Craig, "Ouiatanon, A Study in Indiana History," Indiana Historical Society, *Publications*, II, 319 ff.

[31] Rochemonteix, *op. cit.*, III, 527; V, 52, 66; Thwaites, *Jesuit Relations* . . . , LXVI, 347; LXXI, Index.

[32] *Ibid.*, IV, 66.

you should desire it, for it is the most important after Mishilimak-ina. . . .[33]

The danger was evidently not very real, for Father Chardon is called "missionary to the Poutouatamis" in a report from Vaudreuil to the home government at the end of 1708.[34]

Out of the darkness which envelops the history of the mission, there flashes a charming picture in the closing days of Chardon's ministry. Father Gabriel Marest, missionary at Kaskaskia, decided to visit Mackinac in the spring of 1711 to confer with the Superior of the missions. Holding that office was his own brother, Joseph, whom he had not seen for fifteen years. On the way up, Father Gabriel paid a visit to his confrere at the St. Joseph mission.

Hence I made up my mind to go to the St. Joseph, to the Pouteau-tamis mission which is in charge of Father Chardon. In nine days time I accomplished this second journey which is seventy leagues, sometimes on the swift current of the river, and sometimes cutting across country. . . .

As I approached the Pouteautamis village, the Lord deigned to re-imburse me for all my pains by one of those unexpected happenings which he sometimes reserves for the consolation of His servants. Some Indians who were seeding their land, having seen me from afar, went to advise Father Chardon of my approach. The Father came straightway to meet me accompanied by another Jesuit. What a joyful surprise it was to see my brother, who fell on my neck to embrace me. For fifteen years we had been separated without any hope of ever seeing each other. It is true that I was on my way to meet him; but our reunion was to be at Michillimakinac and not a hundred leagues below. God had doubt-less inspired him to make at this time his visitation to the St. Joseph mission in order to have me forget in a moment all my past distress. We both thanked the divine Mercy which brought us together from such widely separated places to give us a consolation which is better felt than expressed. Father Chardon shared in the happiness of this joyful re-union, and showed us all the attention we could expect from his good-ness. Having stayed eight days at the mission, my brother and I, in his canoe, went on to Michillimakinac.[35]

On his return from Mackinac Father Marest revisited Father Chardon, and remained with him for a fortnight. He thus describes his host.

He is a missionary full of zeal, and with a rare talent for languages. He knows nearly every Indian tongue spoken on the Lakes; he has even

---

[33] *Mich. Hist. Colls.*, XXXIII, 267.
[34] *Ibid.*, 395.
[35] *Lettres Édifiantes*, VI, 289–91.

learned enough Illinois to make himself understood, although he sees these Indians only occasionally when they come to visit his village; for the Pouteautamis and the Illinois are cordial enough and visit each other from time to time. Certainly, their customs are very different; the former are gross and brutal, the latter mild and affable. . . .[36]

Just as Father Chardon, profiting by the efforts of his predecessors, had succeeded in bringing his savage charges through the first steps of civilized life, as denoted by the fact that they were cultivating their land, the western country was thrown into a turmoil by the uprising of the Fox Indians. The English, working through the Iroquois, had nerved them to make a supreme effort to destroy French influence in the Lake country. From their home in Wisconsin they came even as far as Detroit which they besieged in 1712. Chardon found further labors on the St. Joseph impossible, and withdrew to Mackinac. The mission was left without a resident priest for a period of seven or eight years.[37]

Father Chardon continued his missionary career at Green Bay, where he remained until that mission was abandoned in 1728, "the solitary priest on the old mission ground west of Lake Michigan." [38] He was again at the St. Joseph mission for a brief period in 1729. In 1733 we find him in Quebec, carried on the roster of the Society as "old and infirm." He died there, April 11, 1743.[39]

For the subsequent history of the St. Joseph Mission we are indebted to an invaluable source recently come to light, the baptismal register itself. It is not intact, and the patched and water-stained leaves that are left speak unmistakably of the vicissitudes through which they have passed. All the romance of an old register is there. As the entries succeed each other on these pages touched by the hands of priest and soldier, Indian and trader, they conjure up the thrilling history of the Lake region in the half dawn before our national life.[40]

The register as we have it begins with an entry by Father Michel Guignas, dated August 15, 1720. There are good reasons for placing the beginning of his work at the mission about two years earlier. Charlevoix writes in 1721 that the Indians have been for a long time

---

[36] *Ibid.*, 292–93.

[37] *Mich. Hist. Colls.*, XXXIII, 555.

[38] Shea, *The Cath. Church in Col. Days*, 629.

[39] Rochemonteix, *op. cit.*, V, 52.

[40] The original register is in the archives of the Quebec Seminary. Through the kindness of the Seminary archivist, Msgr. Amédée Gosselin, a photostat copy was made for the DCA. This was edited by Milo M. Quaife and George Paré for the *Mississippi Valley Historical Review*, XIII, 201–39.

without a missionary, but that one has lately been sent them. Father Guignas came to Canada in 1716, and made his profession in the Society at Mackinac, February 2, 1718.[41] He was probably assigned to his charge a few months later. There are at least four or five pages missing at the beginning of the register, showing that many entries had been made before the first date mentioned above.

' The first pages of the register disclose that by this time French traders had settled in or near the mission. To Albert Bonne, voyageur, and Marianne Sancer-Ferron is born a son, Joseph. Pierre Pepin Laforce and Michelle Le Ber are blessed with a son, Michael, and to safeguard the interests of some far-off relative, Ange Lafontaine, "a young man from Prairie de la Magdeleine held him over the font taking the place of and acting for another godfather." The fort, abandoned in 1696, had been reoccupied about 1715, and the soldiers had evidently been permitted to bring their wives. Marguerite Faucher, of the parish of Lachine, presents a daughter, Magdeleine, to her husband, Claude Collet, "a soldier in the Troops of the parish of St. Albin, Diocese of Chalon sur Marne."

This obscure soldier and his humble consort were the parents of a son who achieved distinction. Charles-Ange Collet was born and baptized at the St. Joseph Mission on October 1, 1721. As a youth he received his preliminary schooling in Montreal, and in 1744 he began the study of theology at the Quebec seminary. Ordained on September 23, 1747, he was first assigned to Sorel. Some years later he became a member of the Seminary staff, where his zeal and piety soon brought him into prominence. Elected a member of the Cathedral Chapter in 1758, he was one of the three canons who witnessed the interment of Montcalm. A year later he passed over to France, and took up his residence in Thiais, a suburb of Paris, where he was still living in 1793.[42]

For the student of Catholic history in Michigan the Collet family has a particular interest. Charles-Ange was undoubtedly the first native of the state to enter the priesthood. Moreover, it is not unlikely that a pious family on the St. Joseph may have given two sons to the Church as surely as it did one. In 1753, a Recollect was ordained in Quebec, whose name was Leonard-Philibert Collet, and the ordination record states that he was born, November 3, 1715. His birthplace is not given, as it surely would have been had he been a native of France, and no extant Canadian register contains the record of his

41 Rochemonteix, *op. cit.*, IV, 183, 199.
42 See sketch of Charles-Ange Collet by Amédée Gosselin in the *Bulletin des Recherches Historiques* (Quebec), XXX, 389 ff.

baptism. There is a strong probability that the Collet family was already established on the St. Joseph at this date.[43]

After his ordination, the Recollect, now called Father Luke, was destined to spend eight years as chaplain to the troops that France was moving through the West to oppose the British advance. We find him at Duquesne, Niagara, and Presqu'Ile. In 1760 he was twice in Detroit, once on January 14, and again on March 22. On both occasions he signed the baptismal register as "Chaplain of the Ohio river country." The next year he was laboring in the missions along the Mississippi in the neighborhood of Kaskaskia, and in that field he died, September 5, 1766.[44] It is not beyond the bounds of probability that the friar in his grey habit was brother to Charles-Ange wearing the purple of his canonry.

To the little colony on the St. Joseph, although strangely enough he says nothing of the French in it, came Father Pierre Charlevoix in 1721. Ostensibly on a visitation of the western missions, he had really been sent by the home government to gather first-hand information regarding the prospects for colonizing the Mississippi Valley, and the feasibility of opening a path to the Vermillion or Western Sea that still haunted the imagination of the Minister. His previous residence in Canada, his personality, and his talents admirably fitted him for this confidential mission. The record of his travels and observations, published long after his return to France, is one of the most absorbing books of early travel in America.[45]

Father Charlevoix arrived in Quebec in 1720, but did not begin his journey until the spring of the following year. From Mackinac he had intended going to Green Bay, and from there pushing his way westward to the limits of French influence. However, the unsettled temper of the Indians made this so dangerous that he was prevailed upon to choose the St. Joseph route to the Mississippi. To this change of plan we owe his visit to the St. Joseph Mission.

Leaving St. Ignace he coasted along the western shore of Michigan. When at the mouth of the Marquette River, he spent some time trying to locate the grave of Father Marquette. A few days later he was ascending the St. Joseph, his keen eyes noting unfamiliar trees, and

[43] For sketch of Luke Collet see *Ibid.*, 397–400. In 1725 a daughter of Claude Collet was baptized at the St. Joseph Mission. The godmother was Marie Joseph Collet, styled in the record, "a native of this place," hence born there. She had to be at least eight or nine years old to be admitted to the office of godmother.

[44] *Ibid.*, 398. In his mission on the Mississippi, Luke Collet was associated for a time with a Father Hippolyte Collet, another Recollect, but who is known to have come from France.

[45] Louise Phelps Kellog (ed.), *Journal of a Voyage to North America. Translated from the French of Pierre François Xavier de Charlevoix* (Chicago, 1923).

his pleasure at the sight of the ever changing panorama heightened by the perfume of the sassafras growing in profusion.

On August 8, he arrived at the post where, as he writes:

> . . . we have a mission, and where there is a commandant with a small garrison. The commandant's house, which is but a sorry one, is called the fort, from its being surrounded with an indifferent pallisado. . . .
>
> We have here two villages of Indians, one of the Miamis and the other of the Poutewatamies, both of them mostly Christians; but as they have been for a long time without any pastors, the missionary who has lately been sent them, will have no small difficulty in bringing them back to the exercise of their religion. . . .[46]

Father Charlevoix's stay at the mission afforded him a close range study of the Indians assembled there. He mentions a visit to a Miami chief who received him with an impassive hauteur, although minus his nose which had been bitten off during a debauch. He describes the game of lacrosse and the skill with which the Miami played it.

The Potawatomi had a famous old chief named Piremon, and another younger one named Wilamek. "This person is a Christian and well instructed, but makes no exercise of his religion. One day as I reproached him for it, he left me abruptly, went directly to the chapel, and said his prayers with so loud a voice that we could hear him at the missionary's. . . .

Here, as elsewhere, the ravages of the liquor traffic were evident.

> Several Indians of the two nations settled upon this river, are just arrived from the English colonies, whither they had been to sell their furs, and from whence they have brought back in return a great quantity of spiritous liquor . . . every night the fields echoed with the most hideous howlings. One would have thought that a gang of devils had broken loose from hell, or that the two towns had been cutting one another's throats. . . .
>
> Your Grace may from thence judge what a missionary is capable of doing in the midst of this disorder, and how disagreeable it must be to a good man, who has in a manner exiled himself in order to gain souls for God, to be obliged to become a witness of it, without being able to remedy it.

When the Indians are reproached for these disorders they answer that they were taught to drink by the French, and that if no more liquor be forthcoming from them it can always be procured from the English.

The liquor problem thus baldly stated could not be solved by the

[46] Ibid., II, 86–87.

Canadian authorities. The Indian first got liquor for his furs, and later when the very existence of French influence depended upon his loyalty, an ever-increasing supply of brandy was necessary to seal his allegiance. While in no way justifying this course, Charlevoix's national pride led him to soften somewhat his condemnation of the French on the ground that they diluted the liquor destined for the Indians, and thus made it less harmful than the brand supplied by the English. Certain it is that here on the St. Joseph, as in all the other posts, the liquor traffic meant the ruin of the missions.

With this cheerless picture Father Charlevoix closes his account of the mission. His duties called him down the Mississippi and back to France; behind him he left a young missionary soon to leave a lonely post which was from now on to be affected by the general disintegration of the whole Ottawa mission field. Green Bay was about to be abandoned, and from Mackinac the few remaining missionaries were to spend their final years in almost constant wanderings.

There is no report available concerning the future history of the St. Joseph Mission. Some information can be gleaned from the register itself, but it is difficult to decide whether any of the subsequent priests mentioned in it could be considered as attached to the mission.

Shortly after the departure of his famous confrere, Father Guignas was withdrawn from the St. Joseph establishment. The brilliant record of his college days had not been forgotten by his superiors; from the wilderness of Michigan he was summoned to the chair of hydrography at the College of Quebec.[47] His five years of teaching coincided with the current agitation for finding a passage to the Western or Vermillion Sea.

Charlevoix in his report had pointed out that success lay in either of two means: the exploration of the upper Missouri River, or the founding of a mission among the Sioux. The latter plan was adopted but not put into execution until 1727, when Boucher de Boucherville was commissioned to open a trading-post among the Sioux. When he left Montreal on June 16, 1727, he was accompanied by Father Guignas, appointed first missionary to the Sioux, and guarding carefully a case filled with his precious geodetic instruments.[48]

About the middle of September the expedition reached Lake Pepin, and began the building of Fort Beauharnois. The Indians proved to be intractable, and when they appeared to espouse the cause of the Foxes, who had just escaped the punitive forces of De Ligneris, the French sought safety in the Illinois country. Father Guignas returned to the Sioux in 1731 to spend six years in such mis-

[47] Rochemonteix, *op. cit.*, IV, 184.
[48] *Ibid.*, 182.

ery as excited the pity even of his savage hosts. Returning to Quebec in 1738, he passed his declining years in teaching, and died, February 6, 1752.[49]

Father Guignas' immediate successor at St. Joseph became Father Jean-Baptiste Saint-Pé. He could not have remained there long, for he signs but one entry, dated October 1, 1721. He had been on the Ottawa mission since his arrival in Canada in 1719, and was destined to remain at Mackinac until 1737. His name appears again under two entries dated September 19, 1734.

From Mackinac Father Saint-Pé was recalled to Quebec, where he held the office of Superior General of all the Jesuits in Canada from 1739 to 1748, and again from 1754 to 1763. He died there on July 8, 1770.[50]

"In the year one thousand seven hundred and twenty-two, I baptized in the course of the summer 4 Potawatomi children who were at the point of death. They died the same day or shortly afterwards." Thus runs the first entry of Father Charles Guymonneau, the next priest at the mission. We know little concerning him beyond the fact that he was remarkable not so much for his talents as for his indefatigable zeal. He arrived in Canada in 1715, and was soon sent to the West, probably to the Illinois mission, for he was in Kaskaskia when Charlevoix went through in 1721. His last entry in the St. Joseph register is dated May 2, 1723, and he died in the Illinois mission on February 6, 1736.[51]

The succeeding missionary, Father Charles-Michel Mesaiger, extended his ministrations at St. Joseph over a period of seven years. His first entry is dated September, 1724, and his last, January 26, 1731. Four of his entries occur during the winter, and these, together with the order in which several more are found, make it highly probable that he was at the mission the greater part of the time during which it was under his care.

In the spring of 1731 Father Mesaiger was called to Mackinac to undertake a dangerous mission. La Vérendrye and his sons were soon to set out on their historic journeys of exploration in search of the Western Sea.[52] Father Saint-Pé had first been designated as chaplain to the expedition, but now Mesaiger was named in his stead. The explorers pushed on through untold difficulties and hardships as far as the Lake of the Woods, where a fort was built and named St. Charles in honor of their chaplain. Broken in health, Father Mesaiger was

[49] Father Guignas left a Journal, which can be found in Shea's *Early Voyages up and down the Mississippi* (Albany, 1861).
[50] Rochemonteix, *op. cit.*, V, 181.
[51] Rochemonteix, *op. cit.*, IV, 268.
[52] See Parkman's *Half Century of Conflict*, Chap. XVI.

obliged to return to Quebec, where he taught mathematics for some time. He was returned to France in 1749, and died at Rouen, August 7, 1766.[53]

After Father Mesaiger's departure from the mission there is no record of priestly ministration until 1734, when Father Saint-Pé, as previously noted, performed two baptisms. In the following year came Jean Louis de la Pierre, a missionary of whom we have only the scantiest details. Arriving in Canada in the summer of 1734, he returned to France between 1746 and 1749, and died there some time after 1756. His first entry in the register is dated July 25, and his last September 11, 1735.[54]

Coming after a lapse of almost three years, the next entry in the register is dated June 21, 1738, and is signed by Pierre Du Jaunay. He had been in the western missions since 1735, and was destined to labor there with but slight intermission for thirty years. The register indicates that he officiated at the mission at various intervals from the time of his first entry up to his last, which is dated April 22, 1752.

There is a melancholy interest attached to the name of Father Du Jaunay. Year by year he witnessed the decline of the Ottawa mission. The natural inconstancy of the Indians coupled with the demoralizing influence of contact with an increasing number of unscrupulous traders had almost undone the work of the saintly pioneers. For a time there were only two missionaries left in the entire Ottawa mission field. The return to Quebec of Father Marin-Louis Le Franc about 1761 left Du Jaunay alone, the last of the Jesuits in Michigan. A remnant of the Ottawa had established themselves at L'Arbre Croche, near the present town of Harbor Springs. Here the missionary seems to have lived during the final years of his ministry until his recall to Quebec in 1765. He spent his declining years as spiritual director of the Ursulines, and died June 16, 1780, "full of virtue and good works." [55]

In 1825, Father Vincent Badin, curate of St. Anne's, Detroit, made a visitation of the old mission field. The Indians of L'Arbre Croche were overjoyed to see a priest once more. An ancient of the tribe dwelt lovingly upon his memories of Father Du Jaunay from whom he had received his first communion, and pointed out the forest path along which the missionary was wont to recite his breviary prayers.[56]

Over a space of twenty years a familiar figure at the mission was

53 Rochemonteix, op. cit., IV, 204–11.

54 Ibid., 213.

55 Ibid., V, 54, 218.

56 P. Chrysostomus Verwyst, O.F.M., Life and Labors of Rt. Rev. Frederic Baraga (Milwaukee, 1900), 60.

Father Jean-Baptiste de La Morinie, who had arrived in Canada in 1738. From the register it is evident that from 1740 he often alternated with Du Jaunay, and that from 1752 to 1760 he was the only priest to officiate at the mission. Some time after his last entry, April 2, 1760, he is known to have gone to the Illinois mission, where he was stationed at St. Genevieve on the Mississippi. Like his confrere who saw the end of missionary enterprise in the lake region he was to witness the destruction of the Illinois mission.

In 1762 the French government decreed the secularization of the Jesuits at home and in its colonies. The Supreme Council of New Orleans put the decree into effect on July 3, 1763.

> The church vestments and plate at New Orleans will be turned over to the Capuchins; the church vestments and plate of the Jesuits living in the Illinois country will be turned over to the procurator of the King in that region; the chapels will be torn down; finally, the above so-called Jesuits shall be put on board the first vessel ready to leave for France. They are forbidden meanwhile to live in common. . . .[57]

We need not go into the distressing details by which this decree was carried out to the letter.[58] The Jesuits were deported in the spring of 1764. The aged Father Meurin was allowed to remain provided he took up his residence at St. Genevieve on the Spanish side of the river. Father de La Morinie was permitted to return to Quebec, and he soon rejoined his brethren in France. The date of his death is unknown.[59]

There come next in the mission register three entries written in the tiny, characteristic handwriting of Father Pierre Potier. They are dated January 8, 25, and June 12, 1761. By a strange coincidence these entries, the last made by a Jesuit, are by the hand of the sole surviving member of the Society in the entire West. At the time they were made, Father Potier was missionary to a group of Indians across the river opposite Detroit. We know him to have been a laborious scholar, who had, moreover, an eager curiosity regarding the western country which led him to travel widely. So methodical an observer never went on a journey without logging his progress, and to this fact we are indebted for several interesting records of his excursions to distant points. One of them describes the trail from Detroit to Fort St. Joseph, and was jotted down, perhaps, on the very occasion of his

[57] Rochemonteix, *op. cit.*, IV, 398.
[58] For an account of the banishment see Thwaites, *Jesuit Relations* . . . , LXX, 212–301.
[59] Rochemonteix, *op. cit.*, IV, 234, 404–05.

replacing Father de La Morinie at the mission.[60] When Father Meurin died in Prairie du Rocher on the Mississippi in 1777, Father Potier became the last of his line. On July 16, 1781, he was found lying dead before his fireplace. The story of the Jesuit missions in the West begins with Brébeuf paddling up the Ottawa River; it ends with the poor, spent figure of Potier dying alone.[61]

The record of the St. Joseph Mission as a Jesuit establishment could be ended here; the mission has been gradually merging into nothing more than a small French settlement clustered around Fort St. Joseph. However, the historic interest attached to the locality has not been exhausted by the foregoing rather summary account.

By her victory on the Plains of Abraham England tore from France her vast colonial empire. The western posts, among them Detroit, Mackinac, and Fort St. Joseph, were regarrisoned by English troops. They had been of strategic value to the French; they were no less so to their new masters.

When the smoldering hatred of Pontiac against the English flared up in open warfare, Detroit alone of all the posts in the West resisted the besiegers. The story of the lacrosse game which ended in the massacre of the garrison at Mackinac is too well known to need retelling here. There were fourteen soldiers at Fort St. Joseph on the morning of May 25, 1763. By night four of them were on the road to Detroit to be exchanged for Indian prisoners. The other ten had been slain.

The fort was not reoccupied at the close of hostilities, although as a center of strategic and commercial importance, St. Joseph continued to command the watchful attention of the British officials in Detroit and Mackinac. With the opening of the Revolution, this watchfulness was redoubled; from a center of Indian trade and diplomacy St. Joseph became for a time the goal of contending white armies, and even a pawn in Old World diplomacy. From Detroit and Mackinac, British expeditions were launched against the colonists in Kentucky and the French Illinois, and against their Spanish allies in St. Louis; and in their turn armed forces from the Illinois towns and from St. Louis were launched against St. Joseph, as one of the few outposts of Great Britain within accessible striking distance. In June, 1779, Major De Peyster at Mackinac dispatched Lieutenant Bennett with a party of twenty soldiers and sixty traders and Indians to St. Joseph to intercept a hostile force which was reported to be en route from the Illinois via St. Joseph against Detroit. Bennett encamped

[60] There are copies of some of these itineraries in the Burton Historical Collection made from the originals now at the College Sainte-Marie in Montreal, where the major portion of Father Potier's extant writings are preserved. The Gagnon Collection in the Montreal Municipal Library has also a few Potier items.

[61] Rochemonteix, op. cit., V, 59–65.

En Mil sept cent 22 le trenteeme du mois daoust ie prestre
de la compagnie de iesus missionnaire a la riviere St
Joseph Jay supplee les ceremonie du bapteeme a Marie
à face deglise elle est né le 19 dece mois et a cause   mort aux
de danger prestant ou elle estoit baptisé le 21 du meesme   cas
mois le Parrain a este le Sieur Esteenne DeVilledoné
capitaine dune compagnie du detachement de la marine
et apresent Commandant du dit poste de la riviere
St Joseph la marraine a este Margaerite Kouk femme
du Sr michel Massé voyageur de la paroisse de Ste
marie en canada la quelle a dalare ne savoir
signer

                    J. C. Guymonneau S. I.

DeVilledonné

Lan mil sept cent 22 le trenteeme du m . . . .
prestre de la compagnie de iesus missionnaire a la   Jacque
riviere St Joseph soubsigné ay baptise le fils de la Parrue
Abnakis demeurant a la riviere St Joseph agé de nviron
deujours le Parrain a este Jacque Dutremble de Champlain
la Marraine Marguerite Kouk

        jacque dutoam béé J. C. Guymonneau S. I.

. . . . il sept cent 22 le trenteeme du mois daoust à prestre
de . . . . vagnie . . . . missionnaire à la riviere St
Jose . . . . Miltra . . . . rise le fils dun abnaxis de la
bon 1424 le . . . . nelle Des Gayots il a este nonime
. . . . des il . . . . A Ange fils de nir St
. . . . la Marine la Maraine
. . . . nir St ange
. . . . onneau

A page from the St. Joseph Mission baptismal register.
Original in the Quebec Seminary Archives.

some weeks at St. Joseph, when increasing disaffection and desertion on the part of his Indian allies caused him to retire in the direction of Mackinac.

The following summer the British conceived an ambitious project for a comprehensive assault upon the American and Spanish strongholds in the West. While most of the project miscarried, a large British-Indian force attacked St. Louis, and although beaten off, caused much distress and considerable loss to the defenders. The British offensive provoked a prompt counterstroke which was to involve the fortunes of St. Joseph. In the autumn, a French force under La Balme was launched against Detroit from the Illinois towns, and another raiding party from Cahokia, led by Jean Baptiste Hamelin, was directed against St. Joseph.

Hamelin arrived early in December, when the Indians were absent on their periodical hunt. In their absence he overpowered the traders, loaded their goods on packhorses, and with a score of prisoners beat a hasty retreat in the direction of Chicago. But the raiders quickly came to grief, for Lieutenant Dequindre, a British officer, reaching St. Joseph shortly after their departure, rallied the natives and set out in pursuit. Somewhere in the vicinity of modern Michigan City, he overtook the Cahokians, killed or captured most of them, and recovered the plunder.

A second and more formidable expedition against St. Joseph, however, was promptly launched, this time by the Spanish governor in St. Louis. Alarmed by the plans the British were making for a renewed attack upon St. Louis in 1781, and inspired, possibly, by the example of Clark's brilliant campaign of February, 1779, against Vincennes, Governor Cruzat at the beginning of January, 1781, dispatched a small body of soldiers against St. Joseph. At Cahokia they were joined by twenty townsmen, eager for plunder and revenge, and en route by a dozen additional Spanish soldiers and a large party of Indians. The motley array ascended the Illinois River in boats as far as Lake Peoria, and there, the river having frozen, began their overland winter march of three hundred miles to St. Joseph. Their sufferings from cold, hunger, and other privations on the three-weeks' wilderness journey only the imagination can picture. On February 12, 1781, St. Joseph was occupied without resistance from the Indians, the traders were plundered anew, and a large supply of corn, gathered for the use of the British in the coming attack on St. Louis, was burned. The Spanish flag had kissed the breeze for twenty-four hours when the invaders, their work of destruction accomplished, began their return journey, reaching St. Louis in early March without the loss of a single man. Governor Cruzat sent to distant Madrid a somewhat imposing relation of his bloodless conquest, and this report, duly published in the Madrid *Gazette,* became a factor in the involved peace negotiations between Spain and France, Great Britain, and the United States which attended the termination of the Revolution.[62]

Through all these turbulent times the little colony in the neighborhood of the fort lived on. Deprived of the ministrations of a priest, perhaps even of a chapel, it is easy to believe that they met for prayer and worship under the guidance of some one of their number. At least, in some rude cabin was sheltered the precious baptismal register against the coming of a missionary, for its final pages are signed with the grandiose signature of Pierre Gibault.

It will be remembered that following the expulsion of the Jesuits from the Illinois missions, Father Meurin remained alone. At the end of 1766 there were only three priests in the entire western country: the Recollect chaplain in Detroit, Father Potier across the river, and Father Meurin on the Mississippi.[63] How could he alone suffice for the demands made upon him? When the Bishop of Quebec, under whose jurisdiction the territory remained, named him vicar general in 1767, the venerable missionary penned these mournful lines:

> I would almost wish that my self esteem might prevent me from telling you, Monseigneur, that I am as unworthy as anyone can be of the honor which you confer on me; and more than ever incapable of such an office, of which I know but the name. I have never been acquainted with any jurisprudence, either notarial, pontifical, or any other. I have been too long left to myself, and I barely know the duties of a simple priest. . . .
>
> My letters of last spring must have omitted to inform you of my age, and of my weakness of body and mind. I retain only a small portion of weak judgment, have no memory, and possess still less firmness. I need a guide for the soul and for the body; for my eyes, my ears, and my legs are likewise very feeble. I am no longer good for anything but to be laid in the ground. . . .[64]

Moved by the aged missionary's request for assistance, Bishop Briand took stock of his seminarians. A hardy, zealous, trustworthy man was needed. Pierre Gibault, thirty-one years old, and a native of Montreal, suited the emergency. The Bishop advanced his ordina-

---

[62] For opposing views of the Spanish capture of St. Joseph, and its significance see Clarence W. Alvord, "The Conquest of St. Joseph, Michigan, by the Spaniards in 1781," *Missouri Historical Review,* II, 195–210; and Frederick J. Teggart, "The Capture of St. Joseph, Michigan, by the Spaniards in 1781," *ibid.,* 214–28.

[63] For sketch of Father Sebastian Meurin, S.J., see Charles H. Metzger, "Sebastian Louis Meurin," *Illinois Catholic Historical Review,* III, 241–59; 371–88; IV, 43–56.

[64] *Ibid.,* III, 385.

tion, fortified him with extraordinary faculties, and sent him off as vicar-general of Quebec in the Illinois country.

In July, 1768, Father Gibault arrived in Mackinac. The voyageurs, some of whom had not been to confession for years, availed themselves of his ministry as did the Ottawa who had lived in Father Du Jaunay's mission. Although every inducement possible was held out to him to remain in Mackinac, the priest, in obedience to his orders, tarried but a few days and then resumed his journey.

The French settlement on the St. Joseph now claimed his attention. His first entry in the register dated August 17, 1768, records the baptism of a child born five years previously.[65] Two days later he conferred seven baptisms, five of them conditionally. One of these, in the case of a child born in 1762, indicates that no priest had officiated at the post from the time of Potier's visit.

Father Gibault went on to the Mississippi, and fixed his residence in Kaskaskia. We cannot here go into the long story of his priestly life, of his missionary journeys from Vincennes to Mackinac. On March 7, 1773, he was again in St. Joseph, signing himself "Vicar-General of the Illinois country and surrounding territory." He performed a few baptisms, and witnessed two marriages. His last entry, and the final one in the mission register, is dated March 21, 1773, and is the record of a burial.

We cannot dismiss Father Gibault without alluding to the title by which he deserves to be known in American history, "The Patriot Priest." By his influence over the French population in the Illinois country he made it possible for George Rogers Clark to bring the Northwest Territory under the American flag without bloodshed. He induced his people to furnish supplies to the Americans, as he himself did, in return for worthless Continental paper money instead of the current Spanish dollars. When many of the "Big Knives" themselves deserted Clark because they had not been paid, Father Gibault enlisted a company of his own people for the retaking of Vincennes from Governor Hamilton.

In later years when he and his people were poverty-stricken, Father Gibault petitioned the government to which he had given such whole-hearted allegiance for some recompense for his losses. There is no evidence that the petition was ever listened to. He retired to New Madrid on the western side of the Mississippi, and there he died, it is commonly supposed, about the year 1804.[66]

[65] In the register as published, see preceding note 40, the first entry is erroneously given as being April 17, 1768.

[66] The reader will find an exhaustive account of Father Gibault in the several volumes of the *Ill. Cath. Hist. Review.* Every volume beginning with the first (1918) should be consulted.

This sketch of Mission St. Joseph and the priests who attended it can perhaps best be closed with some details about the population to which they ministered. The French inhabitants were typical of many a frontier post. In the beginning there were a few soldiers and their wives. However, the number of soldiers at the fort at any time must have been insignificant compared to the colonists and traders who came in increasing numbers. Between 1740 and 1750 there were probably about fifty-five families living in or near the post. The register records the baptism of seventy-nine French children, and mentions the names of thirty-five French couples. Other names of both men and women scattered throughout the entries indicate the presence of a considerable floating population.

The register is filled with the names of the hardy adventurers, who making for some time at least their headquarters at the mission, roamed up and down the western country in quest of furs. Starting out from the towns along the St. Lawrence, their trails crossed in all the outlying posts of the lake region. Later on, they and their families settled down to form the nucleus of the little communities that lay dormant until another people urged on by land-hunger really began the development of the great West.

There are doubtless hundreds of French-Canadians living in Michigan at the present time whose ancestors lived clustered around the St. Joseph mission. Glancing over the faded register we notice Louis Metivier, the master carpenter, François Ménard, the interpreter, Jean Le Fevre, the farmer. Antoine Deshêtres moved to Detroit in 1751. René Bourassa followed him in 1765 with a large family. Louis Dequindre, who later became a colonel of militia in Detroit, lived for some years on the St. Joseph. The names Chevallier, Dumay, Levêque, Hamelin, occur frequently in the register. Little by little, following the British occupation, the number of French families declined. In 1780 there were eight families comprising forty-one persons, and seven individuals, "each one in his house." [67]

During the palmy days of French influence the place of honor at the post was held by the commandant, who had other duties than the keeping of the Indians under subjection. He was in great demand as a godfather, and in many instances conferred baptism in the absence of the missionary. The register names seven officers who were in command for varying terms from 1720 to 1755. One of them, the Sieur De Muy, was a botanist as well as a soldier, and on a visit to France he carried with him to Versailles a collection of the flora found in the valley of the St. Joseph River. He later commanded at Detroit, where he died in 1758. His epitaph is found in the records of St. Anne's:

[67] *Mich. Hist. Colls.*, XIII, 58–59.

"He died after having received the sacraments with all the piety we could desire, at the end of a life that was always most useful." [68]

Another notable figure was Coulon de Villiers, in charge of the post from 1725 to 1730.[69] He had married in 1706 Angelique, the sister of the heroine of Verchères.[70] From this union were born seven sons and six daughters, a goodly family that made its mark from Acadia to New Orleans. When the sire was appointed to Fort St. Joseph he brought along his sons to initiate them in the profession of arms. They were mere boys, the oldest being seventeen. In the campaign of 1730 against the Fox Indians, engineered by their father, the sons saw active service. Three years later at Green Bay, when De Villiers himself was killed fighting against the Sauk, a son fell with him.

The boys who played along the banks of the St. Joseph in the course of time became officers, and took part in the struggle between France and England for the possession of the West. One of them, Joseph, surnamed Jumonville, while leading a party of soldiers near the forks of the Ohio, was surprised by an English force and killed. His brother, Louis, started out from Fort Duquesne with an avenging force of French troops and Indian allies. The enemy, who were Virginia frontiersmen, took refuge in Fort Necessity. At the end of a one-day siege their position became untenable, and the Virginia colonel in command who surrendered his sword to Louis de Villiers was George Washington.[71]

Living alongside the French traders, farmers, and soldiers at St. Joseph was the Indian population of the mission. As stated in the beginning the mission had been founded to care for the Miami and Potawatomi who were gradually returning to an area from which the Iroquois had driven them. For many years there was a village of each tribe at the mission, but later on the Miami seem to have moved into Ohio and northern Indiana. In 1763 there were one hundred Potawatomi warriors at the post, ten Miami, and ten Illinois Indians from Kaskaskia.[72] Thirty years later, we find Ottawa and Potawatomi, but no Miami.[73] As a consequence of almost constant warfare, and of the roving habits of the Indians, there was scarcely an Indian settlement without its externs belonging to other tribes. A few such inclusions are disclosed by the mission register.

[68] *Ibid.*, XXXIV, 335.

[69] For the history of this family see L'Abbé Amédée Gosselin, *Notes Sur La Famille Coulon de Villiers* (Levis, 1906).

[70] The story of this young girl's heroic defense against a band of Iroquois may be read in Parkman, *Count Frontenac and New France under Louis XIV*, Chap. XIV.

[71] Reuben G. Thwaites, *France in America* (New York, 1905), 162–63.

[72] *N.Y. Col. Docs.*, IX, 10.

[73] *Ibid.*, VII, 583.

Father Guymonneau, for instance, baptized two Abnaki boys. We know that when La Salle made his second venture to descend the Mississippi he brought a band of Abnaki from the French settlements along the St. Lawrence. The original home of this tribe was in Maine, where they came in contact with Jesuit missionaries as early as 1613. The Abnaki mission proved to be a fruitful field, and the majority of the tribe was converted. Many of them came to settle at Sillery, a few miles above Quebec. The Abnaki at the St. Joseph mission were undoubtedly a remnant of the band which La Salle had taken west.[74]

From Father Mesaiger's entries it is evident that a number of Sauk Indians were domiciled at the mission. "In the year 1730 I baptized a dying child of the White Cat, and named him Pierre, the twenty-ninth of June. He died the next day." When the French first knew them the Sauk were a Wisconsin tribe, but in later years they were intimately affiliated with the Fox Indians. The White Cat was a noted Sauk chief, very friendly to the French, who acted as peacemaker between them and the Fox. It may be interesting to read a typical entry from the mission register dealing with Indian converts.

> Today the twenty-second day of the month of april of the year one thousand seven hundred and fifty two I solemnly administered Holy Baptism to two converts who desired it and who seemed sufficiently instructed. the first of the ottawa nation about 45 years old, the second of the Miami nation about 35 years old the daughter of pierre mekabekanga; the first pi8ssik8e took in Holy Bap. the name of marianne, her godfather was Sieur Bolon and the godmother the wife of dumay; the second 8abak8ik8e took the name of Marie, her godfather was Louis chevalier and her godmother the wife of jutras after which I received the mutual marriage consent of pierre mekabikanga, widower of Marie who died two years ago, and marianne pi8ssik8e. all this in the presence of the undersigned witness the year and day as above at St. Joseph.
>
> p. du jaunay miss of the soc of jesus [75]

The passing of the western country into English hands, and the conspiracy of Pontiac threw the Indians of the lake region into a general turmoil. A few years later came the slow American advance into the Northwest Territory. Again the tribes were torn by conflicting loyalties until the issue was decided by the War of 1812. During this whole period all missionary activity, save perhaps the efforts of the Moravian brethren, ceased. The return of peace brought strange

---

[74] For the history of the Abnaki mission see Shea, *Hist. of the Cath. Miss.,* Chap. II.

[75] The missionaries used a character resembling the Greek omega, or the figure 8, to designate a sound in the Indian languages approximating a guttural "ou."

changes. In the old Jesuit mission field on the St. Joseph, the Baptists, with government help, built their Carey Mission. But the Potawatomi longed for a Black Robe, and were not satisfied until one was sent them. During all the turbulent years that had elapsed since the closing of the St. Joseph mission, the memory of their spiritual fathers had not been effaced. A missionary who ministered to the last remaining band of Potawatomi in Michigan, and who gathered up their traditions, wrote the following passage that can serve as the epilogue of the St. Joseph mission.

There is no doubt that the greater part of the Potawatomi then on the St. Joseph were Catholics, for some three or four hundred headed by the wife of the former Naw-maw-qua-bee went to Quebec for the sole purpose of going to their paschal duties, to which place they were told that their good fathers, the Jesuits, had been exiled. Some wended their way to Vincennes for the same purpose; those who went to Quebec remained in the lower province for three years, at the end of which they returned merely a remnant, having fallen victims to that of all diseases most fatal to the Redman, the smallpox. After this from time to time they visited the following posts: Vincennes, Kaskaskia, and Detroit, after the death of the principal chief who annually had sent them as it were from post to post for the purpose of serving the God of the Jesuits. . . .[76]

[76] This passage is taken from an anonymous manuscript history of what was once the parish of Bertrand in Berrien County, Michigan. It was evidently written by one of the first Holy Cross fathers to labor in the district, and is preserved in the Notre Dame University Archives. References to this important archival source will henceforth be designated NDA.

CHAPTER VI

Policies in Conflict

WE HAVE seen that the beginnings of Catholic life in Michigan took place in an area lying about the Straits of Mackinac, termed by the Jesuits the Ottawa Mission, and served by them from the focal point at St. Ignace. As the Indians began their return to the southern peninsula the St. Joseph Mission was established. Viewing the increasing Indian population, the missionaries may have been planning new centers in suitable locations on the lower waterways; but any such hopes were definitely dispelled by the founding of Detroit.

The erection of this new post meant that the French government was taking a fresh hold on the western country. The palmy days of the fur monopoly were over. English traders had reaped a harvest at Mackinac as early as 1685 during a temporary absence of the garrison. Through the Iroquois the eastern colonies maintained a constant, irritating pressure against the French pretensions to the Lake region and the Mississippi valley. At the beginning of the eighteenth century France realized the growing menace of English infiltration, and began to choose strategic locations on the long curved line from Quebec to New Orleans that was intended to keep the enemy within bounds. In the new order of things the center of importance was shifted from Mackinac to Detroit.

This change had an important bearing on our religious history. The French plan contemplated the concentration of the Indian populations around the future posts, where they were to be taught agriculture, the French language, and French customs. Thus inoculated they were expected to be proof against foreign contagion. Consequently, as soon as the little stockade had gone up at Detroit the call went out to the Michigan tribes to settle in its neighborhood. The greater number obeyed, and as a result the missionaries in the north found themselves with depleted congregations. They might have followed their converts to Detroit had anyone but Cadillac been in command. They had known him too well to hope that anything was to be accomplished within the sphere of his authority.

This stand taken by the Jesuits broke the continuity which might otherwise have linked the history of Detroit with their missionary activity in the northern area of the state. They cut themselves off from what was destined to be the permanent center of Catholic stability and growth in Michigan. It was a Recollect who came as pastor with the hardy band that first attempted to fulfill the prophecy of his garrulous confrere, Hennepin. The rather confusing background against which this turn of events took place must now engage our attention.

We might begin with the violent antagonism shown by Cadillac, the founder of Detroit, to the Jesuits. It is evident from the scorching arraignments found in his letters that he came to have no love for them.[1] What the Jesuits thought of Cadillac is not so plainly shown, and the little correspondence which is accessible is couched in a more calm and dignified strain. The reasons for the antagonism have not been detailed adequately, at least for the English reader. Local historians, extolling the picturesque figure of Cadillac with pardonable pride, have not always been able to free themselves from a tincture of old religious controversies. For them there is something indefinably vexatious in the Jesuit. He appears to move in a mysterious half-light, pursuing aims which are but dimly apprehended. Insensibly our sympathies are drawn to Cadillac boldly defying the dictates of a powerful Society. Such a complex is obviously fatal to discrimination.

The clash between Cadillac and the Jesuits arose primarily neither out of personal animosities, nor out of extravagant pretensions by either side. Both parties were heated in the friction of conflicting theories, we may say, policies, which were sound and out in the open, but which needed a more ideal field than New France for their successful reconciliation.

In its larger aspect the issue involved the respective rights of Church and State in the management of the colony's affairs. That the issue should have arisen was not due to extraordinary claims or lust for power on the part of churchmen. To picture them acting from such motives is really to misunderstand them. The influence they sought and the things they fought for were deemed to be plainly within their rights. There was ample justification for their zealous protests. They cannot be judged without reference to a scheme of society and government with which we are entirely unfamiliar.

In the seventeenth century France was a Catholic country wherein Church and State were closely bound together. The administration of the Canadian colony naturally reflected the essential features of such an arrangement. The Church, and the reason for her existence,

---

[1] The Cadillac Papers, a collection of documentary material bearing on Cadillac and his period, make up Vol. XXXIII, and a large portion of Vol. XXXIV of the *Mich. Hist. Colls.*

were officially recognized. In theory, at least, even legislation and policies might be colored by her influence. She was entitled to the support and protection of government in the prosecution of her aims. The place of the Church is plainly shown in the composition of the provisional bodies set up for the colony's government. In the first council, created by the King in 1647, sat the Governor, the Superior of the Jesuits, and two influential citizens. The Bishop was a member of the Sovereign Council created in 1663, and exercised appointive powers concurrently with the Governor.

The legislation enacted by these bodies ranged over practically the whole of the colony's activities. The line of demarcation between matters purely religious and purely civil was often blurred. There was no reason why the churchmen, as members of the legislative councils, should not use their legal privileges to further the interests of religion as they saw them. They were placed there for the very purpose of carrying out the earnest desires of the French monarchs, so evident in their instructions, to promote morality and religion in the colony.

It may be interesting to glance at a few incidents showing the interplay of Church and State during the years that Cadillac nourished and carried out his great project. The Curé of Beaupré lodges a complaint against some of his parishioners, not with the bishop but with the Intendant, the highest civil officer in the colony. Two of his flock have attended Mass in an intoxicated condition, and more of them have walked out on him during his sermon to smoke their pipes outside the door. There may be read today in the register of the Supreme Council the ordinance by which Intendant Raudot remedied such a condition of affairs. Anyone selling liquor on Sundays and holydays, except for the use of the sick, is henceforth liable to a fine of ten livres. Anyone leaving a church to smoke during the sermon is likewise fined ten livres, to the profit of the parish strong box. When attending divine service all parishioners shall be mindful of the reverence due to the holy place wherein they worship.

The same Intendant conceives the idea of giving some recognition to the captains of the militia. He issues an ordinance that in future processions they are to walk immediately following the parish trustees. The Bishop protests, claiming that the laws of precedence make no mention of militia captains, and that the ordinance is an unwarranted intrusion on his authority. The case goes to the French court, and the Bishop is informed a year later that it is His Majesty's pleasure that the ordinance be obeyed.

The King had issued an order that no soldier or officer was to marry without the Governor's permission. Despite the opposition of their commander, Bishop Saint-Vallier officiated at the marriage of an officer and several soldiers. Again the complaint went to the French court that he was meddling in civil affairs. The Bishop stood his ground, pointing out the moral dangers incident to deferring marriage for a long period of years, and maintaining that the soldiery belonged to his flock as much as did the colonists, and that he was going to do his duty by them. This time the Bishop was sustained, and the Governor was told that he might inflict such penalties on the soldiers as he pleased as long as he kept in mind that his penalties bore no comparison to the eternal punishment to which he was exposing his soldiers by enforcing a strict compliance with his orders.[2]

These instances, and others like them which could be adduced, may appear trivial but they illustrate a condition of affairs which must be borne in mind when passing judgment on the activities of the bishops and the clergy. They also indicate the anomalous intervention of the King, that benevolent despot who could decide a knotty problem of theology as easily as some affair of state. Conflicts that arose between the Church and the civil authorities came not so much from arbitrary assumption of power on either side as from ignorance of what was His Majesty's will in the matter. Yet, all disposed as he was to further the religious interests of the colony, the King was jealous of his authority. Accusations against the bishops and the missionaries that they had transgressed their proper limits found a ready ear in Louis XIV. He had a subservient church at home, and he was not minded to let any body of churchmen gain too great an ascendancy. Hence we find a whole series of instructions to the governors and intendants reminding them that the zeal of the clergy was to be kept within bounds.

Obviously, we cannot here go deeply into the vexing problem of Church and State as it existed in the colony. For our purpose it is enough to know that there were serious difficulties, and that they did not arise from undue pretensions to dominance on the part of the clergy. Their aims and course of action were pursued with the full knowledge and consent of royal authority. When they were checked the missionaries were only the victims of those compromises which men in high places can so easily effect. We shall see this confirmed in the phases of the problem with which the history of Detroit is linked.

We have already pointed to the religious aspirations which brooded over the birth of New France. It is not necessary to demonstrate what every Christian must admit, that the origin of such ideals, as indeed of all missionary movements in the Church, is found in the

2 Abbé Auguste Gosselin, *L'Église du Canada* (Quebec, 1911), Part I, Msgr. de Saint-Vallier, 309–19.

command of the Divine Master himself. It is more pertinent to recall that the missionaries represented the insistence of Catholic France that a new field of evangelization be opened, a pressure that prevailed, and that they were officially delegated by royal authority to be the agents of that crusade, and hence were entitled to expect sympathetic assistance from every agency of government. There is no need to labor this fact. A cursory reading of the *Edits et Ordannances* shows many a passage conceived in the same spirit as the instructions given to Governor Callières as late as three years prior to the founding of Detroit.

> The principal and essential duty, and the one which His Majesty desires that the Sieur Callières fulfill with the greatest care, is to satisfy the interests of religion, whence come the blessings we expect from Heaven, and without which nothing can have happy issue. His Majesty desires that the Sieur Callières, as far as in him lies, will use the authority committed to him to the end that God may be served throughout the colony, and that the Christian religion may be spread among the surrounding tribes.[3]

The settlers and the priests who came to the colony following its restoration to France in 1632 were drawn from the mass of French Catholics who felt that somehow Providence had delivered New France into their hands for a holy purpose. The earlier missionaries had been too few and had remained too short a time to do more than prepare the way for their successors. The full tide of the missionary ideal came with the Jesuits. Its power is revealed by their sufferings, their heroisms, and their martyrdoms. Only with a full appreciation of the crusading zeal by which they were driven can we understand and sympathize with their protests when confronted with the obstacles presented by succeeding phases of the colony's development.

Unfortunately, the ideal conditions under which the missionaries began their labors in 1632 were of rather short duration. The reason lay in the defection of the very agencies by which evangelization was to prosper. Founded ostensibly to further missionary enterprise and colonization, the three successive trading companies to whom New France was entrusted were too prone to submerge their idealism in the tide of new-found wealth. Even the Hundred Associates soon dampened their zeal. Canada was looked upon as a region to be exploited; there was not so much concern about its welfare as about the wealth that could be drawn out of it. The trading companies had to make their own profits besides paying a percentage to the royal coffers. There was little or no incentive given to industry

---

[3] Gosselin, *op. cit.*, 302.

for this would have interfered with the business of the French manufacturers who furnished all supplies to the colony.[4]

New France was apparently the inexhaustible source of a luxury which all Europe was greedy to absorb, and that was fur. The economic life of the colony was bound up in the fur trade to such an extent that furs passed for currency. At first, the Indians brought their stocks to trading centers on the St. Lawrence like Montreal and Three Rivers. However, as adventurous traders gradually blazed their trails into the interior, the trade was carried on in the Indian country itself. The peculiar nature of the fur trade made it difficult to control. The government tried to regulate it by issuing licenses to a definite number of traders every year, forbidding unauthorized traffic under severe penalties. The system never worked, and the Indian country was soon overrun by a swarm of unlicensed traders, the Coureurs de Bois. Technically outlaws, and yet often in collusion with dishonest officials, irresponsible and unrestrained, they haunted the streams and trails of the western country.

It is not difficult to understand the powerful attraction which this kind of life held for the Canadian youth. In contrast to the scanty rewards of agriculture, won at the cost of hard labor, was the easy life of the woods. Equipped with a canoe and a stock of trinkets obtained on credit, any young man might slip away from the settlements to spend months among the Indians, living as unconventionally as he cared until he had accumulated a profitable load of furs to be disposed of through underground channels. The fur trade weaned the best blood of the population from the more prosaic occupations of pioneer life, and begot a distaste for labor and the restraints of social life. It substituted for an orderly and substantial development of the colony a fever of prosperity feeding on an ever increasing demand for fur.

Whether the liquor traffic originated with the English or the French is not as important as the fact that it became an indispensable adjunct to the fur trade. It was early discovered that the Indian had an insatiable craving for liquor. When a deep kettle or a shining axe could not move him, a pot of brandy invariably softened him into a profitable deal, from the traders' standpoint. To the Indian liquor was a veritable poison; he had not the tolerance for alcohol developed in the European by centuries of use. Moderation was impossible; whenever able he drank until he was sodden. It would have been difficult enough to civilize the Indian had he not learned the white

[4] A popular account of conditions in the colony may be found in Bennet Munroe, *Crusaders of New France*, in the Chronicles of America Series (Yale University Press, 1921).

man's vices. Once addicted to liquor he was hopeless. Whatever desirable native qualities he possessed were drowned in degeneracy.

The Indian, fur, and liquor were the bases on which the prosperity of New France was raised. Wealth flowed into the mother country, and a generous portion of it into the royal treasury. A powerful and well-placed group of merchants and officials who battened on the fur trade resented any interference either with its spread or with its methods. In the race for profits they were not particularly interested in the moral problems that arose.

In 1663 there occurred a significant change in the status of the colony. It now became a royal province; the mother country was now definitely committed to the acquisition of an overseas empire. To further colonization the last of the trading companies, the West Indies Company, was established. It functioned no better than the others, and its charter was revoked in 1674. The maintenance of the colony, its extension into the interior of the continent, and especially its preservation against English encroachment now became the direct concern of the home government.

It is against this background that the policies of the missionaries must be viewed. A body of men cherishing a purpose like theirs was bound to come to grips sooner or later with the civil authorities over the Indian problem. If the colonial officials and the home government were interested in his conversion they were at the same time faced with the necessity of making nice adjustments of this interest to the exigencies of trade, and to such measures as they deemed necessary for the defense of the colony. Their position was admittedly a difficult one, and it is not surprising that their course was marked by a series of irritating compromises which did not solve the problem. Before long, the missionaries realized the serious menace to their success that lay in the fur trade as it was conducted. Two aspects of it, as already mentioned, were peculiarly harmful. The Coureurs de Bois, hundreds of miles removed from the police power of the colony, may have been noted for their courage and hardihood but, if we are to believe the missionaries, not all of them for their virtues. Living for months with some Indian group they often undid, by their vices and bad example, the results of months of patient instruction. Later on, when troops were stationed in the several western posts, moral conditions became still worse.

But the greatest menace to the missions came from the increasing flood of liquor that debauched and degraded the Indian to the extent of destroying in him whatever made him even susceptible of conversion. When the allegiance of the Indian became a matter of the greatest consequence to the colony, and the government frantically insisted on the necessity of competing with the stream of English liquor, the missionaries could not bring themselves to assent to such a policy. It might be advantageous to the government; in the end it meant the ruin of their missions. Their viewpoint is admirably expressed in the words of Bishop Saint-Vallier, who while visiting the Jesuits at Montreal had a conference with Governor Vaudreuil on this burning issue. The governor advanced his most telling argument.

> Do you want to see this country lost to the King and handed over to our neighbors? They are attracting the Indians by giving them all the liquor they desire. Before long this colony will go up in flames.
> Shall we preserve this colony to the King of France by offending the King of Heaven? Our monarch is too pious to wish to be master of Canada on such conditions. If we must die at the hand of the Indian, to whom should always be refused what cannot be given without sin, it is better to die innocently than to live in guilt.[5]

The bishop's words were spoken in 1714 but they echoed a long established conviction. As a result of their missionary experience the Jesuits held two well defined policies which were deemed necessary to counteract the two evils that wrought havoc with their missions. The first was an unalterable opposition to the liquor traffic. In this they had the entire support of the bishops, who had an added reason for their opposition in the disorders which they witnessed in the colony itself. The details of the liquor controversy, and the record of the successive victories and defeats gained and suffered by the missionaries need not detain us. They are found in every book dealing with the period. The second policy of the missionaries, which along with the first one has some bearing on the history of Detroit, is not so often mentioned.

We have already seen that Richelieu had granted citizenship to the Indian with baptism as the only condition. For all practical purposes that was a magnificent gesture and no more. However, it probably paved the way for a rosy romanticism concerning the Indian which soon became current. The Indian was to be completely Gallicized. To the charms of his sylvan existence were to be added the graces of French customs and speech. By a close contact with the French he was to absorb the culture needed to make him fit for citizenship. The idea caught on at court, and the Jesuits were ordered to begin the program by opening an Indian school at Quebec. This they did in 1635. Despite their earnest efforts for five years they could make no progress, and the project was abandoned. Later, Bishop Laval was commanded to resume the work, but he too could succeed no better.

[5] *Gosselin*, op. cit., 273–74.

Talon and Colbert were both hearty advocates of the Gallicizing policy, and did their best to further it.[6]

Meanwhile, the Jesuits had been living in close contact with the Indian for many years. They had no illusions about him, and knew from accurate first hand knowledge that he could never become a Frenchman. What often happened when the two races lived together in too close contact was that the Frenchmen became Indians. The Jesuits gradually arrived at the conviction that the salvation of the Indian lay not in the fusion of the two races, but in a very definite segregation of the Indians from the French. In the pursuit of this policy they, of course, drew down upon themselves the charge of wanting to keep the Indian under their control for the glory, and even the enrichment, of the Society. We need only reflect upon the degree of assimilation that has taken place in the United States between the white and Indian population, and the methods of our own government in dealing with the Indian problem, to realize the wise foresight of the missionaries. When the fur trade brought the Coureurs de Bois with their vices in too intimate contact with the Indian in the most isolated outposts, the Jesuits were more than ever convinced that they were right, and determined at any cost to make their policy prevail. The French expansion westward with the consequent necessity of establishing French groups at strategic points in the Indian country provoked the open expression of what had hitherto been only an earnest conviction. In the West the missionary ideal with its attendant policies took its last stand against political expediency.

It is easy to see that the missionaries could hardly have acted otherwise. They had dedicated their lives to the conversion of the Indian, an endeavor fully in accord with the wishes of their King and his government. When they protested against conditions which they judged to be prejudicial to their aims they were wholly within their rights. Had they not done so they would have proved recreant to their ministry. We may ponder the wisdom of their policies, their opposition to the Gallicizing of the Indian, for instance, but we may judge them only by drawing upon an experience gained from three hundred years of subsequent history. To them the evils were very close, and they pressed for solution. To see anything mysterious or baleful in the activities or policies of the Jesuit missionaries is to disclose an ignorance of historical facts, or worse, a prejudice that would deny a meed of glory to a band of men who struggled against the most adverse conditions to realize a Christian ideal.

[6] For the Jesuit opposition to the Gallicizing policy of the government see Rochemonteix, *op. cit.*, I, 280–94; II, 177.

Thus far we have engaged in a statement of policies which were more or less operative throughout the whole of New France. We must now confine ourselves to the interplay of these policies in the history of Michigan during the years preceding the founding of Detroit. It will be remembered that the first Jesuits to visit Michigan, Fathers Jogues and Raymbaut, came to the Sault in 1641. However, as they remained but a few days, we must date the beginnings of missionary activity there from the arrival of Father Marquette in 1668. On his departure for the mission at La Pointe, which owed its origin to Father Allouez, he was replaced by Father Dablon. In the meantime Gabriel Druilletes had also been assigned to the Sault, and through the zeal and untiring enery of the two missionaries remarkable progress was made among the Chippewa and other Algonquins who frequented the St. Mary's River.

The *Relation* of 1671 gives a stirring picture of the Indians' response to the work of the missionaries. Coincident with the arrival of Father Druilletes some sort of epidemic had broken out. The medicine men were powerless, but the priests, while ministering to the physical ills of the sick, taught them confidence in the Great Spirit and in prayer. Such a surprising number of cures followed that on a day in October, 1670, the Indians decided to proclaim their gratitude publicly. They thronged the mission chapel to declare officially that the Sault was thenceforth Christian, that the God of their prayer was the Master of life. An aged Indian stood up to give his testimony. He had believed at one time in the incantations of the medicine men, but now he acknowledged that he had been deceived by the evil Manitou. At the point of death he had used the prayer of the Black Robe, and had been straightway cured. His wife had been stricken also, and all one night he had prayed for her thus: "Jesus, you healed me. I was dying and you gave me life. My wife is in extremity. You are good, and you can do as much for her as you did for me. I love her, and she will love you. She will be a Christian." At dawn she had been cured. When he ended his testimony the crowd broke out into applause and deafening shouts, "The Sault prays; the Sault is Christian." Within a year more than three hundred were baptized.

In 1671 Father Marquette established the mission of St. Ignace. The Huron built their village near the mission chapel, and later the Ottawa. The former, a remnant that had escaped the disaster of 1650, are thus described in the *Relation* of 1672.

> At present they show great fervor. They fill the chapel every day, and during the day they often visit it. They sing the praises of God with a devotion that has surprised the Frenchmen who have witnessed it. Adults are there baptized, and old men by their example teach the chil-

dren to be fervent in their prayers. In a word, they practice all the exercises of piety that one could expect from a body of Christians formed upwards of twenty years ago, although for the greater part of that time they have been without church or pastor, and with no other Master than the Holy Ghost.

Because of its favorable location, and of the number of Indians who settled in its neighborhood, St. Ignace became the center of the Ottawa mission. The Jesuit superiors resided there, and to it for rest and retreat came the priests from all the outlying missions, namely, Manitoulin Island, Green Bay, St. Joseph Mission, and the several missions of the Illinois mission. The Sault maintained its importance for some years but was abandoned before 1700.

The same circumstances which determined the choice of the Sault, and later of St. Ignace, as mission posts were no less operative in making these localities succeeding centers of French influence. The first white man to visit the Straits of Mackinac was most likely Etienne Brulé, who had been a companion of Champlain.[7] In 1634 Jean Nicolet halted there on his way to visit the People of the Sea. There is no more bizarre picture in the annals of western exploration than that of Nicolet, arrayed in a voluminous robe of China damask "strewn with flowers and birds," advancing to meet what he confidently supposed to be an Asiatic people. They turned out to be the Winnebagoes of Green Bay, the "Nation of Stinkers."[8] The domination of the Iroquois over the approaches to the West following their outbreak in 1650 made trading quite impossible for some years. Chouart and Radisson managed to get through as far as Green Bay in 1658.[9] A number of traders accompanied Father Ménard to Lake Superior two years later. In 1667 the famous Nicolas Perrot, beloved of the Indians, began his operations in the lake region. Three years later Dollier de Casson and Galinée report a crowd of traders at the Sault.

The year 1671 definitely closed this period of desultory trading. Jean Talon had come to Canada as Intendant for the King over what was now a royal domain. One of the great figures of Canadian history, a man of energy and vision, he was deeply interested in the welfare of New France. During the seven years of his administration, from

[7] Justin Winsor, *Narrative and Critical History of America* (Boston, New York, 1884), IV, 165.

[8] The French called Green Bay, *La Baie des Puants*. Father Vimont in the *Relation* of 1640 give the following explanation. "Some Frenchmen call them the Nation of Stinkers because the Algonquin word *Ouinipeg* signifies 'stinking water.' They thus call the water of the sea. Therefore these people call themselves 'Ouinipegons' because they come from the shores of a sea of which we have no knowledge; and we must not call them the Nation of Stinkers but the Nation of the Sea."

[9] N.E. Dionne, *Chouart et Radisson* (Quebec, 1910), 48.

1665 to 1672, he aroused the colony to an activity which it had never before known.[10] The acreage of land under cultivation was largely increased and new crops introduced. Factories were opened at Quebec for the manufacture of hats, shoes, and cloth. Shipbuilding, fisheries, stock-raising, and tanneries were other ventures sponsored by the tireless Intendant. He planned to develop the mineral resources of the country, particularly the copper deposits on the shore of Lake Superior. With all these major projects in mind, he found time to open a brewery in Quebec hoping that the inhabitants would thereby be weaned from strong drink.

Meanwhile, Chouart and Radisson had transferred their allegiance to the English, and had interested Prince Rupert in the profits to be made from trade with the northern Indians. In the fall of 1668, the Nonesuch, piloted by Chouart, came to anchor in Hudson Bay. She returned to England the next year having amply satisfied the expectations of everyone concerned.[11] When the news reached Talon, he realized that measures had to be taken to keep the English out of the lake region, and to attach the Indians to French interests. Nicolas Perrot, the man best fitted for the task, was engaged to summon every tribe within his reach to the Sault. At the same time, Simon François Daumont, the Sieur St. Lusson, was commissioned to represent the majesty of the French government before the Indians, and to take possession of the western country in the name of France.

Fourteen Indian tribes gaped with astonishment at the ceremony unrolled before them on June 14, 1671, "the most solemn proceeding," relates Father Dablon, "that was ever gone through in these countries." He thus describes what took place.[12]

Everyone having gathered for a great public council, and (St. Lusson) having chosen as suitable for his purpose an eminence that rose above the village of the Saulters, he had a cross erected, and then the arms of the King, with all the splendor he could think of. The Cross was publicly blessed with all the ceremonies of the Church by the superior of these missions, and when it was raised up ready to be fixed in the ground, the *Vexilla* was chanted. To the admiration of the Indians a goodly number of the Frenchmen who were present took up the hymn, and there was mutual joy at the sight of this glorious standard of Jesus Christ that seemed lifted up so high in order to reign over the hearts of these poor peoples.

After that, the shield of France having been affixed to a cedar post, was raised above the cross while we sang the *Exaudiat*, and in this cor-

[10] Talon's policies were not interrupted during a sojourn in France from 1668 to 1670, while Bouteroue replaced him.

[11] This expedition was the genesis of the Hudson Bay company.

[12] The *Relation* of 1671, introduction to Part III.

ner of the world prayed for the sacred person of His Majesty. Then Monsieur de Lusson, with all the forms prescribed on such occasions, took possession of these countries, and the air resounded with redoubled cries of "Vive le Roy" and the discharge of musketry, to the joy and wonderment of all these peoples who had never seen anything similar.

Then a hush fell on the tribes as a man whom the Indians knew and respected arose to speak. It was Father Allouez. With thoughts and words suited to his hearers he proceeded to impress them with the meaning of the double sovereignty under which they were henceforth to live.

Look at that cross so high above your heads. On it Jesus Christ, the Son of God . . . willed to be fastened and to die to satisfy the Eternal Father for our sins. He is the Master of our lives, of heaven, and of earth, and of hell. It is of him that I am always speaking to you, and his name and words that I have carried to all these regions.

But see this other post to which are attached the arms of the great Chief of France whom we call the King. He lives beyond the sea, and is chief over all other chiefs; he has no equal in the world. All the other chiefs that you have ever seen or heard are like children compared to him; he is like the big tree, and they like the little plants that you step on when walking. When he says the word, "I am going to war," everyone obeys, and ten thousand chiefs each raise companies of a hundred soldiers on land and sea. . . . When he attacks he is more terrible than thunder. The ground trembles, the air and the sea are on fire from the discharge of his cannons . . .

The Relation goes on to say that Father "added many other things in a similar vein, so that the Indians were struck with admiration and surprise that there should be on earth a man so great, so rich, and so powerful." St. Lusson followed with a harangue on the benefits to be derived from the new alliance. As night came on, bonfires flamed up projecting against the darkness feathered and painted braves, and the compact group of Frenchmen singing the *Te Deum* to bring the ceremony to a close.

The presence of Father Allouez on this momentous occasion was only another example of the services rendered to the colony by the missionaries. They might differ with the governmnt over policies to be pursued, but there was never question of their loyalty and wholehearted devotion to the colony's welfare. The colonial authorities frequently acknowledeged with gratitude their dependence on the good offices of the missionaires. In the conduct of Indian affairs their cooperation was indispensable. Their knowledge of Indian languages and character, the respect, and often the affection in which they were held by the tribes, made them the undisputed representatives of French influence.

By the scene enacted at the Sault, Talon intended to make that influence felt in the West as the first step in the realization of a great colonial empire. Before proceeding further he had to solve the mystery of the "Great Water" in the interior that led to the sea. But what sea? Did the river run across the continent into the Pacific, or down through the continent into the Gulf of Mexico? Both Spain and England were anxious to find out. Tremendous claims could be based on the first accurate knowledge, and Jolliet's expedition of 1673 was to furnish it.

Although the matter was not definitely settled by the partial exploration of the Mississippi, new Indian tribes were discovered, and a new impetus was given to missionary zeal. During the next ten years there were probably as many as twelve Jesuits going back and forth through St. Ignace on their apostolic journeys covering the territory from the Illinois country to the shores of Lake Superior. The missions were in the heyday of their vitality. Slowly but surely the missionaries were making headway. And just as surely were gathering the elements that would destroy the gains made by such unparalleled, self-sacrificing devotion.

The missionaries had been favored by the comparative peace that had reigned in the West dating from the punitive expedition of the Marquis de Tracy against the Iroquois in 1665. But he had only scotched them. Their spirit remained unbroken; they were only biding their time for revenge. Their hatred of the French was fomented by the English and Dutch traders longing to get into the rich fur country in the basin of the Great Lakes. If the Iroquois could strike fear into the tribes of that region who were friendly to the French, the fur trade could be diverted from Quebec. In the summer of 1680 the blow fell. The famous town of the Illinois Indians, situated near the present Utica, Illinois, was cruelly ravaged.[13] For the next twenty years the western tribes were in a turmoil. Torn between fear of the Iroquois and the allegiance which the French pressed upon them, distracted by continuous efforts to maneuver themselves into some position of safety from the dilemma that pursued them, the Indians were not in too receptive a mood for the preaching of the missionaries.

Meanwhile important changes were taking place in St. Ignace. Favorable as the location was to the missionaries it proved none the less attractive to the fur traders, who flocked there in growing numbers, introducing characteristic evils to the Indian population. Fol-

13 Parkman, *La Salle*, Chap. XVI.

lowing the outbreak of hostilities with the Iroquois it became necessary to station troops in such a strategic location, to protect trade in some measure, and to forestall any move at possession on the part of the English. St. Ignace was given its first garrison in 1683, when La Durantaye was sent there with thirty soldiers.[14]

The commander was a religious man, and much in sympathy with the missionaries. Together they strove against the rising tide of disorder that menaced not only the work of the mission but French interests as well. We catch a glimpse of the situation in a report of the Canadian governor to the French minister.

> In spite of the King's edicts, the coureurs de bois have carried a hundred barrels of brandy to Michilimackinac in a single year; and their libertinism and debauchery have gone to such an extremity that it is a wonder the Indians have not massacred them all to save themselves from their violence, and recover their wives and daughters from them. This, Monseigneur, joined to our failure in the last war, has drawn upon us such contempt among all the tribes, that there is but one way to regain our credit, which is to humble the Iroquois by our unaided strength. . . .[15]

A year after writing this letter, Denonville embarked on his famous expedition against the Iroquois, which resulted merely in the destruction of the Seneca villages.[16] Through the untiring efforts of the missionaries, and of Nicolas Perrot, a large number of Indians from the lake region had been persuaded to align themselves definitely with the French by joining Denonville. On the way down from Mackinac to the rendezvous at Niagara, the Indians, led by La Durantaye, and accompanied by Father Enjalran, passed through the Detroit River. Although time was precious, the war party halted long enough to take formal possession of the region in the name of the King of France. The record of this ceremony has been preserved, and is here given both for its intrinsic interest, and for the fact that it records, to the best of our knowledge, the first time that any priest of the Ottawa mission was in the vicinity of Detroit.

> Ollivier Morel Esquire, Sieur de la Durantaye, Commandant for the King in the lands of the Outaouax, Miamis, Poutouamis, Cioux, and other tribes, under the orders of the Marquis de Denonville, Governor-General of New France.
>
> This seventh day of June, one thousand six hundred and eighty-seven, in the presence of the Rev. Father Angeliran, Superior of the

---

[14] *N. Y. Col. Docs.,* IX, 203.

[15] Letter of Denonville to the Minister dated June 12, 1686. Quoted in Parkman, *Count Frontenac and New France,* 127.

[16] *Ibid.,* Chap. VIII.

missions to the Outaouax at Missilimackinac de Ste. Marie du Sault, to the Miamis, to the Illinois, to the Puans of the Bay, and to the Sioux; in the presence of M. de la Forest, formerly commandant at the fort of St. Louis with the Illinois; of M. de Lisle our lieutenant; and of M. de Beauvais, Lieutenant of the fort of St. Joseph at the strait between Lakes Huron and Eries, We declare to all whom it may concern that we came to the margin of the St. Denys River, situated three leagues from Lake Errier on the strait between the said Lakes Errier and Huron to the south of the said strait and lower down towards the entrance to Lake Errier on the north, on behalf of the King and in his name to repeat the taking possession of the said posts, which was done by M. de la Salle to facilitate the journeys he made, and had made by barge from Niagara to Missilimaquinac in the years . . . at which said stations we should have had a post set up again with the arms of the King, in order to mark the said re-taking possession, and directed several dwellings to be built for the establishment of the French and savages, Chaouannous and Miamis, for a long time owners of the said lands of the strait and of Lake Errier, from which they withdrew for some time for their greater convenience. The present deed executed in our presence signed by our hand and by the Rev. Father Angeliran of the Company of Jesus, by MM. de la Forest, De Lisle and de Beauvais. . . .[17]

After the campaign, during which Father Enjalran was wounded, La Durantaye with his motley followers returned to Mackinac. Two years later, Denonville was recalled, and Frontenac for the second time became governor of Canada. During his first tenure of office he had been an avid abettor of the fur trade, and, of course, a bitter opponent of the Jesuits. His ill will had driven him to such a point that he could write to the Minister a malicious falsehood like the following: "To speak frankly, the Jesuits think as much of the conversion of beaver as they do of souls; their missions are for the most part pure mockeries." [18] He was not alone in trying to cover up his own illicit trading by casting suspicion on the Jesuits.

Shortly after his return, Frontenac removed La Durantaye from his command to replace him with de Louvigny.[19] The Jesuits felt that the removal of La Durantaye was a result of his friendship for them,

[17] Margry, Découvertes, V, 31–33; Mich. Hist. Colls., XXXIII, 41. Just where the pole bearing the royal arms was erected is open to speculation. In the map accompanying the original edition of Charlevoix's travels there is a Riviere St. Deny, but from its location it must be either the Huron or the Raisin, and it does not empty into the strait. The only river fulfilling the conditions must be the Rouge. This is confirmed by the report of a French traveler who passed by Detroit in 1753. "We continued our route through the Detroit River which we followed and ascended for its whole length of thirty-two leagues; we found on our left the Saint-Denis River, and then Lake Sainte-Claire. . . ." J. C. Bonnefons, Voyage au Canada (Quebec, 1887), 69.

[18] Rochemonteix, op. cit., III, 134.

[19] N. Y. Col. Docs., IX, 470.

and that it was really a blow to their influence.[20] Unlike his predecessor, de Louvigny made no effort to prevent the orgies and debauchery that raged around the mission, although he seems to have been politic enough in his dealings with the missionaries, and to have treated them with respect. He tendered his resignation in the fall of 1694 to make way for a personage who came with the seal of Frontenac's benediction, Antoine Laumet de Lamothe, Sieur de Cadillac.

The new commandant owed his appointment as much to his talent and abilities, as to his friendship with Frontenac. He had come to Canada in 1683, at the age of twenty-five, and had soon made a place for himself.[21] As a former lieutenant in a French regiment, and with a knowledge of seamanship, well educated and facile in expression, he was a valuable addition to the colony. Taking up his residence at Port-Royal, Cadillac seems to have spent the greater part of the next five years in trading operations along the Atlantic coast. In 1689, he was accorded a land grant which took in part of the coast of Maine, including the present Bar Harbor. Meanwhile the Canadian authorities were urging on the home government as a solution of all their difficulties a surprise attack on New York and Boston, which should once for all end British claims to supremacy in North America. Cadillac strongly believed in the feasibility of such a venture, and had recorded his observations of the coast as far south as Boston. In 1692 he was summoned to Versailles as the man best fitted to furnish accurate information and plans. The government dallied with the project and finally abandoned it; but Cadillac's ability had been recognized, and it is interesting to speculate as to what the course of history might have been had his plans and advice been followed.[22]

On his return from France Cadillac became an officer in the troops stationed at Quebec, and enjoyed the patronage of Frontenac. The

[20] Charlevoix, *op. cit.*, (Shea ed.), IV, 137–38.

[21] For the most recent and exhaustive treatment of Cadillac see Jean Delanglez, S. J., "Cadillac's Early Years in America," in *Mid-America* (Chicago) for January, 1944; "Antoine Laumet *alias* Cadillac, Commandant at Michilimackinac," in the same periodical for April, July, and October 1945. The series continues: "The Genesis and Building of Detroit," in the same periodical for April, 1948; "Cadillac at Detroit," in the two numbers for July and October. For family details and coat of arms see J. Edmond Roy, *Rapport sur les Archives De France*, Publication of the Archives of Canada, No. 6, (Ottawa, 1911), 998–1000. See also Edouard Forestié, *Hommages à la Memoire du Chevalier de Lamothe Cadillac* (Montaubon, 1905), and his curious explanation of the origin of Cadillac's spurious coat of arms in *Notes Complementaires sur Lamothe Cadillac* (Montaubon, 1907). Consult also the same author's *Notes Historiques ou Ephemerides Montalbanaises* (Montaubon, 1882). These are all in the Burton Historical Collection. This unique and enormous collection of material bearing on the history of Detroit, and housed in the Detroit Public Library, will be designated BHC in all future references.

[22] *N. Y. Col. Docs.*, IX, 530; 659.

bluff old count was no doubt attracted by the verve and wit of his young subaltern, and his estimate of Cadillac is attested by the words in which the appointment to Mackinac was reported to the Minister: "Sieur de la Motte Cadillac . . . is a man of rank, full of capability and valor; and I have just sent him to Missilimakina to command all those posts of the upper country. . . ." [23]

However, there are other things to be reported about Cadillac besides his valor and undoubted talents. When he married Therese Guyon in Quebec in 1687, he was inscribed on the register as "Antoine de Lamothe, Esquire, Sieur de Cadillac . . . son of Mr. Jean de la Mothe, sieur of the place called Cadillac of Launay and Semontel, counsellor of the parliament of Toulouse . . ." [24] Most of this was pure invention. His father, Jean Laumet, was a lawyer and petty magistrate of St. Nicolas de la Grave, while his mother was descended from a long line of merchants. There is no evidence to show that the seigniory of Cadillac ascribed to Jean Laumet ever existed. Cadillac, feeling the need of a coat of arms, and not being entitled to any, appropriated the arms of the barons of Lamothe-Bardigues belonging to the family of Esparbes de Lussan. Such pretensions are clearly indicative of a Gascon running true to type. His nimble imagination always embroidered the truth; exaggerations and extravagant statements came natural to him. It is not easy to conceive Cadillac as ever doing anything temperately. His restless and impetuous disposition kept him always in a ferment. Domineering and avaricious to the point of cupidity he lived in an atmosphere of real and fancied antagonism. His failure as commandant of Detroit, and later as governor of Louisiana, testifies to the resentment that he invariably engendered in those subject to his authority. [25]

That Cadillac throughout his life was a faithful son of the Church is beyond question. However, that did not keep him from expressing his opinions about its representatives. On that subject he could write page after page of bitter invective. His association with Frontenac naturally inflamed him against the Bishop and the Jesuits, but he could include diocesan clergy as well. Just before leaving Quebec for Mackinac he wrote a typical seventeen page letter to France setting forth the clerical oppression under which the colony was groaning. How extravagant Cadillac could be when indulging in his favorite pastime appears from the following extracts. The Bishop had for-

[23] *Mich. Hist. Colls.*, XXXIII, 72.
[24] *Ibid.*, 308.
[25] For estimates of Cadillac see Ferland, *op. cit.*, II, 366; Benjamin Sulte, *Histoire des Canadiens Francais* (Montreal, 1882), VI, 107–13. Margry in the introduction to his fifth volume of *Découvertes* . . . is most sympathetic.

bidden as improper two plays which the garrison intended to stage, a step Cadillac could not ignore.

"The clerics already began preparing for battle. Behold them armed from head to foot, taking their bows and arrows . . . The numerous party of sham religious people flocked together in the streets and squares, and afterwards got into the houses, to confirm the weak in their error or to try to instill it into those who were stronger . . . but, as their schemes were almost entirely unsuccessful, they thought it necessary at least to conquer or die, and persuaded the Bishop . . . to have a charge delivered in the church by which the Sieur de Mareuil, Lieutenant on half-pay, was forbidden the use of the sacraments . . ." [26]

Cadillac then flays the Curé of Batiscan, who had been ordered to deny the sacraments to a member of his parish.

I will not speak of the many extravagances of this rector, upheld by the authority of his prelate, even to preaching from the pulpit that no one but wretches and damned souls could depose to Madame Debrieux being a respectable woman; that if anyone were bold enough to do so, he would beat him to death, and that he would have them put into irons for six months on bread and water; that the Comte de Frontenac had not long to live, but the Bishop was young and would lead them a fine dance one of these days; that he laughed at the complaints made against him to the Supreme Council; that all he did was by the order of his bishop, who recognized no one in this country as above himself, and that there was no judge of his actions except the Pope. Who would not think, at first sight, that this account is full of prejudice? Yet it is just as true as that there is a sun in the heavens.[27]

After detailing many other incidents calculated to show the bishop in a bad light, Cadillac closes his letter with a eulogy of Frontenac.

Fortunately we have a happy, wise, and most enlightened government, the protector of the liberty which the King grants to his subjects, the enemy of an odious, ecclesiastical, and intolerable domination. One must be here to see the plots which go on every day to upset the designs and projects of a governor. A head as firm and level as that of the Comte is required to hold out against the snares laid for him everywhere. If he wishes for peace, that is enough to make them oppose it, and cry out that all is lost. If he wants to make war, they tell him the Colony will be ruined. He would not have so many troubles on hand . . . if he did not oppose the excommunications which they cast at random and the scandals which arise from them; if he would forbid wine and brandy to the Indians; if he appointed no officers except through the communities; if he did not say a word about the fixed

[26] Mich. Hist. Colls., XXXIII, 54.
[27] Ibid., 57.

livings and patronage rights. If the Comte were of that mind, he would certainly be a man without an equal; and he would soon be on the list of the greatest Saints, for they canonize them in this country cheaply.[28]

The Jesuits were soon to meet this redoubtable opponent, for a postscript to the letter states: "I am setting out today to go to the Outavois."

[28] *Ibid.*, 70.

CHAPTER VII

Cadillac and the Jesuits

WHEN Cadillac arrived to take up the duties of his new appointment he found four Jesuits stationed at St. Ignace: the Superior, Father Henri Nouvel, and Fathers Etienne Carheil, Julien Binneteau, and Pierre Pinet. The first named, a man now seventy-three, had spent years in the rigorous missions of the Saguenay region before coming to the Sault in 1672.[1] The second, noted for his literary talent, his zeal, and his sanctity, had labored for twenty years among the Iroquois before his transfer to Mackinac in 1683.[2] Father Binneteau, with two years service among the Abnaki, was just beginning his missionary career. He was to end it five years later, consumed by fever contracted on a Missouri prairie.[3] Pinet, the youngest of the group, and destined to begin the first mission within the present limits of Chicago, had arrived shortly before Cadillac.[4]

For a while the new commandant lived in perfect accord with the missionaries, and seems to have given them no reason for complaint. With characteristic energy he set to work to destroy the web of intrigue spun by the English and the Iroquois in the effort to lure the tribes in the lake region from French allegiance. It was in the performance of this task that the first open break with the missionaries occurred.

A party of Ottawa and Potawatomi had been instigated to attack a band of Iroquois who had been hunting in the Saginaw valley. The intruders were too surprised to offer much resistance, and thirty scalps and as many prisoners were brought in triumph to St. Ignace. Onnaske, the Ottawa chief, formally presented the spoils to Cadillac with the following speech:

Father, I shall not tell you what I have done. The French who have wintered at the Saguinan, have doubtless informed you of it . . . I listened to you, Father; I have performed thy will; I have fulfilled thy word; . . . let the warriors have some brandy to drink; I pledged my-

[1] Rochemonteix, op. cit., II, 407–10.
[2] Jesuit Relations . . . (Thwaites), XLVII, 317.
[3] Ibid., LXV, 263.
[4] Ill. Cath. Hist. Rev., I, 14.

124

self that they should have some; I will not taste of it; I promised it to them. They did as you desired; they told me no lies; they have killed the Warriors and made no prisoners. Do not lie to them. Give them to drink.[5]

Cadillac acceded to the chief's demand, and ordered ten pots of brandy to be distributed to the Indians who had taken part in the attack. The account of this affair, sent to France, goes on to say:

It was but little among two hundred men who were very dry, and unused to drink. They found means to get some (more) from the French (so as to continue) singing through the night, but there was no disorder. The Missionaries, however, found fault, and complained of it to Sieur de La Mothe who answered, That the action the Indians had achieved ought to serve as their excuse; if a little hilarity grieve you so much, how will you be able to endure the daily exposure of these Neophytes, for whom you feel so much affection, to the excessive use of English Rum and to the imbibing of Heresy.[6]

The scene presented by two hundred drink-crazed Indians holding an all night celebration around the palisades of St. Ignace must be left to the imagination. Whether Cadillac understated, or the missionaries exaggerated the night's happenings is not clear, but, at any rate, Father Pinet preached two sermons, aimed in no unmistakable terms at Cadillac, denouncing him as the cause of the disorders that had taken place.[7] Cadillac, stung by this defiance of his control over the Indians, was furious. He threatened to prosecute Father Pinet for his immoderate language, and demanded a written retraction. Either to conciliate Cadillac, or to acknowledge that his subordinate had gone too far, Father Nouvel agreed to give it, excusing Father Pinet on the ground that his zeal, on the spur of the moment had led him into unguarded words. Some time later, while making his confession, Cadillac was requested to destroy the report of the incident which he had drawn up. On his refusal to do so he was denied absolution.

The breach between Cadillac and the missionaries continued to widen. How strained their relations had become is shown in the following episode. Father Carheil, whom Cadillac described as the most violent and seditious person he had ever known, felt it his duty to reproach the commandant for his conduct.

(He) told me, one day, that I neither obeyed the orders of the King nor had them obeyed; that I permitted the liquor traffic, and the scandalous relations between Frenchmen and squaws, in defiance of the prohibitions of His Majesty. I answered him that I took orders from my

[5] *N.Y. Col. Docs.*, IX, 647.
[6] *Ibid.*, 648.
[7] Margry, *Découvertes* . . . , V, xciv.

superiors, and that I knew my business too well to change or modify them. He told me that I would have to answer to God, and not to the government, when it commanded me to act against the will of God, and that the permission to engage in the liquor traffic was against His will. The knowledge of that opposition which I had necessarily obliged me not to obey the government which permitted the liquor traffic. The Indians might desire to drink to excess; it was certainly God's will that they be deprived of liquor. I had no right to obey theirs in preference to His. The Indians had no right to liquor for the beaver which they bartered, for it belonged to God who had given it to them for a good purpose. Consequently, when I knew they were using it for an evil purpose, that is for liquor, I should not barter with them no matter what my orders were.

I answered that this was seditious language that smelled to heaven, and I begged him to desist. Again he told me that I was not obeying the orders of the King, and that I was putting on airs, and at the same time he shook his fist under my nose. I tell you, Monsieur, that I almost forgot that he was a priest, and was on the point of breaking his jaw. But, thanks be to God, I contented myself with taking him by the arm, and leading him out of the fort, telling him to stay out of it in future.[8]

An incident like this shows how bitter the conflict had become. Unfortunately, we must depend entirely on Cadillac's account; the version which the missionaries must have given is not available, and hence we cannot determine how highly colored the narrative really is. To be told, for instance, that a man like Father Carheil could descend to a desire for personal encounter with Cadillac taxes our credulity to the utmost. Cadillac was on his favorite theme, and we may be sure that whatever happened did not suffer in the telling. If his absolute veracity be granted, and the missionary be convicted of a sad display of unbecoming rage, it is evident that in the scene we are witnessing the protagonists of the divergent policies outlined in the preceding chapter. Cadillac was carrying out the orders of Fontenac, who believed that the security of the colony depended upon fortified centers of French influence, and that if moral evils were entailed they could not be helped. The *coureurs de bois* and the soldiers were not angels, but they served a useful purpose, and much that could not be countenanced in the colony itself would have to be tolerated in the outlying wilderness. On the other hand, the Jesuits were unmoved by considerations of statecraft. If the western posts were to render the realization of their ideals impossible, then the missionaries would bend every effort to have the posts abandoned. Judging the matter from our knowledge of the course of history, and

[8] *Ibid.*, ciii-iv.

on the ground of practical objectives to be gained, we shall most likely decide that Frontenac was right, and that the Jesuits were too severe. Yet, we must admit that there are more admirable motives for human action than expediency, and that the missionaries for their stand deserve the honor which the world always has accorded even to a futile idealism.

The last word on the mission problem deservedly belongs to the men who were most affected by it. In a long letter, called by Cadillac a "poisoned memoir," Father Carheil detailed to the Governor the evils from which the missions were suffering, and urged the only possible remedy.

> . . . But even if I had never written to you, it was only necessary to have seen all that is to be seen every day at Montreal, and that you yourself have only too often seen, to enable you to carry back to France enough to give information to His Majesty, and to constrain him to succor our missions. These are reduced to such an extremity that we can no longer maintain them against an infinite multitude of evil acts —acts of brutality and violence; of injustice and impiety; of lewd and shameless conduct; of contempt and insults. To such acts the infamous and baleful trade in brandy gives rise everywhere, among all the nations up here . . . where it is carried on by going from village to village, and by roving over the lakes with a prodigious quantity of brandy in barrels, without any restraint. Had His Majesty but once seen what passes, both here and at Montreal, during the whole time this wretched traffic goes on, I am sure that he would not for a moment hesitate, at the very first sight of it to forbid it forever under the severest penalty.
>
> In our despair there is no other step to take than to leave our missions and abandon them to the brandy traders, so that they may establish therein the domain of their trade, of drunkenness and of immorality . . .[9]

The impossible situation at St. Ignace was relieved, at least temporarily, by a rather unexpected move on the part of the home government. By a decree dated May 21, 1696, the King suppressed every post in the West except one in the Illinois country. This drastic action was due partly to the sympathy which the Jesuits had been able to enlist among their influential friends, and partly to economic reasons.[10] It had been brought about largely through the efforts of the Intendant, Champigny, who, besides favoring the Jesuits, had all along opposed Frontenac on his western policy, and who aimed at a more intensive development of the Quebec colony itself.

[9] *Jesuit Relations* . . . (Thwaites), LXV, 189–253. This letter was written in 1702, but was intended to recapitulate previous letters which apparently had not been delivered.
[10] Kellogg, *The French Regime* . . . , 257.

The sweeping terms of the decree stunned the colony, and in the moment of his triumph Champigny realized his mistake. The court was petitioned to restore the posts at Mackinac and the St. Joseph River with such modifications as were deemed necessary to prevent the former abuses. To this request the court acceded in 1697, but now Frontenac proved obdurate, and made no move to carry out the permission. He satisfied himself by retaining Fort Frontenac, in which he was more vitally interested.

As the result of these proceedings the Jesuits finally achieved what they had so long desired. The wilderness with its wandering tribes was now their undisputed field. Cadillac was recalled, and arrived in Quebec in the first days of September, 1697.[11] But, although overruled, Frontenac was still to be reckoned with. He resolved to make a final effort to present his side to the home government. His choice of an emissary who entered into his views, and who could be depended on to present them skillfully, was inevitable. While Cadillac was approaching the shores of France at the end of 1698, all unknown to him, his patron, Frontenac, lay dying in Quebec.[12]

When the news came to Cadillac, and he found himself freed from the obligation of representing and defending Frontenac, he seized the opportunity to propose a project of his own. He addressed a typical memorial to Count Pontchartrain, wherein he modestly states that Lamothe has never failed in any undertaking, and will not fail now if the court accords him its protection. Of course he knows that he has many enemies, but they are only curs snapping at his heels. He has never tried to please everyone; it is enough that his superiors are satisfied with his conduct. All this is introductory to his project for the establishment of a new post in the western country, designed to obviate all the evils that led to the decree of 1696. First of all, it will control trade in a more satisfactory manner. Secondly, it will unite all the wandering tribes in one emplacement destined to be as large as Montreal, and will thus successfully cope with the English and the Iroquois. Thirdly, all the Indians will be civilized to the point that the majority will be speaking French in ten years, and will thus be transformed from heathens to children of the Church, and consequently good subjects of the King.

The memorial goes on with various provisions calculated to bring about these very desirable results. Cadillac's views on the missionary problem are thus stated.

As there are (will be ?) several missionaries on the spot, they must have a house within the fort, to preach and teach the Faith, to instruct

11 *N. Y. Col. Docs.*, IX, 671.
12 Margry, *Découvertes* . . . , cxxxvii.

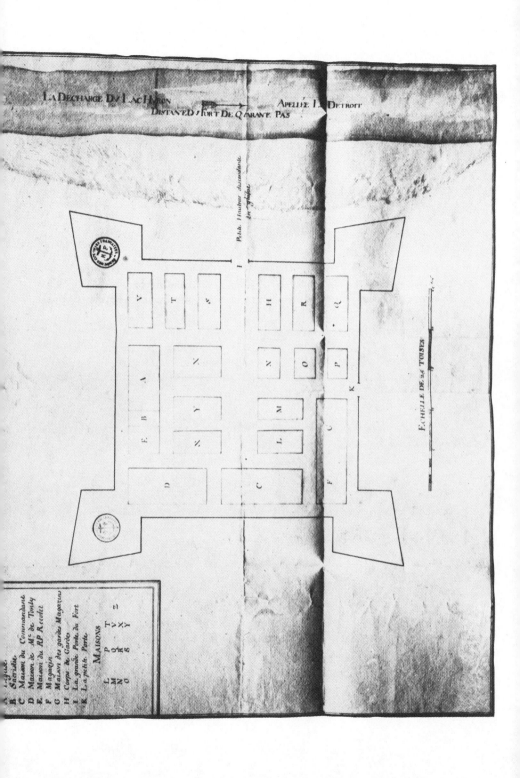

LA DÉCHARGE DU LAC HURON — APELLÉE LE DÉTROIT
DISTANTE DU FORT DE QUARANTE PAS

Petite Hauteur descendante en glacis

ECHELLE DE 25 TOISES

MAISONS

The earliest known map of Detroit. This may well be the plan alluded to in a
letter from Cadillac, dated September 25, 1702, to the French Minister. Copy in
the Burton Historical Collection.

the young, and to teach them French, for which the Indians, especially the children, show great aptitude . . . The missionaries must be straightforward in this question of language, and His Majesty should be good enough to order them to it in the most positive manner, and that for several reasons. The first and strongest is that whenever Religious or other ecclesiastics take hold of anything they never let go. The second is that by this means they make themselves necessary to the King, and to local governors, who need them to explain their intentions to the Indians, as well as to find out the sentiments of these peoples on certain occasions. The third is that if all the Indians spoke French every kind of ecclesiastic could instruct them, and hence (the missionaries) would lose the subsidies they receive for their instruction. For, in a word, although these Reverend Fathers betake themselves to these parts only for the glory of God, one aim does not exclude the other . . . They are the seigneurs of three quarters of Canada . . .

In his enthusiasm Cadillac sees his school system already in operation, and he makes the following recommendations.

It would be well for the Governor, with his officials, to visit the classes from time to time and give prizes to the children. This will make them ambitious, and will greatly please their parents.

It would be well for the King to create a fund for Indian boarding children to be entrusted to the care of the missionaries, provided this be done in concert with the governor. This would keep the Indians in check, for they would never dare start anything while their children were in the French fort, and suspicion would be aroused were they to try to take them out . . .

It would be necessary also to establish a house of Sisters, or Ursulines, to teach French to the Indian girls, and to instruct them in our religion. There need be no fear that they will not be able to speak sooner, and perhaps more than is necessary; parrots and magpies speak (French), why should not rational creatures do the same?

Thus, the Indian children, thrown together with the French children, will engage in conversation, and the same thing will happen that has happened everywhere namely, the Indians will speak French, and the French Indian, for if ten children, each speaking a different language were often together, every one of them would learn the ten languages.

Then follow several recommendations concerning the fur trade, and the memorial ends with the following passage.

The Sieur de Lamothe humbly begs you, Monseigneur, to be persuaded that he has put nothing in this project which he does not believe to be useful to the service of God, and the King, and that to find means to preserve a country that has cost His Majesty so much, and at the same time to preserve the good will of the Farmers he should like the chance to manage their interests.[13] He would do his utmost to content them, and he is certain that he can make a success of this project if he is looked upon with favor. It would be indeed distressing to him, if, after he had beat the brush, someone else should catch the rabbit. He can give assurance of this, that to hope to convert these peoples by any other plan than the one he has mapped out is like knocking one's head against a wall, for the only fruit the missionaries have reaped is the baptism of children and of those who died before coming to the age of reason.[14]

To the practical reasons urging the adoption of his plan Cadillac added others intended to captivate the imagination of the young Minister to whom they were submitted. The site of the new establishment was to be, not at Mackinac, whose climate was too severe, but south of the pearl-like Lake St. Clair upon a deep, clear river. On both banks stretched fine, open plains where roamed herds of graceful deer, and bear, and wild duck, and every variety of game could be found in abundance. In the river were islands covered with fruit trees, and in the fall the wild grape vines could scarcely hold up their sweet burden. This fair locality, this veritable paradise, known hitherto only as Le Detroit, and seen only by an occasional *coureur de bois*, was the real hub of the Lake country, the one spot best suited to hold the English in check.[15]

The answer to Cadillac's memorial is found in a letter to Callières, Frontenac's successor, written at Versailles on May 27, 1699. His Majesty has considered the project, and believes that the reasons supporting it are plausible. Before putting it into effect, however, His Majesty believes that it should be submitted to the leading citizens of Quebec. If they approve there should be no hesitancy in carrying it out.[16]

Cadillac returned to Canada to confront this final obstacle to his plan. He has left us a report of the meeting which took place pursuant to the King's wishes. It is evident that the session was rather heated, and that opinions were freely expressed about the disinterestedness of Cadillac. However, he makes it plain that the power of his logic was irresistible, and that he swept away every objection. To

[13] King's Farmers, a trading company to which was entrusted the collection of the King's revenues.
[14] Margry, *Découvertes* . . . , V, 138–53. Cadillac's venomous estimate of the results obtained by the missionaries is refuted by even a cursory reading of the *Relations*. In this memorial he insinuates, and on other occasions he plainly charged, that the Jesuits profited greatly from an illegal fur trade with the Indians. The answer to the charge which Cadillac was not alone in making, will be found in Rochemonteix, *op. cit.*, I, 343 ff.
[15] Burton, *op. cit.*, I, 83.
[16] Margry, *Découvertes* . . . , V, 154–56.

the mind of Cadillac the most determined opponent of his project was the Intendant, Champigny, who, of course was only a tool in the hands of the Jesuits. He was not impressed by the roseate claims that the Indians could be transformed within ten years, and he objected that they were so vicious that the Jesuits themselves could never employ them as servants, and were obliged to hire Frenchmen. Cadillac disposed of this objection with characteristic vigor.

> This objection does not come out of Champigny's bag; he has made it only because he trusts too much those who desire to destroy this project. Naturally the Jesuits have never employed the Indians as domestics because this is contrary to their views. They hold that the French language should never be taught to the Indians because it makes them more corrupt . . . that all intercourse and relation between the French and the Indians is dangerous, and corrupts their morals . . . These are three illusions rather than three reasons for, if the French language debauches people, and corrupts their morals, kings committed a great wrong in using it, and are responsible for the evil of having permitted its use in Languedoc, Guyenne, and in all the other provinces. If this be true, there should be a prohibition against printing, reading, and writing French outside l'Isle de France. . . .
>
> Jesus Christ did not tell his Vicar, "I will give you the key of the Kingdom of Heaven"; He said "the keys" to make him understand that, able fisherman as he was, he would need help and assistance in his fishing, and that the other apostles and disciples would be like so many pass-keys to open the same gate to the Kingdom. This is confirmed by this other passage: "Go and teach all nations." This term is general and not restricted. Why then should a Jesuit be preferred to another priest, and this priest to another religious. The Vine belongs to the same Master. . . .[17]

Whatever one may think of Cadillac's ability as a scriptural commentator, it is plain that he intended to have a free hand in Detroit, unfettered by the restrictions which the missionaries had attempted to enforce in St. Ignace. He had learned from Frontenac, who, as we have seen, had not been moved entirely by zeal for religion when urging the return of the Recollects to Canada. Moreover, Cadillac must have been aware of the recent sending of the Quebec Seminary priests to the Illinois mission, which the Jesuits protested against as an intrusion.[18] All these prepossessions are mirrored in the final draft of the project, from which the following quotations are taken.[19]

> We must establish at this post missionaries of different communities, such as the Jesuits and other Fathers, and ecclesiastics of foreign mis-

[17] *Ibid.*, 157–66.
[18] The Jesuit position is set forth in Rochemonteix, *op. cit.,* III, 529–89.
[19] *Mich. Hist. Colls.*, XXXIII, 202.

sions; they are laborers in the vineyard, and should be received without distinction to labor at the vine of the Lord, with orders in particular to teach the young savages the French language. . . .

It would be important that there should be a hospital for sick or infirm Savages, for there is nothing more urgent for gaining their friendship than the care of them in their illnesses. . . .

It would be absolutely necessary also to allow the soldiers and Canadians to marry the savage maidens when they have been instructed in religion and know the French language which they will learn all the more eagerly (provided we labor carefully to that end) because they always prefer a Frenchman for a husband to any savage whatever, though I know no other reason for it than the most ordinary one, namely, that strangers are preferred. . . .

We shall find in the execution of this scheme, not only the glory of His Majesty but also that of God magnificently extended; for by this means his worship and his religion will be established in the midst of the tribes, and the deplorable sacrifices which they offer to Baal entirely abolished. . . .

The document containing the preceding passages is dated Quebec, October 18, 1700. In it we are told that the project has finally been approved, and is to be put into execution as soon as possible. Impatient as he was to embark on his venture, Cadillac was obliged to wait a year longer. The Montreal merchants opposed him on the ground that he would ruin their trade.[20] Moreover, negotiations were under way for a final, definitive peace with the Iroquois, and their attitude towards this proposed French center in their neighborhood was uncertain. By the spring of 1701, it was believed that they would probably acquiesce, and on August 4, at Montreal, the peace was signed to the accompaniment of much ceremony and rejoicing. The Indians were, in effect, compelled to consent to the establishment of Detroit, for Cadillac had already left Montreal on June 5 with fifty soldiers and as many *coureurs de bois* to begin the new post.[21] In order not to roil the susceptibilities of the Iroquois he was ordered to take the Ottawa River route, and thus came down through Lakes Huron and St. Clair into the Detroit River. On July 24, the canoes were beached at the foot of a steep bluff which at that time stretched along the river bank between the present Griswold and Wayne Streets, and the party was soon busily engaged in erecting the first structures of Fort Pontchartrain.

Two priests accompanied Cadillac, one, a Recollect, who was to serve as chaplain to the post, the other a Jesuit, Father François Vail-

[20] For the Memorial of the Montreal merchants see Margry, *Découvertes* . . . , V, 180–87.
[21] *Mich. Hist. Colls.*, XXXIII, 202.

lant de Guelis, a distinguished member of the Society who had been in Canada since 1670. He had labored for years among the Seneca, had represented the Canadian government in negotiations with Governor Dongan at Albany, and had been appointed Superior of the Jesuit house opened at Montreal in 1692.[22]

The association of Father Vaillant with Cadillac's project presents a perplexing situation which has never been satisfactorily explained. In the light of past events the Jesuits knew that accord with Cadillac was impossible, and there is no evidence that they had as yet given up their conscientious stand, and were now ready for the sake of cooperation and harmony to come to Detroit on any other terms than their own. Cadillac, as might be expected, had a ready explanation.

> The Jesuits, having had information by the first vessel that you (Count Pontchartrain) had resolved to have Detroit settled, came to the water side and showed me much courtesy. I returned it as far as I could; and finally, when they learned the confirmation of this settlement, they busied themselves effectively, in their usual manner, with the Governor-General and the Intendant in order to establish themselves there alone to the exclusion of all other ecclesiastics and monks, which was at first granted them, and they nominated Father Vaillant to go and take possession of it.[23]

Cadillac could not have written the foregoing in good faith, for the simple reason that it was not true. The Superior of the Jesuits, the Governor, the Intendant, and Cadillac himself all knew that Father Vaillant was to return to Montreal as soon as the establishment should be under way. The very reason for the presence of the Recollect was that the post should not be left without a priest after Vaillant's departure.[24] If his coming to Detroit had been sanctioned by both the Society and government officials he could have been making a gesture of friendly interest in the new project, or he might have been deputed by the officials to make a realistic appraisal of it to counterbalance the founder's enthusiasm. It is hard to believe that his sole purpose was to wreck the whole enterprise, as Cadillac states in his well known imaginary dialogue between himself and Count Pontchartrain written in 1704. Cadillac was in trouble, and his optimism regarding the new establishment that was soon to surpass Montreal had been rudely jolted. In his anxiety and disappointment he relieved his feelings by writing a prolix account of the difficulties he

[22] For details concerning Father Vaillant see Rochemonteix, *op. cit.*, II, 413; III, 200, 365, 386, 410; *Jesuit Relations* (Thwaites), LX, 315; *N. Y. Col. Docs.*, IX, 762.
[23] *Mich. Hist. Colls.*, XXXIII, 201.
[24] Letter of Father Germain to Cadillac in *Mich. Hist. Colls.*, XXXIII, 104–05.

had met. In it he accuses the Jesuit of underhanded attempts to bring about the collapse of the government sanctioned venture.[25]

Q. Apparently Father Vaillant contributed greatly by his exhortations to advancing the works.

A. He exerted himself for this so well that if the soldiers and Canadians had believed him they would have set out after two days to return thence to Montreal on the promise which this Father made them that he would get their wages paid to them by the Intendant for a whole year, although they had been employed only six weeks.

Q. How did you manage to learn his ill-will, and to combat this intrigue?

A. I perceived it from the discouragement everyone showed as to the works, which gave me occasion to sound a few of the most worthy men in private about it; and these frankly confessed to me what this Jesuit had told them in order to persuade them to leave that post and return with him. . . .

The document goes on to describe the scene wherein Cadillac openly accused the Jesuit of his perfidy, and the latter's "running his hardest" into the woods to hide his shame and confusion.

Q. But did you not point out to him his wrong-doing by some reprimand, or by some other means that would be disagreeable to him?

A. Not at all; I thought it was for the good of the service to keep silent. I showed him as much courtesy as I could have done to an Archbishop, contenting myself with informing the Governor-General, and with giving you an account of it. . . .

In the absence of any contrary evidence we must take Cadillac's account for what it is worth. However, we do know from other sources that a complaint against the Jesuit reached the home government, and that the King asked the Jesuit Superior to send Father Vaillant back to France.[26] Evidently, some satisfactory explanation of whatever was involved must have been made, for Father Vaillant remained in Canada as missionary to the Seneca, and did not return to France until 1715.

On the other hand, it is scarcely credible that Father Vaillant, even if opposed to Cadillac's establishment, would have acted in such a tactless manner, and given Cadillac such an opportunity for charges against himself and the Society. There is a letter of Cadillac to Count Pontchartrain, in which this passage occurs.

I have carried out submissively what you did me the honor to write to me concerning the Revd. Jesuit Father Vaillant; that was done after

[25] *Mich. Hist. Colls.*, XXXIII, 198–241. The extract is from p. 202. That this dialogue is wholly imaginary is proved from the fact that it is dated Quebec, November 14, 1704. and the further fact that Count Pontchartrain was never in Canada.

[26] See supplement to the *Report of the Canadian Archives for 1899* (Ottawa, 1901), 349.

my letter was written in the presence of his Superior and of the Revd. Father Germain, Father Vaillant having set out four hours after the arrival of the King's ship. This Father has gone to the Senountoüan. Therefore, as this matter has just been arranged by the Chev. de Calliere, together with various things for the future which have been drawn up in clauses, we may trust you will receive no more complaints from them against me; and I do not think I shall be obliged to carry mine to you . . .[27]

The word "submissively" is an unusual one in Cadillac's vocabulary, and one could read into the passage that he had offered an apology of some sort.

From Father Vaillant himself we have nothing but the letter which he wrote to Cadillac while on his way back to Montreal. Madame Cadillac had left Montreal in the beginning of September to join her husband at Detroit. When she reached Fort Frontenac she found Father Vaillant and Chacornacle, the guide, whom Cadillac was sending back with the report of his safe arrival. The Jesuit used the opportunity to write to Cadillac, and his letter is far from implying that there had been any disagreement between them.

At Fort Frontenac, this 23rd Sept. 1701.
Sir.

Our fortunate meeting at Fort Frontenac with Madame de la Mothe gives me a good opportunity of thanking you very humbly for all the courtesies with which you have overwhelmed me all the past summer both on our march and at Detroit. I beg you to be so good as to continue to grant them to me in the person of the one of our Fathers who is to come down from Missilimakinak to Detroit, for I have no doubt you will have one there very soon, for, on Lake Erie I met Quarante Solz, the Huron, who assured me that the Hurons were going to settle near you after this autumn, without fail. As regards the Iroquois whom we met on the way, we did not find them much opposed to your settlement; some even testified to me their joy that, when going hunting on Lake Erie, they will find at Detroit (in exchange) for the skins of the roebuck, stag and hind, all they want . . . I do not tell you the news we have learnt here because it is Mad. Lamothe who has informed us of it, and she will tell it to you exactly as I could write you word of it. I beg you to accept here my very humble service, and to believe me, Sir, very sincerely your very humble and obedient servant.

François Vaillant. J.[28]

Although Cadillac had been deprived of the services of Father Vaillant, he was not a man to give up so easily. He kept on urging the necessity of Jesuit missionaries at Detroit, and finally succeeded

[27] *Mich. Hist. Colls.*, XXXIII, 151.
[28] *Ibid.*, 106.

in pinning down the Society to a definite agreement. A meeting was held in Quebec on September 25, 1702, attended by the Governor in the role of peacemaker, who induced both parties to draw up an agreement that would be mutually satisfactory.

The second article stipulated that the missionaries "instead of preventing the Indians from going to Detroit, should induce them to settle there by every means possible." In the third article it was agreed that Father Joseph Marest, then at St. Ignace, should go to Detroit the following spring to take up his work among the Ottawa already there. The next article bound the missionaries to obey all the orders of Cadillac, and to refrain from opposing them on any pretext whatsoever, although they retained the right of appeal to the Governor. Both parties agreed to refer their differences to the Governor, and not to the home government. The final article empowered the Governor to reject all complaints that had not first been submitted to the party through whose fault they had arisen.[29]

The second article is the crux of the whole situation. As we have seen, the essential point of Cadillac's plan was that all the Indians of the lake region were to be gathered around Fort Pontchartrain, to do all their trading there, and to be civilized and educated by the agencies there established. The Jesuits, on the other hand, were convinced that such a policy far from hastening the conversion of the Indian could only be harmful to their neophytes, and their subsequent course of action shows that while they gave in to the government policy sufficiently to avoid an open rupture, they were determined to follow the light of their own experience.[30]

In 1703 there were already three Indian villages in the neighborhood of the fort, and trusting in the terms of the agreement, Cadillac sent a canoe to Mackinac to bring Father Marest, who was there with Father Carheil. The missionary refused to come. He was convinced that his superior had been imposed upon, and that in view both of the traditional policy of the Society and of Cadillac's conduct and character, he could not have really meant what Cadillac's order conveyed.[31] Father Marest determined to go to Quebec to find out for himself just what was behind the agreement with Cadillac. In the meantime, Governor Callières had died, and had been succeeded by

[29] Rochemonteix, *op. cit.*, III, 521–22. The document will be found in full in the *Archives de la Province de Quebec*, 1924: *Ordonnances, Commissions, etc., des Gouverneurs et Intendants*, II, 310.

[30] In justice to Cadillac it must be noted that individual members of the Society were friendly to him and willing to take up the work in Detroit. Father Germain was one of them, and Father Enjalran had once been taken off the Ottawa mission and sent back to France because of his lack of sympathy with the views of his confreres. See Rochemonteix, *op. cit.*, III, 512.

[31] *Ibid.*, 522–24.

the Marquis de Vaudreuil, who was not too sympathetic towards Cadillac. As a result of conferences between the Jesuits and the new governor the agreement of 1702 was abrogated, and the Society was thenceforth free to follow its policy of abstention.

From this time on, Cadillac's indignation knew no bounds. If the Jesuits would not come to him, they could at least persuade the Indians to settle around Fort Pontchartrain, and not try to keep them away. It is quite likely that the missionaries did attempt to dissuade their converts from joining Cadillac, although there is plenty of evidence to show that the Indians were dissatisfied with the treatment they were getting from him, that they suffered from his cupidity, and that left to themselves they would never have fulfilled his expectations. Cadillac was now determined to wreck the St. Ignace mission. In August, 1703, he wrote to the Minister: "Thirty Hurons from Missilimakinak arrived here on the 28th of June to incorporate themselves with those who have settled here. Thus only about twenty-five of them remain at that place, where Father de Carheil, their missionary, remains ever resolute. This autumn I hope finally to tear this last feather from his wing; and I am convinced that this obstinate vicar will die in his parish without having a parishioner to bury him." [32]

The Miami and the Potawatomi, who were included in Cadillac's plan, were not coming from the St. Joseph Mission to Detroit fast enough to suit him. There was no doubt in his mind that this was due to the efforts of Father Aveneau, and he determined to oust him from his mission and replace him with a Recollect. The Minister very properly admonished Cadillac that the transfer of missionaries was to be left to their respective superiors.[33] Vaudreuil, commenting on the incident, wrote to the Minister: "It is certain that this missionary by his influence would have diverted the savages of his mission from doing anything contrary to the welfare of the service. The Sr. de la Mothe will not agree to that, for, far from doing that, he defames them to your Highness as far as he can, and injures them in the minds of the French and the Savages." [34]

There is nothing to be gained by going further into the mass of correspondence dealing with the efforts of the Jesuits to defend themselves, and Cadillac's determination to castigate them at every opportunity.[35] A careful reading of it only accentuates the issues at stake as we have outlined them. The result of the controversy was, not that

[32] *Mich. Hist. Colls.*, XXXIII, 162.

[33] *Ibid.*, 338.

[34] *Ibid.*, 396.

[35] The letters of the missionaries accompanied by Cadillac's comments are in the *Mich. Hist. Colls.*, XXXIII and XXXIV passim.

the Jesuits ruined Detroit, but that Cadillac succeeded in ruining St. Ignace. Judging their usefulness to be at an end, the two remaining missionaries, in 1705, set fire to their mission buildings to save them from profanation, and with aching hearts returned to Quebec.[36] The King, however, would not countenance such a departure, and ordered them to return. "His Majesty has been surprised to learn that the missionaries who had been at Mackinac abandoned their missions, and burned their house and chapel. They could have had no good reason for doing so, and His Majesty desires that they return there. Under no pretext is the reestablishment of this mission to cost him anything, or to be made at his expense."[37] The Jesuits, of course, obeyed, and in the late summer of 1706 Father Marest came back alone.[38]

Although pursuant to the King's orders he took up his residence at Mackinac, and not at Detroit, Father Marest was still odious to Cadillac. An Indian council met at Detroit the following year. By symbolic wampum strings, and in the style of diction calculated to persuade the Indian mind, Cadillac stripped the aged missionary of the last shred of honor.

Monsieur de la Mothe, with three strings of porcelin, speaks to the Outtavois; this porcelin represents the black robe, as if he were present at the council.

Speak then, black robe of Michilmakina; you dissuade my children the Outtavois from coming to settle at Detroit; you tell them that I want to make them my slaves, you speak thus to them aside, and in secret, by stealth. This is a proof that you are a liar; for, if you were telling them the truth, you would tell it at a council where there would be Frenchmen and chiefs. But you would not dare, for you well know that the King wishes the Outtavois to come and settle at Detroit. Would you state the contrary before me, black robe? Speak; you dare not; for if you did I would send you to the King for disobedience.

What are you meddling with, black robe? Are you a man of war, have you a sword at your side? You are all tied up with your long robe that reaches down to your heels. Is it for you to settle matters? Speak of prayer and I will hearken to you; the Outtavois may hearken. Go and enter your church and pray to God, you are the director of prayer; go into the huts, clasp your hands and teach them to pray; this is your duty. Prayer is your concern, but not the affairs which there are between the tribes. Onontio is the ruler of all the land, and I am ruler here.[39]

---

[36] *Charlevoix* (Shea ed.), V, 182.

[37] Margry, *Découvertes . . . ,* V, 345.

[38] He writes a letter from St. Ignace dated August 14, 1706. *Mich. Hist. Colls.,* XXXIII, 262. For the further history of St. Ignace see Rezek, *op. cit.,* Vol. II.

[39] *Mich. Hist. Colls.,* XXXIII, 349. Onontio was the Indian name for the governor of New France.

Cadillac was in truth the master, for the Company of the Colony, a stock company formed by the leading merchants of Canada, which had hitherto enjoyed exclusive rights to the trade of Detroit, had released its hold in 1705. Cadillac's exclusive tenure lasted for five years more; but they were not happy years. The salient features of his project did not materialize. The Indians, disgusted alike by his exactions and by the high price and poor quality of French goods, traded more and more with the English. The few settlers who had been induced to come to Detroit found Cadillac every ready to levy on their land or their toil. To his credit it must be said that there was little debauchery or drunkenness in Detroit while he controlled it. He had a better plan. All the liquor he could buy, and sometimes the traders were obliged to sell it at a loss, he placed in a central warehouse, where any one could buy a very small drink for a very high price. The opposition of the Montreal merchants was always active, the *coureurs de bois* still roamed the forests, and he could not enforce the trade monopoly which was rightfully his. The reoccupation of Mackinac began to be entertained, and the return of the license system.[40]

Now that the Jesuits were no longer worthy opponents Cadillac found new enemies to the success of his enterprise in the persons of Vaudreuil and Raudot, the Intendant. He reiterated his complaints to the home government until the Minister sent him a sharp letter with this tenor. It is evident that Cadillac is behaving as if he recognized no superiors. He had better change his ways or he will be withdrawn from his post. He has acted wrongly and imprudently in his dealings with the Jesuits. Let him cease his opposition to them. His demand that his post become an independent governorship cannot be granted. If he shows such lack of subordination as simple commandant, his actions as governor can easily be presumed.[41]

The eventual result of Cadillac's bickerings and complaints was his transfer to the governorship of Louisiana in 1710.[42] Unchanged by his experiences in Detroit, his fretful, irritating, and complaining temper aroused enmity, and ended his usefulness. He returned to France in 1717, and some time later was confined in the Bastile for several months, most likely for his unguarded denunciation of John Law and his Mississippi River scheme, which at the moment intoxicated the French populace with hopes of untold wealth.

From the time of his return to France, Cadillac engaged in determined efforts to obtain compensation for the losses in both real and

[40] See d'Aigremont's report on Detroit in *Mich. Hist. Colls.*, XXXIII, 424–52.

[41] Letter of the Minister to Cadillac, June 6, 1708. See supplement to Canadian Archives mentioned in note 26, p. 402.

[42] Parkman has touched on Cadillac's career in Louisiana in his *A half Century of Conflict*, Chap. XIII.

personal property which his sudden transfer to Louisiana had caused him. From the correspondence available to us it is evident that the government had forgotten all the real services which he had rendered to the Canadian colony, and he seems never to have recovered what was rightfully his. Mellowed by time and misfortune he tried to recoup his fallen fortune not by law but by favor.

> . . . It is not at all fitting for old officers to go to law, more especially since the Governor-General and the Intendant would be necessarily involved in this trial; and that it would be more beneficial to both parties that His Majesty should accord a favor to the petitioner by granting him a pension of a thousand livres on the Order of St. Louis and a pension of a like amount to his family on the navy or elsewhere by prefrement; and in default of the two pensions named, an abbacy or a benefice for M. Joseph de La Mothe who was born at Detroit, son of the Petitioner, aged 21 years, and an ecclesiastic . . . And as there is now vacant the priory of St. Beat in Begorre, by the death of M. de Villes-passau, provost of the Cathedral of St. Etienne de Thé, which yields an income of about two thousand livres, if H.R.M. had the kindness to grant it to the son of the petitioner, the pension asked for, for his family, might remain at one thousand livres; and this would be a recompense for the services rendered to the King by the petitioner and his children.[43]

In 1722 Cadillac was appointed Mayor and Governor of Castelsarrasin, a town in the same department wherein he was born, and about twelve miles from Mantauban. Here, at seventy-two, he died on October 16, 1730, and his remains were laid in the cemetery of the Carmelite monastery adjoining the town.[44] In his last days the old soldier must surely have mused over the fair domain across the sea that had once been his, too feeble perhaps to care, if he knew it at all, that in the very emplacement for the Hurons he had once staked out a Black Robe was again shepherding a distracted flock.

[43] *Mich. Hist. Colls.*, XXXIII, 613. The son referred to in the petition may have been studying for the priesthood at the time, but it is quite certain that he was never ordained. Two daughters of Cadillac became nuns, one in Canada, and one in France.

[44] Burton, *op. cit.*, I, Chapter V. The burial record is in Forestié *Notes Historiques* . . . , 178.

CHAPTER VIII

The First Church in Detroit

THE story of Cadillac's difficulties with the Society and with Father Vaillant has led us far afield. We must now focus our attention on the affairs of the tiny settlement perched high above the river. For a year or two its extent will be no more than one square arpent surrounded by a palisade twelve feet high.[1] Later, the picket line will extend from seven to eight hundred feet frontage on the river, but for the next hundred years or more Detroit will not outgrow a rectangle bounded by the river, Cass Avenue, Congress, and Griswold Streets. The first street to be laid out bisects the enclosure, and leads to gates on the east and west sides. It is twenty feet wide, is called St. Anne's, and will always be the main thoroughfare until the fire of 1805. Two streets, St. Joachim and St. Joseph, parallel it on the north, and St. Louis Street runs below it.[2] In the early days there are only little alleys running north and south, but another street evolves bisecting St. Anne's almost on the line of the present Shelby Street, and called St. Honoré. Around the interior of the palisade runs an elevated platform on which the defenders can stand to peer over the top. The space beneath is the promenade, the Chemin de la Ronde. The enclosure is dotted here and there by primitive habitations built of logs standing upright, and thatched over with grass and straw. The log cabin, as we know it, is a luxury that will be enjoyed only in later years.

It is in this rude setting that the history of the Catholic Church in Detroit begins. It has already been stated that Cadillac, in founding his settlement, was accompanied by a Recollect acting as chaplain for the soldiers. Having recounted how the Jesuits had practically forced him to take Father Vaillant, Cadillac adds: "On the 12th of May I arrived at Montreal where a change was made, the Franciscans having obtained permission for one of their fathers to accompany me and to remain at Detroit as Almoner of the troops, with the Jesuit

---

[1] For details concerning early maps of Detroit and the beginning of the settlement see Clarence M. Burton, *The Building of Detroit* (Detroit, 1912); Silas Farmer, *The History of Detroit and Michigan* (Detroit, 1889). The French arpent was .85 of our acre.

[2] St. Joachim Street appears on the later maps as St. James Street.

as missionary. This outrage, as it were, against the Society in that country set it in commotion, for it was persuaded that I had done it this bad turn. . . ." [3]

It has been generally assumed that the Recollect who accompanied Cadillac to Detroit was Father Constantin Delhalle, and that he remained there until his death. The only certain item in this assumption is that Father Delhalle did die in Detroit. We do not know who came with Cadillac, and if it was Father Delhalle, he cannot have remained much longer than Father Vaillant. The baptismal register in the drowsy little parish of Batiscan, lying halfway between Three Rivers and Quebec, proves conclusively that Father Delhalle, styling himself pastor, officiated there from November 15, 1701, until June 5, 1702.

That his transfer to Detroit occurred immediately following his last entry is evident from a statement of Cadillac's. Although the Company of the Colony had taken over the trade of Detroit in 1701, Cadillac was unaware of the move until Arnault and Radisson, the company agents, arrived in Detroit July 18, 1702, to present their credentials.[4] The commandant, at the same time received orders to present himself in Quebec to settle the details of the new arrangement. He left Detroit July 21, and from Quebec he sent to the Minister a report of his activities dated September 25, in which this sentence occurs: "I am well satisfied with the reverend Father Constantin, the recollect who officiates at Detroit, that is to say for the garrison." [5] If we remember that the journey from Quebec to Detroit consumed ordinarily from four to six weeks, the Recollect must have left Batiscan very soon after his last entry to be in Detroit for some time prior to July 21, in order to occasion Cadillac's favorable estimate.[6]

It is possible to infer from Cadillac's remark that there had been an unsatisfactory Recollect previously. In that event, the Recollect

---

[3] *Mich. Hist. Colls.*, XXXIII, 201–02.

[4] Burton, *City of Detroit*, I, 89.

[5] *Mich. Hist. Colls.*, XXXIII, 150.

[6] It would be tedious and unnecessary to list the instances in which writers on Canadian church history, including Tanguay in his *Répertoire Général du Clergé Canadien* (Quebec, 1868), have confused two priests with somewhat similar names. Patient investigation proves conclusively that about 1700 there were in Canada two Recollects, one named Nicolas Bernadin Constantin, and the other Constantin Delhalle. Their signatures are characteristic and dissimilar. Personal inspection of original registers in various parishes in the Province of Quebec is the basis for the statement here and in the text. There is no authority for giving Father Delhalle any other name than the one here used. The marker erected by the Catholic Study Club of Detroit to commemorate the site of the first church of St. Anne is an instance of the confusion. There may be question of the spelling of the surname. It has been transcribed as De Halle, Del Halle, De Lhalle, and even De Chasles. The form used here is the one in St. Anne's baptismal register.

would be someone whose name has completely escaped the notice of historians. We might hazard the conjecture that it was Father Nicolas Bernadin Constantin, who signs the Batiscan register immediately following Father Delhalle on July 27, 1702. His movements for many months preceding are not known, and it is barely possible that he succeeded the priest who had been ordered to replace him.

The presence of a priest officiating in Detroit in 1702, but prior to Father Delhalle's arrival, seems to be confirmed by a letter of Father Carheil, the Jesuit at Mackinac, to Alphonse de Tonty who had been associated with Cadillac in the founding of Detroit, and who later succeeded him as commandant. The letter is dated at Mackinac, June 17, 1702, and begins with the following passage. "The good evidence which you have been good enough to give me of the diligence of Monique in constantly fulfilling, every Sunday and every saints-day, the requirements of Christianity could not but be very agreeable to me, not only because it assures me that for her part she desires her true welfare, but also because it assures me consequently also for your part, that what you value most in her is also what you most value in yourself. . . ." [7] The passage can hardly mean anything else but that Monique, Tonty's convert Indian servant, is faithful in her attendance at Divine worship on the days prescribed.

If St. Anne's baptismal register had not been burned in the fire of 1703 the identity of the first priest in Detroit could easily be determined. Unless new evidence appears we are left only with conjectures. We may suppose that a Recollect, whose name is unknown to us, came to Detroit with Cadillac and remained but a short while or, because of Carheil's letter, that he remained until the arrival of Father Delhalle. One thing is certain, that Delhalle was not in Detroit from at least the beginning of October, 1701, until the middle of July, 1702.

With the problem we have been considering is necessarily involved the beginning of St. Anne's, the oldest parish in Detroit. There is a pretty tradition to the effect that Cadillac's party on landing began the construction of a chapel, which was completed two days later on the 26th of July, the feast of St. Anne, and dedicated in her honor. Certainly, the priests on the ground with Cadillac said Mass as long as they remained, but that is precisely the uncertain point. There are other reasons for doubting the tradition. Cadillac's first care was undoubtedly the completion of the palisade, which stood between him and disaster in case the Indians took his proceeding amiss. At the same time he had to attend to the sheltering from inclement weather of the large store of supplies he had transported, and whose good con-

[7] *Mich. Hist. Colls.*, XXXIII, 124.

dition was vital to the success of his undertaking.[8] These inferences are confirmed by such reports as are available concerning the beginning of the establishment.

The Canadian governor on October 5, 1702, informed the home government of Cadillac's success.

> The Sr. de Chacornacle has just arrived now from Detroit with five men, and has brought us letters from the Srs. de la Motte and de Tonty; the former notifies us that he arrived at the mouth of that river on the 24th of July with all his detachment in good health, and that after having looked for the most suitable place to establish himself, he built a fort with four bastions of good oak stakes 15 feet long, three of which are in the earth, each curtain being thirty fathoms long; that he has placed this fort three leagues from Lake Erie, and two from Lake St. Clair at the narrowest part of the river towards the west south-west; that he began by building a warehouse in order to put all his goods under shelter; that he is setting them to work at the necessary dwellings, and that they are not yet in a very forward state, which has obliged him to keep nearly all his people trying to complete them before winter.[9]

Cadillac himself, in the letter of 1702, to which we have already referred, gives an account of his first activities.

> You will see annexed the plan of Fort Pontchartrain which I have had built at Detroit. I have thus named it by order of the Chev. Calliere, and the map of Detroit. The houses there are of good timber, of white oak, which is even and hard and as heavy as iron. This fort is in no danger provided there are enough people here to defend it.
>
> Its position is delightful and advantageous; it is at the narrowest part of the river, where no one can pass by day without being seen . . .
>
> After the fort was built, and the dwellings, I had the land cleared there and some French wheat sown on the 7th of October, not having had time to prepare it well . . . There are at Detroit a good fort, good dwellings, and the means of living and subsisting . . .[10]

In neither of the foregoing passages is a church mentioned, and it seems strange that Cadillac in his evident desire to impress the Minister with the advantages of his settlement should neglect to mention this most necessary feature. Undoubtedly, some sort of shelter must have been erected in the first days of the encampment for the celebration of Mass, but it did not deserve to be called a house for divine

---

[8] A complete inventory of the supplies which Cadillac brought to Detroit will be found in the BHC among the transcripts used by Farmer in the compiling of his *History of Detroit and Michigan.*

[9] *Mich. Hist. Colls.,* XXXIII, 110.

[10] *Ibid.,* 140.

audit fort ... le 13...
1703 frere Constantin delhalle —

(1704)

Constantin delhalle frere mineur ...
et ... du fort de pontchartrain du détroit
... ces deux feuilles de papier, être le véritable
... des batêmes du sudit fort et afin de luy
donner toute force necessaire, jay prié ... ...
antoine de la motte cadillac commandant pour
Roy au dit fort de pontchartrain de lhone ...
... son paraphe. fait audit lieu le 14...
febvrier 1704 frere constantin — comme des...

... antoine de lamothe cadillac comman
de le Roy au fort pontchartrain du détroit
... que le present extrait est conforme
... des baptemes qui a été brulé, ...
... arivée le 5 octobre 1703 et que le...
... compris dans ce present livre ...
... pour les baptemes, mariages, et mortuaires
que le r.p. constantin delhalle ...
... dans les ... ...
... pontchartrain le ... ...
de lamothe cadillac

First page of St. Anne's baptismal register. Note Father Delhalle's signature at the top, and Cadillac's at the bottom.

worship. It is more likely that a church was not built until Father Delhalle had definitely taken up his post in Detroit.

It is interesting to note that the designation "parish of St. Anne" appears in the parish registers for the first time on July 17, 1722. Father Delhalle signs himself merely as chaplain to the fort. A register begun after his death is called the book of "Baptisms of Frenchmen at Fort Pontchartrain of Detroit." A succeeding missionary called himself "Pastor of the Royal Fort of Detroit." Father Bonaventure, on the date given above, is the first to use the name St. Anne.

The mists of uncertainty that cover the origins of our religious history begin to clear with the arrival of Father Delhalle in the first days of July, 1702. The same letter of Cadillac's that announces his presence in Detroit provides a pleasing digression from the tedious details with which we have been engaged. It purports to be an account of Detroit, and is written in glowing terms. Through the Detroit River the waters of the northern lakes flow gently. Its banks and its islands are adorned with groves of trees, "marvellously lofty." There are apple and plum trees in abundance "so well laid out that they might be taken for orchards planted by the hand of a gardener." On all sides grow red and white grapes, "the skins of which are very thin, full of good juice." There is a strange tree bearing a fruit like the citrons of Portugal, whose root is a subtle and deadly poison; but it is a sovereign remedy against snake-bite. Another tree is well defended by prickles half a foot long, which pierce wood like a nail; it bears a fruit like the kidney beans.

Fifteen leagues from Detroit at the entrance to Lake Erie are boundless prairies which stretch away for a hundred leagues. It is there that the buffalo, "these mighty oxen covered with wool, find food in abundance." Forty leagues from this lake straight to the south lies a land of perpetual summer, where ice and snow are unknown.

Game of every kind swarms around Detroit. There are quails, woodcocks, pheasants, rabbits, and every variety of wild ducks. Turkeys are so plentiful "that twenty or thirty could be killed at one shot." There are curious wood rats, large as rabbits and sometimes white as snow. "The female has a pouch under her belly which opens and shuts as she requires, so that sometimes when her little ones are playing, if the mother find herself pressed, she quickly shuts them up in her pouch and carries them away with her at once and gains her retreat."

Across this charming panorama of river and trees flit birds of rare beauty. Some have plumage of a beautiful red, others are yellow, with tails longer than their bodies and spread out like peacock plumes. There are birds blue as the sky, and some curiously marked like great butterflies. "I have observed that a pleasant warbling proceeds from all these birds, especially from the red ones with large beaks. Strangest of all are those immobile cranes, both grey and white, that stand higher than a man."

Is it any wonder then that "this country, so temperate, so fertile, and so beautiful that it may justly be called the earthly paradise of North America, deserves all the care of the King to keep it up and to attract inhabitants to it, so that a solid settlement may be formed there which shall not be liable to the vicissitudes of the other posts in which only a mere garrison is placed."

Cadillac has not been idle. He has erected his fort and dwellings, and he has cleared the ground for the sowing of wheat. He has built a ship of ten tons burden and will soon build more, not only for trading purposes but to make some discoveries "which perhaps will be no less lucrative than glorious to France." At some distance from the fort there is already a village of Hurons to whom he has granted land. They are very tractable, and would soon become Christians if the effort were made. "They are very caressing; they dress like the French as far as they can; they even make rough attempts at our language." Half a league farther four tribes of Ottawa have begun a village. "Thus within the space of one league there are four forts and four hundred men bearing arms, with their families, besides the garrison. . . ."

The final proof that Cadillac is in earnest with his plans for the settling of Detroit is that his wife and Madame de Tonty have come there to live with their husbands.

> Last year, my wife and Mme. Tonty set out on the 10th of Sept. with our families to come and join us here. Their resolution in undertaking so long and laborious a journey seemed very extraordinary. It is certain that nothing astonished the Iroquois so greatly as when they saw them. You could not believe how many caresses they offered them, and particularly the Iroquois, who kissed their hands and wept for joy, saying that French women had never been seen coming willingly to their country. . . . If these ladies gave favorable impressions regarding us to the Iroquois, those our allies received from them were no less so. They received them at Detroit under arms with many discharges of musketry . . .[11]

She was indeed a brave and resolute woman, this virtuous wife and loving mother who graced the first home in Detroit. On hearing of

[11] *Mich. Hist. Colls.*, XXXIII, 138. A tablet was unveiled to the memory of Madame Cadillac by the Women's Bicentenary Committee on May 30, 1903, giving no date for her arrival but implying that she came in 1703. Cadillac's statement just quoted, as well as Father Vaillant's letter in the preceding chapter, prove conclusively that she came to Detroit in the fall of 1701.

Madame Cadillac's determination to join her husband some of her friends attempted to dissuade her, wondering how she could bear living so far from civilization. "She very discretely replied that a woman who loves her husband as she ought has no attraction more powerful than his society, in whatever place it may be; all the rest should be indifferent to her. . . ." [12]

We have now some idea of the field into which Father Delhalle came to exercise his ministry. The soldiers, the traders, the two white women and their children, the few Indian converts who spoke French, comprised his parish. He could not have been versed in the various Indian dialects required to minister to the mixture of tribes living in the vicinity of the fort. A church and a dwelling were built for the chaplain, most likely differing little either in size or workmanship from the other structures already erected. Although the site of this first church cannot be determined accurately, the succeeding parish buildings as well as the cemetery were always at the southeastern corner of the enclosure, corresponding roughly to the center of Jefferson Avenue between Griswold and Shelby. That the church stood inside the enclosure seems to follow from the meager account of the first fire in Detroit.

The account is found in the famous imaginary dialogue from which we have already quoted. The purpose of the long document was evidently to assemble every possible fact to prove the deep-dyed villainy of the Jesuits, and the lengths to which they would go to ruin the infant establishment. Cadillac marshalled twenty facts and twenty observations on them to prove his point. The seventh fact is concerned with the fire which occurred on October 5, 1703. [13]

The 7th fact is that the fort of Detroit was set on fire, the fire having been set in a barn which was flanked by the two bastions and was full of corn and other crops; the flame by a strong wind burnt down the church, the house of the Recollect, that of M. de Tonty, and mine which caused me a loss of four hundred pistoles, which I could have saved if I had been willing to let the Company's warehouse burn, and the King's ammunition. I even had one hand burnt, and I lost for the most part all my papers in it. . . . The garrison of a hundred men which had been given me at the beginning had been reduced to fourteen; it was therefore impossible for me to guard the four bastions of the fort. I could only guard two of them . . . However, the savage who set fire to the barn was shot; we have never been able to learn who it was. . . . All of the tribes settled at Detroit assert that it was a strange savage who did this deed, or rather—they say—some French-

---

[12] A letter of Father Germain to Cadillac, *Mich. Hist. Colls.*, XXXIII, 104.
[13] The date is fixed by Cadillac's attestation to be quoted presently.

man who has been paid for doing this wicked act; God alone knows. . . .[14]

But the greatest loss from our viewpoint was the burning of the original baptimal register. However, it appears certain that an attempt was later made to reconstruct the record, and it is due only to someone's carelessness that we have lost the precious information these few pages would have conveyed. As the records are at present bound the third page should really be the first. Along its top run what are evidently the concluding words of an entry made on a leaf no longer extant: "at the said fort and it is to this that I certify this 13 of (month illegible), 1703. frere Constantin delhalle."

Immediately below these words is written the following: "frere Constantin delhalle friar minor Recollect and Almoner of fort pontchartrain of Detroit declares these two leaves of paper to be the veritable book of baptisms of the said fort; and in order to give it all the necessary validity I have besought Monsieur Antoine de la Motte Cadillac commanding for the King at the said fort pontchartrain to honor it with his signature. done at the said place this 14th of February, 1703."

Cadillac's attestation follows, and it will be noted that he seems not only to be ending a set of entries which has preceded, but to be authorizing a new register which now begins. As a matter of fact the verso of the leaf on which the attestation is written begins with the entry which is usually taken as the first in the St. Anne records, namely, the baptism of Cadillac's own daughter on February 2, 1704.[15]

We Antoine de Lamother Cadillac commanding for the king at said fort pontchartrain of detroit certify that the present extract conforms to the book of baptisms that was burned in this fort in the fire which occurred on October 5, 1703, and that the leaves comprised in this present book shall serve for the baptisms, marriages, and deaths as the r. father constantin del halle, almoner of the said fort, performing there the parish functions has declared to us. done at fort pontchartrain the 14th february, 1704.

Lamothe Cadillac.

[14] *Mich. Hist. Colls.*, XXXIII, 233–34.

[15] "I brother Constantin Delhalle, missionary, Recollect, and chaplain at Fort Pontchartrain, certify that I have conferred holy baptism on Marie Therese, legitimate daughter of Monsieur Antoine de la Mothe Cadillac, commanding for the King, and of Madame Therese Guion, the father and mother. There was for Godfather Bertrand Arnauld, and for Godmother, Md'lle Genevieve le Tendre. In testimony thereto we have signed, this 2nd of February, 1704."

The oldest continuous Catholic parish records are those of the Cathedral of St. Augustine, Florida, which date from 1594. The St. Anne records come next. Seven months later the Mobile, Ala., records begin.

Although we have no precise indication as to when the church was rebuilt, we may reasonably infer that the damage caused by the fire was soon repaired. Two years later, we have a reference to the poverty and bareness of the humble house of worship.

> As Divine service is held at the said Fort Pontchartrain in a church containing no ornaments and this is unseemly and inconsistent with Christian piety and gives a bad example to the savages, I also beg you to be good enough to make some outlay on the King's account on behalf of this church. Monsieur de Beauharnois had purchased a piece of tapestry, but when he learned that the church had been burned down he did not give it.[16]

When Cadillac penned these words he had been absent from Detroit since the fall of 1704. He had detected Tonty and two clerks of the trading company in the act of embezzling furs, and had preferred charges against them. As the clerks were related to some of the company's directors, the latter had retaliated by making charges against Cadillac which demanded his presence in Quebec. He was eventually vindicated, but was not allowed to return to his post until the summer of 1706. Meanwhile the Company of the Colony had grown tired of its bargain, and in September, 1705, turned over to Cadillac all its rights to the trade of Detroit. The arrangement was confirmed by the Court, and Cadillac now held Detroit directly under the King. Buoyed up by his success he began making extensive preparations for his colony's advancement. Soldiers were carefully selected, supplies gathered, and prospective settlers interviewed.[17] The religious interests of the colony were not forgotten. Cadillac petitioned for "another Recollect to come with me in the convoy which will start this spring, who will serve as missionary at the said place Detroit, for this is necessary for that Settlement. . . . Two Recollects are therefore necessary at the said post, until their Superior can grant more." [18] Father Delhalle being almoner of the post, the other Recollect was to devote himself to the Indian population surrounding it.

Thirteen years later, when Cadillac was making strenuous efforts to be reimbursed for his losses at Detroit, he lived over again the memorable day in the summer of 1706, when his convoy set out for Detroit.

> MM. Raudot, senior and Junior, having come to Lachine to view my detachment of two hundred soldiers, eight officers, two almoners and

[16] *Mich. Hist. Colls.*, XXXIII, 254–55.
[17] About forty-eight settlers accompanied Cadillac to Detroit in 1706. The Lecuyer brothers brought ten head of cattle and three horses, the first domestic animals in the area.
[18] *Mich. Hist. Colls.*, XXXIII, 255.

missionaries, and forty families which I took with mine, were witnesses of this large equipment of cutters and the troop boats, having taken to Detroit animals of all kinds, all sorts of grain and seeds, even to fruit trees in boxes, all tools for carpentry, for journey, axes, locks of all kinds, and even the materials for building a windmill which in truth cost a thousand pistoles, a barge, in a word, all the ironwork for the fort, which I had built with eight bastions, all the lodging places for the troops, a church, a very suitable building and well ornamented, a fine warehouse, another for powder, a pigeon house, a very fine ice-house, a brewery for beer, a barn eighty feet long. I took a hundred Canadians to work all this transport besides workmen and the soldiers whom I paid thirty sous a day when they worked for me. . . .[19]

Writing so long after the event Cadillac's remembrance of certain details may have been somewhat hazy. He mentions bringing two almoners to Detroit, whereas there are good reasons for thinking that only one accompanied him.[20] As the long procession of heavily laden canoes glided swiftly up the St. Lawrence driven by the eagerness of Cadillac to see again the little domain he had carved out of the wilderness, the missionary thought of the joyful reunion with his confrere at the end of the journey, and the harvest of souls that awaited him. But, somewhere along the route a Frenchman, or a friendly Indian, paddling vigorously with the current, stopped Cadillac and his convoy to pour out startling tidings of the tragedy lately enacted at Detroit.

Cadillac's plans for an Indian Utopia at Detroit were foredoomed to failure. Had there been only one tribe to deal with the results might have justified his hopes. At it was, his grandiose conceptions had led him to invite and install there a heterogeneous population that simmered with intrigue, and could not forget its tribal differences and animosities. By the skillful maneuvering of one band against another some appearance of concord could be maintained; but the fires of hate and revenge only smoldered, ready to break out

---

[19] *Ibid.*, 617.

[20] Cadillac's statement is apparently verified by a passage found in the review of Cadillac's claims for indemnity written by Vaudreuil in 1721. *Mich. Hist. Colls.*, XXXIII, 682–83. "The same year, 1706, he brought two recollets who lived within the fort, one of whom, Dominique de la Marche, now commissioner of the recollets of this country, set himself to learn the Huron language, and passed the winter hunting with them. He returned to Quebec at the end of three years, and from that time there has been only an Almoner at Detroit." As will be noted in the text later on, Father Dominique de la Marche signs the baptismal register continuously from August, 1706, to October, 1707, and hence did not leave the post to winter with the Indians. Another Recollect, Father Deniau, begins to sign the register in November, 1707, and Father Dominique does not appear again until April, 1708. The writer prefers to believe that the latter was alone during his first year. Hence Vandreuil's statement cannot be true, nor is the length of time during which Father Dominique remained in Detroit correct. He returned to Quebec in the fall of 1708.

at the first opportunity. Something of the kind had happened in 1703, and had again flared up three years later with much more serious consequences.

There are two accounts from which we can reconstruct the story of the outbreak. The first is from the testimony of Miscouaky, one of the Indians implicated, and the second is taken from the report of d'Aigremont, who was sent to Detroit in 1708 to investigate the situation in response to the numerous complaints that had come in from the settlers.

The Miami had begun their settlement in Detroit as early as 1703, and some time later became embroiled with the Ottawa. The latter tried to enlist the help of the French in obtaining redress but failed. Uneasy over this refusal, the Ottawa felt that trouble was brewing for them and bided their time until they discovered that a Huron chief, presumably with French consent, had induced the Miami to wipe out the Ottawa village while most of the warriors were to be away on a raid against the Sioux. On the discovery of the plot the Ottawa decided to take matters into their own hands by falling on the Miami without asking the permission of the French, but with no intention of harming them.

According to the decision we had come to, to attack the Miamis, we took our way back to our fort; and, just as we came near to the fort of the Hurons, we found eight Miami chiefs who were going there to a feast. As we met them, Le Pezant said to us "There are our enemies; these are the men who want to kill us . . . On that he uttered a cry to serve as a signal, encouraging us not to let one of them escape. The first time no one moved; but Le Pezant having uttered a second cry, just as we were walking on both sides of the road while they were in the middle, they were fired at and only Pacamakona escaped, who withdrew to the French fort . . .

After those had been killed, our young men began running to carry off whatever might remain in the huts; and as Le Pezant and Jean le Blanc could not go as fast as the others, I was one of the first who got there, so as to prevent any misunderstanding from arising between the French and us, as the Miamis were encamped near their fort. On my arrival I found that the Miamis had withdrawn into the fort of the French, and that one of our young men was killed, who had been recognized as a chief two days before; while our young men in despair at his death were determined to burn down the fort. I threw myself into their midst and wrested from several of them the arrows, on which they had put tinder to carry out their purpose, showing them that they must not do harm to the French who were not at all included in the quarrels we had with the Miamis. While this was going on I heard a voice shouting that the yellow robe had been seized. I ran there and saw my brother, who was sending the Recollect Father back to the fort, having unbound him and begged him to tell the Sr. de Bourmont not to fire on us, and not to give the Miamis any ammunition, but to put them out of his fort and let us alone. We did not know until the next day, my Father, that the Recollect Father and the French soldier had been killed, for those who fired on them did not boast of it.[21]

From d'Aigremont's report we learn a few more details concerning the death of Father Delhalle. After recounting the beginning of hostilities, which agrees substantially with Miscouaky's version, the report continues:

> . . . The missionary, Father Constantin, who was in his garden outside the fort and knew nothing of what was going on, was seized there and bound by the Outaois and taken into their camp. Jean le Blanc unbound him and said to him—"Go and tell bourgmont not to let them fire at us, that we have no designs against the French." As the Father was returning, it happened that a young Outaois was shot dead by the Sr. Bourgmont or some other Frenchman, and at that moment another Outaois, a relative of the one who was killed, shot the Father as he was about to enter the fort, from which he instantly died.[22]

It was on June 2, 1706, that Father Constantin fell dead against the gate of the fort.[23] Not knowing what to expect, de Bourgmont made preparations to withstand a siege. The warehouse, the chapel, and the almoner's house were stripped of their thatched roofs and covered with deer hides to minimize the danger from flaming arrows. There was desultory firing against the fort for two or three days, and then the French were left alone while the Indians settled their own feud.

The Ottawa were not long in realizing that they would be held accountable for the serious consequences which their hasty action had precipitated. "After we had been three days in council Jean le Blanc rose and said to Le Pezant, 'What sayest thou now? It is thou who hast caused the troubles that have fallen upon us; what dost thou think? As for me, I say we are dead men, and it is we who have slain ourselves by falling on the Miamis at the palisades of the French.' All the Kiskakons and the Sinago said the same." [24]

The Ottawa withdrew from Detroit and decided to throw themselves on the mercy of the Governor. Cadillac meanwhile had arrived

---

[21] This is Miscouaky's account as given to Vaudreuil at Montreal on September 26, 1706. *Mich. Hist. Colls.*, XXXIII, 289-90.

[22] *Mich. Hist. Colls.*, XXXIII, 435-36. Cadillac in a letter to Vaudreuil states that the missionary was stabbed before being released, and was dragging himself to the gate of the fort when shot down. The governor declares that witnesses do not corroborate this detail. *Ibid.*, 273.

[23] *Ibid.*, 445.

[24] *Ibid.*, 290.

at Detroit, and immediately advised the raising of a punitive expedition to crush the Ottawa at Mackinac, where they had taken refuge. The Governor wisely doubted the success of such a measure, and, besides, he knew very well that he could not afford to do without their friendship. He contented himself with accepting the slaves which they offered, and by laying down as the unescapable condition of their pardon the delivery to the French of Le Pezant.

> The Recollect father and the soldier you have killed, they are my blood, my own blood. With us the blood of a Frenchman is generally to be paid for by blood. You see that I cannot be contented with what you have done, and that it is, as it were, impossible to satisfy me, after the loss I have sustained, without bringing me as a sacrifice the head of the man who has been the whole cause of it . . .[25]

Le Pezant, so called because of his obesity, wielded so much influence among his tribesmen that it was more than a year before they could nerve themselves to deliver him up to Cadillac. Finally, in September, 1707, a council was held in Detroit at which the portly old chief was led out to stand in silent abjection before the piercing gaze of the commandant.

> There you are, however, Pesant, before your father and your master. Is this the great chief that was so well related and so highly esteemed? It was you, then, that ate of my white bread every day at my table, that drank of my brandy and of my wine. Was it not you who had an incurable disease, of which I had you healed by my physician? Was it not you whom I helped in all your needs, and whose family I took care of? And, because of all these benefits you have killed my people.
>
> You hide yourself and droop your eyes. Was it not you also, who went every day to the grey robe who used to caress you, who made you eat with him, and taught you? Yet it is you who have killed him.
>
> These are reproaches, Pesant, which slay you; there is no longer life in your heart, and your eyes are half dead; you close them, they dare not look at the sun again . . .[26]

Despite these ominous words the old chief was not really in danger. Before leaving Mackinac he had been assured secretly that he would not be executed. Cadillac, in whose hands the final disposition of the matter lay, was merely staging a tense scene, whose climax would prove the magnanimity of the French. The chief was led into the fort as a prisoner, but with the connivance of Cadillac he conveniently escaped during the night by scaling the palisades, a feat which he was too fat to have managed alone. Thus the honor of the French was saved, and the resentment of the Ottawa allayed.

[25] *Ibid.*, 322.
[26] *Ibid.*, 347.

The innocent victim of Le Pezant's outbreak had been buried without priest or funeral service under the primitive chapel wherein he had ministered. But neither the tragedy of his death nor the memory of his kind and saintly life were ever forgotten by the French inhabitants of old Detroit. He was enshrined in their traditions, and there grew up around him a cult which disappeared only when alien races, ignorant and contemptuous of the past, became dominant. Seventeen years after his death the remains of Father Delhalle were disinterred and solemnly reburied. The record of the translation as found in the St. Anne register reads as follows.

> In the year one thousand seven Hundred and twenty-three, the thirteenth day Of May, at the Request of the Reverend father Bonnaventure Recollect Mission.ʳᵉ of the post of detroit on lake Erié We the undersigned Declare that we have been on the spot where was formerly the church in which was buried the late Reverend father Constantin de L Halle Recollect fulfilling likewise the functions of Mission.ʳᵉ for the said post; where after having Examined the place where his Body could be according to the information that the Sr. Delisle who had helped to bury him had given us the said Father Bonnaventure having engaged Two men to dig in the ground they found During the day the casket of the said deceased Reverend Father, the which they recognized as his Body by the Signs that any one Could See; Which are his Cap, several Pieces of the Cloth of his habit, signs Of a cord on his Body and Of a Hair Shirt very Apparent, where after this examination the said Reverend father Bonnaventure had the Body Removed and carried to the Church. In testimony whereof we make to whomsoever it may concern Our veritable attestation. done at the post Of Detroit on Lake Erie The Fourteenth of May, one Thousand seven hundred and Twenty-three.
>
> H. Campau   Pierre Hubert   Bonaventure [27]
> Chas. Chene   Lacroix

Many years later, when the growing importance and population of Detroit called for a new and larger church, the remains of Father Delhalle were transferred to a new location, and in the official record of the translation we catch a glimpse of the veneration in which he was held.

> In the Year of Our Lord One Thousand seven hundred and fifty-five the third day of July, we priest, recollect, chaplain of the King in the

---

[27] The burial was thus recorded: I the undersigned Recollet priest exercising the parochial functions in the church of ste. Anne of detroit certify that I have buried the body of Reverend Father Constantin de lhalle Recollet missionary of the said post, under the platform of the altar of the said church and in the presence of Monsieur de Tonty commanding for the King in the said post and of Monsieur de Rocquetaliade who have signed with me this fourteenth day of may 1723.
Tonty   Rocquetaliade   fr. Bonaventure   R. Mis.

fort of Detroit Heriez and there performing the parochial functions in the parish of Ste Anne, in conformity with the resolution made the twenty-ninth of december of the preceding year, 1754, have transferred from the ancient church to the new one first the remains of the venerable father constantin de Halle heretofore recollest Missionary of this same mission, who had been killed by the Indians in the exercise of his ministry and who from the year (1723) had already been transferred to the said ancient church under the altar steps by Father Bonaventure lionnard our predecessor, we have again placed them under the Steps of the altar of the new church until the contemplated apse and addition to the building permit us to give him a final resting place in keeping with his merits and with the Miracles that several persons worthy of belief have reported to us as having occurred through his intercession in favor of the whole parish. secondly we have likewise transferred to the new church all the other bodies and remains which were found in the ancient church and we have performed a general funeral service for the repose of their souls this day and month as above.

fr. Simple Bocquet Recol.

The church referred to in the preceding entry was the one destroyed in the fire of 1805. In 1817 a certain number of bodies lying in the churchyard which surrounded it were transferred to the succeeding burial ground on Congress Street, and consigned to two common graves.[28] No special mention is made in the record of this reburial of the remains of Father Delhalle, or of any bodies lying on the site of the church itself. The first priest to live and die in Detroit lies in an unknown grave, but most likely under the feet of the unwitting thousands who make up the traffic that roars along Jefferson Avenue over the once quiet spot where stood the altar of a vanished time and people.[29]

Father Delhalle's immediate successor was the confrere who arrived with Cadillac, probably the first week in August, 1706. We know as little of him as we do of his predecessor, save that a later missionary is careful to write him down as a "sometime Lector in Theology." Instead of being free to concentrate on missionary work among the Indians Father Dominique de La Marche found himself compelled to take up the duties of Father Delhalle. His first entry in the register is dated August 16, 1706, and the succeeding thirty-three entries up to and including that of October 21, 1707, are signed by him alone.

Meanwhile, and probably in answer to Cadillac's repeated requests

[28] Burton, op. cit., II, 1424.
[29] Of Father Delhalle we know practically nothing beyond the details in the text. We shall have to wait for the published results of the diligent study of their early history which has engaged the Canadian Franciscans for many years.

for an Indian missionary, a second Recollect had come to Detroit. We cannot fix his arrival with certainty, but his first entry in the register is dated November 7, 1707. It is most unlikely that Father Dominique should have undertaken the journey back to Montreal so late in the season as the time indicated by his latest entry already noted, and the further fact that he signs the register again as early as April 26, 1708, warrants the assumption that during the winter of 1707–1708 there were two priests living in the settlement. Father Dominique signs for the last time on July 29, 1708, and that he returned to Quebec in the fall of that year appears from an extant document dated January 20, 1709, wherein he is called Vicar of the Recollect convent in Quebec.[30]

The priest who came to assist Father de La Marche is not as obscure a figure in his antecedents as were his confreres who served in Detroit. Father Cherubin Deniau came from a French family which could boast of some churchmen in high places.[31] He entered the seminary at Angers in 1695, when the Sulpicians had just assumed its charge. One day while handling a firearm in the courtyard he accidentally shot and killed one of the institution's charwomen. Panic stricken he fled to Paris, where he hid for a while and then enlisted in the army. He happened to be included in a military detachment which was sent to New France in 1697. About the time of his arrival the Quebec Seminary was planning a preparatory school for the youth of the colony, and in the course of making arrangements with Frontenac the rector mentioned the pressing need of a suitable teacher. The Count suggested that he had just the man, one of his troopers an ex-seminarian, whom he would willingly release from military service. The teacher became attached to the Recollects in their adjacent convent, and by them was persuaded to continue his studies for the priesthood. He was ordained by Bishop Laval on December 3, 1700, and was about forty years old when he began his ministry in Detroit.[32]

The coming of Father Deniau coincided with Cadillac's energetic development of what had now become his own domain. On his arrival in August, 1706, Cadillac had set to work repairing the damage done by the Indian uprising. The hides covering the church and house of the missionary had deteriorated on account of the unusual

<hr>

[30] Odoric-M Jouve, O.F.M., *Actes Du Frere Didace* (Quebec, 1911), 52. Father de La Marche died in France in 1738.

[31] Tanguay, *Répertoire* . . . , spells the name Deniaux but the signatures in the St. Anne register are plainly Deniau.

[32] The foregoing biographical details are taken from a sketch of Father Deniau by Msgr. Amédée Gosselin in the *Proceedings and Transactions of the Royal Society of Canada*, Second Series, Vol. II, Sec. I (Montreal, 1896), 59–63.

rains of that summer, and they were now replaced by long bark strips which the soldiers were sent into the woods to cut.[33] No modern real estate operator could make more out of a parcel of land than did Cadillac in subdividing the enclosure into building lots averaging 25x25 feet, for every one of which he received a yearly rent and other payments in lieu of his seigneural rights. In 1708 the white population of Detroit consisted of sixty-three inhabitants living in small houses built of stakes plastered with mud, and thatched with grass.[34] Twenty-nine of the settlers had been granted farm lands outside the fort, but the finest grant of all was the one enjoyed by Cadillac's own daughter.

> To Demoiselle Magdalaine de La Motte a stretch of land with three leagues frontage to the great river of Detroit, to extend from the river Ecorse inclining towards Lake Erie, with Grosse Isle and other islets which there are in the front of the Concession, and in depth five leagues in a straight line; the right of hunting, of fishing and trading; the whole as a fief, with right of the intermediate (and) lower jurisdiciton.[35]

The growing importance of Detroit justified a more fitting house of worship than the rude structure which had hitherto served that purpose, and in 1708 Cadillac began the construction of the first building in the settlement that deserved to be called a church. As usual he complained to the Court about the expense it caused him, and attempted to saddle its cost on the King. The answer to his petition gave him little comfort.

> However, as His Majesty has decided that he will bear no expense on account of that settlement, it will be very necessary that you should in future undertake those which are indispensably necessary such as the maintenance of the almoner, that of the surgeon and of the medicines. It is not right that His Majesty should defray expenses at a place which is not to yield him any return.
>
> The building of the fort, and that of the church are in the same category. It can be nobody but him who has the right to receive the profits of the country, who should be bound to do this building; and that must serve you as a rule in all that may concern this country in the future. You possess undoubtedly, the patronage of the church you are having built.

Fortunately, we have a brief description of the first real church in Detroit, and of its contents. When Cadillac learned that he had been transferred to Louisiana, he proceeded to safeguard his property

---

[33] *Mich. Hist. Colls.*, XXXIII, 446.
[34] *Ibid.*, 426.
[35] *Ibid.*, 381.

rights in Detroit. An inventory of his personal property was drawn up and signed by Father Deniau on August 25, 1711. No mention is made in the document of the almoner's residence, but the item referring to the church reads as follows.[36]

> Also a building, used as a church, thirty-five feet long, twenty-four and a half feet wide, ten high; boarded entirely above, with oak joists in a good ridge, and below of beams with square joints; with doors, window and shutters, and sash frames between of twenty squares each; The whole closing with a key. Also a heavy bell.

The inventory continues with a long itemized list of furnishings and accessories for divine worship, down to the last "6 hand towels, half worn." From it we might try to reconstruct the sanctuary of the primitive chapel. It boasts a green carpet, on which stands an altar "of French walnut-wood with steps . . . and a tabernacle closing with a key." Over the tabernacle is a turning box, draped with velveteen "with a fringe." Usually it presents "a small crucifix of copper or brass" but on occasion it can be revolved to bring to the front "a monstrance of silver without a stand." On the altar stand "large candlesticks of painted wood," to which are added on feast days "eight bunches of artificial flowers, old and worn" inserted presumably in "four pots of red wood." At one side stand "two small credence tables of French walnut-wood, closing with a small bolt," and behind the altar hangs "1 large picture of the Blessed Virgin of gilded wood." Suspended from the ceiling to serve as sanctuary lamp is "1 lantern of tin."

From a census of Detroit drawn up in 1710 we learn another detail of the church erected in 1708. It is located within the palisade, and is constructed of logs "laid one on the other" as is the warehouse. These are the only buildings differing from the others; even the commandant's lodging is still of the upright log type. The chapel, we are told, also serves as residence for the missionary.

The congregation that worships in this primitive log chapel is also revealed in the same document. Delorme, Langlois, Parent, Des Rochers, La Jeunesse, Malet, "are all married and have their wives and children at Detroit. St. Aubain, Lafleur, De Lisle seem to be the only soldiers at the post, and their wives are with them. Vin Despagne is a widower, and Chesne and St. Onge are virtually that, for after their names comes the comment: "Their wives will not go to Detroit." In addition to those already noted there are seven married couples in the post, four men whose wives have not accompanied them, and twelve "bachelors." If we add an undetermined number of

---

[36] *Ibid.*, 452; 519–20.

children, probably fifteen to twenty, and a group of Indian converts increasing slowly in number since 1707, the picture of the little congregation is fairly complete.[37]

The year 1710 was a trying one for the settlement and its founder. The tide of his fortunes had turned. His high-handed dealings with the settlers, and his grasping exactions had aroused their resentment, and a stream of complaints had poured in to the Quebec officials. D'Aigremont had been sent to Detroit in 1708 to make an exhaustive investigation of conditions there, and his report was anything but favorable to Cadillac. As we have seen the King had refused to help Cadillac in the erection of the church, and now he took the further step of withdrawing the soldiers from the post. This was equivalent to a lack of interest in the new establishment, and a cooling of the royal favor. The move had an interesting repercussion on the affairs of the church.

The Recollects officiating in Detroit were here by virtue of appointment as chaplains to the soldiers, and had not been sent directly by church authorities. Father Deniau had most likely come to Detroit on orders from his superior to minister to the Indians at the post, but automatically became chaplain to the soldiers when Father de la Marche returned to Quebec. This seems to be the only explanation of the condition which faced the settlers when the news of the King's order arrived, and of the steps which they took to remedy it.

This day, the 7th of June, 1710, M. de La Mothe, the commandant for the King of the Fort Pontchartrain of Detroit, having called together the inhabitants of the said place to inform them that His Majesty was withdrawing his troops to Montreal on his having refused to supply them with food, and that therefore His Majesty would defray no expense at the said place; and M. de La Mothe having, on this, set forth to his settlers that it was absolutely necessary to have a priest to officiate in the parish (it was decided) firstly, that M. de La Mothe should write to the Lord Bishop of Quebec or, in his absence, to his vicar-general, both on his behalf and in the name of all the inhabitants and others, to beg him to be good enough to grant them a priest or a friar, to come and administer to them the sacraments of our Holy Church. 2nd that M. de La Mothe, the inhabitants and others of Detroit, will pay every year the sum of five hundred livres to the priest and the friar who shall be sent to them by the Lord Bishop, or by his vicar-general, during the time they are inhabitants of Detroit. 3rd that the said inhabitants bind themselves to bring to Pontchartrain the articles necessary for the sustenance and maintenance of the said priest or friar every year, at their own cost and expense, and this to the sum of five hundred livres.

[37] Mich. Hist. Colls., XXXIII, 492–94.

4th that the tithe shall be paid to the said priest or friar irrespective of the said sum of five hundred livres, in accordance with the rules which are made at Quebec about it.

5th that M. de La Mothe binds himself to pay, as his personal share of it, the sum of one hundred livres, so that only the sum of four hundred livres will remain to be paid by the inhabitants; which said sum of 500 livres shall be sent this year to M. Grandmenil, the agent of M. de La Mothe, resident at Montreal, and the following years as ordered by the priest or friar who officiates in said parish.

6th that all the voyageurs and others who may come to trade at this place shall be bound to pay proportionately towards the said five hundred livres for the said priest or friar, and this before beginning their trading; for it is right that, since they share in the profits of the place, they should take part in the expenses of all that concerns the spiritual. Executed in triplicate at Fort Pontchartrain on the day and year as above.

Names of inhabitants Robert, Lafontaine, Joseph Parant, François Fafart, Pierre Roy, Francois Picard, Francois Livernois, Antoine Defrene, Alexis Germain, Joseph Trudaux, Toussain, Dardene, Jacques Gaudet, Michel Campaut, Guillaume Boucher, Jacques Campaut, Jean Chevalier, Pierre St. Yoe, Baptiste Trudaux, Mathieu Perrin, Paul Guillet, Antoine Magnan, Pierre Mallet, Chesne, Jacques Hubert, Antoine Carriere, Laurens Trubo, Alexis Lemoine, Pierre Lebeuf, Nicholas Vozé, Garvan, Jacques L'Anglois, Jacques Cardinal, Jean Casse, Jean Tabant, Jean le Scieur, Jean Paquet, André Chauvet, Michel Bizaillon, Francois Bienvenu, Pierre Esteve, Jacques Demoulin, Ducharme, St. Servin, L'Espagnol, De Martal, Michel Massé, Jean Baptiste Turpin.[38]

We do not know just what change was made in the status of Father Deniau, but from the entries in the register it is evident that he remained four years longer. This later period of his ministry was apparently not a happy one. He seems to have been attached to Cadillac, and when the latter was removed in 1710, the lack of his strong hand was felt, and a great deal of disorder appears to have crept in. The high hopes of Cadillac had not materialized, the settlers eked out a bare existence, and the rotting palisade was a symbol of the fate come upon a once possible rival to Montreal. In discouragement and dejection the missionary, perhaps reflecting the sentiments of his peo-

---

[38] *Ibid.*, 478–79. From the names appended to this document, and those mentioned in the census of 1710, it appears that there were approximately sixty-three men in Detroit in 1710. The reader is warned not to undertake counting them unless he is familiar with the usage of double names so current among the French Canadians. Thus Casse and St. Aubin are interchangeable, so are Delisle and Bienvenue, and Fafart and Delorme. For a complete census of early Detroit cf. Burton, *op. cit.*, Chap. LII. The same chapter quotes an observation by Father Christian Denissen, a noted worker in the genealogy of the early French families, on the custom of double names.

ple, penned the following passage, with which we end the first ten years of our history.

In fact, Sir, Detroit is all in commotion, both within and without; order and subordination, whether spiritual or civil no longer exist, nor respect for authority, political or ecclesiastical. M. Dubuisson has had the fort cut into halves, has turned Madame (Cadillac) out and also the Church, and, consequently, me with the six chief families here, namely deLorme, Parent, Mallet, Roy, Robert and Campos. I have forgotten the surgeon, who is not less necessary than the interpreter. It seems, from the bearing this M. Dubuisson adopts toward us, that he is infallible, invulnerable, and invincible. I do not say more on the subject, for if I were to tell you all, and sketch the portrait of Detroit for you as it is, it is terrible, it would affright you. As for me, I no longer live there. I languish and suffer there beyond everything that could be imagined, seeing its desolation and being unable to get away from it. Yet God be praised for all things, since nothing happens to us in this life but by the will of adorable Providence, and for our sanctification, when we do not oppose its designs.[39]

[39] A letter of Father Deniau dated August 24, 1711, to Cadillac then at Quebec. *Mich. Hist. Colls.*, XXXIII, 517.

CHAPTER IX

War and the Liquor Traffic

WHEN Cadillac had been named governor of Louisiana, his successor to the post of Detroit became François La Forest. Unable to discharge his duties on account of illness, La Forest dispatched a subordinate, Charles Regnault, Sieur Dubuisson, to administer the post temporarily.[1] His arrival coincided with a surge of unrest among the Indians of the Lake region. The rivalry between France and England for the control of the West had not abated. Detroit was a thorn in the side of the English, for it dominated the fur trade of the Lake basin, and radiated French influence over the western Indians. Iroquois emissaries were constantly at work, often successfully, endeavoring to lure their western neighbors to English trading posts, and to weaken their loyalty to the French. The Canadian authorities could not afford to antagonize the Iroquois openly, and at the same time could maintain their hold only by keeping their Indian allies at peace with one another. The English policy was to sow dissensions among the tribes to prevent their acquiring a sense of solidarity through a long period of peace under French management.

In 1711, Vaudreuil, well aware of what was going on under the surface, had deemed it necessary to summon all the tribes to Montreal to fortify their loyalty by personal contact with Onontio. Dubuisson, when taking charge of Detroit, was no less aware of the importance of his position in the event of Indian hostilities. To Father Deniau the steps taken by the new commander were arbitrary and insupportable, but subsequent events show that Dubuisson was a capable officer making the most out of a bad situation. The palisades were rotting away, and in its extent the fort was too large to be defended by the small number of men at his disposal. The commander therefore decided to shorten the north and south sides, and to connect the ends by new palisades. The church was now for the first time in an exposed position outside of the stockade, and Father Deniau had reason to be worried.

In the light of ensuing events it is evident that Dubuisson was making preparations for an inevitable outbreak of Indian warfare which menaced the security of his post. There was one tribe in the

[1] For sketches of Dubuisson and La Forest see *Mich. Hist. Colls.*, XXXIV, 307–10.

Lake region which the French had never been able to entice into the fold, and which was a fertile field for Iroquois propaganda. Living in central Wisconsin, and feared and hated by their neighbors, were the fierce and warlike Outagami, or Fox Indians. Father Allouez had come in contact with them early in his missionary career, and he had written in 1667 that, "whenever they come upon a man alone they kill him, especially if he be a Frenchman, for they are roused to fury at the sight of a beard." Underlying the founding of Detroit had been the hope that in this strategic location the Indians of the Lake region would be concentrated under French influence and control. Cadillac had been successful in realizing this design with nearly all the tribes subject to his jurisdiction. But the Fox, and their allies, the Mascouten, kept sullenly aloof. Finally, in 1710, when Cadillac—the one man who might have been able to manage them—was transferred to Louisiana, about eight hundred warriors with their wives and children came down by land around the end of Lake Michigan, and proceeded to install themselves in the vicinity of Fort Pontchartrain. No one seemed to know why they had come. Their past dealings with the Iroquois, and their traditional hatred of the French, seemed to forebode some sinister design. At all events, their advent shattered whatever comparative peace had reigned at Detroit. They treated the small number of French with contempt and insolence, and lorded it over the other tribes.

In the following year their representatives went down to the general Indian conference held at Montreal with the Governor, Vaudreuil. He told them plainly that, since they had been the cause of so much disturbance at Detroit, it was his will that they return to their old home in Wisconsin. But the Fox paid no heed, and the situation at Detroit grew tense. The breaking point came in the spring of 1712, when a band of Ottawa led by their renowned chief, Saguina, attacked and killed a number of Mascouten, who were hunting along the St. Joseph River. At this news the Fox flared up, raided the Ottawa camp at Detroit, and captured Saguina's wife. In the turmoil that followed Dubuisson probably saw his chance to end once for all the Fox menace. He took sides with the Ottawa, dispatched messengers to all his Indian allies, and thus provoked the open hostility of the Fox. The succeeding weeks witnessed a series of events as thrilling as any in the history of Indian warfare.[2]

[2] For a fuller account of the Fox Indians see Louise Phelps Kellogg, *Wisconsin Historical Society Proceedings* (1907), 142–88; Milo M. Quaife, *Wisconsin, Its History and Its People* (Chicago, 1924), 143–54. It has been intimated that the hostilities at Detroit were the result of a deliberate plot, on the part of the Canadian authorities, to exterminate the Fox. No proof has yet been found. The actual description of the fighting quoted here is from a report sent to the Canadian governor sent by Dubuisson, and printed in the *Mich. Hist. Colls.*, XXXIII, 537–52. Parkman in his *Half Century of Conflict* devotes Chapter XII to the same event.

The Fox began to fortify a position about fifty paces from the fort, while the commander's first concern was to gather in all available food supplies. The corn which the Indians had harvested lay stored in the church, and in another building outside the stockade. With a great deal of skirmishing the greater part of the supplies were brought into the fort.

> But the most important matter was to pull down, as quickly as possible, the church, the storehouse, and any other building alongside of my fort, which was also so near that the enemy would have had it in their power to set our buildings on fire whenever they wished; and moreover it was a matter of importance to make some clearance so that we might defend ourselves better in case we were attacked, which in fact happened. We have returned thanks to the Lord a thousand times, but for whom we were irretrievably lost. . . .[3]

On May 13, when the commander was still anxiously awaiting some word from his allies, a Huron, all out of breath, ran into his quarters. "My father, I ask to speak to you in secret; I come from our old men." Six hundred Huron and Potawatomi would soon arrive, and their chiefs were already in the Huron village. Reassured by this news, Dubuisson saw an opportunity for trying out the traditional French policy. He sent Vincennes, who had just arrived from the Miami country, to parley with the friendly chiefs. Why should there be unnecessary warfare? Would it not be enough to compel the Fox to retire to their own territory? But the chiefs had old scores to settle, and, allured by the prospect of a glorious encounter, were in no mood for such proposals. Vincennes returned dejectedly to the commander to report: "It is useless to speak of any arrangements."

Then the gates of the fort were closed, and the Frenchmen assigned to their posts. Arms were inspected, and ammunition apportioned. The blacksmith hammered out iron wedges with which to load the two cannon that the fort boasted, and fitted swords into long shafts. While these preparations for battle were going on, "our reverend Father, for his part, busied himself holding himself ready to give general absolution in case of need, and to succor the wounded if perchance there were any; he also prepared the consecrated host."

When the suspense was at its height, the commander received word that help was at hand.

> I got up on a bastion, and casting my eyes in the direction of the wood, I saw the army of the tribes from the South coming out, namely, the Illinois, the Missouri, the Osages and other tribes still more distant; with them also was Saguina, the Outtavois chief, and also the Poutoua-

---

[3] The pulling down of the church marked therefore the destruction of the third house of worship in the settlement.

tamis, Sakis and some of the Malhominy. Detroit has never seen so many people; it is a surprising thing how strongly all the tribes are incensed against the Mascoutins and Outagamis. This army was marching in order, with as many flags as there were different tribes; it made straight for the fort of the Hurons, who said to the chief of this army 'You must not encamp, the matter is too pressing. You must enter into the fort of our father and fight for him. As he has always had pity on us, and loves us, it is but just that we should die for him. Do you not see that smoke? It is three women of your village, Saguina, that they are burning, and your wife is among them.' There was no need to say more, they uttered a great cry, and at the same time attacked with all speed, the Hurons at their head, as well as the Outtavois of this place. The Outagamis and Mascoutins also shouted their cry, and about forty of them came out of their fort all naked and painted, with ther arms waving everywhere, to come and reconnoitre our men and defy them so as to make them believe they were not afraid of them. . . .

The commander distributed powder and shot to his Indian allies, and the battle began. For nineteen days the firing went on continuously day and night. The two cannon were .mounted on platforms overlooking the Indian fort and fired with such good effect that the Fox were forced to burrow into the ground. But they had no thought of surrendering, and hung scarlet blankets from their palisade as token that they would fight till the earth was dyed with their blood.

At last there came a lull in the fighting, and a Potawatomi chief asked leave of the commander to parley with the enemy. He mounted one of the gun platforms to begin his harangue.

Wicked tribes that you are! You think to make us afraid with all this red you are putting on your village, but be sure, if the earth is dyed with blood, that it will be with yours alone You speak to us of the Englishman; it is he who is the cause of your loss for you listened to his evil counsel. He is the enemy of prayer, that is why the master of life chastises him as well as you, evil men that you are. Have you not learned, as well as we, that the father of all the tribes who is at Montreal, continually sends parties of his children to the English to make war on them and brings back prisoners in such large numbers that they know not where to put them? The English, who are cowards, defend themselves only in an underhand way by killing men with that evil drink, brandy, which has made so many die a moment after drinking it. We shall see, therefore, what will become of you for having listened to their words.

Dubuisson soon perceived that the enemy were using this respite only to strengthen their position, and he gave orders to resume firing. Undaunted, the Fox gained the shelter of some buildings outside the fort, which had not been demolished in time, and for days kept up a murderous fire on the defenders. At length the cannon, firing the blacksmith's wedges, brought the structures tumbling down.

> They were so terrified by these cannon shots that we heard them giving vent to terrible cries and howls, and in the evening they cried out and asked whether I would consent to grant them permission to come and speak to me.

What the Fox demanded was permission to retire peaceably; but when Dubuisson put the proposal to his Indian allies they would not hear of it. The fighting became fiercer than ever. Up to this time the French seem to have had the better of their savage foes, but when hundreds of flaming arrows began raining into the fort setting many of the houses on fire, they began to think seriously of abandoning the stockade to seek safety in a flight to Mackinac. The commander had barely succeeded in overcoming their fears when a new menace arose. The enthusiasm of his allies was beginning to burn itself out, and they were tired of battling an obstinate enemy whom they could not conquer. What this meant to Dubuisson is plain from the desperate energy with which he faced the crisis. "I was four days and four nights without any rest, or food or drink, applying myself solely to attaching all the young war chiefs to my interests, to make them stand firm with me and encourage all the warriors not to retire until our enemies had been destroyed utterly."

Although the Fox met the new attack with the courage of despair, they had had enough. On a dark and rainy night they silently abandoned their positions, and entrenched themselves on Windmill Point near the mouth of a small creek, that, in memory of their last stand, bears their name to this day. Here on the banks of Fox Creek there were four more days of fierce encounter, and then the Fox surrendered. No quarter was given, and when the slaughter was over more than a thousand Indians had perished in their disastrous campaign. The French allies, however, were not yet satisfied. One hundred and fifty warriors were saved for further refinements of torture, and brought back to Fort Pontchartrain. "All the tribes allied to us returned to my fort with all their slaves . . . Their amusement was to shoot four or five of them every day; the Hurons did not give quarter to a single one of theirs. That, Sir, was the end of those two wicked tribes, with such evil designs, who disturbed the whole land." [4]

Through all these exciting days Father Deniau calmly exercised

[4] The Fox continued to worry the French for many years. Finally, reduced to a remnant of their former strength they allied themselves with the Sauk, and played an important part in American border warfare. The famous chief, Black Hawk, was a Fox Indian.

his ministry. Despite the almost constant firing, and the hideous clamor of the fighting braves, the offices of the Church were carried out, and the record of them inscribed as carefully as if the missionary had been officiating in a quiet little parish on the St. Lawrence. Here, for instance, is the burial record of a Frenchman who was killed during the siege.

> Today, the 21st of May, 1712, was buried in the cemetery of this place with the ceremonies of the Catholic, Apostolic, and Roman Church the body of deceased Alexis Germain, son of Robert Germain, and native of the parish of Pointe aux Trembles near Quebec. He died yesterday at 4 o'clock in the afternoon from a gun shot inflicted on him by the Outagamies against whom the nations of the South were battling in this Fort Pontchartrain. Before dying he gave us signs of sorrow for his sins and seemed to us to be dying with the sentiments of a true Christian. Wherefore we accorded him the grace of absolution, and at the same time the sacrament of Extreme Unction. In testimony thereof we have signed the same day and year as above.
>
> Ch. Deniau ptre. Rt.

On the morrow following the final defeat of the Fox at Windmill Pointe there was great rejoicing at Fort Pontchartrain. The long days of tense anxiety and danger were over. Like good Christians the French felt that their deliverance had come from above. In gratitude they assembled around their simple altar where, in the words of Dubuisson, "Our reverend father celebrated high mass to give thanks to God for having preserved us from this enemy."

Having escaped the horrors of an Indian massacre, the little colony on the Detroit River instead of progressing entered into a period of slow decay. The decade beginning with 1712 comprises the lean years of Detroit's history. The fear of Indian attacks, the maladministration of commandants, the growing interest of the government in the reestablishing of Mackinac, which rendered the continuance of Detroit more or less problematical, were all factors contributing to the dwindling importance of Cadillac's foundation. The settlers who could get away ventured into more promising fields, and there was nothing to attract newcomers.[5] Our knowledge of the whole period is decidedly meager, and particularly so in the details of its religious history.

For instance, we do not know with certainty when the church was rebuilt. The thanksgiving Mass offered by Father Deniau took place most likely in the house of one of the settlers. Farmer states that when the inhabitants began to leave, one of the unoccupied houses was used as a church, and this condition obtained until the arrival in

---

[5] Farmer, *op. cit.*, I, 333.

1732 of Father Bonaventure, who completed the building of a new church within a year.[6] This seems quite probable, both because of the low estate into which Detroit had fallen, and of the further inference that the translation of the remains of Father Delhalle, the record of which has already been quoted, indicates the completion of a formal house of worship. On the other hand, the pastoral letter, to be quoted presently, sent by the Bishop of Quebec to the inhabitants of Detroit in 1720 refers to their "temple" that they have allowed to fall into disrepair. It seems unlikely that the prelate, doubtless fully acquainted with the situation in Detroit, should have dignified with such a term some primitive cabin belonging to a departed settler. It is more reasonable to suppose that he is urging the inhabitants of Detroit to erect a suitable church building instead of being content with some primitive structure which they had been obliged to provide after the events of 1712. Since it is not certain whether the church of 1723 was a distinctly new building, or simply the restoration of an older one, it is likewise doubtful whether it should rank as the fourth or fifth church of St. Anne.

Father Deniau continued to act as chaplain to the post until the summer of 1714; his last entry in the register is dated June 29. In 1715 he was stationed at Beaumont, near Quebec, and was pastor of Louiseville in the diocese of Three Rivers from 1718 until his death in 1733.[7]

The Indians in the neighborhood of Detroit seem to have claimed a large share of Father Deniau's attention. In the second register of Indian baptisms, begun by him in 1709 and closed May 11, 1714, there are approximately one hundred and forty entries. Many of these neophytes are inscribed as being the slaves of their French masters, and this is true especially in the period following the Fox de-

[6] *Ibid.*, 529.

[7] This detail, not mentioned in Tanguay, *Répertoire* . . . supplied by Msgr. Amédée Gosselin, Archivist of the Quebec Seminary. It might be well here to notice Father Deniau's connection with the St. Anne records. An examination of them as they exist at present, besides raising seemingly unsolvable problems, shows that they are not complete, and that whoever put them together in their final form did so very carelessly. The opening page is a declaration by Father Deniau, signed January 15, 1709, that with thirteen sheets of paper he is beginning the "veritable first register of baptisms and funerals at Fort Pontchartrain." The reverse of this sheet is blank, and the next sheet begins with Delhalle's attestation as in the text. The 18th sheet presents a peculiar difficulty. It is again an attestation by Father Deniau that with twenty-two sheets of paper he is beginning the *third* register of baptisms of the French at Fort Pontchartrain, and it is dated November 9, 1707. The thirty-sixth sheet begins the *third* register of Indian baptisms at Detroit, and is dated May 12, 1714. The forty-seventh sheet begins the *second* register of Indian baptisms, and is dated November 14, 1709. There is no remnant of a first register for the Indians. It might be added that the entire set of records down to 1832 has been translated and transcribed, and is available in the Burton Collection.

feat. There is extant an interesting description by an unknown observer of the Indians at Detroit, which although written some time after his departure mirrors his interest in them and their customs.[8]

> The village of the Poutouatamies adjoins the fort; they lodge partly under Apaquois, which are made of mat grass. The women do all this work. The men belonging to that nation are well clothed, like our domiciled Indians at Montreal; their entire occupation is hunting and dress; they make use of a great deal of vermilion, and in the winter wear buffalo robes richly painted, and in summer, either red or blue cloth. They play a good deal at La Crosse in summer, twenty or more on each side. Their bat is a sort of little racquet, and the ball with which they play is made of very heavy wood, somewhat larger than the balls used at tennis. When playing, they are entirely naked, except a breech cloth, and moccasins on their feet; their body is completely painted with all sorts of colors, Some, with white clay, trace white lace on their bodies, as if on all the seams of a coat, and at a distance it would be taken for silver lace. They play very steep (for heavy stakes) and often. The bets sometimes amount to more than eight hundred livres. They set up two poles and commence the game from the center; one party propels the ball from one side and the others from the opposite, and whichever reaches the goal, wins. . . . They often play village against village; the Poux against the Outaouacs or the Hurons, and lay heavy stakes. Sometimes Frenchmen join in the game with them.
>
> The women cultivate Indian corn, beans, peas, squashes and melons, which come up very fine. The women and girls dance at night; adorn themselves considerably, grease their hair, put on a white shift, paint their cheeks with vermilion, and wear whatever wampum they possess, and are very tidy in their way. They dance to the sound of the drum and Sisiquoi, which is a sort of gourd containing some grains of shot. Four or five young men sing and beat time with the drum and Sisiquoi, and the women keep time and do not lose a step; it is very entertaining and lasts almost the entire night. . . .
>
> The Hurons are also very near; perhaps the eighth of a league from the French fort. This is the most industrious nation that can be seen. They scarcely ever dance, and are always at work. . . . They construct their huts entirely of bark, very strong and solid; very lofty and very long, and arched like arbors. Their fort is strongly encircled with pickets and bastions, well redoubled, and has strong gates. They are the most faithful nation to the French. . . .
>
> The Outaoues are on the opposite side of the river, over against the French fort; they, likewise, have a picket fort.[9] They are well dressed, and very laborious, both in their agriculture and hunting. . . . Their

[8] Memoir on the Indians between Lake Erie and the Mississippi, *N. Y. Col. Docs.*, IX, 885–92. The memoir is dated 1718, and is anonymous.

[9] The Ottawa village stood on the river bank about in the center of what was Walkerville before its incorporation into the city of Windsor, Ont.

game of Bowl consists of eight small pebbles, which are red or black on one side, and yellow or white on the other; these are tossed up in a bowl, and when he who holds the vessel tosses them and finds seven or the whole eight of the same color he gains. . . .

The Hurons number one hundred men; the Poux, 180; the Outaouaes about one hundred men and a number of women. . . .

Although Father Deniau made many converts no considerable body of Indians embraced Christianity until long after his time, and then it was the Huron who were the most responsive. In all their wanderings they had preserved some remnant of the teaching that had been brought to them in their old home, Huronia, at the cost of so much sacrifice. The Black Robe had left an indelible impression upon them, and his ministration alone answered to and satisfied their traditions. When he returned to Detroit his ministry was addressed to the Hurons as a matter of course, and they, just as naturally, submitted to his influence. The Huron mission will be dealt with in its proper place; we must now return to the course of events in Detroit.

As far as can be determined from the registers, the post was without a priest for at least a year following Father Deniau's departure. The succeeding Recollect, Father Hyacinthe Pelfresne, makes his first entry on August 20, 1715. Of his ministry in Detroit we know nothing beyond the fact that he remained for about three years, as his last entry is dated March 25, 1718.[10] That he was gone by midsummer is the logical inference from a number of interesting entries that follow his last one.

In 1698, the priests of the Seminary of Quebec, which had been aggregated to the Foreign Mission Seminary in Paris by Bishop Laval, felt that the time was ripe for them to begin missionary work among the Indians.[11] In May of that year they were authorized by Bishop Saint-Vallier to establish a mission in the Illinois country, which had heretofore been confided exclusively to the Jesuits.[12] The three priests first sent out from the Seminary began their labors among the Indian tribes living along the lower Mississippi, but the most important center, and the only one maintained until the withdrawal of the Seminary priests from the Indian mission field, was the Tamarois mission. Its site is marked today by the hamlet of Cahokia lying about four miles south of East St. Louis.

[10] Father Pelfresne was pastor of Three Rivers from 1719 to 1724. He died in France in 1737.

[11] The Seminary priests were a band of diocesan clergy united in a distinctive organization established by Bishop Laval. For its history see Gosselin, *Life of Bishop Laval*, Chap. XIII.

[12] In Rochemonteix, *op. cit.*, III, 550 ff., the Jesuit protest to this action of the bishop is discussed.

As the years went on the Seminary sent new workers into the field, some of whom by their zeal and heroism lived up to the glorious traditions of missionary enterprise left by the Jesuits.[13] On the 10th of May, 1718, there set out from Quebec to join their brethren on the Mississippi a little band of three secular priests. It was headed by the middle-aged Goulvin Calvarin who, in his fervor for the cause, had just laid aside the purple and the dignity of his canonry in the cathedral chapter at Quebec. Of his two associates one, Dominique Thaumur de la Source, the son of a Montreal physician, had been ordained just a year before, and the other, Jean Baptiste Mercier, had been a priest but two days when the convoy started.

We have no details of their journey nor of the route they followed, but we do know that they were in Detroit for the first three days of August, 1718. Father Pelfresne was evidently gone by this time, and the settlers must have been glad to profit by the ministrations of the three missionaries. Father Calvarin, styling himself Vicar-General of the Tamarois mission, performed a number of baptisms on the first two days of August, and all three baptized again on the third.

When they pushed away from the river bank below Fort Pontchartrain, the three missionaries passed out of our history and into that of the missions along the Mississippi. Fifteen months later Father Calvarin succumbed to the hardships he could not endure. Father Thaumur de la Source remained ten years in the Tamarois mission, and then returned to Quebec to die three years later.[14] So great had been his reputation for sanctity that at his funeral crowds tried to touch their rosaries to his body. Father Mercier labored along the Mississippi until his death in 1753. Ten years later, when the Jesuits were expelled from Louisiana, the last of the Seminary priests seeing the general confiscation of church property all around him hastily sold off the houses and lands belonging to the Seminary, and made his way to France with the exiled Jesuits.[15]

The record of priestly ministration performed by the Seminary priests in Detroit serves to complete our affiliation with all the missionary movements in New France. Franciscans, Jesuits, and Sulpicians were in the vanguard, and their history is intertwined with the

---

[13] Father Nicolas Foucault, for instance, left his parish of Batiscan just a year before Father Delhalle was stationed there to go on the Seminary mission. He was killed by the Arkansas Indians in 1718. Father St. Cosme, cited by Shea as the first priest of American origin to die at the hands of the Indians within the territory of the United States, was murdered in 1706 about fifty miles north of the mouth of the Mississippi. Shea, *Cath. Church in Col. Days,* 550.

[14] He evidently passed through Detroit on his way back, for he witnessed a marriage at St. Anne's on May 25, 1728.

[15] An account of the Cahokia or Tamarois Mission is given in the *Illinois Catholic Historical* Rev., Vol. V, Nos. 3, 4; VI, No. 3.

origins of our Catholic life. The names of Calvarin, Thaumur de la Source, and Mercier hidden away in the records of St. Anne remind us that the diocesan clergy as well were inflamed with zeal for the gaining of Indian souls, and that among them there were likewise heroes who dreamed of martyrdom. Their history has not yet been written.

After the departure of Father Pelfresne there was again a period of more than a year during which the settlers were without a resident priest. In the fall of 1719 another Recollect came to fill the vacancy. He was Father Antoine Délino, and his first entry is dated November 12, 1719. Conditions in Detroit were most likely as bad as his predecessor had found them, and it must have been the newcomer's complaints to the Bishop of Quebec that drew episcopal intervention in the form of a pastoral letter to the inhabitants of Detroit.[16]

Jean, by the grace of God and the favor of the Apostolic See, Bishop of Quebec.

To our most dear Children, the Inhabitants of Detroit, Health and Benediction in Our Lord.

The great distance that separates me from you, our most dear Children, joined to the great difficulty that I have in finding priests to administer the sacraments to you, oblige me to bring before you in this pastoral the indispensable obligation resting upon you to lead pure and Christian lives, free from all the sins that can separate you from the grace of God, and from his love. If perchance you were to be deprived of a missionary for a long period how could you reestablish in you the reign of God which you had once destroyed? For this reason you should preserve with great care the grace of God, and his living Temple which are your hearts.

It is only right that we should exhort you to take proper care of His material temple which we understand is in a lamentable condition, and also of the cemetery which you leave unguarded exposed to dishonor because of the cattle which enter it, and which for this reason alone deserves to be interdicted. But above all we recommend that you show a veritable obedience to your pastor whom it is to your interests to preserve, and to use well since there is no priest here, secular or religious, available to succeed him. To bind you more surely to this duty I place before your eyes these words of St. Paul in his first epistle to the Thessalonians: *Rogamus vos fratres ut noveritis eos qui laborant inter vos.*

With this Apostle we pray for you, our most dear Children, to have great consideration for the one who governs you in the name of the

---

[16] *Mandements des Évêques de Quebec* (Quebec, 1887), I, 498. Bishop Laval resigned from the Quebec see in 1684, and died in 1708. His successor, Jean Baptiste de la Croix-Chevrières de Saint-Vallier, began to administer the diocese in 1685, but was not consecrated until 1688. He died December 26, 1727.

Lord, and who warns you of your duties. You should have a particular veneration for him who is working for your salvation, and you should always obey him in everything that he exacts from you for the welfare of your souls. We pray you not to sadden him by perverse opposition nor make him bewail the heavy burden of his charge. By so doing you would lose every advantage to be derived from his zeal and his labors. If you do your duty you will draw down the blessings of God, and will truly console a father who loves you as much as you can desire *in visceribus Christi,* in the bowels of Our Savior Jesus Christ.

Given at Quebec under our signature, and that of our secretary, and sealed with our coat-of-arms this 8th of June, 1720.

Jean, Bishop of Quebec.

Something of the results effected by this pastoral, or some mention of the reasons which prompted it might have been furnished us by the distinguished Jesuit writer and traveler, Father Charlevoix, when he visited Detroit in 1721. The post was as important as Mackinac and St. Joseph, and his failure to make any reference to priest or church or religious conditions is inexplicable and inexcusable. However, he touches upon the state of religion among the Indians enough to tell us that there are no Christians among the Ottawa, and few among the Potawatomi, but that the Huron are all Christian although they have no missionary. In seeming contradiction to this statement regarding the Huron, the reason assigned for their lack of a missionary is that a few of their principal men have no religion, neither will they permit the demands of the others to be satisfied.

Father Charlevoix was in Detroit from June 6 to 18, 1721. His impressions of the post may be gathered from his statement that it had been reduced to almost nothing, and his evident anxiety to get out of it as soon as he could. Here, as at St. Joseph, he seems to have been more interested in the Indians than in anyone else. With a few deft touches he describes an Indian council which he attended.

> The first view of these assemblies give you no great idea of the body; try to imagine to yourself half a score savages almost stark naked, with their hair disposed in as many different manners as there are different persons in the assembly, and all of them equally ridiculous; some with laced hats, all with pipes in their mouths, and with the most unthinking faces.

These same stolid figures, however, could give vent to bursts of oratory that made the onlooker forget their grotesque appearance.[17] During the time of Father Charlevoix's visit Father Délino was

---

[17] *Journal of a Voyage.* . . . Kellogg ed., II, 6–13.

still at his post although his existence is completely ignored in the former's account.[18] He remained until the spring of the following year, and his last entry is dated March 9, 1722.[19]

The immediate successor was a young Recollect who had been ordained at Quebec on July 14, 1720, and who was destined to spend the greater part of his priestly life in Detroit. The name of Father Bonaventure Liénard occurs in the St. Anne register for the first time on June 28, 1722. With slight interruptions it is subscribed to every entry until the latter part of 1754.[20]

It is quite probable that with the arrival of Father Bonaventure a change took place in the canonical status of the little church body at Detroit. Whereas his predecessors had always been content to sign themselves almoners of the post, he recorded his third baptism on July 25, 1722, as acting pastor of the parish of St. Anne, the first time this designation appears in the registers. The stimulus of this new dignity by which what had hitherto been only a missionary station was now raised to the status of a parish might naturally find expression in the building of a new church which, as we have seen, is implied in the transfer of Father Delhalle's remains.

Unfortunately, the long years of Father Bonaventure's ministry are shrouded in obscurity. However, there is extant a charming vignette written by one of his confreres, Father Emmanuel Crespel, who had been sent as chaplain to Fort Frontenac in 1729. Letters passed between them, and some time after Easter of the following year, Father Crespel decided to visit his brother priest.

> In the spring I made a journey to Detroit on the invitation of a brother of our order, who was there on a mission. In seventeen days I reached Detroit, and was received by the priest I went to visit with a warmth which showed the extreme pleasure we experience in meeting one of our countrymen in a distant region; besides, we are brothers of the same order, and quitted our country for the same motive.
>
> I was therefore welcome to him on many accounts; nor did he omit any opportunity of convincing me how pleased he was with my visit. He was older than I, and had been very successful in his apostolic labors. His house was agreeable and convenient; it was, as I may say, his own work, and the habitation of virtue. His time which was not employed in the duties of his office was divided between study and the occupations

[18] Father Délino records a baptism on June 17, 1721.

[19] According to Tanguay, Répertoire . . . Father Délino served in several parishes in the vicinity of Quebec until his death at Chambly in 1740.

[20] The name has often been given as Leonard. As was the case with Father Delhalle, Father Bonaventure had a double whom writers on Canadian history insist on listing among the pastors of St. Anne. The double was Father Bonaventure Carpentier, who was never stationed in Detroit. The signatures in the St. Anne register are definitely Liénard.

of the field. He had a few books, the choice of which afforded a good idea of the purity of his morals and the extent of his knowledge. With the language of the country he was familiar; and the facility with which he spoke it made him very acceptable to many of the Indians, who communicated to him their reflections on all subjects, particularly religion. Affability attracts confidence, and no one was more deserving of the latter than this good man. He had taught some of the inhabitants the French language; and among them I found many whose good sense and sound judgment would have made them conspicuous even in France, had their minds been cultivated by study. Every day I remained with this man I found new motives to envy his situation. In a word, he was happy, and had no reason to blush at the means by which he became so.[21]

But Father Bonaventure's home was not always as peaceful as when visited by his confrere. There were violent quarrels at Detroit, especially in the earlier years of his ministry, between the settlers and the commandant over trading privileges. Alphonse de Tonty, who had been associated with Cadillac in the founding of Detroit, was appointed to the command of the post in 1717. To help defray his expenses, which included the salaries of the chaplain, the surgeon, and the interpreter, and presents to the Indians, he had been granted the exclusive right to the trade of Detroit. This curtailing of their opportunities was bitterly resented by the settlers, who claimed the right to sell to the Indians not only the produce of their farms but also whatever merchandise they could have brought down from Montreal. When Tonty sold his monopoly to a company formed to exploit it, the men of Detroit kept up their complaints and charges against Tonty until they brought about his recall.[22]

During this long-drawn quarrel, Father Bonaventure was more or less a disinterested observer, and there are indications that he acted the role of peacemaker. The presbytery was neutral ground, and there is at least one authenticated instance in which he presided over a meeting wherein grievances were freely aired.

It is quite true, Sir, that, upon certain disputes on the part of the settlers against the Sr. Gastineau and his partners on the matter of the trade, the Revd. Father Bonaventure and the Sr. de Belestre induced them to meet together at the presbytery to agree with the said Sr. Gastineau and his partners on the price of goods, but they had no share

21 Father Crespel's experiences in Canada in the form of letters to his brother first appeared as *Voyage au Nouveau Monde* (Amsterdam, 1752). It was edited by Shea in a collection of missionary journals entitled *Perils of the Ocean and Wilderness* (Boston, 1857).

22 Tonty was spared the humiliation of a recall by his death which occurred at Detroit, November 10, 1727. *Mich. Hist. Colls.*, XXXIV, 313–16.

in that as is proved by the certificate of the said Revd. Father Bonaventure and the Sr. de Belestre. . . .[23]

It is not difficult to imagine the tonsured friar in his grey Franciscan habit trying to soothe the vehement, gesticulating men crowded in the living room of his humble dwelling. There was another matter, however, in which Father Bonaventure played quite a different role. As pastor and moral guide of Detroit he was obliged to take cognizance of the old problem that was as acute in his day as it had been in the time of Frontenac: the fur trade and the liquor traffic. In 1717 the licensing of voyageurs had been attempted, but so many abuses had followed that the licenses had been revoked. Nine years later, in order to counter the stiff competition it was meeting, the government returned to the only system it thought workable, the restoration of trading licenses. As usual, the Canadian officials were trying desperately to counter the growing infiltration of the English into the region of the Great Lakes.

> . . . The Missionaries did by their zeal obtain several years ago the prohibition of the article among them (the Indians), but as the English supply them with as much Rum as they please, the same evil is produced that was expected to be avoided by its prohibition. . . .
>
> The Missionaries will complain that this permission destroys the Indians, and the Religion among them. But apart from the fact that they will always have Rum from the English, the question is, whether it be better that the English penetrate into the Continent by favor of that Rum which attracts the Indians to them, than to suffer the French to furnish them with Liquor, in order to preserve these nations, and to prevent them declaring eventually in favor of the English. . . .
>
> It would appear expedient, nevertheless, to suspend the absolute permission of trading in Brandy until the reception of the news expected at the end of the year, by leaving M. de Beauharnois at liberty to allow Voyageurs to carry a certain quantity with them . . . It is proper also, that he speak of it to the Superior of the Missions, in order to reconcile this affair, which requires a great deal of management. . . .[24]

It did indeed, and the missionaries refused to be managed. Jesuits and Recollects alike were loud in their outcry against this formal acquiescence of the government in the furnishing of liquor to the Indians. So strongly did they represent to the bishop the glaring abuses they witnessed that in 1730 he renewed the censures by which his predecessors had stigmatized the liquor traffic.

> We cannot sufficiently deplore the blindness of those who, in spite of reiterated prohibitions against supplying intoxicating liquors to the

[23] *Ibid.,* 45.
[24] *N. Y. Col. Docs.,* IX, 953–54. Report on the Affairs of Canada, dated May 7, 1726.

Indians, nevertheless continue this disreputable commerce. The temporal and spiritual penalties with which the King and the Bishops have threatened them should have made them realize the gravity of this crime, and should have stopped the course of this torrent of iniquity that swells from day to day, and runs on more rapidly than ever. . . .

To sustain your zeal, my dear Brothers, against the horrible disorders caused by drunkenness among the Indians, we shall employ every means belonging to our ministry . . .

For these reasons we forbid every confessor in this diocese to absolve those who directly or indirectly contribute to drunkenness among the Indians; we mean those who themselves or through others furnish intoxicating liquor to the Indians, knowing the use they will make of it. We reserve to ourselves the power of absolving from this sin, and to forestall any ignorance of this our present decree we order a copy to be sent to every pastor and missionary to be read at the parochial Mass.[25]

This vigorous pronouncement of Bishop Dosquet profoundly stirred the Canadian colony, and as the clergy under his jurisdiction proceeded to put it into effect, none was more literal minded than Father Bonaventure in Detroit.

. . . The Sieur de Boishebert, commandant at Detroit, informed the Sieur de Beauharnois, in a letter dated the month of January last, that the missionary had refused the sacrament of penance generally to those who had sold brandy to the savages, even in exchange for provisions and that had led to such a great scarcity of victuals, which was all the more injurious to the settlers at Detroit since they had only corn enough left, French and Indian, for two months, the drought having greatly diminished their harvests, and the savages had refused to go hunting because they had been refused this liquor . . . We, on our side, informed the Coadjutor of this difficulty, and he told us that he would write to the missionary to give way on the subject of his order in view of the necessity of this trade to the French people of the place for their living, and of the course which all the savages were taking of going to the English. . . .[26]

The bishop went to France some time later, and was called in to confer with the Minister concerning the wisdom of his pronouncement. Father Bonaventure's action at Detroit was brought up as a particularly glaring example of the clergy's intransigeance and interference with government policy. The bishop chose to explain his stand thus:

It is well for you to know that I issued my order only when forced thereto by all the missionaries who complained that I did not walk in

[25] The order, dated November 26, 1730, was written by Pierre-Herman Dosquet, coadjutor of Quebec, serving for Bishop Louis-Francois Duplessis de Mornay. *Mandements des Évêques* . . . I, 535.
[26] *Mich. Hist. Colls.*, XXXIV, 102.

the steps of my predecessors who had forbidden and publicly denounced the liquor traffic. I did not wish to do so because I knew that the King tolerated it in certain posts; but in reserving to myself simply the abuses that might enter into the traffic I endeavored to find a middle ground wherein I could content the missionaries, and not disapprove what His Majesty permits . . .

When they ask me for support in their zeal, I can moderate what I perceive to be indiscreet; and I assure you there is no reason why they should ignore the meaning of my order. I explained it personally wherever I made my visitations and by letter in the distant posts. I might add that I am not responsible for any lack of discretion in my missionaries.[27]

The prelate's compromising attitude bore little resemblance to the fearless stand taken by his predecessors, Laval and Saint-Vallier. Stifled by the growing complexities of the colony's development the flame of religious enthusiasm and spiritual conquest kindled by the pioneers of New France was growing dim. But it was still alive in men of Father Bonaventure's stamp who face to face with crying evils in the far-flung outposts of the colony, followed the dictates of conscience, and must have found it hard to temper them with discretion.

As the years of Father Bonaventure's zealous ministry went on he had the satisfaction of seeing his little parish outgrow the marasmus in which he had found it. By 1730 the importance of Detroit as a bulwark against English penetration into the Lake region and the Ohio valley had been definitely recognized.[28] Voyageurs in growing numbers made Detroit their headquarters. Every year witnessed a few immigrants and discharged soldiers taking up lands in the vicinity of Fort Pontchartrain, and the concessions made to them begin to figure in the official dispatches as early as 1734.[29] In 1749 a determined effort was made to increase the population of Detroit. The following proclamation emanating from Governor Galissonnière was read in every parish along the St. Lawrence.

Every man who will go to settle in Detroit shall receive gratuitously, one spade, one axe, one ploughshare, one large and one small wagon. We will make an advance of other tools to be paid for in two years only. He will be given a Cow, of which he shall return the increase, also a Sow. Seed will be advanced the first year, to be returned at the third harvest. The women and children will be supported one year. Those will be deprived of the liberality of the King, who shall give themselves up to trade in place of agriculture.[30]

[27] Auguste Gosselin, *L'Eglise du Canada* (Quebec, 1912), Part II, 182–83.
[28] *Mich. Hist. Colls.*, XXXIX, 70.
[29] *Ibid.*, 70.
[30] Farmer, *op. cit.*, 333.

These prospects must have proved so alluring that the same year a large number of emigrants took advantage of them. A contemporary document acquaints us with their names and interesting family details. The following is a typical entry.[31]

Louis Plichon was sent from Montreal and arrived at Detroit the 26th of July, 1749, with his wife and two children to take up the land assigned to him. It is 3 arpents long by 40 arpents deep, and is situated on the south side abutting (the land of) Louis Gervais on the north, and the lands not yet conceded on the south. The fifth ration here mentioned was accorded to one of his wife's brothers who rejoined him in 1750.

He received as a donation:

4 rations from July 26, 1749, to the same day, 1750, and from July 26, 1750, five rations up to Jan. 26, 1751.

2 roebucks for meat	2 augers
2 (?) of flour	1 sow
1 hoe	7 chickens
1 axe	80 roofing nails
1 ploughshare complete	4 lbs. powder
1 scythe	6 lbs. lead

He received to be returned or paid back:

20 bushels of wheat	1 cow
1 bushel of corn	1 ox.

The list goes on with the names so familiar in the old French life of Detroit. Jean-Baptiste Drouillard comes with his wife, five boys and two girls. There are the Le Beau's, Pilets, Le Ducs, Godfroys, and Tremblays, all with their wives and children. In one instance, the Royal notary must have been unwilling to spill over the one well-ruled page that was assigned to every settler, for, in the case of Jacques Bigras the only reference to his children is that they are "a numerous progeny." The settlement acquires a shoemaker in the person of Francois Mallet, with his wife and son. According to the notarial document about seventy-five souls were added to the population in the fall of 1749.

Many of the entries, similar to the one quoted in full, state that land is granted on the "south side." All through the French period there was no distinction made between what we know as the American and Canadian sides of the Detroit River. The voyageurs called the connection between Lake St. Clair and Lake Erie not a river, but a strait, Le Detroit. All lands lying along this strait were said to be at

[31] The document mentioned is commonly known as the Cicotte Book, and is one of the treasures of the BHC.

Le Detroit. What we now call the Canadian side was to them the "south side"; the American side was the "north side." The farm grants of 1749 began not only the active development of the Canadian side, but also extended the limits of the parish of St. Anne, which was not confined to the American side until 1768.

By the end of Father Bonaventure's pastorate there were about five hundred souls under his care. They must have taxed the capacity of his tiny church to the limit, and it is no wonder that his successor, the good, kindly soul, Father Simple Bocquet, found himself obliged to erect a new house of worship.[32]

[32] The BHC has a photostat copy of a little known census of Detroit which lies among the Gagnon papers in the Montreal Municipal Library. It is dated September 1, 1750, and was most likely drawn up by François Navarre, the Royal Notary. Since it included neither the priest nor the soldiers at the fort it is evidently a census of just the landholders of Detroit. It is too long to be more than summarized here but even the totals are interesting enough. There are 96 men and 80 women, and several of the families own slaves to the number of 33. Of the children fifteen years of age or over there are 49 boys and 33 girls. Below that age there are 97 boys and 95 girls. There are 1070 acres under cultivation which have yielded 56,200 sheaves of wheat and 2681 sheaves of oats. In addition there are 94 acres planted to corn. The farm stock shows the following totals: horses, 160; oxen, 211; cows, 471; hogs, 251. The fowl number 2187.

CHAPTER X

The Jesuits in Detroit

W E HAVE already seen under what circumstances the Jesuits re-turned to St. Ignace. This post continued to be the center of missionary activity in the Lake region, and the missionaries who made it their headquarters have already been mentioned in connection with the history of St. Joseph Mission. But the establishment of Detroit and the universal unrest among the Indians prior to and following the Fox upheaval cast a blight upon the northern missions from which they were destined never to recover. When Charlevoix visited St. Ignace in 1721 he reported his findings as follows:

> I arrived the 28th in this post which is much fallen to decay, since the time that Monsieur de la Motte Cadillac carried to the Narrows the best part of the Indians who were settled here, and especially the Hurons; several of the Outawaies followed them thither, others dispersed themselves amongst the beaver islands, so that what is left is only a sorry village, where there is notwithstanding still carried on a considerable fur-trade, this being a thoroughfare or rendezvous of a number of Indian nations. . . .
>
> The fort is still kept up as well as the house of the missionaries, who at present are not distressed with business, having never found the Outawaies much disposed to receive their instructions, but the court judges their presence necessary in a place where we are often obliged to treat with our allies, in order to exercise their functions on the French who repair thither in great numbers.[1]

As long as Cadillac remained in control of Detroit a Jesuit mission in its vicinity was out of the question. Even after his departure we have no evidence that the Jesuits contemplated such an establishment, although Charlevoix's comment on the Detroit Huron may imply a velleity in that direction. In the absence of any information bearing on the subject we know nothing of the preliminary negotiations which doubtless took place between the Jesuits and the government regarding Detroit, and which culminated in the founding of a Jesuit mission within the limits of the present city.

[1] *Journal of a Voyage* . . . (Kellogg ed.), II, 39.

The settlers at Detroit who chafed against Tonty's trade monopoly used every means to have him removed. If we are to believe Tonty himself, the malcontents, playing upon the government's concern for Indian allegiance, had stirred up resentment against him among the Huron of Detroit to such a point that they determined to send a deputation to confer with Onontio in person.

The interview with Beauharnois was held at Montreal in August, 1727. With the Indian complaints against Tonty we are not here concerned. After they had been detailed, as may be read in the extant report of the conference, the Indians brought up the matter of obtaining a missionary.[2]

> My father, you know the reason which brought us here last year, with regard to a missionary, and changing our village. It still exists now, and we await your reply as to that.
>
> Beauharnois countered with this answer:
>
> The establishment of the Sioux was the reason why a Missionary was not sent you. We are expecting some this autumn, and one will be sent to you next spring. But I do not advise you to move your village, because you will find everything to suit you in the old place from the arrangements I shall have made there.

Satisfied with this definite assurance the Indians returned to Detroit. The governor kept his promise, and in his report to the home government, dated October 1, 1728, he announced that, "The reverend Jesuit fathers have sent a missionary to the Hurons of Detroit, who appears well fitted to carry on this mission and to curb the proud spirit of this tribe." [3]

The priest selected for this difficult mission was a Frenchman, a native of Perigueux, in the Dordogne. A member of the Society from 1703, he arrived in Canada in 1725, and was sent to the Huron mission at Lorette, a few miles outside Quebec, to learn the language. Father Armand de La Richardie had made a brilliant course of studies in France, and the intelligent application which he brought to bear on his new task fitted him in two years for the work to which he was destined.[4]

When Father de La Richardie arrived in Detroit, the Huron village occupied the river bank somewhere near the foot of the present Third Avenue. The neat rows of bark cabins, each housing several families, were surrounded by a palisade, and stretching back toward

[2] *Mich. Hist. Colls.*, XXXIV, 49–51.

[3] *Ibid.*, 63.

[4] Father de La Richardie was born January 4, 1686, at Périgueux, and entered the Society at Bordeaux, October 4, 1703. Rochemonteix, *op. cit.*, V, 56.

Michigan Avenue were fields of rustling Indian corn. Here in the very midst of his flock the missionary took up his abode.[5]

From the missionary's own account we learn the heart-breaking failure of his first years among the Huron. The Indians had retained some traditions of the past but had wholly forgotten the exercise of Christian practices. Father de La Richardie paced up and down the beaten paths between the rows of cabins soliciting and exhorting, but all to no purpose. Sometimes in the dim stifling interior of a long house he baptized the dying child of some stolid mother who barely suffered his ministrations. At last, grace moved the heart of Hooisens, a chief. He became as fervent as he had hitherto been obstinate," and set such an example to all his relatives that not even a single one of his kindred resisted the Holy Ghost."

The missionary was overjoyed with this little band of converts, but in spite of all his efforts he could not add to their number. When the chief died some time later, Father de La Richardie despairing of success decided to return to Quebec.

"Wherefore, not realizing the depth of God's wisdom, I had nearly prepared for my departure, thinking that when once this chief, who had been the untiring protector of the Christian interests was dead, dead also was the hope of promoting God's glory. While my mind wavered thus, uncertain and spent with weariness, the goodness of our Savior appeared in this, that the savages of both sexes and of all ages, after several fruitless suggestions and attempts, flocked joyfully to the exposition of the Christian doctrine and to the public discourses delivered in the thoroughfares. Furthered by His grace, God's work made such progress that barely three years had elapsed from the death of that praiseworthy chief when not even one person in the whole nation remained obdurate." [6]

[5] It has been generally assumed by writers on Detroit history that Father de La Richardie began his missionary labors on the Canadian side of the river, and in the church yard of Assumption parish there is a monument commemorating the landing of the Jesuits there in 1728. There is no evidence to support such a claim. Boishebert while commanding in Detroit, that is, from 1730 to 1733, drew up a map of his post. The copy in the Burton Collection places the Huron village at the mouth of the Savoyard Creek, the location given in the text. The ground on the Canadian side of the river, which later became the site of the mission is labeled, "Fields of the Hurons." The Potawatomi village is located on the American side halfway between the fort and the Rouge River, and the Ottawa village on the site of Walkerville.

[6] *Jesuit Relations* . . . (Thwaites ed.), LXIX, 51–52. The letter is dated June 21, 1741. The dating is most likely incorrect. The religious conditions portrayed at the end of the letter, and which will presently be given in the text, do not at all square with our knowledge gained from other sources of the troubled years between 1738 and 1742. The missionary in this letter states that he is nearly sixty. If he were born in 1686, and there is no reason for questioning this date, he would be only fifty-five at the time of writing, and hardly "nearly" sixty. By the time the missionary had reached that age

With the help of his eager converts the missionary proceeded to establish the mission on a firm basis. We have no details concerning the building of the church and presbytery, but it is fairly evident that they were up by 1733. In that year, probably to provide an income for the mission, Father de La Richardie drew up a contract with Jean Cecile, a blacksmith at the post.

> The said cecile, Toolmaker and armorer, binds himself to work constantly and assiduously at The forge of the said Reverend father at detroit, in The huron village, for all The needs of the french and of the savages, in all matters connected with his trade.

In return for tools and materials supplied by the priest, Cecile binds himself in the 5th article to furnish without charge all the iron-ware needed by the priest either for himself or for the church. In the 10th article the blacksmith agrees to build himself a house near the forge instead of lodging with the missionary as his predecessor has done.[7]

All these indications point to a settled and prosperous condition of the mission with church and presbytery erected, and a source of revenue established. In 1735 there were six hundred fervent neophytes under the ministration of Father de La Richardie.[8] But the mission was not destined to enjoy for long this serene existence. The old tribal animosities which had been the bane of so much missionary endeavor broke out afresh.

The Indians of Detroit had been in the habit of raiding the Flatheads, or Cherokees, who lived far to the south. In 1738, the Huron, for some obscure reason, informed the other tribes that they were now at peace with the Flatheads, and would warn them in advance against any further attack. Their threat was ignored, and a raiding party was soon organized. The Huron were as good as their word, and not only warned the Flatheads but helped them to repulse their foes, of whom only three escaped. When the survivors reached Detroit with the news the Indian population was in an uproar. With every man's hand against them the Huron barricaded themselves in their fort fearful of the vengeance that they knew awaited them.[9]

Under such conditions there was only one thing for Father de La

---

the mission was in a flourishing condition on Bois Blanc Island. Moreover, the missionary mentioned in the letter as having been sent to help Father de La Richardie must have been Father Degonnor, and he came to Detroit in the summer of 1743.

[7] *Jesuit Relations* . . . (Thwaites, ed.), LXIX, 241 ff.

[8] *Ibid.*, LXVIII, 268. Letter of Father Nau to Father Bonin, October 2, 1735.

[9] *Mich. Hist. Colls.*, XXXIV, 151 ff.

Richardie to do; he withdrew into the French fort until the crisis should be over.[10] The French used every effort to reconcile the Ottawa with the Huron, and managed to avert hostilities. At the first opportunity the Huron abandoned their village at Detroit, and withdrew to a favorite spot of theirs known, in that times as it is today, as Sandusky.

From there they began a long series of negotiations with the authorities at Quebec relative to the selection of a new home for the tribe. They were afraid to return to Detroit, and professed a desire to be united with their brethren who were living at peace in the missions near Montreal and Quebec. At the same time they desired the invitation to come from the authorities, and in a form which would not wound their tribal pride, and make it appear that they were leaving Detroit from motives of self-preservation.[11]

During all this troubled period the missionary activities of Father de La Richardie are rather obscure. He wrote in 1740 that he had met with no success in trying to persuade the Huron to return to Detroit. The impression which his teaching made upon them may be gauged from the fact that in spite of their isolation the Huron remembered the dates of the more important feasts of the Church, and made their way to Detroit to observe them, although they left as soon as their devotion had been satisfied.[12] In the fall of 1739 the missionary undertook to visit his converts at Sandusky, and spent the winter with them.[13]

The government dallied with the Huron's request until the Indians became discouraged, and felt that they were not wanted on the St. Lawrence. Father de La Richardie seems to have been at first in favor of their removal there but as time went on, and the government did nothing, he began to formulate plans of his own. When, finally, Beauharnois had decided on the removal of the Huron to Montreal, and had sent his nephew to Detroit to carry it out in 1741, he found unmistakable opposition to his orders. Father de La Richardie had been corresponding with his superiors, and we can infer that the contemplated move did not meet with their approval. To predicate their disapproval upon the grounds mentioned in the following letter is most likely unjust, but the letter is, at least, an interesting view of the situation.

[10] The document quoted in the preceding note states that the "Fathers" withdrew into the French fort. We have no knowledge of any Jesuit assistant to Father de La Richardie at the time.

[11] *Mich. Hist. Colls.*, XXXIX, 195 ff.

[12] *Ibid.*, 201.

[13] *Ibid.*, 182.

Father de La Richardie wrote to Father Du Jaunay from Detroit, in December 1741: [14]

My Reverend Father:

I would have executed, with much pleasure, the commission with which you had entrusted me for the Chevr. de Beauharnois if he had been here; but, after a stay of about a month—which is not of much use in this country—he decided to go to Sandoske, as he had not been able to induce the Hurons to come here to listen to the message from his uncle. I could not omit making this journey with him, although I had reason to be sure that I was not pleasing him by doing so.

It is an extraordinary thing that measures are taken nowadays which accord so ill with authority and dignity as those they are taking for removing the Hurons from Detroit. They might have seized the moment when the Hurons were asking them to do so, and not have refused them so constantly as they did in order to invite them afterwards in a manner which is burdensome to the French nation without being able to gain anything from them.

The success of his mission will be limited to take with him three of the old men, who will not say a word, whom he had great difficulty in persuading (to go).

It is easy to see that the Chev. wanted to take this mission away from us, that it might fall to his friend M. Piquet who has already begun to have clearings made and huts built for receiving them; but, happen what may, the Hurons would never have any missionaries but us. [15]

The Revd. Father Superior acting in concert with the General, had sent me word to settle them on Grosse Isle, where they would have been better off than anywhere; I do not know from what this change arises. I shall patiently await the orders he may send me on this matter.

Father de La Richardie went on with his plans for the Huron, leaving the governor pretty much in the dark, and extremely annoyed at what he termed the missionary's interference. [16] The matter was finally settled by bringing the Huron in 1742 not to Grosse Isle but to Bois Blanc Island.

Here the mission was reestablished on a more imposing scale. Besides the church, a building almost one hundred and fifty feet long, there was the priest's house, a forge, a house for the smith, another for the domestics, a refectory, barns, a home for the farmer, Jean Baptiste Goyau, and a store or tradingpost presided over by a lay-brother. The farm itself was of several hundred acres, sufficient to support this large establishment. Thus it will be seen that the mission had as-

[14] *Ibid.,* 210.
[15] Father François Piquet was the famous Sulpician missionary. See Shea, *Cath. Church in Col. Days,* 614.
[16] *Mich. Hist. Colls.,* XXXIV, 211.

sumed respectable proportions, and must have presented a prosperous appearance from the river.[17]

We can easily imagine the good father's happiness over the improved condition of his beloved flock. The tribe was once more living together in one place, secure from its enemies, and he had only to keep alive the faith he had implanted in their hearts. In his letter to the Superior General, already quoted, he tells us of the manner in which he conducted his work. Three times a day he assembled the Indians in the church where he recited public prayers and preached to them. On feast days he did this four times. The rest of the day was spent in visiting the sick, settling disputes, admonishing delinquents, teaching catechism to the children, and administering the sacraments. To crown his contentment, the Huron repaid his devotion with the liveliest sentiments of gratitude and affection, and venerated him as their father.[18]

The account book of the mission has been preserved containing a mass of interesting detail.[19] There was evidently a brisk trade between the mission and the fort in lumber, iron, grain, and hides, and the various transactions in these commodities make up the greater part of the record. The cows and the horses are named, the petty details of storekeeping and building are carefully noted, as well as the obligations contracted by various individuals. The conditions of Goyau's six-year lease of the mission farm are duly entered, as well as the contract by which his thrifty spouse, in a laudable desire to increase the family income, bound herself to do all the laundry work and baking for the mission, beginning with St. Michael's day, 1743, for one hundred livres per annum. It is perhaps indelicate to pry into her affairs, but here is what Madame did with her year's salary.

Madam goyau has received a shirt, 3 livres 10 sols; a Quart of brandy, 3 livres; a Quart of brandy, 3 livres; a Quart of brandy, 3 livres; a pair

[17] It is fairly well established that the mission maintained another farm on the mainland somewhere near the site of Amherstburg. See William L. Stone, *Life and times of Sir William Johnson* (Albany, 1865), II, 456.

[18] These details copied almost verbatim from a history of Assumption parish written by the Rev. J. C. Plomer, while a teacher at Sacred Heart Seminary, Detroit. The source is, of course, the 1741 letter of Father de La Richardie already referred to. Father Plommer's history was intended to be merely the introduction to a critical edition of the letters of Father Marchand, pastor of the parish from 1796 to 1825, and was not only written but printed by his own hand. Just as he was beginning the body of the work he died on June 16, 1926. After his death only four complete copies of the introduction could be found. One has been deposited in the Burton Collection. He was the author of the article on the Basilian Fathers in the Catholic Encyclopedia.

[19] *Jesuit Relations* . . . (Thwaites ed.), LXIX, 241 ff. The account book was also edited by Richard R. Elliott in the *15th Report of the Bureau of Archives for the Province of Ontario* (Toronto, 1920).

of mitasses, leggings made of molleton; a Quart of brandy; 2 minots of pease, 18 livres; 6 blankets, 54 livres; a pair of mitasses, 3 livres. Madame goyau is paid in full for the first year.[20]

Father de La Richardie was now nearly sixty, and the strain of his labors was beginning to tell on his health. He wrote to his superiors asking for an assistant; but Beauharnois, in whom the memory of the missionary's independent action still rankled, managed that he should get not an assistant but a successor. The priest chosen to be pastor of the Huron mission was Father Nicolas Degonnor.[21] He had spent some years among the Huron at Lorette, and had resided for a few months at Mackinac following his association with Boucherville's expedition to the Sioux. When he arrived in Detroit in the summer of 1743, Father Degonnor was an invalid utterly incapable of taking charge of the mission. Writing to the minister in October of the next year Beauharnois reported the return to Quebec of Father Degonnor, and the fact that Father de La Richardie was still at his post.[22]

Strangely enough, the governor, while penning this message, made no mention of the priest who had already reached Bois Blanc Island in the place of Father Degonnor, and who had been appointed to succeed Father de La Richardie. Leaving Quebec on June 26, 1744, Father Pierre Potier saw the first dim outline of the mission buildings against the dawn of the 25th of September.[23] He was soon hard at work perfecting himself in the language which he had already begun to study at Lorette, and learning the multitudinous details involved in the operating of the mission. On the departure of Father de La Richardie at the end of July, 1746, Father Potier assumed complete charge.

The Indians who had learned to love and revere Father de La Richardie through the eighteen years of his ministrations among them were not much attracted to his successor. He was of the cold, scholarly type, and lacked the magnetism and bonhomie so necessary to control his charges and to hold their affection. Even three years after his arrival in the mission, he stood powerless in the face of what might have proved a sanguinary tragedy.

Among the Huron there was one chief, known to us only by his

[20] Ibid., 257.

[21] For details concerning Father Degonner see Rochemonteix, op. cit., IV, 201–03.

[22] Idem, V, 50–58.

[23] Father Pierre Potier, a Fleming by birth, was born April 21, 1708, at Blandin, in the Hainaut. Entering the Society in 1729, he was sent to Canada in 1743, and spent eight months at Lorette, the Huron refuge near Quebec, studying the language before coming to Detroit. The date of his arrival in the text, as well as the date of his birth, is established from his itineraries in manuscript and preserved at St. Mary's College, Montreal. These papers were most likely unknown to Rochemonteix for he is uncertain as to the date of Father Potier's arrival in Detroit.

French name Nicolas, who had always been a trouble-maker, and little changed by the influence of the missionaries. On May 20, 1747, Chief Nicolas while in the vicinity of Sandusky with a party of braves surprised five Frenchmen transporting a load of furs, and murdered them. This was only the first stroke in a carefully planned uprising, fomented by the English, if we are to believe the Canadian governor, and which had for its object nothing less than the complete extermination of the French at Detroit, including the missionary.[24] Not only Huron were involved, but a number of Iroquois, and as many disaffected Indians as could be drawn into the plot.

Committed to their course by this initial crime, the conspirators met, presumably in a cabin at the mission, to discuss the final details. The commandant was in the habit of permitting visiting Indians to spend the night within the fort. The conspirators laid plans to take advantage of his generosity on the holyday following the feast of Pentecost. In the middle of the night, the French startled from their beds by fiendish yells would rush out to meet death before they were fully awake.

But the walls had ears, in this instance a Huron squaw who had come for a supply of corn stored in a loft directly overhead. She brought her story to a Jesuit lay-brother, who immediately informed de Longueuil at the fort. When the Indians sought admittance at the gate, they discovered that the commandant's conception of hospitality included a complete search of his guests, and of their blankets.[25]

The news soon spread, and the population of Detroit throbbed with excitement. Judging his exposed position unsafe, Father Potier retired to the fort accompanied by the majority of the Huron. The latter not only deplored the perfidy of their brethren but urged the return of Father de La Richardie as the one person capable of straightening out the Indian difficulties. There was nothing to do but to send for him and great was their joy when he landed in Detroit on October 20, accompanied by the chiefs who had gone to Montreal to escort him back.[26]

In the interim Nicolas and his band had destroyed the mission buildings on the island, and Father de La Richardie was faced with the necessity of choosing another suitable location. After some negotiations with the government, and with the aid of a grant of 5,000 livres, he reestablished the mission a little below Detroit on the opposite side of the river at a spot called La Pointe de Montreal. The mission lands were approximately those occupied today by the parish

[24] New York Col. Docs., X, 83.
[25] Ibid., 114.
[26] Ibid., 142.

of the Assumption, in Sandwich, and the road which now passes alongside the church, called the Huron Line, marks what was once the eastern boundary of the Indian village.

The exact date of the removal to Sandwich cannot be ascertained, but that it had taken place before October, 1749, is evident from the reference made to it by Father Bonnecamps, the scientist of the Céloron expedition.[27] With the completion of the church in the fall of 1750, Father de La Richardie was free to begin his final task, the bringing back to the fold of the recalcitrant Huron. He seems to have spent a great deal of time with the outlaws at Sandusky, and as Nicolas had died in the meantime, the missionary's exhortations were again all-powerful. In the spring the Huron were once more united, and the mission entered upon another period of peace and prosperity. His work accomplished, Father de La Richardie returned to Quebec, where he died on March 17, 1758.

The further history of the Huron mission need not detain us.[28] In time it became a distinct parish with Father Potier as its first pastor. That tall, gaunt figure whose scholarly mind and attainments might in other circumstances have brought him fame and distinction, spent thirty years in the service of a rude and often ungrateful flock. He did achieve the melancholy distinction of being the last Jesuit in the West.[29]

Neither the Detroit nor the Sandwich mission was in any sense an outgrowth of the Jesuit center at St. Ignace. In its decadent condition, as witnessed by Father Charlevoix, this mission continued to exist more as a headquarters for travelling missionaries than for any good that could be accomplished in its vicinity. Consequent on Father Charlevoix's visit the fort was transferred from St. Ignace to the tip of the lower peninsula, and located approximately where Mackinaw City now stands. The date of this removal is uncertain, but can probably be linked with the transfer of the mission itself to the same spot; the missionaries could not have remained for long in their exposed position. A careful study of the extant baptismal register proves that the transfer must have occurred some time in 1741.[30]

---

[27] Céloron in 1749 was sent by Governor Galissonière to the Ohio River to take formal possession of the territory lying west of the Alleghenies. Father Bonnecamps accompanied the expedition as hydrographer. Both his and Céloron's accounts are edited in the *Ohio Archeological and Historical Publications* (Columbus, 1920), XXIX.

[28] For the later history of the parish see Father Plomer's work already mentioned.

[29] Father Potier left numerous manuscripts, the more important of which are reproduced in the Report mentioned in note 19. They include the account book of the mission, a Huron grammar and dictionary, and a collection of sermons in Huron. The Montreal Municipal Library has a census of the Indians on Bois Blanc, and a map of their village.

[30] See Rezek, *op. cit.*, II, 113–15.

From this time down to 1766, when the mission was finally abandoned, only four priests are known to have officiated at Mackinaw. Their entries may be summed up as follows:

> Father Jean-Baptiste de La Morinie, 1741–1752.
> Father Pierre Du Jaunay, 1741–1765.
> Father Claude Godefroy Coquart, 1742–1744.
> Father Marin-Louis Le Franc, 1753–1761.[31]

In the chapter dealing with St. Joseph Mission, Father Du Jaunay was referred to as the solitary survivor of the Ottawa mission, his favorite residence being at L'Arbre Croche. The Canadian government had begun to plan for the removal of the Ottawa to this less accessible location in 1741.[32] Two years later Beauharnois reported: "The Outaouas of Missilimakinac have fixed their residence at Arbre Croche, and Sieur de Vercheres advises me that they have made their clearances in the resolution not to quit that place."[33] It was this spot rather than St. Ignace or Mackinac that remained the last typical Jesuit mission in Michigan. In a future chapter we shall see how the current of Catholic life, broken by the departure of Father Du Jaunay was resumed.

We must now return to the history of Detroit proper to salvage what details we can from the obscurity which covers it during the period we have just been considering. Of Father Bonaventure's relations with the Jesuit mission we know nothing. There are entries here and there in the account book of the mission recording the mass intentions with which he supplied the missionaries out of his own evident abundance. In the period between the general conversion of the Huron, and the troubles which ended with the removal of the mission to Bois Blanc Island, Father Bonaventure was absent from Detroit. His place was taken by a confrere, Father Prisque Daniel. The latter's signature is the first found in the St. Anne register on August 31, 1735, and all entries are signed by him up to June 19, 1738.[34] Within a month from this date Father Bonaventure was back in his parish.

It plainly appears from the parish registers that the Jesuit missionaries were fully occupied with their duties among the Indian population, and that they had little to do with the Frenchmen of the post. Father de La Richardie's name occurs only twice, once in 1741 and

---

[31] For an interesting description of the Mackinac register see Edwin C. Wood, *Historic Mackinac,* (New York, 1918), I, Chap. VI.

[32] *New York Col. Docs.,* IX, 1072.

[33] *Ibid.,* 1098.

[34] This Recollect is practically unknown. He is not even mentioned in Tanguay's *Répertoire.*

once in 1743.[35] In September of the latter year Father Degonnor's signature appears once. Father Potier's only entry is the record of a funeral held on October 11, 1773. To the foregoing we add the name of Father de La Morinie who, although he had no connection with the Huron mission, performed a baptism in 1739. As his missionary career does not begin until 1740, he was probably on his way to Mackinac when he availed himself of Father Bonaventure's courtesy.[36]

Although his name does not appear in the St. Anne records, mention must be made of another famous member of the Society who visited Father Bonaventure. In 1749 Governor Galissonière determined to clinch the claims of New France to the Ohio country. He sent Céloron, a brave and capable officer, with a detachment of two hundred and fifty men to take formal possession of the territory in the name of the King, to drive out English traders, and to form alliances with the Indians.[37] In the report of his action to the minister, the governor wrote that the chaplain of the expedition was Father Pierre Bonnecamps, "Jesuit and mathematician, who will give us more exact and detailed knowledge than we have hitherto not only of that country but of any other through which the detachment will pass going and coming." [38] When its mission had been fulfilled, the detachment cutting straight across Lake Erie from the mouth of the Maumee returned to Montreal. The chaplain received permission to leave the main body for a flying trip to the fort at Detroit. He entered the river on the 6th of October, and spent the next day inspecting the post and the Jesuit mission across the river. Like other travelers before him he was captivated by the charm of the locality. Compared with the forbidding regions along the St. Lawrence it was like Touraine to the rest of "La Belle France."

> . . . I remained too short a time at Detroit to be able to give you an exact description of it. All that I can say to you about it is, that its situation appeared to be most charming. A beautiful river runs at the foot of the fort; vast plains which only ask to be cultivated extend beyond the sight. There is nothing milder than the climate, which scarcely counts two months of winter. The productions of Europe, and especially

[35] Father de La Richardie has sometimes been included in the list of priests serving St. Anne's, as has Father de La Morinie. Neither of them were ever affiliated with the parish.

[36] Father Jean-Louis de La Pierre signs as witness to a wedding on January 27, 1737. He is another of the obscurely known Jesuits, who must have been for some time at Mackinac. He came to Canada in 1734, and returned to France some time after 1746. See Rochemonteix, op. cit., IV, 213; Jesuit Relations . . . (Thwaites ed.), LXXI.

[37] Céloron was twice in command of Detroit. See sketch in Mich. Hist. Colls., XXXIV, 327 ff.

[38] Rochemonteix, op. cit., V, 74.

the grains grow much better than in many of the cantons of France. It is the Touraine and Beauce of Canada. Moreover, we should regard Detroit as one of the most important posts of the Colony. The Fort of Detroit is a long square. I do not know its dimensions, but it appeared large to me. The village of the Hurons and that of the Outaouas are on the other side of the river,—(where father La Richardie told me, the rebels were beginning to disperse and the band of Nicolas was diminishing day by day).[39]

Father Bonnecamps soon turned to the practical purpose of his visit. A hushed little group stood in Father Bonaventure's garden watching the Jesuit as he peered through his sextant trying to determine, probably for the first time in its history, the latitude of Detroit.[40]

That Father Bonaventure enjoyed the luxury of a quite pretentious court yard is revealed to us by what is commonly accepted to be the first detailed map of Fort Pontchartrain.[41] At the same time that he was sending out the Céloron expedition, the Canadian governor determined to ascertain the actual condition and strength of the two important western posts, Mackinac and Detroit. Chaussegros de Léry, a military engineer, was selected to draw up a report on Detroit. His map is a detailed plan of the fort as it was on August 20, 1749.[42] The church is seen to occupy its traditional spot just inside the eastern wall of the stockade. It stands in the southeastern corner of a fairly large square apparently fenced in, and set aside as church property. In the northwestern corner is located the residence of the missionary. Adjoining the west side of the church stands a small structure which unfortunately is not designated in the legend accompanying the map. The temptation to call it a school is strong, but it represents most likely the house of the parish beadle. Still the possibility of there having been some kind of attempt made to provide at least elementary schooling for the children of the post before 1749 is not so remote. We know that for some years prior to 1749 the settlers at Detroit had shown concern regarding the education of their children. The Bishop of Quebec writing to the minister on November 10, 1746 stated that he was considering the matter of sending to Detroit some Sisters of the Congregation, "who would be useful for the instruction of youth, and might induce the inhabitants to settle permanently." However, he did not wish to take definite steps until assured of the minister's approval.

[39] *Ohio Arch. Hist. Pub.* . . . . XXIX, 412.

[40] According to his reckoning he gives the latitude as 40° 38′. It is actually 42° 19′.

[41] The BHC has a map of Fort Pontchartrain which must antedate the de Léry map of 1749. Its authorship and its date have not been determined.

[42] The maker of the Detroit map was Chaussegros de Léry the younger. His father was also a military engineer.

The minister, who was more interested in keeping down expenses, would not commit the home government to the expenditures involved in the proposal. Three years later, during which there had certainly been correspondence in the matter between Father Bonaventure and the Bishop, the question was broached again. The Bishop wrote to the Colonial Minister on November 4, 1749 as follows:

> Several of the inhabitants of Detroit are begging me to give them three Sisters of the Congregation for the instruction of their daughters, and offer to provide them with everything necessary. Thus they will be no expense to his Majesty. I had proposed this four years ago to M. de Maurepas; but he did not seem disposed to consider the project. I propose it to you with entire disinterestedness. I cannot refuse these persons the opportunity to make known to you their desires.

The minister replied that the matter was not urgent, and that nothing could be done without the concerted action of the intendant and governor. There, as far as the government was concerned, the project died. But Bishop de Pontbriand could not forget the appeal that had come to him out of the wilderness.[43]

Through his agents in France the bishop succeeded in drawing the attention of an eminent personage to the religious needs of his vast diocese. Louis, Duke of Orleans, was the son of the Regent during the minority of Louis XV. A gentle, cultured prince, he was as renowned for his virtuous life as his father was notorious for his profligacy. In 1749, three years before his death, he made over to the Bishop of Quebec a fund of twenty thousand francs to be administered in the interests of the most needy places under his care. When the bishop came into actual possession of the fund in 1756, it is noteworthy that he assigned one-tenth of the income resulting therefrom to the Sisters of the Congregation for their proposed establishment at Detroit. But by the time that this donation could have been used Canada was in the throes of the final struggle with England, and there were weightier matters to think about than the beginnings of a parish school in the interior of the continent.[44]

These unsuccessful efforts aimed at the supplying of a need for instruction in secular branches. Whether the chaplains of the post ever gave such instruction is a matter of speculation. But it must not be lost sight of, that the children were never deprived of schooling in the most important branch of all, religion. The successive priests

[43] These extracts quoted from Abbé Etienne Michel Faillon's *Vie de la Soeur Bourgeoys* (Villemarie, 1853), II, 372. Marguerite Bourgeoys founded the Sisters of the Congregation of Notre-Dame at Montreal in 1657. The Sisterhood is today one of the largest in Canada with the Motherhouse in Sherbrooke St., Montreal.

[44] Gosselin, *L'Église du Canada*, III, 194.

at the post could not have been derelict in this most essential duty of their ministry. We may take for granted that from the time of Father Delhalle no child ever went without a course of catechetical instruction, and this even without such a delightful bit of intimation as that found in Chaussegros de Léry's journal: "A stag entered the fort through a breach in the palisade at 4 o'clock this afternoon, and wandered about. The children coming out of catechism class chased after him until he got out by another breach and made for the woods." [45]

Father Bonaventure's long pastorate came to an end in 1754. On the 10th of August his successor arrived in the person of Father Simple Bocquet.[46] Five days later the whole parish assembled to celebrate in a fitting manner the feast of the Assumption.

We are told by an eye-witness that the day was calm and beautiful. From early morning canoes had been gliding along the sparkling river from Grand Marais and La Petite Côte, all converging at the landing place below the fort. The women in their gaily colored kerchiefs, and marshalling their little flocks ahead of them made directly for the church, while the men stayed behind to smoke a last pipe against the inevitable lengthy sermon. In his long red gown, not long enough to hide his clumsy shoepacs, the beadle brandishing his staff of office gave notice that Mass was about to begin, and soon the traditional chant of the Church soared from out the willing throats that had known it from childhood.

Later in the day came the procession. A military detachment merely passing through Detroit stayed long enough to hear Mass, and take part in the solemnity. First the women and children fell into rank, then the men. As the two priests came out of church into the crowded little square the soldiers presented arms, and then took their position as guard of honor. Out of the fort and eastward along the river bank the column proceeded, while over the quiet waters rang hymns of praise in honor of the Virgin Mother. When the procession had returned to receive the final Benediction, the gala day was over and the river was quickly dotted with canoes homeward bound.[47]

On the 11th of September Father Bonaventure left Detroit to re-

---

[45] The Journals of Chaussegros de Léry are published in the *Report of the Archivist of the Province of Quebec for* 1926–27 (Quebec, 1927), 334–405; *Report . . . 1927–28,* 355–429. The quotation is from the second Report, 416.

[46] *Report . . . 1927–28,* 399. Father Bocquet came to Canada in 1743. We know nothing of him between this date and his arrival in Detroit.

[47] Chaussegros de Léry Journal, entry for August 15, 1754. "Jour de l'Assomption, beau temps calme. La procession de la Vierge se fit hors du fort. Le détachment prit les armes. Il n'était resté ce jour que pour la solenité."

turn to Montreal.[48] Father Bocquet remained alone to begin his long pastorate unaware of the thrilling days ahead, and the momentous changes he would live to see.[49]

We are fortunate in possessing a fairly accurate description of Detroit as it was when Father Bocquet took charge. Strangely enough it comes from an American colonist, and it epitomizes the sanguinary border warfare that marked the last phase of the French and Indian War.

In 1755 a band of Indians raided a settlement near the present McConnellsburg in Fulton County, Pennsylvania. Among their captives was Charles Stuart, with his wife and two small children. The prisoners were hurried westward through Ohio and around the end of Lake Erie up to Detroit. Here Stuart and his wife, who had meanwhile been despoiled of their children, were handed over to the French commander and by him compelled to work for Father Potier and Father Bocquet until their labor was the equivalent of the sum that would ordinarily be paid for their ransom. In 1757 they were sent as prisoners to Quebec, were later carried to England, and finally landed back in New York. On his return Stuart evidently dictated a statement of his observations to the military authorities from which the following pertinent passages are extracted:

> From Lake Erie up to the Strait that Emptys Lake Huron there are no French or Indians Settled on Either Side Till you get ab[t] 11 miles up where is one Family Settled on the East side; then 2 miles Higher up Begins the French Settlements w[ch] extend ab[t] 4 miles in Length along the Strait or river, their Plantations are Laid out on the River 3 Acres in Breadth and 100 Acres in Depth from the River, Each Plantation Containing 300 French Acres w[ch] Seemed rather Larger than the English Acres—a Square Cont[g] 10 Perches on Every Side is a French Acre—a French Perch is 7 Ells Long. Each Ell is a yard & Quarter English measure—The French that are Settled in said 4 miles amount to ab[t] 27 or 28 Familys—the Wondot Corn Feilds are Higher up the river and Join on the Side next the French to Cap[t] Jarvis's Plantation (S[d] Jar-

[48] *Ibid.,* entry for September 11.

[49] We must deal here with a difficulty that qualifies this statement. According to Chaussegros de Léry, entry of August 10, Father Bocquet arrived "to relieve Father Bonaventure, also a Recollect, who for a long time had ministered in Detroit as chaplain and pastor." Father Bocquet's first entry in St. Anne's register, dated September 18, is signed in the capacity of pastor. On August 18, 1755, Father Bonaventure is again in Detroit, for he signs the register as pastor, and Father Bocquet signs the same day as assistant. This condition of affairs continues until the middle of October, when both of them sign as pastors. On March 2, 1756, both priests sign the same entry. On September 5, 1756, Father Bocquet signs as assistant, and Father Bonaventure goes on signing as pastor until his last entry, July 8, 1757. What all this means can only be conjectured. At any rate Father Bocquet does not seem to have been in peaceful possession of his parish until Father Bonaventure's departure.

vis is a French Capt of Militia). ab^t 2½ miles Higher up than Capt Jarvis's is the Wondot Town Containing ab^t 60 or 70 Houses and at the Upper End of the Town Towards Lake Huron Stands their church, and Joining to it is the Priests House Garden and Plantation. . . .[50]

About 2 miles above the Wondot Town Stands the Tawaw Town. between These Two Towns Lives Three French Familys—there are also Three Plantations in this distance Belonging to three French Merch^{ts} who live in Fort de Troit—The Tawaw Town Contains ab^t 90 Houses or Indian Cabbins But No Church for the Tawaws are a Heathen Nation & not Proselyted to the Roman Catholick Religion—. . . .

On the DeTroit or West Side of the Strait that Emptys Lake Huron there are no Inhabitants Either French or Indians Till you come within ab^t 1¼ miles of Fort De Troit or ab^t 16¾ miles From Lake Erie and at s^d Distance of 1¼ miles from the Fort Stand on Outotoway Town Containing ab^t 32 Houses. . . . the Above are all the Indian Towns that are any Way near De Troit. . . . The Fort DeTroit Is a Stockade. Its a Square with Bastions and the Side next the Water had Three Bastions, But they have no Cannon In the Fort or Settlement Except a Small Mortar wch its said they have in one of their Stores—The Fort Takes in ab^t 4 (or 5) Acres of Ground and Contains ab^t 70 Houses wch are Built of Loggs & Coverd with Boards of ab^t an Inch Thick, Cut at a Saw Mill But have No defence ag^t Bombs and the Side of the Fort Next the Water is Very Weak and may be Easily Thrown Down By Mens Pushing against it. . . . the Houses in the Fort are Built in Streets and are a much Better defence than the Fort itself—The French have 18 Familys Settled Between De Troit Fort and the Outotoway Town and their Settlements On the North of the Fort Extend ab^t 6 miles up to Lake Huron—the French are Settled in a String along the Water Side But have no Settlements off of the river—Mr. Stuart Thinks the whole Number of French Familys In the whole De Troit Settlements will Amount to But ab^t 360 Familys, and he has seen their Militia under arms at their general Muster wch Amounted to Only ab^t 220 Men.[51]

[50] At this time, and perhaps for a year or two Father Potier had a confrere in his mission, Father Jean Baptiste de Salleneuve. He records a baptism on May 31, 1756. When the Jesuits were banished from the Mississippi area in 1764, Father de Salleneuve was in Kaskaskia, and Father Watrin in his account of the banishment raises a problem as yet unsolved. "Above all, they (the people) were indignant at the seizure made of the sacred vessels of a chapel belonging to the Hurons of Detroit which Father Salleneuve, missionary of that nation had brought to the Illinois country when he had taken refuge there two and a half years before . . ." See Jesuit Relations. . . . (Thwaites ed.), LXX, 277. Rochemonteix adds a comment that the sacred vessels had been removed to guard them from profanation at the hands of the English. Op. cit., IV, 403. Certainly neither Father Potier nor Father Bocquet were ever reduced to such a course of action, and why Father de Salleneuve should have felt obliged to fly to the Illinois country with the sacred vessels at the beginning of 1762 is a mystery. A brief sketch of Father de Salleneuve will be found in Rochemonteix appended to the citation just referred to.

[51] See the "Captivity of Charles Stuart" in the Mississippi Valley Historical Review, XIII, No. 1.

From Stuart's account it is evident that the population of Detroit had grown considerably in the years following the serious attempt of the government to strengthen the post in 1749. It is worthy of notice that the majority of the French lived not in the stockade itself but strung out for miles along both sides of the river. After the English occupation there followed a gradual exodus so that at one time there were only six Catholic families within the enclosure. From this period up to the beginning of American immigration the bulk of St. Anne's parish comprised the farmers who lived up and down the river, and not the townspeople.

On his arrival in Detroit, Father Bocquet must have been struck by the inadequacy of the church building, and profiting no doubt by the presence of Chaussegros de Léry he began to lay plans for a new edifice. From the record already quoted dealing with the translation of Father Delhalle's remains we gather that the church, while not completed, was in use as early as July, 1755. In the preceding fall the old rectory had been torn down and replaced by a new structure into which Father Bocquet moved on the 24th of December.[52]

With these evidences of material prosperity the parish entered upon its final years under the French regime. There was no doubt now as to the importance of Detroit; it was the western base of operations in the closing years of the struggle for supremacy in North America. Through it moved a kaleidoscopic procession of supply trains for French positions less fortunately situated, of troop columns resting between long stretches of hardships, of Indian raiding parties with their spoils, of care-worn, fearful prisoners. But this backwash of the conflict in the East that was swiftly coming to decision seems to have had little influence on the stable population of the settlement. The farmers went on tilling their ribbon farms, and the routine of parish life continued undisturbed.

This was largely true even under British rule. The transfer of Detroit was accomplished without bloodshed, and its inhabitants calmly accepted the inevitable. But before we go on to this momentous change in the history of Detroit it may be of interest to glance at some of the characteristic features of the old French parish life which must have been established by the time of the surrender, and

[52] Chaussegros de Léry's Journal, *Report . . . 1927–28,* 407. He was in Detroit working on the strengthening of the fort in 1754. At this time he made a second map of Detroit differing little from the 1749 map. Farmer, *op. cit.,* 530, is apparently responsible for the assertion copied by Shea that the new church was consecrated by the Bishop of Quebec who spent several weeks in a visit to Detroit. There is no proof either in Detroit or Quebec for such a statement, and it is denied by Bishop de Pontbriand's biographer. Gosselin, *Église du Canada,* III, 334.

which persisted well into the nineteenth century. The development of the Church in the Canadian colony had been molded naturally by the Canon Law of the mother country modified to the extent necessary to meet exceptional circumstances. As a parish in the Diocese of Quebec, St. Anne's exhibited the peculiarities of organization and liturgy current at the time, and which still exist with some modifications in the province of Quebec.[53]

For the administration of its temporalities the parish, already duly constituted in the cononical sense, functioned only through a parish corporation known as "La Fabrique." This was made up of the pastor and a number of laymen called "Marguilliers," a term approximately translated by the English word "churchwardens." To the corporation was entrusted the collecting and guarding of all revenues accruing to the parish as well as the satisfying of all obligations from whatever source incumbent on the parish. In lieu of a convenient bank the parish possessed a "coffre," or strong box, closed by two dissimilar locks, and which could be opened only in the presence of the pastor and the chief marguillier since each held his respective key.[54]

As may be imagined, the office of marguillier was an important one, and marked its possessor as a person of some consequence. There were generally three marguilliers in active service. A new one was chosen every year at a parish election held on the last Sunday of December and the oldest in point of service retired to join the ancient and honorable body of "past marguilliers." On extraordinary occasions when the fabrique was faced by some problem which the active marguilliers could not settle, it was perfectly legal to admit all who had ever held that office so as to profit by their wisdom.

Such high office was not without its compensations minutely regulated by ordinance and custom. The marguilliers had a pew of their own on a higher level than the others, and facing the pulpit. In it they took their places with scrupulous regard to seniority. The blessed bread was offered to them first, and when ashes, or candles, or palms were distributed, the marguilliers were privileged to receive theirs in the sanctuary. In all processions they immediately preceded the clergy, and if the Blessed Sacrament was carried it was their honor to hold the canopy.

[53] The reader desiring a complete description of a Canadian parish, past and present, may consult P. B. Mignault, *Le Droit Paroissial* (Montreal, 1893).

[54] The parish organization is not to be compared with the lawless trustee system that disgraced the beginnings of the Church in the United States. In the French system there was never any doubt concerning the scope of the bishop's or the pastor's authority and rights, and the extent of the laity's participation was minutely regulated.

The parish revenue administered by the marguilliers and the pastor came from various sources. Collections were taken up on Sundays and holydays, cemetery lots were sold, and the pastor received the smaller share of all the fixed charges for weddings and funerals. But the largest and most dependable income was realized from the rent of the sittings in the church. When a pew became vacant, the fact was announced for two or three Sundays, and the pew was then auctioned off at the door of the church to the highest bidder. The price bid became the annual rent, and the pew was held as long as the rent was paid.

Occasionally the parish income was augmented by the unexpected donation of a generous parishioner. The liberality of Pierre Labutte, for instance, lives long after him in this grateful tribute from "La Fabrique."

> Today, the thirteenth of July, one thousand seven hundred and fifty-five, we, the Franciscan missionary and the churchwardens of the parish of St. Anne of Detroit-Hérié, having assembled in the customary manner, Warden Beaubien, who was in the chair, having represented to us that Mr. Pierre Labutte, Sr., moved by a holy and religious good will for the glory of God and the decoration of his temple, has resolved to give alms to our church in the sum of a thousand livres in merchandise, to be taken from his warehouse at our selection at the rate of thirty per cent profit, touched by a just thankfulness for so signal a favor and remembering his great and continued alms which he has made before and will continue to make to our church, after having betwen us duly deliberated, we have concluded and resolved in order to give him efficient testimony thereof and to make his charity public that we bind ourselves and our successors to pray continually to the Lord for the preservation and the lasting prosperity of the said Mr. Pierre Labutte and his family, and that when God should call him to Him in order to reward him for his religious alms, we shall cause to be celebrated at the expense of the vestry, both for him and for Louise Barois, his wife, immediately upon the decease of either of them, a solemn service for the repose of their souls. Thus deliberated, concluded and resolved on the day, month and year above stated.
>
> (Signed) fr. Simple Bocquet, Recollet
> Beaubien.
>
> This extract is a true copy of the original, collated by us, a Franciscan priest, missionary in the said church, this 15th day of January, 1756.
>
> (Signed) fr. Simple Bocquet, Recollet [55]

[55] The French often used the term Detroit-Hérié, meaning Detroit in the neighborhood of Lake Erie. The original record is in the Burton Collection, and is evidently a copy from the vestry book made by Father Bocquet for presentation to the La Butte family. The vestry book itself is missing from the existing records of St. Anne's church. The record is printed in the *Mich. Hist. Colls.*, IX, 458, but the date of Father Bocquet's collation has been misread as being 1760.

The foregoing refers to parish revenue, and has nothing to do with the support of the pastor. He was taken care of by the duty and the generosity of his parishioners toward him. His first means of support were the tithes which his parishioners were legally bound to render. Although the word properly means a tenth, the first ordinance dealing with tithes in the colony, and dated 1663, gave the tithe a value of one-thirteenth. Four years later, in view of the poverty of the colonists, a second ordinance reducing the tithes was issued. The term was definitely established to mean one twenty-sixth part of the grain harvest. Every farmer brought in to his pastor at Eastertime one twenty-sixth of the grain that had been harvested the preceding summer. This was stored in what was necessarily a valuable adjunct to the presbytery, the priest's granary, and from its content he supplied his needs by sale, or, what was usually the case, by barter.

The pastor's second source of income was the "quête de l'Enfant Jesus," the Child Jesus collection. It was the warm, friendly forerunner of our modern impersonal Christmas collection. During the days from Christmas to Epiphany the pastor made the rounds of his parish. The first marguillier called for him every day with his best horse and sleigh, and ensconced in their fur robes the pair started out to the merry accompaniment of the jingling harness bells. Theirs was no unforeseen visit. In a certain section of the parish the children had been scrubbed and arrayed in their best, the houses had been tidied, and a little refreshment provided to fortify the visitors on their arrival. The curé was met at the door by the head of the house and his good helpmate, who both knelt to receive a blessing. Then came the children each in turn, from the oldest down to the veriest toddler. This ceremony was followed by mutual inquiries about health and welfare, and mutual good wishes. Now the children advanced to the curé's chair, and upon each shy promise to be good and helpful during the coming year he bestowed a holy picture or medal. But time was pressing; there were so many more to be visited that day. Amid a chorus of farewells the priest took his place in the cutter and was soon flying down the road to his next stopping place.

Scarcely had he disappeared in the distance when the second marguillier drove up in his sled, a mute reminder of a duty which the pastor had tactfully passed over. Into the sled went a present offered according to the giver's means. It might be a few hands of tobacco, some triumph of home cooking, or a suckling pig. The second marguillier was fortified against the weather, and he too set off to follow the leader.

But this was not all. Along came the third marguillier with the sides of his sled boarded up to thrice their usual height. It was his business to collect what amounted to a voluntary tithe. The householder inquired about the generosity of his neighbors, poured in a few bushels of grain, saw the marguillier off, and went back to his house satisfied that the curé had been well done by.

All the contributions thus gathered were laid away in the pastor's storehouse. They were his own to do with as he saw fit, and like the tithes were generally sold off or exchanged to satisfy his particular wants. In those days of simple living the pastor's needs were few, and with his modest fees and his well-stocked granary he could live content.

The liturgy as carried out in old St. Anne's was regulated by the Ritual of the diocese of Quebec written by Bishop Saint-Vallier, and printed in France in 1703. Its prescriptions present no marked variations from our present practice except in the set instructions which were to be read every year on the appointed Sundays, and in two other points which deserve special mention.

The first is the number of holydays to be observed. According to the first official list issued in 1694, the ecclesiastical year comprised thirty-four holydays of obligation excluding Sundays, and among them were the two days succeeding both Easter and Pentecost.[56] In 1744 Bishop de Pontbriand realizing, as he said, that this large number of holydays was burdensome to the people, transferred nineteen of them to the nearest Sunday.[57] This revision was observed to the end of the French regime. In addition to the feasts in our present calendar which need not fall on Sunday it listed the following: Corpus Christi, the Patronal Feast of the parish, Epiphany, the Annunciation, the feasts of SS. Peter and Paul, St. Stephen, St. John the Evangelist, and four days already mentioned.

The second noteworthy variation in the liturgy lay in that interesting survival of medieval church customs in France, the Blessed Bread. Traces of the usage are found as far back as the seventh century, but it appeared for the first time in the colony in 1645. In the course of time the custom became universal, as did the abuses which grew up around it. These were seen to outweigh its religious significance, and the Blessed Bread as an institution was allowed to die out in the last half of the nineteenth century.

Every parishioner who was a householder was found according to the French law to give, or rather to render, as the expression ran, the blessed bread in his turn, and at the same time make the offering of a candle of its value, that is from ten to fifteen sous. For the majority it was a pleas-

[56] Têtu, *Mandements des Eveques de Quebec,* I, 335.
[57] *Idem,* II, 42.

ure and an honor to fulfill this duty; but for others it was onerous and a cause for complaint. This was true especially among the poor, who at the cost of privation could offer only one or two loaves of ordinary bread.

To many the custom gave occasion for self-glorification, for there was often keen rivalry among the parishioners as to who would offer the finest loaf, not for the greater glory of God but for his own. . . .

In many parishes the blessed bread was ten or twelve stories high; that is, there were ten or twelve layers supported by smaller pieces, and ornamented with stars affixed to the sides by small wooden pegs. The edges of the layers as well as the smaller pieces were often silvered or gilt. The whole was bedecked with little flags of various colors, and this brilliant pyramid was crowned with a pastry ostensorium often surrounded by lighted candles.

The person offering the blessed bread brought it to church before Mass, and placed it in the sanctuary just inside the altar rail. At the conclusion of the Gloria, the beadle, if he could possibly do so, lifted the precious burden to his shoulder and advanced to the altar steps to present it to the celebrant for his blessing.

This done the blessed bread was carried to the sacristy to be attended to by the beadle, often with the help of an assistant. There was no time to lose since the distribution had to be made during the Credo. The beadle cut off a cantle destined for some parishioner as a sign that it would be his turn to make the offering the following Sunday, another portion for the Curé, and the remainder into pieces large and small. Meanwhile he could not help tasting it a bit, just to make sure that it was palatable and fresh. Some compensation was due him for this duty which took him away from his prayers and the hearing of Mass. . . . As soon as the Credo was intoned the beadle or his assistant issued from the sacristy with his basket filled. The large pieces were given to the marguilliers, the highest officer, and the parents and friends whom the donor wished to honor. The smaller pieces, just a mouthful, were distributed to the rest of the congregation.[58]

The portions thus distributed could be eaten in church or carried home. This disadvantage attended the practice, that many a parishioner who intended to receive Communion realized with a start that he had broken his fast in a moment of absent-minded nibbling.

Such was the rite of the "Pain Benit," a survival most likely from the Apostolic age when every one present at the Sacrifice shared in it by Communion. In the time of which we write the religious meaning had become obscure, and the ceremony did little more than make existing social differences too acute. For this reason it may well have been abolished.

[58] Abbé Charles Trudelle in the *Bulletin des Récherches Hist.*, XVIII, 151 ff.

CHAPTER XI

The Coming of the English

I T IS far beyond our scope to deal with the outcome of the struggle between France and England for the possession of North America. As far as Canada is concerned historians have long since marshalled all the factors that contributed to the inevitable victory; but these are only the embroidery on the fact that England was more determined to acquire Canada than France was to retain it. Quebec surrendered on September 18, 1759, but the Canadians were not yet conquered. Their last resistance was broken at the surrender of Montreal, September 8, 1760, when Lévis broke his sword rather than hand it to the surly Amherst who refused his prisoners the honors of war.

The Canadian people had not too much reason for complaint against the conditions imposed upon them either then, or later in the actual transfer of Canada by the Treaty of Paris in 1763. An oath of allegiance by which they became subjects of His Britannic Majesty was prescribed, their property rights were respected, and they were left free to live their lives pretty much as they had before. What properly concerns us here is their religious rights under the new allegiance, and this we must consider in some detail.[1]

The sixth in the Articles of Capitulation proposed by de Ramesy before his surrender of Quebec read as follows:

> That the exercise of the Catholic, Apostolic and Roman religion shall be maintained; and that safeguards shall be granted to the houses of the clergy, and to the monasteries, particularly to his Lordship the Bishop of Quebec, who, animated with zeal for religion, and charity for the people of his diocese, desires to reside in it constantly, to exercise, freely and with that decency which his character and the sacred offices of the Roman religion require, his episcopal authority in the town of Quebec, whenever he shall think proper, until the possession of Canada shall be decided between their Britannic and most Christian Majesties.

[1] For a convenient study of this question see William R. Riddell, Justice of the Supreme Court of Canada, "The Status of Roman Catholicism in Canada," *Cath. Hist. Rev. (New Series)*, VIII, No. 3.

At the surrender of Montreal Article XXVII dealt with religious freedom in much the same terms as the article just quoted. However, in its last sentence it provided that, "These people shall be obliged, by the English government, to pay their Priests the tithes, and all the taxes they were used to pay under the government of his most Christian Majesty." The English answer to this was, that the obligation of paying tithes would depend on the King's pleasure.[2]

In the Treaty of Paris, the King of France by Article IV ceded Canada with all its dependencies to the King and Crown of Great Britain, and "His Britannic Majesty . . . agrees to grant the liberty of the Catholick religion to the inhabitants of Canada . . . and to give the most precise and most effectual orders, that his new Roman Catholick subjects may profess the worship of their religion according to the rites of the Romish church, as far as the laws of Great Britain permit."

To anyone acquainted with the body of anti-Catholic legislation in England from Elizabeth to William III, the foregoing declaration does not appear to have granted much. However, it was well understood that the declaration was to be taken, not in the light of England's internal policy regarding her Catholic subjects, but of the measure of religious liberty she was willing to grant to conquered colonies. By the Treaty of Utrecht in 1714, Spain had ceded to Great Britain the Island of Minorca. Its inhabitants were guaranteed their religious freedom, and England thereby set up a precedent for the management of her colonial accessions which was taken as applying to her conquests ratified by the Treaty of Paris. In the case of Florida, however, wrested from Spain by the same treaty, although assurance identical to that given the Canadians formed part of the stipulations, the provisions were ruthlessly ignored.[3]

Happily for the Canadian people the rigors of English law were never introduced into the conquered province. The government realized that its hold at best was still precarious, and that it had to proceed with caution. Canada was indeed to be made Protestant, but that by peaceful means. It was fondly imagined that the Canadians would refuse to change their allegiance, and that the majority of them would gladly return to the mother country. Every opportunity was given them to facilitate this move on their part, and at the same time strong inducements were held out to Protestant colonists, both from the American Colonies and from England, who were expected to replace them. These expectations were not realized. The Cana-

[2] It was by the capitulation of Montreal that Detroit, Mackinac, and the other western posts came into British possession.
[3] Shea, *Life and Times of Archbishop Carroll* (New York, 1888), 89-92.

diàns, with but few exceptions stayed on, and there was not enough immigration to dilute them. In 1766 there were only nineteen Protestant families in the Province of Quebec, and the rest of the newcomers, mostly blatant fanatics from the American Colonies, were styled by Governor Murray himself as "the most miserable collection of men I ever knew." [4]

The home government was, moreover, fortunate in its selection of the men charged to work out the Canadian problem. Both Murray and Carleton were sympathetic in their attitude toward the Canadians, determined to insure them justice and fair play, and always ready to act as buffers between them and the insensate bigotry both in England and New England that would have crushed them.

In 1763 the western boundary of the new "Government of Quebec" was fixed on a line drawn from the southern end of Lake Nipissing to the point where the 45th parallel crosses the St. Lawrence. The territory lying west of this boundary, including Michigan and the rest of the Upper Country, was to be kept as "an Indian Country, open to Trade but not to Grants or Settlements," and, moreover, was not affected by the legal provisions for the Province of Quebec laid down in 1764. Bitterly resenting the inferiority into which many of these provisions would have held them, the Canadians waged a successful ten year struggle for their modification which was ended by the famous Quebec Act of 1774. This monument of Catholic liberty in Canada freed Catholics for all time from civil disabilities on account of their religion, dissipated their fear of being obliged to take the Test oath, a threat which had been held over them, reestablished the French civil law to which they had been accustomed, and gave them parliamentary government. [5]

The Act also extended the boundaries of the Province of Quebec to the Ohio and Mississippi Rivers, thus bringing Michigan and the Indian reserve within its provisions. It is safe to assume that the liberties accorded by the Act, and their range, were not prompted by any sudden devotion to religious liberty. The American colonies were on the verge of revolt, and the home government was craftily hemming them in by a population that had no cause for grievance, and that could be counted on, at least, to remain neutral in the event of actual rupture. At any rate, the Quebec Act made the American Colonies seethe with indignation. Protestant divines worked themselves into a frenzy with the immortal calumnies of their stock in trade, and the newspapers followed suit. The old bogies that every

[4] Riddell, *op. cit.*, 318.

[5] "The Treaty of Paris, 1736, and the Catholics in the American Colonies," *American Catholic Quarterly Review*, X, 240–55; "The Quebec Act and the Church in Canada," *idem*, 605–15.

generation of Catholics knows so well were trotted out with their usual success. For instance, this one: "We may live to see our churches converted into Masshouses and our lands plundered of tythes for the support of a Popish clergy. The Inquisition may erect her standard in Pennsylvania, and the city of Philadelphia may yet experience the carnage of St. Bartholomew's day." [6]

The strength and extent of this indignation is apparent from the fact that it was embodied in the Address to the People of Great Britain emanating from the first Continental Congress of October, 1774.

> Now mark the progression of the ministerial plan for enslaving us . . . by another Act the dominion of Canada is to be extended, modelled, and governed, as that by being disunited from us, detached from our interests, by civil as well as religious prejudices, that by their numbers daily swelling with Catholic emigrants from Europe, and by their devotion to Administration so friendly to their religion, they might become formidable to us, and on occasion, be fit instruments in the hands of power, to reduce the ancient free Protestant Colonies to the same state of slavery with themselves . . .
>
> Nor can we suppress our astonishment, that a British Parliament should ever consent to establish in that country a religion that has deluged your island in blood and dispersed impiety, bigotry, persecution, murder and rebellion through every part of the world. . . .[7]

Such a declaration, known to be typical of sentiments which had long preceded it, had a decisive effect on a possible union with Canada in the struggle for American freedom. The American invasion of Canada, at first successful under Montgomery, was stalled by its failure in the siege of Quebec. In this crisis the Continental Congress sent a deputation, of which Father John Carroll, the future archbishop of Baltimore, was a member, to the Canadians in a final effort to swing them over to the American cause.[8] It accomplished nothing. Yet, at the same time, there was a widespread desire to join the Americans, outspoken, and in many cases translated into action. But it could never get under way for the simple reason that, despite defections, the clergy held their parishioners in line, and the bishop held the clergy.[9]

[6] Shea, Life and Times . . . , 131–140. See also Charles H. Metzger, S.J., "The Quebec Act, A Primary Cause of the American Revolution," in the U. S. Cath. Hist. Society, Monograph Series (New York, 1936), particularly Chap. VII.

[7] Journal of the Continental Congress, Library of Congress ed., (Washington, 1904), I, 87–88.

[8] Shea, Life and Times . . . 148–52.

[9] The relations between the British Government and the Canadian Church are treated at length in Gosselin, L'Église du Canada aprés la Conquête (Quebec, 1916), Vol. I. For Bishop Briand's efforts to hold his diocesans see idem, II (Quebec, 1917), Chaps. I–VIII.

Bishop Briand used every spiritual weapon of the Church to enforce his decision. There was no uncertainty regarding his reason for it. First, the Canadians had taken an oath of allegiance to the English King, a sacred obligation which they could not break. Second, they had been granted and now enjoyed religious freedom. No Catholic was justified in jeopardizing that freedom by aligning himself with a people who hated and despised him for his religion, and who, presumably, after such a statement as the Address to the People of Great Britain, would have made its exercise impossible to him. How far religious bigotry served as a catalyst to precipitate the American Revolution is a question deserving more study than it has hitherto received. There is matter for profound reflection in the following statement from a student of the problem.

> It may, I think, be fairly concluded that if the British King and his Government paid nearly as much attention to the wishes of the Old Subjects in the Protestant Colonies as they did to those of the New Subjects in the Catholic Colony, there would have been no American Revolution, no Declaration of Independence; and, on the other hand, had they paid as little attention to the wishes of the New Subjects as they did to those of the Old Subjects, Canada would not have continued British, and the United States of America would have stretched from the Gulf of Mexico to the Arctic Ocean.[10]

We have briefly outlined a crisis in the life of the Canadian Church which forms the necessary background for the period of our history into which we now enter. Had the Canadians been obliged to come to open conflict in defense of their religious liberties even a distant outpost like Detroit would have been involved. As it was, the current of religious life went on almost as placidly as before.

Four days after the surrender of Montreal, Major Robert Rogers with two hundred Rangers was sent by Amherst to take possession of Detroit. He had advanced as far as Lake Erie before the French commander received any tidings of his coming or his mission. Unaware of the surrender of Montreal, de Bellestre took the report of Rogers' column to be just one more wild Indian rumor. To show his contempt for it he erected a pole on top of which was fastened an effigy representing a crow feeding off a human head. The significance was obvious, and he only scoffed when the Indians affirmed their opinion that the head might prove to be his own. But there was nothing imaginary about the message he received on the 29th of November from Major Rogers, who, waiting about two miles below

[10] This is Riddell's own summary of his study previously referred to. For a dissenting view see R. Coupland, *The Quebec Act* (Oxford, 1925), 105-22.

the fort, gave him until four o'clock in the afternoon to turn it over. With his summons the English officer had included a copy of the Montreal capitulation, and a letter to de Bellestre from Vaudreuil sanctioning the surrender of Detroit. There was nothing to do but submit.

> The French garrison laid down their arms. English colors were hoisted, and the French taken down, at which about 700 Indians gave a shout merrily exulting in the prediction being verified that the crow represented the English.[11]

Pursuant to his orders Major Rogers proceeded to administer the oath of allegiance according to the formula dictated by Amherst. The inhabitants of Detroit were all summoned to swear their assent to the following declaration.

> I . . . swear that I shall be faithful and that I shall behave myself honestly towards His sacred Majesty George the Second, by the Grace of God King of Great Britain, France and Ireland, Defender of the Faith and that I will defend him and his in this Country with all my Power, against his or their enemies; and further I swear to make known and reveal to His Majesty, His General, or their assistants in place present, as much as depends of me all Traitors or all conspirators that could be formed against his Sacred person, his Country or his Government.[12]

From the available records of the time there is nothing to indicate that the residents of Detroit were molested for their religion or restricted in its exercise. When Sir William Johnson, the Indian Commissioner, visited Detroit in the fall of 1761, the inhabitants headed by Father Bocquet came to pay their respects. They were assured of his Majesty's protection "as long as they continued to behave as good subjects . . . and went away extremely well pleased, their priest at their head." [13] During his stay both Father Bocquet and Father Potier were invited to dine with him along with the prominent men of the settlement, an invitation which was cordially accepted and as cordially enjoyed.[14]

One effect of the English occupation was to bring, for the first time, a Protestant element into the population of the settlement. The troops, for a while at least, were quartered on the inhabitants, and being neither better nor worse than any soldiers would be under the circumstances, such association was not at all desirable from Fa-

[11] Franklin B. Hough (ed.) *Journal of Major Robert Rogers* (Albany, 1883), 197.
[12] *Mich. Hist. Colls.*, XIX, 42.
[13] W. L. Stone, *op. cit.*, II, 458.
[14] *Ibid.*, 463.

ther Bocquet's standpoint. Unaffected by the social and religious inhibitions hitherto operating in the community, the newcomers were bound to be a disturbing element. They introduced a round of social gaiety to which the more susceptible members of Father Bocquet's congregation were irresistibly drawn, and which he must have viewed with alarm. During Sir Johnson's visit, for instance, two occasions are recorded on which the English officers disported themselves.

> This day I am to dine with Captain Campbell, who is also to give the ladies a ball that I may see them. They assembled at 8 o'clock at night to the number of about twenty. I opened the ball with Mademoiselle Curie, a fine girl. We danced until five o'clock next morning.

This was on a Sunday. A little more than a week later there was another party. "In the evening the ladies and gentlemen all assembled at my quarters and danced the whole night until 7 o'clock in the morning." [15]

Following the soldiery into Detroit came a swarm of traders and merchants, Irish, Scotch and English, from Montreal and Quebec, and from the American colonies, making the post their headquarters for their western operations. Many of them were in search of wives, and occasionally they found them. Mixed marriages, hitherto unknown in Detroit, made some inroads into Father Bocquet's flock, and entailed the usual consequences in a large percentage of the progeny.[16]

The English occupation of Detroit so calmly and philosophically accepted by its French inhabitants was soon to meet determined resistance from an unexpected quarter; it had yet to reckon with the original owner of the soil, the Indian. When the French came into the western country they treated the Indian as a friend, and that not only because of their "pliant and plastic temper" as Parkman puts it, but from religious motives as well. If they held part of his land for their own use, they made themselves appear as profiting from his condescension. Their dealings with him were conducted on the basis, apparent at least, of his having some rights and some native dignity. They endeavored to temper their authority by an understanding of

---

[15] *Ibid.*

[16] A cursory reading of the genealogical material in the *John Askin Papers* (Detroit Library Commission, 1928), points to quite a number of mixed marriages in the twenty-five or thirty years following the English occupation. For instance, George Anthon, German by birth, came to Detroit with Major Rogers as surgeon's mate. During his years in Detroit he married two French women. His son Henry, by his second wife, died as Episcopal rector of St. Mark's-in-the-Bouerie, New York. See *Burton Historical Leaflets,* Vol. III, No. 3.

his character, and accommodated their treatment of him to the knowledge thus gained.

To the English, on the other hand, the Indian was merely a "native," worthy of nothing but contempt. When he was strong enough to be feared they truckled to him; when his strength was dissipated he was utterly disregarded. Once his usefulness was over in the struggle against France the Indian began to realize the disdain in which he was held by his new masters. The old camaraderie he had known with the French, the generous presents, the complaisance of officials, all these were no more.

Even these bitter thoughts rankling in the Indian breast might not have stirred him to open rebellion had there not been other causes nerving him to a supreme effort to restore the old order of things. A wave of immigration was spilling over the Alleghenies, determined men who took choice spots wherever they found them, and stoutly defended them. The French element in the West played upon the Indian's disillusionment, and fed his regret until it became dangerous resentment.

Such were the antecedents of the Indian uprising fomented by Pontiac. The great Ottawa chief had perspicacity enough to foresee the inevitable decline of his race unless it presented a determined front to the invaders. This it could not do until the tribes in the Lake region could be made to forget their mutual animosities, and unite in a common cause. By the sheer strength of his powerful personality Pontiac welded them together, and then committed them to his daring plan. This was nothing less than the simultaneous destruction of every English post in the Indian country: Detroit, Mackinac, St. Joseph, Fort Pitt, Venango, Le Boeuf, Presque Ile, Sandusky, Green Bay, and three posts among the Miami in Indiana.

There is no need for retelling here the story of Pontiac's initial bloody successes, or of his eventual failure; the story of the siege of Detroit, whose capture he had reserved for himself, is too well known. Our interest here lies in the bits of information pertaining to our religious history that can be gleaned from the accounts of this momentous period in the city's life.

Had Pontiac's stratagem succeeded on the morning of May 7, 1763, when his warriors stalked after him into the fort hiding sawed-off guns beneath their blankets, there would have been a sudden chorus of fiendish yells, and then swift certain massacre. But Major Gladwin had been forewarned, and Pontiac holding his rage in iron control left the fort to begin the historic siege that lasted for one hundred and twenty-three days.

How Major Gladwin knew of Pontiac's design has always been a matter for conjecture.[17] The Indians would certainly have revenged themselves on the informant, had he become known, and so the secret was carefully kept. There are a number of sources from which Gladwin might have obtained his information, any of which are more probable than the story of the beautiful Ojibwa maiden popularized by Parkman.[18] We have room here for only one, that which centers around the figure of Father Potier.[19] In the Huron mission across the river, presided over by the Jesuit, the forge and the mission blacksmith were still maintained, as appears from entries in the missionary's account book. One essential detail of Pontiac's stratagem was that his warriors bring their guns into the fort undetected, something that could be managed only by filing off a length of the barrels. To do this hardened steel files were needed, and the only place to procure them was the mission forge. An unusual demand for such articles coming from any quarter would have caught Father Potier's attention, and coming from the Indians would have aroused his suspicion. In that event he may have communicated his forebodings himself to Gladwin, or charged one of the French settlers to do so. It is significant that in Father Potier's diary, found after his death, the pages dealing with the period of the siege were missing.

The French population of Detroit was in a difficult position. It must have been almost entirely in sympathy with Pontiac's purpose, and had it joined with him he might have succeeded. But friendly contacts with the English had already been established, and the French shrank from the possibility of a general massacre which they might have been powerless to prevent. Nor must the influence of the two priests in the settlement be forgotten. Both Father Bocquet and Father Potier had their course of action marked out for them by the Bishop of Quebec; the oath of allegiance taken by the residents of Detroit must have been held up to them as a sacred obligation they were bound to respect. Hence, throughout the siege while Pontiac levied on the French for provisions and supplies, many of them were secretly supplying the desperate needs of the garrison.

Actual hostilities began on Monday, May 9. In the words of the Pontiac Manuscript, "this being the first day of Rogations, according to the custom of the church, the curate and all the clergy had a procession outside of the fort quite peaceably. Mass was celebrated in the same way, after which everybody went home to see how the

---

[17] See Burton, op. cit., II, 887, for various conjectures. Major Basset's letter there quoted is in Mich. Hist. Colls., 310–11.

[18] Parkman later doubted the veracity of this story. See his Conspiracy of Pontiac, I, 228.

[19] This conjecture was broached by Richard R. Elliott of Detroit. See Ross and Catlin, Landmarks of Detroit (Detroit, 1898), 172.

day should pass, knowing well that Pondiak would make some other attempt." [20]

The chief appeared before the fort with a band of warriors about eleven o'clock, and demanded admittance on the pretense of a strong desire to smoke the pipe of peace. When entry was denied him he threw all caution to the winds. Mrs. Turnbull and her two sons who lived at some distance behind the fort were killed, and the half-burned bodies were left in the ruins of their dwelling. The Indians then hurried to Belle Isle, where James Fisher, an ex-sergeant of the British army, was living with his wife and children. The parents were killed, and the children carried off as prisoners.

For some obscure reason a legend grew up around the Fisher tragedy. The Frenchmen who had buried them both in the same grave returned the next day, only to see the man's hand sticking out through the earth. Their good offices were repeated, but returning to the spot a few days later they again found the hand exposed. Faced with this uncanny phenomenon they turned to the only man competent to deal with it, Father Bocquet. He visited the grave, blessed it with the prayers of the Church, and the mute gesture of supplication was seen no more.[21]

Along with the Fishers died poor Gosselin, who brought his death upon himself. He was felling trees when the Indians first rushed upon the island. They put him into a canoe, and told him to stay there, that he had nothing to fear. But, when he heard the Fishers shrieking in their agony he lost all confidence in Indian promises, and jumping to shore ran to hide in the woods. Seeing only his back, and thinking him another Englishman, the Indians brought him down.[22]

The next day, although the Indians kept up a furious fire on the fort from four o'clock in the morning until ten, Father Bocquet carefully inscribed the following record.

> In the year of Our Lord one thousand seven hundred and sixty-three, the 10th of May, was buried in the cemetery of this parish the body of Francois Goslin reported to us as having been a native of the parish of

---

[20] *Mich. Hist. Colls.*, VIII, 278. The Pontiac Manuscript is a contemporary account of the siege written perhaps by Francois Navarre, who had been Royal Notary under the French Regime, and was continued in office by the English. It has sometimes been ascribed to some mythical priest in Detroit, but besides bearing no internal signs of such authorship it is in the handwriting of neither Father Bocquet not Father Potier. The original manuscript is in the BHC. Translated by R. Clyde Ford, of Ypsilanti, it was published by Clarence M. Burton under the title of *Journal of Pontiac's Conspiracy, 1763* (Detroit, 1912).

[21] *Mich. Hist. Colls.*, VIII, 360.

[22] *Ibid.*, 280.

St. Thomas, in the diocese and government of Quebec, in Canada. He died yesterday on Hog Island where he was killed by the Ottawa, aged about thirty years. The circumstances of the siege having prevented us from being present at the said interment, he was buried by some charitable persons, who being requested thereto, declare they are unable to sign the register.

On former occasions the church, as we have seen was the vulnerable spot in the fort's defenses. But Pontiac, although not a Christian, feared the God of the Christians enough to respect the building dedicated to His worship. The church in its traditional location was nearer than any other building to the pickets enclosing the fort. It was in Pontiac's plans to set it on fire with flaming arrows, but before doing so he asked one of the settlers to find out from Father Bocquet whether the Christian God would punish him for such a deed. Without troubling the priest on such a matter the settler assured Pontiac that God would be highly offended at this desecration, whereupon the warrior abandoned his design, and the church passed through the siege unharmed.[23]

The mission buildings on the other side of the river were not in the same danger, but Father Potier was certain to become involved with Pontiac. From the *Pontiac Manuscript* it is evident that there were still two bands of Huron, one Christian, and the other as intractable as in the time of Chief Nicolas. The Christian Huron, no doubt through the efforts of Father Potier, seem to have been the only Indians to refrain from joining Pontiac. Three days after the opening of hostilities the chief made a determined attempt to win them over, and gave them plainly to understand what would happen to them should they fail to fall in with the other tribes. The Huron solved the dilemma in characteristic fashion. It was the eve of the Ascension, and they promised that the next day they would join in the attack. "They could not do so sooner, because it was too high a holiday and it would not do to go into a fight without having heard Mass." [24]

The manuscript goes on describing what took place the morning of Ascension Thursday.

Teata and Baby, both chiefs of the good band of Hurons which had until then kept neutral, and which would have kept so longer, seeing themselves forced by threats, assembled their band, which numbered about sixty men, and said to them: "My brothers, you see, as well as we, the risks that we all run, and that in the situation of affairs, we have no other resources than either to join our brothers, the Ottawas and the

[23] *Ibid.,* 345.
[24] *Ibid.,* 287.

Foxes, or else to abandon our band and to fly with our women and children, which will never do, for we will hardly have gone before the Ottawas and the Foxes, and even those of our own nation will fall upon us, kill our wives and children, and force us to do like them; while if we do so now, we shall be assured that our families will be safe in our village. We do not know what are the designs of the Master of Life toward us; perhaps it is he who inspires this war to our brothers, the Ottawas. If he does not order it, he will know how to let us understand his will, and we will be able to retire without being stained by the blood of the English."

Immediately after this address they took their tomahawks, chanted the war-song, and ordered their men to do the same until the hour of mass, which their women chanted, and to which they listened very devotedly. Mass being over, each went to his tent, took the arms necessary for attack, and they crossed the river in twelve canoes, going directly to the Foxes, who uttered cries of joy to see them arrive.[25]

The Huron fought only two days, and by Saturday Father Potier again had them in control, and held them by threatening to refuse all ministrations of the Church to those who dared disobey him. He sent them off to a distance out of harm's way, doubtless telling them that he had enough influence to shield them from Pontiac's vengeance. As far as we know they were not molested further.

The siege went on. Some days were quiet, when both besieger and besieged rested from exhaustion. On other days the settlers up and down the river could hear the rattle of incessant gunfire, or, as on the 30th of May, when a number of captured English soldiers were brought to the Ottawa camp, could catch the exultant screaming of the eight hundred Indians as their victims writhed under slow torture.[26] One quiet day, the 16th of June, not a shot had been fired. Suddenly the warm stillness was broken by a voice that had long been hushed, and over the water and the countryside rang out from St. Anne's belfry the age-old message, "The Angel of the Lord declared unto Mary." Perhaps the commander wisely felt that his men would be cheered and comforted through the living nightmare of the siege by this brazen note of sanity, for it was he who had ordered it.

The Indians were quiet all day. It is usual in all places besieged or surrounded by the enemy that silence be observed, the church bells not be sounded for any purpose, lest the enemy should know the hours when the people go to church, and the bell of the parish church of this place had not been tolled since the beginning of the siege for any church ex-

[25] *Ibid.*, 288.
[26] According to the Pontiac Manuscript the number of soldiers was from twenty to thirty. The account of the siege by Charles Gouin, who witnessed the torture of the prisoners places the number at sixty-four. *Mich. Hist. Colls.*, VIII, 347.

ercise. The commander, having learned from the curate why the bell was no longer tolled, permitted to have it tolled for all church purposes, and it commenced its function at noon by tolling the Angelus.[27]

Two days later, during a lull in the fighting, the watchers in the fort were surprised to behold a party of Indians whom they did not recognize come paddling down the river escorting an unknown Black Robe. The canoe was beached at the foot of the bluff, and out of it stepped Father Du Jaunay. He himself had lived through days of excitement and carnage. On the 2nd of June the Chippewa at Mackinac had begun that famous la crosse game with murder in their hearts. So unsuspecting was the English garrison that the commander had laid a bet on the game, and stood watching it near the gate of the fort. At a given signal the ball sailed through the air towards the gate, the warriors rushed after it, went on through, snatched weapons from their waiting squaws, and in a few minutes had slain seventeen men and taken the rest prisoners. The Ottawa of L'Arbre Croche, Father Du Jaunay's mission, who had not taken part in the attack, had later managed to get hold of two English officers and eleven men, and had brought them to the mission. To what lengths he had gone in his humane efforts on their behalf was evident from his presence now in Detroit.[28]

Father Du Jaunay was the bearer of a letter from Captain Etherington of Mackinac to Gladwin announcing the disaster that had befallen him, and asking for help. He had heard rumors of an attack on Detroit, but had no idea of the desperate straits to which it had been reduced. In his letter he did not fail to mention the kindness and good offices of the missionary: "a very good man, and had a great deal to say with the savages hereabout." [29] Father Du Jaunay's mission under the present circumstances was useless. He remained for a few days with Father Potier, and during that interval had an interview with Pontiac in an endeavor to secure the release of the English prisoners. His plea unheard, he returned to L'Arbre Croche where his influence was recognized. His task of guarding the English captives grew easier as the Indians gradually realized the consequences of their action. By the middle of July all the English in the neighborhood of Mackinac were allowed to depart for Montreal, and the little garrison at Detroit, still besieged, was the only body of English troops remaining in the region of the Great Lakes.

Long days of comparative inaction followed until the arrival of

[27] *Ibid.*, 315.
[28] Wood, *Historic Mackinac,* Chap. XI.
[29] Etherington's letter is in Appendix C to Parkman's *Conspiracy* . . . Pontiac.

Captain Dalzell with his two hundred and eighty men from Niagara on July 29. He lost fifteen of them before he could gain the shelter of the fort. Then came his rash attempt to inflict a crushing defeat on Pontiac. That historic battle on the banks of the Bloody Run cost the life of the brave captain, and of some twenty of his men.[30] During August and September there were skirmishes of minor importance, but the fort was now well supplied and could hold out indefinitely. The Indians began to tire, and during October some of them sued for peace. At the end of the month, Pontiac himself, as implacable as ever in his hatred for the English, withdrew to the Ohio country and Detroit was safe after having passed through the most tense and critical days of its history.

We know nothing of religious matters in Detroit for the next three years, but we are in fortunate possession of a series of letters written by Father Bocquet to his bishop, which begin in 1766 and extend over a ten year period.[31] They reveal him to be a simple, kindly old man, endowed with a sense of humor, scrupulous in carrying out liturgical details, seeing the good and the evil in his people, gentle towards the sinner but testy in claiming his rights, dismayed by this new race bustling around him, whose language he could not understand, and whose evident determination to dominate everything nettled him.

His first letter, addressed to Bishop Briand, opens with the expression of his joy at hearing that the Canadian Church has again a bishop. The see of Quebec had been vacant since the death of Bishop de Pontbriand in June, 1760, and a candidate chosen by the Cathedral Chapter in 1763 had been rejected by the British Government. The next year, Jean-Olivier Briand, who had all along been vicar-general, and who had won the esteem of the English officials, was named to the see by the Chapter; but it was not until June, 1766, after two years' residence in Europe that he was able to take possession.

Father Bocquet's letter was therefore in the nature of a report to one who might reasonably be ignorant of conditions. Here is a characteristic passage.

> The English are ruining everything with their rum, even their own trade. Can it be possible that they will never open their eyes to their

[30] The ravine in Elmwood Cemetery marks a portion of the course of Parent's Creek, renamed Bloody Run to commemorate the battle which took place where the creek crossed the present Jefferson Avenue.

[31] Father Bocquet's letters, seventeen in number, are in the Archives of the Chancery in Quebec. For reference purposes, they as well as all succeeding material obtained from that source will be designated by the letters QCA.

own interests? The amount of fur that has gone out of the post this year is surprisingly small. The Indians are destitute, nearly all sick, think of nothing but drink for which they give up everything they have, and go hunting only when their supply of liquor is exhausted. Many of them have already died. What bothers me most is that a few Frenchmen have begun to engage in the traffic, and flatter themselves with the thought that you will have no objection to it. I gave them such a sermon on that score last Sunday that they are angry at me. I am worried about it. I cannot presume on you by going into a recital of the troubles I have had to bear in the last three years. With the kind of people I am dealing with, one needs to have a head of iron. Nevertheless, I must in justice say that I have a good number of true Catholics who are my consolation. What can one do under a form of government where there is no other law but the will of the commander? I hope that our lot will be changed. We have a new commandant, the Sieur Turnbull, who seems to like the French, and tries to please them. He has a particular esteem for Yourself. What is best about him is that he speaks French, unlike his two predecessors who besides their dislike for the French needed interpreters—and such interpreters.[32]

Despite Father Bocquet's eulogy of Captain George Turnbull, the commandant did not improve on acquaintance, and before long he and the priest were at loggerheads. The issue reflects to some extent the unsettled period of adjustment between conqueror and conquered, but more the arrogance and pretensions of petty commanders entrusted with almost absolute power in posts remote from control.

Two members of Father Bocquet's parish, first cousins, came to him to be married. On his refusal to act without a dispensation from the impediment, the couple sought out Captain Turnbull with the result that the priest received this curt notice:

> At Detroit, Jan. 6, 1767.
> I certify that Sieur Le Gras and Mademoiselle Gamelin, although first cousins, have my permission to marry whenever they please.
> George Turnbull, Capt. 2nd. Battn. 80 Reg.

At this invasion of his authority the priest called upon the commandant to protest against his meddling in a matter of church discipline, citing the fact that the government had officially recognized the Church, and by permitting the bishop to take his see had recognized the exercise and extent of his jurisdiction. To all these remonstrances the commandant turned a deaf ear. The sole reason for having a bishop in Quebec, to his notion, was to provide against the extinction of the Church by having priests ordained. There was no

---

[32] This letter is undated, but from the context it was certainly written in the fall of 1766.

use arguing the matter; he had given his orders, and unless the priest obeyed he was laying himself open to punishment.[33]

All the Canon Law that Father Bocquet knew had never anticipated such a contingency. In his isolated situation he had only an inkling of the adjustment that was going on between the Church and the new government. Perhaps the commandant was right. Indeed, as the priest states, no one could be so headstrong in maintaining a position unless he were right. In his quandary he decided to proceed with the wedding, and then lay the whole case before the bishop.

His misgivings were only partly justified. The bishop did blame him for his spineless attitude, acknowledging, however, that it was palliated to some extent by the regrettable circumstances of his isolated position. But the bishop's mild rebuke was not without compensation. To forestall such occurrences in the future Father Bocquet was not only granted wider powers, but was named a vicar-general, a title he used for the first time in St. Anne's register on July 20, 1768.[34]

As for the commandant it is hard to decide whether his action sprang from conceit or plain ignorance. Certainly his interference in such a matter exceeded his powers, and that he was censured for it is implied in a letter of the Bishop to Father Bocquet stating that he had brought the matter to the attention of Governor Carleton, who had blamed the officer and had promised to acquaint the Commander-in-Chief, General Gage, with his abuse of power.[35] Something of the kind must have brought about the change referred to by Father Bocquet when he wrote:

> As for the English I get along well with them all, especially with the commandant; but he is so petty that I must always be on my guard against him. There was a coldness between us for some time, but a certain happening brought us together. He needed me, I obliged him, and since that time he has never known a man of such parts, or so useful as myself. He said it again just a few days ago. Perhaps while I am writing to you he has changed his mind. Nevertheless I know what course to take, and I am getting along famously.[36]

The foregoing misunderstanding was related at some length because there is a full record of it in Father Bocquet's correspondence. However, it was neither the first nor the last instance of such interference on the part of the English officers commanding at the post.

[33] Letter to Bishop Briand, dated April 27, 1767. QCA. The original order signed by Captain Turnbull accompanies the letter.

[34] It was not unusual for the Bishop of Quebec to make any number of his outlying missionaries vicar-generals with wider powers.

[35] Letter of Bishop Briand to Father Bocquet, August 7, 1767. QCA.

[36] Letter to Bishop Briand, May 12, 1769. QCA.

In 1763 Father Bocquet was constrained by Major Gladwin to perform a marriage which he had refused to countenance on account of the written opposition of the bride's father. In his record of it the priest notes that the compulsion was based on the usages and laws of England, "to which it has pleased Divine Providence to subject us." [37] In 1775 there is another record of a marriage performed in deference "to the decision of the Commandant."

There is much in Father Bocquet's letters regarding that notorious character of early Detroit history, Phillip Dejean, a creature of Turnbull's, and the first judge under English rule. How his currying of English favor aroused the animosity of the French element, and his high-handed administration of justice finally brought him to disgrace have been narrated elsewhere.[38] The details furnished by Father Bocquet complete the picture, and do not belie the traditional estimate of Dejean's activities.

In 1787, Dejean, who spoke both French and English, was appointed judge by Turnbull, and empowered to establish a court. To give this new dignity adequate expression he lost no time in demanding for himself a position in the church comparable to that held by high civil authorities under the French regime. His demands are best expressed in the following letter of complaint addressed to Bishop Briand.

> My Lord:
> The most humble of your servants, although not having the honor of being known to you, takes the liberty of addressing you, praying that you will clear up a matter for him, and render him the justice which he believes is his due. In 1767, on my arrival in this post, being known to the English and speaking the two languages, I had the honor of being appointed judge. The French, in concert with their pastor, set aside Pentecost as the day on which I was to offer the Hallowed Bread, and the wardens allowed me to carry one pole of the canopy on Corpus Christi. Today they have deliberately deprived me of this last privilege on the ground of my having no right to it. That may be true. However, I should like to ask you to be good enough to grant me the rights pertaining to a judge, which are: a pew, a candle when following the Blessed Sacrament, the Hallowed Bread after the Wardens, likewise the adoration of the cross after them and before the beadle. If the church is

[37] St. Anne register, December 11, 1763.

[38] See reference to Dejean in Burton, *op. cit.*, I, 167; 910. *John Askin Papers*, 105. The climax of Dejean's arbitrary dispensing of justice was the infliction of the death penalty on two persons accused of robbery in 1776. For this he was indicted by the grand jury at Montreal along with Hamilton, the civil governor of Detroit. They were both taken prisoners by George Rogers Clark in his capture of Vincennes, and spent some months in prison at Williamsburg, Va. Dejean later returned to France and is then lost sight of.

too poor, I will pay for the pew of honor that the judge held in the time of the French. If he had one why not I? I dare to believe that my demands are just, and that you will be good enough to grant them. Believe me, Monseigneur, with profoundest respect your most humble and obedient servant.

P. Dejean.[39]

The bishop acknowledged receipt of the Judge's "polite and amiable" communication, but was very sorry that it was not in his power to grant his demands.[40] They were not rights which he could claim by virtue of his office. If the wardens had offended him that was regrettable, but wardens have their prerogatives, and judges have theirs. "Voilà tout." Father Bocquet soon heard of the bishop's reply and proceeded to give him inside information. The matter could be easily explained. A disaffected warden had been cajoled by one of Dejean's fellow topers into stepping aside at the right moment to let the judge take his place in the church processions. The strategy had succeeded twice, but this year, with a new chief warden handling matters, the judge had been just a few seconds too late. Hence his discomfiture and his complaint.[41]

Some time later, the judge, who still hankered for the privileges he had been denied, visited the bishop in Quebec in a final effort to obtain them. The prelate entertained some doubts touching his Catholicity, and on his return to Detroit the judge demanded a certificate of good standing from Father Bocquet. It was granted readily enough, but with the notation that court fees in Detroit were so exorbitant that few of the inhabitants could afford to have their wrongs redressed. This was more than the judge had asked for, and gave his recommendation an uncertain value. He showed it to some of his English friends, and Father Bocquet seems quite happy to report that for his pains the judge got more chaffing than sympathy.[42]

Enough about Dejean. Reverting to purely religious matters we find in Father Bocquet's letters many interesting points connected with his priestly ministrations. Perhaps the most important is the record of the first division of the parish. Father Potier on the other side of the river was officially only missionary to the Huron, and had no jurisdiction over his French neighbors. About 1765 they petitioned the vicar-general in Quebec for the erection of a separate parish on their side of the river. Although Father Potier was at first in favor of the division, when the petition was provisionally sanctioned

[39] Letter dated Detroit, June 22, 1770. QCA.
[40] The bishop's reply is interlined on the preceding letter, evidently for the guidance of his secretary.
[41] Letter to Bishop Briand, October 2, 1770. QCA.
[42] Same to same, March 1, 1773. QCA.

pending the arrival of a bishop, he refrained from acting on it lest he hurt the feelings of his Indians, who could not but realize that they would henceforth have only a secondary position. However, he administered the sacraments to the French on his side of the river, and they, through the favor of Father Bocquet, paid their tithes to him. Father Bocquet writes that the Jesuit was satisfied with this arrangement, but he cannot help adding, "He ought to be." [43]

In 1767, the Recollect himself petitioned the bishop for a division of his parish. His first reason was the size of his territory. The parish was eighteen miles long, and to make matters worse, it was divided by a dangerous river. The priest avowed that there was nothing which he as a Parisian was less able to cope with than a stretch of rough water. His second reason was the fact that Father Potier derived no support from his Indians, and could not subsist without the alms and tithes of the French. For his third reason he advanced the utter impossibility of being able to instruct all the children of his parish. "For the last few years nearly every house in the town has been occupied by English traders, and I am obliged to keep in my own home children of both sexes preparing for their first communion. I lodge them, feed them, and for the most part clothe them, and the majority of them come to me without knowing even how to make the sign of the cross." [44]

Deeming these reasons sufficient the bishop erected the settlement on the south side of the river into a distinct parish on August 7, 1767. Father Bocquet formally conferred upon the Jesuit his new charge, and reported his action in October of the same year.[45]

One of the few extant letters of Father Potier is the one wherein he acknowledges his appointment, and for its local interest it is here quoted.[46]

My Lord.

I have received Your Lordship's letter confiding to my care the South Side of Detroit. This new parish consists of some sixty odd families of whom about one third paid their tithes last year. The Hurons whom I have served during the past twenty-four years pay no dues. The new chapel which I have built with the help of the people is in debt, and I have been obliged to sell the mission land to pay for it. I furnish the wine for the Mass, and the candles. Your Lordship will see from this that the establishment of a fabrique is useless for the present; but they have elected wardens to assist me, and as soon as I have paid off the debts on the chapel, they will begin their duties. The late Bishop Pontbriand

43 Same to same. Undated but from context evidently in 1766. QCA.
44 Same to same, June 30, 1767. QCA.
45 Same to same, October 21, 1767. QCA.
46 Father Potier to Bishop Briand, September 6, 1768. QCA.

gave me permission to use the blessings reserved to the Bishop, and I beg your Lordship to renew this faculty. I pray that Our Lord will preserve your sacred person for His glory, and for the salvation of souls. I have the honor to be, etc.,

Pi. Potier, J. M.[47]

Some time later Father Bocquet reported to the bishop a transaction involving a most precious relic of the early Jesuit missions. He informed him that Father Du Jaunay on leaving his mission at L'Arbre Croche in 1765 had brought the sacred vessels to Detroit, and had left them in the care of Father Potier. There were in all two chalices, two ciboria, and two monstrances. Father Bocquet being in need of a monstrance, as his was unfit for use, borrowed one of them and later purchased it for the parish. He describes it as bearing an inscription of which he could read only the following: ". . . by Mr. Nicolas Perrot in. . . ." There is no mystery in the inscription for us. We know that it reads: "Ce Soleil A Este Donne Par Mr. Nicolas Perrot A La Mission De St. Francois Xavier En La Baye Des Puants. 1686." [48] It may be read today on the base of the famous Perrot monstrance once the property of St. Anne's parish, and now resting in the Neville Public Museum at Green Bay.[49]

Father Bocquet's letters afford us several glimpses into the devotional life of his parish. For instance, he describes his observance of the Jubilee granted to the Canadian Church in 1767. The ceremonies opened with the whole parish going in solemn procession to a cross erected at some distance from the fort. This was repeated for five days, after which the ceremonies were confined to the church.

[47] It will be noticed that the original mission building gave way to a second structure, and hence did not form part of the remnants torn down about 1912.

[48] Letter to Bishop Briand, July 18, 1771. QCA. The extract referring to the monstrance is the following. "Father Potier received a letter from Father Du Jaunay, who stated that he wrote at your suggestion. There is question of the sacred vessels of Mikelimalinak which were left with Father Potier by Father Du Jaunay. Do they belong to the mission parish or to the Society? I do not know, but I presume to the former. The Sieur Bourassa who had been charged with the care of the church after the departure of the priest came here, and begged Father Potier not to dispose of the said vessels because they belonged to the residents of the place, and they hoped, when the times became better, that they could obtain a missionary. . . .

[49] How or why the monstrance was removed from Detroit is a mystery. A workman, in 1802, while digging a foundation trench for a house in Green Bay unearthed the identical monstrance described by Father Bocquet. It remained in the possession of the Grignon family, and was used by traveling missionaries until a church was built in 1825. When the church burned in 1828, Father Vincent Badin, curate at St. Anne's, brought it back to Detroit. Ten years later, Father Bonduel, then in charge of Green Bay, saw the monstrance in Detroit and bought it from Father Badin for $26. It was loaned for many years to the State Historical Society of Wisconsin before coming to its present resting place. See J. D. Butler, "A Seventeenth Century Ostensorium" (*Wis. Hist. Colls.*,), VIII, 199 ff.

There was a sermon every morning and evening, and Benediction of the Blessed Sacrament. On the last day the parishioners, all shriven and happy, made their final procession to the cross chanting the Te Deum.[50]

Rogation Days were observed by processions to similar outlying crosses. That they were crosses and not chapels is evident from a letter written in 1773. The pastor is now seventy years old and infirm. He finds it almost impossible to walk in procession to these crosses, and then be obliged to return to the church for the celebration of Mass. Bishop de Pontbriand had given him permission to build two outlying chapels, but the coming of the English has forced him to abandon the project. He now seeks a renewal of the permission.[51]

How early the Forty Hours Devotion was established in Detroit is uncertain, but Father Bocquet implies that it had been introduced at least by his predecessor. The traditional time for it was on the three days preceding Ash Wednesday. In the course of time the priest found this period most unsuitable. As the English population within the palisade increased the French moved out, so that in 1770 he had only four families on whom he could count to take their turns before the Blessed Sacrament. Moreover, at that time of the year there was little snow, and the conditions of the roads were such that his people living up and down the river had great difficulty in attending. He petitioned therefore to have the time of the devotion transferred to Christmas and the two days following, and was granted permission to make the change in 1770. The good pastor worried about the fact that exposition for two hours at midnight Mass and for three successive periods of twelve hours totalled only thirty-eight hours, and he professed his willingness to make up the deficit by staying up alone during the night. The bishop does not appear to have required it.[52]

The bane of Father Bocquet's ministry was the number of irregular marriages which which he had to deal. In nearly every letter he had difficulties on that score to lay before the bishop. This is not surprising in view of the fact that from 1765 to 1775 there were never more than four priests in the West from the Great Lakes to the Mississippi: two at Detroit, and two, Fathers Meurin and Gibault, working in the scattered missions in the vicinity of St. Louis. Here and there throughout this vast expanse of territory were isolated groups

---

[50] Letter to Bishop Briand, October 2, 1770. QCA. This was the Jubilee proclaimed by Clement XIII on his accession in 1758. The war had made its observance impossible in Canada, but the Bishop obtained the extension of its favors to the Canadian people for the year 1767.

[51] Same to same, March 1, 1773. QCA.

[52] Same to same, October 2, 1770. QCA.

of Frenchmen living perforce in primitive fashion, and cut off from all contact with civilization and the Church. Young people desiring to be married pronounced the marriage contract in the presence of witnesses, or dispensed with the witnesses. Traders and merchants from the civilized centers along the St. Lawrence, who sometimes spent years in the wilderness, occasionally forgot the ties they had once contracted. Many of these came within the purview of Father Bocquet who, sometimes half-convinced of the futility of his efforts, struggled nevertheless to maintain respect for law and morality.

In his own parish, while Father Bocquet did not have the same evils to contend with, he had to reckon, as we have seen, with the interference of English commandants, and with what we know to have been the growing number of mixed marriages. In his letters he writes at length of only one such marriage, and it is interesting to note that his anxiety about it springs from the fact that the Catholic party is forced to engage in the liquor traffic, and not that she is is exposed to the loss of her faith. Regulations of the bishops regarding the liquor traffic were still in force in 1770, but not too zealously observed. The person referred to in this instance was undoubtedly Angélique Cuillerier who married James Sterling in 1765. She has been advanced as a possible informer who forestalled Pontiac's stratagem. The story is that fearing for the safety of her lover she warned Gladwin against Pontiac, and hence much romance has been woven about her and her gallant Irish sweetheart. The thumb sketch drawn by Father Bocquet is not quite so romantic.

> A French girl has married an English merchant, and consequently a trader in liquor. He uses her as an interpreter, and he is an absolute master who must be obeyed. I understand that he even makes her handle it. My heart is moved to compassion for her. The general law is positive; however, as she has yet demanded nothing from me I am keeping quiet. One day, before knowing that she was engaged in the liquor traffic, I saw her standing in her doorway. I said to her: "Well, my daughter, have we abandoned our religion altogether?" I saw the tears running down as she answered me; "He has not said so, yet." He permits her to come to Mass and the other services, but that is all that she can obtain. I think nevertheless that if she were more determined she would obtain everything; but the liquor question keeps me from pressing her.[53]

With his own people Father Bocquet seems to have been fairly well content. We do not need his testimony to believe that the majority must have been a simple, pious, God-fearing folk, differing little

[53] Same to same, September 22, 1767. QCA.

from their brethren in the province of Quebec, then and today.[54] The ever present source of evil of which he often complained was liquor. In a homogeneous population under the laws civil and ecclesiastical of the French regime the evil was amenable to some control. The intrusion into the population of a masterful, hard-drinking set of soldiers and merchants who led the social life of the settlement was not calculated to better conditions. It was to be expected that some of the inhabitants in their desire to ingratiate themselves with their conquerors should have thrown off restraints which, in the old order, would have been powerful enough to hold them.

Father Bocquet testifies to a sensible diminution of fervor in his parishioners following the advent of the English. He laid this to the extraordinary amount of social gaiety that was thus introduced. In his own graphic way he thus commented on the situation.

> Now is the time for pleasure; how can they refuse their masters to take part. People fear to displease them, and the passion for balls has never been as active as this year. Old women eighty years old who had never been to a ball before have given them, and what is more, have danced more vigorously than the others . . .[55]

Then as now there were social climbers in Detroit, who could forget principle for favor. One of them is thus pictured by her pastor.

> I had the honor to report to your Lordship last year that a child of a Protestant father and Catholic mother was baptized by one of our merchants who, although not a minister, acts as one. This does not bother me as much as the fact that a Catholic woman, married to an English officer, offered her services and actually assisted as godmother, stoutly maintaining that such is the usage in Montreal. She succeeded in attracting a number of our people who were present with her. These functions are generally followed by a big meal, and so I am not surprised that they went. But the return of this dame into our midst has caused disquiet and restiveness. She saw everything that there was to be seen at Montreal; she is the last word on everything; and a lot of sillies, even though they despise and hate her, cannot help listening to her and believing her. I am consoled by the fact that a large number of Protestants are scandalized at her conduct, and have asked me how a Catholic woman can in conscience publicly engage herself to have a child brought up in the Protestant religion.

Thus in Father Bocquet's letters we catch glimpses of some of the results following the merging of an entirely Catholic population

[54] Shea, *Life and Times* . . . , 109, makes this statement: The libertines at Detroit were especially anxious at this time to compel him (Father Bocquet) to withdraw, and molested him greatly . . . In proof he quotes the letter of August 16, 1773. There is nothing in the letter to support the statement.

[55] Letter to Bishop Briand, May 12, 1769. QCA.

with an adventitious racial and religious element. The human weaknesses responsible for the inevitable lowering of standards were in evidence then as they are now.

And now we must come to the last days of Father Bocquet himself. In 1771, when he was sixty-eight years old, there was some talk of removing him; but the old man protested that he would never leave until the bishop obliged him to. He knew that he was afflicted with infirmities, but, as he wrote, the old hulk was still staunch. Two years later he suffered some sort of accident which incapacitated him for a few days, during which several parishioners sent off a letter to the bishop petitioning for a curate. When the priest had fully recovered there were some embarrassing explanations to be made, as he duly records. His last letter is dated June 8, 1775, but his entries in the parish register go on into 1780.[56]

Towards the end, although he grew very feeble, he managed to say Mass.[57] While standing at the altar he was subject to long fits of abstraction, which became so frequent that Jean-Baptiste Roucout, the parish schoolmaster, was appointed to stand beside him to nudge him back into reality. Some time in the summer of 1782 the order came for the tottering old man to return to Quebec. There in the midst of his few remaining brethren, who had been permitted by the British authorities to live together until death should dissolve their little community, he passed away peacefully on March 24, 1787.[58] He was the last of the Recollects in Detroit.

[56] His last record is signed January 10, 1780.

[57] The Moravian missionaries in Detroit in 1781–82 refer to Father Bocquet as being old and unable to preach. See *Diary of David Zeisberger* (Robert Clarke: Cincinnati, 1885), I, 35; 98. "November 4, 1781. We remained quiet in our lodgings. People went in the street to mass, but since we had come in very wretched clothes, torn and ragged, we held it best not to go out much . . . Many officers, English and German, and also many Frenchmen, came to visit us, had compassion with us that we had been so illtreated, and promised to help us, so far as lay in their power. The French priest also called upon us, quite an old man, with whom, however, we could not speak, for he knew not English . . . It is something wonderful here and pleasant if any one is found who shows a desire for God's word, for the place here is like Sodom, where all sins are committed. The French have indeed a church here and a priest, who, however, is quite old, and never preaches but merely reads Mass. On the other side of the river are also a church and a priest, where both French and Indians go, there to be seen in their heathenish garb, with painted heads in full war-array. But the English and Protestants have neither church nor preacher, and wish for neither, although they could have them if they would . . ."

[58] Tanguay, *Répertoire . . . Canadien.*

CHAPTER XII

Priests in a Changing Order

BEFORE going on with the march of events in Detroit we must
pause to record a passing contact with that interesting figure in
history of the Old Northwest, Father Pierre Gibault. His career has
already been sketched in a preceding chapter. Had we Father Bocquet's full correspondence we might expect to find some mention of
Father Gibault, as there frequently is of Father Meurin; but in the
extant letters there is only one passage that might be taken as referring to him.

As far as we know, none of the Recollects stationed in Detroit ever
left the settlement to do missionary work in the state; indeed there
were only two centers where they might have done so: the Straits of
Mackinac and the St. Joseph Mission. As we have seen, Father Potier
visited the mission in 1761, and there is no entry in the register between that year and Father Gibault's first visit in 1768. Nor is there
any entry in the Mackinac register between the retirement of the last
Jesuit in the northern missions, Father Du Jaunay, until the coming
of Father Gibault.

It was in answer to the despairing letter of the aged Jesuit alone
on the Mississippi that the young priest left Montreal in the beginning of June, 1768, and took the Ottawa River route to reach the
Great Lakes.[1] The letter describing his work at Mackinac deserves to
be quoted in full.

At Michillimakina, this 28th July, 1768.
Monseigneur:
    In the moment of my departure from this post I have the honor to
assure Your Lordship of my respect, and to render you an account in
as far as I am able, despite the confusion in which I find myself, of
what I have done in this post. Up to now our journey has been slow and
difficult on account of the rain that we have had from Montreal to
Michillimakinac. There were twenty-two days of downpour, to say nothing of the wind. We had one consolation namely that we were not in
want for anything and did not have to be sparing with our provisions,

[1] His permit to make the journey is signed by General Gage, dated June 1, 1768, and
is preserved in the Archives of the Chicago Historical Society.

228

although the canoes that preceded and followed us were reduced to eating "tripe de roche." Arriving at this post, and having dined with the Commandant, I entered the confessional and did not leave it until ten o'clock, and yet that is the only day on which I left it as early. I have performed several baptisms, but only one marriage. My little stay has brought me sorrow and sadness, but consolation too. My sorrow is due to the fact that I could not stay long enough to satisfy the importunities of a tremendous number of voyageurs who desired to make their confessions covering a period of from three to ten years. They made every possible offer to retain me, even to supplying my people as far as the Illinois country, and accompanying me later with two canoes. But since your Lordship has ordered me to the Illinois country, I fear lest something happen there which would be my fault.

Tomorrow there are starting with us four canoes whose destination is a hundred leagues away, and who have delayed eight days purposely to make their confessions. In a word God is not yet entirely forgotten in these places; there is a need of laborers determined to endure hunger and thirst, and to observe a perpetual Lent.

As M. Despains has remained with me up to the present, and would be put out not to arrive in the Illinois country with me, I have been able to stay here only eight days. I hope to be well received there, as I have reason to believe from news that has reached me. The Spaniards have driven Father Meurin from their villages; the English commandant kindly took him in. Otherwise he would have been on his way to the sea in twenty-four hours. For myself, I am pleased that he is on my side (of the river).

The Indians of Father Du Jaunay have come to visit me in this post. They miss him as much as the first day he left them. Some of them came to confession as they spoke French. Others would have liked to do so, but we could not get into communication. With all my heart I desire to arrive at my destination to fulfill the designs of God and those of your Lordship of which I am, etc.,

Gibault, priest.[2]

On his way down from Mackinac the young missionary stopped for two or three days at the St. Joseph mission, which had not been visited by a priest for seven years. Arriving at length on the Mississippi he took up his residence at Kaskaskia, and with untiring zeal began to reach out in every direction to retrieve the souls that had suffered for years the lack of priestly ministrations. Vincennes had been without a priest since the banishment of Father Julien Dever-

[2] Letter to Bishop Briand, July 28, 1768. QCA. Father Meurin had begun his labors on the western or Spanish side of the Mississippi. He became *persona non grata* when it was known that he held his faculties from the bishop of Quebec, and to escape deportation he crossed over to the English side, where he was well received. See Shea, *Life and Times* . . . 113–30.

nai in 1763.[3] In his place Phillibert, a layman, administered baptism and conducted funerals. There is no more affecting scene in the annals of the American Church than that presented by the arrival of Father Gibault at the little settlement on the banks of the Wabash in the spring of 1770.

> In this post deprived of a priest for seven years all restraint had broken down; libertinage and indifference had come in. But when I arrived everyone crowded down to the banks of the river to receive me. Some of them fell to their knees, too overcome to speak; others could speak only through their sobs. Some of them cried, 'O Father, save us; we are almost in hell.' Others exclaimed, 'Truly God has not abandoned us, for it is He who has sent you to us to make us do penance for our sins.' [4]

Father Gibault remained at Vincennes for two months, and then returned to Kaskaskia. Three years later he went on another long missionary journey during which his presence in Michigan is attested to by the final entries in the register of the St. Joseph mission. In 1775, he again made a tour of the western posts, this time going as far north as Mackinac. From here he wrote his bishop a most despairing letter. Disgusted and disheartened by the sins and the ingratitude of his people, weighed down by the responsibilities which rested on his shoulders alone, broken in health by the hardships of his missionary life, he asked again, as he had asked before, to be returned to the Quebec area. If that were not possible, he offered to serve one or the other of the parishes presided over by the two venerable priests at Detroit.

> Father Potier has testified to me his eagerness that I go to live with him. 'Then,' he told me, 'I shall have only my Indians to think about, and it will be easier for you to do missionary work in the north out of Detroit, and with less fatigue and danger than out of the Illinois country.' Moreover, Father Simple is on the brink of the grave.[5]

Having waited in vain for an answer to his letter, Father Gibault took a desperate resolve. Rather than winter in the desolation of Mackinaw he ventured to begin on the 4th of November a perilous journey by canoe to Detroit.

> I preferred to risk perishing on Lake Huron than to pass the winter at that place. Therefore, in a little canoe made of bark, with one man

---

[3] There are variant spellings of this missionary's name. The one given here is in Melançon's list.

[4] The majority of Father Gibault's letters have been published in the first three volumes of the *Illinois Historical Collections,* Virginia Series.

[5] Letter to Bishop Briand, Mackinaw, October 9, 1775. QCA.

and a child, on their first voyage, I myself having been across but once, having had no experience with a boat for sixteen years, asleep during the nights and often during the day, and consequently knowing nothing of the dangerous places, which are not uncommon, . . . in this miserable conveyance, resolved to overcome every obstacle, steering the canoe myself, through ice, in snow, of which there were eight inches in the level country, amidst high winds and tempests, at a season when no one in the memory of man has ever ventured forth, in twenty-two days I reached Detroit. That was ten days ago. The river, since before my arrival, has been covered with ice and can be crossed as is done in winter from Quebec to Point Levis. I am therefore frozen up here. Perhaps I may get away this winter, perhaps, as the oldest inhabitants tell me, not until March. God be praised . . .

Father Potier told me that the Hurons want him to keep me and teach me their language so that I may be their next father. They came to his houses to greet me ceremoniously. I say this only in passing because I would much prefer to return to Canada than to stay in Detroit . . .[6]

Unfortunately, we have no details concerning Father Gibault's stay in Detroit, which must have been prolonged until the end of April, 1776.[7] The last extant letter of Father Bocquet was written in June of the preceding year, and there is no existing correspondence from either of the Detroit parishes from that time until 1783. Although unable to overcome his repugnance to the Illinois mission Father Gibault returned to the scene of his first labors with no intimation of the undying fame that awaited him. Had he remained in Detroit his life might have been as placid and uneventful as the career of Father Bocquet. His return to Vincennes and Kaskaskia involved him in the initial struggles of the American Colonies to wrest the Northwest Territory from British control. Henceforth his name would go down in American history indissolubly linked with the successes of George Rogers Clark, and no story of the growth of the American Republic is complete without tribute to the activities of Father Gibault the "Patriot Priest."

On his departure, the two old men in Detroit were left to continue their ministry as best they could. The first one to go was the aged Jesuit, found dead before his fireplace on July 16, 1781. His parish was not vacant for long. Three years before, the Bishop of Quebec had sent a visitor to the Illinois mission in the person of Jean-François Hubert, a priest of the Seminary. On his way through Detroit he

[6] Letter to Bishop Briand, Detroit, December 4, 1775. QCA.
[7] Father Meurin to Bishop Briand, Prairie du Rocher, May 23, 1776. QCA. "I am patiently waiting the arrival of M. Gibault. He arrived today, May 22, full of dislike for his parish, which he desires to quit as soon as he can arrange his affairs."

had been captivated by the charm of the locality. Returning to Quebec he had severed his connection with the Seminary to engage in parish work. When the news of Father Potier's death arrived, he offered himself as successor, was accepted, and reached Detroit about three months later.[8]

For the next few years conditions in Detroit were so unsettled that Father Hubert often ministered to the parishioners of St. Anne's, and his name occurs repeatedly in the parish registers.[9] His priestly zeal had led him to beg for a distant post like Detroit, where nothing could be expected save poverty and hard work. But his long and honorable career in responsible positions in the diocese could not be forgotten. In 1785 while immersed in the cares of his pastoral labors, he was notified of his appointment as coadjutor to the Bishop of Quebec. Consecrated the next year, he succeeded to the see in 1788 and ruled it wisely and honorably until his resignation in 1797, the year of his death.[10]

Only a few months after the arrival of Father Hubert, the tottering pastor of St. Anne's, as we have seen, was recalled to Quebec. Halfway on his homeward journey he was met by the young priest who was coming to replace him, Father Louis Payet.[11] What he found in Detroit in the wake of an old man who could barely perform the most necessary functions is set forth in his first report to Bishop Briand.[12]

> These are my observations. I noticed that the people had not been governed with a firm hand, but seemed to have governed themselves. The old man often let himself be taken in; he had friends whose influence often extended even to the functions of his ministry. A certain party wanted the Mass at an unusual hour, and he got it. Another wanted to receive communion before Mass, another during Mass, and another after Mass. No one was refused. People were married morning or night, with or without banns, and this simply to please them and without necessity. A thousand abuses of various kinds have grown up in this locality . . . However, the inhabitants are not as ignorant as those to be found in many sections of Canada. They are more intelligent, but at the same time more indifferent towards their religion, and there is

[8] Jean-François Hubert, born February 23, 1739, at Quebec. Ordained July 20, 1766. He was for many years secretary to the Bishop of Quebec, and for five years Superior of the Seminary. Went to the Illinois missions in August, 1778, and returned to Quebec the following summer. He left for Detroit in September, 1781.

[9] His signature occurs from September 5, 1782, in scattered entries.

[10] He died at l'Hôpital-General in Quebec, October 17, 1797.

[11] Louis Payet born at Montreal, August 25, 1749. Ordained February 26, 1774. Died August 26, 1801, and was buried at Verchères.

[12] Letter to Bishop Briand, Detroit, January 8, 1783. QCA.

very little decorum and recollection in church. It is true that mine is in such dilapidated condition that it inspires disdain rather than veneration.[13]

A few months later Father Payet wrote that he was still struggling against old abuses which had crept in, and which were hard to eradicate. Despite the high cost of materials, and the difficulty of procuring them, he had built a new rectory, had repaired the church, and had opened a new cemetery.[14]

Although we have few details concerning his missionary journeys, we know that Father Payet did not confine his labors to Detroit. In 1784 we find him at Vincennes, which Father Gibault had not visited for five years. He remained from July to September validating marriages, and supplying the ceremonies of Baptism to the many children whom Phillibert had baptized.[15] The next year Father Gibault himself took up his residence in Vincennes.[16]

Early in 1786, Father Payet reported to his friend, Father Hubert the bishop-elect, the satisfactory condition of his parish.[17]

> Things here are in good order, thanks be to God. We have recently found means to add eight new pews to the church by rearranging the communion rail. We have established a marguillier as overseer in the rear of the church, where perched up in a sort of pulpit he preaches by his silence and demeanor to the irreligious whose number diminishes every day.[18]

In the same letter the priest expressed his determination to retire from Detroit on account of ill health, and to return to parish work in Canada. Whatever the answer to his request was, Father Payet remained until the summer and then betook himself to another long neglected spot, the post at Mackinaw, which had not seen a priest

[13] Father Bocquet wrote in 1771 that the steeple of the church had been struck by lightning and severely damaged. He went on to say that two years before the church had been almost in ruins, and had been repaired. In 1773–74 the building of a new church was contemplated, but nothing was done.

[14] Letter to Bishop Briand, July 13, 1783. QCA.

[15] Shea, *Life and Times* . . . . , 472–73.

[16] Letter to Bishop Briand, Vincennes, June 8, 1786. QCA.

[17] Letter to Father Hubert, February 20, 1786. QCA. The letter contains much interesting Detroit gossip. Quite a few English children have died from scarlet fever. Major Ancrum has lost two, McGregor two, Macomb two, and Dr. Anthon his oldest son. Mr. Hay and Mr. Williams have died of gout. An Englishman named Christie, a former schoolteacher in Canada, and an unnamed companion, have been killed at the Rouge by Indians.

[18] In the passage referred to in note 15 Father Payet is said to have built a new church. Shea is mistaken. The priest is reporting the progress of the Assumption church which Father Hubert had begun before his recall to Quebec.

since the last visit of Father Gibault in 1775.[19] In the course of time important changes had taken place there. The pressure of the slow American advance northward from the Ohio River was beginning to make itself felt by the British in the lake region. Alarmed by the capture of Vincennes they began feverish preparations to strengthen their posts in Michigan. At Detroit this activity lay behind the construction of Fort Lernoult. At Mackinaw it showed itself in the abandonment of the post at the tip of the southern peninsula, and its transfer to what was believed to be a much safer location, the island of Mackinac itself.

The island was purchased from the Chippewa on May 12, 1781, for five thousand pounds, but this was only the final transaction fulfilling an agreement which had been operative for more than a year.[20] In the views of Patrick Sinclair, Governor of Mackinaw, the island was to be fortified, a part of it devoted to the growing of the necessary foodstuffs, and the trading population of the Straits was to reside there. Apparently there was some opposition to the plan, particularly from the French, who were averse to giving up their long-established homesites in the old location; but Sinclair prudently won them over, especially by making provision for the transfer of the church. The building was taken down in sections early in 1780 and pushed across the ice to the island. The record of this unusual procedure is found in a letter of Sinclair to Captain Brehm.

> As this place was never the seat of industry I had to Combat with some Difficulties which nothing, to tell you the truth, but very strict attention to the King's Previcions enabled me to overcome . . . and, now, with all these works going on pretty well & regular, I have all the Traders, their servants, . . . employed in carrying over the Church to the Island, which will be I expect completely rebuilt about the latter end of March. The French Church will stand where the Traders will be hereafter fixed, not in the Fort. By this removal the Worship & work of the Canadiens will be drawn to the Island next year . . .
>
> But from the attachment of two or three People to their good Houses, on this side, some artful insinuations were sliding among the Indians, which, with several advantages attending the removal of the Church, were soon silenced. The Priests House will follow . . .[21]

---

[19] Since he does not mention it in his letters Father Gibault was probably unaware that his presence in Mackinaw occasioned a petition for a resident priest sent not to the bishop but to Governor Carleton, who was to use his influence with the bishop to have the petition granted. It was accompanied by a subscription list in which seventy-three persons, several of them non-Catholics, promised a total of 2,398 livres for the support of a priest. See the *Mich. Hist. Colls.*, X, 286–88.

[20] The document conveying the ownership of the island is reproduced in the *Mich. Hist. Colls.*, XIX, 633.

[21] Letter of Sinclair to Brehm, February 15, 1780. *Mich Hist. Colls.*, IX, 539.

It was therefore to the little church on the island of Mackinac that Father Payet came in the summer of 1786.[22] We have no letter of his describing his labors on this occasion; following his stay on the island he returned to Quebec instead of to Detroit, and therefore made his report to the bishop in person. However, that his labors were fruitful is apparent from the tenor of a document which he was deputed to present on his arrival in Quebec, a petition from the French at Mackinac for a resident priest.[23] Apart from its historical interest the petition has a pathetic side. We are accustomed to picture the voyageurs and traders as rude, illiterate individuals, little above their Indian companions either in ideals or conduct. The handwriting of the petition is perhaps the most beautiful to be found in any document bearing on the early history of Michigan, and its contents reveal a depth of religious feeling, a hunger for the consolations of religion, and a striving to maintain the ideals of Christian living against the pressure of wilderness life and customs.

REQUEST OF THE VOYAGEURS OF MICHILIMAKINAC IN 1786 TO HIS LORDSHIP THE LORD BISHOP OF THE PROVINCE OF QUEBEC IN CANADA,
My Lord:
Deprived for the last eleven years of any spiritual help in this region, it is with the liveliest satisfaction that we have welcomed M. Payet, missionary of Detroit, who on his way to Canada has been pleased to pass through this place to minister to us. This worthy priest, in addition to the troubles which he has already undergone for us, is willing to present to your Highness our most humble petition for this most distant portion of your flock that seeks a pastor.

All the citizens and inhabitants of this region unite under the respectable name of Christians to unanimously supplicate you to send them a wise director to guide them in the way of salvation. The innocence of the children, the weakness of the aged, the sins of the most vicious, all these demand the favor of your pastoral charity; nor can your generosity fail to be moved by this powerful motive, that the lustre of religion must be preserved in the midst of savage tribes. Wherefore they earnestly pray you to consider, not the bad impressions of their morals that you may have received, but your paternal charity in order to forestall the sad results of a flock straying without a shepherd.

The preaching of M. Payet has stirred every heart, has touched and converted many, and they hope that the report presented to you by this

[22] His first entry in the baptismal register is dated July 15, 1786.

[23] Rezek, *op. cit.*, II, 169, states that Father Payet remained at Mackinac until the end of August, 1787. The language of the petition as well as the priest's correspondence prove that the missionary made two distinct visits to the island, one in 1786, and another in 1787. The same volume in Chap. XVII gives the further history of the church on the island, and reproduces a sketch of the church as Father Payet must have seen it.

faithful minister will effectually move you in their regard. Consequently they offer you their facilities and their purses for the passage of the missionary who shall be confided to them. If on account of the dearth of priests the one sent cannot remain more than a few months, he shall have in the spring everything fitting to his person and his character, and in the fall he shall be conducted to his home with the same care and attention. If the stay of the desired missionary is to be permanent and uninterrupted, his annual support is herewith guaranteed in the annexed subscription list. To the rest of your diocese we join our sincere wishes for the preservation of your Lordship. We hope, with your paternal benediction, to obtain a director for our souls, zealous, expert, charitable, and prudent as is M. Payet, at least to open our mission, and to begin things on a proper basis. Such is the expectation of those who have the honor to be with the most profound respect, of your Lordship, the most humble and most obedient servants and children in Jesus Christ our Lord.[24]

From the extant parish register we learn that a definite parochial organization was set up on July 23, 1786. Two trustees, Jean-Baptiste Barthe and Louis Carignant, were elected wardens after having sworn to administer the affairs of the church "upon their souls and conscience." His priestly duties fulfilled, and the congregation organized, Father Payet went on to Quebec bearing the hopeful request of the men whose good will and veneration he had won.

In the early summer of 1787 Father Payet again visited the island mission, and remained at least until the 20th of August. An extant letter from him at this time mentions various repairs that are being made to the church, and the number of devout parishioners who have remained faithful despite a good deal of wickedness surrounding them.[25] As the result of his two visits to Mackinac the register of the mission records sixty-five baptisms, among them that of an Ottawa chief, four marriages, and one funeral.[26] Unfortunately, the bishop was unable to accede to the wishes of the Mackinac traders for a resident pastor. It was fully seven years after Father Payet's departure before another priest set foot on the island.

When Father Payet was preparing to start out on his first visit to Mackinac he was still pastor of St. Anne's in Detroit.[27] In the parish across the river Father Hubert had been succeeded by Father Pierre Fréchette, who had arrived at the end of October, 1785.[28] Evidently, the plea of ill health advanced by Father Payet to justify his recall to

[24] Original in QCA.

[25] Letter to Bishop Hubert, Mackinac, August 14, 1787. QCA.

[26] Rezek, loc. cit., 169.

[27] His last entry in St. Anne's register is dated June 22, 1786.

[28] Pierre Fréchette, born at Quebec July 21, 1758. Ordained December 18, 1784. Died at Beloeil, January 3, 1816.

Canada must have been accepted, for, during the time of his first visit to Mackinac his successor was already on his way to Detroit. In the second week of October, François-Xavier Dufaux, who had been in the Sulpician house at Montreal, arrived in Detroit to replace Father Payet.[29] Surprisingly enough, his pastorate lasted for just three days and this is the explanation of what happened.

> I remained three days at the fort and said Mass twice. Many persons were present, but no one even wished me good day, or offered me the least assistance. Where was I to lodge the two missionaries? [30] In the fort I would have been obliged to pay one hundred dollars rent, besides their other household expenses. They would have needed a man to take care of them, and living and clothing are frightfully dear. What income could they have received to supply their wants? In the fort there are four or five schools containing both boys and girls, the most of them English, for they alone are desirous of educating their children, and can afford to do so. I saw very well that I was in a sorry plight, and that I had given up a most tranquil life to engage myself in many troubles. I sought out M. Fréchette and told him my worries and difficulties. He gave me the tale of his own, and assured me truthfully that he had shed more tears than he could hold in his hat. What a situation! Nothing on one side of the river, and everything all wrong on the other. He seemed disposed to take the parish in the fort, where he is now getting along fairly well, rather than remain at Assumption to charge himself with the care of the two missionaries. As for myself I remained in his place . . .[31]

Father Dufaux proved to be a better correspondent than Father Fréchette, and were we concerned with the history of Assumption parish it would be easy to find many intimate details to lighten the dry recital of facts. For instance, there was Mouton, the priest's "boy," who had served Father Hubert, and who looked askance at his successor. The Indians brought presents of game to Father Dufaux, but when he sat down to table in pleasant anticipation he found two wings of a wild turkey, and onion soup. After ten days of nothing but onion soup the pastor's patience was exhausted, and Mouton was obliged to seek employment elsewhere. Undaunted, he presented a document purporting to have been signed by Father Hubert authorizing him to dispose of all the former pastor's possessions which had been left behind. No one but himself knew just what belonged to Father Hubert, and at the end of eight days when he had finished

[29] François-Xavier Dufaux, born at Montreal January 16, 1752. Ordained August 16, 1778, and stationed in the Sulpician seminary at Montreal. Signs the Assumption register for the first time October 13, 1786. Died at Assumption parish September 11, 1796.

[30] Father Dufaux acting on the orders of Father Hubert brought two young women with him to begin a school in Assumption parish, Miss Ademard and Miss Papineau. They are the missionaries referred to.

[31] Letter to Bishop Hubert, August 24, 1787. QCA.

trundling household goods out of the rectory in a wheelbarrow there remained nine plates, two dishes, three worn tablecloths, one water bottle and two glasses.[32]

As a result of the exchange Father Fréchette became pastor of St. Anne's, a position he was to hold for ten years. He is described by Father Payet as being of small stature, a zealous and pious priest, "but a man of superlative tranquillity." [33] Perhaps this characteristic accounts for the fact that there are only two extant letters of his, one of which will be quoted later.

Father Fréchette deserves further consideration as the founder of the first outgrowth of St. Anne's parish on Michigan soil. The beauty and fertility of the country watered by the Raisin River could not long remain unnoticed. How early migration thither from the Detroit colony took place cannot be decided with certainty. François Navarre is said to have been the first settler in what is now Monroe, and to have taken up land along the river in 1780.[34] In the next five or six years the number of colonists grew to such an extent that Father Dufaux interested himself in making some provision for their religious needs. He reported the situation to Bishop Hubert as follows.

> The River Raisin is being settled by people who are at a loss what to do. Thirty-two inhabitants have already built cabins along the river; many propose to join them in the spring. At present more than a hundred farms have been staked out there. I really believe that in a short time a pastor will be necessary. I intend to go there this spring to mark out a piece of land for a cemetery; but I will not bless it until a chapel or a house has been built for the priest who may be sent there. Who will be charged with this little mission? The pastor of Assumption or of St. Anne's? I should like to know your Lordship's wishes in that regard. Poor Jean-Baptiste Drouillard, who was just getting started in the new settlement, died there. Those who brought his body to the fort nearly perished on the way. I chanted a funeral service for him a few days ago. Fortunately, he made his Easter duty last fall on his arrival from Sanduskey.[35]

Although Father Dufaux brings up the subject of having a priest on the Raisin River only in 1788, and speaks of the settlement itself as being quite recent, it is certain that some one had been advocating the building of a church at least two years earlier. There was a band of Potawatomi living along the river, and through the good offices of

[32] *Idem.*
[33] From letter quoted in note 19.
[34] *Mich. Hist. Colls.*, IV, 318; VI, 362.
[35] Letter to Bishop Hubert, January 28, 1788. Easter duties are not made in the fall. Perhaps the good priest meant that the man had gone to the sacraments at the time.

some unknown promoter the chief, who if not a Christian still retained the traditions of earlier days, was induced to deed a parcel of Indian land for religious purposes. The interesting document by which the transfer was effected, dated September 14, 1786, and attested by the totem sign of the chief himself has recently come to light.[36]

> I Eskiby Pouteouatamis Chief of the Raisin River both in my name and in the name of my nation & of the families of my tribe who dwell there, I declare that I have reserved a plot of ground three arpents wide throughout its length to build there the house of prayer,[37] the said land situated on the rising ground on the right side of the river abutting the concession of Francois Navarre Hutrau; this location destined to become a place of prayer in perpetuity shall be occupied for no other purpose, and only by the master of life; wherefore all persons of any nation whatsoever are expressly forbidden to use the said place for settlement or tillage under penalty of seeing their efforts wasted and the fruits of their labor destroyed. For this reason I have affixed my signature in order that no one may doubt our resolution which is and always will be irrevocable. At Detroit the 14th of Sept. 1786. And the concession of lands which we have given to the brothers & children of Robiche as well as to those of Marie, widow of Alexis Campau, shall likewise be in perpetuity for them and their children so that no one can disturb them for any reason whatsoever.

It appears that the chief's generous gift was not used when the parish was established. Father Dufaux's question must have been answered by the bishop's ordering Father Fréchette to undertake the organization of a parish in the new settlement, for on October 18, 1788, we find him presiding over a meeting of the settlers assembled for that purpose. The official record of their deliberations on this occasion has been preserved, and in it we read that the farm of Sieur Montminni, Sr., was unanimously chosen as the most suitable location for the church. "We have bought one acre and two perches of the said farm for four hundred francs, and a half acre has been given us of his own free will by Joseph Hyvon . . . the whole forming an acre and a half and two perches which will serve for the location of the church, presbytery, etc. . . ."[38]

Fully aware of their extreme poverty, the settlers went on to state that for the present they could not support a resident pastor, but were prepared to erect a structure to house the priest on his occasional

[36] The original deed in French was recently acquired for the archives of Marygrove College, Detroit.

[37] The ribbon farms of Detroit were duplicated in the Monroe colony. Frontage on the water was all-important, depth meant little.

[38] The extract is translated from the manuscript record of the parish assemblies.

visits, and to serve as a chapel. They further promised to pay tithes to Father Fréchette, and to store them according to his orders. In return for their good dispositions as "veritable followers of the Lord," they hoped that the bishop when informed of their action by Father Fréchette would allow them to participate in all the favors and indulgences which it was in his power to accord.

There were fifty settlers at this initial meeting of whom ten signed the minutes, and forty affixed their marks. According to the traditional organization of a French parish, a number of syndics [39] were chosen, and before long the first parish building arose on what is now the Trinkley farm on the North Custer Road, about two and a half miles west of the present St. Mary's church in Monroe. All available records seem to indicate that no building exclusively devoted to divine worship was erected until about 1797.[40] Although it is only reasonable to suppose that Father Fréchette must have visited the settlement at least once a year, there is no existing record proving the presence of a priest at the River Raisin between the time of the first parish organization and the arrival of the first resident pastor in the person of the restless, impetuous Irishman, Father Edmund Burke. His activities in this section of the country were not confined exclusively to his priestly duties. To explain them we will leave Fathers Fréchette and Dufaux in the peaceful round of their parish ministry while we rapidly sketch the salient facts of this period in Detroit's political history.

As we have already stated the Quebec Act of 1774 did not mean that the British government had been suddenly converted to the principle of religous freedom. It could conveniently forget its own code in the more important business of stalking the American Colonies slowly drifting towards revolution from the time of the Stamp Act. Open conflict began with the skirmish at Lexington and ended with the surrender of Cornwallis, October 19, 1781. With the military operations in the Colonies along the Atlantic seaboard we are more or less familiar. What is still imperfectly known is the cruel, inhuman warfare in the rear of the Colonies, foreseen and fostered by the Canadian authorities.

Despite the efforts of the British government to keep American set-

[39] According to the Canadian parish organization all church building and repair work was entrusted to a committee distinct from the wardens, whose members were called "Syndics."

[40] Father Camillus Maes, one time pastor of St. John's Church, Monroe, and later Bishop of Covington, wrote *A History of the Catholic Church in Monroe City and County, Mich.* The brochure bearing neither place nor date of publication has become a rare item. Father Maes states that his history was written at the urgent request of John Gilmary Shea. He dates the building of the church from "soon after" the meeting of 1788. The time was actually much later.

tlers out of the territory behind the Alleghenies, their land hunger could not be denied, and at the opening of the Revolutionary War there were settlements in western Pennsylvania and New York, and along the Ohio River in West Virginia and Kentucky. The little clearings in the wilderness were far from the eastern battle lines, and there were no English troops to harass them; but they were exposed to the greater horror of ruthless warfare. Even in his failure Pontiac had taught his conquerors a lesson, and furthered in a sense the interests of his people. British agents became assiduous in cultivating Indian friendship with abundant liquor and liberal presents. When the time was ripe, they had only to unleash their Indian allies.

The limits of pioneer advance were strung along the arc of a great circle swinging down from Niagara to Cincinnati, whose geographical center was Detroit. It therefore became the base from which Indian warfare in the rear of the Colonies was directed. Here were the headquarters of the Indian Department in the West, and the depot for the distribution of Indian presents, supplies, and ammunition. Hundreds of prisoners were brought in, either to be put to work on the fortifications, or sent down to Montreal and Quebec. There is no need of a detailed account of the atrocities for which the Indian Department was responsible.[41] One writer has thus summed them up:

> White, half-breed, and Indian agents went through the forests inciting the natives to deeds of horror; prices were fixed on scalps—and it is significant of the temper of these agents that a woman's scalp was paid for as readily as a man's.
>
> In every corner of the wilderness the bloody scenes of Pontiac's war were reenacted. Bands of Savages lurked about the settlements, ready to attack at any unguarded moment; and whenever the thin blue smoke of a settler's cabin rose, prowlers lay in wait. A woman might not safely go a hundred yards to milk a cow, or a man lead a horse to water. The farmer carried a gun strapped to his side as he ploughed, and he scarcely dared venture into the woods for the winter's supply of fuel and game. Hardly a day passed on which a riderless horse did not come galloping into some lonely clearing, telling of a fresh tragedy on the trail.[42]

Probably no one was more responsible for such conditions than Henry Hamilton, Lieutenant-governor of Detroit, who assumed office on November 9, 1775. It was George Rogers Clark who first called him the 'Hair-buyer,'' and from what we know of him the charge was justified. Under his orders Indian war-parties spread out

---

[41] All the historians of Detroit give various details.

[42] Frederic Austin Ogg, *The Old Northwest* (Chronicles of America series; Yale University Press. 1921), 46 ff.

fanwise in every direction led by choice spirits like the Tory Frenchmen, the Dequindres, or by Alexander McKee, Matthew Elliott, and
William Caldwell. The Indians who perpetrated the Wyoming Valley massacre were drawn in large part from Detroit.[43] The Kentucky
settlements at Boonesville and Harrodsburg were raided, and Daniel
Boone himself was brought to Detroit a prisoner.

The first blow struck in retaliation by the Americans was the capture of Kaskaskia by George Rogers Clark on July 4, 1778. Through
the intervention of Father Gibault, Cahokia and Vincennes surrendered without resistance. At a stroke the boundaries of the future republic had been extended to the Mississippi, and northward to the
Illinois River.

Hamilton, who had long been planning some decisive blow against
the Americans, now saw his chance. He decided to retake Vincennes.
However, there was more than a desire for military glory behind his
decision. He had to offset the unsavory reputation gained by his administration of civil affairs at Detroit, in which he had been aided
and abetted by Phillip Dejean. They had both been indicted by a
Montreal grand jury, Dejean for having "acted and transacted divers
unjust and illegal, tyrannical and felonious acts contrary to good government and the safety of his Majesty's liege subjects," and Hamilton
on the charge that the "said Hamilton hath not only remained at Detroit aforesaid and been witness to the several illegal acts and doings
of him, the said Phillip Dejean, but has tolerated, suffered, and permitted the same under his government, guidance, and direction." [44]

Having arranged all the details of his punitive expedition, Hamilton was ready to start on October 7, 1778. Mistrusting somewhat the
loyalty of the French militia who formed the greater portion of his
troops, he proceeded to strengthen it by the means most calculated to
impress them.

> Pere Potier, the Jesuit missionary, a man of respectable character and
> venerable figure, came to the head of our little encampment on the
> common of Detroit, and having attended to the reading of the Articles
> of War, and the renewal of the Oath of Allegiance to His Britannick
> Majesty, he gave the blessing to the Catholics present, conditionally
> upon their strictly adhering to their oath, being the more engaged
> thereto as the indulgence and favor of their prince merited their best
> Services & had exceeded their most sanguine expectations. The subse-

[43] Farmer, op. cit., 249.

[44] See Burton, op. cit., II, 919. Among the many charges in the presentment was one
dealing with the illegal execution of one, Jean Constantineau. The Frenchman and a
Negro accomplice, Ann Wiley, were found guilty of robbery and sentenced to death.
Dejean gave the woman her freedom on condition that she hang Constantineau. This
she did readily enough.

quent behavior of these people has occasioned my recalling this circumstance.[45]

The result of Hamilton's expedition is a matter of common knowledge. A few days before Christmas he retook Vincennes. Dejean, to be with Hamilton, went down in February just in time to be included in Hamilton's surrender to Clark. The latter had determined to push Hamilton out at any cost, and in the face of untold hardships he accomplished his purpose on February 24, 1779. Dejean and Hamilton were sent as prisoners to Virginia, and confined at Williamsburg. After a few months of rather harsh treatment they were released; the first, to sink into oblivion, the second to hold in after years the honorable position of Governor in Bermuda, and to give his name to its capital city.

The Indian scourge was in a measure abated by Clark's victory, and although he was ready to push on to Detroit itself, he was given no encouragement, and Detroit remained in British hands. By the Treaty of Paris it became American—but only on paper. Justifying their action by alleging certain treaty obligations unfulfilled, the British held on to the lake region and its strongholds. At the end of the war immigration poured into the Ohio Valley, again meeting sullen Indian resentment. This time the Indians were aroused to fighting mood not because they were British allies, but because they were struggling against dispossession of the lands that had been theirs from time immemorial. Another wave of Indian hostility broke over the creeping line of American advance. Again Detroit became the center from which British agents fomented and instigated Indian atrocities, and supplied and rewarded their perpetrators. If the Americans could be stalled off long enough treaty obligations might never have to be lived up to.

When Washington became President under the Constitution in 1789 he determined to end this intolerable situation. Numerous attempts at peace-making with the Indians had been frustrated by British intervention, and the time for action had come. Harmar set out with his punitive expedition in 1790, but was badly defeated. The next year St. Clair with an augmented force was completely routed. In this crisis Washington's last hope was Anthony Wayne. By the battle of Fallen Timbers Wayne justified the choice of the Commander-in-Chief; the Indians could not recover from that blow, nor could their instigators fail to realize that their dishonorable tenure was at an end.[46]

[45] *Mich. Hist. Colls.*, IX, 491.
[46] The battle of Fallen Timbers took place on August 20, 1794, and was fought on the banks of the Maumee River, a short distance from Toledo, Ohio.

At the beginning of 1794 John Jay had reopened negotiations in London for the final settlement of the boundary line, and the disposal of matters that were still unadjusted. In June he wrote that the British government positively refused to surrender Detroit and Mackinac. But the news of the victory at Fallen Timbers could not be disregarded. In November the boundary line was definitely determined and the pledge given that the western posts would be evacuated not later than June 1, 1796. Still sparring for time to see what could be done with Indian help the Canadian authorities did not authorize the transfer of Detroit until June 2, 1796, when an order to that effect was signed at Quebec.

During the years that Detroit was the center of opposition to the American advance its own existence was peaceful enough. In the town itself groups of jaded prisoners came and went, and the streets were often cluttered with bands of victorious Indians who had come to claim their rewards, and lay sleeping off their drunken orgies. Up and down the river the French population went about its accustomed occupations content to be, in great part at least, merely the spectators of the game of empire that was being played over their heads. That there was a strong undercurrent of sympathy with the Americans is evident from the official correspondence of the period, as well as the fact that the two priests in Detroit knew that they were being counted on to exercise their influence in the right direction. Father Fréchette, who was accused of some disloyal act whose details at this distance are unknown to us, drew a stiff though apparently undeserved rebuke from his bishop. Perhaps the Canadian authorities felt the need of a more militant clerical direction of the French population radiating from Detroit, for this was undoubtedly one of the reasons underlying the coming of Father Edmund Burke.

A native of Ireland, and with the record of a brilliant course of studies in Paris, Father Burke was a welcome addition to the Canadian Church when he arrived in Quebec in 1786.[47] He was immediately assigned to teach philosophy in the Seminary, and in course of time became one of the directors of the institution. Because of his nationality and his talents he was soon on intimate terms with the most influential officials of the government, whose friendship he

---

[47] Father Edmund Burke was born at Maryborough, County Kildare, in 1753, and following his ordination was stationed at Kildare. His alignment in certain controversies making a foreign residence desirable, he applied to the bishop of Quebec and was accepted. There is a biographical sketch in the Catholic Encyclopedia. It is of rather doubtful value and more eulogistic that extant documents warrant. Many of these will be found in the *Memoire sur Les Missions de la Nouvelle-Ecosse* (C. Darveau; Quebec, 1895). The book is anonymous, but is known to be the work of Abbé Casgrain, who wrote it in answer to a flattering sketch of Father Burke entitled the *Memoirs of Bishop Burke*. It will be quoted simply as *Memoire*.

deemed it worth while to cultivate. Tiring of seminary life, and convinced that in Quebec his energies were cramped, Father Burke began to long for wider fields. He offered his services to Bishop Carroll, but was not accepted. Having expressed his preference for parish work he was named to one of the best pastorates in the gift of Bishop Hubert, situated on the Island of Orleans, and remained there until the fall of 1794.

Meanwhile Father Burke had been carrying on a correspondence with his friend and protector, Archbishop Troy of Dublin.[48] He had much to say about the great Northwest, and the wonderful opportunities it offered for evangelization. In his opinion it had been very much neglected by the Church authorities, and he suggested that if it were confided to him, and he were given certain privileges, for instance, that of conferring the sacrament of Confirmation, he could soon bring this section of the diocese of Quebec to a flourishing state. The archbishop used his influence in Rome, and in 1791 Bishop Hubert was notified by the Propaganda Congregation that it was ready to further Father Burke's proposal.[49] The bishop made known his willingness to accept the plan both to Father Burke and to the Congregation; but as the former had decided to take the parish on the Island the matter was dropped for the time being.

In 1794 the Canadian authorities felt a growing alarm over the inroads made by the American emissaries among the Indians in Ohio, and especially among the French population lying between the Raisin River and the mouth of the Maumee. Lieutenant-Governor Simcoe communicated to Lord Dorchester the necessity of combating this propaganda, suggesting the following means:

> It may be worthy of Your Lordship's consideration whether some trusty loyal Clergyman might not be of use to us in the settlement of the River au Raisin to counteract any improper opinions and transactions, if such a person may be found in Lower Canada.[50]

Simcoe need not have been so dubious; within a month the suitable person had been found. Of this we are assured in a petition written some years later by the person himself.

> The humble Petition of Edmund Burke one of the Vicars Gen. of the Diocese of Quebec. Most humbly showeth
> That in the month of September, 1794, on the application of Lord Dorchester then Governor General of British North America in consequence of a requisition from His Excellency John Graves Simcoe then

[48] See Peter Guilday, *Life and Times of John Carroll* (New York, 1922), for other references to the interest of Archbishop Troy in the affairs of the American Church.
[49] *Memoire*, 102.
[50] *Mich. Hist. Colls.*, XXV, 130.

Lieutenant Governor of Upper Canada, your Petitioner was removed from the United Livings of St. Peter and St. Lawrence in the Isle of Orleans by the Right Revd. John Francis Hubert then R.C. Bishop of Quebec to the River Raisin in the Miamis Country expressly to counteract the Machinations of Jacobin emissaries whose influence amongst the Settlers and numerous Tribes of surrounding Indians, might, not to say infallibly would, have caused an Insurrection, the consequence of which might prove fatal to the King's 24 Regiment then stationed in the Forts of Detroit & the Miamis about eighty miles distant one from the other, the strong settlement of the River Raisin midway between them.

That your petitioner by persevering diligence and at the risque of his life happily succeeded in suppressing the flames which were already kindled by a resolution of the settlers to refuse obedience to the Militia laws. . . .[51]

While the petitioner states bluntly enough that the sole reason for his coming to the River Raisin was political, it is only fair to believe that the bishop had other motives in transferring him. In his loyalty to the government the bishop was willing to accede to a perfectly legitimate request; but at the same time he must have welcomed the opportunity of ministering to the religious needs of this distant portion of his flock, and of trying out, to some extent at least the plan of 1791.

Just before leaving Quebec for the West, Father Burke wrote to his friend, the Archbishop:

My Lord:

Tomorrow, I set out from Quebec with provisions from the Bishop as ample as possible, and with orders from the Governor to all the Officers at the different posts to furnish the necessary conveyances to the Upper Country: *A Domino factum est istud.* Government here is more zealous in the support and extension of the Catholic religion than in any other country on earth; in sound policy they act judiciously; but 't is yet astonishing that a Protestant Government should pay the expenses of sending Catholic Missionaries, and supporting them, not only amongst the Indian Nations, but even amongst the civilized people; yet 't is not more surprising than true. I must request that Your Grace will please to let Cardinal Antonelli know that a more favorable occasion of sending a Missionary to the Upper Country has happened, and the Bishop, in compliance with His Eminence's orders, has immediately appointed your humble servant. Many in the Diocese would have filled the place with greater advantage. I now begin to feel the folly of having desired so great a field: 't was an act of levity. I'm not equal to the task; may God, of His infinite mercy, support me. Many different Nations, whose

---

[51] The passage is an extract from a petition addressed by Father Burke to the "Right Honorable Lord Hobart, one of His Majesty's principal Secretaries of State & &" and dated Halifax, December 19, 1803. See *Mich. Hist. Colls.,* XXV, 212.

languages I don't understand, expect instructions: *Parvuli petierunt panem, et non erat qui frangeret eis.*

The Indians and Americans are at war: a battle was fought about a month ago at the Miamis: the Indians lost 50 Warriors, the American about 300 soldiers. Our Government does not interfere, at least ostensibly. We had some Democrats who made a noise—a most despicable rabble: some few were imprisoned, and that settled the business. . . .[52]

Bearing the title of Vicar-General of Upper Canada and commissioned to exercise a general supervision over church affairs in the Detroit district Father Burke arrived about the end of October, 1794. After a stay of a few days in Detroit he went on to the River Raisin settlement to establish himself there as the first resident pastor. On November 16, the assembled congregation chose St. Anthony of Padua as patron of the parish, and accepted from Joseph Iracque the gift of an eighty acre farm. Later on, wardens were elected, and the traditional parish organization initiated by Father Frechétte in 1788 was completed.[53]

When Father Dufaux, writing from Assumption, reported to the bishop the arrival of Father Burke, with whom he had had a few days' conversation, he expressed his misgivings about what would happen in the new parish. Father Burke might suit the settlement, but the converse could not be true.[54] After three months' residence Father Burke thus described his situation.

Alas, My Lord, how sad is the state of religion in this distant portion of your diocese. On arriving, I found the people of the River Raisin in revolt against M. Fréchette. If they demanded a missionary it was not a Catholic missionary. The emissaries of General Waine put them up to demanding the notorious, or rather the infamous Le Dru, who did a great deal of harm in Detroit.[55] These same scoundrels engaged the

[52] Letter dated Quebec, September 14, 1794. Letter is in the Georgetown University archives, but has been printed in the *Records of the Amer. Cath. Hist. Soc.*, XVIII, 392.

[53] From the original entries by Father Burke in the parish records.

[54] Letter from Father Dufaux to Bishop Hubert, Detroit, November 7, 1794. QCA.

[55] Le Dru is a shadowy figure in the early Catholic history of America. Before 1788 he had been a missionary in Nova Scotia and New Brunswick. In that year he was sent by Bishop Carroll to the Illinois missions. See the *Illinois Cath. Hist. Review*, I, 209, 334. In 1794 he was at Mackinac from May 8 to July 9 signing himself Missionary Apostolic. Father Dufaux's letter just quoted has this passage concerning Le Dru: "M. Ledru remained for some months at Michillimack-inac. He exercised his ministry there without recognition from the government and without any jurisdiction. He wrote me, and as soon as he received my answer he ceased his ministrations. He came on to Detroit where he became known as an out and out republican. He was shipped to Fort Herier (Fort Erie), from there back to Detroit, and from Detroit to Fort Herier; from there he was conducted by four riflemen to Niagara. I think he is now on his way through Oswego to the colonies." Just what Le Dru did in Detroit is unknown to us, and he was certainly gone before Father Burke arrived. Bishop Carroll writing to Bishop Hubert in 1796 thus referred to him. "I do not think that any objections will be raised by the government of the United States regarding the detention of priests laboring in the Detroit missions unless

people to make and sign a convention that they would hold out against civil authority, and would have pushed them a good deal farther if by some mischance I had been delayed a week longer. On the very day of my arrival the men from the lower end of the Parish were to meet at the rectory to fight those of the upper end who were steadfast under the guidance of Captain Reaume, a man of probity whom Your Lordship knows better than I. God gave me the grace to bring back a large number to their duty. . . .

The rectory is not yet completed. I spent my winter half in the open air, without any other servant than the man I brought with me. The upstairs I use for my church whose vestments and sacred vessels are those of my travelling kit. . . .

I must warn Your Lordship that my stay here is not without danger. The Sansculottes of Lower Canada are worthy fellows and saints if compared to the sansculottes of this place.[56] They are a band of outlaws; murder, theft, violence . . . have their center. . . . If anything happens to me I hope that Your Lordship will replace me with a man of firm character; a timid man has no business here unless he wants to make money, and in that case he might succeed. . . .[57]

As everywhere the liquor traffic was a scourge in the settlement. Father Burke had strict orders from Simcoe to do everything in his power to repress it, and from his letters it is evident that despite the enmity incurred in consequence, he did his duty faithfully in this regard. But the ameliorations of moral evils does not seem to have been as important to Father Burke as the other activity for which he had been selected by the government; he was first and foremost a Loyalist clergyman.[58] Hence his letters continue in much the same strain as the first one already quoted, and reveal the real or fancied tribulations which such a course of action brought him.

The blindness of the Canadians is almost incredible. Wayne is making them believe that Frenchmen are going to help him get possession of Detroit, and it is almost impossible for Father Burke to make them see how foolish and preposterous such pretensions are.[59]

---

in the case of Rev. Mr. Burke, whom ill-intentioned persons and especially an apostate Dominican named Le Dru have succeeded in imbuing some of the officers of the American troops posted near Fort Detroit with prejudice against that Priest as the one who endeavored to foment and excite in the hearts of the Indians great animosity against the States. . . ." Letter dated March 2, 1796. QCA.

[56] The Sansculottes, a term originally applied to the mob in the French Revolution, here designates American sympathizers.

[57] Letter to Bishop Hubert, Raisin River, February 2, 1795. QCA.

[58] There is no intention here of blaming Father Burke for his loyalist activities. As a British subject it was within his rights to take the position he did. There is nothing to be gained by questioning how far his zeal in this matter was compatible with his priestly activities. We are concerned merely with the fact that Father Burke played a part, if only a minor one, in the political events of the times.

[59] Letter to (?), River Raisin, February 3, 1795. QCA.

Disloyal scoundrels are insinuating themselves everywhere, trying to sap the allegiance of the Canadians; they are ready to murder anyone who opposes them. He himself dares to sleep only on the floor away from windows.[60] On his frequent journeys he goes about disguised, and always with a bodyguard. He would like to visit Mackinac and St. Joseph, but fears for his safety.[61]

We catch an interesting glimpse of the cross currents of intrigue that seethed around Detroit in the period from 1794 to 1796 in a letter from Father Burke to Colonel McKee, the head of the Indian Department at Detroit.

My dear Sir:

Notwithstanding all the exertions of Wayne's Emissaries & his numerous adherents in and about Detroit, he has not been able as yet to assemble any Indians except some young fellows who have been dragged by Sans Crainte, Pepin, Williams, McDougal & La Chambre; Francois Navarre is indefatigable in the service, the Ottawas have sent four young fellows, no chief, the Wyandots have sent nobody, I cant learn that the Poutawatamies or Chipawas have sent a chief, thay all wait the orders of their Father.

I wrote a second letter to the Poutawatamies of St. Joseph's, it fell into the hands of Sans Crainte & Pepin, and they joined to my letter a certificate of which I send you a copy. You'll see the Moderate terms in which these fellows speak of Government, you and your humble servant. My letter was Cautiously drawn up, Contained no political matter. I have sent the original to Lieut. Governor Simcoe & a Copy to you for his Lordship's inspection, 'twill prove to them the necessity of Curbing these fellows before they find means of turning the Tomahawk against us. Macomb is to us an absolute pest he torments the Indians more than any other man. McDougall has been disappointed in bringing the Yankees to Sandusky. Wayne was near being taken in a trap, however he artfully evaded it. If the men were sent at all they did not come near Sandusky, a Delaware came in with the Alarm whoop, the Indians were in a state of intoxication, yet instead of receiving the Yankees in a friendly manner as was expected. they armed to a man and prepared for battle. I believe Wayne will not make a second experiment. Francois Navarre expects to bring a Detachment to the River Raisin, that peasant's impudence deprives me of all patience. Johnie Askin has given Bullocks and Rum for a large tract of land . . .[62]

[60] Letter to (?), River Raisin, February 3, 1795. QCA.
[61] Same to same, October 5, 1795. QCA.
[62] *Mich. Hist. Colls.*, XII, 171. The letter is dated Detroit, June 17. The certificate mentioned is appended and reads thus:

"My comrades, You know that I have always spoken to you as a brother & this time I am incapable of lying to you, he who writes to you is neither a Frenchman nor a Priest but a rascal who has been chosen by the English to deceive you & blind you as McKee has always done. . . ."

A few months before writing this letter Father Burke had himself gone to Sandusky in an attempt to hold the Indians assembled there to British interests. The speech they made in answer to his was not too respectful in tone, and he does not seem to have accomplished more than any of the other Indian agents.[63] In the months following the battle of Fallen Timbers Wayne was able to persuade the confederated tribes who had opposed him to assemble for the signing of a treaty of peace. Conferences began on June 10, 1795, and the Treaty of Greenville was concluded on the 3rd of August. Just as the final negotiations were in progress Wayne received an authenticated copy of Jay's Treaty, wherein the British agreed to evacuate Detroit. The Indians realized that they could no longer count on British support, and that further resistance was useless.[64]

To the pair of staid and conservative priests at Detroit Father Burke's conduct was distasteful and imprudent. Father Fréchette expressed his feeling about it in a letter to his bishop.

> Your Lordship will not take it amiss that I inform you of the following concerning M. Dufaux.
>
> It is a truth too well known that M. Burke, Vicar-General of Upper Canada, since his arrival has evinced in his letters and conversation an unbounded jealousy and rivalry against M. Dufaux. On every occasion the latter has certainly by his conduct merited the esteem and the affection of the public in Detroit in the two parishes; (not that I have any complaint against M. Burke, for I can say that since he is in Detroit he has always shown me the highest regard. He stays with me almost as much as he does at home), but M. Dufaux has to suffer a great deal.
>
> It is a patent fact that M. Burke has brought trouble to our parishes. In his own he has alienated the greater part of his parishioners from their Christian duties by his words, his violent discourses, and by his conduct somewhat too relaxed for this section which you knew before I did.
>
> For the last five or six months he has been acting as commissary in his parish; he distributes at home, or has distributed, provisions and clothing to more than fifteen hundred Indians for the government. He cares little for the Hurons and has done nothing for them, something that has given rise to many complaints. These things are public, and Your Lordship can presume the sad consequences in our present circumstances. . . . Government officials themselves have told me that he would be better off minding his parish affairs than meddling in government business. He wants me to pray from the pulpit for the King and the Governor in the words of a prayer composed by a Scotch bishop, and

---

[63] *Mich. Hist. Colls.*, XX, 392.

[64] See Utley and Cutcheon, *Michigan as a Province, Territory, and State* (Pub. Soc. of Mich., 1906), II, Chap. VII.

which he found in a gazette. M. Montigny refused to translate it as I refused to say it; and I told him that I was not bound to make any un-accustomed prayer without the order of Your Lordship. He has not spoken of it since.

He tried to oblige me to give holy water and the Blessed Bread to M. Jacques Baby in his capacity as Lieutenant of the County; I answered that I was not bound to do so. He has preached a few times in my church, but he uses such violent terms, for instance, "scoundrels, blackguards, monsters," terms that I would never think of using, that many of my parishioners have told me they would not come back to hear themselves treated in like fashion.

Please believe me, My Lord, when I say that I am not complaining against M. Burke. I am only telling what is going on in this locality.[65]

For some months prior to his letter Father Burke had already planned the abandonment of his exposed position at the River Raisin for a more secure retreat at Detroit. When it became evident that Detroit was actually to be surrendered to the Americans, Father Burke decided that he would be in a safer position on the other side of the river. "It is evident to Your Lordship that I cannot remain in a post subject to the Yankees. I do not like them, nor do they like me." [66] He was quite right, for while the negotiations leading to the Treaty of Greenville were in progress, Colonel John Francis Hamtramck, himself a Catholic, had written to General Wayne.

Father Burke continues in his exhortations. He assures the inhabitants that if any of them should be so destitute of every principle of honor and religion as to advise the Indians to come to the Americans, they shall be anathematized. He is now a commissary, and issues corn to the Indians. Mr. Le Chanvre informs me that Burke is going, in the spring, to Michilimackinac. Of consequence we may easily judge his mission. He will, no doubt, try to stop the nations from coming in to the treaty. How would it do to take him prisoner? I think it could be done very easily. . . .[67]

If Father Burke were to be stationed in Assumption parish Father Dufaux would have to be transferred. Despite importunate appeals the bishop refused to consent to this, and in seeming disregard of Father Burke's earlier letters he informed him that Father Fréchette had already received orders to quit St. Anne's for Quebec on the arrival of the Americans, and that he could replace him in Detroit if he wished.[68]

From the fall of 1795 Father Burke's movements are not easy to

[65] Letter to Bishop Hubert, October 23, 1795. QCA. *Memoire,* 126.
[66] Letter to Bishop Hubert, Detroit, May 19, 1795. QCA.
[67] *Mich. Hist. Colls.,* XXXIV, 736.
[68] Letter of Bishop Hubert to Father Burke, December 22, 1795, in *Memoire,* 125.

follow. He seems to have spent more of his time in Detroit than in his parish. His letters speak of contemplated visits to Mackinac and to St. Joseph, but there is no evidence that he actually undertook them. An attempt has been made to show that he did missionary work among the Indians of northern Ohio, and therefore deserves to be considered as the successor of the Jesuit missionaries in that area. He is said to have been stationed near Fort Meigs on the Maumee, a military post erected by the British on American territory, and the authority for the statement is a letter which he wrote to the Archbishop of Dublin, and which is dated February 2, 1796.

Without emphasizing the fact that Fort Meigs was built by the Americans in 1813 we are not disposed to believe that the letter was written in any other spot than the River Raisin settlement. Father Burke writes that he is in a parish on the western side of Lake Erie, a few miles from Fort Miami. His appreciation of his location varies little from the sentiments expressed in his other letters concerning the parish to which he was definitely assigned, and which answers to the geographical position indicated. This is the letter on which the claim is based.

> I wrote from Quebec, if I rightly remember, the day before departure for this country; am now distant about five hundred leagues from it, on the western side of Lake Erie, within a few miles of the Miami fort, lately built by the British government. . . . I'm here in the midst of Indians, all heathens. This day a grand council was held in my house by the Ottawas, Chippewas, and Pottowatomis. These people receive a certain quantity of Indian corn from the government, and I have been appointed to distribute it. That gives me a consequence among them I hope will be useful, as soon as I can speak their language, which is not very difficult.
>
> This is the last and most distant parish inhabited by Catholics on this earth; in it is neither law, justice, nor subjection. You never meet a man, either Indian or Canadian, without a gun in his hand and his knife at his breast. My house is on the banks of a river which falls into the lake, full of fish and fowl of all sorts; the finest climate in the world, and the most fertile lands. . . . Next summer I go on three hundred leagues towards Mackina, or Lake Superior, where there are some Christian Indians. . . .[69]

It is certain that Father Burke did not carry out this good intention. Writing from Detroit on June 7, 1796, he announced to his

[69] Rev. George F. Houck, *A History of Catholicity in Northern Ohio and in the Diocese of Cleveland* (Cleveland, 1903), I, 4–5. Shea in his *Life and Times* . . . , 475–78, is much confused in his account of Father Burke. It is hardly necessary to point out that the American attitude to Father Burke would have made a stay of a year on the Maumee impossible.

bishop that he had just received a rescript from the Holy Father authorizing him to confer the sacrament of Confirmation, providing he had the bishop's consent. He was therefore writing to His Lordship to obtain a supply of Holy Chrism and instructions as to the manner of conferring the sacrament.[70]

While Father Burke was waiting for these necessary instruments of his newly received powers, events took a sudden turn. The order for the evacuation of Detroit was signed at Quebec. American soldiers were watchfully waiting in Ohio for word to take possession. On July 7, 1796, Colonel Hamtramck, then stationed near the present Perrysburg, Ohio, sent a detachment of sixty-five soldiers under the command of Captain Moses Porter to receive the surrender. Exactly at noon on July 11, the British colors were hauled down, and the Stars and Stripes unfurled. From this moment Detroit, and the whole Northwest Territory actually belonged to the American nation.

Father Burke had departed seven days before, having suddenly discovered that he was badly needed by the small English-speaking Catholic groups at Kingston and Niagara. Father Dufaux could not have meant to be uncharitable when he wrote to his bishop:

> Mr. Burke left Detroit for good the day before yesterday. He is regretted neither at River Raisin, nor at St. Anne's, nor at Assumption; and he is regretted by no one save myself who did everything I could to retain him. He is gone; God be praised.[71]

Later on when Father Dufaux had met General Wayne and Colonel Hamtramck in pleasant social intercourse, and the long days of stress and uncertainty were over, he made this final reference to Father Burke:

> The General and all the officers detest Mr. Burke for the horrors that he occasioned through the instrumentality of the Indians while he was in the Indian Department. He did well to leave, and I do not think that it will ever be profitable to him to return to this section. . . .[72]

Thus passed Father Burke out of our history. Although his career in Detroit was rather unfortunate, he was, after all, only following what he conceived to be his duty. Had his sympathies been on the other side there is no telling what niche he might be adorning in our national history. That he was a man of talent and abilities is evident from his further career. Appointed in 1801 by the Bishop of Quebec as Vicar-General of the missions in Nova Scotia, with residence at Halifax, he found himself surrounded by a population more tempera-

[70] Letter of Father Burke to Bishop Hubert, Detroit, June 7, 1786. QCA.
[71] Letter of Father Dufaux to Bishop Hubert, Detroit, July 6, 1796. QCA.
[72] Same to same, September 2, 1796. QCA.

mentally suited to him, and was free from the complications that had
thwarted his efforts in Detroit. In 1816, he was named Vicar-Apostolic of Nova Scotia, and was consecrated at Quebec, July 5, 1818. He
lived only two years in this office, dying at Halifax on November 29,
1820. Although Monroe and Halifax are far apart, they have a common bond in Father Burke, first pastor of the one, and first bishop of
the other.

CHAPTER XIII

American Jurisdiction

THE passing of the Northwest Territory out of British control, marked by the American occupation of Detroit, was bound to effect momentous changes in ecclesiastical jurisdiction.[1] Heretofore, what little church organization, authority, and even government existed in the Territory derived from Quebec. Henceforth, they were to be grafted on a new stock which had been planted in the American nation itself. The old affiliations were to be sundered in a new orientation parallel to the course of our national history. It is desirable, therefore, to acquaint ourselves with the beginnings of the ecclesiastical jurisdiction which, in its successive subdivisions, now spreads over the United States.

Whether there existed a sprinkling of Catholics in the American Colonies prior to the foundation of Lord Baltimore's establishment is a question which has been too little studied to permit a well-founded judgment. Certain it is that the Colonies had been brought to the notice of Roman officials as early as 1625, but this was done more with reference to the possibilities they presented for the establishing of missions for the Indians. In that year Father Simon Stock, an English Carmelite, wrote to the Propaganda Congregation regarding the Puritan emigration to New England. It appears that he himself was thereupon ordered to America to make at least a tour of investigation. Finding it impossible to comply with the order he addressed, in 1626, the following letter to the Propaganda.

> I have sent you the map of America, from which you may see that there is probably a passage to Japan and China through North America, so that it is not necessary to pass through the equinoctial or tropical stream or the temperate zone, what would be a great benefit to the Holy Church and an easy voyage. You may see also that the English heretics possess the best part of North America, namely the one which corresponds to Italy, Spain, Hungary, France, and so forth, lying in the temperate zone; there the pagans are more mild, humane, frank, brave,

---

[1] The Northwest Territory comprised the present states of Michigan, Ohio, Indiana, Illinois, Wisconsin, and about half of Minnesota. See B. A. Hinsdale, *The Old Northwest* (New York, 1888).

agile and accustomed to endurance than the others, and they are pretty nice and well proportioned in their build. They are all white, when they are born, but they become dusky later as a result of not protecting themselves against the rays of the sun and of painting themselves to look more terrible in war. Some men and squaws have been brought over here to England and they are not different from those of Europe, and one of them took part in the last wars of Bohemia. Our Holy Faith is all that is missing to make them like the Italians.

Among the other plantations which the heretical Englishmen have established in North America on the same line, the Polar elevation and latitude of Rome, a town was built upon hills like those of Rome and a fort, where three years ago two ministers or preachers were stationed, but lately some others have gone there to corrupt that tribe by their heresy. On the above mentioned map that town is called Plimouth. Your Most Illustrious Lordships will find that place looking at the latitude of Rome and the longtitude of degree 32. You will see the island of which I have written before and notice, how convenient a place it is to commence the conversion of this part of the world which is as large as that of Europe. . . .

As a result of this and similar correspondence the Church formally extended her jurisdiction to the American Colonies. On November 22, 1630, the Propaganda Congregation resolved that "Catholic missionaries should be sent into that New Land as soon as possible who shall impede the progress of Puritans and minister to the Catholic Settlers, and that, therefore, the Procurator General of the Capuchins be charged to arrange with Father Joseph of Paris that a mission of French and English Capuchins be established in New England under the usual conditions, viz., that the said Pere Joseph is prefect of the mission and must send a list of the names and numbers of the missionaries and report some future time about their progress."

The Capuchin, Father Joseph, chosen as the head of this new Prefecture Apostolic was none other than the famous "Gray Cardinal," the shadow of Richelieu.[2] However, missionary work when actually undertaken by virtue of this authorization was confined to Acadia, and it is still a matter of conjecture whether Capuchins labored in New England.[3]

Four years after this step on the part of Propaganda came the foundation of Lord Baltimore's colony in Maryland. Directed by Leonard Calvert, brother of the Lord Proprietary, the Ark and the Dove

[2] There is a biography in the *Catholic Encyclopedia* under Father Joseph's real name, Leclerc du Tremblay.

[3] See John M. Lenhart, O.M. Cap., "An Important Chapter in American Church History," *Catholic Hist. Rev.*, New Series, VIII, No. 4. Thomas Hughes, S.J., *The History of the Society of Jesus in North America* (Longmans, Green, 1908), I, 181 ff.

sailed from Cowes on November 22, 1633. "On the day of the Annunciation of the Blessed Virgin Mary in the year 1634," says the journal of the voyage, "we celebrated the first Mass on that island; [4] never before had it been offered in that region. After the holy sacrifice, bearing on our shoulders a huge cross, which we had hewn from a tree, we moved in procession to a spot selected, the governor, commissioners and other Catholics, putting their hands first unto it, and erected it as a trophy to Christ our Saviour; then humbly kneeling, we recited with deep emotion, the Litany of the Holy Cross." [5]

Maryland thus became the cradle of Catholicism in the English-speaking colonies, and for a century continued to be the only Catholic center. We need say nothing here of the vicissitudes of the Maryland colony, nor of the sad requital meted out to these English Catholics in return for their adherence to the principles of religious toleration which they were the first to bring to these shores. The record of it makes another dismal chapter in the history of Protestant intolerance.

Under pressure of unbearable conditions in Maryland some of the settlers moved to Pennsylvania, where a greater measure of religious freedom was accorded them. Mass was said openly in Philadelphia in 1707. About thirty years later, in consequence of a considerable German Catholic immigration to Pennsylvania the Commonwealth was dotted here and there with small Catholic settlements. The brutal deportation of the Acadians by the British in 1755 suddenly threw about six thousand Catholics into the colonies from Massachusetts to Georgia. This unlooked for accession was not destined to contribute much to the growth of the American Church. The majority of the Acadians made their escape to regions beyond English control, or were hounded out of the colonies. Hundreds died from want and privations, and of those who remained numbers were lost to the Faith through a deliberate campaign of perversion. Only in Maryland and Pennsylvania could they find priestly ministrations, and the only gain to the Church in the American Colonies resulting from the advent of the Acadians was two small groups, one in Baltimore, the other in Philadelphia. It may fairly be said that as late as the Revolutionary War the Church in the colonies consisted of a handful of Catholics in New York, New Jersey, and Virginia, and about fifteen thousand living in scattered settlements in Maryland and Pennsylvania.

[4] St. Clement's Island in the Potomac River. A few days later the first permanent settlement was begun at St. Mary's. The writer was apparently unaware that more than sixty years before Spanish Jesuits had said Mass, and had been martyred in the same neighborhood. See Shea, *The Cath. Church in Col. Days*, 147-50.

[5] Quoted in Shea, *ibid.*, 41.

The priests chosen to accompany the settlers in the foundation of the Maryland colony were two Jesuits from the English province. As the needs of the colony increased additional members of the Society were sent over, and thus it came about that down to the Revolution the only priests in the American colonies, with but few exceptions, were English Jesuits. In 1641, as a consequence of differences between Lord Baltimore and the Jesuits regarding land holdings, an attempt was made to supplant the Jesuits by the introduction of secular clergy. However, the Society weathered the storm, and the two seculars, who spent some years in Maryland, ended by aligning themselves on the Jesuit side of the controversy.[6] Beginning with 1672 the Jesuits shared their mission field with the English Franciscans, who sent two of their number to Maryland in that year. During the whole course of this endeavor the number of priests sent over from time to time did not exceed ten. The last Franciscan in the Colonies died about 1720.[7]

The Church in the Colonies, for at least the first hundred years of its existence, is seen, therefore, to have been in reality no more than a Jesuit mission. The first priests coming to Maryland obtained their faculties from their Provincial, and the practice continued without the question being raised of whether any other source of authority was to be consulted. In fact, one would be hard put to find any recognized jurisdiction during this period, and in later years even Rome itself professed ignorance as to who really held jurisdiction over the American Colonies.

The reason for the strange status of the Church in America was, of course, the collapse of the hierarchy in England resulting from the era of persecution. No Catholic bishop could subscribe to the Oath of Supremacy exacted by Elizabeth in 1559. The hierarchy dwindled away in exile or in prison, and the last English bishop died in 1580. Cardinal Allen for a few years longer was recognized unofficially at Rome as the representative of the English Catholics, and then from 1598 to 1623 Rome appointed simple clergymen as arch-priests or prefects to manage church affairs in England. The people were thus deprived of the special ministrations which only a bishop could bring them, and their courage and hope waned. In 1623 a bishop was consecrated for England, but he lived only a year. A successor followed immediately, but he was exiled in 1631. After his death in 1655 jurisdiction developed upon an Episcopal Chapter which his predecessor had established, and which he himself had maintained. Its authority, doubtful as it was known to be, was the only one in England for

6 See various references to Fathers Gilmett and Territt in Hughes, *op. cit.*, Vol. I.
7 See references to Franciscans in Hughes, *op. cit.*, Vol. II.

thirty years down to the appointment of John Leyburne as Vicar-Apostolic of all England. In 1688 the country was divided into four vicariates, one of which was the vicariate of London.[8]

In a foregoing chapter we had occasion to refer to the presumptive jurisdiction of the Archbishop of Rouen over New France. Something similar now developed in regard to the American colonies. There was nothing that could be construed as referring to them in the Brief which erected the four vicariates. A Jesuit wrote in 1695:

> When I was sent by my Superior to those missions (Maryland-Pennsylvania), there were not as yet any Catholic English Bishops. Afterwards, four such were created under the Catholic king, James. But to which one of them the aforesaid countries (the American Continent and the West Indies) are subject, I do not know. At all events, when I was in those missions, there was no vicar-apostolic there; but all the missionaries depended upon their regular superiors alone.[9]

Without any one troubling very much to account for it the presumption gradually arose that the colonies were subject to the vicariate of London. In 1714 a Maryland missionary wrote to his superior regarding some difficulties in applying the canonical marriage laws, and the matter was finally brought to the attention of Propaganda by the Rector of the English College in Rome. The solution of the problem evidently called for the intervention of some episcopal authority, for the Maryland Provincial suddenly found himself in a quandary when confronted with the issue thus definitely raised. He wrote: "It will be hard to find under which Vicar-Apostolic Maryland is. London too far. Quebec are foreigners." [10] Some years later Bishop Giffard, the Vicar-Apostolic of London, although he made no positive claims regarding the colonies, nevertheless conferred on the Jesuits certain favors and privileges which they complacently accepted.[11] Out of this pleasant intercourse, which the bishop's successors continued, grew the supposition that the London vicariate had a measure of jurisdiction over the American missions, a supposition which had not the slightest canonical foundation.

In 1753 the Roman authorities decided to settle the question of jurisdiction over the colonies. Some of the pertinent documents reveal a curious state of affairs. When Challoner, then coadjutor to Bishop Petre the Vicar-Apostolic of London, and destined to succeed

---

[8] The question is treated at length by Peter Guilday. *op. cit.,* Chap. X.

[9] *Ibid.,* 139.

[10] Hughes, *op. cit.,* II, 587.

[11] Bishop Giffard's relations with the Jesuits began in 1721. Two years later he did state that Maryland was "part of and belonging to the London District." Guilday, *op. cit.,* 140.

him in 1758, was asked to justify the claims of the London vicariate he answered:

> All our settlements in America have been deemed subject in spirituals to the ecclesiastical Superiors here, and this has been time out of mind, even, I believe, from the time of the Archpriests. I know not the origin of this, nor have ever met with the original grant. I suppose they were looked upon as appurtenances or appendixes of the English Mission. . . . Whether the Holy See has ordered anything in this regard, I cannot learn. . . .[12]

The Propaganda Congregation after a diligent search of its own archives was obliged to report:

> No document is found in these archives to show that the charge of despatching missionaries to the islands or mainland of America was ever invested in the Archpriests of England prior to the foundation of this Sacred Congregation; nor again in the Vicars-Apostolic who were appointed for that kingdom after the said date; nor that any superintendence over the missionaries or the missions was ever committed to them. . . .[13]

The investigation resulted in the formal grant of jurisdiction over the colonies to the London vicariate for renewable periods of six years. However, long before its putative authority was thus solidated the London vicariate had endeavored to rid itself of the burden imposed by the care of the American colonies. It was in the course of clearing the ground for the appointment of a vicar-apostolic for America, a proposal set forth by Dr. Challoner, that the foregoing decision was rendered. Shortly after it became operative new complications ensued. Canada passed under British rule, its bishop died, and the conquerors showed little inclination to permit any one to replace him. The British colonies now extended from Florida to Newfoundland. Was this whole extent of territory to be administered by the London vicariate? When the question was submitted to Rome its gravity was so apparent that no hurried decision was possible. The problem was simplified to some extent by the appointment of Bishop Briand to the see of Quebec in 1766. Rome might then have proceeded to provide for the American colonies had not opposition arisen from an unforeseen quarter.

The colonies, for some years back, had been in the throes of a most violent anti-Catholic agitation. In Maryland particularly, a group of prominent Catholics had contemplated the advisability of emigrating into French territory, and Charles Carroll actually began negotia-

[12] *Ibid.,* 144.
[13] *Ibid.,* 145.

tions with the French court for a grant of land on the Arkansas River.[14] Driven to extremities by fanatical hatred, their priests proscribed, their property crushed by taxation, the Catholics felt that the appointment of a bishop for them would be an overwhelming calamity. With mens' passions at white heat it was no time to appear to flaunt the growth or prestige of the Catholic Church. Two hundred and fifty-nine leading Catholics of Maryland signed a remonstrance against the appointment of a vicar-apostolic. Their position is made plain in the following extracts:

1. The legislative power of this colony is so disposed with regard to those of our persuasion, as to have made many attempts of late years to put the most pernicious penal laws in force against us, and are still, every convention aiming more or less at something of yt kind. Would not the presence of An Apostl. Vicar afford a new and strong argument for further deliberations on this head?

2. Amongst the sundry motives alledged for putting the penal laws in force, one of the most urged was the too public exercise of our Divine worship, in so much that one of the gentlemen was obliged to quit the colony to avoid being summoned for a fact of this kind. Would not the functions of an Apostl. Vicar be deemed a more public, & open profession thereof than anything of that kind that could have been hitherto?

3. The Genln. have no farther liberty for exercising their priestly functions yn a private family, & that by a particular grant of Queen Ann suspending during the Royal pleasure ye execution of an act of Assembly, by wch. it was made high treason for any Priest to reside in the colony, wch, act still subsists, & will of course take place whenever the above grant is repeald. Would the functions of an Apostl. Vicar be interpreted functions of a Priest in a private family?

4. Neither this province, nor indeed any one of the British American colonys has ever hitherto had one of that Ecclesiastical rank & dignity. Would not our setting the 1st. example of yt kind appear very bold & presuming, if not also even dareing and insulting? Reflecting on these reasons amongst several others we cannot but judge the above of sending us an Apostl. Vicar in the present situation of affairs would necessarily draw after it the utter destruction & extirpation of our H. religion out of this colony, & consequently compel us to either forfeit a great part of our estates & fortunes in order to retreat to another country, or utterly give up the exercise of our H. religion. . . .[15]

The remonstrance doubtless had its effect, for the matter remained in abeyance. Later, Bishop Challoner interested Rome in the possi-

[14] Guilday, *op. cit.*, 153. For details of the persecution in Maryland consult Hughes, *op. cit.*, II, 529–50.

[15] The Remonstrance was dated July 16, 1765, and was addressed to the English Jesuit Provincial. It is quoted entire in Guilday, *op. cit.*, 154–55.

bility of having the Bishop of Quebec visit the colonies to administer Confirmation, and to regulate ecclesiastical affairs. When Bishop Briand was ready to accept the mission in 1772, he was dissuaded from doing so by the Jesuit Father Farmer, then residing in Philadelphia, on the same grounds as those set forth in the remonstrance. In the following year the Society of Jesus was suppressed; two years later came the Revolution; and in the tangled uncertainties of those trying days there was nothing to do but wait.

The Revolution, the struggle in a common cause, welded the diverse elements in the colonies as nothing else could have done. Catholics fought side by side with those of other faiths, and were often placed in positions of honor and trust. The French alliance, the friendly interest of Spain, the help given by Father Gibault in the West, all these contributed to a new. respect and tolerance for what had hitherto been a despised and downtrodden element in the colonies. A symbol of the changed order of things was the attendance at Mass, in Philadelphia, of George Washington and the members of the Continental Congress on the third anniversary of the Declaration of Independence. Despite the disabilities that were to linger in the codes of several States for years to come, it was evident to the leaders of the time that religious equality was to be written in the fundamental law of the nation.

One of these leaders was John Carroll. No man was better fitted than he to initiate a new era of the Church in America. A native of Maryland, and a member of a cultured and distinguished family, his natural abilities had been developed by years of study in European schools.[16] After his preliminary years at the famous college of St. Omer, in France, he had become a Jesuit novice in 1753, had been ordained in 1769, and had made his profession three years later. He had lived in an atmosphere wherein he could not help familiarizing himself with the political thoughts and movements of his time. He had traveled, and had been in close contact with persons of social distinction. On the suppression of the Society he had refused a position of ease in England in order to return to America from which he had been absent for twenty-six years. He arrived in 1774, a man of forty, an amiable and cultured priest, but one who had signed away his inheritance on his entrance into the Society, and who was now faced with a precarious existence.

Father Carroll was at heart a patriot, and the outcome of the Rev-

[16] John Carroll was born at Upper Marlborough, Maryland, January 8, 1735. Since the colonies lacked suitable schools for Catholic youth, parents who could afford to do so sent their sons to Europe. John Carroll began his studies at the Jesuit college of St. Omer in 1748. He entered the novitiate at Watten, a few miles distant, in 1753, made his philosophy at Liege, taught for a while at Bruges, and was ordained in 1769.

olution convinced him that the Church in America could no longer remain the appanage of a foreign jurisdiction. His brother priests had been willing to continue recognizing as their local superior a vicar-general chosen by the London vicariate. Father Carroll refused to do so, and for his action he was cut off from sharing in the revenues derived from the Jesuit estates.

Alone among his brethren Father Carroll seems to have had the breadth of outlook to survey the distressing conditions of the times, and to have foreseen the possibilities opening up before the Church. Around him he saw nothing but inaction and stagnation. The Jesuits in the Maryland-Pennsylvania missions, crushed by the blow that had fallen upon them, went about their priestly work in a listless routine. As Father Carroll himself wrote:

> The clergymen here continue to live in the old form. It is the effect of habit, and if they could promise themselves immortality it would be well enough. But I regret that indolence prevents any form of administration being adopted which might tend to secure to posterity a succession of Catholick clergymen, and secure to these a comfortable subsistence. . . .[17]

To the betterment of these conditions Father Carroll now devoted himself. His Plan of Organization was brought forth in 1782. Speaking of it he outlined its purpose thus:

> We are endeavoring to establish some regulations tending to perpetuate a succession of laborers in this vineyard, to preserve their morals, to prevent idleness, and to secure an equitable and frugal administration of our temporals. An immense field is opened to the zeal of apostolical men. Universal toleration throughout this immense country, and innumerable R. Catholics going and ready to go into the new regions bordering on the Mississippi, perhaps the finest in the world, and impatiently clamorous for clergymen to attend them. . . .[18]

The body of the clergy was now moved to action. They met in 1783 to discuss the details of Father Carroll's plan, and at the same time drew up a petition to the Holy See to have one of their number invested with episcopal dignity, and constituted head of the Church in the United States. At a meeting held the following year to perfect their organization the clergy received formal notice that Father Carroll had been named Prefect Apostolic. Something had been gained, but it was still inadequate. Succeeding years proved clearly the absolute necessity of a superior vested with the plenitude of episcopal jurisdiction. By a Brief issued November 6, 1789, John Carroll was

---

[17] Hughes, *op. cit.*, Part Second (Documents), I, 609.
[18] *Ibid.*, 615.

appointed Bishop of Baltimore with authority over all Catholics in the United States. He was consecrated in England, at Lulworth Castle in Dorsetshire, on August 15, 1790, and in the following December he arrived in Baltimore to take possession of his see.[19]

The newly erected Diocese of Baltimore was as coextensive as the new Republic. With the exception of the East and West Floridas, which after their return to Spain remained in her possession until 1819, it extended from the Atlantic to the Mississippi, and northward to the Canadian boundary of 1783. Within this vast territory there were approximately fifty thousand Catholics, and from thirty-five to forty priests.

The extent of Bishop Carroll's jurisdiction was in reality no greater than it had been under his Prefecture. His first contact with the Diocese of Quebec was concerned with the Illinois country won for the Republic by George Rogers Clark. In 1786 Father Carroll sent as his vicar-general to the missions along the Mississippi Father Huet de la Valinière, a Sulpician who had been ejected from Canada on account of his pro-American sympathies.[20] To Father Gibault this was an unintelligible invasion of his authority, and he complained to Father Carroll that he was the only rightful vicar-general, having held that position for nineteen years under the Bishop of Quebec. In his quandary Father Carroll submitted the matter to Bishop Hubert.

> My Lord: I find myself compelled to ask your Lordship for some light upon a rather delicate matter, and this necessity at the same time gives me an opportunity to assure you of the esteem I entertain for your character and episcopal virtues.
>
> Encouraged by the favorable recommendations with which M. Huet de la Valinière was supplied by his ecclesiastical superiors in Canada, I gladly accepted his offer to go to the Illinois, and have appointed him my vicar general there. Since he left, I have received letters written at Post Vincent (Vincennes) by another priest named Gibeau, who tells me that for nineteen years he himself has been vicar general in that section of the bishops of Canada. It is about this matter, my Lord, I wish to be informed, and upon which I presume to ask you to throw some light; especially since reports have reached me concerning M. Gibeau's conduct which are very unfavorable to him.
>
> I learnt some time ago that your Lordship was dissatisfied with me because I meddled in the ecclesiastical government of the Illinois country. I did so because I thought it was included in my jurisdiction, and I had no idea that your Lordship extended your pastoral care to that region. No motive of ambition actuated me; and if you propose to pro-

[19] This is, of course, the barest outline of the development. For the story of the interesting complications which attended it see Guilday, *op. cit.*

[20] For Father de la Valinière's activities in the neighborhood of St. Louis see Rev. John Rothensteiner, *History of the Archdiocese of St. Louis* (St. Louis, 1928), I, 161–64.

vide for the spiritual needs there, you will save me from great embarrassment and relieve my conscience of a burden which weighs heavily upon it. In such an event, my only anxiety would be that probably the United States will not allow the exercise of power, even of a spiritual nature, to a subject of Great Britain. . . .[21]

The bishop's answer, although not decisive, was entirely in accord with Father Carroll's views.

It is true that they (the missions) are incontestably in the diocese of Quebec according to our original grant, and also that the Seminary of Quebec for that reason long had the right to nominate a superior among the Tamarois, a prerogative which the said seminary resigned only in favor of the Bishop of Quebec. Be that as it may, I believe it is prudent for us under the circumstances to accommodate ourselves to the new order of things, although I be not at liberty to assent to the dismemberment of this part of my diocese without the consent of my coadjutor and of my clergy. Divine Providence having permitted that the Illinois, etc., should have fallen into the power of the United States, the spiritual charge of which is confided to your care, I urgently beseech you to continue in the meantime to provide for these missions, as it would be difficult for me to supply them myself without perhaps giving some offense to the British Government. . . .

True it is that Mr. Gibeau was nominated twenty years ago as vicar general for the Illinois country. But since that time the episcopal see of Quebec has twice changed its incumbent without his faculties having been renewed. Complaints of various kinds, especially a suspicion of treason towards the government, caused my predecessors to entertain some antipathy towards him, so much that I propose to give him no employment in the future. . . .[22]

While Father Carroll thus continued to administer the Illinois country, the problem of jurisdiction there was submitted to the Propaganda Congregation. Its decision was announced on January 29, 1791.

All the faithful living in communion with the Catholic Church, both ecclesiastics and lay persons, whether they dwell in the provinces of federated America or in the neighboring regions outside the provinces, so long as they are subject to the government of the Republic, even though they belonged heretofore to some other diocese, will be and shall be hereafter under the jurisdiction of the Bishop of Baltimore, nothing to the contrary availing. . . .[23]

[21] Letter of Father Carroll to Bishop Hubert, May 5, 1788, quoted in the *Records of the American Cath. Hist. Soc.* (Philadelphia), XVIII, 155–56.

[22] *Ibid.,* 157..

[23] *Ibid.,* 162. This decree abolished as well the jurisdiction which the Bishop of Havana was still exercising over Natchez.

It would have been almost impossible for Bishop Carroll to provide for this new territory, now his indubitable responsibility, had not the Sulpicians made their providential appearance in the United States. From the time that he had been placed in a position of authority, the head of the American Church had realized that to promote further progress two things were indispensable, a Catholic college, and a seminary. The first he had been able to accomplish by the founding of Georgetown College, which opened its doors in 1791.[24] The second project, which had so long seemed beyond possibility, was destined to be realized in the same year. As Guilday writes: "There are indeed few events in the history of the Church in this country which show more plainly the hand of God."[25]

In a foregoing chapter the beginnings of the Society of St. Sulpice were alluded to. Its saintly founder, first influenced by a desire to contribute a new body of missionaries to the evangelization of the Indians, had ended by founding a Society whose sole purpose was to be the training of candidates for the secular priesthood. The Society became a group of retiring and conscientious scholars, who in time directed sixteen seminaries in France, and stamped their virtues on thousands of priests.

When the bishop-elect of Baltimore, early in the summer of 1790, sailed to England to be consecrated, France was on the verge of the Revolution and the Terror. The Sulpician superior, Father Emery, was only too well aware of the storm that was soon to break upon the Church, and he was casting about for some haven of refuge. Just then, the Papal Nuncio at Paris informed him that Bishop Carroll was in England, and that he was deeply concerned with the immediate necessity of a seminary in America. Here was an unexpected opportunity. A delegate was sent to London to interview Bishop Carroll, and a few days later the Bishop reported to the Propaganda Congregation the outcome of the meeting.

> These past few days, at the request of the illustrious Nuncio, there came from Paris the learned and worthy priest, Father Nagot, the Superior of the Seminary of St. Sulpice; with whom, after our conference, I decided to establish the episcopal Seminary of Baltimore. Certainly this is a wonderful mark of divine providence in our regard, that such excellent priests should be incited to confer upon us such valuable assistance. . . .[26]

Through the generosity of the Sulpician superior all financial impediments were cleared away, and on July 10, 1791, the first band of

[24] Georgetown College, although to a large extent made possible by the generosity of the Jesuits, was not under their ownership or direction until 1806.
[25] *Op. cit.*, 466.
[26] Quoted in Guilday, *op. cit.*, 467.

Sulpicians, Fathers Nagot, Levadoux, Garnier, and Tessier arrived in Baltimore. Five seminarians accompanied them, and on October 3 the regular work of the seminary was begun. In March, 1792, came Fathers David, Flaget, and Chicoisneau, and in June of the same year Fathers Maréchal, Richard, Matignon, and Ciquard.[27]

The seminary begun in America with such high hopes came to the very brink of failure. Ten years later, when affairs in France had mended somewhat, the Paris superior was on the point of recalling his priests, and it was only by the personal intervention of Pius VII that they were allowed to remain in America. The reason for this contemplated withdrawal was very simple; there were no students to be taught. The Church in America had not yet arrived at the stage where it could furnish enough vocations to make the Sulpician effort worth while. In view of the special purpose of the Society, its priests could be used to better advantage in France, where the Revolution had made inroads into its ranks.

But the failure of the seminary during those early years proved to be of inestimable value to the Church in the United States. With no outlet for their teaching abilities these learned, highly trained, and pious priests were at the disposal of Bishop Carroll at a time when priests were sorely needed, and with the consent of their superior many of them were assigned to the ordinary duties of the secular priesthood. Thus it came about that when Bishop Carroll had been fully assured of his jurisdiction over the Illinois country he had competent, efficient priests to send there. In June, 1792, Fathers Levadoux and Flaget set out for the West, the first assigned to Cahokia, with the faculties of vicar-general, and the second to Vincennes. Three months later, Father Gabriel Richard started westward to assist Father Levadoux, and took up his residence in Kaskaskia.[28]

The two Sulpicians were close friends, united in the spirit of their Society, and looking to each other for comfort in this strange, unsheltered life in which they found themselves. They were together for four years ministering to the French settlements on the eastern side of the Mississippi namely, Kaskaskia, Cahokia, and Prairie du Rocher.[29] They both had a hand in building a church at Cahokia, which is still standing as a monument to their zeal.[30] But there is lit-

---

[27] A useful although quite inadequate history of the Sulpicians in America is Charles G. Hebermann, *The Sulpicians in the United States* (New York, 1916).

[28] Shea, *Life and Times* . . . , 407.

[29] Father Richard begins to sign the Kaskaskia register on February 17, 1793, as "pretre curé de la paroisse." On May 1, 1793, he signs the Prairie du Rocher register as "Pretre curé de St. Joseph." The original registers are in the archives of the St. Louis University.

[30] Rothensteiner, *op. cit.*, Chap. X. A description of the church and a photograph will be found in the *Ill. Cath. Hist. Rev.*, I, 459.

tle else than their entries in the respective parish registers from which we may reconstruct these first missionary years.

Meanwhile, far to the northeast of them, the British flag was still flying, and Father Fréchette sat in judgment with Father Dufaux over the strange proceedings of Father Burke. Although the Bishop of Quebec in answer to Father Carroll's first letter had recognized the latter's jurisdiction over the Illinois country, he was not ready to do so regarding Detroit. He had written: "As for Detroit, I shall continue to send missionaries there as heretofore." [31] But now, the American advance as outlined in the preceding chapter was to have its effect on the Church in Michigan and the Northwest Territory. On January 14, 1796, the Bishop of Quebec dispatched to Baltimore this significant letter.

> Monseigneur Carroll,
> Bishop of Baltimore.
> My Lord: According to the treaty which has been concluded between the United States of America and Great Britain, the missions of Upper Canada are to be restored and will in consequence become a portion of the Baltimore diocese. The city of Detroit and its outskirts form a large enough parish of Catholics to deserve to have a resident priest. The one who has had charge of it for nearly ten years is a Canadian named Mr. Fréchette, and he has asked me to bring him here,[32] I could not refuse him this favor after his long and edifying services. Raisin River, now in charge of Mr. Burke, my vicar general, will also be transferred to your jurisdiction; and as Mr. Burke has for several years past manifested a desire to serve under your Lordship, I give him the liberty of changing his diocese, either by retaining his present mission or by occupying any other place to which you find it suitable to assign him. I have notified him of my intentions; now it is an affair to be arranged between him and your Lordship. If he prefer to remain in my diocese, he will be stationed at Kingston or Kenty Bay. . . .[33]

We have already seen why Father Burke did not care to accept the pastorate of Detroit. Faced with the necessity of filling such an important post, Bishop Carroll, writing on March 30, 1796, proposed it to Father Levadoux. However, with his usual kindness the bishop did not insist on acceptance, and asked the Sulpician at least to visit the place so that he could forward first-hand information concerning the new missions about to come under the bishop's jurisdiction.

The touching friendship of the two Sulpicians on the Mississippi

---

[31] *Records of the Amer. Cath. Hist. Soc.,* XVIII, 158.

[32] Father Fréchette left Detroit to return to Quebec on July 6, 1796, two days after Father Burke's departure. St. Anne's was thus without a pastor until the arrival of Father Levadoux.

[33] *Records of the Amer. Cath. Hist. Soc.,* XVIII, 172.

is evident from Father Levadoux's answer. He is going to write plainly, like a son to his father. He can see how useful to the bishop is the proposed tour of inspection, and he is ready to make it. But, as for remaining in Detroit, he wishes that the bishop would not ask it, and his first objection is that such a step would separate him from Father Richard. They have both pondered the bishop's letter, and they both sign this answer.[34]

The outcome was that Father Levadoux did set out for Detroit, and the following letter to the bishop is the interesting recital of his journey.

My Lord: I am profiting by the first opportunity to inform you of my arrival in this post. As I wrote you I left Cahokia on June 15. On the 24th, I arrived at pey-houryas [Peoria], a little village about 100 leagues from the Illinois, and on the river of the same name. The village consists of about eighteen to twenty French families, all very poor. I remained there three days, said Mass every day, and preached the word of God. I heard a number of confessions, performed some marriages, and administered baptism to several children. Continuing my journey I arrived on the shore of Lake Michigan, at a village named chicagou [Chicago]. My stay there lasted a day and a half, but during it I was visited by a great Indian chief, and a large number of his warriors. On July 6, I set out to cross the lake, a trip lasting sixteen days. It was a most painful experience, and it would take me too long to narrate what I suffered during it. Finally, I reached michilimakinac. It is a fort where the English have always kept a strong garrison, and is the centre of all the trade in the northwest, or, as the inhabitants call it, the upper country. At the time of my arrival there were two to three thousand persons engaged in the trading. It is also the great Indian center, and the Kings of France had always maintained there a mission of the Jesuit Fathers, whose memory is still held in benediction.

I cannot tell you how gladly I was welcomed in that post. Everybody, Englishman, Frenchman, and Indian, all tried to surpass themselves in expressing the joy my coming gave them. Major Day, commanding for the King, loaded me with attentions, as did all the traders. I remained there for three weeks, and I assure you that I have never exercised my ministry with more consolation. It is absolutely necessary for the good of religion that a missionary be stationed there. The Indians are to demand it from the Governor, who is there at this writing. When he returns I shall take up the matter with him, and will inform you of my observations.

I reached here Detroit on August 14, some time after nine o'clock at night. The day before, we were still forty leagues away, and beating against the wind, and I was saddened at the thought of not being able

[34] Letter to Bishop Carroll from Cahokia June 4, 1796. Baltimore Chancery Archives. This source will hereafter be designated BCA.

to say Mass on the feast of the Assumption. But God heard my prayer, the wind changed during the night, and we arrived sooner than we expected. Early in the morning I had my presence announced by the ringing of the bells, and it gave joy to every one. Then I called upon the Colonel in command, who is a Canadian and a Catholic, and whom I had met at the post he was commanding in the time of Mr. Flaget.[35] He received me with much civility, and I begged him to introduce me to General Wayne, who had arrived the preceding evening. When he hastened to do so, the General received me honorably, expressed his pleasure that I was to minister at the post, and his satisfaction with you for having thought to send me. I took the liberty of telling him that on that very evening after vespers, I and my parishioners would sing a solemn Te Deum in thanksgiving for our union with a free people, and at the same time would pray heaven to preserve the hero who so wisely presides over the United States, and who by his victories has delivered us from the fury of a barbarous people. He thanked me very civilly. I thought, my Lord, that you would approve of this action on my part. It has been well received by all my people.

The town of Detroit itself is not very much. English traders form practically the entire population. But the shores of the river are inhabited for twelve leagues on both sides making this parish extremely difficult to care for. I have already partially covered it. The River Raisin is a new establishment on both sides of the river of this name, which empties into Lake Erie. The nearest of its settlers are at least fourteen leagues from Detroit. There are about 110 families, nearly all farmers. They came to bring me there, and gave me a very kind reception. A plot of 120 acres has been set aside for the use of the priest on which they have built a pretty rectory whose upper story serves as a church. They have already written you concerning their ardent desire to have a priest sent them.

The letter goes on with various details referring to the temporalities of the River Raisin parish, and of the church in Detroit. Then Father Levadoux announces his decision.

I see that I cannot return to the Illinois. I hope that my letter reaches you early enough to enable you to replace me before winter. If you could only replace Mr. Richard so that he would be free to join me! I need his help badly. . . . The people here are better instructed and much more religious than in the Illinois country. I can not but praise their piety and good manners. I do not dare give them to hope that they shall have the pleasure of seeing you. For them, as for their pastor, that would be the height of happiness. They have charged me to convey to you their gratitude for having been provided with a pastor. Please, my Lord, accept mine for all the kindness you have shown me, and believe

---

[35] The reference is to Colonel John Francis Hamtramck.

that it will last as long as the life of him who is with most profound
respect, of your Lordship, the most obedient servant.

Levadoux.[36]

Thus with the joyful ringing of bells, and the mutual expression
of respect and good will between representatives of government and
church, the new era was ushered in. One hundred and twenty-six
years before, the Sulpician, Dollier de Casson, had seen Detroit only
as an Indian sanctuary in the primeval wilderness. He could never
have foreseen that one day a confrere of his would rule here a well-
established parish under a government that had not yet been born.

Father Michael Levadoux, the first priest assigned to Detroit by
an American bishop, was born at Clermont, in the diocese of Limoges, April 1, 1746. He joined the Society of Saint-Sulpice in Paris,
and in 1774 was sent to Limoges as director of the seminary. Chosen
by Father Emery for the Baltimore foundation, he acted as bursar for
the struggling institution until his appointment to the Illinois mission.[37] It is regrettable that we know so little concerning him, but we
have, at least, the satisfaction of seeing him through the eyes of Father Dufaux, who must have subjected this stranger to close scrutiny.

I profit by this opportunity to inform your Lordship that the Bishop
of Baltimore has provided a pastor for Ste Anne of Detroit. He has
sent as his vicar-general Mr. Levadou, a Sulpician, who for the last
three years and a half has been serving in the Illinois country. He is
a dignified, and a worthy little man, 50 years old. He seems very much
attached and devoted to the American government, and to his bishop—
as I am to mine. We hear each other's confessions in all confidence. As
good confreres, we hope to live in harmony even though we belong to
different dioceses, and observe their proper ceremonies and customs.
He appeared surprised that in this section we abstained during Lent,
and on Saturdays. I assured him that this year two thirds of my parish
had observed Lent perfectly. There are differences also in the matter of
feasts and their solemnization. Over on his side, *Domine, salvum fac
regem,* is no longer the prayer. It is now, *Domine, salvum fac populum.*
. . . There are no more fees for dispensations. They are granted gratis,
if he so desires. In his diocese, persons may be married at any hour, and
confessions are heard even in the houses. Priests, and even bishops, dress
as laymen. However, he has not as yet changed any of our usages save
that on the day following his arrival, Assumption day, he sang a high
Mass, and at Vespers a solemn *Te Deum* in thanksgiving for the entry
of General Wayne, and for the delivery of the posts. After this came

[36] In BCA.
[37] These details are taken from manuscript notes on several Sulpicians written by a
confrere, Philpin la Riviere, and preserved in the archives of St. Mary's Seminary, Baltimore.

benediction of the Blessed Sacrament, which he imparted by chanting, and making the sign of the cross three times, as a bishop does. . . .[38]

We have seen how Father Levadoux paid his respects to the military authorities. Father Dufaux was no whit behind his neighbor in expressing the general good feeling, and he writes an amusing passage describing his relations with the Americans. He had called on Colonel Hamtramck as soon as he was settled, but had found him absent. The Colonel, on being apprised of the priest's visit, went to Sandwich accompanied by several officers to return it. When General Wayne made his appearance, both priests went to greet him, and received an invitation to dinner.

> We accepted the honor of his invitation. After the meal, as is the custom, the General began to call out the toasts. He then placed me on his right, and asked me to propose one. I immediately responded thus: May we all live together in peace, and then together we all downed a bumper. After this I arose, and announced myself the humble servant of the General and his company. . . . All this passed off very respectably. . . .[39]

Unfortunately, Father Dufaux was not destined to enjoy for long the cordial relations so happily begun. Nine days later, on September 9, he died in the arms of Father Levadoux, leaving behind a reputation for kindliness, and holiness of life. It is evident that Father Levadoux felt his loss keenly, and deplored the isolation in which he was left. Reporting Father Dufaux's death to Bishop Hubert, he begged for an immediate successor.[40] But mails were slow, and travel difficult, and it was not until Christmas night that Jean-Baptiste Marchand, likewise a Sulpician, made his appearance in Assumption parish.[41] By virtue of faculties he had received, on his arrival, from Father Dufaux, Father Levadoux had been privileged to extend his ministrations to the members of the Sandwich parish, and the death of its pastor had placed a heavy burden upon him.[42]

The pastor of St. Anne's had plenty to do on his own side of the river. His people were strung up and down its shore for miles, and small groups were already pushing northward a considerable dis-

---

[38] Letter to Bishop Hubert, Detroit, September 2, 1796. QCA.

[39] *Ibid.*

[40] Letter to Bishop Hubert, September 15, 1796. QCA.

[41] Letter of Father Marchand to Bishop Hubert, January 31, 1797. QCA. This is the first of an interesting series of letters written by Father Marchand, which occasionally throw some sidelights on Detroit history. Father Marchand was a Canadian, born at Verchères in 1760. Ordained in 1786, he was principal of the Sulpician college in Montreal until his transfer to Assumption parish.

[42] Down to Bishop Lefevere's time, at least, priests on either side of the river had faculties for the adjoining diocese.

tance. Thus, in 1797, he speaks of going to the St. Clair River to afford the settlers there an opportunity of making their Easter duties.[43] Although he does not mention it, he must have attended the Catholics who had begun to live along the Clinton River. But the largest group, and the one which demanded the most attention, was the Raisin River settlement. The parish records still preserve the minutes of the first meeting presided over by Father Levadoux.

> In the year 1796, August 31, M. Michel Levadoux, vicar-general of his Lordship, the Bishop of Baltimore, and of the entire United States, having called together the parishioners of St. Anthony's at the River Raisin, has propounded to them the following questions: 1. Do they desire to have among them a minister of their faith who would procure them all the spiritual help which the Holy Church grants to her children? 2. What measures can they take to support him in a suitable manner? They agreed: 1. To pay into the hands of three syndics, nominated for that purpose, one twenty-fifth part of all that they shall harvest on their farms, and every individual one cord of wood to be delivered at the pastoral residence. . . . 2. To pay the aforesaid tithe this year whether the priest arrive or not, in order to defray the necessary expenses of the church; the balance to constitute a church fund. Three syndics were then appointed: for the lower side of the River Raisin and Sandy Creek, Mr. Antoine Campeau, acting trustee, unanimously; for the upper side of the River Raisin, Mr. Jean Dussault; for Otter Creek, Mr. Pierre Fourerault. . . . 3. It has been resolved to distribute the blessed bread as a sign of union every Sunday, the bread to be offered by every family in turn, and on holydays of obligation by those who volunteer to give it on such days. . . .

In an abandon of generosity ninety-eight settlers affixed their signatures or their marks to these proceedings. Father Levadoux reported them to his bishop as an earnest of the request for a resident priest, which the trustees themselves had previously forwarded to Baltimore. As a result the trustees received a personal letter from Bishop Carroll, which deserves to be reproduced here as the only extant piece of correspondence linking the Church in Michigan with the first bishop in the United States.

Baltimore, October 19, 1796.

Gentlemen:

The request which you were good enough to address me on May 10, did not reach me until the month of August. I saw in it, with real satisfaction, that you are aware of the inexpressible advantages of the

---

[43] "I have already heard more than 1500 Easter confessions, and I leave tomorrow for Raisin River, and then for the St. Clair river distant 25 leagues from here . . ." Letter to Bishop Carroll, April 24, 1797. BCA.

true religion, and of a ministry of salvation which corresponds to her holiness, and is worthy of her. Conscious of the heavy burden of my pastoral charge, I am comforted at having its weight lessened by the Christian dispositions of those who are the objects of my solicitude. I did not answer your request at once because, having already charged Monsieur Levadoux, my vicar-general in that portion of my diocese, to report to me the condition of the religious establishments in the territory lately ceded to the United States, I decided to wait for his statement. It has just come to hand, and in what relates to you, I find that it confirms the favorable conception I had formed of your dispositions. Consequently I am writing him today to arrange for your being given an excellent priest at present living in the Illinois country; or, if that be impracticable, to advise me as promptly as possible so that I may have one start from here as soon as I have the means to defray the expenses of his journey.

The principles of your religion, your behavior, your industrious habits, and your love of order are to me a real assurance that you will be peaceful citizens, obedient to the laws of the government and the state of which you are a part; and that you will never abuse the liberty in which you participate to make of it a pretext for living without the restraints of religion, or of civil authority.

I prize highly your assurances of respect for your Fathers in the order of salvation, and your good wishes for my well-being. In return, I beg of you to think of me as having for you the most paternal affection, as desiring ardently to see you, and as uniting myself with you before the altar of the Most High, praying him to shower on you, on all Catholics, and on our erring brethren his choicest blessings. I am, Messieurs, with esteem, and I dare say, with gratitude for what you have done for the good of religion,

Your most obedient Sevt. and Father in J. Christ,

J. Bishop of Balt.[re 44]

From the parish records it appears that the settlers made earnest efforts to provide means of support for the priest thus promised them. But Father Levadoux, who continued his occasional visits for two years more, describes them as living in the most abject poverty, and their church as lacking even the most necessary articles for divine worship.

There is little to be gathered from Father Levadoux's letters concerning the details or the extent of his priestly ministrations in Detroit; but there is much about his troubles. As in Father Bocquet's time, the advent of a new element in the parish, in this instance rough and burly pioneers drafted into Wayne's army, had caused an-

[44] The original letter, in French, is preserved in the archives of Marygrove College, Detroit.

other epidemic of mixed marriages, some of which were adulterous as well. In the original French settlements such unions would have entailed social and religious ostracism. Now, in the presence of an alien population in which resided authority and influence, the old sanctions were not so potent. As a result, Father Levadoux was obliged to exclude from his congregation several of his parishioners who had contracted civil marriage even after his arrival in the parish.[45]

There were difficulties of another nature involving the strong Tory sentiment still existing. One of the parish wardens, for some reason or other, signed a declaration to the effect that he was still a British subject. Hearing of it the civil authorities notified Father Levadoux that the warden should be replaced by an American citizen. The warden promised his resignation if it should prove agreeable to the parish assembly convoked to consider it. He had evidently counted on strong support, for, much to his surprise, the resignation was accepted. He immediately recalled it, and Father Levadoux brought his action to the attention of the court. An order was issued that no British subject could hold office in Wayne County. Armed with this order, Father Levadoux called another meeting, which proceeded to the election of a new warden.

. . . Instead of submitting, the very next day he and the English ran from one house to another, and held a meeting in his home wherein they repudiated everything that had been done, and without notifying me or the wardens, put him back in office.

Then the court cited the warden, and two of his abettors, presumably for contempt, and this time the retraction was final.[46]

Father Levadoux himself was the butt of criticism from the element that professed to be offended at the zeal with which he had embraced American ideals. What they hoped to gain is not clear, but nevertheless he was denounced to his confreres at Montreal as a dangerous "sans culotte," and an enemy of royalty. He complained bitterly that for this reason not one of his confreres had written him, and that his friends, even Father Flaget, had deserted him. He was certainly mistaken in his judgment of the attitude taken by the American Sulpicians, but what he believed to be their studied neglect only intensified his own sentiments.

[45] Letter to Bishop Carroll, April 14, 1797. BCA.

[46] This incident is an example of the excitement caused in Detroit by those who wished to retain their British citizenship. No legal provisions had been made for such a status, and the attempt to establish a *modus vivendi* was the source of much agitation. See Burton, *op. cit.,* I, 242. For a study of the period the indispensable work is F. Clever Bald, *Detroit's First American Decade* (Ann Arbor, 1948).

I am a member of the United States. I would be a wretch to abandon their interests to sustain those of a crown whose yoke they have thrown off. I seek to do my duty honorably and conscientiously. . . . My conduct is lawful and approved, I dare flatter myself, by every one not blinded by prejudice. General Wayne honored me with his esteem, as did Colonel Sargent, vice-governor, as long as he was here. Colonel Hamtramck, at present in command, honors me with his friendship, as does Major Rivard, and all the other officers of the post. I have reason to believe that up to the present my conduct has been approved by all my parishioners.[47]

In this connection, Father Levadoux deserves to be remembered for his share in the first patriotic celebration ever held in Detroit. In 1797, as Washington's birthday grew near, the officers and soldiers in the post decided to celebrate the day in a fitting manner. The military features of the program were not deemed sufficient; the day was too solemn to be allowed to pass without religious observance. On Tuesday evening, a committee waited on Father Levadoux asking him to hold a special service on the morrow, at which all the officers could be present. While professing entire willingness to do so, the priest pointed out that if the celebration were deferred to the following Sunday, when his congregation could be present, added solemnity would be given it, and a deep impression made upon his people. To this the officers assented, and the news ran through the parish.

On Sunday, the church was filled to overflowing. To the strains of martial music officers and officials filed into St. Anne's to the places of honor, and the crowd pushed in after them. When Mass was over, Father Levadoux, ascended the pulpit, abashed somewhat perhaps, but strong in the consciousness of the duty before him. He would express not only his own sentiments, but he would endeavor to strengthen the loyalty of his people to the American government. In the traditional style, he went to the Old Testament for his introduction, to the story of Samson smiting the Philistines. As he warmed to his subject the transition grew easy, from Samson to the modern savior of his people, George Washington. In sonorous periods the priest brought out his hero's greatness as a man, his valor as a general, and his wisdom as a statesman. In a final apostrophe he exclaimed:

Pardon, O Great One, the temerity of a stranger who has undertaken to eulogize you. Although born on foreign soil, he is no less an admirer of your virtues. O! that he could implant into the hearts of every one of his hearers the sentiments of admiration and veneration with which his own is filled! O, that he could inspire them with the highest degree

[47] Letter to Bishop Carroll, February 8, 1797. BCA.

of attachment to the government which you have created, and which you have directed to the present with such wisdom and glory!

Then Father Levadoux, flushed by his effort, descended to intone the *Te Deum* in which every one joined. As the congregation filed out, the officers crowded around the preacher to congratulate him, and to beg for a copy of his eulogy which they wished to send to the Secretary of War. But Father Levadoux demurred. His bishop should see it first; nothing could be circulated without his approval. The eulogy went on to Baltimore despite the admission that it was "a very feeble effort," a "mere throwing together on paper of some ideas." If it was just that, the yellowed manuscript bears few traces of corrections or revisions. It is as worthy a testimony as any of the loyalty taught by the Catholic Church at the very beginning of the Republic.[48]

As time went on, Father Levadoux realized that he could not adequately minister to the Detroit district. His letters to Baltimore became more and more insistent on the need of additional priests to share his burden. They should preferably be Sulpicians, because their union in the Society would insure harmony, and help them to bear their common poverty. Always, he desired Father Richard, if he could possibly have him. Bishop Carroll, hard-pressed as he was to satisfy the calls that came from every quarter, could not neglect the representations of his vicar-general in the western country. At one time he was ready to send Father Jean-Louis Cheverus. It is interesting to speculate on what would have been the future, in Detroit, of the priest who became first bishop of Boston, and who died Cardinal Archbishop of Bordeaux.[49] Finally, in 1798, Father Levadoux had the happiness of welcoming to Detroit two Sulpicians, one of whom was his bosom friend, Gabriel Richard.

[48] The eulogy written in Father Levadoux's characteristic microscopic characters fills seven manuscript pages and lies in the BCA. It was edited under the title *Eulogy on George Washington* by Edward B. Ham (Ann Arbor, 1944).

[49] In a letter dated May 27, 1797, Father Levadoux advises Bishop Carroll to use the $200 sent from Detroit to defray the traveling expenses of Father Cheverus, and gives directions for reaching the town. BCA.

CHAPTER XIV

The Fire of 1805

WHILE Father Levadoux was begging Bishop Carroll for reinforcements there were only three priests in the whole Northwest Territory: himself at Detroit, Father Rivet, a secular, at Vincennes, and Father Richard at Prairie du Rocher on the Mississippi. On the western or Spanish side of the river Father Gibault was stationed at New Madrid, Father Maxwell, an Irishman turned Spaniard, was in charge of St. Genevieve; and Dom Didier, the Benedictine who had almost been bishop of the Gallipolis colony, puttered over his fragrant herbs in the little churchyard at St. Louis.[1] In Kentucky, Catholic immigration from Maryland had begun as early as 1774, and Father Stephen Badin spent his days on horseback attending the three or four hundred families scattered through the various settlements.[2]

From his station at Prairie du Rocher Father Richard attended Cahokia and Kaskaskia. Describing his situation he wrote.

As for me I am fairly content with my little village of Prairie du Rocher, although at times there are grave scandals in it. I derive my greatest consolation from 5 or 6 English-speaking families who live from 10 to 15 miles from my place of residence. They are surrounded by other families who are Protestant, but among whom I could doubtless make some converts if I had greater facility in speaking English. A suitable book for this purpose would be the account of Mr. Thayer's conversion, and I beg you to send it to me.[3] You would oblige me as well as these

[1] Rothensteiner, op. cit., I, 212. Following the organization of the Northwest Territory in 1787 came the notorious land-grabbing operations like the Ohio, and Scioto Companies. The Scioto Company sold most of its holdings in Paris, and in 1790 a body of French immigrants of the better class came to America, and settled in the present Gallipolis, Ohio. The colony did not prosper but its breaking up spread through America a superior type of French Catholic. Peter Audrain, the lawyer, and Peter Desnoyer, honorable figures in Detroit history came from the colony. For a good account see Laurence J. Kenny, S.J., "The Gallipolis Colony," Catholic Historical Review, IV, 415 ff. Dom Didier had been proposed as bishop of the colony, but Rome respected the jurisdiction of Bishop Carroll. See Guilday, Life and Times . . . . , 392–406.

[2] For beginnings in Kentucky see V. F. O'Daniel, O.P., The Right Rev. D. Fenwick (Washington, 1920) Chap. IV.

[3] John Thayer was the first American convert from the Protestant ministry. He published an account of his conversion in 1787. See Guilday, op. cit., 420.

English-speaking families if you could send me a book of English hymns set to music.[4]

Kaskaskia gave Father Richard little consolation. He speaks of it as a place where drunkenness and indolence reigned supreme, and where scarcely any one attended Mass on Sunday. A priest, Father Pierre Janin, had tried to live there for a while, but had been supported only by the generosity of a Protestant resident.[5]

At Cahokia there were many fervent Catholics headed by that sterling character, Nicolas Jarrot, with whom Father Richard boarded when in the settlement.[6] But even there we catch a glimpse of the factious, unruly spirits who held lightly their religious obligations. During an absence of Father Richard, a certain Thomas Brady, who could not wait until the priest's return to be married, had the ceremony performed in the church by the magistrate. The following Sunday Father Richard made some appropriate comments on such unheard of conduct, and the parties, smarting under his rebuke, carried a garbled version of his remarks to the magistrate. That same afternoon he was cited to explain his supposed defamatory utterances, and was finally ordered to apologize. Whether he did so or not is uncertain, but Jarrot, reporting the incident to Father Levadoux, wrote: "As he (Father Richard) stays with me, he asked my advice regarding his visit (to the offending parties). I told him that he should not go, and that if he did he would be doing irreparable harm to religion." [7]

The affair was duly reported to Bishop Carroll, who may have judged that Father Richard's prestige had been impaired, and that it would be just as well to send him to Detroit to help Father Levadoux. Two young French priests, the brothers John and Donatien Olivier, had offered their services, and could be sent to the Illinois country, as they actually were. Early in 1798, Father Richard received orders to repair to Detroit. On the way he reported his progress to Bishop Carroll. He had been making earnest efforts to learn English, and the following is a faithful transcript of his letter.

Post Vincennes   20th April   1798

Most Reverend Sir

As I am in way to go to Detroit in pursuance of the orders I received from you, I will send you words from this place. I started from Illinois

[4] Letter to Bishop Carroll from Prairie du Rocher, January 24, 1796. BCA.

[5] Father Janin had come to Kaskaskia in 1795, but was leaving at the time of Richard's writing. He was pastor of St. Louis in 1800. Rothensteiner, *op. cit.*, 213.

[6] For the history of the Jarrots see Margaret E. Babb, *"Transactions of the Illinois State Hist. Society"* for 1924, 78–93.

[7] Letter from Father Levadoux to Bishop Carroll, April 24, 1797, in which he quotes a letter received from Jarrot. BCA.

the 21st of last months and I came here by Ohio and Wabache Rivers. It is of my duty to give you some notice of event that has happened in the performing my mynistry as pastor of the Illinois country. Conformably to your directions I did give the benediction of marriage to tow certain persons, both Catholics which had been married by a justice of the County of Randolf where Kaskaskia is. This same judge (Cownel yohn Edgard is his name) made me some reproaches about it, however very civilly, and said to me he was obliged to write on that subject to the Secretary of the States, alledging that my conduct was contrary to the Laws which should be vane if a second marriage as he said before Catholic priest be necessary. I have explained to him our opinion on the present matter in the better maner I could, and with the most fit politness and the most suitable to the freinship that has allwais existed between him and me. I have distinguished the Sacrament from the contract and moreover the civil contract from the Ecclesiastic contract, so that the civil contract could have all its effects, though at the same time the ecclesiastic contract might be invalid before our church. No more upon that matter.

I found Reverend Mr. Rivet but little better. Since fifteen months he has been almost allwais sick, and I am affraid very much that he will never live long while.

I will set of from this place immediately and I hope to be at Detroit at least in a month. There is already a month I left Prairie du Rocher. The Ohio was rising so much and the wind blewd hard so often, that I could not go fast. Before I may conclude this letter, I must beg you as much earnestly as I can, to provide a good pastor to Prairie du Rocher. It was a little flock but grateful and faithful. I was too much happy with that people, but alas! what do I say? I must resing me entirely to the supreme will of God. I rely on his promises, and I hope he will not cease to assist me and to be my comfort. I beg you the assistance of your prayers, I have never been in a so much need of (them) as I am and I will be in the new poste where you send me. I remain your most obedient and perfectly devoted servant.

Gabriel Richard.[8]

Father Richard reached Detroit on June 3, much to the pleasure of Father Levadoux, who wrote to Bishop Carroll that the arrival of his assistant had brought joy to the whole parish. "Since that time he has won the confidence of all, and I hope that his services here will be of the greatest value. His knowledge of English, which he speaks passably well, will entitle him to much consideration." [9]

While Father Richard was coming in from the West, another priest

[8] BCA.
[9] Letter to Bishop Carroll, July 20, 1798. BCA. The date of Father Richard's arrival in Detroit is established by a report of his work sent to France in 1826, and published in the *Annals of the Propagation of the Faith*, Vol. III. See note 14.

was on his way to Detroit from Baltimore, sent by Bishop Carroll in answer to Father Levadoux's petition. He was Father Jean Dilhet, a Sulpician who had landed in America the previous January.[10] He arrived in Detroit in the last days of June, and finding that Father Levadoux was away on his periodic visit to the Raisin River settlement he went on to meet him there. On Sunday, July 1, he said the parochial Mass, and at a parish meeting held immediately afterwards he was presented as the resident pastor.

To Dilhet's methodical care we owe the preservation of such church records as he found on his arrival. It is seen again in his attempt at the very beginning of his incumbency to give an accurate delimitation of his parish. His enumeration gives an interesting insight into the lines of development from the original settlement.

> The parish of St. Anthony, on the River Raisin, embraces the settlements on the River Raisin, those on Otter Creek and Sandy Creek, those on the Miamy and Portage Rivers, those on Huron Creek South, those at the little Lake Sanduské, at the little and the great Sanduské village, at the Glaise, at Fort Wayne or Miami, at the Huron River North, at the Huron village, at the Grosse Roche, at Mont Wagon, at St. Joseph's, etc.[11]
>
> In a word it extends North to the Riviere aux Ecorces, South to the Illinois, Kaokias, and Post Vincennes, East to Lake Erie, and to the West it has no limits.
>
> This parish has within its limits people who belong to different civilized nations, and many savage tribes. The former, citizens of the United States, are either French, Canadians, American, English, Irish, or Scotch. The Indians are: Hurons, Outouais, Ouatomis, Sauteux, Chouanons, Wolves, Foxes, etc.
>
> Among these, many have been baptized, especially those born of parents belonging to civilized nations; most of the Huron tribe have also been baptized. But all are not Catholics. By baptism they belong to the church; but by creed they belong to different heterodox sects. . . .[12]

Father Dilhet's parish was surely large enough, and the pride

[10] Father Jean Dilhet was born at Toulouse, November 10, 1753, and completed his studies in the Sulpician house at Issy. He arrived in Baltimore January 13, 1798. He wrote a sketch of the Church in the United States, which was edited by Rev. Patrick W. Browne under the title: *Beginnings of the Catholic Church in the United States* (Washington, 1922).

[11] Otter Creek and Sandy Creek are still local designations. The Miamy is the Maumee emptying into Lake Erie at Toledo, and the Portage River empties into the lake at Port Clinton. The Huron Creek South, now Huron Creek, meanders through two Ohio counties, Huron and Erie. The Glaise is the French name for the creek near Clay Junction, Wood County, Ohio. The Huron River North, and the Huron Village, designate the Huron River running through the town of Rockwood, Michigan. The Grosse Roche is Flat Rock, Wayne County. Mont Wagon is Monguagon, and St. Joseph is St. Joseph Mission.

[12] The whole passage is a preface to the baptismal register.

which he occasionally displays must have been amply satisfied with its extent, particularly to the West. It is quite probable that he visited the settlements which he locates in northern Ohio, but there is no mention of pastoral work there in his meager, extant correspondence.[13]

However, we have ample evidence of the energy and zeal which the priest displayed in the management of his parish. His first care was to establish the ownership of the lands held by the parish. These had been the gift of parishioners who themselves had no more secure title than a mere verbal donation from the original Indian owners. The donations were reiterated in the presence of witnesses, and quitclaim deeds were secured and registered.

For the administration of the parish Father Dilhet proceeded to lay down all the detailed regulations of the French system. The rights of "La Fabrique," the parish corporation, the convocation and authority of parish assemblies, the election, duties, and privileges of wardens, the role of the Syndics, the humble tasks of the sacristan, all these are minutely provided for. As support the pastor is to receive a tithe, one twenty-fifth of all farm products. Then there is the schedule of fees for various services rendered. A funeral with High Mass and *Libera* deserves an offering of twelve shillings, one dollar and a half. The lowest fee is for a churching, and the highest, two dollars and a half, for a wedding.

If we are to believe Father Dilhet, there were five hundred families in the settlement, surely enough to maintain the parish in a flourishing condition. Yet, their poverty and parsimony made his lot, as well as that of his immediate successors, anything but pleasant. As a typical instance, the parish records reveal that when the pastor petitioned to have another room added to his rectory that would serve as a granary, the wardens, after mature deliberation, voted to provide the extra room by a new partition somewhere in the house.

Meanwhile, Father Richard was attending the scattered Catholic groups to the north of Detroit. All the early French settlements in Michigan were located either some distance up its inland waterways, or along the shores of the surrounding lakes. Roads, other than Indian trails, were as yet unknown, and the only facilities for communication were by water. The French Canadian was not too interested in agriculture, and was not actuated by the land hunger which drove the later immigration to develop the interior resources of the state. As we have seen, the trend of the Canadian colony from the very beginning had been away from the serious business of tilling the land to the easier, freer life of the fur trade. As a consequence, and ex-

---

[13] Browne, *op. cit.*, xii and 108.

cluding the urban centers along the St. Lawrence, the average individual was disposed to be satisfied with the necessities of life. With his little patch of ground, and with access to the water for hunting and fishing, he could supply his humble needs, and bring up his generous family in contentment.

The French population of Detroit spread out therefore in two directions. To the south it found suitable conditions along the Rouge, Ecorse, Huron and Raisin Rivers, and in the curve of Maumee Bay. To the north there were inviting spots like L'Anse Creuse, the Clinton River, Anchor Bay, Swan Creek, the St. Clair and Black Rivers. All these were Father Richard's first missionary field, and by the end of 1779, a log chapel had already been erected on the Clinton River.[14]

There remained another Catholic group which had not been visited from the time that Father Levadoux had stopped there on his way to Detroit in 1796. Accordingly, Father Richard left Detroit on June 20, 1799, in a government vessel of the same name, bound on a missionary journey to Mackinac. The following extracts are taken from the long report of his activities sent to Bishop Carroll.

On the 29th of the same month I did meet there in that place with great many people. It may be said that near a thousand men come there in the Summertime. It is the grand Rendezvous of several traders of Lac Michigan, Mississippi, and Lac Superior, etc. There are about 50 houses; I found a great number of Children, I supplied the Ceremonies of Baptism to 30 and better who were above seven years. However it is very sorrowful to see so many poor creatures quite abandoned without instructions. Several of them Know scarcely to do the sing (sic) of the cross. And I was told that there were Good many in the same condition in different places, that they call hivernement viz. at River St. Joseph, at Wisconsing River, Prairie du Chien, at Green Bay, at St. Mary's Falls, and several rivers of lac Superior, at Grand Portage, and many for the countries in the North West of lac Superior where the Grand-N.W. Company of Montreal keeps annually seventeen hundred men, almost all of them Canadians. . . .

During tow first months I was making Catechism for children every

---

[14] Father Richard refers to his building of this log chapel in a letter to the head of the Society for the Propagation of the Faith, dated December 22, 1825. This chapel was the second outgrowth from St. Anne's, and makes the Mt. Clemens parish the third oldest in the Diocese of Detroit. The Society just mentioned was a missionary association organized at Lyons, France, in 1822. Its periodical, the *Annales de la Propagation de la Foi* printed the letters of the missionaries who wrote to it for assistance, and it is thus an invaluable source for the details of missionary activity in many parts of the world. References to it will henceforth be denoted by the word "Annales." The authoritative monograph in English on the history and work of the Society is by the Rev. Edward J. Hickey, *The Society for the Propagation of the Faith* (Catholic University Press, 1922). In the course of his researches Father Hickey copied hundreds of letters in the archives of the Society which are not printed in the *Annales*. References to these will be entitled the Hickey Transcripts.

morning, and in the evening I said the Evening-prayers in the Church, after which I was used to give a familiar explanation of the different parts of Christian Doctrine. Commonly a pretty good number of people particularly of the travellers was meeting then in the Church, which is only forty-five feet in length and 25 in breath; as it is a cedar building, tho it is very old, it will dure many years yet. It is very well furnished with Ornaments and linen and books for the divine worship. only it wants a Chalice and a Pix. . . .

The 3rd day of September I went to pay a visit to the Wtawas who live on the Michigan Lac side at 45 miles only from Makina Iland. the late Genl. chief who died tow years ago was baptized. But among 1300 persons, men women and children, there is only one I could be ascertained had been baptized. I saw the place called La Mission where the Fr. Dujaunai their missionary lived. There remains only a large Cross, on the shore which is there near three hundred feet high. it is situated at five miles from the beginning of the Wtawa village on the way to Makina. However I asked in your name if they were willing to have a priest to instruct them or at least their children. . . .

But until the 24th of September I started from that place I did not receive a word on the subject, tho many were coming to the Iland on one day or another. To tell you the truth they are so much abandoned to drink spirit, that they do not care much about religion. when I was at their village they were drinking, and I saw some of them drunk. In the Iland every day some of them were to be seen drunk in the street or in the shore. the most part of the trade consists only of liquors. As long as it will be so, there cannot be any hope of making them Christians. the traders themselves confess that it would be better for their own profit to not give rum to the Indians, but as the Indians are very much fond of it, every trader says that he must give them rum not to lose all his trade. So that it should be necessary that all traders might agree on it, but the covetousness and cupidity shall never permit such agreements. God knows how many (evils?) will flow from that trade. Some have observed that English rum has destroyed more Indians than ever did the Spanish Sword. . . .[15]

Leaving Mackinac on September 24, Father Richard visited St. Joseph Island and then went on to the Sault. There he found several Frenchmen living with Indian consorts. He would have liked to legitimize these unions, but was deterred by the crass ignorance of religion evident in the women. "I wished many times in my travell that I could marry at least civilly that is to say without making sacrament, and consequently without saying the words *Ego conjungo vos*, etc. in order to take off the scandal and to legitimate so many innocent children who are born every day from such illawful conjunctions . . ."[16]

[15] Letter to Bishop Carroll, November 6, 1799. BCA.
[16] *Ibid.*

The crying need of this portion of the territory assigned to Father Levadoux made a profound impression on Father Richard. During his stay at Mackinac the traders had proposed that he take up his permanent residence among them. This he was quite willing to do provided he had Father Levadoux's consent, and he wrote to lay the matter before his superior. How uncomplicated and detached were the lives of the great pioneer missionaries; in the event of an affirmative answer he stated that nothing more need be sent him than the second half of his breviary, and his winter cassock that was in the trunk behind his bed.[17]

But Detroit could not spare Father Richard, and to it he returned in October. He wrote to Bishop Carroll that he confidently hoped to repeat the missionary tour in the near future, adding that he could thereby perfect himself in the use of English. He complained that Detroit offered him so little opportunity for practice that he was likely to forget what he had already learned.

> . . . There are but very few Roman Catholics amongst the English people of this place. Five or six of them only are used to come to Confession. There is maybe a dozen of our profession, but most part of them are certain perpetual travellers from Ireland some of whom only recollect of hearing their father or mother to be Romans, and know nothing of Catholic Doctrine nor care much of being instructed in it. They are of different trades viz. taylors, tavern keepers, soldiers, etc. You know very well how much it is easy to make such people good Christians! I am very sorry for it, but what is to be done? However I will invite them to meet together at certain days in order to deliver them a clear explanation of our belief. The offers I made by one of them who was to advise them has been unsuccessful. . . .[18]

The fewness of English-speaking Catholics in Detroit at the time of Father Richard's writing is borne out by the record of a most important event, the presence, for the first time, of a bishop in Michigan. Bishop Hubert had resigned from his see in 1797, in favor of his coadjutor, Pierre Denaut. Writing to Baltimore a year later Bishop Denaut expressed his intention to visit the outposts of his diocese in Ontario, and his willingness to be of service within Bishop Carroll's jurisdiction. A portion of his letter referred to a rather

[17] Letter to Father Levadoux from Mackinac, July 19, 1799. BCA.

[18] Letter to Bishop Carroll, May 19, 1800. BCA. A search through the St. Anne register for the first three years of Father Richard's ministry reveals less than ten names which are not French. In 1798 Susan Atway and Peter Cook are baptized. A year later occurs the name of Theophile Fallman, whose father is said to be an artillery officer, and Francois Jones. The next year appear the names of William Johnson, Alexander Cooper, and John Grant, a man of twenty-five, who as a child had been ransomed from the Indians by Alexander Grant. In 1800 the names of James Condon and John Kane appear as designating sponsors.

disturbing American novelty which Father Dufaux had already reported Father Levadoux as practicing, the granting of dispensations gratis.

> The present vicinity of your diocese to mine has led me in my late instructions to missionaries sent thither to ratify everything that might be done by those under your jurisdiction. In order to obviate all difficulties, do you not think it would be well for you to give your sanction to those who labor under mine? . . .
>
> Before the Americans took possession of that portion of Detroit which now belongs to your diocese a certain fixed sum was received by way of alms for dispensations from Banns, relationship and affinity. This custom, established for all time and authorized by the Sovereign Pontiff, having been put a stop to by your order requiring all dispensations hereafter to be given gratis, I have thought it necessary to forbid all compensation therefor, in order to preserve uniformity of praxis, as any divergence therein would lead to bad feeling and murmuring. I should likewise wish to confer with your Lordship about the norm to follow in regard to marriages contracted between Catholics and Protestants, which your missionaries, it is said, have permission to witness. Without doubt you have been thus empowered by the Pope, and he has refused similar powers petitioned for by my predecessors. . . .[19]

Bishop Denaut had conditioned his visitation upon the appointment of a coadjutor, which he expected in the spring of 1799. But it was not until January 25, 1801, that he was able to consecrate him in the person of Joseph-Octave Plessis. In the following April the bishop wrote to the pastor of Assumption parish that he was ready to begin his long-deferred visitation.[20]

From the bishop's diary we know that he arrived in the parish on June 16. He was accompanied by Father Payet, the one time pastor of St. Anne's, whom he had brought along as his secretary. The religious exercises of a mission were immediately begun, and the faithful were prepared for the reception of Confirmation. According to the bishop's figures, five hundred and twenty-nine were admitted to the sacrament.

Unfortunately we have no account of the bishop's entry into Detroit. The record inscribed by Father Richard reveals that Confirmation was administered in St. Anne's church on June 25, 26, 28, and on July 2. On these four days five hundred and fifty persons were confirmed, and there is a notation to the effect that thirteen more belonging to the parish had received the sacrament in the other

---

[19] Letter to Bishop Carroll, October 10, 1798. *Records of the Amer. Cath. Hist. Soc.,* XVIII, 179.

[20] The bishop's letter as well as extracts from his journal pertaining to Detroit will be found in the *Bulletin . . . Historiques,* I, 97 ff.

parish. In the entire list of names there are less than ten that are not French.

The bishop then went on to the Raisin River settlement. Father Dilhet was no man to record such an important event with mere names and figures; he gave all the details.

On the 18th of June, 1801, Mgr. Peter Denaut, Catholic Bishop of Quebec, arrived towards 3 P.M. at the River Raisin, and disembarked in front of J. B. Réaume's house, where Mr. J. Dilhet, pastor of the parish, received him without any solemnity, the Bishop having refused the offer of being received in due form. He was introduced into the said house by the Pastor, and entered it with Mr. Michael Levadoux, Vicar-General of the Bishop of Baltimore, Mr. Marchand, pastor of the Assumption of Detroit, and Mr. Payet, his secretary. Mr. Hubert La-croix welcomed the Bishop in the name of all the parishioners, after which the many people present fell on their knees to receive the Bish-op's blessing. Having entered the carriages which were in readiness for the party, they started for the church escorted by nearly fifty men on horseback, and by a great crowd on foot. . . .

The next day being Sunday, the Bishop of Quebec, after a discourse on Confirmation, administered the sacrament to those who presented themselves at the communion railing. He did the same the next two days. . . .[21]

Exactly a month from his arrival the bishop sailed down the river on the return journey to Quebec. To the spiritual blessings resulting from his ministrations in Detroit we must add the evident awakening of the parishioners to the material needs of the parish. Under the pastor's direction Father Richard drew up a preamble to a subscription list for the building of a new church, and proceeded to turn good will into signed promises.

The large white pages, tied with bows of green silk ribbon, were irresistible; one hundred and forty men, presumably family heads, displayed their generosity in the presence of witnesses. It is significant that only about thirty of them were able to write their signatures; the rest could only scratch a cross. Colonel Hamtramck, as the most prominent parishioner, led off with thirty pounds New York currency. Michael Levadoux and Gabriel Richard both promised a fifth of that year's tithe, which they estimated to be worth forty pounds. Cajetan Tremblay agreed to furnish baulks of French walnut, thirty-

[21] The account is in the parish register. There is something very wrong with the date given by Father Dilhet. The bishop, arriving in Assumption parish on June 16, was certainly not at the Raisin River parish on the 18th. From the bishop's diary it is plain that he remained on the Canadian side until he confirmed in Detroit on the dates given. The only Sundays on which he could have been at the Raisin River fell on the 5th and 12th of July.

five feet long, and sixteen inches square. Joseph Rivard put himself down for four thousand shingles, and Antoine Cecile for one hundred pounds of iron. Many parishioners undertook to bring canoe loads of stone, and Alexander Ouellette pledged himself to labor at the lime kiln. One man donated a horse, and several others grain and cider. Those who had nothing bound themselves to so many days of labor. Only one non-French name appears in the entire list, that of John Shaw. He made the substantial donation of one thousand bricks.[22]

Despite this imposing array of promises the new St. Anne's was not built. At Detroit, as at the River Raisin settlement, the factional spirit was always strong. There were petty bickerings and jealousy. The French-Canadian loved to talk things out, and the system of parish deliberations gave him full opportunity. As a result the men who had been so eager to promise talked the whole project into a froth of words, However, the church was repaired and embellished, and Father Richard reported his progress to Bishop Carroll the following year.

> You may have been informed by Mr. Levadoux that I was trying to repair our Church of Detroit. I have now the pleasure of informing you that it has not been without success. The roof excepted, it is now almost entirely a new Church. . . . A new steeple is to be erected this week. . . . The clear revenue of our Church will be at least 400 dollars per annum by the addition of 30 pews. You may see easily that such an undertaking could not be done without some difficulties and contradictions. Some objected me that I had meddled with it too much, some, but few, not enough. . . .[23]

For Father Richard, however, when he wrote the foregoing lines the brunt of parish criticism was all the harder to bear in that he was now alone. Father Levadoux in consequence of ill health had requested that he be relieved of his duties in Detroit. He received a favorable reply from his superior, Father Nagot, probably early in 1802, but the date of his departure is uncertain.[24] Most likely, it occurred soon after his last entry in the baptismal register, April 17, 1802. Returning to Baltimore Father Levadoux took residence at the Seminary; but the following year he was sent to France and appointed director of the seminary of St. Flour in the department of

---

[22] The original subscription list is preserved in the archives of the Detroit Chancery. This documentary source will be designated by the letters DCA in all future references.

[23] Letter to Bishop Carroll, October 20, 1802. BCA.

[24] There is a letter from Father Emery to Bishop Carroll referring to Father Nagot's withdrawal of Father Levadoux in the BCA.

FATHER GABRIEL RICHARD. This is a reproduction of the engraving in Sheldon's *The Early History of Michigan*.

Cantal. In 1814 he was transferred to the directorship of the seminary at Puy, and there he died January 13, 1815.[25]

On May 3, 1802, Father Richard for the first time appended to his signature in the St. Anne register the title, Curé. He was just on the threshold of that long and unique career which ranks him among the great pioneers of the Church in America. For our local history he represents the transition period linking the old French life in Detroit with the beginnings of the diocese. A man of tremendous physical energy coupled with a keen, active, and well-trained mind, he displayed a diversity of interests and a range of activities that are astonishing. His greatness lies not so much in what he accomplished as in what he visioned. His life was a succession of failures. There is no enterprise in the diocese today which traces back to him. The state university which he helped to found has, until recently, striven to disclaim relationship with him. Years of agitation could not give his name to the great highway through the state which he fathered. For thirty years as pastor of St. Anne's, sometimes in seeming dishonor, often in the midst of discord, always in extreme poverty, he struggled for the betterment of a backward and lethargic community that would not follow where he led. His renown need not suffer from his failures; they prove only that he was ahead of his time and superior to his setting.

Father Gabriel Richard was born at Saintes, in the department of the Charente-Inférieure, on October 15, 1767.[26] He was the third son of François Richard, a retired officer from the naval base at Rochefort, and Mary Genevieve Bossuet.[27] In the deeply religious home life which they fostered the restive and flighty disposition of their little Gabriel gave the parents much concern. At the age of eleven he was entered as a boarder at the College of Saintes, which was conducted by a number of diocesan clergymen. For the first few months he showed no inclination to study, and school meant just a splendid opportunity to indulge in a series of schoolboy pranks. One of these, the climbing of a ladder to throw stones at some workmen repairing

[25] Details from the Philpin de Riviere manuscript in the archives of St. Mary's Seminary, Baltimore.

[26] The year of Father Richard's birth is sometimes given as 1764. This is an error and there is good documentary evidence for the date in the text. The best, and indeed the only printed source for details of Richard's early years, is the biography by Pierre Guérin entitled Le Martyre de la Charité (Lefort; Lille, 1850). The volume is rare, but a manuscript copy obtained from France is the basis for the statements in the text. Another biography by N-E Dionne (Quebec, 1912), is not too accurate.

[27] Scarcely anyone has written on Father Richard without mentioning his enate relationship to the great Bossuet. Researches undertaken by the Rev. E. Levesque, librarian of St. Sulpice in Paris, and communicated to the writer do not support the assertion.

the college building, had an almost fatal termination. The ladder fell, and among the boy's injuries was a permanent facial disfigurement which earned him the nickname of "wrymouth." The danger from which he had escaped had a sobering effect, and from that time onward he was a model of deportment and application. At his first communion, in 1781, his teachers could scarcely believe that the fervent serious-minded youth had grown out of the little madcap whom they had threatened to expel during his first year at school. In 1784, at his graduation he led his class, and was awarded three prizes out of a possible four.[28]

Meanwhile the youth had been maturing the idea of a priestly vocation, and to the joy of his parents he entered the Sulpician Seminary at Angers in October, 1784. Here he threw himself with intense ardor into his studies, and at the end of two years he gained his Master's degree for a thesis in physics. To a copy of the dissertation sent to his father the young man added a letter which foreshadowed his lifelong interest in education.

> I am amazed at all the sacrifices which you have made for my education. Impossible as it is to be worthy of such goodness, I can only promise that by hard and continued application I shall give you all the satisfaction that lies in my power. As a proof of my gratitude, and of my tender and respectful devotion, I beg you to accept this thesis which bears as its dedication: *Patri familiam edocenti.* You are truly a virtuous father, zealous for the education of your children. . . . How wise you were to realize that learning was above wealth, and that it was the best heritage you could leave us. I esteem it a hundred times more than anything you could will me, for worldly goods can be lost, but learning and education are a lasting possession. I shall be grateful to you all my life for these gifts above everything else. . . .[29]

At the end of his third year of theology the seminarian decided to join the Society of St. Sulpice. To continue his preparation for the priesthood he was sent to the Sulpician house of studies at Issy, a suburb of Paris, at the beginning of 1790. In the terminology of the Society such a house was called a Solitude. But, at that moment in France there was no solitude so deep as to keep out the dull rumble of the approaching storm that was to shake the nation and the continent to its foundations. The Bastille had fallen on the 14th of July, 1789. Five weeks later came the Declaration of the Rights of Man. In November the Church was despoiled of her property, and her clergy became salaried functionaries. The succeeding February re-

---

[28] The documents conferring the awards are in the DCA.

[29] Guérin, *op. cit.* The author evidently had access to the Richard family papers. He quotes several letters.

ligious vows were dissolved by law, and the Civil Constitution of the
Clergy was voted in July. When its enforcement began in November,
every priest in France had to swear allegiance to a State Church or be
deprived of his office, his citizenship, and his liberty. The year 1791
was one of tumult, and the massacres of priests in July, 1792, were a
prelude to the Terror.

In such circumstances the young Sulpician approached his goal.
His biographer tells us that in view of the dangerous situation the
ordination was not only advanced, but was hidden from public observation. At some distance from the church of St. Sulpice, but still
within the parish limits, stood a private house owned by the Sulpicians, which contained a private chapel. Here on October 9, 1791,
Gabriel Richard was ordained by de Bonal, Bishop of Clermont, in
the absence of the Archbishop of Paris, who had already sought a less
exposed position.[30]

According to his biographer, Father Richard returned to Issy for
his first Mass, and remained there until his superiors decided to send
him to America. Nothing is said about his having been in any personal danger during this time, and it is difficult to determine how
much truth there is in the highly colored recollections of an old
resident of Detroit. As a youth he had taken French lessons from
Father Richard, and had wondered at a large scar which the priest
bore on one cheek. To satisfy the youth's curiosity Father Richard
gave this explanation.

> I was a priest in France at the time of the Revolution directed by
> Robespierre. I saw some of the soldiers near my house one day, and
> heard them asking for me. I knew what they meant, and I jumped out
> of a rear window. As I landed on the ground a woman in an adjoining
> house threw a teapot at me. It broke on my cheek inflicting a deep
> wound. I ran out on the street until I was exhausted. Seeing some men
> digging a ditch, I jumped into it. They were friends and covered up my
> priest's garb with their coats and vests. I was not seen, and my pur-
> suers passed by. I worked in that ditch until I got a chance to leave for
> America in a vessel.[31]

Granted that the second-hand account of Father Richard's prolonged concealment in a ditch is hard to believe, it is very probable
that in the first months of 1792 he, as well as all the non-juring
priests, were in hourly danger of violence. However, whatever happened did not interfere with the plans made to send a second band of
Sulpicians to Baltimore, and on April 9, 1792, Richard with three
companions, Maréchal, Matignon, and Ciquard sailed from Hon-

[30] Copy of ordination certificate procured through the librarian of St. Sulpice in DCA.
[31] Recollections of Levi Dolsen, *Mich. Hist Colls.*, XXVIII, 608.

fleurs. After a stormy voyage their ship entered Chesapeake Bay on June 19, and five days later, on a Sunday morning, the four priests came ashore at Baltimore.[32]

The little group was soon separated. Father Ciquard went to the Abnaki Indians in Maine. Matignon, who was not a Sulpician, began his fruitful labors in New England from his headquarters in Boston. In Maréchal Baltimore had a future archbishop. The insistent needs of the West drew Father Richard from a position he was at first expected to fill, that of professor of mathematics at the nascent Georgetown College.[33] His six years on the Mississippi and his first five years in Detroit bring us again to the beginning of his pastorate.

Father Levadoux had been gone but a few weeks when Father Richard received a heartening letter from Bishop Carroll. In answer to it he wrote.

> I suppose your intention was to give new strength to my courage. However, I may tell you that though there is much good to do which remains undone, I receive great comfort from several of my parishioners; I feel my wishes for the salvation of the whole increasing, as by their docility and some success my flock becomes every day dearer to me. Pray the Almighty that I may remove all obstacles I have daily opposed to his benevolent designs, that the Holy Ghost may be diffused upon all flesh. . . .[34]

Even while thus expressing himself as fairly satisfied with his parish, Father Richard was having difficulties with his parishioners over certain minor matters of discipline which he was trying to bring into accord with the provisions of the First National Synod convened by Bishop Carroll in November, 1791.[35] But his troubles were light compared to those experienced by Father Dilhet in the Raisin River settlement. All his efforts to arouse the people to a sense of duty to him and to the Church were met by an unfeeling spirit against which he was powerless. Convinced that further trying was useless Father Dilhet sent his resignation to Bishop Carroll in the summer of 1802, but stayed on until the middle of March, 1804, waiting for a successor. Before leaving he read to his people a letter from Bishop Carroll

---

[32] The details of the voyage contained in a letter of Father Richard to his Paris Superior from Baltimore, July 7, 1792. In archives of St. Sulpice.

[33] The Philpin de Riviere manuscript is the authority for the statement that Richard was first destined for the professorship of mathematics at Georgetown.

[34] Letter to Bishop Carroll, July 28, 1803. BCA.

[35] In the preceding letter Father Richard writes: "I must give you an account of a small difficulty between me and my parishioners. It was the custom here that the oblations of the faithful were collected by a young girl who presented the holy bread to the priest who gives her to kiss an image of the Blessed Virgin called La Paix. Last Christmas I refused one for her indecent dress, and several persons told me I had done rightly, except her relations."

promising to send them another priest provided they paid his traveling expenses. He then came to Detroit to live with Father Richard, who, in writing to his bishop assigned a rather unusual reason for Dilhet's failure: "Though there are many who are much addicted to him, nevertheless several of them do not desire to have for their pastor a man of so extensive abilities and learning . . ." [36]

Having Father Dilhet as his disposal Father Richard was now able to investigate the outlying mission that had been giving him much concern. No priest had set foot on Mackinac since his own visit there in 1799. The religious sentiment of its long-neglected population was so nearly extinct that no one had protested against conditions and happenings such as he communicated to Bishop Carroll.

> I have been informed lately that the summer before last, a dead dog was found on the altar where it had been put in mockery by a young Protestant called Maxwell, and that the priest's house which is joined to the church was a public brothel. I shall write to the trustee about this last, and will notify him not to let the rooms (there are but five) but to honest persons. . . . I want to be authorized by you to give orders if you believe it convenient, for to send to Detroit the ornaments, books, portable altar, chalice, etc., which things are very much exposed to get spoiled or abused.[37]

Father Dilhet arrived at Mackinac on June 9, and remained on the island for six weeks. On leaving Detroit it had been his intention to extend his ministrations to the northern shore of Lake Superior, but there is nothing in his own account to indicate that he went farther than the island. Here, as he relates, he performed a large number of baptisms, assisted at several marriages of Canadians and Indians, and prepared quite a number, among whom were a few Indians for First Communion. New churchwardens were elected, and an inventory of the church property drawn up. Again the residents signed a petition for a resident priest, which was forwarded to Baltimore. Nothing came of it, and fourteen years elapsed before a priest again visited the island.[38]

On Father Dilhet's return, Father Richard saw a chance of realiz-

[36] Letter to Bishop Carroll, February 8, 1804. BCA.
[37] Quoted from the letter of July 28, 1803, already mentioned. Whether the articles named were brought to Detroit then, or at some later time is not known. Certainly, they were in Detroit at some time or other. The museum at Notre Dame University proves that Bishop Borgess listened to the siren voice of that indefatigable collector, Professor Edwards, and gave him precious relics of the old mission.
[38] Browne, op. cit., 123–28. Rezek, in his history of the Diocese of Sault Ste. Marie and Marquette mentions a record in the Mackinac baptismal register dated September 9, 1818, and signed by a priest unknown to him, Joseph Crevier. Father Crevier was assistant to Father Marchand in the Assumption parish, and in 1818 he made a four months' missionary tour along the Canadian territory bordering on the Great Lakes.

ing a project which the two priests had been studying for some time. He thus outlined it to Bishop Carroll.

> Since the taking possession of Louisiana by the U. S. we have had opportunity of being more convinced of the necessity you will be in of providing this additional part of your immense diocese with a few pastors. The probability that a great number of parishes will come under your care has conduced us to look for young children in my parish that could be brought up to be priests. Of course Mr. Dilhet, finding his zeal too much constrained at River aux Raisins, seems to be disposed after his return from Makina, to stay at Detroit with me in order to teach Latin to a few young boys. During his station here last week he has examined eight or ten whom I thought more able for this purpose. They are from 9 to 15 years old; but few of them know to read well, and scarcely two know to write. It is a hard undertaking indeed, as these children belong to parents who are scarcely able to provide them for ink and paper. However, if you approve our design Mr. Dilhet is disposed to do all his exertions to make it succeed. . . .[39]

Father Richard's first educational venture, of which we have any details, was therefore a preparatory seminary.[40] It is hardly necessary to point out the foresight and courage of the man who amid the pressure of his daily cares preserved his breadth of outlook, and was winning to struggle almost singlehanded to prepare for the future. In the beginning of October, 1804, Father Dilhet opened what he calls the "College or clergy school." Rooms were fitted out in the rectory for the purpose, and nine boys began their instruction in Latin, Geography, History, Sacred Music, and the practice of mental prayer.[41] In the detailed financial statement of the parish for the years 1804–05 no allusion is made to the school, and it is therefore quite certain that whatever expenses it entailed were met by Father Richard personally.

Notwithstanding the enthusiasm and sacrifices of the two priests, the little seminary was destined to a premature end. In March, 1805, Father Richard wrote to the bishop that "We have met great difficulties and oppositions to the establishment of a school for the latin and the sciences. The most material difficulty is the scarcity of Scholars. The school of the French gentleman, Mr. Serrières is yet going on.[42] . . . The number of our own scholars is at present but four who are learning pretty well . . ." [43]

[39] Letter to Bishop Carroll, May 1, 1804. BCA.

[40] A more detailed account of Father Richard's educational activities will be given later.

[41] Browne, op. cit., 117.

[42] According to Farmer, op. cit., I, 715, Serrier, as he names him, had been a soldier during the French Revolution. An old sabre cut, or the too liberal use of alcohol, caused him at times to act rather queerly.

[43] Letter dated March 14, 1805. BCA.

In the very next paragraph of his letter Father Richard apprised the bishop that his withdrawal from Detroit was imperative for reasons that would be communicated to him by the Baltimore superior, Father Nagot. A return to France had been offered by the Paris superior, and he would take advantage of it as soon as his successor arrived. No explanation of such an unexpected move is available, but there is ground for inferring that his action was due to some serious disagreement with the trustees. In September he had evidently received permission to leave, for he said farewell to his congregation, and consigned it to Father Dilhet. Immediately, legal proceedings were instituted to prevent his departure.[44] In his trouble Father Richard sadly writes.

> I am prevented from going off by a writ which is to be issued tomorrow against me. I need not state that it is grounded only upon a false and calumniatory report. . . . This year I have experienced many contradictions, but at the same time I have obtained greater successes, if I am not deceived by my self love. In general there are good dispositions, and I conceive that a clergyman of a moderate temper with patience and time would be very useful. . . .[45]

Father Dilhet had consented to remain in Detroit only during the emergency caused by Father Richard's departure. He also had received an invitation from the Paris superior to return to France, and when he saw his confrere's predicament, he decided to leave. In his own narrative he states that he set out for the East in September, 1805, and he does not forget to add that his departure caused great regret in the parish, and created a sensation that was still vivid after a lapse of fifteen months.[46]

Again Father Richard was alone, and this time in utter desolation, for he had neither church, nor rectory, nor school. The town had lived unscathed through changes of government and the vicissitudes of more than a hundred years of frontier life. What neither the Fox nor Pontiac himself had been able to accomplish came to pass through the lee of a lowly baker's pipe.

On the morning of June 11, 1805, John Harvey, with a lighted pipe in his mouth, went out to the stable behind his bakeshop to hitch up his French pony. The smoke proving bothersome he tapped out his pipe and went on with his work. A few moments later the stable was ablaze, and despite the efforts of the townsmen who ran to the scene, the fire was soon beyond control. The two hundred or more wooden

---

[44] Dilhet states that these proceedings were brought by the trustees. Browne, *op. cit.*, 117.

[45] Letter to Bishop Carroll, September 10, 1805. BCA.

[46] Browne, *op. cit.*, 118. Father Dilhet returned to France, and died suddenly at Puy on October 31, 1811.

houses fronting on streets only twenty feet wide, and all packed within an area of three acres, offered an easy prey to the flames. In the late afternoon not a vestige of Detroit was left but a few stone chimneys standing out of the smoking embers, and an old warehouse down by the river bank. Father Dilhet, as an eye witness, penned the following description.

> The celebration of the jubilee was about over, and the town was filled with people who had gathered from the distant settlements to participate in this great event in a fitting manner by assisting regularly at the instructions, at Holy Mass and the other exercises, and by approaching the Sacrament of Penance The fire began while I was engaged with Mr. Richard. I was interrupted by a person who came to inform me that three houses had already been burned, and that there was little hope of saving the others. I exhorted all those present to help one another, and I went to say Mass with only one server. It was a low Mass, and when it was over we had hardly time to save the church furniture, the vestments, the household effects and provisions in the presbytery which adjoined the church. The flames spread with great rapidity, and soon enveloped both, though they were located on the outskirts of the town. In three hours (from nine o'clock to noon) the town was burned to the ground, and nothing could be seen but live embers, and chimneys which seemed to rise like pyramids. At the time of the fire there was no wind, the flames and smoke rose to a prodigious hight, and the entire town looked like a huge bonfire. It was the most wonderful, and at the same time the most horrible sight I have ever witnessed. . . .[47]

This was Detroit's darkest hour. When night came, the homeless residents sat in little groups around their household goods piled along the river bank and on the commons. Mothers stilled their whimpering children while fathers discussed the dubious possibility of the town's rebuilding. Almost a third of the six hundred residents, convinced that Detroit would never rise from its ashes, decided to seek fortune elsewhere.

The one thing that mitigated the extent of the disaster was the cheerful charity of the French farmers up and down the river. Father Richard was everywhere, gathering up the food supplies which were readily tendered, and arranging for the shelter of the homeless.[48] Soon every house was crammed with refugees, while those who had decided to remain on the spot improvised shelters out of whatever odds and ends they could find. For many years Detroit had been supplied with lumber from the neighborhood of Port Huron, and the town might soon have been rebuilt on its old lines, as was the intention of the

---

[47] Browne, *op. cit.*, 111. Every historian of Detroit has written the story of the great fire. The accounts differ only in minor particulars.

[48] George B. Catlin, *The Story of Detroit* (Detroit, 1923), 117.

townsmen who were determined to stay. But a set of circumstances intervened which modified the future development of Detroit, and had a bearing on matters proper to our story.

The Northwest Territory was created by the "Great Ordinance" of 1787, nine years before a large portion of it had actually come into American possession. In 1800 occurred the first dismemberment into the Territory of Indiana, and the Eastern District including the eastern half of the present state of Michigan. When Ohio was admitted to statehood in 1803, the whole of Michigan was attached to Indiana Territory. Two years later Congress established the Territory of Michigan, giving it boundaries differing little from those of the future state.[49]

The civil government of the original Northwest Territory had been vested in a Board composed of a governor and three judges. Succeeding divisions of the Territory were to be so governed, and when they had attained a certain level of population were to be entitled to a legislative assembly. Accordingly, the President entrusted the government of Michigan Territory to the following officials: Governor, William Hull; Judges, Augustus B. Woodward, Frederick Bates, and Samuel Huntington who resigned to be replaced by John Griffin. They were the first members of the body called the "Governors and Judges" which was to rule Detroit and Michigan, sometimes tyrannically, until the first legislative assembly held in Detroit in 1824.

Arriving in Detroit a few days after the fire, Judges Woodward and Bates found the population clearing the site, and going ahead with plans to rebuild the town on its original lines. With some vision of the future the Judges induced the people to defer their plans until the arrival of the Governor himself. He made his appearance on July 1, and Father Dilhet describes what followed.

The new governor, William Hull, arrived at Detroit two or three days after this disastrous occurrence. In his inaugural address, delivered in an orchard where an altar had been erected, the governor spoke most sympathetically to the people of the loss which they had sustained, and inspired them with comforting hopes for the future. Two or three days later, before the same altar, he administered the oath to the deputy-governor, or secretary, to the chief justice and other officials. The chief justice, Mr. Woodward, being a Catholic, had asked my permission, and the governor who had great respect for the Catholic religion was pleased that the others do likewise. On this occasion he made another

---

[49] In 1818 Michigan Territory was increased by the addition of what is now the State of Wisconsin. In 1834 it was further enlarged to include all of the present states of Iowa and Minnesota, and a large portion of South Dakota.

address in which he discussed the principles of the present government, and outlined the regulations he had drawn up for the government of the territory. As most of those present did not understand English very well, I repeated his speech in French, and it was received with great applause for the governor. He faithfully carried out what he promised to these good people. He set to work immediately to shape plans for a new town. This plan was drawn up by Judge Woodward on the lines of the City of Washington, enlarged and improved. Within three or four weeks I saw twenty houses in course of erection in this new town, and building has gone on continuously ever since. . . .[50]

The foregoing account would lead us to believe that under the benign rule of Governor Hull the happy citizens fell to work in something approaching a holiday spirit. In reality there were long and vexatious delays, and frequent displays of arbitrary power to compel adherence to the new plan of reconstruction. Property holdings in the old town were commuted for sites in accordance with the new plan by methods whose details need not detain us.[51] This, however, is pertinent, that Jefferson Avenue as now laid out ran straight through the hallowed site where succeeding churches had stood from the time of Cadillac. Father Richard petitioned for a new location, and on October 4, 1806, the Governor and Judges passed the following resolution.

Resolved, that the Roman Catholic Church be built in the center of the little military square, on section No. 1, on the ground adjacent to the burying ground; the said lot fronting on East and West Avenue two hundred feet wide and running back two hundred feet deep, and bounded on three sides by three other streets.[52]

The ground thus described, which lay between Bates and Randolph Streets, and fronted on Cadillac Square, had been in possession of the parish since 1798, and had been given to it by Colonel Strong, then in command of Detroit, for burial purposes. On April 6, 1799, the parish assembly came to this decision. "Having obtained the one arpent of land from the commandant for a Roman Catholic cemetery, each citizen of our church is to furnish ten stakes, and the accounts agreed upon, L.13, 5s., are allowed for the work of Joseph Coté and Charles Labadie." [53]

---

[50] Browne, op. cit., 112. There are some inaccuracies in the passage. Hull did not arrive until July 1. Father Dilhet most likely wrote down his recollections after his return to France, and his memory sometimes deceived him. His statement that Judge Woodward was a Catholic is surprising, and most likely untrue. Historians of Detroit are generally agreed that hardly any building took place during 1805; conditions were too unsettled. See Mich. Hist. Colls., XXXI, 510 ff.

[51] For the methods by which this commutation was accomplished the interested reader may consult Farmer's and Burton's histories of Detroit, and especially the Proceedings of the Land Board of Detroit (M. Agnes Burton, ed., Detroit, 1915).

[52] Farmer, op. cit., I, 532.

[53] Burton, op. cit., II, 1420–21.

Apparently Father Richard was satisfied with the arrangement, but to the parishioners it meant the desecration of their ancient churchyard. This difference of opinion was the genesis of a long period of misunderstanding between priest and people which grew increasingly bitter, and which could be terminated at the end of ten years only by interdict. A parish committee defending its position brought to bear on the Governor and Judges all the resources of an impassioned rhetoric.

> . . . That after having maturely considered the proposal of the Legislature respecting the relinquishment of the ground held by the Inhabitants of this country from the date of the earliest settlement, by their French ancestors as a public Burial and Church Ground Lot, in consideration of other ground delineated by the appellation of the little square near the Fortress of Detroit, we acknowledge the intrinsic value of the ground proposed to us, but owing to the strongest natural ties which spring from sources that imperiously bind our sensibilities as civilised men, must and do by these presents decline any alienation of such soil. . . .
>
> We appeal to the humanity of our fellow citizens to decide whether it would not evince in the highest degree a want of those humane and charitable qualities which are and ought to be the peculiar characteristic of Christians were we to abandon for the purpose of a common highway the earth in whose bosom reposes the remains of our fathers, our mothers and common kindred. O Sympathy! O Nature! where are thy Godlike Virtues by which the great Author of the Universe has distinguished Man! . . .[54]

The matter dragged on until 1816 when the Corporation of St. Anne, in exchange for that portion of its former property lying in Jefferson Avenue, was given a deed by the Governor and Judges to the remainder of the property fronting on the Avenue, to the ground mentioned in the resolution of 1806, and to as much more as was needed to complete the plot now bounded by Cadillac Square, Bates, Larned, and Randolph Streets.[55] In addition a deed was given for a new cemetery, which comprised the greater portion of the ground within the lines of Broadway, Madison, Witherell, and John R. Streets.[56]

[54] The entire petition is quoted in Burton, as in the preceding note. It is dated April 22, 1807, and is signed by Charles Moran, Joseph Campau, and John R. Williams. The last named, who is most likely the composer, abandoned his faith some years later. He became the first mayor of Detroit, and John R. Street is named after him.

[55] It is to be noted that the deed to this property was contingent upon use for church purposes only. The property was conveyed in fee simple to the Corporation of St. Anne in 1834 in exchange for the opening of Congress Street from Bates to Randolph. See the *Proceedings of the Land Board,* 253.

[56] This ground was never used for cemetery purposes, and was included in the settlement of 1834.

While the Governor and Judges were parcelling out land immediately following the fire, Father Richard was confronted with the necessity of providing accommodations for divine worship. From Father Dilhet's account it seems likely that for a few Sundays at least Mass was said in the open air. Before very long, however, Father Richard had rented for church purposes the old warehouse which had escaped the flames, and which stood near the southeast corner of Wayne and Woodbridge Streets. The parish account book for 1806 mentions payments for planks to be made into pews, and the pew-rent list for the year names the occupants of twelve pews on the Gospel side and eleven on the Epistle side. Whatever meager evidence is available points to the continued use of this improvised church for about three years, or until the acquisition of the Spring Hill farm to be mentioned later.

Typical of Father Richard's courage in adversity, as well as of his piety is the small manuscript volume begun amid the distressing circumstances resulting from the conflagration.[57] Perhaps he felt that with the destruction of all outward incentives to worship an extraordinary means was necessary to keep his people bound to the Blessed Sacrament now abiding in such an uncouth dwelling. It took the form of a Confraternity of the Blessed Sacrament erected in the parish on September 8, 1805.[58] The purpose of the Confraternity presented an interesting variation of the Holy Hour now general in the diocese. Each associate was to make his hour of adoration by himself, but in so doing was to represent the entire parish. The hours were so arranged that throughout the year the Presence should never be left without a worshipper.

In the book referred to above the aim and practices of the Confraternity are detailed, and then follows a list of the associates with the hours assigned to them. Here surely was the flower of Father Richard's flock. There were young boys and girls like Archange McDougall, and Peter Beaubien, both twelve years old, youths and maidens, fathers and mothers, old patriarchs like Jacques Boulai. Heading the list are the names of the four young women who were to consecrate themselves to their pastor's educational enterprises. He puts himself among his people, and his hour of adoration reveals the man, and shows where he found strength and peace throughout his troubled life. It is from one to two o'clock in the morning.

[57] Manuscript preserved in the DCA.
[58] Father Richard copied the articles of a Confraternity printed at Baltimore in 1794 "with the approbation of Mr. J. Carroll, Bishop of the same city."

CHAPTER XV

Father Richard and the War of 1812

FATHER RICHARD'S decision to retire from his parish in favor of Father Dilhet has already been noted. When the pressure of circumstances forced him to remain he was above repining at his responsibilities. Here begins a long period in his life, characterized by restless energy, wherein he is not only the devoted pastor of his flock but a public spirited citizen spending much unthanked effort to raise the cultural level of an apathetic community. The history of the Church in Detroit for the next twenty years is little more than his biography.

Naturally, Father Richard's foremost task was the rebuilding of St. Anne's, and the protection of its property under the new system of government. On April 3, 1807, the Governor and Judges passed "An Act concerning Religious Societies." Its provisions empowered any religious organization to hold and administer real and personal property, and to vest such ownership in any person or persons chosen according to its own polity. The Act is in three sections, and that it was inspired by Father Richard is more than likely. The second section is the longest, and refers exclusively to the "Church usually denominated Catholic, Apostolic, and Roman." [1] No mention is made of any Protestant organization; in fact none existed at the time. [2]

Under this Act Father Richard twelve days later filed articles of incorporation for his parish. The first designated the official title: "The Catholic, Apostolic, and Roman Church of St. Anne of Detroit." Next, the personnel of the Corporation was described as composed of the Pastor and four Trustees. The third and final article read: "The regulations for the interior policing of the Church and

---

[1] The Act is found in the first compilation of Michigan laws made in 1816, and printed by Father Richard. This was the last book to issue from his press.

[2] It is interesting to note that a few days after Father Richard filed his articles, a number of Presbyterians applied for a location, but were denied. Without intending to promote church unity the Governor and Judges understood only two terms, Catholic and Protestant. The Presbyterians obtained their grant in 1819, but only after they had incorporated under the title, "The Protestant Religious Society of Detroit." See Burton, *op. cit.*, II, 1248.

Schools will be made by the Bishop alone, or by the Pastor of the parish. The latter shall have the nomination of male and female teachers." [3]

The rebuilding of the church was another matter. As early as June 30, 1805, the wardens had broached the question, and had decided to build a combined church and rectory as soon as the Land Board should assign a location. By the 29th of December they had advanced to the vision of a church 100 x 40, and a rectory 30 feet square, both to be constructed of logs. A year later they began to toy with the prospect of brick or stone structures. But the building of a church was an alluring topic which had to be considered from every angle, and the more it was discussed the more hopeless became its realization.

Unfortunately, the situation was soon complicated by more serious factors than a mere lack of decision. As we have seen, the majority of the parishioners were opposed to the surrender of the old site lying in Jefferson Avenue. But the town people, and their neighbors to the west and south, while they differed as to the precise location of the church, were agreed that it should be built in the town. Another section of the parish would not make even that concession. From an early date the river shore, beginning at about St. Antoine Street and stretching up to Gaukler's Point, had been called the Côte du Nordest, or the Northeast Shore. At the period we are dealing with it was thickly settled, and its population formed the most prosperous portion of the parish—and the most belligerent. They opposed the rebuilding of the church in the town, refused to contribute to such a purpose, and demanded that the church be rebuilt in their section, or that they be given a church of their own. To justify their opposition they alleged the small number of Catholics in the town, their own distance from the church, and the impossibility of reaching it in bad weather. But there was another reason the consideration of which brings us to the origin of the famous Church Farm case of later years.

A Frenchman by birth, and a silversmith by trade, Francois Paul Malcher came to Detroit about 1792. He did a thriving business turning out the silver trinkets so prized by the Indians, and when he died in 1810 his estate included more than a thousand ear bobs and ear wheels, and four snuff boxes filled with the jewelry he had been making for Walk-In-The-Water, the Huron chief.[4] In 1802 he purchased a farm which lay just east of the present Belle Isle bridge approach.

[3] The articles of incorporation were inscribed by Father Richard in the Register of Parish Assemblies. As may be gathered from the third article, Father Richard was in the thick of his school activities.

[4] All these details concerning Malcher and the Church Farm are borrowed from the careful study of the whole matter made by Burton, op. cit., II, 1268 ff.

It had a frontage of 960 feet on the river, and extended back almost three miles. There was a small log house on the property, which was no fit home for a man who had made his fortune, and now boasted a country estate. Therefore Ignace Moross, the master builder, was called in to furnish specifications and to erect the two-storied structure that soon arose, 20 feet wide by 30 feet deep, and connected by a covered passageway with the primitive log house.

It is no unheard of thing for rich men to tire of their achieved ambitions, and gradually it became known that Malcher would deed his estate to any one guaranteeing him a life pension. Came the fire of 1805, and the consequent agitation for the rebuilding of the church and the controversy about its site. Someone saw the possibility of taking over the Malcher farm for church purposes, and the Northeasterners were quickly organized. The following agreement fortified by eighty-eight signatures was drawn up.

> We, the undersigned inhabitants living on the northeast shore . . . authorize Messrs. Louis Beaufait and Joseph Cerre dit St. Jean, to purchase the farm of Paul Malcher situate in the said northeast shore in the said district and territory, with all its improvements, agricultural implements and animals at the lowest price that will be possible, and upon such conditions as they may judge convenient, and we each promise to approve such bargain as they can make with said Malcher. . . .
>
> We consent that said Beaufait and St. Jean shall have entire charge of the management of the revenue of the church which will be built on the farm of the said Malcher, and make such arrangements as they deem proper with the priest who will officiate in said church, and will receive each year from each of us the proportion which will be allotted to each to pay of the said annuity, for which they hold themselves responsible, and for the payment of which they have mortgaged all of their property, real and personal. We consent and agree that the said Beaufait and St. Jean shall have exclusive charge of the revenues and the management of the said church during the natural life of the said Malcher and after that there will be one or more trustees, according to the custom of the country, and the said Beaufait and St. Jean will have authority to make with Mr. Richard such bargain as they may deem reasonable, even to selling him the said farm, or of transferring to him the bargain that they have made with the said Malcher.[5]

Negotiations with Malcher were terminated by the deed which he executed on April 5, 1808. In return the Northeasterners bound themselves to pay him an annuity of $250, and to discharge some incidental obligations.[6] That Father Richard had anything to do with this arrangement is extremely doubtful. It was not in accordance with his

[5] Burton, *loc. cit.*, 1274.
[6] Burton, *ibid.*, 1275.

plans, and neither he nor the Corporation of St. Anne had any control, but apparently were deliberately excluded.

Thus provided for, the dwellers on the Northeast shore paid a deaf ear to Father Richard's appeals. They had a farm, a building that could be used as a church, they saw no reason why they should contribute to another, and they could bide their time until Father Richard came around to their views. But he was not so easily compelled, and his determination to resist them seems to be the only explanation of his next move.

Just at this time the Federal government was offering for sale or lease a farm which it had obtained in a judgment against a defaulting customs collector in the port of Detroit. Only twenty days after the Malcher deed was signed Father Richard leased this property which became known as the Spring Hill farm.[7] It lay just east of Fort Wayne, and the present Morrell Street cuts through it. There was a large house and a barn on the property, and the priest's purpose in acquiring them is set forth in a report of the transaction sent to Washington.

> Mr. Richard's object is to establish a prominent school for the education of youth of both sexes, and wants to acquire this property as it is deemed an eligible situation for the purpose. . . . By this lease Mr. Richard has the privilege of occupying a large Barn as a temporary church. He would not rent the property unless this privilege was granted, and I considered that the using of it for that purpose could not materially injure it. . . .[8]

Here, in a place of his own choosing, and unhampered by interference, Father Richard had not only facilities for Divine worship but an opportunity for a large scale development of his long-cherished educational projects.[9] We can imagine with what ardor he threw himself into so congenial a labor. For weeks he reveled in reckless expenditures for boards and shingles, nails, glass and ironware.[10] Then there were his precious looms and spinning wheels to be installed, and a hundred details to be attended to for the opening of the Spring Hill Academy.

Thus engaged, perhaps Father Richard sometimes forgot his more serious troubles, for in town the wrangling about a church site still went on. The faction in favor of the traditional location had by this time signified its determination by planting a row of pickets along

---

[7] The original lease is in the DCA.

[8] Letter of Solomon Sibley to Gabriel Duval, May 14, 1808. BHC.

[9] Apparently the old warehouse in the town remained in use as a church until some time in 1809. This will appear from a letter of Father Marchand to be presently quoted.

[10] Sibley papers. BHC, Vol. 934, 157.

THE
CHILD'S SPELLING BOOK;

OR

Michigan Inſtructor:

BEING

A COMPILATION,

FROM THE MOST APPROVED AUTHORS.

SELECTED BY A TEACHER.

PART I.

DETROIT:
PRINTED BY JAMES M. MILLER.
1809.

The first issue of Father Richard's press, and the first book printed in Michigan. From the Burton Historical Collection.

the line of the old cemetery in Jefferson Avenue. Father Richard has a sly note in the Assembly Record Book to the effect that the town marshall had a hand in the sudden disappearance of the obstacle.

It must not be forgotten that during the period we are dealing with, and for many years to come, Father Richard's educational and other enterprises were added to a tremendous burden of pastoral work. He was as yet the only priest in Michigan, and his sick calls took him from Port Huron to Monroe. For some years following the fire he was the only clergyman in Michigan, a fact which had somewhat unusual consequences. Perhaps we might never have heard of them, they seemed so natural to him, had not his tight, conservative neighbor across the river instilled a scruple. To allay it he had recourse to Bishop Carroll.

This letter is to have you advise me on a point of my present conduct that seems somewhat irregular on some respect. About the end of August last, I have been invited by our Governor and some other Gentlemen to try to preach in the English language. Although I was sensible of my incapacity, as there is no other English minister of any denomination, I thought it could be of some utility to take possession of the ground. In order to prevent any irreverence towards the Blessed Sacrament, I have found proper to hold our English meeting not in our chapel but in the Council House.[11] As there are many prejudices against our Society particularly among the people of the lower class, or mechanics, (N.B. in the whole town there are no more than two English persons of the Roman Cath. Society), I found that it would be a great point if I could obtain that they would be willing to hear me. For that reason I have chosen for the subject of my Discourses to establish the General Principles of the Christian Religion, that is to say the Principles used in the discovery of truth, the several causes of our errors, the existence of God, the spirituality, immortality of our souls, the Natural Religion, and the several evidences of the Christian religion in General; I have avoided to make any other ceremony but a Discourse or familiar conference. To make an experiment, that Plan may take more than a year before I should enter into any discriminating point of the Cath. faith. Every Sunday since the 30th August I have met about twelve o'clock in the Council House for the above purpose. Last Monday, Mr. Marchand, the priest of the British side, advised me to write to you as that matter of preaching seemed to him a little strange and it is to comply with his direction that I now pray you to direct me on this important affair. . . .[12]

---

[11] The Council House was a one story building on the southwest corner of Jefferson and Randolph. It was used for every variety of public assembly, and in 1826 a second story was added to serve as a Masonic lodge room. The building was destroyed by fire in 1848.

[12] Letter to Bishop Carroll, October 8, 1807. BCA.

We do not know what Bishop Carroll answered, nor how long Father Richard continued his lectures. At all events his letter testifies as much to his priestly zeal as it does to the respect and esteem in which, throughout his life, he was held by the non-Catholic population of Detroit.

The opening of the Spring Hill Academy, and of another school in the town, had exhausted Father Richard's resources. He had received no encouragement from the Governor and Judges. His own people, partly from poverty and as much from indifference, were little disposed to help him even had they not been split up into factions. A certain amount had been subscribed for the rebuilding of the church, but had then been withdrawn at a turbulent parish assembly. Confronted by such a state of affairs he decided to seek assistance not only in the East, but in his native country as well. For his schools he hoped to enlist the patronage of the Federal government, and the generosity of his well-to-do relatives and friends in France. Appeals in behalf of St. Anne's were to be circulated in the prosperous centers of the East.[13]

Accordingly, Father Richard left Detroit on November 28, 1808, much to the distress of Father Marchand, who saw himself obliged to minister to the vacant parish. Like Father Bocquet he seems to have had a fear of the water, and he thus complained to his bishop.

My neighbor, Mr. Richard, left for Baltimore the 28th of last month, and expects to be gone for three months. . . . You can see the trouble I am in; I promised to do what I could for his parish. Considering the extent of his parish, the inconstancy of the weather, and the difficulty of crossing the river this time of year, and the further fact that I have as much territory of my own to cover, I fear that I cannot do much for him. Moreover, he has only a wretched church building, a dilapidated warehouse serving as a church, no sacristy, no rectory. He lodges wherever he can. In this season when the days are so short how can I say two masses that will benefit the two parishes? How can I risk crossing

[13] One such appeal is extent in the DCA. It was written from Albany, May 10, 1809. After mentioning the fire of 1805, and the consequent impoverishment of the townspeople the appeal continues. "The Town of Detroit is now built up again on a very Elegant and much improved plan. The inhabitants having at last a shelter for their families, are now disposed to make new exertions to erect a Building of public worship that might be an additional ornament to their rising city. In order to succeed in so important and Laudable undertaking they want the Assistance of their fellow citizens in the U. S. with whom they share the Blessings of their Liberal Government. . . . The Subscriber, Mr. Gabriel Richard, Rector of St. Ann of Detroit (The name of the Parish Church Consumed by fire) in the name of all the inhabitants of the City of Detroit and the adjacent Country living on the Borders of the beautiful Strait (in French Detroit) between Lake Erie & Lake Huron, humbly & Earnestly sollicits the assistance of all Liberal & Religious persons in Albany and its Vicinity, and all through the United States of America."

a river that is covered only with thin ice, and doing it after mid-day? . . .[14]

Father Marchand would have had more reason for complaint had he known how long he was to continue these double duties, for Father Richard did not return until the end of July, 1809. His eastern trip had proved rather barren of results. Circumstances had compelled him to abandon his proposed visit to France. The government had made promises regarding his schools, which it later made no move to fulfill. Nor is there any evidence that the Catholics of the East were deeply touched by the plight of their fellow religionists in Detroit. However, Father Richard carried back with him to Michigan something that proves the ardor of his ambition to promote the cultural advancement of his community, and his unerring discernment of the most potent force to bring it about. It was a printing press, from which issued the first newspaper, and the first books to be printed in Michigan.

While in the East Father Richard had gone over the situation in Detroit with Bishop Carroll, and the latter addressed to the malcontents of the Northeast shore a letter whose contents are unknown, but wherein he doubtless tried to break down their intransigeant attitude. On his arrival in Detroit the pastor made a supreme effort to unite the factions in some concerted action. How stubborn and unamenable they were, and how hopeless his endeavor is best set forth in the minutes of the assembly held on August 1.

The question was brought up concerning the letter written by the Bishop of Baltimore to the residents of the Northeast shore. Louis Beaufait answered that the parish being no longer under the Bishop of Baltimore, the letter was of no value to the assembly. On the motion of Gabriel Godfroy, it was unanimously resolved that the wardens make their accounting this week. The Pastor proposed to the residents of the Southern shore (below Detroit) that they enter in joint possession (with the holders) of the farm on the Northeast shore, and that thus united all parishioners immediately build the church of Detroit. The proposition was rejected. Mr. Godfroy proposed that the chapel on the Northeast farm be moved to the town, and that the expense be shared by everyone. This was rejected by the residents of the Northeast shore who declared that their investment in the farm, and the subsequent improvements made upon it were too valuable to be abandoned, and that people living in the end of the district would be too far from the church.

[14] Letter to Bishop Plessis, December 5, 1808. QCA. A census of Father Richard's parish as of July 15, 1808, is inscribed on the cover of the parish assembly record. "Ecorce River, 20 families; Rouge River, 30 families; Southwest of Detroit, 35 families; In the City of Detroit, 35 families; Northeast shore, 95 or 100 families; L'Anse Creuse, 25 families; Huron River, 22 families; Salt Creek, 5 families; St. Clair River, 28 families; Total, 300 families."

Mr. Pierre Chene then proposed to the residents of the South shore that they buy the Malcher farm, and while waiting for the erection of the church of St. Anne in the town, that they consent to attend Divine service in the Northeast chapel instead of in George Meldrum's warehouse. The motion was rejected.

Nothing daunted, Father Richard kept on pressing for a solution. More meetings were held, and on September 13 it is recorded that a number of parishioners believed that a subscription should be taken up, and that the church should be rebuilt on the site donated by the Governor and Judges. The whole matter was back where it started. There is not another word in the record about rebuilding until 1814.

Louis Beaufait was neither the first nor the last lay canonist in Detroit, but there was some truth in the point he made in the minutes just quoted. Although Bishop Carroll had contemplated the division of his vast diocese as early as 1792, the question was not seriously entertained in Rome until ten years later. Apparently the bishop would have been satisfied with the erection of one new see, but in 1802 Propaganda expressed its opinion that the only adequate provision for American needs lay in the creation of an ecclesiastical province whose four of five suffragans should depend on Baltimore as the metropolitan see. To Bishop Carroll was entrusted the selection of the new sees as well as of the priests whom he judged worthy to occupy them. Following his recommendations the Holy See, on April 8, 1808, erected the dioceses of Boston, Philadelphia, New York, and Bardstown.[15]

In the wording of the brief *Ex Debito,* which marked such an important advance in the history of the American Church, the fourth diocese was thus delimitated. "Bardstown, that is, the town or city of Bardstown, and thereto we assign as a diocese the states of Kentucky and Tennessee, and until otherwise provided by this Apostolic See, the territories lying northwest of the Ohio, and extending to the great lakes, and which lie between them and the diocese of Canada, and extending along them to the boundary of Pennsylvania . . ."[16]

At first sight it may seem strange that the little town in Nelson County, Kentucky that today lies dozing over its past, should become the first episcopal see beyond the limits of the original colonies. The tide of westward expansion that followed the close of the Revolutionary War flowed naturally into the territory now known as the States of Kentucky and Tennessee. The latter state drew a majority of its population from the Protestant Scotch and Irish colonists of North Carolina. Kentucky, on the other hand, from the very beginning of

[15] Guilday, *Life and Times . . . Carroll,* Chap. XXIX.
[16] Shea, *Life and Times . . . Carroll,* 622.

its settlement attracted an increasing number of Catholic families from the impoverished farms of Maryland although the stream of Catholic immigration did not assume large proportions until 1785. In that year twenty-five families from Maryland settled on Pottinger's Creek. In quick succession small Catholic communities arose, especially in Nelson, Marion, and Washington Counties, and in 1793 there were at least three hundred Catholic families in Kentucky. Ten years later the number of familes had risen to seven hundred, and in 1807 a careful estimate revealed nine hundred and seventy-two families living in twenty scattered settlements.[17]

The first missionary to the Kentucky Catholics was Father Charles Whelan, a Franciscan, who arrived in 1787. He was followed in 1790 by Father William de Rohan, who remained only a few months but long enough to build the first Catholic church in the state. In May, 1793, Bishop Carroll ordained a young Frenchman who had finished his studies with the Sulpicians in Baltimore. He was Stephen Theodore Badin, the first man raised to the priesthood in the United States, and destined to be the apostle of Catholicity in Kentucky. He arrived in his mission field in December of the same year to begin the herculean task of ministering to the scattered Catholics of the state. Although helped occasionally by travelling missionaries he bore the brunt of the labor himself for the next ten to twelve years. With the coming of the Dominicans to St. Rose, Washington County, in 1806, a new era of flourishing development began.

From the foregoing outline it is evident that when the matter of dividing Bishop Carroll's diocese arose, if a bishop were needed anywhere in the West, it was in Kentucky in the midst of a large Catholic population, and in the stream of westward immigration. Michigan was still a wilderness, off the beaten trail, and Ohio, although filling up rapidly, had as yet an insignificant number of Catholics. All this was well known to Father Badin, and in 1807 he had gone to Baltimore to urge upon Bishop Carroll the necessity of a bishop in Kentucky. He also proposed a candidate for the office in the person of Father Benedict Joseph Flaget, a Sulpician, who on his arrival in America in 1792 had labored for two years in Vincennes, and had then returned to Baltimore where he was engaged in teaching. The outcome of his representations is seen in the division of 1808, which made Father Flaget bishop of Bardstown, the center of the mission field in Kentucky.[18]

But the humble Sulpician, frightened at the thought of the re-

[17] O'Daniel, op. cit., Chap. IV.
[18] M. J. Spalding, Sketches of the Early Catholic Missions in Kentucky (Louisville, 1846), 181.

sponsibilities such an office would lay upon him, refused to accept the nomination. In an effort to have it recalled he even went to France to enlist the support of his superior. However, Pius VII would hear of no refusal, and in August, 1810, Father Flaget returned to America bringing the official documents bearing on the division of the Baltimore diocese and the consecration of the new bishops, which Rome had been unable to forward to Bishop Carroll for two years. He was consecrated on November 4 of the same year.

How to reach his diocese was Bishop Flaget's first problem. He himself had no money, and Archbishop Carroll was unable to relieve his necessities. But the bishop's numerous friends in Baltimore rallied to his assistance so that in May, 1811, he was able to set out for Bardstown. He thus describes his entry into his see.

> It was on June 9, 1811, that I made my entry into this little village, accompanied by two priests, and three young students for the ecclesiastical state. Not only had I not a cent in my purse, but I was even compelled to borrow nearly two thousand francs in order to be able to reach my destination. Thus, without money, without a house, without property, almost without acquaintances, I found myself in the midst of a diocese two or three times larger than all France, containing five large states, and two immense territories, and myself speaking the language very imperfectly. Add to this that almost all the Catholics were immigrants, but newly settled and poorly furnished. . . .[19]

Three years elapsed between Bishop Flaget's nomination to the see of Bardstown and his entrance upon his duties. During this time there is no indication of his having given any thought to the situation in Detroit. Indeed, while Father Richard was making every effort to unite the warring factions the bishop-elect was in Europe trying to throw off his burden. As we have seen, the Northeastern faction, when it suited its purpose, cited the division of 1808 to nullify the effect of Bishop Carroll's letter. But they were shifty antagonists, and it was not very long before they were quite willing to solicit his intervention. On March 23, 1810, they addressed to Baltimore the following petition.

> Your Lordship.
> We again appeal to you in the name of the signers, and of the wardens of the Côte du Nord Est, to establish our church as the church of St. Anne, and to give it this name in view of the fact that it is the only church in the parish and that there is no likelihood of our having another. Moreover, the site of our church is within the corporate limits of the town, and in the middle of the parish which extends for ten miles on either side. We hope that your Lordship will bear in mind that we

[19] Spalding, *op. cit.*, 188.

are more numerous than those gentlemen below the town who have
no place of their own in which to offer the Holy Sacrifice. At several
meetings in the presence of Mr. Richard we have invited them to join
us, insisting that we had acquired the property only for the general welfare of the parish. They not only refused but opposed Mr. Richard in
his ministry to us. Mr. Richard, for whom we have infinite respect, began to say Mass in our church the first day of the present year. He has
continued to do so every fortnight, and we have testified our generosity
by offering him the tithe, a house 60 × 30 for his lodging, many other
buildings on the said farm, a splendid orchard, and a plot of ground
such as he desires for the building of a college. . . .[20]

The petition goes on in the hope that its proponents will be given
a share of the furnishings of the old church. The ancient custom of
having women take up the offerings in church is evidently dear to at
least this section of the parish for permission is asked to continue it
"provided the women are modestly dressed." The final demand is for
a priest of their own who shall live near their church.

Meanwhile, Father Richard was holding on to the Spring Hill
farm, not worried much about the terms of his lease because of the
promises made to him in Washington. But his confidence was destined to be rudely jolted, and the following self-explanatory letter
reveals his chagrin and disappointment as he sadly surveyed the ruin
of his hopes.

To His Excellency the President of   Detroit, Oct. 12, 1810.
the United States.

> Will you be so good as to hear me once
> more? Pardon me if I take so much of
> your time.

Sir:

Mr. Atwater has lately called on me for the Rent of Spring-Hill's
farm during the year 1809 to the amount of $205, & Besides he told me
that he would call again after the first day of 9ber next for the rent of
the present year during ten months in proportion. I have been extremely surprised for these reasons. I was in Washington on the 7
January, 1809, and it was then agreed by the Government, and promised
by Mr. Jefferson, then President of the U. S., that some kind of Agreement should take place between the Dept. of the Treasury & the Dept.
of War, in order to make the school of Spring Hill enjoy the premises
without paying any rent. This was solemnly promised to several Indian
Chiefs at the same time. I have always understood that no rent should
be required from the time the agreement was made, especially as I had
incurred great Expenses in travelling to Washington from so great

[20] The original in BCA. It is a fine example of phonetic French, and is rather difficult
to decipher. The text is an approximate translation.

Distance for the very purpose of settling our affairs with the Govt. relative to our institution. It is true that no kind of writing properly signed was executed at the time, but minutes of the transaction were kept by Mr. Smith, first Clerk in the dept. of war. . . . In case I could not obtain a Passage (which was really the case) for France, my affairs with the Governt. were to be adjusted by letters. Therefore I have written several from New York and from this place. But nothing final was done; which obliged me at last to write that I would prefer to have the farm sold at auction rather than to remain any longer in the uncertainties I have been in the two years past. You have already been informed by Mr. Atwater of the consequences; Mr. James Witherell has bought the premises for the sum of 5000 doll. This sum was above my means. Therefore I have now to move with great expenses. . . .[21]

The great quantity of affairs I have under my direction prevented me from completing this letter in the autumn. I am induced to finish it now by the opportunity offered by Mr. Greely, the Surveyor of public lands, a very respectable Gentleman. . . . I have moved pro tempore to a farm I have rented about middle distance between Spring Hill & town of Detroit. . . .

My present situation is extremely painful. When we were moving from Spring Hill I said to myself; It is then in vain I have worked so hard, travelled so far, and struggled against so many obstacles. . . . It is in your power, Sir, to approach your benevolent hand near the walls of the Edifice I have erected under your patronage.

With the greatest esteem and respect I am, Sir,
Your most humble Servant,
Gabriel Richard.[22]

For all we know to the contrary Father Richard's letter was referred to some government bureau, and there buried. The disheartened priest started all over again in a new location known as the Loranger farm. Approximately, it included the land running back from the river between Twentieth and Twenty-second Streets. Somewhere along the river bank lay a building which was converted into a combination church and school. But these were not its only uses, for Father Marchand, writing at the end of 1811 thus referred to it: "The church, the rectory, the convent, and the boys' school are all one building . . ."[23]

While Father Richard was thus desperately struggling against adverse conditions Detroit entered upon another gloomy period of its history, the War of 1812. The actual declaration of war, made by

---

[21] At this point the letter was laid aside, and the following paragraph was begun under the date of January 28, 1811.

[22] There is a photostat copy of this letter in the BHC. It is known to be in Washington, but its precise location is not indicated.

[23] Letter to Bishop Plessis, November 26, 1811. QCA.

Congress on June 18, was no surprise to the people of Detroit. From what was happening under their eyes they were well aware that the British had never given up hope of recovering at least some portion of the old Northwest Territory. They resented a long series of incidents marked by a contemptuous disregard of American rights. Above all they feared the growing menace of an Indian uprising fomented by British influence, whose center was at Amherstburg, or as it was then called, Fort Malden. As early as 1806, Tecumseh, almost as great a figure as Pontiac, had begun his campaign with British backing. The Shawnee chieftain, aided by his half-mad brother Elkswatawah, "The Prophet," slowly built up an Indian confederacy for the purpose of massacring the American garrisons at Detroit, Chicago, Fort Wayne, St. Louis, and Vincennes. Then would follow the raiding of the settlements, and the expulsion of the Americans from the Indian country. Every year the Indians in greater number made pilgrimages to Fort Malden where they were loaded with presents, and refreshed by assurances of British friendship. As the alienation of Indian lands steadily proceeded the anger of the dispossessed mounted to culminate in the battle of Tippecanoe.[24] It was an American victory, but it did not destroy the Indian menace. Fresh depredations against the settlers began early in 1812, and the British hand was easily discernible.

The record of the military operations around Detroit must be quickly passed over. The town itself was surrendered on August 16 by General Hull, not a traitor but a scapegoat. For its recovery volunteers from Kentucky and Pennsylvania were sent to Ohio to be welded into a fighting force. Early in 1813 one section of it began to move northward under the flabby, old, incompetent General Winchester. On the morning of January 22, a surprise attack deliverd by a body of British troops and their Indian allies crushed the Americans at the River Raisin. A day later ensued the massacre of the wounded who had been left behind, supposedly under guard. In May, the British along with Tecumseh and his warriors, attacked the American base in Ohio, but were beaten off. On September 10, Perry won his famous victory at Put-in-Bay, and it was now the American turn to advance. The British fell back, abandoning Fort Malden and Detroit, and made their last stand at the Battle of the Thames, near Chatham. There was no resisting the onslaught of the Kentuckians exacting revenge for the Raisin River massacre. The British commander got safely away, but Tecumseh died bravely. There was no more fighting in the neighborhood of Detroit, and the

[24] The battle was fought on November 7, 1811, near the present village of Battle Ground on the Tippecanoe River in Indiana.

war was ended by the Treaty of Ghent, concluded December 24, 1814.

The war brought great hardship to the people of Detroit. During the British occupation they were terrorized and plundered by the Indians who lorded it over them in their role as British allies. Supplies of every kind were scarce, and with hundreds of soldiers and prisoners to feed the necessities of life were at a premium. The streets of the town were filled with harrowing sights. Indians roamed about hawking prisoners to the highest bidder, or gleefully exhibited the bundles of bloody scalps for which they collected a bounty. For months following the victory at the Thames, although the Indians were no longer to be feared, conditions were not much better. The British had burned everything they could not carry off. Hundreds of American soldiers were quartered around Detroit, and obliged to forage in every direction. In the rude barracks which had been hastily constructed cholera broke out, and spread to the townspeople. Seven hundred soldiers died in a few weeks time.[25] It was not until the end of 1815 that Detroit began to recover from its war-time afflictions.

During this whole period any activities looking to the rehabilitation of St. Anne's parish were necessarily abandoned. Of Father Richard himself we catch only occasional glimpses. From the very beginning of hostilities he must have engaged in some sort of relief work, as appears from the following certificate.

This is to certify that there is due the Revd, Gabriel Richard by the United States for one month's rent of an Hospital, ten dollars, and I do promise to pay him the same whenever I shall have received from the U. S. money for that purpose.

Detroit, 29 Aug. 1812.
James Abbott.[26]

In the general distress of 1814 when the military requisitioned all food supplies, and rationed even the civilian population, the needy instinctively sought the intervention of Father Richard.[27] Even Congress took cognizance of the deplorable conditions in Michigan, and made a relief appropriation. When it became available, Governor

[25] Catlin, *op. cit.*, Chap. XXXVIII.
[26] Original in DCA.
[27] There is extant some manuscript evidence of this intervention. On November 8, 1814, Father Richard sent this note to the "Commanding officer of Fort Detroit." Sir: These are to pray you to make an exception in favor of the most distressed person existing in the territory, Francis Pepin. He is afflicted with a palsy, and Dysnry, he can scarcely utter a few broken words. . . . BHC, Vol. 943, 210. On the next day he sent this appeal: Since you are a friend of humanity, see this poor woman burdened with a family, who for eight has had no food but corn soaked in water. To accord her a ration is to render her a great service. *Idem.*, 221.

Cass had no hesitancy about naming the man to whom its distribution should be entrusted.

Your letter of May 25, authorized me to distribute to the distressed inhabitants on the River Raisin fifteen hundred dollars. Presuming that the expenditure of this sum was confined to the people there, because it was supposed that the principal scenes of misery and distress were there to be found and having satisfactorily ascertained that the proportion of suffering and indigent persons was no greater nor the means of subsistence less easily obtained than in the other parts of the Territory, I determined to render the bounty coextensive with the subjects requiring it. In extending it to the people of the Territory, I consulted with the Catholic Rector whose ecclesiastical Jurisdiction comprehended the whole country, and whose character as well as office gives to his representations upon this subject great weight. To him I have committed the task of distribution, and the accounts shall be forwarded as soon as practicable . . . .

Permit me, Sir, to state that the resources of this country are totally inadequate to support the number of indigent and helpless people in it. I am told by the Catholick priest that in the immediate vicinity of this small place there are not less than forty widows with families. They are in a state of actual want, and unless the arm of the General Government is extended for their relief, their sufferings must be extreme. . . .[28]

When the trying times were over Father Richard called upon his people to express their thanks to the government. At a parish meeting held on January 14, 1816, it was resolved that the Governor, "who is himself entitled to the Gratitude of the Inhabitants, be respectively requested on behalf of the said inhabitants of the said territory Michigan to express to the President of the U.S. the high sense they entertain of the innumerable favors received from the Bounty of the Government during his administration, and especially in procuring provisions and seed wheat to the poor, in the said territory. Resolved 2 ly, by the said inhabitants of Detroit and its vicinity that a copy of this Resolution shall be forwarded to the President of the U.S. as a token of their approbation and as a merited tribute of their acknowledgment of his truly paternal benevolence, and as a perpetual testimony of their attachment to a Government always just and generous."

To Father Richard as he penned these resolutions the words "attachment to a Government" were more than a formal phrase; he had suffered for his attachment. General Brock, to whom Detroit had surrendered in 1812, was soon succeeded by the detestable Henry Procter. As far as he dared he gave his Indian allies free rein, and the efforts of the townspeople to mitigate the sufferings of the Ameri-

28 *Mich. Hist. Colls.*, XXXVI, 383.

can prisoners that kept pouring in only angered him. Sensing both the defiant opposition to his rule, and the contempt in which he was held for his inhumanity, he resorted to the extreme measure of exiling some thirty leading citizens of Detroit.[29] They were compelled to return to the East, leaving their families to an uncertain fate.

If anyone could be counted as an influential citizen it was Father Richard, and his conduct must have been closely watched. To Father Marchand from his vantage point across the river it was clearly reprehensible. He wrote his impressions to Bishop Plessis.

> Yesterday, the two of us called upon the new commandant, Colonel Procter. He (Father Richard) was received with politeness; but I am uncertain as to the outcome. Richard has always shown himself extremely republican, and even anti British, a sentiment from which, as I have often told him, he might well refrain. All this is no secret to our Government, and day before yesterday, one of our officers speaking to me about him said, 'We know that gentleman. His principles are too much at variance with ours.' I fear that all this will prove dangerous for him. He loves to talk politics, and if things are not conducted according to his ideas, he is neither slow nor gentle in expressing his opinion. That sort of thing, especially on the part of the clergy, is distasteful to us. If his place happened to be vacant, either because our Government found him objectionable, or that he retired voluntarily, or that he was recalled by his Superior—for he is a Sulpician from the Baltimore house—What should I do? I have all I can do to take care of my own parish. I see nevertheless that this portion of God's people must not be abandoned. What is most disheartening is that there is neither church nor rectory; the furnishings of the ancient church are so dispersed that it would be difficult to bring them together; and what is worse, there is division among the inhabitants, and the headstrong are numerous. . . .[30]

The citizens deported by Procter's orders left in the first days of February, 1813. Although Father Richard was a marked man he was allowed to stay on. We do not know the nature of his final offense that roused Procter's ire, but on May 21 he was ordered out of Detroit and committed to the custody of Father Marchand to await his deportation to Lower Canada. Father Marchand thought of interceding in his confrere's behalf, but Procter seemed so determined that he did not dare. However, for reasons which we can only surmise, Procter did not carry out his threat, and Father Richard remained virtually a prisoner in Father Marchand's rectory until the evening of June 16, when a strange scene was enacted. Procter strode into the

[29] Details will be found in any of the histories of Detroit, and in the *Mich. Hist. Colls.*, XXXVI, 283 ff.
[30] Letter to Bishop Plessis, August 18, 1812. QCA.

low-roofed living room accompanied by Jacques Baby, the leading citizen of Assumption parish, and offered Father Richard the choice of exile, or of signing a declaration that he would henceforth keep his opinions to himself. Thinking only of the welfare of his people Father Richard signed while the candle light flickered on Procter's red face set in its half circle of beard, and on Baby and Father Marchand waiting their turn to sign as witnesses. Father Richard was now free to return to Detroit, and Procter was not much longer in a position to enforce his demand.[31]

With the advent of peace, and some measure of recuperation from the ravages of war, Father Richard devoted himself again to healing the division in his parish.[32] But the parishioners were still unwilling to sink their differences, and he struggled along as best he could on the Loranger farm. Yet, despite adverse circumstances this period of his life was one of intense activity. When Bishop Plessis came to Assumption parish on an episcopal visitation in 1816, he wrote in his journal this striking characterization of Father Richard.

> This ecclesiastic is, moreover, thoroughly estimable on account of his regularity, of the variety of his knowledge, and especially of an activity of which it is difficult to form an idea. He has the talent of doing, almost simultaneously, ten entirely different things. Provided with newspapers, well informed on all political matters, ever ready to argue on religion when the occasion presents itself, and thoroughly learned in theology, he reaps his hay, gathers the fruits of his garden, manages a fishery fronting his lot, teaches mathematics to one young man, reading to another, devotes time to mental prayer, establishes a printing press, confesses all his people, imports carding and spinning-wheels and looms to teach the women of his parish how to work, leaves not a single act of his parochial register unwritten, mounts an electrical machine, goes on sick calls at a very great distance, writes letters and receives others from all parts, preaches every Sunday and holyday both lengthily and learnedly, enriches his library, spends whole nights without sleep, walks for whole days, loves to converse, receives company, teaches catechism to his young parishioners, supports a girls' school under the management of a few female teachers of his own choosing whom he directs like

---

[31] These details are condensed from two letters of Father Marchand to Bishop Plessis, May 28 and September 24, 1813. QCA. It has often been asserted that Father Richard was a prisoner for a time at Malden, and that he was released through the good offices of Tecumseh. No contemporary evidence in proof has yet been found. The story seems to have first appeared in the Detroit Catholic Vindicator for May 5, 1855, and purported to be the testimony of a well-educated Indian then living at Mackinac. See Verwyst, *op. cit.*, 54.

[32] In 1814, John R. Williams, while in Albany, wrote to Father Richard that he would be willing to collect in eastern cities for the rebuilding of St. Anne's church, and would make up the balance from his own private means. His offer was duly accepted and inscribed in the parish register. His letter is in the BHC, Vol. 451, 227.

a religious community, while he gives lessons in plain-song to young boys assembled in a school he has founded, leads a most frugal life, and is in good health, as fresh and able at the age of fifty as one usually is at thirty.[33]

The bishop remained for some time in the neighborhood of Detroit, and on June 30, with the consent of Bishop Flaget, he confirmed about 200 persons in the chapel of the Northeast shore.[34] During his stay he was introduced to all the notables of the town by Father Richard, and he has left us a rather amusing account of a social function as it was carried out by his host. The formalities began with a visit to General Macomb, the military commander of the post.

The Bishop on arriving at the gate of this garden was received by the first aide-de-camp. On one side of the garden the guard was under arms; a band of musicians a little farther off began playing a national air, while the General in full dress and surrounded by his staff awaited the prelate under the portico to besiege him with attentions. . . .

The visit lasted about half an hour, and was entirely spent in mutual ceremony and civilities. The General showed his guests his apartments, his library, the environments of his house, and when we retired to continue our route as far as Mr. Richard's, who lives a mile lower down, on the same bank, and where we were to dine, the General would not consent to let us go there otherwise than in his boat, prepared expressly and manned with an elegant crew. He accompanied us as far as the embarkation. The guard was still under arms, and the musicians lined the steps to play a flourish just as we walked down.

The visitors thought they had done with ceremony, at least for the

---

[33] Bishop Joseph-Octave Plessis, who traveled extensively throughout his vast diocese, kept a journal, written in the third person, and preserved in the QCA. There is a copy of the portion relating to Detroit in the BHC.

[34] The Northeast chapel was most likely better suited for this function than Father Richard's establishment on the Loranger farm. Bishop Plessis thus describes both locations:

"They (the parishioners) are divided between two chapels; the one situated on the northeast shore about two or three miles above the city, and the other a league below. The latter, which is directly opposite the Church of the Assumption is nothing more than the house occupied by Mr. Richard and belonging in reality to an individual by the name of Laselle who lets it to him as well as the entire piece of land. The house being spacious, Mr. Richard has changed one of its apartments into a sanctuary, using another as a sacristy. A third and a fourth form the nave, without counting that a certain number of parishioners can attend divine service at the windows, at least during the fine season, by means of a covered gallery in front of the house.

"The parishioners do not like this chapel and would prefer to assemble in that of the Northeast Shore. It is nothing better than a barn with a ceiling and windows and an entrance at one end, and a small sanctuary at the other. They are attached to this chapel on account of its being placed on a lot which they have acquired in the hope of having there one day a parish church. They are Masters there and suffer to see the priest, by occupying a lot and house for which he pays rent, enjoying an independence at which they are offended. . . ."

remainder of that day, and hoped to dine freely and fraternally at M. Richard's house where they were expected. On the contrary, while they were going there by water, the Governor and the General arrived by land. . . .

The Abbe Richard, who had summoned all these guests without the participation of the Bishop of Quebec, placed him simply between the Governor and the General, and served them on a rather badly disposed table a dinner too abundant in meat, too scant in vegetables in too small an apartment, whose windows he had had the precaution of removing to give more air to his company. A shower of rain driven by the southerly wind, which occurred during the repast, sprinkled the chief guests. They would have desired to have the windows closed; but there were none to close. . . . Toasts or healths had to be drunk; The first was in the Bishop's honor. He proposed one to the President of the United States, expecting that it would be returned by another to the King of England. Not at all. Governor Cass proposed his to our Holy Father, the Pope, and the General's to the prosperity of the Catholic clergy. It must be remarked that these two dignitaries had quite recently received from Mr. Richard an honor that the Catholic clergy do not ordinarily grant to Protestants, which was that at the solemn procession of Corpus Christi, the 13th of the same month, he had invited them to hold the ribbons of the canopy under which was the Blessed Sacrament, and had had the procession accompanied by an American regiment under arms. The parishioners had not been, in general, edified by such a mixture, and had justly complained of this novelty. The Abbe Richard justifies his conduct by what the Bishop of Baltimore had given as a principle to his clergy: to do towards Protestants all that might draw them to the Catholic Church, an excellent principle as long as it does not violate the rules in essential points . . .[35]

Bishop Plessis had long been in correspondence with Bishop Flaget concerning the situation in Detroit, and was expected during his

[35] In the days of Father Richard the Corpus Christi procession was an event of civic importance. Farmer quotes an order addressed to a captain of the militia.

"In the interim you are requested to appear with your company on the General Parade ground in the rear of this city on Saturday next at 2 o'clock P.M., with a view to prepare your men to attend as a military escort at the celebration of the anniversary of the institution of the feast of the blessed sacrament of our Lord Jesus Christ." *Op. cit.*, I, 533.

Referring to the same celebration the *Detroit Gazette* on June 20, 1820, carried this advertisement:

According to ancient custom, the solemn Procession in commemoration of the Blessed Sacrament, commonly called the Lord's Supper, will take place on Sunday next at 5 o'clock P.M., within the enclosure of the Church of St. Anne. A short address explanatory of the ceremony will be delivered at half past four. Christians of all denominations are welcome. It is expected, however, that they will conform to all rules observed by Catholics on such occasions by standing, walking and kneeling. The Military on duty may remain covered. It is enjoined on all persons to preserve profound silence during the whole ceremony. N.B. A collection will be made, the proceeds of which will be employed in completing the steeples of the Church of St. Anne, and covering them with tin.

visit to heal the division between the parishioners.[36] He secured from the Northeast group a half-hearted agreement to concur in the plans of Father Richard, and then advised him to raise funds for the immediate rebuilding of St. Anne's by auctioning off the parish property in Jefferson Avenue. On July 17, 1816, just as the sale was about to begin, a crowd of malcontents headed by an attorney appeared on the scene and stopped the proceedings. The bones of their dead should never be desecrated, and moreover, their interest in the property was not sufficiently safeguarded by the inadequate representation which they had in the Corporation of St. Anne. For the remainder of the year nothing more was done despite two letters from Bishop Flaget urging peace. In one of them he promised to make the Northeast shore a separate parish if its residents withdrew their opposition to the sale of the old property. For answer they organized themselves into a distinct corporation.[37]

Meanwhile, the town authorities desirous of opening up Jefferson Avenue were standing by awaiting a settlement of the wrangle. If the site donated by the Governor and Judges were not soon used for church purposes there was danger of its being lost. In this crisis Father Richard wrote a complete history of the controversy to Bishop Flaget so that with all the facts in his possession the Bishop could give a final decision.[38] It was issued on February 23, 1817.

The Bishop began by reminding the dissenters of his patient and conciliatory treatment of them. In spite of it, "one of the adherents has been insolent enough to raise his hand in threatening violence against your worthy pastor who, for more than twenty years, has watered with the sweat of his brow this ungrateful land, sacrificing his own comfort and tastes that you might not be left without the ministrations of a priest, with no other thing to his reproach than an excess of goodness which I might call weakness. . . ."

Then came the bishop's positive declaration. St. Anne's was to be erected on the site donated by the Governor and Judges. The Corporation was empowered to abandon the old cemetery after transferring its contents to the new one adjoining the site of the new church. All property belonging to the Corporation could be disposed of for "the greatest good of the said Catholic Church of Detroit." Finally, seven ringleaders of the Northeast faction were declared excommunicate, and their chapel laid under an interdict.[39]

---

[36] Most of the correspondence between Bishops Flaget and Plessis is printed in Vol. XVIII of the *Records of the American Catholic Historical Society* (Philadelphia).

[37] Detail from the Parish Assembly Record.

[38] Father Richard's report and other documents bearing on the controversy lie in the NDA.

[39] Burton, *op. cit.*, II, 1287.

Submission was still a long way off. In the first week of May, Father Richard began the removal of the bodies from the old graveyard. The rebels rallied to the scene, and began shovelling the earth back into the open graves. One of them, Charles Gouin, began an altercation with Father Richard, who dubbed him "a perjured man." Gouin promptly brought suit for defamation of character, and was awarded a verdict of twenty dollars.[40]

Father Richard was in despair. He asked Bishop Flaget to remove him. During the late war he had met many people from Ohio, and he would be glad to begin a parish in Columbus or Chillicothe. He would do missionary work in Ohio, or he would go back to teaching, either in the Bishop's seminary in Kentucky or in Baltimore. Before the fire the Detroit parish had been all that one could desire, but now it needed a better and stronger man than he.[41]

Realizing that only his presence in Detroit could put an end to such disgraceful condition, Bishop Flaget started from St. Thomas, Kentucky, in the middle of May, 1818. He was accompanied by two young priests, John Bertrand and Philip Janvier, whom he had borrowed from the diocese of Louisiana.[42] Traveling on horseback the party reached the Raisin River at the end of the month. Here the bishop remained for three days, but the church was in such ruinous condition that he could not say Mass.[43] On June 1, the bishop entered Detroit surrounded by a mounted escort that had gone to meet him ten miles below the town.

After paying his respects to Governor Cass and General Macomb, who received him with the greatest courtesy, the bishop entered upon the serious purpose of his visit. His kindness and tact displayed in numerous conferences soon broke down all opposition. The factions were united, and the froward, making repentant submission, were relieved of the censures hanging over them.[44] There remained only the lifting of the interdict from the Northeast chapel, and this was accomplished on June 9 amid general rejoicing. Cannons

---

[40] The legal papers in the case are among the May Papers in the BHC.

[41] Letter to Bishop Flaget, May 5, 1817. NDA.

[42] There are several references to these two clergymen in Rothensteiner, *op. cit.*

[43] Maes, *op. cit.*, 33.

[44] In the document announcing the interdict Bishop Flaget devoted a postscript to Joseph Campau. He was in no mood for submission; he had abandoned the practice of his religion many years before, and had become a Mason. "Campau, to hold his followers in line and to dishearten Father Richard, attempted the building of a church near the old site. The foundation was laid and the cornerstone was blessed by himself, mockingly, with a bottle of whiskey. At least so says tradition." From Denissen manuscript in the BHC quoted by Burton, *op. cit.*, II, 1286. Father Christian Denissen, pastor of St. Charles, Detroit, from 1890 to 1911, because of his interest in the Church Farm property made extensive researches in Detroit history. His genealogy of Detroit families, an immense work still in manuscript, is indispensable to all local historians.

boomed to mark the hour of assembly, and the music of the military band swelled the chorus of the chanting crowd as it moved up the river bank.

It was a gala day for the little city, and everyone turned out to do honor to the Bishop, and to the occasion. We can see them now as they form in procession in Larned Street in front of the future home of their church. Everyone enthusiastic as if on a Fourth of July celebration, and yet few of them comprehending that they were taking part in one of the most impressive ceremonies of the Catholic Church, the removal of an interdict. Slowly they marched down Randolph Street to Atwater Street, and thence up that road along the margin of the river, for Jefferson Avenue was not then opened, picking their way in many places where the road was not well graded, past the houses of the Beaubiens, and Morans, and Gouin, and Riopelle, Dequindre, and Jacques Campau, St. Aubin, Dubois, and Chene, across the little bridge that spanned Parent's creek, where, half a century before, was fought the disastrous battle of Bloody Run. . . . Their destination reached, with impressive ceremonies, with tears in the eyes of many, with repentence expressed by all, absolution was granted and the church reopened. [45]

In the afternoon the procession returned to the town, and there, on the site donated by the Governor and Judges, the bishop performed the final act symbolic of the accord that now ended years of contention. He laid the first stone in the foundation of another church of St. Anne that was planned to eclipse all its predecessors. Firm in his judgment of the future, the bishop had overruled the cautious dimensions proposed by Father Richard, and had himself staked out more ample lines for the edifice that would one day become the first cathedral of the Diocese of Detroit.[46]

A few days later, Bishop Flaget, leaving Father Janvier as assistant to Father Richard, undertook a journey to Montreal accompanied by Father Bertrand. He returned at the end of July, and after a month's rest set out to visit Sault Ste. Marie. On October 11, the bishop and Father Bertrand were back in Detroit, both suffering from a fever contracted on the voyage. The latter recovered so slowly that he was of little service in Detroit, and as a consequence he re-

---

[45] Burton, *op. cit.*, II, 1290.

[46] To Father Richard the final dimensions of St. Anne's were enormous. The building was 116 feet long, 60 wide, and 30 high. "My first plan had been to make it 29 feet shorter, but the Bishop of Bardstown . . . arrived in Detroit as we were beginning to dig the foundations. He himself laid the first stone, and impelled me to lengthen the structure to its present size, announcing to me—it was in 1818—that it would be the cathedral of the proposed diocese of Michigan. God alone knows what straits this excessive size left me in." Letter to the Society for the Propagation of the Faith, December 22, 1825.

turned to his diocese some time in 1820. He died at New Orleans in the fall of 1824.[47]

By the 1st of November Bishop Flaget was well enough to begin an arduous round of pastoral duties. On that day two hundred persons were confirmed, and the bishop began the exercises of a mission for the residents of the Northeast shore. He next turned his attention to the Raisin River parish. Here, six weeks were spent in determined effort to remedy the results of long years of neglect. Public sinners did public penance, the children were prepared for first communion, and their elders were given a course of instructions.[48] Returning to Detroit on December 30, the bishop spent the winter in wiping out the last traces of insubordination among the parishioners, and in correcting abuses. To his friend, Bishop Plessis, the prelate sent the following account of his occupations.

> At present I am engaged in winning back the inhabitants of the Northeast shore. They are a people deeply embittered, suspicious, and extraordinarily susceptible. In general they show me much confidence, and at different times have assured me that their hearts were free from all discord. . . . It is in large measure due to these worthy gentlemen that I am passing the winter in Detroit, in order to secure peace, nor surely will my time have been lost should I have the happiness to succeed . . .[49]
>
> After having visited the different stations that form the Catholic Church of Detroit, I have reason to believe that the people's inordinate love of social pleasures, evening gatherings and dances, was the cause of their immorality, idleness, and extreme poverty. I protested with all possible vehemence against balls in particular . . . Thus far this peremptory action has succeeded, and last week a fiddler of my diocese refused an offer made to him of thirty dollars if he would play for two nights at a dance in Malden . . .[50]

To prevent the recurrence of further trouble the bishop published a set of regulations designed to provide for the expansion of the Church in the district around Detroit. After a lengthy preamble in which the bishop called upon the faithful to preserve the fruits of his visit, he laid down the following provisions.

> Convinced by a long and sad experience that churches to which lands are not annexed at the time of their erection are always poor and unable

[47] "Yesterday a Mass was sung for the repose of the soul of Mr. Bertrand who died at New Orleans a short while ago. . . ." Letter of Father Marchand to Bishop Plessis, October 7, 1824. QCA.

[48] The first children of Irish parentage, whose names appear in the Monroe register, Mary Jane O'Rorke and Mary Lynch, were baptized during the visitation. The bishop was again in Monroe to give Confirmation in April, 1819.

[49] Letter to Bishop Plessis, January 22, 1819. QCA.

[50] Same to same, February 21, 1819. QCA.

to provide for the needs of their respective priests, and the support of schools, if there are any, we flatter ourselves that henceforth no church will be established as a parish unless it is provided with 200 acres of land or a house whose value would equal or surpass the above mentioned.

The Church of St. Anthony of Padua, situated on the banks of the Riviere aux Raisins, will include, until new ones are built, all the Catholic Establishments from 15 to 18 miles around.

The two banks of the Riviere aux Hurons together with those of the Riviere aux Ecorces will form a third parish, the center of which will be near the town they are founding, and the church they intend to build there shall be under the vocable of Holy Mary.

The two banks of the Rouge River as far as Milk Creek, or the Milk River, shall make a fourth division of which Detroit, where St. Anne's chapel is, shall be the center.

From the Milk River to the Pointe a Guignolet there shall be a fifth division, the center of which shall be at Grosse Pointe; the church they will build there shall be under the vocable of St. Peter, the Apostle.

From the Riviere aux Hurons to the St. Clair River, this shall, for the time being, form the sixth division of which the church of St. Francis de Sales on the Riviere aux Hurons shall be the central point.

As, in a future time, there will be a church between Lake St. Clair and Lake Huron, the inhabitants on the St. Clair River shall be separated from the parish of the Riviere aux Hurons, and the church they shall build there shall be under the vocable of St. Agnes.[51]

During his stay in Detroit, the bishop was a frequent visitor to the Canadian side of the river. In Assumption parish he confirmed and gave a mission. He also visited the two congregations which by this time had grown out of the mother parish, namely, Amherstburg, and Prairie Siding on the Thames.

When Bishop Flaget was satisfied with the salutary effects of his stay in Detroit he decided to heed the insistent calls from Kentucky for his return. On May 29, he left Detroit for Erie, two days earlier than he had planned, in order to feel the thrill of riding that marvelous new means of transportation, the Walk-in-the-Water, the first steamboat to ply the lakes. To lighten Father Richard's burden, he allowed Fathers Bertrand and Janvier to remain in Detroit.

With two assistants to look after his outlying missions, Father

---

[51] The document is published in the *American Cath. Hist. Researches*, XV, 103. Although not dated it was certainly written at Detroit early in 1819. In a second section the bishop makes particular reference to the Northeast chapel, which he calls St. Joseph's Church. St. Anne's is to be clearly recognized as the parish church, and St. Joseph's is tolerated only to facilitate ministry to the parishioners. "If the gentlemen of the Northeast coast are not satisfied with these arrangements, if they renew their complaints and murmers, we declare, at once, their church closed *forever*, in order to terminate finally scandals which have lasted already too long. . . ."

Richard devoted himself to the rebuilding of St. Anne's. The erection of a stone building on the scale proposed by Bishop Flaget was a tremendous undertaking for those days. His people had little more than the necessities of life, and the old French system of parish administration with its well-defined methods of raising revenue promoted a sense of satisfaction with a certain level of duty accomplished rather than a spirit of generosity. But Father Richard had enough money to start with, as the advertisement in the Detroit Gazette attested.

> Great Bargain! Offered by Gabriel Richard, rector of St. Anne. 200 hard dollars will be given for twenty toises of long stone of Stony Island delivered at Detroit on the wharf of Mr. Jacob Smith, or two hundred and forty dollars if delivered on the church ground. 100 barrels of lime are wanted immediately. Five shillings will be given per barrel at the river side, and six shillings on the church ground.[52]

In those early days currency was scarce, and barter was the prevailing method of trade. As the work progressed Father Richard's cash was exhausted, and he resorted to the common practice of issuing scrip to pay his workmen. Before long someone flooded the merchants of Detroit with counterfeits of Father Richard's due bills, and when the fraud was discovered he could do no more than write the following letter to the public.

> The undersigned returns his thanks to the merchants and other citizens of Detroit and its vicinity for the liberal assistance given him in erecting the Church of St. Anne, and for having given free circulation to his small notes.
>
> With sorrow and displeasure he has discovered that many of his small notes are counterfeited, and that several of his neighbors have suffered by reason of the counterfeit. It appears that more than 200 fifty cent bills have been within the past fortnight put in circulation in this city . . .
>
> The public are warned that every possible exertion will be made by the undersigned to redeem his bills without delay, and in order to do away with any fears that may exist as to his capability to do so, he deems it proper to state that besides three sections of land of the finest quality, and three valuable lots in the city, the Corporation of St. Anne holds a very valuable and extensive spot of ground which surrounds the Church, worth ten times more than the whole amount of the bills now in circulation . . .[53]

By the end of 1820 the basement had been roofed over, and was in use as a temporary chapel. The superstructure rose slowly accord-

[52] The *Detroit Gazette,* August 19, 1818.
[53] *Ibid.,* April 23, 1819.

ing to Father Richard's means, and it was not until the Christmas of 1828 that the completed church was used for the first time. A two-story wooden rectory was built adjoining the church, and first occupied in May, 1822.[54]

The rebuilding of St. Anne's came at a most opportune time. The American pioneers on the way to the virgin lands of Michigan were just over the horizon. Soon they would be followed by the pilgrims from foreign lands to whom America meant freedom and opportunity. In the polyglot mass that was to build up the city and the state, the original French population was to be slowly submerged. Sermons in strange tongues would soon be heard in St. Anne's, and Bishop Flaget's predictions would come true. The old mother parish was ready to cradle all the alien children that Providence had on the way to her doors.

[54] Farmer gives this description of old St. Anne's. "The size of the church is sixty by one hundred and sixteen feet. Originally there was in the center an octagonal dome, thirty feet in diameter and thirty feet high, and two small cupolas in the rear. The center dome was surmounted by a representation of the sun, on which was a human face, and over it a cock. On the smaller cupolas were representations of the moon and a fish. The center dome and the cupolas were removed in 1842. The next year the towers were fully enclosed, and the front porch erected. In the spring of 1850 the brick extension in the rear was added, and it with a wing extending out to Bates Street, was used for school purposes, and a school with several hundred pupils maintained here up to 1864." *Op. cit.*, I, 533.

CHAPTER XVI

Father Richard in Congress

IN THE years following his missionary journey to Mackinac in 1799 Father Richard's pastoral ministry had been confined to the town of Detroit and the French settlements along the eastern shore of the state from Maumee Bay to Port Huron. Much as he wished it, he had never been able to investigate personally the greater portion of the Territory in which he was the only priest. But in 1821 the long awaited opportunity presented itself. The rebuilding of St. Anne's was progressing favorably, and he could take advantage of the services of Father Janvier who was still in Detroit.

Although Father Richard would most likely have made a missionary tour on his own initiative there were other reasons why he undertook the journey at this time. The Potawatomi Indians of western Michigan were about to meet in Chicago to cede to the government the remainder of their lands lying south of the Grand River.[1] They had invited Father Richard to be present at the negotiations to aid them in making provisions for the establishment of a Catholic mission which they had long desired.[2] Moreover, he had been commissioned, presumably by Bishop Flaget, to report on the religious conditions in the Territory, and to make recommendations for the placing of priests where they were most urgently needed. Such a commission reflected the development which had been taking place in the Bishop's own diocese. We must pause here to consider certain aspects of it bearing on our history which our preoccupation with affairs in Detroit obliged us to forego.

Distressing as were the conditions under which Bishop Flaget began his ministry in Kentucky, his own zeal and energy together with the labors of the devoted priests whom he directed soon brought about remarkable results. Within a few years the Church in Kentucky gave every evidence of fervent and vigorous life. The seminary at St. Thomas was opened in November, 1811. The following year

---

[1] The cession was signed at Chicago in August, 1821. See *Mich. Hist. Colls.*, XXVI, 275.

[2] Letter of Father Richard, August 25, 1827, in *Annals of the Propagation of the Faith*, III, 336.

witnessed the beginnings of two native Sisterhoods: the Sisters of Loretto, and the Sisters of Charity. On August 8, 1819, the cathedral at Bardstown was dedicated to divine worship, and a week later Father John Baptist David was consecrated as coadjutor to Bishop Flaget. In 1821 there were about twenty-five scattered parishes, some of them with schools, ministering to approximately twelve thousand communicants.[3]

The tremendous burden imposed upon Bishop Flaget by the extent of his diocese is apparent in the report which he made to the Holy See in 1815.[4] Yet, the document has no reference to the dividing of this vast territory. Some time between the writing of the report and his visit to Detroit in 1818 the bishop began to plan for the dismemberment of his diocese. This is evident in the directions which he gave to Father Richard for the rebuilding of St. Anne's. It is likewise plain that he had taken counsel in the matter with his friend Bishop Dubourg of Louisiana, for the latter wrote to Archbishop Maréchal of Baltimore on May 7, 1819, asking him to petition Rome for the erection of a see at Detroit, and perhaps a second one in Ohio.[5] In December of the same year Bishop Flaget expressed to the Archbishop the necessity of sees at Vincennes, Cincinnati, and Detroit. Three months later, he reiterated his recommendations for sees at Cincinnati and Detroit, and moreover suggested likely candidates for them.

Had Bishop Flaget's desires been acceded to at the time, Detroit would have been linked with another illustrious pioneer of the Church in America. The Bishop's first choice for the contemplated see was Prince Demetrius Gallitzin. Scion of one of the oldest and wealthiest families of Russia, the prince began, at seventeen, to practice the religion of his Catholic mother. Five years later, he came to America in the course of his foreign travel, and here he made a momentous decision, nothing less than the plighting of his life and fortune to the advancement of the Church in America. He entered the Sulpician seminary in Baltimore, the year after it was founded, and in 1795 was ordained to the priesthood.[6] For his field of labor he chose the mountainous country of western Pennsylvania, and there

[3] Details *passim* from Spalding, *Sketches. . . . Missions in Kentucky.*

[4] *Catholic Historical Review*, I, 305–19.

[5] Rev. John H. Lamott, *History of the Archdiocese of Cincinnati* (Cincinnati, 1921), Chap. II.

[6] Father Stephen Badin, the first priest ordained under American jurisdiction came to Baltimore from France as a subdeacon. Prince Gallitzin was the first man to receive both minor and major orders in the United States. For many years, in order to avoid publicity, he bore the name of Father Smith. There is an excellent biographical sketch in the Catholic Encyclopedia.

he spent forty-one years of arduous ministry. His personal fortune was devoted to the upbuilding of Catholic colonies in his mission field. Within a radius of fifteen miles from his original establishment there are today twenty-one flourishing parishes.

The Bishop's second choice for Detroit was a Canadian confrere, a Sulpician at Montreal, Jean-Jacques Lartigue. But while Father Lartigue was being proposed for Detroit, the Roman authorities were considering him for the post of auxiliary to the Bishop of Quebec, with special charge of the Montreal district. He was consecrated to this office in 1821, and became the first bishop of Montreal on May 13, 1836.

The candidates just named were the choice of Bishops Flaget and Dubourg. But the former was studying the matter from every angle and he proposed an alternative arrangement. Father Gallitzin, on account of his knowledge of German, would perhaps be needed more in Ohio, and in that event the Bishop proposed for Detroit his original candidate for Cincinnati, Father Benedict Fenwick, S.J.

His is another honored name in American Catholic history. A descendant of one of the first Catholic families of Maryland, he began his studies with the Sulpicians in Baltimore. On the restoration of the Society of Jesus in the United States in 1806, he entered as a scholastic, and was ordained two years later. After being twice president of Georgetown College he was consecrated second bishop of Boston in 1825. During the twenty-one years of his episcopacy his educational interests were to the fore, and he was the founder of Holy Cross College.[7]

In the meantime Bishop Dubourg had written to the Roman authorities on his own initiative suggesting the erection of sees at Cincinnati and Detroit, and proposing still another candidate for the latter see in the person of Father John Grassi, S.J.[8] He was a learned Italian who had come to the United States in 1811, and who was rector of Georgetown College from 1812 to 1817. When proposed by Bishop Dubourg he had returned to Rome, and there he held many important offices until his death in 1849.

After the flurry of letter writing had subsided, and the Roman authorities were in possession of all needed information, they decided to follow the advice given by Archbishop Maréchal in 1820 that the erection of a see at Detroit was inopportune. However, they recognized the imperative need of relieving Bishop Flaget, and of providing for the interests of the Church in Ohio. Accordingly, the

[7] See Robert H. Lord, John E. Sexton, Edward T. Harrington, *History of the Archdiocese of Boston* (New York, 1944).

[8] Lamott, *op cit.*, 43.

diocese of Cincinnati was erected on May 21, 1821, with Edward Dominic Fenwick as its first bishop. The diocese proper embraced only the State of Ohio, but to Bishop Fenwick was entrusted the administration of Michigan Territory.[9]

Again, the territory wherein the Church had been established for over a hundred years became the appanage of a jurisdiction outside its borders. It had not yet been sufficiently quickened by the stream of immigration that still preferred the Ohio valley route as the outlet to the West. In 1800 Ohio had a population of 42,000. After its admission to statehood in 1803 development was rapid. By 1810 the population had grown to 230,000, and at the end of the next decade this number had been more than doubled.

When the diocese was erected there were approximately 6000 Catholics in the state.[10] With the exception of the Gallipolis colony, which was now in a decadent condition, the Catholic settlers were largely Irish from the Atlantic states, and German from Pennsylvania. Indeed, the history of the Church in Ohio, after the long silence that followed the intermittent visits of the French Jesuits, begins with the sturdy German pioneer, Jacob Dittoe, writing in 1802 out of the Ohio wilderness to Bishop Carroll for a priest. On land which he had given for that purpose near Somerset, Perry County, the first Catholic church in the state was built, and dedicated on December 6, 1818. The Irish Catholics in Cincinnati besides their poverty had intense bigotry to face, and it was not until Easter Sunday of 1819 that they were able to worship in a church of their own.[11]

The nurture of the Church in Ohio had been the work of one man, who was now its bishop.[12] Born in St. Mary's County, Maryland, in 1768, he was sent abroad to study, and made his religious profession as a Dominican in 1790, in the house of that Order at Bornheim, Belgium. Ordained three years later he was obliged to flee to England with his brethren when the French Revolutionists advanced into Belgium in 1794. During his years in England, serving in several

[9] Nearly every Catholic writer speaks of Bishop Fenwick as being administrator of Michigan and the Northwest, and the Roman authorities, no more precise here than they were in some other instances, used the same terms in erecting the diocese. As a matter of fact there was no such entity at the time as the "Northwest." The Northwest Territory after the creation of the Territory of Indiana in 1800 consisted of only half of Michigan, and what was later to be the State of Ohio. When Ohio was admitted in 1803, the whole of Michigan was attached to, and became a part of Indiana Territory. Indiana was admitted to statehood in 1816, Illinois in 1818, and the rest of what had once been the Northwest Territory became simply Michigan Territory. For a good study of these changes see the *Wisconsin Historical Collections*, XI, 451 ff.

[10] Lamott, *op. cit.*, 118.

[11] *Ibid.*, 31.

[12] O'Daniel, O.P., *op. cit.* The details in the text are taken *passim* from this scholarly biography.

houses of his Order, Father Fenwick conceived the project of a Dominican establishment in America. Encouraged by Bishop Carroll and authorized by his superiors he came to the United States in 1804. He had hoped to make his foundation in Maryland, but bowing to the wishes of Bishop Carroll he repaired to Kentucky. In December, 1806, Father Fenwick with two confreres founded the first convent of the Dominicans in the United States near Springfield, Washington County.

Jacob Dittoe's prayers were answered in 1808 by the arrival of Father Fenwick in the tiny German settlement. To the care of his missions in Kentucky the zealous missionary now added semiannual visits to Ohio. Alone, on horseback, he often rode a thousand miles or more seeking out isolated members of the Faith.

In Kentucky, the early Catholic colonists ordinarily sought to form settlements composed principally of those belonging to their church. In Ohio, there was little of such concerted action among this class of pioneer settlers. They came from all places, and made their homes in all directions. This not only necessitated long and frequent journeys for their pastor, but often deprived him of all the companionship of those of his own faith, and caused his life to be at once more trying and solitary than had been that of Kentucky's lone missionary (Father Badin). . . .

Describing his labors in 1818 Father Fenwick wrote:

It is now two years since I have lived in the Convent of Saint Rose in Kentucky, having become, as they call me here, an itinerant preacher. I am continually occupied in traversing these immense tracts of country, either in search of stray sheep or to distribute the "bread of angels" to thousands of persons who live scattered about in these our vast solitudes. The whole state of Ohio and a part of Kentucky, from Frankfort, Lexington and Richmond to Cincinnati, Canton, and on to Cleveland on Lake Erie, are the places to which I make my apostolic travels not neglecting the adjacent counties and cities. In the State of Ohio, which has a population of 500,000 souls, there is not a single priest (that is, not a single secular priest, or a priest with a home of his own). There are Germans and Irish who know no English at all. . . . It often happens that I am compelled to traverse vast and inhospitable forests, wherein not a trace of road is to be seen. Not infrequently, overtaken by night in the midst of these, I am obliged to hitch my horse to a tree; and making a pillow of my saddle I recommend myself to God . . .[13]

A short time before writing this letter Father Fenwick had been joined by his nephew, Father Nicholas Young. Together they blessed the first Catholic church in the state, St. Joseph's at Somerset. It was

[13] *Ibid.*, 211, 214.

with full knowledge of their missionary labors that Bishop Flaget had petitioned the Holy See for a bishopric in Ohio. When the diocese was erected the two Dominicans were still the only priests in the state.

Father Richard in Detroit was abreast of all these developments taking place to the south, and his journey of 1821 was dictated by them in addition to the particular reasons already stated. He left Detroit on July 4 in a sailing vessel bound for Mackinac.[14] His stay on the island lasted three weeks during which he made heroic efforts to remedy the evils resulting from long years of neglect. Several marriages were blessed, and the baptismal register shows forty-seven entries in his handwriting.[15]

After Mackinac the place which most interested Father Richard was the Indian settlement at L'Arbre Croche, the site of the old Jesuit mission. He had not seen it since his first tour of the missions in 1799. But this time as he aproached it Lake Michigan was in so wild a mood that landing was impossible. As the ship beat down the eastern side of the lake Father Richard assuaged his disappointment by studying the geological formation of the shore line. Finally, he arrived at the mouth of the Marquette River, which he had long been eager to visit in order to discover the burial place of Father Marquette. From here he wrote an interesting letter to one his confreres in Montreal.

> . . . There are about ten Ottawa families living here. I had them brought to me to find out where the celebrated missionary of the Society of Jesus had been buried. . . . The Ottawa led me to what had been the mouth of the river in 1675 when Father Marquette entered it on the 8th of May, and died on the 9th. At present the river empties into the lake at least three thousand feet above, or to the south, (for Lake Michigan has been discharging its waters for many centuries through the Straits of Mackinac into Lake Huron), between two hills more than sixty feet high that appear to have been separated by the combined action of wind and water. The spot pointed out to me by the Indians is about 240 feet from the actual shore of the lake on the southern bank of the old bed of the river named after Father Marquette, which is 2800 feet north of the river as it is today. There I erected a cross in the presence of eight Ottawas and two Catholics, Frederick Countryman who made the cross, and Charles Rousseau a young Canadian from Montreal who is known to you. I placed it directly over the spot where the Indians told me a cross had been standing, erected by the Canadians, until blown down by the winds three years ago. With my pocket-knife I carved the following inscription in English:

14 Letter dated August 25, 1827. See note 2.
15 Rezek, *op. cit.*, II, 174.

Fr. J H Marquet
Died Here 9 May, 1675.[16]

On the following Sunday I celebrated the sacred mysteries under a tent at the mouth of the river, and in the afternoon we went in procession from the altar to the cross erected over the grave of Father Marquette. There were fifty of us, English, Canadians, and Indians, and we walked along the level sandy beach, two by two, singing the Litany of the Blessed Virgin. You can well imagine that it was easy to be eloquent in that lonely spot, and at the grave of a missionary to whom tradition attributes the working of miracles. Then we sang a Libera, and we returned to our camping place chanting the Litany of the Saints. . . .

Whether Father Richard in paying this touching tribute to Father Marquette felt that he was venerating the actual remains of the saintly missionary is not clear from his letter. He was undoubtedly familiar with Charlevoix's account, and must have known that the Indians had transferred the remains to St. Ignace in 1677. If he was unaware of their final resting place so was the world at large until 1877, when Father Edward Jacker, pastor of St. Ignace, discovered the fragments of Father Marquette's body on the site of the old mission chapel.[17]

Continuing his journey down Lake Michigan Father Richard experienced such unfavorable weather that he was delayed in reaching Chicago. When he arrived the Indians had already completed their negotiations, much to his disappointment. At the time, Chicago was nothing more than a cluster of rude dwellings in the shadow of Fort Dearborn. In one of them lived Jean-Baptiste Beaubien, a trader and a descendant of the early Beaubiens in Detroit. Father Richard remained with him for a few days, saying Mass in his house, and on Sunday he preached to the soldiers of the garrison. He was most likely the first priest to offer Mass in Chicago from the time that the Jesuits abandoned in 1700 the Guardian Angel mission which they had founded there four years previously.[18]

[16] The date as printed in the *Annales* is probably a printer's error. Father Marquette died May 19.

[17] Many references to the burial of Marquette, and the result of a search for his grave will be found in the *Illinois Cath. Hist. Rev.*, Vol. IX. For Father Jacker's account of his discovery see *Catholic World*, XXVI, 267 ff.

[18] "The Canadian in whose house Father Richard said Mass on this occasion was, in all probability, Jean Baptiste Beaubien, Indian trader and agent of the American Fur Company at Chicago, who settled there permanently shortly after the Fort Dearborn massacre. His home at the period of Father Richard's visit was in the so-called 'Dean House,' which he purchased in 1817 from a Mr. Dean, sutler to the Fort, and which stood south of that structure and near what is now the intersection of Randolph Street and Michigan Avenue. Here, then, was apparently offered up the first Mass in Chicago

From Chicago Father Richard had intended returning to Detroit, but on discovering that it would be forty or fifty days before he could engage passage home he decided, as he says, "to descend the Illinois River, and make the great circle by way of the Mississippi and the Ohio. I hoped in this way to arrive in Detroit sooner than by waiting for a chance sailing vessel." He reached St. Louis on October 5, and spent some days with Bishop Dubourg whom he had known in Paris. After visiting his old mission field along the Mississippi he started out from Kaskaskia on horseback on his way to Vincennes. The first day out he was thrown from his horse and so severely injured that, although he was able to reach Vincennes, he had to remain there fifteen days to recuperate. He then went on to Bardstown, where his injury compelled him to stay for two months.

To the priest from Michigan who had been struggling for so long, alone, to build up the externals of religion in his territory, Bardstown and its neighborhood was a delight. He records his admiration of the "divers and astonishing establishments" of Father Nerinkx and Bishop Flaget. Here he saw cathedral and seminary, convent and school, the realization of all that he had planned for Detroit. He witnessed again what he must often have hungered for, the stately ceremonial of a pontifical Mass in the cathedral. More than that, he was privileged to participate in a historic function, and writing about it years later he could not forbear mentioning that "at the consecration of Monseigneur Fenwick I read the Mandatum of the Holy Father. . . ."[19] The ceremony took place on January 13, 1822, at the hands of Bishop Flaget, who, by papal dispensation, was assisted by two confreres of Father Fenwick.[20]

During his sojourn in Bardstown Father Richard became acquainted with a young priest, and a seminarian in major orders, who expressed their willingness to work with him in Michigan. Bishop Flaget generously consenting to their release, Father Richard began his homeward journey in March accompanied by Father Anthony Ganilh, and Francis Badin, brother of the pioneer priest of Kentucky. In Cincinnati the party tarried just long enough for the ordination to the priesthood of Francis Badin by Bishop Fenwick.[21] Then

---

after it had become a settlement of white people. As to the discourse preached by the missionary to the garrison, it may safely go on record as the first sermon preached in modern Chicago. . . ." Gilbert J. Garraghan, S.J., *The Catholic Church in Chicago* (Chicago, 1921), 30. For a history of the Beaubien Family see Charles P. Beaubien, *Ecrin D'Amour Familial* (Montreal, 1914).

[19] The Mandatum is the official order of the Holy See to proceed with the consecration.

[20] O'Daniel, *op. cit.*, 243.

[21] Francis Vincent Badin was born in France, August 2, 1784. The ordination took place on Holy Saturday, April 6, 1822.

came days of laborious travel northward through Ohio, and across the Michigan line as far as the River Raisin settlement.

The parish had been without a resident priest since the departure of Father Dilhet in 1804. Thereafter, it had been visited four times a year by Father Richard save for the troubled period from 1812 to 1815, and Father Janvier had replaced him in 1820 and 1821. Now it was to have its third resident pastor in the person of Father Ganilh. The parish register thus records his solemn installation.

> This twenty-eighth day of the month of April, A.D. 1822, Mr. Anthony Ganilh, priest, has taken possession of the church of St. Anthony of the River Raisin, of which he has been nominated pastor by Monseigneur Edward Dominic Fenwick, Bishop of Cincinnati, and administrator of the Michigan and Northwest Territories, in the presence of the inhabitants assembled to assist at the holy mysteries, in the presence of Mr. G. Richard, Vicar-General, and of Mr. Vincent Badin, assistant priest of St. Anne's parish, Detroit, who have signed the present act.

If Father Richard imagined that the care of the settlement had now been shifted to other shoulders, he was soon to be disappointed. The old lay trustee system that had always made the lot of the pastor so difficult was not dead. Father Ganilh asked for a small addition to the rectory, and a cord of wood from every family. The addition demanded long deliberation, and the matter of firewood was a nice problem. After much debate it was agreed that the pastor had a right to ask for wood, and everyone promised to supply him provided he did not sell it, and that the parishioners were entitled to warm themselves at his fire before and after every service. This was more than the pastor could stand. Less than three months after his installation he shook the dust of the settlement off his feet, leaving this entry in the parish register.

> Today being the 17th day of July, 1822, I, Anthony Ganilh, who had been nominated pastor of this parish, happily got rid of it after having suffered hunger, thirst, sorrow, and abandonment for three or four months, and every kind of misery. . . . Farewell, poor church and still poorer presbytery; may I never lay eyes on you again . . . Poor Kentucky! Why did I leave thee? [22]

Evidently not of the stock out of which pioneer priests are made, Father Ganilh left for Ohio, and Father Richard and his young as-

[22] Father Ganilh came as a seminarian from France to Bardstown. Letter to Archbishop Maréchal, January 19, 1823. BCA. After serving in various stations in the diocese of Cincinnati, and for a while pastor of Wheeling, W. Va., he became an apostate and wrote thrillers about the confessional to delight his non-Catholic readers. Letter of Bishop Bruté to Bishop Rosati, January 20, 1838, in St. Louis Chancery Archives. He later returned to France and died there.

sistant were now the only priests in Michigan Territory. On their arrival in Detroit they had found Father Janvier making preparations for his departure. He had been ordered by Bishop Dubourg to leave on a singular mission. The Ursuline convent in New Orleans, a French foundation dating from 1727, was in urgent need of sisters. An appeal had been sent to the Canadian houses in Quebec and Three Rivers, and four religious had volunteered their services. To Father Janvier had been committed the charge of meeting them in Montreal to conduct them to their destination on a ship sailing from New York. He left Detroit about the end of June, and accomplished his mission in December.[23]

Father Richard and his assistant had barely organized their labors when they were gladdened by the visitation of Bishop Fenwick. He came about the middle of July, and must have remained for some weeks.[24] From the following letter written to Archbishop Maréchal the bishop's purpose is evident. He was making a first hand study of Michigan Territory with the intention of ridding himself of it. In his opinion the time was ripe for a see at Detroit.

> . . . I can assure your Reverence, 1. that nothing could now afford me more pleasure and relief of mind than the erection of the Bishop's See in Detroit, whose jurisdiction should extend over the Michigan and Northwest Territories, containing an extent of country equal to all Europe, tho a great part of it is as yet unexplored and only inhabited by Indians and wild beasts; 2. that there are at least seven thousand Catholics through that wilderness, besides an unknown number of Indians who were once christianised by the good Jesuits, but are now void of all Christianity for want of Priests among them. 3. In the town of Detroit there is a large, elegant church, not quite finished, 130 feet long by 50 or 60 wide, well calculated for a cathedral, built of stone and brick. A Bishop who could gain the confidence and esteem of the people would, I think, soon finish and pay for it. That church and a new two story frame house, large and convenient, stand on a lot of five or six acres well enclosed. At about three miles, I believe, from town is a tract of land of 300 acres or more and a church enclosed with three acres—all church property. 4. I should think an American speaking French would be most suitable and conformable to the character of the people. The French language becomes in a manner daily less used, and in twenty years will, I suppose, be scarcely spoken at all.

[23] There is some correspondence relating to Father Janvier and the Ursulines in the *Records of the Amer. Cath. Hist. Soc.*, XIX, 190–213. Father Janvier later returned to France, and was in the ministry in the Diocese of Lyons in 1835. Letter of Father Janvier to Bishop Rosati, April 10, 1835. St. Louis Chancery Archives.

[24] "The Honorable Bishop Fenwick is arrived at Detroit. I hope to have the pleasure of seeing him before he goes away. . . ." Letter of Eliza Ann Godfroy to Bishop Flaget, July 19, 1822. Photostat in Dominican Archives, Washington.

When I was at Detroit last fall, I confirmed about 300 souls in only two congregations, not having it in my power to visit more on account of the lateness of the season, and the want of means to travel or defray expenses. It requires nearly six months to make the visit of my diocese of Ohio, not allowing myself more than a week or two to spend in each congregation or settlement of Catholics. Hence you will readily conclude on the necessity of a Bishop at Detroit as I have absolutely more to do in Ohio than my ability and circumstances enable me to do, and where no provision was made, nor enquired into, for a Bishop. No earthly resource or asistance is afforded me but the cooperation of three of my confreres, whose precarious subsistence depends on our good conduct and zeal among the people, who, I believe, will not let us starve or go naked. . . .[25]

To reinforce his position the bishop had asked Father Richard to furnish Archbishop Maréchal with accurate statistics from which a decision could be arrived at. The report gives an interesting survey of the Church in the Territory at the close of 1822.

Detroit, Dec. 22, 1822.

Your Lordship:

I have received your letter of Dec. 2. I hasten to answer your questions in the order in which they were proposed.

1. I begin at the boundary between the Territory of Michigan and the State of Ohio. At Fort Meigs, situated at the foot of the rapids of the Miami of Lake Erie, and in the neighborhood, the French or Canadian Catholic families number approximately 16

8 miles to the north, at St. Joseph on Miami Bay 54

6 miles to the north, at Otter Creek 27

In the town of Monroe on the River Raisin, there are 40 Protestant, American families. Canadian Catholic families at the said river 110

3 miles to the north, at Sand Creek 15

6 miles to the north, at Swan Creek 7

8 miles to the north, at Huron River 8

15 miles above the Huron River there are 20 American, Protestant families.

From the mouth of the Detroit River for a distance of twelve miles up there are 30 Amer. Prot. Families.

8 miles below Detroit at the River Ecorces 25

5 miles below Detroit at the River Rouge, about 32

On the same River 50 Amer. Prot. fam.

On a strip 18 miles long beginning 3 miles below the town of Detroit, and following up the large river here called the Detroit River 160

[25] Letter of Bishop Fenwick to Archbishop Maréchal, February 9, 1823. BCA.

In the town of Detroit 150 Amer. Prot. fam.

30 miles to the northeast of Detroit in the interior	80

Those who bought lands last summer and fall, and who will come next spring, number about 200 Amer. Prot. fam.

20 miles from Detroit along Lake St. Clair	30
9 miles further north on the River Huron of Lake St. Clair there is a chapel of St. Francis de Sales	25
From the River Huron to the mouth of the River St. Clair which is the continuation of the Detroit or St. Lawrence River	10
Along the River St. Clair to Fort Gratiot	40
From Lake Huron to Sault Ste Marie	20
On the island of Michili-makinac, 30 (Amer. Prot. fam.)	80

N.B. In the months of June, July, August, and September, there are every year at M-Makinac 600 Canadian Catholic voyageurs.

At Green Bay	60
At Prairie du Chien	120
At Chicago	5
	926

N.B. There are American garrisons at Detroit, Saginaw, Sault Ste Marie, Mackinac, Green Bay, and Prairie du Chien.

These 926 families at 6 per family make the number of Catholics	5656
Add 150 Catholic Irishmen scattered here and there	150
	5806 [26]

The report goes on to describe the church property in Detroit, and the revenues which will presumably support a bishop. Each farmer gives as his tithe four bushels of grain out of every hundred "according to the Canadian usage." On the four acre plot surrounding St. Anne's houses can be built for investment purposes. The Archbishop is advised that since two thirds of the population are French-speaking the new bishop should have a command of that language; he should be a Frenchman or an American. Father Benedict Fenwick is the ideal man for the office. Being a Jesuit he will bring other members of the Society for the Indian missions which the Jesuits once watered with their sweat and blood, and which they alone are competent to direct. The closing paragraph of the report lists the churches in the Territory.[27]

[26] The report is in the BCA. Fort Meigs was near Perrysburg, Ohio. St. Joseph on Miami Bay was the forerunner of the present parish of Erie, Mich. Swan Creek is the parish at Newport. Huron River is the present Rockwood. The Huron River north is the Clinton.

[27] In the letter coupled with this report Father Richard states that although Father Gallitzin is a likely candidate for Detroit he will probably refuse the offer. That the Archbishop sounded out Father Gallitzin after the receipt of the report appears from the latter's blunt letter of refusal containing a rather tart account of the laity at Detroit and their pastor. Letter dated February 18, 1823. BCA.

We have the chapel of St. Joseph at Miami Bay, the chapel of the Northeast shore two and a half miles from Detroit, the chapel of St. Francis de Sales at the Huron River, the church of St. Anthony at the Raisin River. The church of St. Anne at Mackinac, built by the Jesuits, was destroyed three years ago, and we are engaged in building a church there. To help me in my ministry to this immense territory I have only Mr. Vincent Badin, whereas I should have a dozen priests. . . .

Without a doubt Father Richard believed that Detroit needed a bishop and could support one. Neither Bishop Flaget nor Bishop Fenwick had found as much on their arrival in their respective sees. But Bishop Fenwick's plans for Detroit differed in one important detail from the report just quoted. His candidate for Detroit was Father Richard himself. When he went to Rome in 1823 he importuned the Holy See to erect the diocese of Detroit, and to name as its first bishop the man "of great learning, piety, and zeal" who had been the apostle of Michigan for twenty-five years.[28] To bolster his appeal he had letters from the laity of Detroit. John R. Williams, a pillar of St. Anne's, had written his sentiments to the bishop.

Your diocesans being likewise informed that it is in contemplation to create a separate Bishopric in the Territory of Michigan . . . beg leave respectfully to mention the name of our Reverend and well-beloved Pastor, Gabriel Richard, and humbly recommend him as a suitable person to fill that distinguished station. His long and pious services, indefatigable zeal, and charitable character entitle him to our sincere admiration, respect, and eternal gratitude. He has labored faithfully and eloquently in the vineyards of this country during a period of upwards of twenty-five years, and would consequently be highly acceptable to his flock when clothed with higher dignity and greater powers . . .[29]

Despite Bishop Fenwick's representations the Roman authorities could not be hurried into action. Father Richard's fitness for the episcopacy was not questioned. There were two reasons for their hesitancy. In the first place, they needed more definite assurance than had been given that the Catholics of Michigan could support the activities which the coming of a bishop would entail. Secondly, they wished to ascertain the attitude of the laity towards episcopal authority both in its control of temporalities and in its administrative exercise. Just at the time, the Church in the United States had fairly

---

[28] O'Daniel, op. cit., Chaps. XIV, XV.

[29] Letter to Bishop Fenwick, Detroit, May 29, 1823. Williams Papers, BHC. As the foremost English-speaking parishioner of St. Anne's Williams is the probable writer of another appeal to Bishop Fenwick dated June 4, 1823, and signed by eight parishioners. It is in the Propaganda Congregation Archives, Scritture Originale, Vol. 938. See O'Daniel, op. cit., 281.

entered on a critical period. The very nature of American institutions and life, and the unusual conditions under which the Church had begun her growth combined to give the laity an exaggerated notion of the extent to which their participation in the polity of the Church was justified. Roughly speaking, for a period of twenty years beginning with 1820, the tenure of church property and the right of appointment were claimed by various groups in open defiance of their bishops. There could be only two endings to such a contest: schism, or a recognition of the scope of episcopal authority in the government of the Church. Happily, the latter prevailed.[30] But in 1823, when the erection of a diocese in Detroit was being considered in Rome, and the riots of the previous year at St. Mary's in Philadelphia were fresh in mind, the temper of the Catholics of Michigan, where the trustee system was the only one known, needed to be more fully investigated.[31]

While the Congregation of the Propaganda was thus scrutinizing the situation, events were taking place in Michigan that would decidedly affect the outcome of its deliberations. Spurred on by necessity and zeal Father Richard was venturing into the hazardous crosscurrents of political life. From the time of his arrival in Michigan he had been much concerned about the Indian population of the Territory. His "Outline of a Scheme of Education for the Territory of Michigan" submitted to Congress in 1809 pointed out to the government its obligation to uplift and civilize its Indian wards. But, as a priest, he had even more at heart their spiritual enlightenment. He knew the history of the Jesuit missions, and that at some time or other every Michigan tribe had been leavened by the teachings of the missionaries. If the Indian had any possible affinity with Christianity it was through the Catholic Church. To Father Richard the Indians were as much a part of his flock as were the French, and yet he was powerless to help them. In contrast to his helplessness were the efforts being put forth by the various Protestant Missionary societies. His failure, for instance, to attend the treaty with the Potawatomi at Chicago in 1821, had been taken advantage of by the Baptists with the result that in the following year Carey Mission was established in the very spot on the St. Joseph River which the Jesuits had once cultivated.[32]

To Father Richard casting about for some means of coping with

[30] For a good general account of the trustee problem in the United States see "The Evils of Trusteeism," *Historical Records and Studies* (United States Catholic Hist. Society), VIII, 136 ff.

[31] That these were the reason for delaying the erection of the see of Detroit is evident from the printed *Acta* of the Propaganda Congregation for 1826, 311–14.

[32] For various references to the Carey Mission see *Mich. Hist. Colls.*, V, 145, and Index.

this new phase of the Indian problem out of a clear sky came a novel proposal. An election to choose a territorial delegate to Congress was impending.[33] Two prominent French-Canadian parishioners called upon Father Richard, and urged him to announce his candidacy for the office. In the absence of any worth while study of political conditions in early Detroit the motives underlying the proposal are rather obscure. We may venture the likelihood that the French element of the population was determined to make a final stand against the domination of the rising Yankee invasion with its ill-concealed racial and religious prejudices, and Father Richard was without question the most representative Frenchman in the Territory.

Father Richard's first reaction was to recoil from the proposal. As he himself writes: "Two of the most respectable Canadians of Michigan, two colonels of the Militia, came to ask me whether I would be willing to be the Delegate. Such a suggestion was so utterly unexpected that I bid them be off, telling them that it was folly to think of such a thing. . . ."[34] Naturally, he talked the proposal over with his assistant, Father Badin, and it gradually dawned upon them both that here was the solution of the Indian problem. Father Richard would go to Congress, and there at the seat of government he would be most favorably situated to secure adequate provisions for his projected missions. Moreover, at home the church of St. Anne was only half finished, and the eight dollars a day he would be paid while serving as delegate would go far towards its completion.[35] There is no sign that Father Richard was at all interested in whatever political motives may have animated those who proposed his candidacy. To him it was a splendid opportunity to further the interests of the Church in Michigan, and he determined to grasp it.[36] Fully aware that such a step was without precedent he sought the advice of Bishop Dubourg, and he received the following answer.

[33] By an Act of February 16, 1819, the Territory was allowed representation in Congress, and authorized to send a Delegate, who was to hold the position for two years. In September of the same year William Woodbridge was elected, but resigned in 1820. Solomon Sibley was elected to fill out the unexpired term, and remained in office until 1823. Farmer, op. cit., 102, 111.

[34] Letter from Father Richard to the Sulpician Superior General, dated Washington, January 9, 1824. Archives of Saint-Sulpice.

[35] "My neighbor is getting eight dollars a day. That will make him a good sum, and you know that he needs it. . . ." Letter of Father Marchand to Bishop Plessis, December 11, 1823. QCA.

[36] "You know doubtless that I am going to Washington as Delegate of Michigan Territory. I consulted Monseigneur Dubourg, who urged me to accept the office if I were elected. God knows that my principal motive in accepting such a charge is that I may work more efficaciously for the good of religion, and especially that the knowledge of the Gospel may be brought to the poor Indians. . . ." Letter to Father Rosati of St. Louis dated Sandusky, November 24, 1823. In St. Louis Chancery Archives.

Everything well considered, I believe that you should not hesitate to accept the nomination that has been proposed to you. It seems to me that Providence designs to use this extraordinary means to help you and the Church in your district. I hope that you have decided in the affirmative, and I would rejoice if my letter arrived in time to allay the fears that you might feel in accepting, and to inspire you with the confidence that such duties demand. I thank God for the bright prospects in store for the Church of Detroit. He has made you, my venerable friend, go through fire and water. I have no doubt that He will soon bring you relief . . .[37]

Having announced his candidacy in the early summer of 1823, Father Richard left Detroit to visit the northern missions, and incidentally to work up what support he could in the northern counties.[38] He spent some time on Mackinac Island, and at L'Arbre Croche, and then passed over to Green Bay.[39] His work there is thus described.

. . . For the first time I made an apostolic journey to Green Bay, where I found more than sixty Catholic families. During a period of seven days, ending on the feast of St. Anne, I performed 126 baptisms, 26 marriages, and heard the confessions of nearly everyone. Among those married were seven young squaws, whom I baptized. A squaw seventy-two years old married a white youth of seventy-eight. He said to me, 'I have been here for sixty years, and I have never seen a priest.' The majority of the women are half Indian, and prove to be good wives. They are docile, industrious, and would become good Christians. The people promised to build a chapel that will be ready by next June. When I hear that it is completed, and that a sufficient number have learned the catechism during the winter, I shall feel myself obliged to send a priest to visit them, or go myself . . .[40]

Returning to Detroit Father Richard found himself in the throes of a bitter political campaign.[41] The other six candidates, although divided by their personal rivalries, were united in a common antagonism to the priest who in their eyes was a rank interloper. Detroit's only newspaper at the time, the *Detroit Gazette,* absolutely ignored his candidacy. Even among his own people there were regrettable dis-

[37] Father Richard quotes the bishop's answer in the Washington letter mentioned in note 34.

[38] At the time, Michigan Territory included a part of Minnesota and the whole of Wisconsin in addition to the lower and upper peninsulas of the present state. See William L. Jenks, "History and Meaning of the County Names of Michigan," *Mich. Hist. Colls.,* XXXVIII, 439 ff.

[39] Rezek, *op. cit.,* II, 175.

[40] Passage from letter mentioned in note 34.

[41] Catlin, *op. cit.,* 268–69. Contemporary issues of the *Detroit Gazette* as well as much material in the BHC help to fill in the story of Father Richard's political vicissitudes.

sensions. John R. Williams, the man who had proposed his pastor in such glowing terms for the see of Detroit, was a candidate. The Catholic vote which he might have controlled was hopelessly lost with Father Richard in the field. Baffled in his ambitions Williams launched a broadside against his pastor, too long to quote in its entirety.

The course which for some time past you have thought it proper to adopt merits a public exposure inasmuch as it appears that you have decided to prefer political affairs to those belonging to your profession . . . but it must be acknowledged that you have known well how to disguise your plans and intentions up to the moment when you extend one hand to grasp the Episcopal mitre, while with the other you take measures to secure the seat, and what is more, the pay of a delegate to the Congress of the United States.

I cannot reconcile this apparent incongruity of principle and precept, example and illustration. It is reserved for you to give the most austere rules, in words and sermons, against the honors, riches, and distractions of this world, and to add by example the ablest political manoeuvre to clothe yourself abundantly with them all . . .

Believe me, for you ought to be convinced that you are out of your element when you give up your breviary and your Bible in order to meddle with political affairs which you do not understand; you expose yourself upon the turf which now appears to you covered with flowers and riches, only to gather thorns and brambles . . .

It is possible that your zeal for the establishment of your brethren, the Jesuits, has led you to this false step. Believe me, Congress will not trouble itself with the establishment of Jesuit missionaries at this time in the Territory of Michigan. The time and reign of Louis XIV has passed. The opinions of the 17th century are not fashionable in the Capitol of the United States. . . . Believe me, you have a talent for preaching the Gospel; confine yourself to that and the French language, and you will assuredly be useful to many good Christians; but I do not believe that you can be in the House of Representatives at Washington where they speak English only . . .[42]

It is not surprising that Williams, bitter and disgruntled as this tirade reveals him, left the Church and died out of it.[43] To offset the broadside Father Richard's sacristan and loyal lay-helper issued a counter-blast to the French population.

I address you again relative to the just pretensions of the Rev. Gabriel Richard for the office of delegate to represent you in the Congress of the United States. I would not have written to you today, were it not

[42] Original in BHC.

[43] John R. Williams became the first mayor of Detroit. He died in 1854 and is buried in Elmwood Cemetery. His sister was Elizabeth Williams, one of Father Richard's schoolteachers. See Burton, op. cit., II, 1402.

for a letter signed by John R Williams, of which a great number have
been printed and circulated with the intention of ruining Mr. Richard.
But, friends and fellow citizens, that letter is only the second part of
the one addressed to you a short time since by Mr. May. Neither letter
has any weight or any authority, and they are only calculated to throw
dust in your eyes . . .

We shall finish this letter by observing to you that the probity, the
merit, the zeal, and the integrity of Mr. Richard is so firmly fixed in
your minds as to render you incapable of changing your sentiments,
knowing that he has no greater wish than to serve you.

The election begins next Thursday, September 4, between 9 and 10
in the morning. The friends of Mr. Richard are invited to come to his
house where they will have the goodness to conduct themselves with all
possible order and quiet until they have given in their votes. . . .

As your enemies say maliciously that one can buy 20 French votes
with a bottle of whiskey, show them on that day that it is a black cal-
umny . . .

Monsieur and friend, you will have the goodness to assemble your
friends and ours as speedily as possible, and read this letter to them.
Do not listen to anything further. It is all trickery.[44]

The election returns were slow to come in especially from the
north, and the results were not officially announced until the 24th of
October. Out of a total of 1581 votes cast, Father Richard received
444, Major John Biddle 321, and Austin Wing, the sheriff, 335. The
remainder of the votes was divided among the other four candidates,
and John R. Williams ran last with 51.[45]
Although Father Richard had won the election he was not to take
his seat in Congress without further difficulty. During the thirty-one
years that he had lived in America he had never thought it necessary
to take out naturalization papers until he was building his bridges
for his campaign. On June 16, 1823, he applied for citizenship, and
on the 28th he received his certificate.[46] John Biddle contested the
election on the grounds that the County Court had no authority to
naturalize Father Richard, and even if it had, he should have been
a citizen for a full year before being eligible to hold office. When the
successful candidate left for Washington in November with his credentials from Governor Cass, he was followed by John Biddle carrying his protest to the Congressional Committee on Elections. On
January 13, 1824, the Committee in its report declared that Biddle's

44 The French original is dated August 31, 1823, and lies in the Godfroy Papers. BHC.
45 The *Detroit Gazette,* November 7, 1823. Father Richard's strength lay in Monroe
and Wayne Counties, with some support in St. Clair and Macomb. Not a vote was cast
for him in Oakland nor in any of the northern counties, Crawford, Brown, and
Michilimakinac.
46 See Thomas A. Weadock, "A Catholic Priest in Congress," *Mich. Hist. Colls.,* XXI,
438 ff.

contention was unfounded, and that Father Richard was entitled to his seat in Congress.[47]

The Territorial Delegate from Michigan appeared in the House on December 8, for the opening of the first session of the 18th Congress. In that assembly his profession, his English tinged with a pronounced French accent, and his inexperience were bound to make him a singular figure. The impression was doubtless heightened by eccentricities of dress and manner of which an amusing glimpse has been left us by a contemporary.

> In 1824, as I was wending my way to the humble yet patriotic Capitol of the United States . . . my attention was attracted to a singularly odd-looking gentleman. He was of middle size, sharp features, and wiry frame. His low-crowned, broad-brimmed hat was thrown back on the crown of his head, and a pair of large goggles sat enthroned on the uppermost of an expansive, bulging forehead. He had on the nicest-fitting and best-polished shoes man could ever wear, with silver buckles—but no stockings. He was tapping a fine gold snuffbox, and he appeared in the act of offering a pinch to a friend whom he seemed just to have met . . . In sooth he was the Very Rev. Gabriel Richard . . .[48]

However, the Delegate's oddities were forgotten in view of his mental vigor and attainments, and for his inexperience there was nothing but sympathy and assistance.[49] None of the defeated candidates could have been more devoted to the interests of his constituents; indeed, Father Richard had very decided convictions as to the service that he owed to the people whom he represented. He wrote to one of his Detroit friends.

> I have written a great many letters since I am here, I may say more than 60 in less than a month. My object is to render service to my constituents, not to court their popularity. I might, as perhaps too many do the same, I might offer Resolutions which I would know would not, and could not pass, if I would calculate only to please. But I aim at something more useful, I omit such acts in order to devote more time in paying visits to the members of the committees before whom I have Business, and I may say, perhaps, that I tease the committees by calling too often in order to awaken the petitions that are at rest . . .[50]

[47] For the report in full see the *Annals of Congress* (Washington, 1856), 1001. A copy of Biddle's protest, and Father Richard's defense, both in the latter's handwriting, are in the DCA. Biddle Avenue in Wyandotte is named after John Biddle, who owned the site on which the city lies.

[48] A long investigation has failed to identify the author of this quotation. It is found in the *Illustrated Catholic Family Almanac* for 1871, p. 49. The article from which it is taken goes on to mention the writer's friendship with Father Richard, and he states that he has a sheaf of manuscripts from which the life story of the priest could be compiled. The article is signed merely with the initials, O. D.

[49] James V. Campbell, *Outlines of the Political History of Michigan* (Detroit, 1876), 398; Ross and Catlin, *op. cit.*, 361.

[50] Letter to Alexander Fraser, February 10, 1824. BHC.

While Father Richard was engaged in the routine service of his constituents, he was not forgetting the primary object of his coming to Washington. It is regrettable that there is available so little documentary evidence bearing on this phase of his activities. What to him was the most important project he hoped to foster was necessarily to be forwarded by personal contact in certain quarters, and had no connection with his services as Delegate, which are a matter of record.[51] How much he accomplished in this regard, or to what extent he influenced the subsequent policy of the government toward the Indian is questionable. That he was busily engaged in some project for his Michigan Indians, and that he had at least consulted the government is evident from a passage in a letter to the Sulpician superior at Paris.

> The Indians at L'Arbre Croche signed for me a petition to be presented to our good President (James Monroe) in which they asked for a Catholic priest like the Jesuits from Father Marquette to Father Dujaunais, who took his departure in 1764. This is one of the principal reasons why I am here. The President and the Secretary of War were surprised and delighted to see the hieroglyphic signatures of these poor Indians. Following two or three visits that I paid to each of them, the Secretary of War (in France we would say the Minister of War), Calhoun, wrote to me to be at his office tomorrow to talk over this important matter: the civilization of the Indians and the methods of bringing them to religion. The proposal of the Government I am to communicate to Msgr. Fenwick, who has written me that he can procure Jesuits either in France or in Italy. The Jesuit Superior here, to whom I gave the preference for these missions which were begun by the Jesuits, is to write to the Superior General at Rome, who will conclude the matter with our Bishop . . .[52]

The first session of the 18th Congress closed at the end of May, 1824, and after spending the summer in the East Father Richard returned to Detroit. He came home, not to hear the plaudits of admiring citizens, but to suffer the ignominy of a term in jail. The vengeance of a parishioner had at last found its mark.

In 1816, Francois Labadie secured a divorce in Detroit from his wife then living in Montreal, and remarried. Father Richard felt in duty bound to report the matter to Bishop Flaget, who in due course ordered him to publicly excommunicate the delinquent. Labadie fiercely resented the attendant disgrace, alleged that he had suffered financially because of it, and sued the priest for $5000 as balm for his

[51] *Mich. Hist. Colls.*, XXI, 433 ff. More details may be gathered from the correspondence with Alexander Fraser in the BHC. The DCA has a small manuscript diary kept by Father Richard during the second session.

[52] Another passage from letter mentioned in note 34.

wounded reputation. Describing his plight to one of his confreres immediately following the issuance of the writ against him, Father Richard expressed the conviction, doubtless founded on legal advice, that he could quash all further proceedings by shifting the blame to Bishop Flaget.[53] That he would not do, and he thereupon became the victim of a long series of legal entanglements that paralyzed his activities and blighted his life. The suit was begun on August 29, 1817. Fortunately for Father Richard, a warm friendship had long existed between him and Judge Augustus B. Woodward, a member of that fantastic body that dispensed justice in early Detroit, the Supreme Court of the Territory.[54] It may have been largely through his efforts that the case dragged along for four years, but he was evidently powerless to prevent the verdict given on October 12, 1821. Father Richard was declared guilty of having defamed Labadie, and the latter was awarded damages in the sum of $1116. An appeal for temporary arrest of judgment was entered, and the case was held over until 1823.

The assertion has often been made that Labadie was urged by the political enemies of Father Richard to prosecute and discredit him at the time when his election as Delegate seemed certain. Although they doubtless made capital out of the suit, there is little to prove that they engineered the hearing in 1823. As a matter of fact Labadie had done all the harm he could two years before the priest had any thought of entering the political arena.

The case was reopened on October 4, 1823, before that famous trio of judges who held sway in Detroit from 1808 to 1824, Woodward, Witherell, and Griffin. From the records of the trial it appears that Witherell had always been ready to convict, but from the history of the Court we know that Woodward and Griffin generally took malicious pleasure in dissenting from their colleague. In this instance Woodward's friendship for Father Richard was an added motive for outwitting Witherell. When the time came for a verdict, Griffin was conveniently absent, Woodward and Witherell of course disagreed, and the case was again put over.[55]

[53] Letter of Father Richard to an unnamed Sulpician confrere dated Detroit, August 30, 1817. BCA.

[54] See Sketch of Judge Woodward by William L. Jenks in *Michigan History Magazine,* IX, 515. There is a diverting account of the Supreme Court in Farmer, *op. cit.,* Chap. XXXI.

[55] The sequence of events in the trial, and its dovetailing into Father Richard's political career have generally been incorrectly stated. For the statements in the text the writer is deeply indebted to the researches of the Rt. Rev. Msgr. Edward J. Hickey of Detroit, who has gathered transcripts of all available records of the trial found in the BHC, the County Building in Detroit, the files of the Supreme Court at Lansing, and, for the last stages, the files of the Supreme Court in Washington.

Therefore, when Father Richard went to Washington for his first session in Congress he was still in jeopardy. But he had the lengthy opinion of Judge Woodward in his favor, and he was eager to bolster it up with the authority of the most distinguished lawyers in the East.[56] He had no difficulty in procuring what must have been to him a most precious document. It read in part.

> Words in themselves actionable may nevertheless be spoken under such circumstances and in such connections as that they thereby cease to be actionable; and if in this case it sufficiently appear that the Defendant meant only to impute to the Plaintiff that which the Roman Church considers as an offense, and not that which the municipal Law regards as such no action will lie for such words.
>
> We may add that there are many cases in which words are spoken before Ecclesiastical Jurisdictions, or in the exercise of ecclesiastical discipline, which can not be made the subject of a suit for slander, although they might be actionable if spoken without such cause or occasion, and maliciously. But the chief ground of our opinion in this case is that the words, under the circumstances and in the connection in which they appear to have been spoken, do not charge any offense punishable by the municipal Law; therefore we think they are not actionable.[57]

The lawyers who concurred in this opinion, and who signed it, were Daniel Webster, Henry Clay, Edward Livingstone, John W. Taylor, John Piott, Peter Du Ponceau, and Horace Binney. Never was any document signed by a greater array of legal talent.

Meanwhile, in answer to the repeated protests of the citizens of Detroit, Congress had modified the legal system of the Territory. The terms of the existing judges were to expire February 1, 1824, and reappointments were to be for a term of four years only. Judge Witherell was reappointed, Judge Griffin made no effort to be, and Judge Woodward, despite the strenuous efforts of Father Richard in his behalf, failed to secure a place on the bench. To Father Richard the consequences were inevitable. He wrote to Alexander Fraser.

> Judge Woodward has arrived on the 10th inst. . . . Had he followed, or rather preceded Judge Hunt only one day, his name should not have been erased from the list of the judges . . . He will, I have no doubt, obtain some other appointment, but he will be lost for our Territory. . . . All Gentlemen of the Bar, all the most learned men in jurisprudence to whom I have spoken about it, are surprised even that such a case was ever admitted in the court. They say it is impossible to lose it

[56] Judge Woodward's opinion dated October 7, 1823, is among the May Papers in the BHC.
[57] The document is in the DCA.

unless by the ignorance or prevention or prejudice of the judges, as the two new judges were both parties in the same case, they may perhaps decline to seat in the case, and then if left to the old judge alone, it is easy to anticipate how it will turn . . .[58]

He had gauged the situation accurately. As soon as he had returned to Detroit, a hearing in the case was ordered. The two new judges, Sibley and Hunt, having served as counsel in preceding hearings withdrew from the bench, leaving the disposal of the case to Judge Witherell alone. The outcome was certain. The 1821 judgment was reaffirmed, and for good measure Sheriff Wing, one of the candidates in the election won by Father Richard, was ordered to execute it immediately. What followed is perhaps best described in the open letter addressed to the parishioners by their pastor.

My Very dear Brethren!
No doubt you have all been informed that on September 21 of this year, a judgment was rendered against me in favor of Francois Labadie for having excommunicated him by order of Monseigneur, the Bishop of Bardstown, because having a lawful wife, Apolline Girardin, still living, he married another woman before a civil magistrate, which action is pronounced by the Church as adultery. One hour after the judg-- ment was rendered I was served with its execution by the sheriff, who demanded that I immediately pay the eleven hundred and fifty-four piastres, more or less, or be imprisoned. Persuaded that the judgment is unjust and contrary to the law, besides my inability to procure such a large sum in a moment of time, I chose to come to prison where I am still today, the tenth of October, 1824, at this time of writing. More than six days ago, a sworn surety that I would remain within the limits of the County of Wayne was signed by three worthy citizens of this parish. But, although approved by two justices of the peace, this writing was rejected by the plaintiff's attorneys, who demanded one of a different form. So it has happened that by a special dispensation of Providence I find myself still detained, and although this is the Holy Sabbath day I shall not have the happiness of offering the Holy Sacrifice, and you will be deprived of assisting thereat. We should, each of us, be resigned to the will of God who rules all things in his wisdom for his greater glory, and for our greatest good.
But although I am held a prisoner, I would say to you in the words of St. Paul when he was a prisoner like me for having done his duty: 'The word of God is not bound.' *Verbum Dei non est alligatum.* And although I am separated from you by these walls of four foot thickness and by these iron bars, in which I glory, I can still continue to address to you the word of God . . .[59]

---

[58] Letter to Alexander Fraser, Washington, March 17, 1824. BHC.
[59] The original letter is in the DCA.

There was no lack of courage in Father Richard. The letter goes on to reaffirm the censure passed on Labadie, and, more than that, singles out another individual in the parish guilty of the same sin, and threatens him with the same penalty. On the following Tuesday, Father Richard was released from custody on bail furnished by three of his parishioners. However, he was still bound by court order to remain within the limits of Wayne County.[60] The question now arose: how was it possible for him to attend the second session of Congress? Could he as a member claim immunity from arrest if he violated the conditions of his bail? The local attorneys being unable to furnish a satisfactory answer, he appealed to Henry Clay, who seems to have given him some sort of assurance that he had nothing to fear.[61] He therefore left Detroit on November 4, 1824, and on December 6 he took his seat in the House for the second session.

Father Richard's outstanding service to his constituents while in Congress was in the matter of roads. A public land office had been opened in Detroit in 1818, but the absence of roads into the interior seriously hindered Michigan's development. Indeed, to the pioneers flocking westward Michigan had been pictured as a waste of worthless swamp to be avoided. The real growth of the State began with the knowledge gained from the surveys to which Father Richard had given the impetus.[62] His best known achievement in this matter was his sponsoring of an appropriation by Congress to open a road from Detroit to Chicago. In the support of this measure he made his first and only speech on the floor of the House. The result is the great highway that today links Michigan Avenue in Detroit with Michigan Avenue in Chicago, the sole lasting memorial to the first Catholic priest in the history of the nation to sit in Congress.[63]

The second session ended on March 3, 1825, and Father Richard returned to Detroit to find himself involved in further difficulties. His plea for immunity had not been respected, and Labadie was allowed to sue him and his bondsmen to recover on the bond whose terms he had violated by going to Washington. Under this menace the priest spent the remaining years of his life. The case dragged on for six years, during which Labadie parcelled out portions of the judgment awarded him to several individuals, who never left off

[60] The Act regulating prison limits was passed in Detroit, November 18, 1822.

[61] "When I saw you in Washington in January, 1825, I was by a Bail considered within the jail bounds, which was by our statutes the whole county of Wayne. With the advice of Mr. Henry Clay I went to Washington. . . ." Letter of Father Richard to Bishop Fenwick, Detroit, February 28, 1831. NDA.

[62] George Newman Fuller, *Economic and Social Beginnings of Michigan* (Lansing, 1916), 263.

[63] See *Mich. Hist. Colls.*, XXI, 441. A fairly recent agitation to have U.S. 112 named after Father Richard met with no response.

hounding the priest for payment.[64] On July 27, 1831, court action was again taken against Father Richard, who thereupon appealed to the Supreme Court in Washington. There the case lay at the time of his death.[65]

Curiously enough, the filing of Labadie's suit did not dissuade Father Richard from seeking reelection to the 19th Congress. There ensued another bitter campaign followed by an election tainted by charges of ballot stuffing, and intimidation of voters. The three leading candidates were Father Richard, Austin Wing, and John Biddle. On October 21, 1825, the commission sitting in hearings on the testimony offered by the candidates awarded the election to Austin Wing by a majority of four votes over Father Richard.[66] This time it was the priest's turn to contest the election, and he laid before Congress an elaborate memorial in support of his claim.[67] But the decision was against him and he returned to Detroit to nurse his disappointment, and to remain for the rest of his life within the limits of Wayne County. He entered his candidacy again in 1827, but the announcement created scarcely a ripple on the political situation.[68] His career in politics was definitely over.

We have digressed somewhat from church affairs to follow the career of Father Richard. It must not be forgotten that all this while Rome was studying the advisability of placing a bishop in Detroit. There is some history yet to cover before we come to see why and where the choice fell as it did.

[64] "One circumstance that makes my case unpleasant and doubtful in its results is that Mr. F.L. has assigned all the amount of the original judgment to several individuals, I think, five, among whom is Mr. Jh. Campau, whose share is $640, and he asks the whole without any deduction. . . ." Letter to Bishop Fenwick, Detroit, December 11, 1830. Archives of Mt. Saint Joseph's College, Cincinnati.

[65] Docket of the United States Supreme Court from 1832 to 1834.

[66] A Report of the Proceedings in Relation to the Contested Election for Delegate to the Nineteenth Congress (Detroit, 1825). There is a copy in the BHC.

[67] Proceedings of the Friends of Mr. Richard Relative to the Contested Election (Detroit, 1825). A pamphlet of 19 pages in the BHC.

[68] The Detroit Gazette for 1827, passim.

CHAPTER XVII

Recruits from France

WHEN Bishop Fenwick went to Europe in 1823 it was not for distraction but to find some answer to the three major problems that beset him. Recruits had to be found to swell the number of his clergy, pecuniary assistance had to be solicited for the needs of his struggling diocese, and the Roman authorities were to be urged to take definite action in the matter of a bishop for Detroit who would take over the burden of Michigan Territory. In Rome he was attracted by the personality of a young German priest, Frederic Rese, who expressed his willingness to accompany the bishop to America and to devote himself to the German Catholics of Ohio.[1] On his return journey through France the bishop made the acquaintance of two young French priests interested in the American missions, Jean Bellamy of the Diocese of Rennes, and Pierre Déjean of the Diocese of Rodez. They both volunteered to serve in the Diocese of Cincinnati. Knowing the urgent needs of priests at home the bishop decided to send his recruits on to America while he himself prolonged his stay in Europe. Accordingly, Fathers Bellamy, Déjean, and Rese arrived in New York on September 1, 1824.[2] In obedience to the directions they had received the two French priests came on to Detroit, while Father Rese set out for Cincinnati.

On their arrival the newcomers found Father Richard in jail, and they had their first interview with him there.[3] Father Bellamy was immediately appointed to the Raisin River settlement where he was obliged to install himself on October 10, the same Sunday on which

[1] O'Daniel, *op. cit.*, 263. From all available signatures it is certain that Father Rese always signed his name "Rese" with two grave accents, which are of course meaningless. As will be noted later the family name was "Reese," and the accents were an attempt to approximate the sound for non-Germans.

[2] *Ibid.*, 267. For the date of arrival see letter of Father Déjean *Annales*, III, 303.

[3] Letter of Father Richard to Bishop Fenwick, Detroit, February 28, 1831. NDA. Father Marchand across the river thus commented on their arrival to his bishop. "Two young priests sent to him (Richard) by the Bishop of Cincinnati arrived last week. They seem to be two good lads, and willing enough. Mr. Richard has given each of them a parish. Today, the older of the two, Bellamy by name, about thirty-one, is leaving for the Raisin River. The other one, about seven years younger, named Déjean, is leaving for the Huron and St. Clair Rivers." Letter dated October 7, 1824. QCA.

Father Richard exposed his plight to his parishioners.[4] Despite his strenuous efforts to remedy the conditions which had so disheartened Father Ganilh, little progress was made, and at the end of a year in the parish Father Bellamy thus described his situation.

> My little church is certainly the poorest, and the most wretched of all churches. It has no chalice, no ostensorium, no ciborium, no vestments, no altar linens, no missal. Everything that I have I have borrowed. For an altar I use a sacristy table on which I place an altar-stone. . . . This table is little more than half covered by an old and patched altar cloth. This is my altar on which the Spotless Lamb is offered every day. . . . On Good Friday of this same year, 1825, Mr. Richard, returning from Congress, of which he is a member, stopped here to preach the Passion sermon. Such crowds came to hear him that it is a miracle that the floor of my church did not collapse under the weight. My little church is up-stairs over the room that serves as my rectory. . . . In trying to enter my chamber after the ceremony I could open the door only with great diffi-culty. The ceiling had sunk so far that whereas It was ordinarily two inches above the door it was now touching it. Nevertheless we celebrated Easter in this chapel after having taken the necessary precautions, but on Low Sunday I announced to my people that in order to shield them from evident danger I would no longer hold services until the necessary repairs had been made.[5]

Although the majority of Father Bellamy's parishioners lived along the Raisin River another group had been slowly forming on the shoreline of Maumee Bay. How early its size justified the building of its own house of worship is not definitely known; but it will be re-membered that Father Richard in his census of Michigan for 1822 mentions a chapel of St. Joseph at Miami Bay. From the settlement at "la Baie," as the French called it, grew the present parish of Erie, and, according to local tradition the primitive chapel stood by the water-side directly east of the church now in the village. That St. Joseph's in the time of Father Bellamy was already considered a separate par-ish seems to follow from the fact that on March 4, 1825, he began its proper baptismal register.

Neither the pleadings nor the threats of both their pastor and Fa-ther Richard could stir the parishioners of the Raisin River settle-ment to unite for the building of a suitable church. The town of Monroe, platted in 1817, was growing in importance, and forward-looking parishioners wanted the church there. The conservative por-tion of the parish would brook no change. Convinced that his efforts were useless, Father Bellamy not only surrendered his charge but

---

[4] Bellamy notes the date in the parish register.
[5] Letter in the *Annales* . . . II, 108–09.

made a most unusual decision, that of spending his life in the service of the French missions in Indo-China. He signed the register for the last time August 23, 1827, and October 7, he sailed from New York bound for Macao. A few months later he was at his post in Tong-king.[6]

While Father Bellamy thus passed out of our local history, the young priest who accompanied him to Detroit was busily engaged in the field to which Father Richard had appointed him. As already stated, the French spread out from Detroit in two directions. To the south they clustered along the banks of the Raisin River. To the north they were attracted by the languorous windings of the "Huron of Lake St. Clair," the Clinton River of today. The number of settlers warranted the building of a house of worship as early as 1799, for in that year Father Richard supervised the construction of a log chapel on the north bank of the river, and dedicated it to St. Francis de Sales.[7] The Huron River settlement therefore ranked next to Monroe in importance, and although it had no resident priest it was attended by Father Richard and his assistants. When Father Déjean arrived he was accordingly named first resident pastor of St. Francis de Sales.

Father Déjean thus became the pioneer priest of Macomb and St. Clair counties. We have an interesting series of letters written by him during the five years that he was stationed in this district.[8] He was quite willing to satisfy his friends in France thirsting for the details of his new life. It was all very marvelous to him, and there are signs that he recorded not only his own observations but tales that some old hunter must have fed to the credulous young priest, as, for instance, that tigers roamed through the wilds of Michigan. Here is probably the first letter that he wrote, "From the Huron River, in a log cabin."

I have received with gratitude the books that you were good enough to send me. You would have obliged me very much had you added one or two sacred pictures, some old vestments, elementary catechisms, small crosses for the Indians, and beads of all kinds.

This year the cold has not been severe, nevertheless I have often

[6] Letter of Father Bellamy in the *Annales* . . . III, 404–09. In the DCA there is a letter from Father Bellamy written from his mission field to Father Déjean, and dated July 12, 1829. From the letter it appears that Father Bellamy was allied with the priests of the Paris Foreign Mission Society.

[7] In the memorial booklet commemorating the golden Jubilee of St. Mary's High School in 1921, the location of the first chapel is thus described: "There had been for a long time a little chapel across the river on the Moore farm just above what is now the Trombley farm, and at the head of the road below Joseph Hatzenbuhler's place."

[8] The letters here referred to are in the *Annales* . . . III, 303–25. There are three more in IV, 466–69; 491–96; 545–46.

tramped over the ice, and in a brief period I have made many a league on sleighs and even on horseback. At present I sometimes go twenty-five leagues across Lake St. Clair in a ship made of a single log, and with one companion.[9] Pray for me; we are sometimes in danger of being swamped. I engaged myself to visit the settlers once a month. The first time that I went everyone was transported with joy. On the trip over-land I was escorted by four 'Gentlemen' as if I had been a bishop. Arriv-ing at Fort Gratiot on Lake Huron, where no priest had ever been seen save Father Richard on two occasions, I held public prayer in the eve-ning in an old warehouse. More than forty-five persons were present. After the prayer I said a few words to them to urge the proper fulfill-ment of their religious duties. At the end of my talk made, as you may well believe, extemporaneously and out of my store, I showed them a crucifix. The sight of it produced a deep impression; I could hear deep sighs on all sides. Among the Catholics there were several Protestants, and a few Indians. At six o'clock in the evening I began my session in the sacred tribunal, which lasted until two hours after midnight. I heard the confessions of twenty-seven persons. After Mass on the following day, about the same number came to me. I celebrated the holy mysteries in the shabby vestments I brought from France. Nineteen Protestants came to me after Mass to beg me to give them a sermon in English. My ignorance of the language excused me. . . .

I hope that our little church of the Hurons which will be dedicated to St. Felicity will be completed by summer. I live alone in a little wooden house that I have had built. My ordinary fare is potatoes, chunks of deer and bear meat, ducks which the Indians or whites bring me. For my recreation I dig in a little garden in front of my door. I get along well with the Protestants, and several of them, including Metho-dists, have subscribed towards a church. . . .

As a result of Father Déjean's zealous ministry the congregation outgrew its primitive log chapel, and a new church became necessary. Meanwhile two more Catholic groups had been slowly forming in his district, and in the fall of 1826 we find Father Déjean building three churches simultaneously. He wrote on October 7:

We are busily engaged in the building of three churches in the district that has been confided to me. 1. St. Francis on the Huron River where I reside. I hope to be able to say Mass in it within a month. 2. St. Felic-ity, on the River St. Clair. 3. In L'Anse Creuse a church forty feet long by thirty feet wide. It is already under roof. Dare I recommend to you the church of St. Francis de Sales? If your good friends procured us one hundred dollars, we could have a more suitable building. . . .

[9] Father Déjean could not have meant that he was crossing the lake to the Canadian shore. He was evidently referring to his periodical visits to Fort Gratiot, the Port Huron of today.

Every vestige of these three churches has long since disappeared. St. Francis stood on the Tucker farm, about three miles below Mt. Clemens, just a stone's throw from the new bridge where the Shore Road crosses the river. It remained in use for some years after the center of the parish had shifted to the town, and was torn down some time after 1846.[10] St. Felicity was built on an acre and a half donated by George Cottrell and John Petea, and was situated on the shore of St. Clair River about two miles below Marine City.[11] The church at L'Anse Creuse stood on the shore of the bay at the end of the Rattell farm, a property now designated as 40000 Lake Shore Drive. The site is at present under water some distance from the shore line, and according to local tradition both this church and St. Felicity were destroyed about ten years after their erection when the lake and the river rose to an unprecedented level.[12]

On the departure of Father Bellamy, Father Déjean replaced him for some time in the River Raisin settlement, and was almost persuaded to establish his residence there.[13] But he returned to his parish, and remained until the summer of 1829 when he betook himself to the Indian missions of the north.[14]

While Fathers Bellamy and Déjean were working in their respective parishes, Father Richard could not overstep the limits of Wayne County, and the missionary excursions that had to be made in the Territory fell to the lot of his devoted assistant, Francis Badin. Scarcely anything is known of his first three years in Detroit beyond the fact that, in 1825, he erected a chapel on the shore of the lake, a few miles above the city, and dedicated it to St. Paul.[15] This was the beginning of the present parish of Grosse Pointe Farms. In the same year he was deputed to go over the ground that Father Richard had covered in his journey of 1823.

Leaving Detroit on April 27, 1825, Father Badin sailed for Mack-

[10] Details from source in Note 7.

[11] The deeds to the property in the DCA are dated September 16, 1826. The present church property at Marine City was bought from the government by Father Richard, and the patent was issued on April 1, 1825. The second church was erected on this property in 1846.

[12] "Although the spring of 1836 was very dry, about the 10th of June the rain commenced falling, and in such abundance that the whole country was flooded. . . . This and the succeeding year, 1837, were known as the years when the water in the rivers and great lakes was higher than it had ever been known. Many of the old farms bordering on Lake St. Clair were under water from six inches to two feet." *Mich. Hist. Colls.*, V, 54.

[13] Letter dated November 26, 1827. *Annales* . . . III, 320.

[14] Letter from L'Arbre Croche dated October 29, 1829. *Ibid.*, IV, 491.

[15] "Mr. Badin erected last year a small chapel under the invocation of the great Apostle of the Gentiles. . . ." Letter of Father Déjean dated October 7, 1826. *Ibid.*, III, 320. According to local tradition the chapel stood on the shore of the lake on the Reno farm, a few hundred feet above Vernier Road.

inac. After a few days of intensive ministry on the Island, he passed over to Green Bay. There were eighty-four families to be cared for, a task which engaged Father Badin for the next two months.[16] Of his work in the last days of his stay at Green Bay he wrote:

> Nine boys and eight girls, in age from thirteen to thirty, were admitted to First Communion. This touching ceremony, by which every one was greatly impressed, took place on Sunday, June 26, in the new chapel which was blessed on the same day. Several baptisms were also conferred, and this prolonged the ceremonies of the morning until three o'clock in the afternoon. At five o'clock we sang vespers, benediction, and hymns. Father Richard left to me the baptism of thirty adults, as he was unable to instruct them sufficiently during his short stay. I had only two marriages to bless. For ten days in succession we sang High Mass in the new chapel, and on the day of my departure. When that time came, I was so moved at taking leave of the eleven catechists of both sexes whom I had chosen, that I could scarcely go on with my Mass."

Making Mackinac his headquarters, Father Badin spent the next four months bringing the consolations of religion to the scattered Catholics within his reach. He made two long stays at L'Arbre Croche, where the Indians quickly erected a chapel for him which he dedicated to St. Vincent de Paul. The Indians were overjoyed to have a Black Robe in their midst, and Father Badin extolls their devotion and their fervor in divine worship. There was another colony of Catholic Indians on Drummond Island, which had been cared for occasionally by Father Joseph Crevier of Sandwich, assistant to Father Marchand. Here Father Badin spent several days, giving instructions and administering the sacraments, and marveling at the piety and simplicity that he found. The final weeks of his stay in the north were passed at Mackinac, and on November 14 he sailed for Detroit.[17]

In April, 1826, Father Badin returned to the northern missions.[18] For the next twelve months he scoured the northern lake region in search of those who had long been deprived of priestly ministrations, and then pushed on as far as Prairie du Chien, which at the time was in Michigan Territory. Southward, and at some distance across the Illinois border, lay the rising settlement of Galena, the center of the lead-mining district along the Fever River. Illinois, admitted to statehood in 1818, still belonged to the diocese of Bardstown, but Bishop Flaget had confided its care to the bishop of St. Louis. There were

[16] The number of families is so stated in Father Richard's census to be given later.

[17] In his absence Father Badin was replaced by the Rev. Appollinaris Herman, a young Frenchman who had been ordained in Kentucky. After a stay of six months he left for Martinique. O'Daniel, *op. cit.*, 332.

[18] Father Badin writes that he found at Mackinac twelve vestments that had been used by the Jesuits, a crucifix, and four candlesticks. *Annales . . .* II, 123.

many Irish Catholics among the miners in the Galena district, and Father Badin was anxious to include them in his ministrations. Accordingly, he wrote the following letter to Bishop Rosati from Prairie du Chien.[19]

> I take occasion of the journey of my respected friend, M. Dubois, to ask you for definite information as to whether Fever River, about thirty miles from Prairie du Chien, depends on your jurisdiction or that of the Rev. M. Richard of Detroit; and if, in the former case, I may exercise there the functions of the sacred ministry. It is now the third week since my arrival. I have much work to do, and that is not surprising; for since the days of the Jesuits, that is, since time immemorial, no priest, save the good Trappist Prior, made his appearance at Prairie du Chien. People here tell me that he perished on his voyage to Europe.[20]
>
> The aspirants to first holy communion, thirty-seven boys and men, and forty-six girls and women, making a total of eighty-three souls, keep me very busy. You can imagine how great the number of invalid marriages is, and how many baptisms had to be conferred.
>
> I have conceived the project, dear Father, of going and depositing my conscience in yours, as it is now fourteen or fifteen months since I saw a priest, having been ordered to remain over winter at Sault Ste. Marie, Drummond Island, Michillimackinack Island, Arbor Croche, La Pointe, St. Ignace, etc. But I find my project cannot be carried out for several reasons. All that is left to me, therefore, is to implore the mercy of God and the assistance of your good prayers.
>
> Yesterday, the inhabitants of this place (Prairie du Chien) have commenced to cut down trees for the erection of a chapel, fifty feet long. God grant that I may be able to bless it to His greater glory before I leave the Prairie. I hardly believe that I can hold first communion services here as early as I had hoped. . . ."

With faculties from Bishop Rosati, Father Badin began his ministry in Galena at the end of August, and remained there until some time in November. He then went on to St. Louis before returning to Detroit.

For the next two years, Father Badin's missionary activities are not so easy to follow. He went north again in the summer of 1828, and spent the following winter most likely in Prairie du Chien. The

[19] Letter dated June 9, 1827, *Illinois Cath. Hist. Rev.*, II, 175. Father Badin describes his experiences during the Indian uprising known in Wisconsin history as the Winnebago War. "I suppose the papers kept you informed on what the savages did here. I was filled with terror more than once, more than twenty times; not that I am timid, not that I am afraid of death. . . . All the inhabitants shut themselves up in the fort, where I had established a pretty chapel in the large hall of the hospital. There I sang several High Masses. A few days later they made me move. I was forced to move the altar more than six times, either on account of the war, or of pouring rain . . ."

[20] The "good Trappist Prior" was Father Dunand. For details concerning him and his brethren see numerous references in the volumes of the *Saint Louis Catholic Hist. Rev.*

extant record of his ministrations during this period show him at work in Galena or Prairie du Chien from August 10, 1828 to August 9, 1829. He thereupon returned to Detroit, and was assigned to the district left vacant by the departure of Father Déjean.[21]

Having glanced over the activities of Father Richard's helpers, we must now go back to the affairs of Father Richard himself. Bishop Fenwick returned from Europe at the end of 1824, and remained for a while in Baltimore, where he had frequent opportunities of meeting the priest-delegate from Michigan. To the bishop, the appointment of Father Richard to the see of Detroit was an accomplished fact. The priest wrote his friend Alexander Fraser in Detroit:

I have recd. yr. letter dated 16th Jan. Since more than 8 days I am sick, keeping bed untill this day, inclusive five o'clock P.M. I have read yr. letter in bed and I answer to it. I have the honor to inform you that I approve very much of the method you have concerted with Judge McDonell. In conformity with it I have written a short letter to Mr. Badin inclosed within a short one to Judge McD., all three this same date. This may be to you a sign that I am getting better, although I am very weak. My sickness originated in a cold occasioned by walking in snow 4 weeks ago. I neglected it, and on the day after the Bill for Chicago road passed, I could not go to the H. (House) any more, next day in 6 hours I was bled twice, and 2 days after once more. As this afternoon we have had a great deal of snow, I will be kept at home some days more to get strength. I have seen Bishop Fenwick last Saturday the 5th. He says that every day the official nomination from Rome may arrive directed to the Archbishop of Baltimore, by which I may be bound to give up running candidate as delegate. It is therefore far from being certain that I will be a candidate. If any person wants to know it, you may tell them that they will be able to know it when I will arrive in Detroit sometime before Easter which falls this year on the third of April. I will thank you if you will show this letter to our common friend Mr. McDonell. I cannot write more now. . . .[22]

We have already seen why Rome was inclined to act slowly in the matter, and Father Richard left Washington without the "official nomination." That he was still expecting it after his return to Detroit is implied in the postscript of a letter written to Bishop Rosati:

There is a prospect of an establishment at Arbre Croche by a Catholic priest, and Charity Sisters of Emmitsburg.—If I have to be the Bp. of Mich. I wish to have if possible all priests members of a

21 The baptismal record which Father Badin kept at Galena and Prairie du Chien has been published in the Records of the *Amer. Cath. Hist. Soc.*, XXII, 164 ff. There are entries for 1830 which the editor cannot explain. They certainly refer to baptisms in the Detroit area which Father Badin performed in the parishes established by Father Déjean.

22 Letter to Alexander B. Fraser dated Washington, February 9, 1825. BHC.

Congregation. I wish to know if it would be possible to have priests of the Lazarists. . . .[23]

But no word was forthcoming, and Father Richard remained at home to face the end of his political career, and the cramping effects of his legal misfortunes. In May, 1826, Archbishop Meréchal urged Propaganda to take cognizance of Bishop Fenwick's urgent appeal in behalf of a new see in Detroit, and of the candidate he had proposed.[24] A month later, Bishop Fenwick himself pressed for immediate action. [25]

Before the bishop's letter arrived the Propaganda Congregation had met to consider the matter. On the one hand there was ample testimony to the necessity of a see in Detroit, and to the integrity of Father Richard.[26] On the other hand reports had filtered in of his being heavily in debt, and of his having served a term in prison. The Congregation needed more light on this strange personage. It decided to seek the advice of Father Anthony Kohlmann, S.J., who had spent many years in America, and who was then holding the chair of theology at the Gregorian College. On June 11, he wrote his opinion of Father Richard, which is here summarized:

Gabriel Richard is a man of about 50 to 60 years old. For many years he has exercised his ministry in Detroit, and has always had the reputation of being a zealous and blameless priest. Well versed in theology, he joins pleasing manners to an acute mind. He knows French and English. His election to Congress proves the esteem in which he is held. The writer has heard that he was twice imprisoned for having excommunicated a member of his congregation. He does not believe that the imprisonment has lowered Father Richard in the estimation of his people. His zeal for the glory of God, and his enterprise, have laid on the priest a burden of debt which the writer can not appraise.

The Congregation was still undecided; further inquiries were necessary. What were the facts behind Father Richard's imprisonment? How had his standing in the community been affected by it? Was there any possibility of his being exposed to the same danger again? No action could be taken until satisfactory answers to these questions were forthcoming.[27]

Meanwhile, Father Richard was laboring with unabated activity,

[23] Letter to Bishop Rosati dated Detroit, April 24, 1825. St. Louis Chancery Archives.
[24] Letter to the Propaganda Congregation, May 13, 1826. Propaganda Archives, *Scritture Riferite*, VIII.
[25] Letter to Propaganda Cong., June 16, 1826. Propaganda Archives, *America Centrale*, VIII.
[26] The printed *Acta* of the Congregation for 1826, 311–14, take up the matter of Father Richard's appointment, and give Father Kohlmann's report.
[27] Propaganda Archives, *Ristretto 3050*, June 26, 1826.

alive to his responsibilities and to the needs of the future. In the light of the present reality it is interesting to read his forecast as he communicated it to the *Annales:*

> . . . I hope soon to see the beginnings of this college or seminary that will henceforth furnish the numerous missionaries required for the Indians and for the vast American population that is coming in crowds to settle in our forests. The State of Michigan is certainly destined to be a flourishing region. The air is pure and salubrious, the land excellent. That the Federal Government recognizes its importance is evident from the fact that at the last session of Congress a resolution which I proposed was adopted namely, the opening of a highway from Detroit westward to Chicago, a settlement lying at the southernmost point of Lake Michigan. Three commissioners named by the President, and two surveyors, have explored this vast solitude, 260 miles, and have laid out the course of this important route which will open the interior of our Territory to the immigrants who have been crowding in this last season. Three steamers and more than 150 sailing-vessels plying our lakes have brought us 6 or 7 thousand immigrants who came to buy land. The great canal, 365 miles long, from Albany to Buffalo on Lake Erie has been completed. . . .[28] This summer, in our little city of Detroit, seventy-two houses were built, some of them having two stories, and quite elegant. We expect that a hundred more will be built next summer, and that the canal will bring us twelve thousand immigrants from the East to clear our vast timber lands. It is true that there are few Catholics among the newcomers, but that is all the more reason why we need sterling priests to work for their conversion. . . . Much could be done by having priests travel among the Americans, holding friendly conferences in their homes during the long winter evenings, and answering questions—Americans are inquisitive. . . .
>
> M. Dubois and M. Bruté are training for me, at Emmitsburg, professors for the future college of Detroit. From the large community of Sisters of Charity at the same place six members have been offered to me by the Mother Superior, Sister Rose White, and are ready to found a school at Arbre Croche among the Ottawa Indians.[29] God knows how many other projects, great and small, go through my head, of schools and missions for the Indians, for the deaf and dumb, for poor children, etc., but means are lacking in a new country where everything must be created out of nothing. . . .[30]

In 1826 Father Richard again wrote to the Propagation of the Faith Society, and this time he endeavored to give fairly accurate

[28] The Erie Canal completed in 1825 diverted much westward immigration from the Ohio River route, and was the greatest single factor in the settlement of Michigan.

[29] The motherhouse of the Daughters of Charity at Emmitsburg, Md., disclaims having any correspondence from Father Richard.

[30] Letter to Didier Petit of the Society for the Propagation of the Faith, December 22, 1825.

statistics of the souls under his care. Father Badin had just returned from an extensive visitation of every Catholic center in the neighborhood of Detroit, and with his help Father Richard drew up the following table representing the condition of the Church in the Territory of Michigan:

	Catholic Families	Individuals	Churches or Chapels
At Prairie du Chien, at Fort Crawford near the mouth of the Wisconsin in the Mississippi	120	720	0
At Green Bay, at Fort Brown, the old St. Francis-Xavier Mission	84	504	1
At Michilli-Mackinac, Mission of Saint-Anne	80	480	destroyed
At Drummond Island	40	240	0
At Sault Ste-Marie	20	120	0
At Clinton River, St. Francis de Sales, and neighborhood	70	420	1
At St. Clair River and neighborhood	55	330	1
At Detroit, on a strip along the river fifteen miles above and twenty miles below Detroit, that is, to Lake Erie	300	1800	2
At River Raisin, St. Anthony	150	900	1
At Miami Bay, St. Joseph	90	540	1
At Miami River and neighborhood	40	240	0 [31]
From the 1st of May to the 1st of October more than 600 Canadian voyageurs come to Michilli-Mackinac to barter their furs		600	
Total	1049	6894	6

[31] This designation refers to the settlements in and around what is now Toledo, O. When Ohio was admitted to statehood in 1803 its northern boundary was not clearly defined. Two years later the southern boundary of Michigan Territory was laid down as a line drawn from the end of Lake Michigan to Lake Erie. In 1817 Ohio drew its present northern line, but Michigan insisted on the line of 1805, and claimed a strip varying from 5 to 8 miles wide along the northern border of Ohio. This led to the Toledo War of 1835. See Burton, *op. cit.*, II, Chap. XLI. In 1837 the State of Michigan was given the upper peninsula in exchange for the disputed territory.

If to these six thousand, eight hundred and ninety four Frenchmen, of Canadian origin, you add three hundred and six English-speaking Catholics, scattered here and there (nearly all poor Irishmen), scarcely twenty of them born in America, you will have seven thousand as the total white, Catholic population. There are also about a hundred colored people. . . .[32]

But Father Richard's major problem centered about the Indians of the Territory. His letters prove abundantly how they engrossed his attention. Had he been permitted, he would willingly have given up St. Anne's to spend his life at L'Arbre Croche, where, as he says, he would have found more consolation than among the whites. His helplessness was only accentuated by the strenuous efforts put forth by the Protestant missionary societies.[33] Hence the burden of his appeals to the Society for the Propagation of the Faith was immediate help for his Indian missions.

Bishop Fenwick, oppressed with his cares in Ohio, felt keenly the plight of Father Richard, and his inability to help him. As he wrote himself to the Society: "His [Father Richard's] situation is painful for him, and heart-breaking for me. He does not cease calling for missioners. If you can send him a reinforcement of some good priests endowed with constancy and ardent zeal, you will relieve him very much and oblige me infinitely. As for myself in Ohio I can employ only those who know English well. To obtain such as these I depend on Fathers Rese and Badin." [34]

In the hope of securing relief for his crying needs, the prelate had dispatched Father Rese to Europe in January of 1827. As agent of the bishop for the settlement of certain questions that had arisen in the diocese of Cincinnati Father Rese was ordered to proceed to Rome at the earliest opportunity. He arrived there at the end of May, just in time to give an unexpected turn to another business that was almost completed.

The Congregation of the Propaganda had at last decided to erect the diocese of Detroit. The result of its deliberations reads as follows:

The urgent representations that have been made by their Lordships, Ambrose Maréchal, Archbishop of Baltimore, and Edward Fenwick, Bishop of Cincinnati, and by others, make it evident that the growth and stability of religion in the province of Michigan and the Northwest, hitherto administered by the Right Reverend Bishop of Cincinnati,

---

[32] *Annales* . . . III, 325–31.

[33] For Protestant missionary endeavor in the neighborhood of Mackinac see Edwin O. Wood, *Historic Mackinac*, I, 394 ff.

[34] O'Daniel, *op. cit.*, 334. The Father Badin here mentioned was Stephen Badin, who had been absent for some years in Europe.

demand that the said province become a distinct diocese whose see shall be at Detroit, and whose boundaries shall be the limits of the said province. In a general meeting held on February 19, 1827, the Sacred Congregation of the Propaganda presided over by his Eminence Mauro Cappelari, Prefect of the said Congregation, agreed and decided, after mature deliberation, to petition the Holy Father to draw up the apostolic letters by which the said diocese should be actually erected.

This resolution of the Sacred Congregation was made known to our Holy Father, Leo XII, by the Most Reverend Peter Caprano, Archbishop of Iconium, and Secretary of the Congregation, in an audience held on March 4, 1827. His Holiness graciously gave his approval, and commanded apostolic letters in the form of a Brief to be issued.[35]

The Congregation had proceeded further to the naming of the first bishop for the see of Detroit, and he was Gabriel Richard. It spoke of him as a priest eminent for his piety, the integrity of his life, his zeal for the ministry, and the length of service he had rendered. In the audience of March 4, the Holy Father endorsed the nomination of Father Richard, and authorized the steps necessary to make it effective.

The routine procedure by which these decisions of the Holy Father were to be promulgated was put into motion, and, on March 20, 1827, the Bull erecting the diocese of Detroit was officially issued.[36] But the appointment of Father Richard which would ordinarily have been issued at the same time did not appear. It had been thwarted at the last moment. In the final attempt to estimate the qualifications of Father Richard the Congregation sought information from a man who knew him, and who had just arrived in Rome, Father Martial, formerly of the diocese of Bardstown, but now affiliated with New Orleans. To his mind the appointment was unwise. Knowing that Father Rese was on his way to Rome, the Congregation delayed action until it could hear his opinion. He corroborated the statements of Father Martial.[37] The weight of this presumably accurate information was enough to abate all further proceedings. Detroit remained

---

[35] Propaganda Cong. Archives, *America*, Vol. 308, p. 192.

[36] The Bull is published in the *Jus Pontificium de Propaganda Fide* (Rome, 1891), V, 681.

[37] The printed *Acta* of the Congregation for 1833, pp. 86–87, contain the following passage: "In regard to the election of a bishop in the person of Gabriel Richard, Vicar General in Michigan, who died last year of cholera. The arrival in Rome, however, of Father Martial, missionary in Kentucky, and shortly afterwards of Father Rese, caused the sending of the Briefs to be suspended. They asserted that the erection of the diocese was still premature; that the small number of Catholics did not demand it; that a bishop would have no means of subsistence; and, finally, that although Father Richard was capable and zealous, he was burdened with debt, and could not with dignity exercise the office of bishop . . ."

a diocese without a bishop; the nomination of Father Richard was suppressed. Apparently the Congregation decided to let this anomalous situation stand until his death should make a new beginning possible, for six years later another Bull erecting the diocese of Detroit was issued without any reference to the action taken in 1827.

To what extent Father Richard was aware of the debates that centered about his nomination we have no means of knowing. It is barely possible that the outcome disappointed him; he most likely rejoiced at his escape from added responsibilities. His burden was heavy enough shared as it was, at this period of his life, only by Fathers Vincent Badin and Déjean. In the summer of 1828 another helper came, who was none other than the proto-priest of the United States, Father Stephen Badin. He was now sixty years of age, and had returned to America, after ten years spent in Europe, to devote the rest of his life to the missions. Father Richard stationed him at Monroe, which had been without a resident priest since the departure of Father Bellamy.[38] He went on to Kentucky in the following year when a successor was appointed during the visitation of Bishop Fenwick.[39]

As we have seen, the bishop paid his first visit to Detroit in 1822. His increasing pastoral labors in Ohio, and his confident expectation of a bishop for Detroit led him to defer a second visit from year to year. But the collapse of Father Richard's candidacy indicated that Michigan would remain under his charge for some time to come. He continued to urge the importance of a see in the Territory, and proposed another list of candidates to the Sacred Congregation.[40] In May, 1829, he began his long-delayed visitation of the northern missions.

The bishop proceeded directly from Cincinnati to Green Bay, where his appearance was most timely. For more than a year the parish had been in the hands of Jean-Baptiste Fauvel, an ex-seminarian from Quebec. He had applied to Father Richard for permission to begin a school at Green Bay; but this was the least of his ambitions. He soon began to preach, went through the ceremonies of the Mass

[38] Letter of Father Clicteur of Cincinnati in the *Annales* . . . IV, 473.

[39] O'Daniel, *op. cit.*, 375. There is a long letter of Stephen Badin, written from Monroe, in the *Annales* . . . IV, 470, and another long letter in the *St. Louis Cath. Hist. Rev.*, V, 172.

[40] Bishop Fenwick proposed three candidates in the following order: Rev. John Acquaroni of Louisiana, Rev. G. Chabrat, who later became auxiliary to Bishop Flaget, and Rev. Simon Bruté, the first bishop of Vincennes. In case none of these could be named, the bishop asked for the transfer to Detroit of the Rt. Rev. Michael Portier, then in charge of the vicariate of Alabama and the Floridas. O'Daniel, *op. cit.*, 358.

attired in priestly vestments, and usurped other functions of the ministry, alleging that he held special faculties from the Holy See. Denunciations from Detroit and Cincinnati had no effect, and only the presence of the bishop ended the scandal.[41]

From Green Bay the bishop crossed the lake to the missions of L'Arbre Croche and Mackinac. Led by Father Déjean, who had lately taken up his residence among them, the Indians received the bishop with all the pomp they could muster. He said Mass in their bark chapel, baptized and confirmed à number of them, and took his meals with the chiefs, sitting cross-legged on his mat.[42] After spending three busy weeks on the Island, he came down to Detroit, where a large Confirmation class awaited him. Visits to the outlying parishes followed, and some time in July the bishop returned to Cincinnati.

By prearrangement Bishop Fenwick had found at Detroit Father Samuel M. Smith.[43] A converted Quaker, ordained for Bardstown in 1826, he had lately been transferred to the diocese of Cincinnati. The growing number of English-speaking Catholics in and around Detroit had determined the bishop to send him to the assistance of Father Richard. However, Father Stephen Badin's desire to return to Kentucky created a vacancy which had to be filled. Accordingly, Father Smith was installed as pastor of Monroe.[44]

Fortunately, the bishop was soon able to carry out his original design. Father Patrick O'Kelly applied for admission into the diocese, was accepted, and was assigned to Detroit.[45] He thus became the first priest of his nationality to labor in Michigan after Father Edmund Burke. Father O'Kelly was born at Ballycallan, near Kilkenny, in 1792. On completing his studies for the priesthood at St. Kieran's

[41] For details concerning Fauvel see the *Wisconsin Hist. Colls.*, XIV, 166. Bishop Fenwick wrote a long letter, April 8, 1829, to the Propaganda Congregation describing the iniquities of Fauvel. Propaganda Archives, *America Centrale*, X. Father Richard wrote to Judge Grignon of Green Bay to have Fauvel removed. Copy of letter, dated April 30, 1829, in BHC.

[42] For an account of Bishop Fenwick's visitation reported by Father Mullon of Cincinnati see *Annales . . .* IV, 486.

[43] The *Detroit Gazette* for Thursday, June 25, 1829, after noting the arrival of the bishop on the preceding Sunday, announces that on the following Sunday "will be delivered by the Rev. Mr. Smith a discourse for the benevolent purpose of obtaining contributions for the benefit of the Sunday School established in this city." According to a sketch of Father Smith in the *Philadelphia Catholic Herald* for October 16, 1834, he was a native of Pennsylvania. As a young man he followed a company of traders to the Mississippi. Later he became overseer of a farm belonging to a Catholic family of St. Louis. Here his eremitical mode of life attracted the attention of Bishop Dubourg, who mistook his singularity for piety and urged him to study for the priesthood. The clergy list in Lamott, *op. cit.*, gives his ordination date as February 18, 1826.

[44] His first entry in the parish register is dated September 7, 1829.

[45] He signs the St. Anne register for the first time on October 8, 1829.

College he came to America in 1821. Whether he was ordained in Ireland before leaving, or by Bishop Connolly of New York on his arrival, has not been determined. At the time, there were only seven priests in the entire State of New York. Father O'Kelly became the eighth, and was given charge of the scattered Catholic population in the western part of the state. He made his headquarters in Rochester, where he built the first Catholic church in 1823. In the imperfect records of the period there is no trace of Father O'Kelly for the next six years, or until we find him at the disposal of Bishop Fenwick in 1829.[46]

What Father O'Kelly's status was during his first months in Detroit is difficult to state with certainty. Besides assisting Father Richard he held most likely a roving commission to attend the Catholics of his nationality who were trickling into Wayne and its adjacent counties. It will be remembered that in his census of 1822 Father Richard mentioned "150 Irish Catholics scattered here and there." In the census of 1826 he gave the number of English-speaking Catholics of the Territory as 306, "nearly all of them poor Irishmen, scarcely twenty of them born in America." A cursory examination of the St. Anne records for a period of three years beginning with 1826 reveals approximately eighteen families that should be classed as recent immigrants. William Daly and Honoria McGrauser brought a child to be baptized. To prove its legitimacy the priest had nothing but the declaration of the parents, duly inscribed in the register, that "they were married by Father Maher in the diocese of Cashel." A like declaration was made by Morris Shauhnessey and Mary Halay; John Enright and Margaret Donovan harked back to Askeaton. Michael Fahey and Catherine Donovan were married at Quebec; James Meehan and Margaret Myer at Kingston; Richard Butler and Bridget Murphy in Newfoundland. James Lonergan and Jane O'Neill were married at Rochester, New York, and Thomas Welsh and Catherine McDonell at Lockport. These entries taken at random are typical of the early Irish immigration into Michigan, much of it immediately from Ireland, but some only after previous residence in the Canadian provinces, and in the Eastern States.

However, when Father Richard speaks definitely of Father O'Kelly's activities, at least in his available correspondence, it is noteworthy that the drift of immigration is into Washtenaw County. Writing to Bishop Fenwick in December, 1830, Father Richard complained

---

[46] For these details concerning Father O'Kelly's early life see Rev. Bernard Leo Heffernan, *Some Cross-Bearers of the Finger Lakes Region* (Chicago, 1925), Chap. VII. It must be noted that Heffernan and the Catholic Directories give the name as "Kelly." Its owner always signed as Patrick O'Kelly, and the name is thus inscribed on his tombstone in the cemetery of Sacred Heart parish, Dearborn, Mich.

that, burdened by his debts, he could no longer support Father O'Kelly, and asked for his recall.[47] In February, 1831, he wrote:

> I have postponed from day to day until now to concluding this letter, expecting the return of Mr. Kelly. He left Detroit on Thursday after the 1st Sunday in lent—to be three Sundays at his visit to Washtenaugh county. It appears that he was much pleased at Ann Arbour and its vicinity. They calculate to build a church there next season for him. There are great many more Irish men there than at Detroit. . . .[48]

Perhaps this very visit of Father O'Kelly decided the final arrangements, for before the summer of 1831 a log church was erected, not in Ann Arbor, but in section 29 of Northfield township.[49] However, for some unknown reason Father O'Kelly now seems to have left off caring for his compatriots, and he was certainly absent from the Territory for the greater part of 1832.[50] In the following year he returned to take up his residence near the first Catholic church in Washtenaw County.[51]

Both Father O'Kelly and Father Smith had been sent to Michigan as a result of the vivid impression of the Territory's needs which the bishop had gained during his visitation of 1829. He saw clearly that Michigan was on the verge of a development paralleling that of his own state. A closer touch had to be maintained, and even at the expense of crippling his own forces more priests had to be supplied. Deeply moved by the progress already made by Father Déjean among the Indians of L'Arbre Croche, the bishop was fired with the prospect of completing the work begun by Marquette and Allouez. Henceforth, there were no souls dearer to him than the Indians of Michigan.

For 1830 Bishop Fenwick had planned another tour of the northern missions but the pressure of cares at home obliged him to forego it, and in his stead he sent Father Rese, now his vicar-general. The visitor was accompanied by Father Stephen Badin, who had again volunteered for service in Michigan. They reached Detroit on July 1, and some days later all the priests in the Territory came together, a

---

[47] "This afforded an imperative motive to remove Mr. Kelly immediately. Had he not been here I might have spared four hundred dollars which would help me much in my distressed situation . . . The best perhaps is for you to call him near yourself in order that you may see for what he is fit . . ." Letter dated December 11, 1830. Archives of Mt. St. Joseph, Ohio.

[48] Letter dated February 28, 1831. NDA.

[49] Samuel W. Beakes, *Past and Present of Washtenaw County* (Chicago, 1906), 772. The location is shown in Bela Hubbard's copies of the Land Office maps in the BHC.

[50] Father Richard wrote two letters to be quoted presently bearing on the number of priests in the Territory in 1832, and in neither of them is Father O'Kelly mentioned.

[51] His name appears in the Catholic Almanac for 1834.

gathering the like of which St. Anne's rectory had never witnessed. Father Richard records it with evident satisfaction: "From the 10th to the 14th we have been here seven priests, Mr. Kelly, Mr. Smith, Mr. Dejean, two Messrs. Badin, Mr. Rese, and me. . . ." [52]

On the very day that this conference closed Father Rese set out across country by stagecoach to visit the Potawatomi living in their traditional location, the neighborhood of the long-abandoned St. Joseph Mission. The Baptist mission forced upon them by the Chicago treaty had made little headway; the Indians were restive under it, and had never given up hope of seeing a Black Robe come to live with them. They had often appealed to Father Richard, who was of course helpless to grant their demand. At the appearance of Father Rese their joy was unbounded.[53] They crowded around him to listen to his instructions, and to ask baptism for their children. Leopold Pokagon, the chief, and his consort, Elizabeth, were baptized on July 22, and then united in Christian marriage.[54] Confronted with such proofs of faith and sincerity, Father Rese could not resist making the promise of a resident priest without delay, although on his way back to Detroit he must have wondered how he was to fulfill it. However, the veteran missionary, Father Stephen Badin, was not to be denied another opportunity for active ministry, and in August he left Detroit to begin four years of zealous labor as the Black Robe of Pokagon's village. With him, as interpreter, went Angelique Campeau, that faithful soul who had devoted herself to the service of the Church from the time that she taught in Father Richard's first school. Bishop Fenwick was immediately notified of the undertaking:

> On this day (August 17) at 5 o'clock Mr. Badin Sen., has left Detroit in company with Sister Angelique Campeau on the stage to go to St. Joseph, where he intends to stay until another priest sent by you will go to take charge of the whites and Indians. (Potowatomies) Perhaps he says he may, if the climate suits his health, continue to reside there.[55]

Having thus provided for the Potawatomi mission, the visitor went up the lakes to complete his itinerary. He touched at Sault Ste Marie, preached a mission at Green Bay, and spent a few days on the Island of Mackinac, and with Father Déjean at L'Arbre Croche. At the end of August he began his homeward journey stopping again at Detroit and at Monroe.

[52] Letter to Bishop Fenwick, August 17, 1830. NDA.
[53] There is an account of Father Rese's visitation in the *Annales* . . . VI, 147 ff.
[54] During his stay Father Rese performed thirty baptisms. They are recorded in the baptismal register of what was later the parish of Bertrand, below Niles, Mich., and which is preserved in the NDA.
[55] This is the opening paragraph of the letter quoted in Note 52.

As a result of the visitation Michigan gained two priests before the end of the year. On September 5, 1830, Bishop Fenwick ordained Peter Carabin, a native of France, born in 1807, who had completed his studies in Bardstown.[56] During Father Rese's stay at Monroe, Father Smith had been dangerously ill, and this circumstance probably directed the bishop in his appointment. Father Carabin was sent as assistant to Father Smith. He notes in the baptismal register that he said Mass in the parish for the first time on the second Sunday in Advent.

Father Carabin's companion in ordination was a young Italian destined to carve out a distinguished career as a pioneer priest in Wisconsin, Iowa, and Illinois. Born at Milan in 1806, Samuel Charles Mazzuchelli entered the novitiate of the Dominicans in Rome at the age of sixteen. When the opportunity for working in the American missions presented itself during Father Rese's European visit, he gladly volunteered. In 1828 he joined his Dominican brethren in Ohio to make his final preparations for the priesthood, and to acquire proficiency in English. His zeal for the missionary life was put to the test immediately after his ordination, for Bishop Fenwick sent him to reside on Mackinac Island with the whole upper lake region as his parish. He arrived at his post in November, and plunged into the life of self-sacrifice and hardship inseparable from such a situation.[57]

There were now, that is, at the end of 1830, eight priests in the Territory. Perhaps, at the time, the number was sufficient. Outside of the traditional French parishes whose origins have been traced there was only one Catholic group within the present limits of Michigan large enough to justify the presence of a resident pastor, the one to which Father O'Kelly was sent. Even in Detroit Father Richard felt that he could get on very well alone. No amount of work could dismay him if only he were freed from the financial worries that oppressed him.

> . . . tomorrow I will begin the exercises of the Jubilee as I have published last Sunday, and on this day major Dequindre has given me notice that the proceedings in the case of Fr. L. are to go on during this term of the Supreme Court open this day, and that my attorney will not

[56] There is a short sketch of Father Carabin in Rev. George F. Houck, *op. cit.*, II, 463. He came from the diocese of Nancy, and his dimissorial letters in the NDA are dated July 7, 1829.

[57] Rezek, *op. cit.*, II, 180. Father Mazzuchelli's first entry in the Mackinac register is dated November 19, 1830. While on a visit to Italy in later life he wrote an account of his labors in America. Translated into English his work is known as the *Memoirs Historical and Edifying of a Missionary Apostolic* (Chicago, 1915).

defend my cause until I pay him fifty dollars immediately, whatsoever may be the result of the Decision of the court.

One circumstance makes my case unpleasant and doubtful in its results, it is that Mr. Fr. L. has assigned all the amount of the original judgement to several individuals, I think five, among which is Mr. Jh. Campau, whose share is $640 and he asks the whole without any deduction. The result is dubious. Should I lose the amount to be paid shall be $1156 with the interest to be paid on that sum from the original judgement in 1824 September, i.e. 6 years and 4 months, that is in toto about 1600 dollars: an exorbitant sum; therefore it will be necessary in such case to appeal to Washington, but the law requires that I should give a security quadruple the amount of the judgement and the probability is that I will not be capable to get any security. This prospect is truly distressing. I want your advice. The hope conceived by my creditors last summer that Mr. Rese was to assume all my debts has only excited their appetite and has made my situation worse than ever before.

This affords an imperative motive to remove Mr. Kelly immediately. had he not been here I might have spared four hundred dollars which would help me much in my distressed situation. I must use the greatest economy in order to make the greatest offer possible to my creditors. I am apprehensive that our Trustees who will have the management of the church affairs in the next year will make no appropriation for his support. The best perhaps is for you to call him near yourself in order that you may see for what he is fit.

The concurrence of the Jubilee with my present affairs is rather unfortunate and perhaps (sic) distressing. at my age of 63 to have so many embarasments is truly discouraging. I have still a very good health and I can do a great deal of work provided I can see the prospect of discharging debts that are sacred. for that object I must remain alone for a few years. then I will have great deal less trouble and will be enabled to pay five or six hundred dollars every year at least by economy. In the name of God permit me to remain alone and you will be surprised at the result. should I fall sick Mr. Badin junior is at hand ready to come to my assistance *au premier coup de soufflet.* Pray God for me and give me your good Blessing. . . .[58]

To some extent Father Richard was justified, for the era of uninterrupted progress was not yet at hand. The year 1831 was marked by changes rather than by gains. In Monroe, Father Smith was not in the best of relations with his parishioners. With the consent of Bishop Fenwick he had broken down the old trustee system that had paralyzed the parish for so many years, and although his action was salutary, it had been carried out in a manner that begot an animosity which he took no particular pains to compose. Father Carabin was more sympathetic, and his attitude created a situation in which

[58] Letter to Bishop Fenwick, December 11, 1830. See note 47.

Bishop Fenwick was bound to intervene.[59] From L'Arbre Croche Father Déjean, worn out by the hardships of his life among the Indians, was asking leave to retire and to return to France.

These matters, as well as his interest in the Indian missions, prompted Bishop Fenwick to visit Michigan for the third time. On the way up to Detroit his travelling companion was a young priest, Frederic Baraga, who had come to Cincinnati in January for the avowed purpose of devoting his life to the service of the Indian tribes in the Territory.[60] His arrival was traceable to a new missionary enterprise that owed its origin to Bishop Fenwick.

When Father Rese was sent to Europe in 1827 his mission, aside from the business transacted in Rome, was to recruit priests and secure financial aid for his diocese. The only organization to which he could look for assistance was the Society for the Propagation of the Faith, founded in France, and which as yet drew its resources exclusively from French Catholics. Bishop Fenwick believed that a similar development of the foreign mission spirit was possible among the Catholics of the German States, and Father Rese was commissioned to attempt to set it in motion. His success was phenomenal. At the end of 1828 he could announce the formation of the "Leopoldinen-Stiftung" in Vienna, and the "Ludwig-Missions-Verein" in Munich.[61] Unlike the French Society these Associations devoted their contributions almost entirely to America, and there is scarcely a diocese in the United States, at least among the older ones, which is not indebted to their generosity.[62]

From the time of his ordination Father Baraga had been at work in his native diocese of Laibach. The accounts of missionary life in the diocese of Cincinnati popularized by Father Rese fascinated him. He felt himself irresistibly drawn to consecrate himself to the conversion of the Indian tribes in Michigan Territory. That such a step meant

[59] There are five letters from Father Smith to Bishop Fenwick in the NDA.

[60] Verwyst, op. cit., 103. Father Baraga was born June 29, 1797, at Dobernig in Lower Carniola, at the time a province of the Austrian Empire but now included in Jugo-Slavia. He graduated in law at the University of Vienna in 1821, and then entered the seminary in Laibach. He was ordained September 21, 1823.

[61] Letter of Father Rese to Bishop Fenwick, December 10, 1828. See O'Daniel, op. cit., 361.

[62] There is a convenient sketch of the Leopoldine Association in the Catholic Encyclopedia (Index Volume). This society issued a publication similar to the *Annales* of the French missionary organization, the *Berichte der Leopoldinen Stiftung im Kaiserthume Oesterreich*. It complements the *Annales* and is invaluable for the study of American Catholic history from 1830 to 1860. The first number was issued in 1831. The *Berichte* are now very rare, and there are only a few complete sets in the United States. A partial list of their contents is given in the *Cath. Hist. Review*, I, 51 ff. Rarer still are the *Annalen der Verbreitung des Glaubens*, a similar publication of the Ludwig-Missions-Verein issued from Munich. A sketch of this association is given in the *Cath. Hist. Review* (New Series), II, 23 ff.

resigning a comfortable living had no weight with Father Baraga, and, on October 29, 1830, he began his long journey to the welcome that awaited him in Cincinnati. A few months spent in the study of English and Ottawa, and he was ready to accompany Bishop Fenwick northward.

The travellers reached Detroit on May 15. Here they met Father Déjean who had already said farewell to his Indian converts, and was waiting for permission to leave the diocese. Although his decision must have given regret to the bishop he was allowed to go.[63] Nothing more is known of him beyond the fact that he departed immediately for France.

A few days later Bishop Fenwick left for Mackinac with Father Baraga, who was straining with impatience to be at the post vacated by Father Déjean. On May 28, he saw L'Arbre Croche for the first time, and the university graduate who had never known poverty embraced the new, hard life before him with these sentiments: ". . . Happy day which placed me among the Indians with whom I will now remain uninterruptedly to the last breath of my life, if such be the most holy wish of God." [64]

There was something in the artless piety of these primitive Christians at L'Arbre Croche that fascinated every priest who knew them. Here in this wilderness the bishop himself seemed to catch a dream of his young priesthood. After installing Father Baraga he wrote:

> During my stay in this mission thirty Indians, three being adults, were baptized. Ten more will be received into the Church as soon as they are fully instructed. I confirmed thirty persons, and on Corpus Christi twenty-eight made their first Communion. On that day we held, after my Mass, the procession with the Blessed Sacrament at which such order and devotion prevailed as can seldom be seen in civilized countries. I believe there was more real piety, manifestation of real faith and devotion, than I have seen on similar occasions among our Catholic Americans. . . . I have never before felt happier and more contented than I have on that day. The poor savages covered the way we passed with mats and shawls, and scattered grass and wild flowers over it. Truly I would gladly exchange my place and my honors in Cincinnati for the hut and happiness of the missionary here among these good savages. . . ." [65]

But this could not be, and the bishop hurried on to complete his visitation. With Father Mazzuchelli he worked strenuously at Mackinac and Green Bay. In both places he was cheered by the prospect of new churches and schools. Coming down from the north he visited

[63] O'Daniel, *op. cit.*, 388.
[64] *Berichte* . . . IV, 8.
[65] *Ibid.*, III, 23.

Father Badin in his Potawatomi missions, and then made his way to Detroit to engage in the pastoral labors he had omitted when bringing Father Baraga.

He found Father Richard unusually disturbed by his financial troubles. The visit of Father Rese in the preceding year had given rise to a rumor that the pastor of St. Anne's would soon be given a sufficient sum to pay off the several holders of the Labadie judgment. Before this they had only annoyed; now they clamored. The trial for having violated the jail limits by going to Washington was about to be heard—with little prospect of a favorable outcome. To alleviate these worries the bishop could do little more than assure Father Richard that he would receive a generous share of the remittances that were expected from the European mission societies.

In the early part of July Bishop Fenwick began his homeward journey, and on the way stopped at Monroe. He had now to deal with the situation to which allusion has already been made. Father Smith had been loud in his complaints that Father Carabin was demoralizing the parish; but the bishop evidently took another view of the matter, for he ended the difficulty by removing Father Smith.[66] His priestly instinct must have divined something insincere in the querulous, captious convert, and the sequel justified his action. Not long after his removal Father Smith renounced his priesthood, and became one of the most notorious defamers of the Church during the Native American movement.[67]

Bishop Fenwick arrived in the episcopal city to witness the consummation of two projects that he had tirelessly promoted. The *Athenaeum,* a Catholic college, was opened on October 17, 1831. Five

[66] In the parish record Father Carabin made the following notation: "Bishop Fenwick arrived here in the month of July, 1831, removed Mr. Smith from the parish and replaced him with Mr. Cummins, an Irish priest. As for myself I chose to retire to the Baie. After a few weeks Mr. Cummins left the parish . . . I unhappily succeeded . . ." Little is known of Father Michael Cummins, so named in a power of attorney given him by Bishop Fenwick, and quoted in *Mich. Hist. Colls.,* IX, 130. He is most likely the person named in a letter from Father Rese to Bishop Rosati, May 27, 1831. St. Louis Chancery Archives. "Our college is almost furnished. We are expecting the professors among whom is the respectable Signor Commins (sic), who was for many years president and director of studies in the Irish college of the Picpus Fathers at Paris. . . ." Father Smith's last entry in the baptismal register is dated July 7, 1831. He remained in Monroe almost ten months longer, but in what capacity is not clear. Father Richard writing to Bishop Fenwick on May 7, 1832, states: "Mr. Smith has left Monroe by the middle of April to go to see his mother."

[67] See the article on *Knownothingism* in the Catholic Encyclopedia. The apostate's contribution was a periodical called *The Downfall of Babylon, or The Triumph of Truth over Popery,* by Samuel B. Smith, Late a Popish Priest. The first issue appeared in New York, November 6, 1834. A file of the first year is in the library of the Centraal-Verein in St. Louis. For Smith's association with Maria Monk see Ray Allen Billington, *The Protestant Crusade, 1800–1860* (New York, 1938). Many more of Smith's publications are there listed.

days later appeared the first issue of what is today the oldest Catholic paper in the United States, the *Catholic Telegraph*. But no complacency in these achievements could efface from the bishop's memory the impressions he had received when visiting the Indian missions. Their needs and their possibilities drove him to further efforts. Lewis Cass, Governor of Michigan from 1813, had just been appointed to President Jackson's cabinet to serve as Secretary of War, thus heading the department which, at the time, had jurisdiction over Indian affairs. A few days after the opening of his college, Bishop Fenwick set out for Washington to present personally to Lewis Cass a report of the Indian schools which had been established, and to solicit from the Government the support to which they were entitled.[68] And he was still at Washington, working for this purpose, in the first months of 1832, a fateful year that made an end of the old order.

[68] O'Daniel, *op. cit.*, 399–404.

CHAPTER XVIII

Last Days of Father Richard

IN 1830 Father Richard had written to Bishop Fenwick that he was equal to the task of caring for the Catholics of Detroit single-handed. But, as time went on, sickness and the increasing number of Catholic immigrants forced him to retract his confident assertion. The tremendous energy that had carried him through the troubled years of his career in Detroit was beginning to run low, and yet even in his decline his zeal ranged as widely as it had in the days of his prime. In May, 1832, he wrote thus to his bishop:

I have received yr. letter written at Washington before your departure for Cincinnati. I did write immediately to Mr. Taney who has not as yet sent me a single line. I trust the case will have been postponed to the next year. Mr. Jh. Campau is not willing to take less than $641 it being his share in the assignment made over to several individuals for the amt. of $1116. The five other asignees are disposed to take some one half, some three fourths of their share and give up the interest.

Mr. Beuffit [sic] and Mr. Rivard have by the advice of Mr. Wood-bridge consented to make a deed of the farm of the *cote* du Nord-est provided the whole due to Mr. Jos. Campau (now seven hundred dollars) be paid by you. I have communicated it to Mr. Rese long time ago, but he did not say a word about it, when he answered my letter. there is a rumor in circulation that Mr. Davis is urging the above-mentioned Trustees to give him a lease for 99 years for the said farm promising to pay Mr. Jh. C. his due and pay a yearly rent. I have dissuaded them from concluding any such contract until you or Mr. Rese will come this spring, when if nothing is done, it will be perhaps impossible to prevent the lease that is contemplated.

Since my last illness, my constitution is broken and much weakened. I want very much one or two assistant priests. Mr. V. Badin has to much to do about his various stations. he is here only *en passant*. Please to bring or send me a good flemish priest who can hear confessions in french. and when you have secured me such an assistant I will be disposed to support also another priest who should be american native a smart preacher as Mr. Mullon.[1] There is since some weeks a disposition among a small part of American populace to recieve Instruction on

---

[1] Father Ignatius Mullon, ordained by Bishop Fenwick in 1825, labored with distinction in the Diocese of Cincinnati.

Catholic Doctrine. Since the Holy Thursday I have given a Lecture every Sunday by candle light to Americans, who have come to hear the explanation of the Cath. principles in sufficient number so as to give me hope that truth will not be preached in vain; with the grace of God. —I am preparing my accounts. . . .

At the request of Mr. Baraga I have caused to be printed small alphabets for the Indians. I have sent him 1000 copies by Mr. Ant. Dequindre last week, 200 do. to Mr. Mazzuchelli, I have a few hundred more for St. Joseph's.

By the exertions of the ladies of the Cath. Charity Society a free school has been opened on the first of this month of May. No less than 38 poor girls will learn gratis to read and to work and to serve God under the tuition of Elizabeth Williams. It is expected that it will succeed. Mrs. Hale and Mrs. Brooks desired me to beg of you to procure some nuns to take care of their infant establishment, i.e. the said free school.

Mr. Smith has left Monroe by the middle of April to go to see his mother.

By all means please to send me or bring me one flemish priest who can speak french: I have to much to do. I cannot stand it. asking your Good Blessing & in union with yr. Holy Sacrifices and prayers, I very respectfully remain forever your most obt. and affectionate servant. . . .[2]

Although Father Richard was unaware of it, help was coming. On the very day his letter was written a ship, pitching violently in a sudden storm off the coast of Sicily, carried among its passengers a little group of priests and lay brothers whose destination was Detroit. They had sailed from Trieste with the zeal of crusaders to open the first house of their order in America, and their project was another fruit of Father Rese's European journey. During his stay at Vienna his recruiting activities brought him to the convent of the Redemptorists that had been established there in 1820. Father Passerat, the successor of the saintly Clemens Hofbauer, listened to the vicar-general with growing interest, and finally agreed to release some of his subjects for the diocese of Cincinnati whenever possible. It was not until March 5, 1832, that the little band of volunteers set out from Vienna.[3]

The Redemptorists arrived in New York on June 20, and the superior immediately dispatched the joyful tidings to Bishop Fenwick. Now that the perils of the sea were past here were good, robust workmen ready for any task.

The enclosed letters from the General Direction of the Leopoldine Society, from our Reverend Vicar-General, Joseph Passerat, and from

---

[2] Letter dated May 7, 1832. NDA.
[3] The journey to the United States is described by Father Saenderl in the *Berichte*, V, 20-23.

the Apostolic Nuncio at Vienna, will acquaint your Lordship with the fact that three priests and three lay brothers of the Congregation of the Most Holy Redeemer at Vienna have been sent to the diocese of Cincinnati, in accordance with your orders. I, the undersigned, have the pleasure of informing you, Most Reverend Prelate, that our voyage over the ocean to New York has been happily accomplished and that in accordance with the appointment of the Rev. Vicar-General Frederic Rese we may go directly to the Territory of Michigan, where in the city of Detroit we shall await a further appointment from your Lordship.

We came from Vienna by way of Trieste because a journey through Germany and France would have entailed long delays on account of the prevalence of that plague called cholera morbus. From the Austrian port we came directly to the port of the United States, a voyage that lasted sixty-six days. We have brought with us a fairly good supply of the articles necessary for divine worship, namely, sacred vestments and vessels, two chalices, a ciborium, ostensoria, a thurible, a small organ of an improved type, and many other church furnishings. These objects were procured for us partly by our Congregation and partly by benefactors.

To have a knowledge of the English language we studied it with the greatest diligence during the entire ocean voyage, and in a short time we hope to be able to use it in the functions of the sacred ministry. French is better known to us, especially to Father Hätscher, who is proficient also in Italian and Dutch.

Our names are: Simon Saenderl, Francis Xavier Hätscher, Francis Xavier Tschenhens, priests. Lay brothers: James Koller, Aloysius Schuh, Wenceslaus Witopill. Of these the second is by trade a blacksmith, but he is also a bookbinder, a tinsmith, and he can plate vessels in gold and silver. Wenceslaus is by trade an expert cabinetmaker.

Finally, I commend myself, and the fathers and brothers of my Congregation, to your paternal affection and benevolence. Deign to receive in your service those who shall strive to satisfy your Lordship in every possible way. . . .

Your most humble and obedient servant,

Simon Saenderl. . . .[4]

While making their preparations to start out for Michigan the Redemptorists heard some disquieting rumors. Father Rese was said to have in mind the breaking up of the little band by assigning some of its members to New York, and others to Philadelphia.[5] There was only one thing to do. They had come to America to labor for Bishop

[4] The Latin original is in the NDA. The *Berichte*, V, 19, announce the departure of the six Redemptorists, and give some biographical details. Simon Senderl, as the name is there spelled, was born at Malgersdorf in 1800, and was ordained in 1825. Francis X. Hätscher, born at Vienna in 1784, was ordained in 1816. Francis X. Tschenhens, born at Nonnenbach in 1801, was ordained in 1831.

[5] Letter of Father Saenderl to the Leopoldine Society, Detroit, August 28, 1832. *Berichte*, V, 23.

Fenwick, and to him they would go. Therefore instead of proceeding directly to Detroit they made their way to Cincinnati, incidentally, having many difficulties with their precious baggage. They reached the episcopal city on July 17, at 2 o'clock in the morning, and later in the day when they went to present their respects they discovered that the bishop had departed for Michigan more than a month before.

Father Rese's hearty welcome made the disappointment less acute, and the orders left behind by the bishop made the travellers feel how eagerly they had been looked for. They were to go immediately to Michigan. But Father Rese, wielding his authority as vicar-general in the absence of the bishop, kept Father Tschenhens in Cincinnati to minister to the German Catholics of the city. In his letter Father Saenderl had made no reference to any special ability possessed by Brother James, who was nevertheless a hidden treasure, a chef. He too was retained to practice his artistry at the seminary where there had been a lamentable dearth of substantial German cooking. The others departed on July 25 for Detroit where they were to meet Bishop Fenwick.

The prelate, now sixty-four years old, worn out by his travels, weakened by illness, had nerved himself to make another tour of the northern missions. He seems to have had a presentiment of what lay before him, but nothing could prevail against his desire to hear again the soft, sibilant accents in the gloom of the bark chapel at L'Arbre Croche, as the worshipers chanted their beads.

> Kitanamikwn Marie moaskinesgagwian onichichiwin kipapakana-wenimik missi kagijitotch, awachamens epitch Sakihintwa kitch ikweg awachamens kiskihigw missi gaie kitchitwa wenindogossi kigwissis Jesos kainintch napitch kaoni chichin Marie Dio kawkwississimatch gagano-tamawiang ketagw. Pematissiwanguen gaie wich nipoiang gaganwtama-winam.[6]

Leaving Cincinnati on June 14 he reached Detroit in the first days of July. His companion was Father Augustus Jeanjean, a priest of the diocese of New Orleans who was on his way to France, but who had consented to accompany the bishop during his visitation. In the city, an outward calm only masked the trepidation of its citizens. There had been a wave of intense excitement in May when volunteers had marched away to help the majesty of the United States teach Black Hawk his final lesson. Some of them had gone as far as Chicago before learning that their services were not needed. They returned

---

[6] The Hail Mary as found in the Indian prayerbook published at Detroit in 1830 by Father Déjean.

home to face an enemy no less redoubtable than the famed Indian warrior. The Asiatic cholera coming out of India in 1817 had scourged the East at successive intervals. In 1830 it broke out in European Russia, and in the next two years it left a trail of death over central and northern Europe. Immigration carried it to America, and in 1832 it swept over the land from east to west.

The plague had not yet reached Detroit when the bishop arrived. On July 4, the *Henry Clay,* bound for Chicago with a body of troops, stopped at Detroit. There was sickness on board, and the next day a soldier died. Ordered away from the city, the vessel tied up for a few hours at Belle Isle, and then went on to Fort Gratiot. In his eagerness to continue northward the bishop, with Father Jeanjean, must have taken passage on the *Henry Clay,* for he wrote to Father Rese from Mackinac:

> We experienced many sufferings and contradictions from Detroit to this place. Before we arrived at Fort Gratiot a soldier died of the cholera and was thrown into the water. The next day, three others were seized with the same sickness, one of whom was a Catholic and made his confession to me. These were landed and died there with eight more. We were detained two days at Fort Gratiot.[7] We arrived at Sault Sainte Marie on the fourteenth, but were not permitted to leave the boat— were held there in quarantine until the sixteenth. We debarqued here on the seventeenth at five A.M. While at Sault Sainte Marie, I was taken with chills and fever. The same thing occurred on the evening of the sixteenth. Yesterday I was indisposed all day. Today I feel pretty well. . . . The air and health on the island being good, the cholera is not feared here. Yet a soldier or so from the *Sheldon Thomson* have died here; fifteen died at Chicago. After two days more, if I am well enough, we will go to Arbre Croche, and from there to Green Bay. My plan is to engage one of the Redemptorist Fathers to go to Green Bay with one of the lay brothers, to have a second remain with Father Richard, and to place the third, with two brothers, near Detroit. . . .[8]

As soon as he could muster sufficient strength the bishop went on with his visitation as he had planned it. When he debarked at L'Arbre Croche the Indians were waiting for him in a double line stretching back from the water's edge. They greeted him with rounds of musket fire, and as he walked slowly through the lines he shook hands with every individual, a ceremony that to the Indian was not

---

[7] *Mich. Hist. Colls.,* XVIII, 672–73. All the troops were landed at Fort Gratiot. "From there the soldiers began to make their way to Detroit, but many of them died on the road, and were devoured by wild beasts; only one hundred and fifty reached the city, arriving here about July 8. . . ." Farmer, *op. cit.,* 48.

[8] Letter from Mackinac, July 18, 1832. Quoted in O'Daniel, *op. cit.,* 413.

a formality but a sign of deep friendship. Thus began a few days of happy ministry crowned by the administration of Confirmation to a large number.[9]

On his return to Detroit Bishop Fenwick sent a report of his visitation to Archbishop Whitfield of Baltimore:

> I have returned thus far from the distant and laborious missions of the Rapids of St. Mary (Saut Ste. Marie), Mackinac, Arbre Croche and Green Bay; at each of which places much good has been done, and there remains yet much to be done. All these are Indian missions, extending to the head of Lake Superior, which I could not reach, being stopped in my progress by sickness. I was sick at Saut Ste. Marie and at Mackinac. Am yet feeble and languid. My strength and health have failed much. I am evidently sinking gradually to the grave, being now sixty-four years old. I was consoled with the progress of religion, and [with the] prosperity of my Indian schools at Mackinac, Arbre Croche, Green Bay, and St. Joseph's River in Michigan. The amount of my good Indians baptized and civilized (most of them confirmed) at all these missions (collectively taken) is about fourteen or fifteen hundred. . . . This is an interesting portion of our flock and diocese. Indeed, I think it is the most interesting and important. At all events, it is the most simple, innocent and humble and docile part. I have stationed a Priest at each of the above missions, except at that of Lake Superior and the Rapids of St. Mary. . . .[10]

The Redemptorists waiting at St. Anne's for Bishop Fenwick were rewarded for all their disappointments by the fatherly welcome which they received. He now disclosed the plans which he had made for them. To serve as a base for the missionary excursions in which they were to be generally engaged throughout the Territory a convent was to be established. Its location could very well be on the Malcher farm which was still held by the corporation which had opposed Father Richard in the rebuilding of St. Anne's. In fact, the dwellers on the Côte du Nord-Est had already entered into preliminary negotiations with the Redemptorists. They would transfer their ownership of the property on these conditions: some outstanding debts were to be paid; Mass was to be said every day; there was to be a French sermon every Sunday; a school was to be erected. To carry out these provisions the Redemptorists were to use their influence with the Leopoldine Association to have it bear the necessary expense. For the time being, however, the bishop desired Father Saenderl to take charge of Green Bay, where a church had just been com-

---

[9] From a report by Father Baraga in the *Berichte*, V, 35.

[10] Letter dated August 22, 1832, and quoted in O'Daniel, *op. cit.*, 420. Bishop Fenwick arrived in Detroit on August 16.

pleted, until the following spring. Father Hätscher would remain at St. Anne's to assist Father Richard. These arrangements were carried out, and the first pastor of Green Bay was soon on his way to the north.[11]

What earnest and hopeful conferences must have been held between the bishop and his little band of priests! The prospects of the Church in Michigan were growing brighter. The Indian missions were flourishing. Money and gifts were coming in from Europe. The newcomers were only the vanguard of the reinforcements that were on the way.

The effect of all this on Father Richard might have been predicted. If he were ever free from the contradictions and misfortunes that had dogged his life, he would gravitate in just one direction. Three days after the bishop's arrival in Detroit he sent the following letter to the Superior-General of the Sulpicians in Paris.

> The favorable opportunity offered by Mr. Jeanjean enables me to repeat a communication that I had already sent to you . . . with the letters that I wrote to my nephew, pastor of St. Jean d'Angely in the Charente Inferieure. . . . My nephew, a young priest twenty-nine years old, was for several years a teacher in the college of La Rochelle, and, from his letters to me, I judged him to be a man of piety and zeal. I invited him to join me in Detroit, and to help me establish a college in Michigan soon to become the 25th State in America. He seemed disposed to come; he obtained the consent of his father, Charles Bossuet Richard. Help him, if necessary, to obtain an exeat from his bishop (of La Rochelle).
>
> I have many things wherewith to begin a college, even on a grand scale: an electrical machine, a pneumatic machine, an organ for the church, an extensive, well-chosen library, a printing-press with 800 pounds of type, a farm of 300 acres adjoining the second city of Michigan, 400 acres of land near Kaskaskia in the state of Illinois, etc. All this will belong to the college, which has been planned for a long time but has never become a reality because I have always been extensively engaged in the ministry, for a long time being the only priest in charge of a large number of missions, and, moreover, because of a prolonged lawsuit with a man whom I denounced and excommunicated by the order of Bishop Flaget. The case is now before the Supreme Court of the United States in Washington city. Bishop Fenwick who has returned here from Mackinac and L'Arbre Croche, and will leave on the 20th, advises me to compromise. He generously offers to help me pay a portion of the amount demanded, and desires me to attempt to stay the payment of the balance, and to leave the matter in the hands of Providence.

---

[11] These details from a letter of Father Saenderl in the *Berichte,* V, 25.

Father Richard then goes on to enumerate the priests who are laboring in Michigan, and the localities which they serve. He continues:

> I hope therefore that I shall soon be able to devote myself to the establishing of a college. For that purpose send two or three Sulpicians along with my nephew, and the college will belong to the Society of Saint-Sulpice. On beholding my nephew you will judge whether he should be affiliated with our Society.
>
> Michigan is already important enough to become a state. Every day since the spring of 1831 we have had a steamboat to and from Buffalo. There are often 200 to 300 passengers aboard, who are coming to settle in Michigan. This year Congress appropriated $64,000 to begin or continue five different roads in various directions, two of which lead from Detroit to Lake Michigan. Judge for yourself. The Americans are asking me for a college wherein French shall be one of the principal branches, and offer to help me with the buildings, etc. Success is certain. . . .[12]

Not so certain; one cause of failure had been overlooked. There is only a postscript in the letter to indicate the doleful time above which this brave planning rose: "Since July 6 there have been 51 deaths, nearly all from cholera, in my parish of St. Anne alone." As soon as the *Henry Clay* had gone, the plague fastened itself upon the city to take its daily toll.[13] Father Richard, the fearless pastor of his flock, was everywhere, nursing the sick, comforting the sorrowing. Although the details of his ministry are not known, his heroism and his service of the unfortunate are enshrined in a tradition witnessed to by every writer on Detroit history.

The letter just quoted was entrusted to Father Jeanjean, who left immediately for New York. But in his enumeration of the priests in

[12] Letter dated August 19, 1832. The original is in the archives of Saint-Sulpice in Paris. The priests named as being at work in Michigan are the following: the two Badins, Carabin, Baraga, Saenderl, and Hätscher.

[13] Farmer, *op. cit.*, I, 49, thus describes the epidemic of 1832. "Meanwhile, on July 6, two citizens died of the disease, and a panic was at once created. Many persons left their business, and fled from the city. In the country the excitement was even greater than at Detroit. On the arrival of the mail coach at Ypsilanti, the driver was ordered by a health officer to stop, that an examination of the passengers might be made. The driver refusing, his horses were fired on; one was killed, and the driver himself had a narrow escape. . . . At Rochester persons from Detroit were turned out of the hotel and their baggage thrown after them, and the bridges were torn up to prevent persons from entering the village. At Pontiac a body of men were armed, and sentinels were stationed on the highway to prevent ingress. One of the citizens of the latter place, Dr. Porter, came here to investigate the disease, but on his return was refused admittance to his own home, and compelled to revisit our city. In Detroit the Board of health issued regular bulletins, and the court and juryrooms in the old capitol were used for hospital purposes. By August 15 the epidemic was practically over. The deaths, ninety-six in number, could be traced in most instances to intemperance and carelessness."

Michigan Father Richard had overlooked Father Mazzuchelli at Mackinac, and to supply the omission he wrote to Father Jeanjean on August 21, addressing the letter "in care of the right Revd. Bishop Dubois near St. Patricks Cathedral Church, New York." His purpose attended to, Father Richard added a series of jottings indicative of the tension under which he was laboring.

> Mr. Carabin arrived last night. The Bishop today confirmed 46 persons. Tomorrow he will consecrate my chalice that has been well repaired. The day after tomorrow, at 4 o'clock, the Bishop intends to leave for Canton. We expect Mr. Badin Junr. tonight. P.S. He has arrived. Father Simon is getting ready to leave for Green Bay tonight with one of the brothers. The man to whom you administered Extreme Unction died yesterday. Two persons died of the cholera during the night and this morning, and several others have been recently attacked. Fear seems to be the principal cause in many cases. That makes 57 Catholics who have died in the parish of St. Anne since July 6.
>
> I resume my letter at 6 o'clock in the evening of the 22nd. The Bishop is not leaving tomorrow. He will take Mr. Carabin with him to New York or Canton. Mr Badin Junior arrived last night to help me, as did Father Francis who has just come in with a mild attack of the cholera. It will not bother him long as he is doing everything to get rid of it. I am better because I take no supper no breakfast; I take only cold liquids. Warm drinks go down immediately and stir up the diarrhea . . .[14]

By the end of the month the epidemic had run its course; only one more victim was to be taken, Father Richard himself. Worn out by his exertions he could offer no resistance to the disease that was daily sapping his strength. How the end came was graphically described by Father Vincent Badin in a letter to Bishop Fenwick, written on September 13.

> . . . Monsieur Richard, my incomparable friend, rendered his holy soul to his Creator this morning at 10 minutes after 3, dying of cholera. Last Saturday he went downtown to transact various matters, and returned toward noon feeling very weak. Nevertheless he began hearing confessions. As I was going to the lower River Huron for three or four days only, I went to say goodbye to him. On Sunday he was taken with violent cramps, and sent for the Doctor. He could not say Mass, and he suffered a great deal during the day and through the night. On Monday Father Francis sang a High Mass for his recovery. The church was crowded. No improvement. He refused to make a confession saying that I was his confessor, and he would have no other. A little wagon was sent off to bring me, and it reached me Tuesday morning. At noon I was

---

[14] Original letter in the archives of Saint-Sulpice in Paris. "Father Francis" is Father Hätscher.

with my venerable dying friend. About two o'clock I had much difficulty in hearing his confession. Fully conscious he received Viaticum between three and four. I was assisted by Mr. Baraga.[15] We as well as the small number of persons present were extremely edified by his sentiments regarding the August Sacrament of the altar, for he wished everything done in silence. He desired that Extreme Unction be put off until later. When the Doctor came, and saw that the calomel had no effect, he prepared a stimulant that we gave the patient every half hour. He took it without difficulty all through the night, and slept after each potion. Wednesday morning, the 12th, he was much better, and a ray of hope animated us. At nine o'clock all hope vanished. I was summoned from the church where I was preparing to sing a High Mass, assisted by Mr. Baraga. I administered Extreme Unction, the last blessing, and said the prayers for the dying. . . . Towards night it became impossible to make him take anything, and all we could do was to wet his tongue with a feather until the moment when his happy soul winged its way to the bosom of God. . . .[16]

Thus came peace at last to Father Richard. There is no life comparable to his in the annals of the American priesthood. The impress that his person and his work made upon his contemporaries and his community may be gauged from this. The façades of the City Hall in Detroit are adorned with the figures of four great men deemed inseparable from the history of Michigan: Marquette, La Salle, Cadillac, and Richard.

Bishop Fenwick was at Canton, Ohio, when he received Father Badin's letter. Although unwell when leaving Detroit he had resolved to visit several parishes in his diocese before returning to Cin-

[15] During his last visit at L'Arbre Croche Bishop Fenwick gave Father Baraga a sum sufficient to bring out another Indian prayer-book to correct the imperfections of the earlier one published by Father Déjean. *Berichte,* V, 36. Father Baraga was in Detroit attending to its printing at the time of Father Richard's death. The book is the *Otawa Anamie—Misinaigan,* a rarity second only to Father Déjean's volume in importance for collectors of this type of Americana. There are copies of both issues in the DCA.

[16] Letter in NDA. Another letter generally quoted, describing Father Richard's death, was written by Father Badin to Louis Grignon of Green Bay. There is a copy in the BHC. The purpose of the letter was to start a subscription for the erection of an "obelisque" to the memory of the departed priest. It is worth noting that the memorial mentioned in the text was erected through the efforts of Bela Hubbard, a non-Catholic. A city school and a public library branch in Detroit are named after Father Richard, and in 1931 the City of Grosse Pointe designated a new school built in the French Chateau style the Pere Richard Elementary School. The only tribute under Catholic auspices is a statue of Father Richard at the Detroit bridge approach to Belle Isle dedicated October 16, 1940. It stands in Gabriel Richard Park, which was set aside by the joint efforts of the City of Detroit and the Public Works Administration.
Father Richard was first buried in a cemetery that occupied the site now known as Clinton Park opposite the Detroit Memorial Hospital. He was later transferred to a crypt beneath the church which he built. When the old church was abandoned in 1886 the remains were removed to the new, where they rest in a vault under the main altar.

cinnati. On Tuesday, September 25, while traveling in a stagecoach to Wooster he was taken violently ill with the cholera. Arriving at his destination he took a room in the village hotel, and lay there shunned by everyone until a Catholic woman who had been a fellow passenger in the coach summoned medical assistance, and sent for Father Henni, who was stationed at Canton.[17] Together with two physicians and a negro servant she spent the night trying to alleviate the bishop's sufferings. In the morning he became unconscious, and at noon he breathed his last. When Father Henni rushed up breathlessly in the evening, the mortal remains of Bishop Fenwick had already been buried.[18]

In the deaths of Father Richard and Bishop Fenwick there is more to be seen than the taking off of two great churchmen. Occurring so closely together in September, 1832, they serve to mark the close of the preliminary period of Catholic history in Michigan which antedates the erection of the diocese of Detroit. In these pages we have seen the varied elements and personalities that colored it: Jesuits, Sulpicians, Recollects, traders, settlers, soldiers, Indians. Cadillac's little colony in the wilderness became of such importance that three nations fought for it, but even when Father Richard came it was still only a palisaded rectangle on the steep river bank, still surrounded by a wilderness. What marvellous changes he lived to see: Detroit a thriving city, steamboats plying up and down the Great Lakes, roads cut through the trackless forests, the wilderness peopled. He came to Michigan at a time when almost its entire population consisted of the French Canadians dwelling on its fringes; before his death it was a cosmopolitan commonwealth ready to take its place in the great family of American states. As a Frenchman he had come to serve a French-speaking community; he lived to hear the vanguard of alien races clamoring for a ministry in their own tongues.

During the long period we have been considering, four ecclesiastical jurisdictions held sway over Michigan. Bishop Laval of Quebec blessed Father Ménard setting out to find the survivors of the Huron mission on the shores of Lake Superior. Bishop Carroll of Baltimore wrote a pastoral to the settlers on the Raisin River. Bishop Flaget of Bardstown laid a corner stone in Detroit, and prophesied future greatness. Bishop Fenwick of Cincinnati risked his life—and lost it— to bring his ministry to the far-flung missions of the Territory. At his death the Church in Michigan was ready to pass from its tutelage to begin its independent existence as a diocese.

[17] Father John Martin Henni became the first bishop of Milwaukee in 1844, and died as Archbishop of that see in 1881.

[18] O'Daniel, *op. cit.*, 424–25.

We have already referred to the successive attempts made by both Bishop Flaget and Bishop Fenwick to rid themselves of the administration of Michigan. An unfortunate set of circumstances had prevented Father Richard from becoming the first bishop of Detroit. It was almost certain that after the withdrawal of his nomination no one else would be appointed as long as he lived. His death, and that of the administrator, left the Roman authorities free from possible embarrassment in reopening the matter whenever it should again be presented to them.

A few weeks before his death, in fact, Bishop Fenwick had again urged upon the Propaganda Congregation the necessity of being relieved from his heavy burden. He advanced as a candidate for the proposed see of Detroit his own vicar-general, Father Rese, provided he could obtain as his coadjutor in Cincinnati Father Peter Kenny, S.J. This we learn from the letter already referred to written from Detroit to Archbishop Whitfield of Baltimore.

> . . . I therefore feel and see the propriety, and even the necessity, of soliciting the common Father of the faithful to grant me a coadjutor who may be prepared to succeed me at my death, and carry on the works I have been entrusted with. . . . Upon serious and frequent reflection on the subject, I find no one in America of my acquaintance so well qualified to succeed me in the See of Cincinnati, as Rev. Mr. Kenny, the Provincial or Superior of the Jesuits of Maryland. . . . If I can obtain his appointment for Cincinnati, I would then recommend Rev. Fréderic Rese, my vicar-general, for the See of Detroit in Michigan, for which he is better qualified than for Cincinnati, being much attached to the Indian missions, and much esteemed by all the clergy and laity of Michigan, and well known to the Propaganda for his talents and zeal and piety and knowledge—of all which I could not say too much. But I could not deprive myself of him and his services without the ruin of my diocese and the destruction of my peace and life, unless Father Kenny is first appointed and associated to me.
>
> Your Grace will please to weigh these subjects, and then communicate to the Holy Father and the Propaganda your opinion and concurrence with my petition, which I have sent to Rome by Rev. Mr. Jeanjean from New Orleans, having expressed myself in the above manner both to the Pope and to Cardinal Pedicini. You will please to favor me with an answer to this when you write to Rome. . . .[19]

The death of Bishop Fenwick removed the necessity for a coadjutor. On December 22, 1832, Father Rese was named administrator of the diocese of Cincinnati, a position which he held until the successor of Bishop Fenwick, in the person of John Baptist Purcell, was con-

[19] *Ibid.,* 421.

secrated at Baltimore on October 13, 1833.[20] But the other recommendation coming as the solution of a problem that had been so long before the Congregation was favorably acted upon. For the second time the diocese of Detroit was erected by a Bull of Gregory XVI, dated March 8, 1833, and on the same day Father Frederic Rese was named as its first bishop.[21]

Ten months elapsed, however, before Detroit could welcome its own bishop. Father Rese desired to be consecrated by Bishop Rosati of St. Louis, and he deferred the event until the latter should pass through Cincinnati on his way to the Second Provincial Council of Baltimore. The consecration took place in the cathedral at Cincinnati on October 6, 1833.[22] After the ceremony the two bishops set out to attend the deliberations of the council. They were back in Cincinnati at the end of November, and Bishop Rese tarried there, winding up affairs, until the end of the year. On January 7, 1834, he made his entry into Detroit to take possession of his see.[23] Bishop Flaget's prediction had at last been verified. The stone church of St. Anne that had cost Father Richard so many years of poverty and labor had finally become a cathedral.

The new bishop was no stranger to the Catholics of Detroit who gazed wonderingly at him in the dignity of his purple. They were familiar with the rather short, well-knit figure, the round and ruddy countenance lighted up by smiling blue eyes, the shock of curly black hair.[24] He stood before them in the prime of life, needing just a month to complete his forty-third year.[25] They did not reflect perhaps on the strange ways through which Divine Providence had brought an erstwhile lowborn orphan to be the first of his race to wield episcopal power in the United States.

[20] Lamott, op. cit., 70.
[21] Both the Bull and a long laudatory letter from Gregory XVI to the bishop-elect are given in full in the Jus Pontificium de Propaganda Fide, V, 70–71.
[22] There is a curious discrepancy in the account of the consecration. Francis X. Reuss, Biographical Cyclopedia of the Catholic Hierarchy (Milwaukee, 1898), states that the assistant consecrators were Bishops Flaget and David, and he is usually careful in his statements. The Very Rev. Charles L. Souvay, C.M., of Kenrick Seminary communicated to the writer a copy of the record which Bishop Rosati inserted in his diary. The date is October 6, the XIX Sunday after Pent. After naming the officers of the Mass the record goes on to state: "acting in the capacity of assisting bishops by a special Apostolic dispensation were the Rev. Fathers St. Th. Badin and . . . Volger." The last named must have been the Rev. Jerome Vogeler mentioned in Lamott, op. cit., 399.
[23] The only authority for this date is Farmer, op. cit., 963.
[24] These details of personal appearance are taken from a manuscript written by Richard R. Elliott of Detroit, who in his boyhood often served Bishop Rese at the altar. Manuscript in DCA.
[25] The baptismal record as quoted by Reuss, op. cit., 94, is as follows: Reese, John Frederic Conrad, born of Gotfried Reese and Caroline Alrutz (leg. conj.), born on February 6, 1791 (in loco) Viennenberg, etc. . . . ."

Bishop Rese was born at Vienenburg, a little village in the former kingdom of Hanover, and in the diocese of Hildesheim.[26] His parents lived in poverty and died early, leaving a family of small children to the care of grandparents. Frederic, a frail and puny lad, was apprenticed to a tailor, and after he had learned his trade he set out on the customary wanderings of a journeyman. During this period of his life Germany was in the throes of the Napoleonic Wars. In 1813 the War of Liberation began with the call to the entire man power of the Germanic States. The tailor became a soldier, and as a cavalryman in a Hanoverian regiment he served under Blücher at the battle of Waterloo.

Now in his twenty-fifth year the soldier determined to become a priest. In his struggle for a livelihood there had been little opportunity for learning, and he was rather advanced in age to begin his preliminary studies in Germany. Some one advised him that his goal could be more easily reached if he offered himself to the Propaganda Congregation as a candidate for the ministry in foreign missions. He set out for Rome on foot, again the impecunious tailor, stopping to work at his trade whenever necessity compelled.

Such persistency did not go unrewarded; the ambitious student found a welcome reception in the College of the Propaganda. Here he displayed an aptitude for languages that made him proficient in French and Italian by the time that he was ready for ordination. He was ordained in 1823, and in consequence of the contract he had made on entering the college, he was immediately sent to a mission field in Africa.[27] Before very long his health gave way, and he was obliged to return to Rome. He was there, waiting for another assignment, when he met Bishop Fenwick in 1824. The prelate was seeking for some one to minister to the German Catholics of Ohio, and his need tallied with the priest's aspirations. Having readily obtained permission to come to America Father Rese, as we have seen, arrived in Cincinnati in the fall of the same year.

Here, Father Rese soon became indispensable to Bishop Fenwick. Besides his work among his compatriots he displayed an administra-

[26] In the absence of any documentary material bearing on the early period of Bishop Rese's life, the only account available is that found in Richard H. Clarke, *Lives of the Deceased Bishops of the Catholic Church in the United States* (New York, 1888), III, 266–67. A sketch of Bishop Rese, differing only in slight particulars from the preceding one, was written by Msgr. F. G. Holweck for the *Pastoral-Blatt* of St. Louis, issue of April, 1920.

[27] According to Reuss, *op. cit.*, the ordaining prelate was Cardinal Zurla, Prefect of the Propaganda Congregation, and the ordination took place in 1822 during the "Trinity ordinations." In that year Trinity Sunday fell on June 2. However, in the Detroit Chancery Archives there is a celebret issued to "Frederico Rese . . . Presbytero hodie in urbe rite promoto." It was given at Rome, March 15, 1823.

tive ability that made him at first secretary and then vicar-general. During his years in Rome he had gained acquaintance with the highest officials in the Church, and had become familiar with the machinery of Church government. His awakening of the missionary spirit that led to the founding of the Leopoldine Association had aroused the charity of a nation to the needs of his diocese, and of the Church in America. When, as a result of Bishop Fenwick's proposal, he came to Detroit as its first bishop, the man who had begun life so humbly could count among his friends Cardinals and Princes.

We must now turn our attention to the diocese over which Bishop Rese came so auspiciously to preside. Let us consider first its territorial extent.[28] According to the wording of the document which brought it into existence the diocese was to comprise "the provinces of Michigan and the Northwest, which had hitherto been subject to the Bishop of Cincinnati as apostolic administrator. . . ." As has already been pointed out, there was no such entity as a "Northwest" province. The term had passed out of existence with the first division of the old Northwest Territory. What was given to Bishop Rese was precisely Michigan Territory.

By an Act of Congress, dated April 18, 1818, this protean area comprised what is now Michigan and Wisconsin, and as much of Minnesota as lies within a line, roughly speaking, drawn from St. Paul to the Canadian Border. This was the remainder of the old Northwest Territory after the States of Ohio, Indiana, and Illinois had been admitted to the Union. The boundaries of Michigan Territory remained unchanged until June 28, 1834—five months after Bishop Rese's arrival—when they suddenly assumed enormous proportions. They included the present States of Iowa and Minnesota, and those portions of North and South Dakota lying east of the Missouri River. When the Territory was admitted to the Union on January 26, 1837, it was given the present boundaries of the State of Michigan.[29]

The ecclesiastical jurisdiction over the Territory in its widest extent is not so easily defined. In 1826 the diocese of St. Louis was cut off from the diocese of New Orleans. Two years later, Bishop Rosati reported the extent of his jurisdiction to the Propaganda as follows:

> The boundary line of the diocese of St. Louis to the East—to the West of which is a desert, there is no need of assigning limits—is con-

[28] There is an article dealing with this matter in the *Mich. Hist. Colls.*, IX, 128–37. It fairly bristles with inaccuracies, and is worthless.

[29] *Mich. Hist. Colls.*, XXX, 1–27. The dispute over the boundary line between Michigan and Ohio caused some friction between Bishop Rese and Bishop Purcell. Rome finally settled the matter in the latter's favor. Lamott, *op. cit.*, 98.

stituted by the Mississippi river; so that the State of Illinois and the so-called North-West territory are outside the diocese. If these regions were properly settled by Catholics, the ecclesiastical division might well be made to coincide with the civil division; but in proportion to the area, the number of inhabitants is quite small, and among these, Catholics are few. . . . In Europe and in countries thickly populated, large rivers are on the outskirts; here in this part of North America, they are centers. On this account both banks of the river are naturally connected together, and would seem to belong to the same diocese. . . . The Bishop of St. Louis himself, going from one to another of the parishes of his diocese, has to pass through several parishes of Illinois, because this is the shorter and better road. . . . For this reason, as soon as the Right Reverend Louis William Du Bourg established his residence in St. Louis, he was asked by the Right Reverend Bishop of Bardstown to take these parishes under his care. At the request of the same prelate and of the Bishop of Cincinnati, I too, continue to take care of them.[30]

Although, perhaps, of only academic interest, the problem presented by the inclusion of Iowa in Michigan Territory must be touched upon. Iowa lay clearly in the diocese of St. Louis with as yet but one important group of Catholics, that in Dubuque. In this case did ecclesiastical jurisdiction follow the civil boundaries? It is certain that Bishop Rosati applied to Bishop Rese for the faculties of a vicar-general, but doubtful whether they were to be used in any definite locality. Bishop Rese answered:

Your esteemed letter reached me at Detroit. I willingly concede to you the faculties of a Vicar-General, and you may subdelegate them to others. I ask you only to keep a record of the dispensations that you shall grant in the Northwest Territory, and that you inform me of their number. . . .[31]

There is a curious bit of evidence tending to show that Dubuque was actually considered to lie within the diocese of Detroit. Father Mazzuchelli was there in 1835 building the modest stone church that became the cathedral when Bishop Loras arrived in 1839. A copy of the document placed in the corner stone was sent to the Leopoldine Association, and was printed in the Berichte.

. . . Gregory XVI happily ruling the universal Church of Christ; Frederic Rese being Bishop of the Diocese in the Territory of Michigan; Andrew Jackson, President of the Free States of North America; Stephen L. Mason, acting Governor of the aforesaid Territory; this corner-

[30] Rothensteiner, op. cit., I, 444. Prairie du Chien, in Wisconsin, was another parish on the east bank of the Mississippi cared for from St. Louis.
[31] The letter in the St. Louis Chancery Archives, is dated September 17, 1833. The bishop-elect was in Detroit negotiating with the trustees of St. Anne's for the settlement of property affairs.

stone of St. Raphael's church in the Town of Dubuque was laid with appropriate ceremonies on the Feast of the Assumption, the 15th day of August in the year of Our Lord, 1835, in the presence of the people by the humble servant of God, Samuel Mazzuchelli, a priest.[32]

We turn now to the clergymen who were affiliated with the diocese of Detroit at the beginning of Bishop Rese's régime. In a brief report on his diocese which he sent to the Leopoldine Association in November, 1833, he listed his priests as follows:

> I have at present twelve priests, and I hope the number will soon be increased. Six of these priests are in the Indian missions. Father Baraga is with the Ottawa; Fathers Saenderl and Hätscher with the Menominee; Father Mazzuchelli, from Milan, with the Winnebago; Fathers Badin, Senior, (a Frenchman) and Deseille (a Fleming) with the Potawatami in the South on the St. Joseph River. The parishes in the civilized communities of Michigan are ministered to by the following priests: Father Badin, Junior, (from France), Fathers Van den Poel, de Bruyn, Bohême, Bonduel (a minorist) from Flanders, Fathers Andreas Viszoczky from Hungary, and Father Carabin from Germany. . . .[33]

The foregoing list, which is neither accurate nor exhaustive, was written not quite fourteen months after the death of Father Richard. It contains several unfamiliar names, and is helpful in following the changes that occurred among the clergy during that period.

When Father Badin had finished describing Father Richard's last moments in the letter to Bishop Fenwick already quoted, he begged that Father Hätscher be appointed pastor of St. Anne's.

> . . . Father Simon has written him to go to Green Bay. This is impossible. As for me, I am unable to take the place of Mr. Richard. 1st. For ten days I have been fighting the cholera. I find great difficulty in keeping my natural heat, and I fear that I shall die too. Fiat. Fiat. 2nd. I can not preach. 3rd. My spirit is weak—little theology, as you know, My Lord. I am good only for small missions. . . .

Nevertheless, Father Hätscher heeded the call of his superior, and in a few weeks joined him at Green Bay.[34] In his place came Father John Lostrie, a Belgian from the diocese of Ghent, who arrived in Cincinnati as the beginning of September.[35] For several months, during which the pastorate of St. Anne's was undecided, he and Father

[32] *Berichte*, XI, 43.
[33] *Berichte*, VII, 3–4. Letter dated November 9, 1833.
[34] His last entry in the St. Anne register is dated October 7, 1832.
[35] His first entry in the register is dated October 8, 1832.

Badin lived together, not always in perfect concord.[36] Some time in August, 1833, he was appointed to Mackinac Island to succeed Father Mazzuchelli who had begun to work among the Indians of Wisconsin.[37] Father Lostrie's ministry here does not seem to have extended beyond the end of October, and at its close he left the diocese.[38]

The Fleming mentioned in Bishop Rese's list was a compatriot of Father Lostrie who had come with him to America.[39] A native of the parish of Slydenge in the diocese of Ghent, Father Louis J. Deseille at the end of ten years of ministry in his own country longed to sacrifice his life to the Indian missions in Michigan.[40] He arrived in Detroit on November 29, 1832, and after a brief stay went to assist Father Badin in the Potawatomi mission on the St. Joseph River.[41] We shall see later how he fulfilled his desire.

Leo Fidelis Van den Poel of the Diocese of Bruges and John De Bruyn of the Diocese of Malines came to Detroit together in the fall of 1833.[42] Although they both spent some time in the Indian missions, the first at Green Bay, and the second at L'Arbre Croche, they were destined to begin the first school of higher learning in the Diocese of Detroit.[43] In that connection they will be dealt with in a later chapter.

Ghislenus J. Bohême left his native Belgium to complete his studies for the priesthood in Cincinnati.[44] In 1832 Bishop Fenwick sent him to assist Father Stephen Badin in the Potawatomi mission, where, besides his duties as catechist, he was to finish his theological course under the direction of the veteran missionary.[45] Following the arrival of Father Deseille at the mission he went to Bardstown to be ordained. He received his priesthood January 20, 1833, at the hands of

[36] Father Badin complains to the vicar-general that Father Lostrie acts without consulting him, and boasts that when he is pastor he will dispose of Father Richard's library. Letter dated November 13, 1832. NDA.

[37] His last entry is dated August 4.

[38] Rezek, op. cit., II, 183. Although Father Lostrie is named among the Detroit clergy, in the United States Catholic Almanac for 1835, as being at Mackinac, he was certainly not there. Nothing further is known concerning him.

[39] "In 1832 we seven missionaries sailed from Antwerp to Baltimore. My companions were: Van der Weyer, Fathers Lostrie, Deseille, Deganquiver, of the diocese of Ghent, and two lay men . . ." The Story of Father Van den Broek, O.P. (Chicago: Ainsworth & Co., 1907), 41.

[40] He was born July 14, 1795, and ordained November 9, 1821. Lamott, op. cit., Clergy List.

[41] Letter of Father Badin to Father Rese, December 2, 1832. NDA.

[42] A copy of Father Van den Poel's dimissorial letters in the DCA is dated September 5, 1833.

[43] The Catholic Almanac for 1835 places Father Van den Poel at Green Bay with Father Van den Broek, but does not mention the whereabouts of Father De Bruyn. In 1836 he is listed as being at L'Arbre Croche.

[44] Born in 1803 according to Lamott, op. cit., Clergy List.

[45] O'Daniel, op. cit., 407.

Bishop Rosati who happened to be on a visit to Bishop Flaget.[46] After some months of itinerant missionary activity in Ohio, Father Bohême came to Detroit about the end of August.[47]

A particular interest attaches to the next name in the list. Florimond Joseph Bonduel was born at Comines, a town of western Flanders, on September 17, 1800. He entered the preparatory seminary at Roulers, and studied theology at Tournai. Before the reception of major orders he decided to come to America, was accepted by Bishop Fenwick, and reached Cincinnati in 1831.[48] He was still unordained when sent to Detroit in the spring of 1833. In all probability, the first exercise of Bishop Rese's episcopal power was the ordination of Father Bonduel, which took place on February 9, 1834.[49] That Father Bonduel took pride in the fact that he was the first priest ordained in the diocese of Detroit is evident from the phrase that he often added to his signature, "Proto-Sacerdos Detroitensis."

In August, 1834, Father Bonduel was sent to Mackinac Island, where he remained as pastor for four years.[50] He was then transferred to Green Bay, and the remainder of his life is identified with the history of the Church in Wisconsin. He died at Green Bay, December 13, 1861.

The last unfamiliar name in Bishop Rese's list is that of Father Andreas Viszoczky. He was born in 1796 at Wallendorf, a village in the diocese of Szepes, then in northeastern Hungary, but now comprised within the boundaries of Czecho-Slovakia. After completing his studies in Vienna, he was ordained, October 20, 1821, and exercised his ministry in his native diocese for the next twelve years. The work of the Leopoldine Association so aroused his interest in the American missions that he decided to offer himself to the diocese of Cincinnati. He landed at New York on August 11, 1833, and reached Cincinnati in time to be present at the consecration of Bishop Rese. However, his transfer to the new diocese was arranged and Father Viszoczky was ordered immediately to Michigan to take up his residence at "St.

---

[46] Date of ordination from Bishop Rosati's diary in the St. Louis Chancery archives.

[47] Bishop Rese writing to Bishop Rosati, September 17, 1833, states that Father Bohême is waiting for his trunk to arrive. Letter in St. Louis Chancery archives.

[48] These details taken from the researches of Archbishop Mesmer of Milwaukee found in the *Salesianum*, a quarterly published by the St. Francis Seminary, Milwaukee, for April, July, and October, 1924.

[49] Father Bonduel gives the time of his arrival in Detroit, and the date of his ordination in a letter to the Society for the Propagation of the Faith, dated April 25, 1855. There is a copy in the Hickey transcripts.

[50] The term of his pastorate is established by the dates given in Rezek, *op. cit.*, II, 184: from August 16, 1834 to August 30, 1838. During this period Father Bonduel visited missions in Wisconsin, and in the home of Solomon Juneau celebrated the first Mass said in Milwaukee. See the *Salesianum* for January, 1919.

Félicité, St. Claire's River," the present parish of Marine City.[51] His first letter to the Leopoldine Association disclosed both his zeal and his courage.

> I found here a wooden chapel and a wooden cabin, one more wretched than the other. Briefly, they were not so much dilapidated as they were absolutely bare. My living was as poor as my abode until January 8 of this year. Potatoes and peas were my daily fare, and water my drink, as it still is and will be. I am living all alone with only rats and mice as my companions. I have no school, no schoolmaster, no sexton, no Mass server. In a word, I have nothing. Yet, in spite of my poverty and destitution, I have completely recovered my health, and by the grace of God I live happy and contented, more so indeed than I was in my native land. . . .[52]

It is curious enough that Bishop Rese in his enumeration of the diocesan clergy left out Father Patrick O'Kelly who was certainly back with his little group of Irishmen at Northfield. More curious still was his omission of a priest whom he had known for some years in Cincinnati, and whom he had sent to Detroit almost six months before, Father Martin Kundig. He was destined to play such a part in the Catholic history of Detroit as makes him comparable to Father Richard alone.

Martin Kundig, a native of Switzerland, was born November 19, 1805, at Schwyz, a town in the canton of the same name. His parents, in lowly circumstances, brought him up in an atmosphere of profound piety. The boy was gifted with a talent for music, and with his sweet soprano voice he sang himself into the affections of influential friends. When 13 years old he was sent to the celebrated abbey of Einsiedeln to study in the monastery academy restricted to forty youths chosen for the beauty of their voices. Here he found his vocation, and four years later he began his studies for the priesthood, first in the seminary at Lucerne, and later in the College of the Sapienza at Rome.

It had never been the seminarian's intention to come to America, but in a chance meeting with Father Rese at Rome in 1827 he was invited to affiliate himself with the diocese of Cincinnati. The prospect at first frightened him and only the persistence of the vicar-general overcame his reluctance. His surrender was complete when his friend, John Henni, volunteered to accompany him. Together they arrived in New York at the end of May, 1828, and a few weeks later, having travelled on horseback from Wheeling to Cincinnati,

---

[51] These details from the *Berichte*, VI, 55: VII, 35.

[52] *Berichte*, VIII, 43. Father Viszoczky arrived in Detroit on October 20, and went to his parish on November 14.

they were welcomed by Bishop Fenwick. As he had yet no seminary of his own the bishop gave them Minor Orders, and sent them to Bardstown to complete their studies. On February 2, 1829, Martin Kundig and his friend were ordained to the priesthood in the cathedral of Cincinnati.[53]

Father Kundig began his ministry with the care of the German Catholics in and around Cincinnati. In 1839 he built himself a log cabin a few miles from Fayetteville, Brown County, and founded the parish of St. Martin.[54] However, Bishop Fenwick had other plans for the young foreigner who displayed such tireless zeal, and, in 1832, Father Kundig was again a roving missionary to the German Catholics of Ohio. No less than Bishop Fenwick, Father Rese was aware of the missionary's worth, and when he received word of his appointment to the see of Detroit he had no hesitancy in transferring Father Kundig to his own diocese.[55]

It may be of interest to supplement the foregoing commentary on Bishop Rese's clergy list with the first published description of the diocese as found in the *United States Catholic Almanac for 1834*. While it is evidently an earlier list than the one we have been dealing with, it supplies information which cannot be gathered from the other.

Diocess of Detroit

Michigan and North-West Territories

Detroit, Cathedral of St. Ann. Right Rev. Frederick Reze, D.D.; Rev. Vin. Badin; Rev. Martin Kundig; Rev. Mr. Bonduel. High Mass at 9 o'clock for the Germans, and at 11 for the French. Sermons in German, French and English.

Monroe. High Mass at 10. Rev. Mr. Carabin.

St. Joseph's. High Mass at 10. Rev. S. T. Badin; Rev. Mr. Deseille. Instruction in Indian and French.

St. Paul,
St. Felicite, } visited alternately. Rev. Mr. Bohême.[56]
St. Francis,

[53] For the latest biography of Father Kundig see the Rev. Peter Leo Johnson, *Stuffed Saddlebags* (Milwaukee, 1942). Another good account was contributed to the *Salesianum* by Archbishop Messmer of Milwaukee in the eight consecutive issues, XIII, No. 2 to XV, No. 1. He edited with critical notes an incomplete biography compiled by Mr. Bernard Durward, a former professor at St. Francis Seminary, who had derived his information from Father Kundig himself. The details in the text are condensed from the first number of the periodical mentioned above.

[54] *Ibid.*, XIII, No. 3, 1–12.

[55] *Ibid.*, XIII, No. 3, 17. "He came to Kundig and said: 'If I accept of this position you must go with me, you must pack up all your things quietly and then go to Cleveland—stay there a few days and then go to Detroit.'" Father Kundig's first entry in the St. Anne register is dated July 17, 1833. Later entries prove an almost continuous residence in Detroit until the coming of Bishop Rese.

[56] The reader will remember that these three names stand for the present parishes of Grosse Pointe, St. Clair Shores, and Mt. Clemens.

St. Felicite, St. Claire's River. Rev. Mr. Visyoyky.
Island of Michillimachinac. Rev. Mr. Lostrie. Instructions in English
and French.
Arbre Croche. Rev. Simon Lauderle. Cong. St. Liguori.[57]
Grand River. Rev. Mr. Boraga. Instructions in Indian.
Ann Harbour. Rev. Mr. Kelly.
Vinebago. Rev. S. Mazzuchelli. Instructions in the Vinebago language.[58]
Green Bay. High Mass at 10. Rev. Mr. Hotsches. Sermons in French
and Menomony.[59]

The location of Father Baraga in the above list deserves particular
notice. From his station at L'Arbre Croche he had been able to reach
many scattered groups of Ottawa, and had established missions at
Grand Traverse, Beaver Island, Manistique, and Little Detroit.[60] But
he had never come in contact with one large band that lived to the
south on the Grand River. In the winter of 1832–33, he sent one of
his converts, his "John the Baptist," as he calls him, to sound the
willingness of the Grand River Indians to receive a missionary.[61]
Assured of a favorable reception Father Baraga arrived among them
on June 15, 1833, and remained about three weeks. He said Mass
daily in the home of Louis Campau, a trader, who had established
his post on the east bank of the river on a spot that is now almost the
center of the city of Grand Rapids.[62]

Father Baraga's zeal was amply rewarded, for eighty-six Indians
were baptized before his return to L'Arbre Croche. This number of
converts together with several Canadian families in the neighborhood
seemed to warrant the presence of a resident priest. Accordingly,
Father Baraga was directed by Father Rese to relinquish the L'Arbre
Croche mission to Father Saenderl, and to begin a new establishment
on the Grand River. After a farewell tour of his scattered missions
Father Baraga rejoined his recent converts at the end of September.

At this time the Grand River, to a point some distance within
Ionia County, formed the southern boundary of the Indian lands in

[57] This is only the printer's weird rendering of Father Simon Saenderl's name.
[58] Father Mazzuchelli left Mackinac to work about two years among the Indians of
Wisconsin. His principal mission among the Winnebago was situated a few miles from
Fort Winnebago, where the city of Portage now stands. See sketch of Father Mazzuchelli by James Davie Butler in the *Wisconsin Hist. Colls.*, XIV, 159 ff.
[59] The Menominee lived behind Green Bay, and Father Mazzuchelli as well as Father
Hätscher labored among them. The principal mission station was in the present town
of Kaukauna. See *Wisconsin Hist. Colls.*, XIV, 191. During the winter of 1833–34 Father
Hätscher lived on Mackinac Island, and Father Mazzuchelli replaced him at Green Bay.
Rezek, *op. cit.*, II, 184.
[60] Verwyst, *op. cit.*, 145–46.
[61] *Ibid.*, 141–42. The author is here merely following Father Baraga's letter in the
Berichte, VII, 10–25.
[62] Albert Baxter, *History of the City of Grand Rapids* (New York and Grand Rapids,
1891), 48.

western Michigan which were to be ceded by the Treaty of Washington in 1836.[63] Father Baraga therefore located his mission site on the Indian side of the river. Although the Leopoldine Association was ready to defray the cost of a mission building he could find no workmen capable of erecting it. Nothing daunted he set out on horseback for Detroit, where he succeeded in hiring two carpenters. On the return journey the three men, with Father Baraga's horse as their sole means of transportation, walked and rode by turns through almost impassable trails until they reached the mission. By the end of the year two or three rude structures had been erected that served as church, rectory, and school for the first parish in Grand Rapids.[64]

To complete our notion of the diocese of Detroit as it was at the beginning of 1834 we should have fairly accurate statistics of the Catholic population within it. However, this is too much to hope for at such an early date. The total population of Michigan Territory in 1830 was 31,640.[65] Four years later these figures were increased to 87,278.[66] The first state census in 1837 gave a population approximating 170,000.[67] Perhaps the earliest attempt to enumerate the Catholics of Michigan is found in Blois' *Gazetteer of the State of Michigan,* published in 1838. "The Catholics have one bishop and 30 priests, and they claim a Catholic population of from 20,000 to 24,000, 3000 of whom are converted Indians, 8000 are English, Irish, German, and American, and the balance is French." [68]

If Michigan doubled its population from 1834 to 1838, the increase was due entirely to immigration from the Eastern States and from Europe; the French element received no such accessions. Hence Blois' estimate of 8000 Catholics, exclusive of Indians and French, might be reduced by half to represent the number of "foreign" Catholics in 1834. Even this number should probably be reduced because the rate of growth was more rapid from 1834 to 1838 than from 1830

---

[63] Alpheus Felch, "The Indians of Michigan and the Cession of Their Lands to the United States," in the *Mich. Hist. Colls.,* XXVI, 274–97.

[64] Verwyst, *op. cit.,* 148–49. Father Baraga's mission building stood somewhere in the neighborhood of Watson and Broadway. In 1837 the parish was relocated on the other side of the river.

[65] Fuller, *Economic and Social Beginnings of Michigan,* 535.

[66] John T. Blois, *Gazetteer of the State of Michigan* (Detroit and New York, 1838), 151.

[67] Fuller, *op. cit.,* 536–39.

[68] Blois, *op. cit.,* 150. This statement was most likely copied from the introduction to the first directory of Detroit, a pretentious novelty published by Julius P. Bolivar MacCabe in 1837. The author names some of the former priests in Michigan, and in a note pays his respects to Father Smith: "This individual some time ago became an apostate, is now one of the noble Trium of the Maria Monk humbug, and reviles the catholics with us much virulence as he formerly did the protestants of every denomination."

to 1834. A fair estimate, therefore, would give 15,000 as the total number of Catholics in Michigan at the beginning of 1834.

The racial distribution of the immigrant Catholics in Michigan calls for some attention. What Blois meant to convey by "English" Catholics is not very clear. There was a small number of Englishmen in Michigan at the time, but if there were any Catholics among them they were so few as scarcely to deserve mention. A like uncertainty attaches to the meaning of "Americans." The bulk of American immigration to Michigan came from New York and the New England States, and was decidedly Protestant. Whatever Catholics there were among them might better be classed as rather recent immigrants whose residence in the East was only a prelude to a further westward movement.[69]

Regarding the distinctively Irish immigration there is little to add to what was said when referring to Father O'Kelly. If his early records were extant it might be possible to conjecture the number of settlers to whom he ministered.[70] Only this much is certain, that a steady growth took place, and that in 1844 Father O'Kelly, as we shall see, divided his time between seven parishes. In Monroe, out of 237 children baptized between 1830 and 1834, perhaps 20 should be classed as the offspring of recent Irish immigration. Although the Irish in Detroit were numerous enough to warrant having their own Mass on Sundays, no report of their number is available. The first accurate statistics are for 1840, and they show 202 heads of families on the roster of Holy Trinity parish.[71]

The first listing of the diocese of Detroit discloses the presence of another group of immigrant Catholics, the Germans, large enough to be accorded a distinct hour of worship in St. Anne's. Although there were a number of Germans in Detroit and Michigan very early in the history of both, nothing approaching group immigration occurred much before 1830.[72] From that time up to the great migration of

[69] "If New York may be called the second New England, Michigan may justly claim to rank as the third. Owing to the great foreign immigration to New England in later times, Michigan represents today more truly the blood and ideals of the Puritans than does any of the New England States. The foreign immigrants who came after 1848, finding Michigan already largely occupied, moved farther west to Wisconsin, Minnesota, and Iowa. As a result of the early immigration from New England and New York, Michigan probably has a larger percent of original New England stock than has any other State in the Union." Fuller, *op. cit.*, 482.

[70] The earliest records so far known kept by Father O'Kelly date from 1843, and are preserved in the parish records of Fenton.

[71] List compiled by Richard R. Elliott, and published in the bicentenary edition of the *Michigan Catholic*, August 22, 1901.

[72] More fortunate than the Irish the Germans found a chronicler for their contribution to the development of Michigan. See John Andrew Russell, *The Germanic Influence in the Making of Michigan* (Detroit, 1927), 66–69.

1848 caused by the revolutionary disturbances in Germany the German element increased to such an extent that, next to the Irish, the
Germans became the most important foreign group in the development of Michigan.[73]

In dealing with the Catholic phase of this immigration we are, as
usual, hampered by a lack of accurate information; nevertheless, we
have a precise starting point. As far as existing records go, they prove
that the first foreign settler in Detroit—and in Michigan as well—
while it was still under French rule was a German Catholic. Thanks
to the French efficiency in keeping records there has been preserved
for us the curious story of Michael Yax.[74]

With the founding of Germantown by Pastorius in 1683, Pennsylvania became the mecca of succeeding waves of German immigration.
From 1710 to 1727 thousands of Germans passed through Philadelphia on their way to the back country. The majority of them belonged to various Protestant sects, and in 1760 there were only 900
German Catholics in Pennsylvania.[75]

In 1747 Michael Yax, a Catholic, living somewhere in Pennsylvania, decided to emigrate. He might have gone to any of the German
colonies that had meanwhile sprung up along the Atlantic seaboard
without much hardship or danger. Whether or not he was actuated
by religious motives does not appear, but at all events he set his face
toward a distinctively Catholic colony, the German Coast of Louisiana.[76] He started out with his wife and child, and was evidently coming down the Ohio to the Mississippi when he was captured at the
mouth of the Scioto by a band of Ottawa from Detroit.[77] The captives
were despoiled of their little possessions and conducted to Detroit,
where the commandant, de Longueil, paid ransom for them. By the
charity of the inhabitants Michael Yax was supported for three years,
and in 1751, when the Quebec authorities were making desperate
efforts to colonize Detroit, he was rated as high as the rest and was

[73] See various references in Fuller, *op. cit.*

[74] The name Yax is the French approximation to the real name, whatever it was. In
his manuscript genealogies in the BHC Father Denissen states that the original name
was "Jacks"; that variant is certainly not German.

[75] Russell, *op. cit.*, 24.

[76] For the German immigration to Louisiana promoted by John Law for his Mississippi grant see J. Hanno Deiler, *The Settlement of the German Coast of Louisiana*
(Philadelphia, 1909).

[77] The determined effort made by the Canadian authorities to colonize Detroit has
already been referred to. Michael Yax is included in the notarial record and the details in the text are taken from the brief sketch appended to his name. The place of
his capture is given as Sonnioto, which was a Shawnee village near the mouth of the
Scioto River.

granted a farm on the Detroit River.[78] Here with provisions from the King's stores he began life anew, and became the sire of a numerous progeny.[79]

His wife, Catherine Herbinne, deserves to be rescued from oblivion. She had evidently been brought up as a Lutheran, and had remained such despite her marriage to Michael Yax. Some years after her arrival in Detroit she was received into the Church, and thus became, in all likelihood, the first convert from Protestantism in Michigan. To the little French Catholic community, and to Father Bocquet, that was an event of a lifetime, and he recorded it in quite the longest entry devoted to an individual in the pages of St. Anne's register.

In the year of Our Lord one thousand seven hundred and fifty-five, on the sixteenth of March, after having examined Catherine Herbinne, wife of Michael Yax, both natives of Germany, who, born and brought up in the errors of Luther, had professed them up to now, and having found her sufficiently instructed in the Distinctive and Eternal Truths of our Holy Religion, and touched by the ardor with which she desired to be joined to the faithful and to make a public and firm profession of the catholic, Apostolic and Roman faith, and likewise edified by the regularity of her conduct for about the five years that she has lived in this parish, we, Recollect priest, performing the pastoral functions in the parish of St. Anne of Detroit Erie, and provided for this end with the faculties of the Illustrious Monsg. Henry Marie du Breil de Pont Briant, bishop of Quebec, dated April 29 of the preceding year one thousand seven hundred and fifty-four, on this day Passion Sunday, at the end of Vespers, we have received the public abjuration which she made between our hands of the above-named errors, and after having given her absolution from the excommunication and other censures incurred on this head, we have solemnly reconciled her to Our Mother the Holy Catholic Apostolic and Roman Church in the presence of M. Dumay, captain of the troops of his Majesty, Knight of the military order of St. Louis and commanding for the King in this fort and its dependencies, and of a great number of other persons of whom the leading ones have signed with us the day month and year as above. The said Catherine Herbinne declared she could neither read nor write.

From this time down to 1830 there is scarcely any trace to indicate the presence of German Catholics in Detroit. In that year six families

[78] The farm, later known as private claim 344, was situated in what is now Grosse Pointe.

[79] According to Denissen's genealogy he left eleven children. The reader may be interested in the list of supplies given to Michael Yax from the King's store: 1 plow, 1 axe, 1 hoe, 1 sickle, 1 scythe, 2 augers, 7 chickens, 1 sow, 8 lbs. lead, 4 lbs. powder, 2 lbs. rice, 6 lbs. flour, 1 pot of wine, 80 nails.

came to Detroit directly from Neustadt.[80] Among their descendants the tradition is constant that the emigration was motivated by the glowing description of Michigan circulated by a fellow townsman who had lived for some time in Detroit. The newcomers immediately took up land on the outskirts of Detroit in an area corresponding to the Grotto parish of today, and before very long they erected a little log church almost on the very site occupied by the present parish buildings.[81] From this humble beginning the number of German Catholics in and around Detroit must have increased very rapidly. Father Baraga, on his way to L'Arbre Croche for the first time, spent five days in Detroit in May, 1831. His only comment on his stay is the following: "There are many German and French Catholics there. During the time I remained there I was busy preaching, and hearing confessions." [82]

It is cause for regret that the two German Redemptorists who were in Detroit in 1832 were not more specific in detailing their impressions. Father Saenderl writes: "During my sojourn in Detroit Germans have come to me daily, of whom the majority have not been to confession for years since there is no priest for them. Here and in the neighborhood the Germans are so numerous that we preach to them in German every Sunday to their great joy. They regret very much that we are not yet established here. They come to us for confession from the woods, and from the adjoining sections of Canada. . . ." [83]

Father Hätscher, who remained in Detroit for some time after Father Richard's death, thus described his ministry among his German compatriots:

> Every Sunday I teach catechism and preach to the Germans living in the woods. . . . Two and a half hours [84] from Detroit, in the woods, there is a parish of Germans of whom the majority come from Alsace, Lorraine, etc., and their number is increasing every day. They too desire us to settle in Detroit, but they are unable to do more than supply lumber for a building. . . . When I go out on a missionary tour five

[80] In 1930 their descendants celebrated the 100th anniversary of what they called "the first organized German immigration to Detroit."

[81] See the interesting booklet published in conjunction with the celebration mentioned above, and held June 15–16. There is a copy in the BHC. The facts concerning the early immigration were compiled after careful investigation by Mr. Frank A. Weber.

[82] *Berichte*, IV, 8.

[83] *Berichte*, V, 26.

[84] The word "stunde" of the original, here translated "hour," when applied to distance means the ground covered by an ordinary walker in an hour, that is about four miles. This statement apparently confirms the tradition of the log church on or near the site of the present Grotto parish buildings.

or six of them accompany me on horseback so that they may freely converse with me about their spiritual welfare. . . .[85]

With the coming of Father Kundig in the following year the German Catholics of Detroit and its vicinity were for the first time definitely organized and adequately provided for. However, no estimate of their number is available. The first recorded census of German Catholics was made ten years later.[86] It listed 1117 communicants, of whom 687 lived in the city proper, and 430 in the outskirts.

[85] *Berichte*, V, 31.
[86] The census, in St. Mary's parish records was made by Father Otto Skolla.

CHAPTER XIX

Bishop Rese

WE COME now to the story of Bishop Rese's episcopate. It is a subject that bristles with so many difficulties that it can hardly be dealt with adequately. Whether or not, in view of the unfortunate termination of the bishop's career, a deliberate effort was made to veil his administration is something which the lapse of time has rendered impossible to ascertain. This much is certain, that there are scarcely any first-hand records of his term of office extant. If for the sake of convenience we group for study the seven years which elapsed between the bishop's arrival in Detroit and the appointment of a successor, we shall gain some knowledge of the period only by making the best of whatever secondary information may be gleaned from various sources. Despite diligent research the figure of Bishop Rese remains only dimly visible, and he plays a barely discernible part in a time wherein we should expect to find him acting the most prominent role.

Naturally, the presence of the bishop in Detroit inspired his little band of priests and the laity. How rosy were the prospects before them may be inferred from a report which Father Bonduel sent to the Leopoldine Association.

> . . . Since the appointment of our Reverend Bishop, the learned and pious Doctor Rese, we have witnessed a flourishing revival of religion. Buildings dedicated to the worship of the Most High have been generally repaired, and new ones have been erected. The church of St. Anne, lying in the center of the city, and at present the cathedral, has been so completely restored that it appears like a new edifice. The adjacent plot of ground will be the site of a new college and seminary, which the bishop will erect as soon as possible. Before long, the St. Clare Institute, which is having great success in this city, will be moved to the vicinity of the cathedral.
>
> More than half of the population of our district is made up of French, German, Irish, and American Catholics. What a magnificent future lies before us! The American and Irish Catholics have lately purchased from the Presbyterians their church building in this city. At the first assembly, presided over by their future pastor, Father Bernard O'Cavanagh, more than $1000 was raised for the purpose. The same

reverend gentleman pushed the matter vigorously for three or four consecutive weeks, and now he and the bishop have the consolation of having opened a second Catholic church in the city of Detroit. I am told that the Germans will soon follow the example of their American and Irish brethren in the Faith. A location for the erection of a German Catholic church has already been secured for them, and with the help of God there will soon be three churches in the chief city of the new diocese: the cathedral for the French, a church for the Americans and the Irish, and finally one for the Germans.

. . . It is reported that in the course of a year, or perhaps sooner, a Catholic paper will be started in this city to support the great cause of truth. The most reassuring feature of this enterprise is that the supervision of the publication will be entrusted to a man who directed a Catholic paper for almost three years from its beginning. We have every reason to hope that under the auspices of our worthy and learned bishop, and the former publisher of the Hartford Catholic Press, all the important interests of the true religion will be powerfully sustained. I have never seen anywhere the unity that here binds the people to their clergy, and the priests to each other.[1]

Perhaps the most interesting detail in the foregoing report is the reference to the St. Clare Institute, the first convent established in Detroit. Its origin must be sought in the endeavors of Bishop Fenwick to procure religious teachers for his diocese when in Europe during 1823–24. At Bruges he had visited a community of Collettine Poor Clares, and had enlisted their interest.[2] Having obtained the necessary permissions, two nuns, Sisters Françoise Vindevoghel and Victoire de Seilles, sailed from France on August 14, 1826, with Cincinnati as their destination. Father Stephen Badin, who was then in Rome, thus announced their coming to Bishop Fenwick:

. . . It may be proper to inform you that the two nuns, Francoise Vindevogle and Victoire de Seilles, have been permitted by their Abbess and the Vicar-General of Ghent to go to the United States to establish their order in the backwoods. The first is the oldest in age and religion. She possesses many good qualities and a sufficiently large property to commence an establishment. . . . A dispensation has been obtained at Rome for possessing and disposing of their temporal property for that object. . . . Sr. Francoise has an income of about 4000 frs . . .[3]

A school was opened in Cincinnati but after two years of teaching the Sisters became dissatisfied, and left the diocese to begin anew in Pittsburgh. Here they attracted a number of postulants, and the little

[1] *Berichte,* VIII, 12–13. Letter dated April 29, 1834.
[2] Lamott, *op. cit.,* 242–45.
[3] Letter of Father Stephen Badin to Bishop Fenwick, Rome, August 2, 1826. NDA.

community conducting St. Clare's Convent was soon flourishing. The first outgrowth of this foundation came to Detroit as a result of negotiations with Bishop Rese while he was still administrator of Cincinnati. He could scarcely have been apprised of his nomination to Detroit when he purchased, April 23, 1833, the southwest corner of Larned and Randolph Streets as the site of the St. Clare Institute.[4] A month or two later the Sisters arrived, and took up their quarters in a two-story yellow house that stood on the property.[5] As soon as the necessary additions had been made the convent became the fashionable school of Detroit. At the end of a year it had an enrollment of one hundred pupils, the majority of whom were non-Catholics.[6]

Father Bonduel's letter likewise discloses the beginning of Trinity parish and the identity of its first pastor. Bernard O'Cavanagh came to the United States about 1823 from the Irish diocese of Leighlin to study for the priesthood. Having finished his course at Mt. St. Mary's College, Emmitsburg, he was ordained in the Boston cathedral on July 19, 1829. A unique distinction was in store for him, that of establishing the first Catholic parish in the State of Connecticut.[7] Some weeks after his ordination he was assigned to Hartford, where a small Catholic group was planning to purchase a church which the Episcopalians of the town were ready to abandon. A year later when the church had been paid for it was dedicated to the Most Holy Trinity, and in 1844 it became the pro-cathedral of the diocese of Hartford.[8]

Father O'Cavanagh's arrival in Hartford coincided with the launching of one of the earliest Catholic newspapers, the *Catholic Press*, the first issue of which appeared July 11, 1829. In addition to his pastoral duties he found time to do editorial work for the publication, and it was doubtless this experience which lay behind the expectation held by Father Bonduel that a Catholic paper would soon be established in Detroit.[9]

[4] See the *Detroit Times and Tribune* for March 18, 1906, for a description of the St. Clare Institute by Robert B. Ross.

[5] In 1834 the City Council planned to open Congress Street through the property belonging to St. Anne's church. Bishop Rese protested, and his protest, a copy of which is in the BHC, is signed also by the Sisters of St. Clare's Institute. Their names are: Sister Mary Frances Vindevoghel, Sister Mary Serafin, Sister Colet Sheehy, Sister Constantia Ghissian, Sister Augustine Conway, Sister Tosiline Hefferen, Sister Celestia Scott, Sister Clarissa Sheehan.

[6] Father Bonduel thus enumerates them: ". . . 20 of them are boarders, 40 are day-scholars from the best families in the city, and 40 are poor children . . ." *Berichte*, VIII, 10.

[7] For details concerning Father O'Cavanagh see the *Cath. Hist. Rev.*, I, 148–52.

[8] *Ibid.*, 153.

[9] Paul J. Foik, C.S.C., *Pioneer Catholic Journalism* (New York; The United S. Cath. Hist. Soc., 1930), XIII. See also the Diocese of Hartford in the Catholic Encyclopedia.

Father O'Cavanagh left Hartford at the end of 1831, and his whereabouts are uncertain until we find him teaching at the Seminary of Cincinnati in 1833.[10] Most likely at the invitation of Bishop Rese he came to Detroit some time in February, 1834.[11] It is interesting to note the parallel between his work here and in Hartford.

The first Protestant church building in Detroit arose through the efforts of an interdenominational organization called the First Protestant Society.[12] It was built in 1819 on the east side of Woodward Avenue about 100 fee north of Larned Street.[13] In 1825 the congregation came under Presbyterian influence, and the church was used by that denomination until the construction of a new edifice on the same site in 1834. The old wooden church was up for sale and removal when Father O'Cavanagh arrived in Detroit to begin an English-speaking parish. He was quick to take advantage of the opportunity, as Father Bonduel notes, and by early summer the church had been moved to the northwest corner of Bates Street and Cadillac Square on a lot purchased by the bishop. After having undergone extensive alterations the church was dedicated to the Most Holy Trinity on June 14, 1835.[14]

In October, 1834, Bishop Rese himself wrote to the Leopoldine Association. His letter is filled with pious generalities which tell us nothing. Only this bit is worth quoting. The Association's wealthy patrons pleased by his elevation lost no time in providing him with a rich assortment of church furnishings for his cathedral, and personal belongings in keeping with his new dignity. Expressing his gratitude he wrote:

> I hasten to present my thanksgiving to my benefactors, and to thank God for having inspired you with a zeal for the decorum of His public worship. The cases came on a day when the good Sisters had assembled in my house to work for the poor. We immediately opened them, and found a variety of beautiful and costly objects. The women of the city come daily to gaze upon your gifts. . . . Now for the first time I can appear in my church as a bishop should. My church was completed just as I received the good news that the amount necessary to defray the

[10] *Cath. Hist. Rev.*, V, 241.

[11] *Ibid.*, 249.

[12] The first Protestant church in Michigan was erected by the Methodists on the Rouge River in 1817. Among its ardent supporters were two daughters of Peter Audrain who married non-Catholics. Burton, *op. cit.*, II, 1245.

[13] Farmer, *op. cit.*, I, 557.

[14] Some local historians have named Father Kundig as first pastor of Holy Trinity parish. This can hardly be true; Father O'Cavanagh clearly began the parish unit. He initiated the first baptismal register, and he alone signs it continuously until the end of June, 1839.

cost had come from the Leopoldine Association, and was in the hands of my bankers in New York.[15] I had not relied on Divine Providence in vain. My church is now seemly and beautiful, but the episcopal residence is still the old, wooden, one-story house that was built for the pastor. I dwell there with three priests, Mr. Badin, a Frenchman; Mr. Kundig, a German; and Mr. O'Cavanagh, an Irishman, and with four seminarians, a cook, a handy man, and a carpenter.[16] I often lodge the missionaries coming back from their missions, some for confession, and others to tell me their troubles. . . . We are often crowded together, and my dear servants of the Lord sleep on the floor in a buffalo robe, or something similar, which they roll up in the morning and throw in a corner . . .[17]

Bishop Rese's first few months in Detroit were evidently happy ones, marked by progress, and by hopeful planning for the future. In the summer he began his episcopal visitation of the diocese, but we have no record of his work in any place save at Sault Ste. Marie. He arrived there at the beginning of August, and was received by Father Hätscher, who had come a few weeks earlier to become the first resident pastor.[18] The congregation consisting of half-breeds and a few soldiers was rather unpromising material, but the Indians in the neighborhood responded eagerly to Father Hätscher's zeal. More than a hundred of them were ready to receive Confirmation when the bishop arrived.[19]

By the middle of September the bishop was back in Detroit, his visitation still unfinished. To Bishop Rosati who expected him in St. Louis for the consecration of the new cathedral he wrote his regrets:

[15] According to the financial statements appended to Vols. VIII and IX of the *Berichte,* the Leopoldine Association had given to the diocese of Detroit by the end of 1835 the sum of $11,000.

[16] Richard R. Elliott in the manuscript already referred to thus recalls the household of Bishop Rese: "The personal surroundings of Bishop Rese included 'Charles,' the chef . . . he was an alsacian, and a famous cook . . . 'Philip,' the German Gardner, and two male servants. There were no women employed in the episcopal household. In the religious staff was included a lay brother, Mr. John Pontius, or, as he was familiarly called, 'Brother John.' He was master of ceremonies, served Mass for the Bishop, and accompanied him on all his episcopal visitations. He was an accomplished linguist, and spoke freely nearly all the European languages, including Latin. He was short in stature, quick of movement, an able organizer of all ceremonials which he managed without friction, and which he conducted on a scale of grandeur. . . ."

[17] *Berichte,* IX, 27.

[18] *Annales Congregationis SS. Redemptoris,* I, 19. This is a printed compilation of the annals of the Redemptorists in America, designed for circulation in the houses of the Congregation.

[19] An extensive visitation of the northern missions is described in the *Annales de la Prop* . . . VIII, 293–97. The bishop is said to have left Detroit on May 12, 1835. This must be an error, for, as we shall see, he dedicated Trinity Church on June 14 of that year. A letter in the St. Louis Chancery Archives dated July 10, 1834, states that the bishop is to start north in a few days.

I must administer Confirmation in ten parishes which I have not yet visited. My regret is increased by the fact that I shall miss the added solemnity, the consecration of the bishop of Vincennes, which will take place in St. Louis, according to the "Catholic Herald." . . . I have the consolation of being able to announce to you that church affairs here are taking on a most favorable aspect, and that I cannot say enough about my priests. During the cholera epidemic Father Kundig merited the applause of the whole city, and in Protestant papers he is compared to the Good Samaritan . . . The city corporation has placed in my charge the county hospital and poor house. Deo Gratias . . .[20]

The bishop was apparently away during the great calamity that befell Detroit in 1834, the return of the cholera. And just as Father Richard had been a tower of strength to his townsmen in previous disasters so again a Catholic priest rose to heights of heroism and self-sacrifice unapproached by any other figure in the city's history.

The epidemic probably began with the death of Governor Porter on July 7. Despite a few intermittent cases, no alarm was felt until the beginning of August, when the plague descended upon the city in full earnest. It claimed approximately seven hundred victims before it spent its force in the last days of September. Business was suspended to such an extent that grass grew in the principal streets. At night the glare of flaming tar barrels designed to disinfect the air lighted up the deserted thoroughfares. The tolling of church bells for the dead was so continuous that it oppressed the living, and they begged for relief from the fearsome sound.[21]

Mayor Trowbridge and the physicians of Detroit were heroic in their efforts to alleviate distress and suffering, and a few prominent citizens volunteered their assistance; but foremost in the work of mercy stood Father Kundig. Farmer says of him: "Tall, strong, brave Father Martin Kundig outshone and outdid all others by his tireless devotion to the sick and dying. . . . He was so much of the time among the patients that he was avoided on the streets lest he should spread the contagion. . . ."[22] The mayor himself afterward paid this tribute to Father Kundig's heroism.

Being in the daily habit of visiting the hospital, my opportunities of observation were of the best kind, and it is impossible to impart to one, who has not passed through similar scenes, the admiration and respect inspired for the man, who, regardless of all personal consequences, was out, day and night, picking up the miserable creatures, who fell in the streets, struck with the dreadful scourge; and having transported them,

[20] Letter in St. Louis Chancery Archives, dated September 19, 1834.
[21] These are only the highlights of the descriptions furnished by the several historians of Detroit. See especially Friend Palmer, *Early Days in Detroit* (Detroit, 1906), 280-86.
[22] *Op. cit.,* I, 49.

in a litter which was constructed for the purpose, to the hospital, brought them in upon his own back, and, leaving them in care of the physicians and attendants, went immediately in quest of other sufferers . . .[23]

The hospital which the mayor visited was none other than the church lately purchased for the Irish Catholics of the city. It had been moved to Cadillac Square and was being remodeled to make it fit for Catholic worship when the cholera broke out. We have Father Kundig's own version of the change from church to hospital.

In the latter part of July, 1834, it (the cholera) made its appearance, and spread with fearful rapidity. Our citizens, as if overcome with fear, had neglected making any arrangements for the direful event—there was no hospital—the common council had failed to obtain the capitol for that purpose.

I then prevailed on the late Mr. Alpheus White to give us the use of the old Presbyterian meeting house, which he had recently purchased, to convert it into a Catholic church.[24] He most cheerfully complied. The house was divided into two apartments, for males and females, and all the necessary arrangements for a hospital of this kind were made.[25]

The ladies of the above-mentioned association did all the sewing necessary for making up the bedding; they were joined by the Sisters of St. Clare, and day and night, through all the horrors of that direful dispensation, they lent their aid to the sick and dying.[26] I would do wrong, did I forget the magnanimous and powerful assistance we received from the never-to-be-forgotten Alpheus White. He neglected his business, and with the assistance of his employed hands, attended, at all times, in my absence, to the care of the sick. My time was much en-

[23] The quotation is from a letter dated February 14, 1837, and addressed by Mayor Trowbridge to the Legislature in behalf of Father Kundig. It is quoted entire in the rare pamphlet issued by Father Kundig, *Exposition of Facts Relating to Certain Charitable Institutions Within the State of Michigan* (Detroit: E. A. Theller, 1840). Copy in BHC.

[24] Alpheus White was perhaps the most prominent layman of his day in Detroit. An architect by profession, and living in Cincinnati, he had been converted by Bishop Fenwick, and had built the Atheneum. As an admirer of Bishop Rese he followed him to Detroit. He was a delegate from Wayne County to the convention which drew up the first state constitution, and he remodeled and enlarged the capitol building to provide space for the meetings of the legislature. He afterwards returned to Cincinnati, where he died. See *Amer. Cath. Hist. Researches*, XV, 145–51.

[25] The account in the *Salesianum*, XIII, No. 4, gives the following details: "They put up a partition right through the middle of the building, knocked out every other pew and made cells or small apartments, the one side for men, the other for women . . . the devoted priest invented a wagon so constructed that the cover could be taken off, put the mattress on a sort of trestle, place it on the wagon, and replace the cover very easily . . . he was going with it up and down the streets of the stricken city day and night . . . all the ladies, both Protestant and Catholic, came to help him . . ."

[26] The "above mentioned association" was the Catholic Female Benevolent Society to be mentioned in a later chapter.

gaged, finding out the sick, and conveying them to the hospital. . . .
Dying parents recommended their children to me, and begged me, in
the name of the merciful God, to interest myself for them. I became
their deputed father, and continued to live for them, until they
were taken from me by circumstances which will hereafter be explained . . .[27]

This is the barest statement of the prodigies of Christian charity
performed by Father Kundig in his hospital, and throughout the city.
Calm and undismayed in the midst of panic he planned and executed
his relief measures. His tireless strength was at the beck and call of
every sufferer, and he shrank from no menial service to the living or
the dead. It was inevitable that he should compel the gratitude and
admiration of every one who survived the dreadful visitation.[28]

However, there is more to the story of Father Kundig than his
heroism during the cholera epidemic. Had his benefactions ended
there he might even now be held in grateful memory instead of being
almost forgotten. It may be that he has been conveniently forgotten
for he is the central figure in a phase of Detroit history of which, to
say the least, the city cannot be proud. It will be dealt with in a later
chapter.

We must now return to the point from which we digressed to view
Father Kundig as the dominant figure in a great emergency. We left
Bishop Rese in the flush of his first episcopal visitation, enjoying the
work that it entailed, praising his little band of devoted priests, facing
the future without misgivings. Certainly, at the moment his optimism
was reasonable; he could not know how little the future would justify
it. For practical purposes his episcopate may be considered to have
covered a span of six years, from 1833 to 1840. During this period the
record of growth is not so large but that it can be here surveyed with
some detail.

In the city itself the first sign of life was given by the English-speak-

[27] Father Kundig's pamphlet, p. 8.

[28] For instance, the Hon. George C. Bates is thus quoted in the *Mich. Hist. Colls.*,
XXII, 336. "So when in August, 1834, the cholera burst upon Detroit with a ferocity
and slaughter that it had never exhibited elsewhere, when in sixty days it had swept
away ten per cent of our people . . . when at early dawn the old French carts could
be seen in line, like the commissariat of the Grand Army, marshalled by sexton Noble,
stretching away to the old cemetery, a fearful line of festering corpses, when all men,
no matter how brave, seemed appalled; when we had no hospital, no asylums, no place
of refuge or safety for the sick and dying, Father Kundig, God bless him, improvised
a hospital on Michigan Grand Avenue and summoned to his aid all the fair daughters,
sweet young girls, of the Desnoyers, the Dequindres, the Campaus, the Morans, and
Beaubiens, and organized them into a splendid corps of Sisters of Mercy . . . and when
the final record shall be made up in heaven of old times and 'bygones' of Detroit, high
upon that scroll will be inscribed by God himself, in letters of living light, the names
of Kundig and his brave and beautiful army of Catholic girls of our city. . . ."

ing Catholics when they emerged from the basement of St. Anne's, where they had been worshipping, into a building of their own. As soon as the cholera epidemic had subsided, Alpheus White set to work changing the temporary hospital back into a church. On June 14, 1835, Bishop Rese solemnly dedicated the one-time Presbyterian house of worship to Catholic purposes under the patronage of the Most Blessed Trinity.[29] It was a proud day for the parishioners, and they noted with pleasure the presence in their little church of Lewis Cass, Secretary of War, and of Governor Mason.

About the same time, a third church in the city was under construction. The animosities that had been aroused by Father Richard's decision to rebuild St. Anne's in the town following the fire of 1805 had long since died down, and the inhabitants of the northeast shore had lost their group identity. While Bishop Rese was still only the administrator of the Church in Michigan he had without difficulty acquired control of the Malcher farm and its buildings.[30] He now decided to restore the chapel which Father Richard had first used in 1810. How a new church resulted is told us by Father Kundig to whom the work was entrusted.

> He, Bishop Rese, ordered me to repair the old shabby church, which I did by taking off the casing and shingles. But the night following, February 22, 1834, the whole concern was, by a great storm, blown to the ground. It had looked as old as if it was Noe's Ark itself. He then put up a new church, he built the additions to the old and worthless house and repaired it, and from that time he took care to have a clergyman remain there.[31]

Dedicated to St. Joseph, the new church must have come into use some time in 1836. Its baptismal register opens with an entry dated November 27 of that year.[32] However, there was really no need at the time for a parish in that locality, and St. Joseph's does not seem to have enjoyed a separate existence for more than three or four years.[33] The church became merely an adjunct to St. Anne's, was attended

[29] An account of the dedication has been preserved in the *Berichte*, X, 24–26.

[30] The trustees holding the Malcher Farm conveyed it to Father Rese on April 22, 1833. Their action laid the foundation for the famous Church Farm case that runs through the history of the diocese. For the wording of the dead see Burton, *op. cit.*, II, 1297.

[31] Farmer, *op. cit.*, I, 532.

[32] The register in the DCA contains the entries of 55 baptisms and 6 marriages. The existence of the register proves the intention of making St. Joseph's a separate parish. Because of its connection with the college the church was later called St. Philip Neri's.

[33] Despite Father Kundig's statement it seems hardly probable that St. Joseph's had a resident pastor. The college was opened in 1836, and the priests there attended the church until the college was closed. After that anyone was likely to be sent to conduct whatever services were held there.

from there for some years, and finally fell into complete disuse. The decaying structure was burned to the ground on July 13, 1861.

A second abortive parish for the French, begun within the present limits of the city, belongs to the same period. For the scattered families living along the Rouge and Ecorse rivers Father Vincent Badin erected a modest structure, which he blessed on June 16, 1835, and named the church of the Holy Cross.[34] It stood in Dick's settlement, about six miles below Detroit, on the bank of Baubee's Creek, a branch of the Rouge River. Although the formation of a parish was doubtless intended, no priest seems ever to have been stationed at Holy Cross, and the trend of development in the district left the church standing idle in the center of its graveyard. Long years afterward, when the necessity of a Catholic cemetery in the southwestern section of the city was evident, the site together with additional ground became Holy Cross Cemetery. The church was used as the cemetery chapel until it was destroyed by fire in 1908.[35]

The German Catholics, like their Irish brethren, worshipped at St. Anne's, and as a group were first cared for by Father Kundig. During the regime of Bishop Rese, no separate organization was effected in the city itself.[36] The only attempt in this direction was made by the colony, mentioned in the preceding chapter, living on the Hessian Road. The *Catholic Almanac for 1839* has this entry: "Chapel of the Assumption, not dedicated (German), Rev. Joseph Freygang."[37] Too temperamental to remain long in one place, the reverend gentleman soon deserted his congregation. However, it continued to be attended from the city until it became the Grotto parish, so well known to the older generation of Detroiters.

This completes the record for the city and its immediate vicinity. We must now try to survey the diocese although, in the absence of any detailed reports of Bishop Rese's several visitations, this can be done only imperfectly.

North of Detroit no progress whatsoever was made. In 1834 there

[34] *Berichte,* X, 26.
[35] The cemetery office on the right of the entrance gate stands on the site of the church.
[36] It is evident from the letter which begins this chapter that a German parish must have been planned by Father Kundig soon after his arrival. He began a separate baptismal register for his German Catholics on July 5, 1835, the date of the first entry in the records of the present St. Mary's register. Two years later the project was again taken up by another German priest not yet mentioned, Father Clement Hammer. Down to 1843 the German Catholics continued to worship in St. Anne's.
[37] "Freigang, Rev. Joseph, a native of Baden; came to this country in 1837; was first stationed at Boston, then at Detroit. From the latter place he came to the diocese of Cincinnati in 1840. . . . Contrary to the wishes of Bishop Purcell he organized St. Peter's congregation in Norwalk, and in doing so caused his bishop much trouble. He was dismissed in February, 1841. No other record of him." Houck, *op. cit.,* 104.

were two priests between Detroit and Port Huron; in 1840 there was one. Marine City was vacant, and was destined to remain so for the next fifteen years. While fairly content with his parish, Father Viszoczky had never given up hope of realizing the ambition that had called him from his native land. When the opportunity presented itself in February, 1835, of replacing Father Baraga at the Grand River mission he eagerly accepted it. The remaining seventeen years of his life were spent in Grand Rapids, where he witnessed the gradual transformation of an Indian settlement into a well-ordered American community.[38]

The next pastor of Marine City was Father Baraga himself. That he left his mission because of the opposition which the Indians themselves offered to his ministry is quite probable.[39] But another reason has been advanced which is just as credible, and which shows Father Baraga in a modern period involved in a situation akin to the dilemma that had confronted the Jesuit missionaries almost two hundred years before him.

The cession of the Ottawa lands north of the Grand River, which took place in 1836, was the result of a process that had begun in Father Baraga's time. To effect the peaceful withdrawal of the Indians the Government was compelled to secure the assent of a large number of petty chiefs. It was not averse to using the time-tried method of extracting concessions from the Indian, namely, giving him his fill of hard liquor. But the agents, and the traders in league with them, met unexpected resistance from the chiefs who had come under the influence of Father Baraga. He had always been particularly uncompromising in his stand against drunkenness, and had been able to instill a stern sobriety into a number of his converts. The Government did the expedient thing. It permitted the demoralization to proceed, and practically forced Father Baraga off the reservation and away from his mission because "he was disturbing the peaceful status of its Indians." [40]

With no thought of forsaking his missionary life, Father Baraga

[38] Father Viszoczky died January 2, 1852. The obituary notice in a Grand Rapids paper states: "Since the year 1835, Mr. Visoisky has been identified with the efforts, growth and prosperity of the Denomination of Believers in this Village . . ." The editor used a rather unusual designation for Catholics.

[39] Verwyst, *op cit.*, 153–56.

[40] The reason here given for Father Baraga's removal is the one advanced by Richard R. Elliott in the *Amer. Cath. Quat. Rev.*, XXI, 106–29. It seems to be well-founded, but the study lacks documentation. See also Rezek, *op. cit.*, I, 63. Before authoritative judgments can be passed on this and similar difficulties in the same field more research is necessary than anyone has thought it worth while to give. There is a mass of material available in Washington to some Catholic scholar who will write the history of the relations between the Government and the Church regarding the Indian missions.

came to Detroit in February, 1835, and was compelled to wait until June before he could begin in a new field. The intervening time he spent as pastor of the Marine City parish, and in the care of the Catholic families living along the St. Clair River up to Port Huron.[41] That there was no likelihood of his being weaned away from his career may be inferred from a reference to the school which his predecessor had started.

> . . . The seminarian, Mr. Kelly whom you sent in place of Mr. Cullen began school Wednesday the 22 of the month. He has 18 scholars but I hope that soon he will have more. The people are very glad that you have permitted me to reduce the price; and I now see that the only reason why they talked against Mr. Cullen's school was that the price was too high.
> Mr. Kelly lives with me in the rectory and boards one week with David Cottrell, another with George Cottrell and the third with Lambert Minnie. He pays a dollar a week for his board and washing and will get 4 shillings a month for each child. It is not very much but he says he is content. It is only on these conditions that scholars can be had in this miserable parish.[42]

Father Baraga's opportunity was not long delayed. In June he left Detroit with permission to devote himself to the Indians along the southern shore of Lake Superior. The location selected for the central mission was a tiny settlement on Madeleine Island in Chequamegon Bay called La Pointe. Here Father Baraga entered fairly upon his life work. For the next thirty-three years he was to live an amazing story of unwavering zeal, of personal holiness, of indifference to hardship that makes him as worthy of veneration as any of the great missionaries who had preceded him, and in whose footsteps he reverently trod.[43]

As a consequence of the missionary's departure, Father Bohême, stationed at L'Anse Creuse, remained the only resident priest north of Detroit. With occasional help from the Detroit clergy he continued to care for the Catholic population living along the shore and the waterways from Grosse Pointe to Port Huron. There is no record of his having gone further north. The Thumb of Michigan during the period we are dealing with was almost untouched by settlement.[44]

[41] Father Baraga writes to Bishop Rese at Pittsburgh that he has been on a ten day mission to Port Huron, and while there has contracted a fever. Letter dater May 21, 1835. NDA.
[42] Letter to Bishop Rese, April 25, 1835. NDA.
[43] Father Baraga died as first bishop of Marquette, January 19, 1868.
[44] The *Catholic Almanac* for 1839 lists the staff of the Cathedral as follows: Rt. Rev. F. Rese, D.D., Very Rev. Vincent Badin, V.G.; Rev. S.A. Bernier, Rev. Mr. Hammer. Father Bernier is stated to be attending Mt. Clemens on the last Sunday of the month, and St. Claire occasionally.

In the line of French settlements extending southward from Detroit to the Ohio border there were only two churches at the beginning of Bishop Rese's episcopate, one at Monroe, and the other at the Bay Settlement. The first addition came through the exertions of Father Vincent Badin. At the end of 1834 he supervised the erection of a small wooden church to serve the French group living near the mouth of the Huron River, and dedicated it to St. Vincent de Paul.[45] Although many years were to elapse before a resident priest lived beside it, Father Badin had taken the first step in organizing what is today the parish of Rockwood.[46]

The Bay Settlement, as the reader may remember, was the forerunner of the present parish of Erie. It appears for the first time in the *Catholic Almanac* for 1836 as a separate parish, and accredited with a resident priest in the person of "Rev. Mr. Terworen." This may have been the intention of the bishop, but was hardly that of the designated incumbent. An inspection of the parish records reveals that Father J. F. Tervooren, as he signs himself, performed a baptism in May, and a marriage in June of 1835. These are his only entries. He was evidently a Belgian or a Hollander, and after his brief sojourn in the Bay Settlement he disappeared into an obscurity as deep as that of his origin. In all likelihood he was not the first resident pastor, for Father De Bruyn, who is not named in the Almanac for 1835, signs a long series of entries in the register beginning with February 2, 1834, and ending March 3, 1835. After the departure of Father Tervooren the Settlement was with a priest for almost a year until Father Warlop came to begin his long pastorate.[47]

In the *Almanac* for 1839, two new parishes appear in the district: "Riviere aux Signes" and "Riviere aux Ecorces." [48] The first, Riviere aux Cygnes, as it should be written, or Swan Creek, designates the French settlement which is today the parish of Newport. A log chapel erected in 1838 justified the entry but there was to be no resident priest in the settlement until 1853.[49] With reference to Ecorse, the

---

[45] *Berichte*, X, 26.

[46] The church surrounded by its graveyard stood on the west side of the Dixie Highway where it intersects the present southern boundary of the village of Rockwood.

[47] He signs the register for the first time June 28, 1836, and ends June 26, 1853.

[48] In the *Almanac* the two places are bracketed as being under the care of "Rev. Mr. Bowens, General Missionary." In 1841–42 he is listed as pastor of St. Philip Neri. He signs some entries as "Charles Bauwens." Elliott was in error when he wrote in the *Amer. Cath. Quat. Rev.*, XXVI, 518, "This young priest of an excellent Belgian family died from malarial fever at the college soon after his ordination." Father Bauwens received dimmissorial letters from Bishop Lefevere addressed to the bishop of Ghent, January 21, 1844.

[49] "Until the year 1838 nothing was done toward the erection of a church, but in that year a modest log house was erected on the farm of Peter Allore, that place being located in the vicinity of the present church north of Swan Creek." John McClelland Bulkley, *History of Monroe County* (New York, 1913), II, 658.

Bishop Frederic Rese. From portrait in Archbishop's residence, Detroit.

building of a church at this date is not so certain. If local tradition is to be believed, the entry in the *Almanac* marks only the organization of a congregation which met at stated times for worship in a private dwelling.[50]

One parish in the district remains to be mentioned, St. Anthony's at Monroe. Father Carabin somehow carried through a project that had balked all his predecessors, the building of a suitable church. Its progress is recorded in the parish register.

> In the month of January, 1834, he (Bishop Rese) arrived, and commanded me to build a new church, promising to help me. The settlers squared timbers all that winter. The greater part of the bricks were burned in the following summer. The foundations were laid in the fall. The walls were erected in 1835, and the roof was placed in 1836. Bishop Rese returned from Rome in 1838, and helped me to finish the church by giving me $2400. In the month of May 1839, the church was dedicated by Rev. Mr. Kundig. . . .

Father Carabin himself was no better off than the priests who had given up the parish before him; he had merely a greater capacity for hardships. At least this can be inferred from the following account of him based on the recollections of eye witnesses.

> . . . The pastor was a Frenchman speaking very imperfect English. The English-speaking members of his congregation were in the minority; they attended Mass on Sundays at eight o'clock, at which hour the pastor always preached. At half-past ten he offered the Holy Sacrifice for the French families, who came swarming in from the prairies in little springless carts drawn by lively ponies, small but strong.
>
> The mother, holding the baby, sat in a chair, which occupied the middle of the cart. The children stood around her holding on to a railing which enabled them to keep an upright position and also kept them from falling out.
>
> The half-past ten o'clock Mass was always served by a venerable Frenchman, who sang the *Gloria, Credo* and *Sanctus* in the old Gregorian chant—and finally made the collection. The rain came through the roof and the snows of winter fell on the fingers of the officiating priest; the cold never shortened his sermons; he preached usually one hour. . . . One gloomy afternoon when it was too cold to snow, Father Carabin called at Mr. Scanlan's comfortable home; he was returning from a sick call eight miles out on the prairie; he had walked there and back; his patched boots were very thin and his flimsy coat was drawn together here and there with black thread by his own unskillful fingers; one of these "darns" had given way. This coat was buttoned up to his chin and Mrs. Scanlan could see no wristbands; evidently he wore no

---

[50] According to local tradition the first house of worship in Ecorse was the old LeBlanc homestead, a log house situated on what is now Jefferson Avenue, in the middle of the block between LeBlanc and White Streets.

shirt; he wore no overcoat. He was smiling cordially, but Mrs. Scanlan saw that he looked ready to faint. She brought her husband's wrapper and asked the exhausted priest to put it on while she repaired the rent in his coat. . . . When Mr. Scanlan came home in the evening he was informed that the pastor was starving and freezing. Without waiting for his supper Mr. Scanlan, taking with him a parcel containing all sorts of necessities, including bed-clothing, which his wife had ready for him, drove quickly in his double sleigh across the river. Father Carabin sat in his desolate room, without fire, or food; wrapped in his one poor blanket, he was reading his office, by the light of a short bit of candle . . .[51]

Although the English-speaking members of the parish were in the minority, they were numerous enough to contemplate starting one of their own, and they may have petitioned Bishop Rese to that effect. At all events, Father Ferdinand McCosker appeared in Monroe in 1834 to organize a separate congregation. Beyond his name nothing more is known of him than is recorded by Father Carabin: ". . . an Irish priest who remained here as pastor of the Irish until 1836, when he was suspended. He left in 1837." Later efforts to revive the project met with no success until St. John's opened its doors in 1873.[52]

The bulk of Irish immigration during Bishop Rese's regime apparently continued in its preference for the district lying about Ann Arbor. In 1835, Father O'Kelly, at Northfield, was given an assistant in the person of Father Thomas Morrissey.[53] Traditional accounts picture the two priests making long missionary circuits on horseback through Washtenaw, Livingston, Ingham, Jackson, Calhoun, and Oakland counties, saying Mass in private houses, and ministering to the tiny settlements that would later grow into parishes. The association was broken in the summer of 1837, when Father O'Kelly again became a pioneer in another section of the diocese. He was sent to organize a parish in Milwaukee, which up to that time had no Catho-

[51] Mary Angela Spelissy, "Sketch of the Life of Philip Francis Scanlan" in the *Records of the Amer. Cath. Hist. Soc.*, XI, 409–10. Philip Scanlan with his family came from Dover, N. H. to Monroe in 1836. Lack of school facilities for his children led him to move to Philadelphia, where he died in 1880. He was a scholarly and zealous layman. The quotation is taken from his reminiscenses as edited by his daughter.

[52] "That reverend gentleman (Ferdinand McCosker) came to Monroe in 1834, Father Carabin having been pastor of St. Mary's Church since 1832. He gathered the English-speaking Catholics, mostly Irish, in the little brick church which had been built in 1827 on the Fair Grounds, in the now Fourth Ward of Monroe City. However, Father McCosker did not succeed in effecting a lasting organization, and left the city in 1836, the Irish returning to St. Mary's church in 1845, when the Redemptorist Fathers built the new sanctuary and residence, and used the materials of the Fair Grounds church." These details from the booklet commemorating the 25th anniversary of St. John's church, Monroe, issued in 1898.

[53] His obituary notice in the Almanac for 1851, states that he was a native of Ireland, born at Maddleigo, Waterford County.

lic church, and had been visited occasionally only by Father Bonduel. Beginning his pastorate with the use of the court-house for Sunday services Father O'Kelly, in the summer of 1839, erected St. Peter's, the first Catholic church in Milwaukee, and the first cathedral of Bishop Henni.[54] His labors in this new field may be gauged from the *Almanac* for 1840, where Milwaukee appears for the first time: "Milvakie. Rev. Mr. Kelly, who visits alternately Racine, Mt. Pleasant, Rochester, Burlington, South Port, Pleasant Prairie, Salem."

Northfield again contributed to the development of the Church in Wisconsin when it was deprived of Father Morrissey, who was sent to rejoin Father O'Kelly, apparently, in 1839. Unlike his confrere, who returned to Detroit as we shall see, Father Morrissey spent the remainder of his life in Wisconsin. He was an indefatigable missionary, and there is scarcely an Irish settlement in the diocese of Milwaukee that was not visited by Father Morrissey in its pioneer days. He died at Spring Prairie, May 19, 1850, and was buried at Burlington.[55]

To replace Father Morrissey came the tall and fair-haired Father Thomas Cullen. A native of Wexford, he had come to Cincinnati as a seminarian in 1832, and had followed Bishop Rese to Detroit, where he was ordained in 1836.[56] He taught in the College of St. Philip Neri until the fall of 1839, when the institution was closed, and he was free to fill the vacancy created by Father Morrissey's departure. Father Cullen was quick to perceive that the most advantageous center for his missionary work was not Northfield but Ann Arbor. Accordingly he took up his residence in the flourishing little town that had become the western terminus of the Michigan Central Railroad in 1839, and the *Almanac* for 1841 named as his charge the towns of Ann Arbor, Northfield, Dexter, and Marshall.[57]

Northfield and Grand Rapids were the only settlements in the interior of the State that had resident priests in 1834. At the end of six years there was one more. It appears first in the *Almanac* for 1839: "Grand River (vicinity of,) German congregation, Rev. Mr. Kopp." The entry marks the beginnings of the church in Clinton County, for the locality so vaguely referred to is none other than that center

[54] Heffernan, *op. cit.*, 44.

[55] Obituary notice as in note 53.

[56] Details taken from a sketch of Father Cullen written by Richard R. Elliott, his personal friend, in the *Researches of the Amer. Cath. Hist. Soc.*, XIII, 177–85.

[57] The Detroit & St. Joseph Railroad was chartered June 29, 1832. It was taken over by the State in 1837, and renamed the Michigan Central. The road was opened to Dearborn in January, 1838, to Ypsilanti a month later, to Ann Arbor on October, 1839, to Dexter in 1840, and to Jackson in 1841. Burton, *op. cit.*, I, 685, 691. Father Cullen held services in private homes until he built a small frame church in 1843. See Louis William Doll, *The History of St. Thomas Parish, Ann Arbor* (Ann Arbor, 1941).

of vigorous Catholic life and piety, almost untouched by modern ways, the village of Westphalia. Its origin has been handed down to us in the microscopic writing of Father Anton, or Anthony Kopp.[58] On August 26, 1836, he and "a large number of farmers" sailed from Bremen, and landed in New York five weeks later. The party pressed on to Detroit and then to Ionia, where, in the recently opened land office, the immigrants could buy the most for their slender means. They had come as a unit, and they bought as a unit the lands on which their descendants live today.

Father Kopp went back and forth between Detroit and the settlement, in the interests of his colonists, and does not seem to have settled permanently with them until April, 1838. Their poverty made his lot a trying one, and he is careful at the end of every year to record the price of the staples of his existence. If we are to judge from his journal, the bright episodes of his life were the occasional missionary visits which he paid to a colony of Irish living on the "Bellevue Road." They were the neglected pioneers of what was long known as Hackett's Settlement, in southeastern Ionia County. He writes: "The Irish do more for the priest than either the Germans or the French."

To the north of Grand Rapids on the fringes of the State lay the missionary centers with which we are familiar. There is little to be recorded of them between 1833 and 1840 save for the changes that occurred among the clergy serving them.

At the Sault, Father Hätscher's success with the Indians so aroused the resentment of two local preachers that they incited their followers to acts of vandalism. After he had patiently repaired the damage his church was burned to the ground on the eve of All Saints, 1834.[59] Having erected a new structure in the summer of 1835, Father Hätscher remained at his post for another year, and was succeeded by Father Francis Xavier Pierz.[60]

Below the Sault lay Mackinac Island to which Father Bonduel was sent, as we have seen, in 1834. When he was assigned to Green Bay in 1838 to begin his long missionary career in Wisconsin, he was replaced by Father Toussaint Santelli.[61] Had he been as hardy as his countryman, Father Mazzuchelli, we might never have known what

[58] Father Kopp's journal covering the years from 1836 to 1840 is preserved in the Westphalia parish records.

[59] Rezek, op. cit., II, 45. This was perhaps a local manifestation of the wave of bigotry that was sweeping over the country at the time. In the preceding August the Ursuline Convent in Boston had been destroyed.

[60] Father Pierz, a famous missionary comparable only to his countryman, Father Baraga, was at L'Arbre Croche from 1839 to 1852, and then went on to the Indian missions in Minnesota. There is a good sketch of him in Rezek, op. cit., I, 344-59.

[61] Father Santelli signs the register from August 2, 1838, to August 5, 1843.

little we do about him. He wrote Bishop Blanc of New Orleans in 1841, asking to be received into his diocese because he could not bear the northern climate.[62] In his letter he stated that he was born in Italy, and was ordained in Milan. For five years he was rector of the Imperial College of Lodi. He was then dragged, as he says, into the missions of Michigan by Bishop Rese, and had been three years in America. His request was not granted, and the southernmost point that Father Santelli reached was Monroe, where he became Father Carabin's successor.

There remains the mission of L'Arbre Croche, where Father Saenderl had succeeded Father Baraga. With the exception of a year spent in Green Bay, whose significance we shall see later, he continued in charge of the mission until August, 1839, when he resigned his post in favor of Father Pierz, and left the diocese.[63]

Across Lake Michigan lay the other half of the diocese, Wisconsin Territory. In 1833 it held two priests, Father Hätscher at Green Bay, and Father Mazzuchelli at Fort Winnebago. When Father Hätscher went to the Sault in 1834 he was replaced by Father Van den Broek.[64] In 1835, Father Baraga began his ministry to the Indians from his headquarters at La Pointe.[65] The Redemptorists returned to Green Bay in 1836, and Father Van den Broek began a new Indian mission at Little Chute, thirty miles to the south on the Fox River. Father Mazzuchelli went to Ohio in the spring of 1835 to visit his brethren in Somerset, and then established himself at Dubuque, where, in the same year, he wrote the document inserted in the corner stone of St. Raphael's church.[66] At the beginning of 1839 there were four priests in Wisconsin, Father Bonduel at Green Bay, Father Baraga, Father Van den Broek, and Father O'Kelly at Milwaukee.

To complete the survey of the diocese we come to the extreme southwestern end of Michigan, to the St. Joseph mission. In answer to the entreaties of Pokagon, Father Badin had gone there, as we have seen, in 1830, to resume the missionary labors that had ceased with the retirement of the last resident Jesuit seventy years before. He took up his quarters in Pokagon's village, and the Indians gladly set to work to provide him with a mission house combining living quar-

[62] Letter from Mackinac, August 5, 1841. NDA.
[63] He returned to the diocese a few years later as we shall see.
[64] Theodore Van den Broek was born in Amsterdam, November 5, 1783. First a Francisan, and then a Dominican, he came from Holland to Springfield, Ky. in 1832. He accepted Bishop Rese's invitation to work in the Indian missions, and went to Green Bay in July, 1834. He died at Little Chute, November 5, 1851.
[65] The Almanacs for 1838-39 list Father Baraga as attending La Croix and Fond du Lac. The first should have been La Pointe.
[66] The Almanacs for the period station him at Prairie du Chien. He paid it only occasional visits.

ters and a chapel, which he solemnly blessed on the 21st of November.[67] The arrival of Father Deseille in 1832 left Father Badin free to enlarge the scope of his ministry. He thereupon purchased a large tract of land just over the Indiana line, and built another mission house and a school. His purchase is today the site of the University of Notre Dame. Some time in 1835, Father Badin retired from the Indian missions to spend his declining years as an honored veteran in the diocese of Cincinnati.[68]

Now that he was alone Father Deseille literally wore himself out in the service of his charges. He went back and forth constantly between Pokagon's village and another important mission center for the Potawatomi of northern Indiana which he established in Marshall County.[69] On one of his missionary tours late in September, 1837, he was taken violently ill at the mission house near South Bend. Certain of his approaching death, and fearful of dying without the last sacraments, he dispatched messengers to the two nearest priests, one at Chicago, and the other at Logansport. But the first was ill himself, and the second was away on distant missions. Father Deseille was at death's door when the tidings came. Summoning his last bit of strength he dragged himself from his bed to the rude altar of the mission house, groped for the door of the Tabernacle, and gave himself the Viaticum. A few of his faithful neophytes witnessed his final agony, and his body lay unattended for a day because, out of reverence, they feared to touch it.[70]

The death of Father Deseille, and the brutal transfer of the Potawatomi to western reservations which followed soon after, brought to an end the missionary phase of the Church in southwestern Michigan.[71] The era of organized parishes was at hand, and on this historic ground it began with the parish of Bertrand. On the east bank of the St. Joseph River, almost opposite Pokagon's village, Joseph Bertrand, a Frenchman with an Indian wife, had established a trading-post at least as early as 1812. After the Potawatomi ceded their lands to the

[67] The date is given in an account of Father Badin's activities in the *United States Catholic Miscellany* for August 27, 1831. A contemporary survey of the county preserved in the Chamberlain Memorial Museum at Three Oaks marks the precise location of Father Badin's mission house. It lay on the west side of the river in the rear of the property later known as the Charles L. Copp farm.

[68] Father Stephen Badin died in the home of Archbishop Purcell on April 21, 1853.

[69] Father Deseille's missionary labors are detailed in a long letter prepared by Bishop Bruté of Vincennes for the Leopoldine Association, but not printed in the *Berichte*. See the *Cath. Hist. Rev.*, I, 58. See also, Thomas T. McAvoy, C.S.C., *The Catholic Church in Indiana* (New York, 1940).

[70] There are varying accounts of Father Deseille's death, but all agree in the main. There is a lengthy article in the *Ave Maria*, I, 474 ff. See also, Rt. Rev. E. D. Kelly, *Correspondence of Rev. Louis Baroux* (Ann Arbor, 1913), 34–45.

[71] See the *Indiana Magazine of History*, XVIII, 258–66; 315–36.

Government in 1833, Bertrand acquired large holdings, and together with some shady associates—who later fleeced him—promoted the visionary city of Bertrand which was to rise around the old trading-post.[72] The project died from a fever of speculation, and only this much of its history concerns us, that the expectations it aroused found expression in the building of a rather pretentious church. There had always been a number of French settlers in the neighborhood, and tradition points to the presence of a log chapel in Bertrand at an early date.[73] But in 1837, when the vision was at its height, the primitive chapel was replaced by a brick structure, which was dedicated to St. Joseph.[74] In the *Almanac* for 1837, the parish appears for the first time, listed as in charge of Rev. Mr. Alwill.[75]

Here ends the survey of the diocese as it was during the episcopate of Bishop Rese. Outside of the city itself the signs of progress that marked the close of the period may be thus roughly summarized: A new center in Clinton County and in Milwaukee; some extension of the Indian missions through the labors of Father Baraga; a few of the old French settlements crystallized into parish organizations; the number of priests increased by, let us say, five.[76] The total is not impressive, but it reflects the conditions of the time, and could hardly have been greater. It must not be forgotten that the first wave of immigration into Michigan brought a predominantly Protestant population from the Eastern States. What little Catholic influx occurred during the period was practically submerged, and was too scanty to form definite groups for religious purposes save in the localities just dealt with. The real growth of the Church in Michigan was to come only from European immigration, and that tide had just begun to

[72] There is an interesting account of the origin of Bertrand in the *Mich. Hist. Colls.*, XXVIII, 128–33.

[73] The manuscript history of Bertrand quoted at the end of Chapter V has this passage referring to the old chapel at the St. Joseph Mission. "A Canadian trader by the name of Leclerc bought the chapel from one of the chiefs who had to flee the country. . . . This church was then torn down and removed four miles up the river to a place called Green Oak, now Bertrand. There is nothing now remaining of the building except two pieces of cedar logs . . . in the possession of Naw-Naw-qua-bee, the principal chief of the Potawattomies. . . ."

[74] "A log church was erected early at Bertrand trading-post, and in 1837 the brick church was erected at that place, which was organized as St. Joseph's church, and on Nov. 5, 1838, Joseph Bertrand, Edward Atherty, and Benjamin Bertrand were chosen trustees . . ." *History of Berrien and Van Buren Counties* (Philadelphia, 1880), 165.

[75] Father Alwill, or Alwell, is said to have come as a seminarian to Detroit, where he was teaching in St. Anne's Academy in 1836. *Amer. Cath. Hist. Researches*, XIV, 154. He was gone from Bertrand by 1840, and his subsequent career is unknown.

[76] The *Almanac* for 1834 gives the total number of priests in the diocese as 17. The same source in 1839 increases the number to 24. Probably neither total is correct. In 1838 Father Vincent Badin, as vicar-general, paid salaries to two priests recorded only by their surnames: Merz and Mills. No other trace of them appears.

flow. No matter how active may have been the zeal of Bishop Rese and his priests, they were thwarted by disheartening circumstances which only time could change.

Of the bishop's personal zeal for the welfare of his diocese there can be no doubt, but it is unfortunate that so little evidence of it can be adduced. While we have no records of his visitations, except the incomplete one for 1834, there are indications that he undertook the laborious task every year. Enough of his correspondence has been preserved to prove his deep interest in the Indian missions, and his persistent efforts to secure from the authorities just treatment of his Indian wards in accordance with treaty obligations. The educational projects which he fostered demonstrate how determined he was to build up a well-rounded Catholic life in his diocese. But of the details of his administration we know scarcely anything. There are no pastorals, if any were ever written, no sermons, no diocesan regulations, no records to shed any light upon the manner in which he exercised the distinctively pastoral duties of his office.

A like obscurity shrouds the problem presented by Bishop Rese's resignation. In April, 1834, Father Bonduel expressing the optimistic outlook of the episcopal household could write the confident letter that begins this chapter; in April, 1837, the bishop was in Baltimore proffering his resignation to the bishops assembled for the Third Provincial Council. He reminded them that he had reluctantly accepted the see of Detroit, and he gave as the reason for his present action that he had been so beset by trials and difficulties that his charge had become an intolerable burden.[77] The declaration is not only vague, but is unsupported by anything of a public nature that occurred during the bishop's tenure of office. Hence, in Detroit at least, there has been much speculation—some of it even prurient—endeavoring to account for the mysterious retirement of Bishop Rese from his diocese. Although we cannot hope to know all the factors that brought about the retirement, it is quite possible to dispel much of the mystery surrounding it by examining two somewhat singular episodes in which the bishop had a part.

The first concerns the Redemptorists whom we have already seen coming to Michigan in 1832. When Father Rese, as the agent of Bishop Fenwick, visited their superior in Vienna he was in search of priestly reinforcements for the diocese of Cincinnati. To Father Passerat, glad to contribute to the needs of a struggling diocese, the sending of his subjects was equivalent to the founding of a Redemptorist house in America. At first sight the antagonism between the

---

[77] The text of the letter of resignation is found in the official minutes of the Council. It is dated April 15, 1837.

two purposes is not apparent, but it was there nevertheless. Bishop Fenwick and his vicar-general planned to assign the newcomers to various posts as the need arose; they, on the other hand, came to America with the definite understanding that they were to live a community life so as to be able to follow the rules of their institute. Bishop Fenwick fell in somewhat with their plans when he offered them the Malcher farm. He consulted his own needs when he sent Father Saenderl to Green Bay, and left Father Hätscher in Detroit. The two priests accepted what they considered a temporary arrangement, but with no thought of abandoning an ideal to which religious obedience committed them.

When Father Hätscher went north to rejoin his companion he was buoyed up by the hope that at last the foundation was possible. One cannot help admiring the holy foolhardiness of the two priests trying to establish a monastery in the half-civilized settlement that was the Green Bay of their time. The attempt was doomed to failure not only on practical grounds but because Bishop Rese was not in sympathy with it. Discouraging letters went back to Vienna until Father Passerat decided to send a visitor to America in the person of Father Joseph Prost. He arrived in Detroit in the late summer of 1835, and on going to interview the bishop found Father Saenderl already there. If Father Prost was prepared to offer opposition to the bishop he was disarmed by the latter's tact and promises, and as a result of the interview he himself set out for Green Bay with Father Saenderl to begin the new establishment. Father Prost's disillusionment was not long in coming, and some rather sharp correspondence was exchanged between Green Bay and Detroit. Convinced that the foundation was impossible he came to Detroit in the spring of 1836 for a final interview with the bishop.[78]

The record of this meeting, preserved in the memoirs of Father Prost, has unusual value for our purpose.[79] It is a first-hand estimate of Bishop Rese written late in life when time should have erased whatever bitterness arose from the controversy.

> . . . I arrived in Detroit. My appearance there aroused great amazement. Still the bishop received me in his home with hospitality. The debates we had conducted in writing were now gone all over again in conversation. He told me that no one had ever spoken to him in this manner. He took his cross in his hand, and said that the crucifix consoled him in all his afflictions. He declared that he always had the best

[78] This summary exposition is merely a condensation of the matter in the Redemptorist *Annales* for the years in question. The same topic is treated in Henry Girouille, *Life of the Venerable Father Joseph Passerat* (London, 1929), 422–34.

[79] Late in life Father Prost wrote a *Relation* of his work in America. It has been printed in a supplement to the *Annales Cong. SS. Redemp.*

of intentions, but that he was always being misunderstood. He was right; not only we but all his clergy began to be dissatisfied with him. One of his best priests, the Rev. Mr. Kundig, told me this. Yet the bishop might notwithstanding have succeeded in softening me but for the warning the Rev. Kundig gave me. "Be steadfast, otherwise he will get the best of you. The bishop has the misfortune of trying to settle everything by shrewd politics. He always follows the crooked path, so that one never knows where he is headed for." This made me determined. . . . I am convinced that Bishop Rese sought only the best according to his own opinion. But unhappily the good man did not always understand what the best was, and often considered as such something which in reality was disastrous. His program was that one should as much as possible accommodate one's self to American ways. "Look here," he said to me, "the contemplative orders are useless for America. Take the poor Clares, for instance, whom I invited to come here from Pittsburg. I have put them to some practical use. . . ."

The second misfortune of this bishop was that he strove to accomplish everything by politics and devious ways. He wished to do good, but his methods were more worldly than apostolic. He preferred to promote the temporal prosperity of his diocese. Everybody became dissatisfied with him. . . . He himself came to see that his entire administration was a mistaken one, that lacked the blessing of God. In 1837 he appeared before the Provincial Council at Baltimore, and resigned his see. . . . Bishop Rese visited me after his resignation in Baltimore, and regretted sincerely that a breach had occurred between us. He came in all humility, and who would not have felt pity for him.

The upshot of the interview was that the Redemptorists left the diocese,[80] and that the first permanent house of the Redemptorists in America was opened at Pittsburgh in 1839.[81] What effect their going had on Bishop Rese's resignation is problematical. However, there are indications that his treatment of them brought him into disfavor with the Leopoldine Association, and that his administration was crippled by its consequent cautious generosity. The funds contributed by the European friends of the Redemptorists through the Society for the American foundation never quite reached their destination.[82] The Fathers kept on complaining, and their benefactors wondered. While Bishop Rese knew his needs better than any one, his withholding of designated gifts for purposes of his own was not calculated to increase the contributions of interested givers.

Apart from his comments on Bishop Rese's policies, the most important fact gleaned from Father Prost's narrative is that somehow

[80] *Relation* of Father Prost, 101–03.
[81] Father Saenderl remained in L'Arbre Croche until 1839, and Father Hätscher in Green Bay until replaced by Father Bonduel in 1837.
[82] *Relation* of Father Prost, 127.

the bishop had forfeited the confidence, respect, and sympathy of his priests. That good, kind Father Kundig could have made, under the circumstances, the remark attributed to him is most significant. A year later he wrote to Archbishop Eccleston: "If our Bishop has gone to Europe, which I have no reason to doubt, I am very uncertain of his intention to continue Bishop of Detroit, for though the Diocese will be the richest in the union, it is the poorest in piety zeal or order." [83] If this reflected the mind of his priests, the bishop may well have felt that his usefulness was, to say the least, seriously impaired.[84]

The second episode to be examined, which seems to bear more directly on Bishop Rese's resignation, is his altercation with the Poor Clares. From the scraps of information available it is hopeless to attempt to reconstruct the whole story, but its outlines are fairly apparent. Let us begin with the fact that at an uncertain date Bishop Rese was appointed Provincial or Superior of the Poor Clares in the United States. He proceeded to use his authority in an arbitrary and imprudent manner, if we can believe the confusing accounts that are extant. According to Father Prost, the bishop was determined to impose his ideas of usefulness upon the Sisters in the mother house at Pittsburgh. They firmly resisted policies which they regarded as an invasion of their rule, and for their resistence "they were driven from the convent as rebellious subjects by means of constables." [85] There may be some truth in this account, but there is another version of the trouble which is better substantiated.[86]

A candidate for admission into the Sisterhood at Pittsburgh had been rejected on account of her eccentric piety. She must have applied for reinstatement to Bishop Rese in his quality of Provincial for she was later teaching in the diocese of Detroit.[87] The storm arose when the bishop attempted her transfer to the mother house. Even under censures the Sisters refused to receive her, and persisting in

[83] Letter dated June 30, 1837. BCA.

[84] Father Stephen Badin in a letter to Archbishop Eccleston, dated March 24, 1840, pillories Bishop Rese in no uncertain terms for his treatment of his priests. Letter in BCA.

[85] Father Prost's *Relation*, 72–73.

[86] Two accounts varying slightly are found in Rev. Andrew A. Lambing, *Foundation Stones of a Great Diocese* (Pittsburgh, 1914), 329–31. Guilday in his *Life and Times of John England* (New York, 1927), II, 386–89, gives a version of Bishop Rese's difficulties which supplements Lambing's and which is founded on documents to which he had access in the Propaganda Congregation archives.

[87] The identity of the person in question is not clearly established in Lambing's account; she is known merely as Clara. If the point be worth establishing, she was most likely one of the Sisters with Father Van den Broek at Green Bay in 1834, and whom he describes as lowering into graves with their girdles the bodies of cholera victims. He states that they had been brought there by Father Mazzuchelli in 1833, and that their names were Clare and Theresa Bourdaloue. *Story of Father Van den Broek*, 50–52.

their refusal, they were forcibly ejected from their convent in May, 1835, by the agents of the bishop, who took over the property. The Sisters lodged a complaint in Rome, and the Propaganda Congregation, evidently not in sympathy with procedures which caused so much scandal, urged the bishop to settle the matter by more gentle measures. However, both sides stood firm, and in 1836 the Sisters were still under interdict, and deprived of the Sacraments, a condition which seems to have resulted from the concerted action of Bishop Rese and Bishop Kenrick of Philadelphia, who had been ordered to intervene.[88] On December 8, 1836, Bishop Kenrick received orders from Rome to remove the interdict, and two months later he was appointed Provincial of the Sisters, replacing Bishop Rese.

The Roman authorities may be presumed to have arrived at some sort of judgment regarding Bishop Rese's exercise of power not entirely favorable to him, and another phase of the trouble brought a sharp reproof. It will be remembered that Sister Francis Vindevoghel was wealthy in her own right, and that she had been dispensed by the Holy See from her vow of poverty to use her means for the establishment of her community in America. Her funds had made possible the houses in Pittsburgh, Detroit and Green Bay.[89] When the community was threatened with dissolution, Sister Francis tried to recover from Bishop Rese the amounts she had entrusted to him for her purpose, but without success. She appealed to Rome on that score, and the bishop was "reminded that such a transaction was sacred in the eyes of God, and would imperil his salvation.[90] As far as the Detroit house was concerned the situation was thus described by Father Stephen Badin in a letter to Archbishop Eccleston.

> The affairs of the Pittsburg convent are very probably known to you better than to me: and I will say nothing about them: but I will briefly relate something about that of Detroit, to which I was, with the Rev. Mr Kundig, an eye-witness. Bp. R. Received $2000 from Sister Frances Van de Voghel to purchase a Lot & houses in Detroit for the establishment of the Clarisses, & he caused the Deed to be made to himself. In order to recover her own property the sister was obliged to go to Rome, & obtained from the Cardinal Prefect of Propaganda an injunction to the Bishop to do her justice—I have read several times the original

[88] Bishop Kenrick was obliged to issue a card of explanation in the various Catholic periodicals. The *Shepherd of the Valley,* for instance, in its issue of August 29, 1835, published the bishop's explanation of the disturbance, which agrees substantially with version given above in the text.

[89] The Green Bay property was deeded to Sister Vindevoghel by Henry L. Baird on November 25, 1833.

[90] Guilday, as in note 86, 389.

letter and the translation in English. The Vic. Gen. refused to have any concern in the affair. The sister remained calm and silent—and finally had, besides the mortification, to bear the fatigues & expences of two sea voyages, to return to her native country, and robbed of her property, equally with a number of professed sisters, turned out in the wide world." [91]

Father Badin's evidently hostile criticism of Bishop Rese is introduced merely as first-hand evidence of a disagreeable situation existing in Detroit. To justify or to blame the bishop in this or in his other difficulties is not our concern. Unfortunately for his memory time has preserved nothing for his defense, but much that is derogatory. It would be neither just nor charitable to judge him from such one-sided evidence. But from the facts presented it is certainly permissible to conclude that the bishop's administration was anything but happy. Apart from the trials inherent in the care of an unwieldy and sparsely settled diocese, he involved himself in predicaments— both known and vaguely hinted at—which cast suspicion either on his motives or on his ability to govern. That he became discouraged and sick at heart, and sought escape is not surprising; his resignation is not so mysterious.

The sequel to Bishop Rese's resignation is an interesting story in itself with its own lights and shadows. A week after the bishop had been heard, the Fathers of the Council sent a joint letter to the Holy See recommending that the resignation be accepted.[92] At the same time they suggested three candidates for the see.[93] But the Roman authorities were unwilling to take action until they could confer with the bishop, and he was therefore summoned to Rome. He apparently met with paternal admonitions and encouragement instead of censures, for his resignation was not accepted, and he was directed to return to his diocese.[94] Before doing so, Bishop Rese spent some months in Europe, and unfortunately again incurred the displeasure of the

[91] The quotation is a postscript to Father Badin's letter already referred to. The Detroit house of the Poor Clares was abandoned in 1839 as well as the other foundations in the United States. As far as is known Sister Francis returned to Belgium with the majority of her Sisters.

[92] Copy in DCA. Many of the details here presented come from a series of documents obtained from the Propaganda Archives by Msgr. Frank O'Brien of Kalamazoo, who had devoted many years to historical research. The documents bear no file numbers, but only a serial number given them by the secretary who transcribed them. They will here be referred to as the O'Brien documents. The joint letter of the bishops is No. 2.

[93] The names proposed, and their order, were as follows: John Mary Odin, later Archbishop of New Orleans; Matthias Loras, first bishop of Dubuque; Peter Richard Kenrick, who died as archbishop of St. Louis.

[94] That Bishop Rese went to Rome, and was told to return to his diocese, is stated in No. 10 of the O'Brien documents.

Holy See by collecting funds for his diocese, something which he had evidently been forbidden to do.[95]

On his return to the United States in July, 1838, Bishop Rese came to Detroit, and resumed his duties by undertaking a visitation of his diocese. He went to the extreme end of it, to Father Baraga's station at La Pointe, and the missionary describes the joy of his people, the majority of whom had never beheld a bishop.[96] Although the bishop's visit was unexpected, Father Baraga's charges were not unprepared for Confirmation, and the sacrament was administered to one hundred and twenty individuals.

But despite this zealous resumption of his work, the chapter of Bishop Rese's misfortunes was not closed. Impossible as it is to explain, the fact remains that the bishop returned to Detroit to find another summons to Rome awaiting him.[97] Perhaps new complaints had been lodged against him, or he may not have complied with certain imposed requirements. It may be that Rome was still unsatisfied with whatever course he had followed in settling his financial difficulties with the Poor Clares. This might be read into the following fragment of a letter written while on his way to Rome.

. . . I have had Mr. Quarter write to you that I have nothing more to do with the convent at Pittsburgh because, as you also know, I had already retransferred the property to the Mother Abbess. I would be losing my head completely if I were still willing to pay the debts that the Mother contracted in Pittsburgh after so much trouble. . . . I leave tonight for Rome from which I hope to return in a few months. My blessing to all my clergy and diocesans, who, I hope are all in good health. . . .[98]

Having appointed Father Vincent Badin to care for the diocese during his absence, Bishop Rese sailed for Europe at the end of May, 1839.[99] In Rome the procedure was almost a repetition of what had happened in 1837. Again the bishop tendered his resignation, and again it was held in abeyance.[100] The Holy See took no action until it could consult for a second time the American bishops assembled

[95] Guilday, as in note 86.
[96] *Berichte,* XII, 72.
[97] The summons was enclosed in a letter from Archbishop Eccleston to Bishop Rese, dated September 15, 1838. NDA.
[98] Only the date of the letter remains, July 17, 1839, and there is nothing indicating to whom, or from what place the letter was sent. NDA.
[99] Bishop Rese wrote a final letter of instruction to Father Vincent Badin from New York, May 20, 1839. NDA.
[100] O'Brien documents. No. 10.

for the Fourth Provincial Council in May, 1840. They reaffirmed the expediency of the resignation, and their decision accompanied the result of the Council's deliberations carried to Rome by Bishops Rosati of St. Louis, Miles of Nashville, and Portier of Mobile.

The oral explanations of the three American bishops brought the matter to a final decision, and Bishop Rese was directed to draw up a formal letter of resignation. Its contents, or the honorable terms on which he was allowed to retire, must dispose effectively of suspicions that he was being penalized for any delinquency. It clearly proves that the Holy See was concerned with the methods or policies of the bishop's administration, and that after its own investigation it did no more than concur in the bishop's own admission that he was unequal to the regimen of a diocese.

Bishop Rese's resignation was signed on August 19, 1840. In it he laid down three conditions: 1. He was to remain bishop of Detroit in fact, but the diocese was to be governed by a coadjutor to whom he would delegate full authority. In return for this delegation he was to be made a titular archbishop. 2. He was to receive an income of a thousand dollars a year from the diocese. 3. He was to be free to live wherever he pleased.[101]

The resignation as proposed was accepted, and thus ended the career that had begun so full of promise six years before.[102] But Bishop Rese had scarcely entered upon the peace and obscurity that he desired when his misfortune, that had been so charitably shielded by the Roman Court, was blazoned to the world from an unexpected quarter. At the time, the Native American Party was lashing itself into the fury that broke out in 1844. A certain Bernadino Castelli, possibly, as has been asserted, a renegade Italian priest, saw in the case of Bishop Rese, of which he must have had some knowledge, a rare opportunity to inflame the fanaticism of the Protestant body. In Washington itself he addressed a letter on July 14, 1841, to Daniel Webster, then Secretary of State, calling attention to the sad plight of Bishop Rese, an American citizen, who was languishing in a Roman prison.

> . . . In 1839 when I made his acquaintance, he was confined in a convent under an ecclesiastical persecution. On the process being completed, he was ordered to resign. This he refused to do; and then he

[101] *Ibid.*, No. 7.

[102] *Ibid.*, No. 6. Although in this document the Holy Father is said to agree to the titular archbishopric, there is no evidence showing that Bishop Rese ever held such a title. The pension was arranged in terms of Italian scudi giving it a value of about $970.

was thrown into a dungeon, perhaps of the Inquisition, where three other Bishops are also lying. . . ."[103]

The Secretary was urged to invoke the intervention of the United States "to cause the Papal government to be called to account for such a scandalous abuse of its spiritual powers." The charges were soon made known to the Press, and the country fumed with denunciations of the Pope and all his works.[104]

In due time the State Department instructed Lewis Cass, then Minister to France, to investigate. He consulted the Papal Nuncio at Paris, who had to do no more than produce the following letter from the Cardinal Prefect of the Propaganda to prove the charge unfounded.

> . . . On receipt of your letter of August 21st concerning the person of Mgr. Rese, Bishop of Detroit, I consider it my duty to inform you that the rumors of the imprisonment of the said prelate in Rome are quite untrue. For, having come to Rome in the autumn of 1837, and remaining a long time in that, and other cities of Italy, Mgr. Rese was always free, and having thereafter traveled in Germany, Flanders, and France, he returned to America in 1839. He came to Rome again in the summer of 1840, and while there was always at liberty, and that he was not deprived of it afterwards is proved by the fact that he has actually been living for several months in his native town of Hidesheim in Hanover . . .[105]

The State Department should have investigated Castelli, and not the Papal Court. How he was prevailed upon to confess his imposture is not known, but at all events he retracted his charges. The *Detroit Daily Free Press* for January 26, 1842, carried the following notice copied from the *Philadelphia Ledger*: "Castelli has recently published another letter, in which he says that his former statement was in no respect true, but was dictated merely by human passion."

[103] Another letter of the same tenor was writen from New York, August 7, 1841. Both letters are in the State Department Archives, and there are copies of them in the BHC.

[104] The story was revived as late as 1872 in an article published in the *Chicago Post*. Burton, *op. cit.*, II, 1305.

[105] Letter of the Cardinal Prefect of the Propaganda to Msgr. Garibaldi, Nuncio at Paris, September 11, 1841. O'Brien documents, No. 8. In the *Philadelphia Catholic Herald* for *July 22*, 1841, appeared the following item, written apparently by the editor. "An absurd tale regarding the Roman Inquisition and the Bishop of Detroit has appeared in some of the daily papers on the authority of an Italian who is stated to be a Catholic priest, but who, although he is said to pass himself off as such, has never received any sacred orders in the Catholic Church. The present writer has seen Bishop Rese publicly in the streets of Rome, and at that time he resided in the convent attached to the church of San Lorenzo in Lucina, where we are confident he still continues, as we have a few months since seen his name mentioned in the Tablet as officiating at the obsequies of the late Princess Borghese in that church."

The letter of the Cardinal Prefect discloses that Bishop Rese was living at Hildesheim toward the end of 1841. There is no further trace of how or where he spent the next eighteen years of his self-chosen retirement. In 1869 a German correspondent of the *Katholische Volkzeitung* of Baltimore having noticed an article referring to the Diocese of Detroit wrote that he could add some interesting information.[106] Six or seven years back he had been visiting in Hildesheim, and on several occasions he had watched a group of Sisters escorting to the cathedral a wizened old man who clutched nervously at a pectoral cross. Upon inquiry he learned that the decrepit invalid was Bishop Rese of Detroit, and he was successful in locating a nephew of the bishop, who gave him what knowledge he possessed concerning his maternal uncle.

The nephew related some details regarding the bishop's early life, details with which we are already familiar. He remembered that his uncle, as Bishop of Detroit, had visited his relations. For a long stretch of years thereafter he had been unheard from. About 1860 word had come from a town in Switzerland that a stranger, who was ill, claimed to be a bishop, and a native of Vienenburg. When his identity had been established he had been sent to Vienenburg, and afterward to Hildesheim. His personal effects had been forwarded from Marseilles, France. Although the family had reason to believe that he had gone to Africa even after his resignation no knowledge of the bishop's past could be gained from conversation with him. He had no sense of time relation, and was continually slipping from one language to another.[107]

Fortunately this account can be officially verified. There is a sheaf of documents relating to Bishop Rese in the Chancery at Hildesheim, and the first in point of time is the following letter from the Royal Notary at Vienenburg to the Chancery, and dated April 13, 1859.

The Bureau of the Rt. Rev. Vicar-General has, by order of this office, already been informed through Mr. Multhaupt, a hotel owner, that the Catholic bishop, Frederic Rese, formerly a legal resident of Vienenburg, has arrived in Hanover from Basle in impaired bodily health, and in a depressed mental state, and that his condition therefore demands care and supervision.

Nothing can be done for him here in view of the lack of medical and hospital facilities, not to mention the fact that the townsmen have protested against such a charge being laid upon them on the ground that

106 The correspondent's letter is in the issue for November 13, 1869.
107 It has been frequently stated that the bishop was already impaired in mind when he left Detroit to tender his resignation, and that it was accepted for that reason. No basis for such a statement is in evidence, and it is more likely a pious fiction resorted to in an effort to cover up a disagreeable situation.

Bishop Rese is no longer a legal resident of Vienenburg. However, it seems highly undesirable that a person who once held so exalted an office in the Catholic Church should be permitted, in his present mental condition, to remain in a town where the population is to some extent non-Catholic.

For these reasons I make bold to presume that the bureau of the Rt. Rev. Vicar-General will be willing, if it be at all possible, to secure accommodations and medical aid for Bishop Rese, either in the monastery of the Capuchin Fathers or in that of the Carthusians. I humbly urge that the steps necessary for this arrangement be taken at once, and that notice of whatever decision is arrived at be sent to me as soon as possible.

I also wish to state further that papers found on the person of Bishop Rese indicate that he is the possessor of several thousand dollars, and that it is probable that a legal guardian will shortly be appointed for him in the person of the hotel owner, Multhaupt.

For the present, Bishop Rese will remain, by order of the Royal Commissioner of Police, in the hospital at Hanover and I most respectfully suggest that your bureau confer directly with the Commissioner regarding the removal of Bishop Rese to Hildesheim.[108]

As the result of this communication Bishop Rese was, within a few days sheltered in the hospital of the Sisters of Mercy at Hildesheim. There for the remaining twelve years of his life he found peaceful asylum from the buffets of an unkindly world. He was almost eighty-one years old when he died on December 30, 1871.[109] His funeral service was held in the Dom on New Years Day, and he lies buried in the cloister-yard so close to the cathedral apse that over his grave drift the fallen leaves of the heaven-sent token to Louis the Pious, the thousand year rosebush of Hildesheim.[110]

[108] On the occasion of a visit to Hildesheim in 1930 Monsignor Edward J. Hickey of Detroit secured transcripts of all available material relating to Bishop Rese in the Hildesheim Chancery archives. This letter is among the transcripts.

[109] This is the date as officially recorded in the Hildesheim Chancery.

[110] As the legend runs Louis the Pious once went on a hunting trip, and in order not to omit his daily devotions he brought along his chaplain and the requisites for the celebration of Mass. On returning to his palace he discovered the loss of a precious reliquary. The chaplain, having been sent into the forest to search for it, beheld it hanging on a rosebush from which it could not be dislodged even by his utmost efforts. The Emperor, interpreting this prodigy as a sign from heaven, built a church near the rosebush, and the site was the same as the one now occupied by the cathedral of Hildesheim. The renowned rosebush, in vigorous life since the beginning of the ninth century is pictured in the Catholic Encyclopedia clinging to the apse of the cathedral. See also R. Herzig, *Der Dom zu Hildesheim* (Hildesheim, 1929).

CHAPTER XX

Bishop Lefevere

THE EPISCOPATE OF BISHOP LEFEVERE

ONCE Bishop Rese had definitely relinquished the government of his diocese the Roman authorities were confronted with the problem of choosing his successor. Of the three nominees presented by the Third Provincial Council only one was available. Father Loras had already became bishop of Dubuque, and Father Kenrick was not yet ready to give up his long-cherished desire to affiliate with the sons of St. Ignatius. There remained Father Odin, whose candidacy was strongly supported by Bishop Rosati.

In the solution of the difficulties arising from Bishop Rese's resignation the Bishop of St. Louis was the dominant figure. He had consecrated Bishop Rese, had been his confidant, and was therefore fully acquainted with the state of affairs in Detroit. When he went to Rome in 1840, as we have seen, the authorities deferred entirely to his judgment and informations regarding the resignation, and the final settlement of the matter was the result of conferences held with the Propaganda Congregation and with Bishop Rese.[1] The vacancy at Detroit gave him the opportunity of championing not only a candidate proposed by the Council but a priest of his own diocese, a Lazarist like himself, and a man whose virtues and abilities were manifest.[2]

Accordingly, John Mary Odin was named Coadjutor Bishop of Detroit toward the end of 1840.[3] At the time, the prospect of such a dignity was farthest from his mind. He had been nearly a year in the Republic of Texas endeavoring to revive the Catholicity which had almost expired under the Mexican regime. In May, 1841, he returned

[1] Rothensteiner, *op. cit.*, I, 787–92.

[2] Father Odin, born in France in 1801, joined the Lazarist congregation in Paris, and came to America in 1822 to complete his studies for the priesthood. After his ordination he was for years attached to the Lazarist house and seminary at the Barrens, near St. Louis.

[3] On December 4, 1840, Bishop Rese conveyed to John Mary Odin, "Coadjutor of the aforesaid bishopric of Detroit," all the property of the diocese. The conveyance was made in the presence of George W. Greene, American Consul at Rome, and was witnessed by Bishop Rosati and Father Joseph A. Lutz. Document in DCA.

to St. Louis for a conference with his superior, and on the way visited Bishop Blanc of New Orleans. To his amazement he was presented with the Bulls for his consecration which had just arrived. But he could not be persuaded to accept them without hearing the decision of his superior. He hastened to St. Louis, and the decision was this:

> Mons. Odin, good men can easily be found for the Bishopric of Detroit, where things are already in a prosperous way; but it would be difficult to find a competent person now to take so poor and difficult a post as yours in Texas; hence I think it more for the glory of God and the good of souls that you send back the Bulls and return to your post.[4]

As the result of his humble obedience Father Odin became the Apostle of Texas.[5] But the vacancy at Detroit was still unfilled, and the Roman authorities must have again taken counsel with Bishop Rosati. No one else could have suggested the obscure missionary who had gone to Europe with his bishop to recuperate his strength, and who was then at home in his native Belgium. On July 23, 1841, Peter Paul Lefevere was named Bishop of Zela, *in partibus*, Administrator of Detroit, and Coadjutor to Bishop Rese with right of succession.[6] His first impulse was to refuse the dignity, and only the peremptory command of the Holy See made him accept what he believed to be an overwhelming responsibility. Late in the fall of 1841 he returned to the United States with Bishop Rosati, and proceeded directly to Philadelphia for his consecration. He received it at the hands of Francis Patrick Kenrick, then Coadjutor bishop of Philadelphia, assisted by Bishops England and Hughes. The ceremony took place November 24, in the church of St. John the Evangelist.

We must now trace the antecedents of the man so providentially chosen to rule the church of Detroit. He was born at Roulers, April 29, 1804, the son of Charles Lefevere, a farmer in good circumstances, and Albertine Muylle.[7] From his boyhood his thoughts were directed to the priesthood by his pious mother, and at sixteen he entered the preparatory seminary of his native town. He left it in 1825 to continue his studies in the Lazarist seminary in Paris. Here, through his acquaintance with the work of the Congregation in the diocese of St. Louis, he decided to devote his life to the American missions. He came to the United States in the spring of 1828, completed his theo-

---

[4] Richard H. Clarke, *op. cit.*, II, 213. The superior who so decided was Father John Timon, who later became the first bishop of Buffalo.

[5] Father Odin was consecrated Vicar-Apostolic of Texas, March 6, 1842. In 1847 the state became a diocese with the see at Galveston. In 1861 Bishop Odin succeeded Bishop Blanc as Archbishop of New Orleans. He was taken ill while attending the Vatican Council, and died in France, May 25, 1870.

[6] Bulls in DCA.

[7] Information from parish records of Roulers.

logical course at the Barrens, and was ordained to the priesthood by
Bishop Rosati, November 20, 1831.[8]

For a year after his ordination Father Lefevere was assistant at
New Madrid, the historic parish in which Father Gibault had died.[9]
He was then transferred to the Salt River Mission, where he began
his pastorate in January, 1833. A considerable number of Catholic
emigrants from Kentucky and Maryland had been drifting into
northern Missiouri, and the largest group was established on both
sides of the Salt River in the extreme northeastern corner of Ralls
County. Here Father Lefevere began his missionary career, seven
years of toil and hardship through which he drove with indomitable
energy and zeal. Nominally pastor of St. Paul's, as the congregation
was called, he was in reality the pastor of a fallow parish a hundred
miles wide and a hundred and seventy-five miles long, split in two by
the broad highway of the Mississippi. St. Paul's lay near the river just
halfway between St. Louis and the northern boundary of the state.
The opposite bank bounded Illinois, whose western half was under
the jurisdiction of Bishop Rosati, and north of a line drawn eastward
from St. Louis there was only one priest, Father St. Cyr at Chicago.
Any Catholic within fifty miles of the Mississippi from Dubuque to
St. Louis had no other priest to send for but Father Lefevere. What
this situation entailed may be gathered from his letters.

> . . . The cholera has been more fatal in Palmyra than in any other
> place I have ever heard from. Out of a population of six hundred and
> odd souls 109 persons have fallen victims to that disease . . . I at-
> tribute it to a special favor of God that I have escaped the disease; for
> during eighteen days I have been continually exposed to all that spell
> of weather, which caused every creek and water-course to be past ford-
> ing, being wet to the skin every day by a hard beating rain, or by swim-
> ming or high fording . . .[10]
> . . . This missionary visit took me about three months, during which
> I never could pass more than three nights in the same place. I went from
> Atlas to the head of the Rapids, forty or fifty miles backward and for-
> ward in the interior of the country, continually hunting after some
> Catholics that were newly come to this section.
> Then I returned on this side of the Mississippi among the Half In-
> dians and in the New Purchase where the Catholics are increasing very
> fast. . . . When I reached Salt River after a mission of 18 days, I had no
> sooner received your letter of the 9th of August . . . but another one
> was handed to me which called me in all haste into the state of Illinois,

[8] Ordination certificate in DCA.

[9] Rothensteiner, op. cit., I, 370–78.

[10] Ibid., I, 570. There is a series of Father Lefevere's letters in the St. Louis Chancery
archives. Many of them are given at length in the volume quoted.

to assist two persons at the point of death. So that, although much fatigued and thinking to be at my journey's end, I was obliged to set out again, and ride in full speed upwards of a hundred miles to the County of McDonough, where, instead of two, I found numbers of Catholics dangerously sick of the bilious and congestive fevers, which complaints were so prevailing there and in the adjacent counties, that I have been all this while so intensively engaged in visiting and assisting the sick in various parts of Illinois, that I could not find leisure, many a time, to say my office, and have often been in danger of perishing in the difficult crossing of swamps and high watercourses . . .[11]

In 1837, Father Lefevere sent to his bishop a detailed report of his missions.[12] He ended by thus describing his work.

Such is the statement, Right Rev. Sir, I can give in answer to the several questions you have asked me. These stations above named, together with the numerous families widely scattered in remote parts of the same and other counties, keep me continually travelling from one part of the country to another, and were I to go whithersoever Catholics dispersed in the country invite and beg me to come, one trip would take me six months steady riding.

And although these Catholics ought to be visited, yet it is absolutely out of my power. For no sooner had I ended one journey, then I have to commence another, and so in rotation; so much so that in the course of the year, I cannot remain one week steady at home. And particularly this last winter, during the coldest weather, at a time when I thought to enjoy a few days for myself, I was called out to the sick; three times into the State of Illinois, once to the River Des Moines, and once into Wisconsin territory, 150 miles north from Ralls County; and that at a time when the snow was about eighteen inches deep on the ground, and I had to ride a distance of twelve miles on the ice on the Mississippi. Then on my return the weather breaking up with a sudden thaw, the waters began to run so swiftly that I was compelled to travel all the night and in full speed in order to get the start of the high waters, and it was then only by lucky circumstances, or the special Providence of God that I, several times, escaped being drowned. I must finish this tale for fear of being prolix. . . .

Father Lefevere went on to remind the Bishop rather bluntly that he had been neglecting this portion of his diocese, and that he had neither confirmed in nor visited any congregation of the Salt River

[11] *Ibid*, I, 579.

[12] *Ibid.*, 581–83. Father Lefevere states that he visits from one to two thousand souls in Missouri distributed through fourteen congregations and eight stations. "In the State of Illinois: 1, in Adams County, in the town of Quincy; 2, in Hancock County at the Head of the lower Rapids; 3, at the Head of Crooked Creek, twenty-five miles east from Commerce; 4, in the northwest corner of Fulton County, on Cedar Creek. In the Wisconsin territory; 1, at Keokuk, in Half Indian tract between the river Des Moines and the Mississippi; 2, on Skunk River, ten miles west from Fort Madison . . ."

Mission. Bishop Rosati's answer was a visitation of the entire field in the fall of 1838. In his diary, referring to the Salt River congregation, he wrote:

"We visited the Church of St. Paul, which is a wooden building, but beautiful in its simplicity and poverty. Near the church there is a cemetery and a garden and the house of the pastor which is very small. Reverend M. Lefevere deserves great commendation for the care with which he keeps all things in church and house in decent, neat, and orderly condition." And when the visitation was completed, the Bishop's final comment was this: "M. Lefevere keeps his Churches and congregations in the best order. The people are very good practical Catholics." [13]

The seven years of arduous missionary labors just described were Father Lefevere's only preparation for the episcopate. At their close he was a man of thirty-six, grave and somewhat taciturn, and inured to poverty and hardship. With his rugged strength and courage he advanced and held a salient in the advancing line of the Church on the western frontier. His absolute faithfulness to the ideals of his calling had ingrained a stern devotion to duty, and a meticulous care in its fulfillment. Herein lay precisely his peculiar fitness for the position he was destined to fill.

Detroit was still in every sense a pioneer diocese. The three shadowy years of Bishop Rese's episcopate had been merely an episode with scarcely any bearing on the development of the diocese, and which left little more behind it than problems for his successor to solve. Whatever may have been the ability and endowments of Bishop Rese, organization and administration were certainly not his forte. His thoughts were so fixed on the glorious future that he neglected to make any solid provisions for it. The effects of his leadership ended with his resignation, and in the period of uncertainty that followed with its sense of failure and its vanished hopes the diocese sank to what it had been in 1833, merely a geographical area containing an indefinite Catholic population.

This was the legacy bequeathed to Bishop Lefevere, a magnified Salt River Mission. His predecessor, gratified with the gifts of the Leopoldine Association, had written, "Now I can appear as a bishop should." Bishop Lefevere had no such concern: under his purple he remained the missionary, who continued to wear the square-toed boots of his hard-riding years along the Mississippi. Although he accepted his charge with trepidation and misgiving, he took hold of it with the same courage, tireless energy, and grasp of detail that had marked his previous labors. His tenure lasted twenty-seven years, and

[13] *Ibid.*, I, 589.

at its close the Diocese of Detroit, in the sense of a compact, well-organized unit of the Church in the United States, was an accomplished fact. Every phase of diocesan activity begins with him. The magnificent growth of today rests squarely upon the solid foundations which he left to his successors.

Bishop Lefevere's first official act, while he was still in Philadelphia after his consecration, was the addressing of a pastoral to his flock. A passage from it discloses his humility and sincerity, and breathes the spirit that animated his episcopate.

> We feel ourselves pressed forward by the charity of Christ, and we are ready to make every sacrifice, and to endure all hardships, to supply in our own person what may be wanting for the application of His sufferings and death to the souls of men. The piety and zeal of our venerable brethren the clergy, who have labored with such fidelity and perseverance, encourage us; and we trust, with their cooperation, to cultivate successfully the portion of the vineyard committed to our care. We shall endeavor with them to be the models of the faithful in word, in conversation, in charity, in faith, in chastity. Having been inured to the labors of a missionary life for many years in a remote part of the diocese of St. Louis, we feel ready to share with you, venerable brethren, all the labors of the ministry; and we are ambitious of no distinction, except that imposed on us by our station, of greater solicitude for the souls entrusted to us, and of greater zeal for our own perfection.[14]

Equally typical of Bishop Lefevere was perhaps his first public act in his diocese. He arrived in Detroit a few days before Christmas, and on the festival he ascended the pulpit, not with joyous greetings to the cathedral congregation, but with a denunciation of intemperance. He wrote to Bishop Purcell:

> Seeing the great & many evils that have resulted & are still daily resulting from even the moderate use of intoxicating liquors, and the immediate necessity of a reform in the clergy as well as in the laity, I delivered my first sermon last Christmas to the French congregation of St. Ann's on temperance & the great necessity of a total abstinence society. . . . In order to give the example and make a start, I with my seminarians, took the total abstinence pledge at the altar immediately after high mass. I had the soul moving pleasure of being followed by upwards of two hundred of the French congregation. I hope to see that society established in every part of my diocese, & with the clergyman at the head of it . . .[15]

[14] The pastoral was printed at Philadelphia in pamphlet form. There is a copy in the DCA.
[15] Letter dated February 24, 1842. Letter Book I, DCA.

The most urgent problem confronting Bishop Lefevere at the beginning of his administration was the necessity for relieving the diocese from the financial embarrassment under which it lay. The correspondence of the period discloses that Bishop Rese, from the time of his entry into Detroit, had had in mind the acquisition of large holdings in land from which the Church was presumably to profit at a later date. At this distance it is impossible to ascertain the details of his plan—if he had one—or the extent to which it was carried out; but this determination on his part is fairly evident.[16] To acquire unproductive land was easy enough; to retain it against mounting taxes was another matter. When Bishop Lefevere, therefore, took charge of what he rightly considered the patrimony of the diocese, he saw with dismay that he could not hope to hold it intact. He poured his troubles into the kindly ears of the French missionary society.

> I have not only the honor but the duty of expressing my gratitude for the interest that you have shown for the welfare of the poor diocese of Detroit by sending me a check for 6421 frs. . . . . I have just been made Administrator of the vast diocese of Detroit, which comprises the State of Michigan and the Territory of Wisconsin, and which for the last three years has been, so to speak, entirely abandoned. Here I am absolutely lacking in everything, and yet every day I am burdened by new debts and new demands for money from every side, and lawsuits against the various churches and their property. I know not what to say or what to do. . . . . I see clearly that without some extraordinary help from the Propagation of the Faith, on which I build all my hopes, I can not even remain here, much less accomplish anything. . . . . In the mission of Mr. Vizosky one of the finest churches of the diocese has already fallen into the hands of the Protestants for lack of means. I can still reclaim it by paying $3000. Many parcels of land belonging to the Church in several localities of the diocese have been confiscated by the government, or have fallen into the hands of others for arrears of taxes. If we do not pay more than $600 in back taxes on these properties we shall lose them all, and be forced besides to pay the cost of legal proceedings. Nearly all of our churches and their properties are in that condition because of extreme negligence. . . .[17]

To make matters worse the bishop's control of even the cathedral parish was insecure. In May, 1834, the Corporation of St. Anne had

[16] Bishop Purcell wrote to Bishop Blanc: "It is said by the two Revd. Badins who were here this week that Bishop Lefevere has given up to the state of Michigan nearly all the lands of the Church as they were not worth paying taxes, which are enormous, on them." Letter dated December 13, 1842. NDA.

Describing his situation to Father Deluol, the Sulpician superior at Baltimore, Bishop Lefevere stated that "the affairs of the diocese at Large, & the so highly boasted land property of Dr. Rese is in a most wretched condition." Letterpress copy, February 24, 1842. DCA.

[17] Letter dated February 15, 1842. Letter Book I, DCA.

leased its properties and the church to Bishop Rese and his successors for a period of 999 years.[18] The transfer was contingent upon certain obligations to the Corporation which the bishop was to assume.[19] These had not been fulfilled, and for some months prior to Bishop Lefevere's arrival the Corporation had been publishing in the daily papers the necessary legal notice for cancelling the lease.

Faced with such discouraging prospects the bishop did not falter. There is no need of going into the long and tedious story of how financial safety was in the end achieved. It is enough to know that by rigid economy and by subsidies from the German and French missionary societies, such church properties as had been in jeopardy were retrieved without serious loss.

It was, no doubt, a legitimate grievance that prompted the action taken by the Corporation of St. Anne. Bishop Lefevere met the crisis with prudence and tact, and his evident willingness to carry out the terms of the agreement allayed the mistrust of those who shied at episcopal control. Consequently, the lease was continued, but the bishop was left with the duty of carrying out one provision, which was as difficult to comply with as it was ardently desired by the Corporation, namely, the establishing of a free school and orphan asylum. This meant the introduction of a Sisterhood, and in his quandary the bishop turned to Father Deluol, who was directing the Daughters of Charity founded by Mother Seton at Emmitsburg, Maryland.

> . . . These conditions, particularly the free school and orphan asylum, have until now been neglected, and have exasperated the trustees so far as to take all the necessary formalities of the law to deprive us of the property. . . . I therefore now apply to you with full confidence that you will not defeat that expectation, and I beg of you for the glory of God, for the good of Religion and society to endeavor that we may obtain some five or six competent Sisters of Charity to commence that institution. . . .[20]

There were months of anxious waiting before assurance came that four Sisters could be spared for the new mission. When the little band was ready the bishop himself hurried to Emmitsburg to meet them, and he hovered over his charges until they were safely landed in Detroit. They arrived May 30, 1844, and were immediately in-

[18] The lease is dated May 1, 1834, and was registered March 29, 1836, in Liber o. 38–40.

[19] The obligations were the following: within two years all debts and liabilities of the Corporation were to be discharged; the church buildings were to be kept in necessary repairs; a free school and an orphan asylum were to be assigned to the church, and a French sermon was to be preached every Sunday and holyday.

[20] Letterpress copy in DCA dated February 24, 1842.

stalled in the house formerly occupied by the Poor Clares. Within a month the school was in operation. The Corporation of St. Anne was at last satisfied.[21]

Bishop Lefevere's experience with the Corporation had two important results. In the first place he determined that the embarrassing situation in which he had found himself should not be repeated. The freedom of action which he needed was not to be trammeled by leaseholds, particularly on his own cathedral. Accordingly he purchased a plot of ground on the northeast corner of Jefferson Avenue and St. Antoine Street, and began the erection of a church and residence that would be free from any vestige of lay control. Thus did the Church of St. Anne lose the primacy that it had enjoyed for almost a century and a half. The corner stone of the new cathedral, dedicated to SS. Peter and Paul, was laid on June 29, 1844.[22] Construction was slow and often interrupted, the bishop, because of his settled aversion to debt, insisting on paying for each stage of the building before authorizing the next. Finally, in the spring of 1848, the structure was ready for divine worship, and it was consecrated on June 29 by Archbishop Eccleston, who came from Baltimore for the purpose.

The building of the cathedral was only the first step toward the accomplishment of the more important aim which the bishop had in mind, namely, the abolishing of trusteeism in his diocese. Detroit had been spared the scandals originating in lay control of church property that had convulsed some of the eastern dioceses. The admonition coming from the First Provincial Council of Baltimore, held in 1829, that the ownership of church property should be vested in the bishops had been only too well warranted. In the French parishes of the diocese conforming to the thorough and rigid code which they had

[21] "We arrived in Detroit on the 30th of May and . . . were conducted to our establishment on the corner of Larned and Randolph Streets. We found a cluster of old wooden houses just vacated by a dozen poor families. We installed ourselves in the one directly on the corner. . . . The good Bishop purchased a barrel of flour, a tea kettle, etc. With all these conveniences we easily prepared our supper, and had high recreation on the strength of it. . . ." Extract from the chronicle of the house in the Emmitsburg Archives.

[22] A copy of the document placed in the cornerstone is in Letter Book I, DCA:

Die vigesima nona Mensis Junii anno millesimo octingentesimo quadragesimo quarto, Gregorio XVI papa nostro doctissimo ac piissimo Ecclesiam Dei regente: Joanne W. Tyler Provintiarum Americae Septentrionalis foederatarum Praeside: Joanne S. Barry Provintiae Michiganensis Gubernatore, & Joanne R. Williams urbis Praefecto, Hunc lapidem primarium Ecclesiae Cathedralis Detroitensis, Deo dicatae sub intercessione beati Petri Apostoli, posuit Petrus Paulus Lefevere Episcopus Zelanus Coadjutor & Administrator Dioecesis Detroitensis. Assistentibus adm. Rev. D. Petro Kindekins, Rev. D. Laurentio Kilroy, & Rev. D. Antonio Kopp, nec non magna frequentia plebis.

Strangely enough only St. Peter is mentioned in the document, but there is no doubt of the bishop's intention to dedicate his cathedral to the two apostles.

inherited from the diocese of Quebec, and which functions there satisfactorily to this day, such troubles were not likely to occur. They would probably mark the later Catholic development in Michigan. If Bishop Lefevere could not undo the past he could certainly dictate a policy for the future. He put it into effect from the very beginning of his administration. Here, for instance, was his answer to a petition from "The Committee of Irish Catholics of Stony Creek, Monroe Co." asking for a church of their own.

> . . . As to the size of the church, I would suggest my opinion that a real & substantial frame building of fifty feet long, by thirty feet wide, would be as much as your means will allow, & would answer the intended purposes of the whole congregation for many years. For what respects the ground gifted for the building: It has been resolved and ordered by the provincial council of Baltimore, approved by the Sovereign pontiff, that, to avoid all difficulties—as unhappily there occurred many—[no churches?] shall in future be built unless the ground be deeded to the bishop of the Diocese in trust for its respective congregation. Therefore it is my wish & imperative desire, that you should not commence the building of that church before that gifted ground be secured according to the provisions of the Council of Baltimore. . . .[23]

The bishop went on to write the wording of a deed that would be acceptable to him. During his administration he had many occasions to repeat the procedure. But his firmness was proof against all opposition, and he left his successors secure from any pretensions of the laity to the ownership of ecclesiastical property.

Oddly enough, despite these earnest efforts to ensure the material welfare of his diocese, Bishop Lefevere is associated with the greatest loss which it ever suffered. The reader will remember that in 1808 Paul Malcher wishing to promote the building of a church in the Côte du Nord Est donated his farm for that purpose. The property was held by a group of trustees, and in 1833 the surviving members conveyed it to Bishop Rese and his successors under the sole condition that the property be held or disposed of "in trust for religious and literary purposes."[24] Evidently, the church of St. Joseph and the college of St. Philip Neri, which have already been referred to, were erected by Bishop Rese to fulfill the terms of the trust. When he resigned there was no doubt as to the ownership of the Malcher, or Church Farm, as it was called. Neither could any one have ever con-

[23] Letter dated February 20, 1842. Letter Book I, DCA.
[24] The story of the Church Farm has been told at length by Burton, *op. cit.*, II, Chap. LI. The reader is referred to this account for a mass of detail which can find no place here.

ceived its potential value, for the Church Farm, as deeded to Bishop Rese, comprised the tract of land now lying between Field and Baldwin avenues, and extending from the river to Harper Avenue, approximately three hundred and fifty acres.

The Church Farm had originally been purchased by Malcher from Hipolyte St. Bernard, and when the former executed his deed of gift to the trustees one of the conditions called for the payment of a certain sum to the son of St. Bernard on his coming of age. In 1824 the condition had not been fulfilled, and the son transferred his interest to Joseph Campau, that astute and doughty antagonist of Father Richard. Seeing the possibility of invalidating Malcher's donation, Campau began working on the cupidity of the dwellers on the Côte du Nord Est. Many of them, persuaded that they had not forfeited their ownership and could share in the proceeds of the farm if it were sold, made over the rights to their advisor. In 1834, Campau and a number of associates brought suit to have the property divided and sold. The partition had already been ordered by the court when Bishop Rese awoke to the danger. He protested against the action of the court, which presumably recognized his ownership, for all proceedings were halted, and the case was not reopened.

As Detroit developed, this large tract of land with a somewhat clouded title was bound to whet the avidity of enterprising lawyers. About 1854, a number of them saw the same vision that had allured Joseph Campau, and the agitation was resumed. Three years later suit was brought against Bishop Lefevere. Unfortunately, all the trustees were dead, and while the bishop urged the right of prescription and had reams of testimony as to the nature of the original transaction, he could not produce the document by which Bishop Rese had acquired title to the Church Farm. The deed given by the trustees to Bishop Rese in 1833 had never been recorded, and could now nowhere be found.[25] In this desperate situation, and faced with the prospect of years of litigation, the bishop did perhaps the best thing possible under the circumstances. In return for undisputed possession of at least a portion of the Church Farm he agreed to relinquish his claim to the rest of it. The court entered a decree that Bishop Lefevere as the owner of the property could dispose of it, and he thereupon conveyed to his opponents all of the Church Farm lying below Gratiot Avenue, with the exception of a narrow strip on the western side containing about twenty-seven acres. "Thus," says Burton, "was the church despoiled of a great estate." All the claimants were not represented in this transaction, and several attempts were made, even

[25] It was discovered in 1915 in a sheaf of old records by C. M. Burton.

as late as 1909, to disturb the results of the 1857 agreement. They were all unsuccessful.[26]

Bishop Lefevere's efforts to set the temporal affairs of the diocese in order naturally implied the beginnings of ecclesiastical discipline. Whether Bishop Rese formulated any set of rules for the guidance of his priests is extremely doubtful. At all events no record of them has been preserved. On the other hand, Bishop Lefevere with his bent for order and system was certain to do so as soon as he had well surveyed his field. The following letter, dated March 12, 1844, and addressed to Father Kundig, then beginning his missionary labors in Wisconsin, discloses that formal diocesan statutes had been issued as early as the spring of 1843.

I have just received a letter from Bishop Loras in which he states that you have written to him about the state of your missions & informed him that, in Wisconsin, 17 Congregations are now already organized; & that 13 new ones will be organized within the course of this year; that, in every direction churches are being built, & that the *debts are increasing.* All this, in Bp Loras' opinion, is alarming, & to me it [is] as queer as it is astonishing. That a number of Congregations be organized, & new ones continually forming is good & laudable, & reflects great credit upon your zeal & courage; but that new churches should be built within the jurisdictional limits of the Diocese without the knowledge of the Ordinary is wrong & contrary to the rules of ecclesiastical discipline, & more particularly so after the promulgation of Diocesan statutes which expressly forbid to *build or attempt to build* any church without having previously obtained permission in writing from the Bishop. . . . Wherefore, sensible of my duty as Bishop Coadj. & Adm. of the Diocese of Detroit under whose immediate jurisdiction Wisconsin yet remains, I do urge & command compliance with the Statutes of the Diocese of which you have received a written copy last spring; & do also request that you contract no debts nor cause any debts to be contracted in any congregation for church purposes or any other purposes more or less connected with the church.[27]

This primitive code was added to as the need arose, and in 1851 there appeared the first printed summary of diocesan legislation.[28]

[26] The diocese salvaged in all about 117 acres, which through the years have been gradually disposed of. The origin of St. Anthony's parish lies in Bishop Lefevere's desire to fulfill the terms of the original grant. Another aspect of the Church Farm controversy connected with Father Christian Denissen was to appear during the episcopate of a later bishop.

[27] Letter Book I, DCA. There is no extant copy of these first statutes available. It is safe to assume that they were not too extensive, and they may have been communicated to the individual pastors in hand copies.

[28] Copy in DCA. The summary was issued December 25, 1851, and consists of four closely printed pages. Its purpose, as stated, was to confirm the statutes of 1843, and to make such minor changes as circumstances dictated.

Finally, in 1859, Bishop Lefevere's efforts in this direction culminated in the holding of the first diocesan synod.

The diocesan clergy to the number of forty-three assembled at the cathedral on Tuesday, October 4, to begin their annual retreat.[29] In the afternoon of the following Sunday the bishop presided at the first session of the synod, and submitted for discussion the subject matter of the proposed legislation. At the same time he instituted and named the personnel of a Board of Consulters which was to aid him in the administration of the diocese.[30] Presumably to allow full freedom of this discussion the bishop absented himself from the three subsequent sessions, but was present at the fourth and last on Tuesday, October 11. After an allocution to his clergy the bishop declared that pastors would be removed only for the gravest canonical reasons, a statement at which, as the unknown transcriber of the proceedings naively writes, "all were greatly pleased." The synod was closed a day later with appropriate ceremonies.

The result of the synod's deliberations was embodied in sixty-three articles, of which the first officially promulgated the decrees of the several Baltimore councils, and of the two provincial councils of Cincinnati, which had been held in 1855 and 1858. The articles range over the dress, residence, and parochial duties of the clergy, the temporalities of the parishes, the administration of the sacraments, the teaching office, the establishment of schools and religious societies. In the course of time additions were made to this basic code, but few alterations. It came at a formative period in the history of the diocese, established its customs, and imposed the uniformity so necessary to weld the divers national elements of the diocese into a compact body.[31]

The second diocesan synod convened in the last three days of September, 1862.[32] Apparently, its main purpose was to put in force the decrees of the Third Provincial Council of Cincinnati, which had been held the previous year. The fourth article of that council, strangely enough, advocated a return to a modified form of the trustee system in the parishes, a step sufficiently important to warrant full explanation and discussion before the synod.[33] The clergy were not

[29] During Bishop Lefevere's regime the annual clergy retreat lasted a full week, and the faithful were called upon to forego Mass on the Sunday during the period.

[30] Seven consultors were named, among them a Redemptorist, Father Theodore Majerus.

[31] The proceedings were printed in a forty-four page pamphlet: *Constitutiones Synodi Diocesana Detroitensis Primae Habitae Mense Octobri* A.D. *1859.* Detroiti Ex Typis Joannis Slater / Via Grinswold, No. 58 / 1859.

[32] *Synodus Dioecesana Detroitensis Secunda, Habita Mense Septembri,* A.D. *MDCCCLXII, Detroit:* Ex Typis Joannis Slater / Via Jefferson, No. 166. 1862.

[33] Lamott, *op. cit.,* 216–17.

unprepared for it, as Bishop Lefevere, two months before, had issued a set of regulations designed to enforce the new privilege granted to the laity.[34]

The two diocesan synods convened by Bishop Lefevere are not the only evidences of his vigilance and zeal in office. They were supplemented by a series of pastoral letters, plain, blunt, straightforward utterances that castigated abuses, or called attention to duty. In this connection mention may be made of a measure which the bishop introduced to provide at least the minimum of religious instruction for his flock. He prepared a rather lengthy epitome of doctrine and devotion, whose contents are sufficiently indicated by the opening paragraph:

> By order of our Rt. Reverend Bishop, we are bound to instruct you in your principal duties, which may be reduced to what you must believe, what you should ask of God, what you should do, and what you should avoid in order to be saved.

Every pastor was obliged to read to his congregation, once a month, this digest of Catholic belief and practice, "slowly and in a loud voice." [35]

We must now turn to another major problem that confronted Bishop Lefevere on his accession to Detroit no less important than the safety of church property, and the inculcation of discipline. The number of priests was entirely inadequate to the needs of the diocese. Just at a period when Michigan was experiencing its greatest development, and Catholic immigration was streaming in, the roster of the clergy progressively declined. In the *Catholic Almanac* for 1839, the last year of Bishop Rese's régime, twenty-three priests were listed as belonging to the Diocese of Detroit. In the *Almanac* for 1845 only thirteen were listed.[36] The seminary, or rather the training of seminarians, which Bishop Rese had begun in his household, was no longer maintained after his departure, nor was it possible for Bishop Lefevere to resume the work until 1846.[37] In his distress the bishop

---

[34] They are found in a rare pamphlet: *Rules and Directions for the Administration of the Temporal Affairs of the Church in the Diocese of Detroit.* John Slater, Book and Job Printer, No. 166 Jefferson Ave. 1862. DCA.

[35] *Rudimenta Fidei Catholicae.* Detroit. Daily Volksblatt Print. Cor. Griswold and Woodbridge St. 1862. The booklet was printed in German, French, and English.

[36] Based on the figures given in the *Catholic Almanacs,* which need some correction, the number of priests in the diocese from 1839 to 1850 was approximately as follows: 1840...18, 1841...17, 1842...15, 1843...17, 1844...15, 1845....13, 1846...18, 1847...23, 1848...26, 1849...28. The low figure in 1845 is due to the fact that Wisconsin had become the diocese of Milwaukee in 1843. Detroit thereby lost Fathers Bonduel, Carabin, Kundig, Morissey, and Van den Broek.

[37] "Our seminary, opened in 1846, has furnished us with three priests, and at present has 9 students in theology who prepare themselves with the greatest zeal for the salvation of their brethren . . ." Letter to the Society for the Prop. of the Faith, February 15, 1848. In the Hickey transcripts.

BISHOP PETER PAUL LEFEVERE. From portrait in Archbishop's residence, Detroit.

could do nothing else but cry out his needs to the Catholic countries of Europe. He wrote to the Propagation of the Faith:

> I told you in the adjoining paper that one day Michigan will be distinguished by the name, The Catholic State; but for that we must soon be in condition to place some fifty missionaries, and furnish them the means of subsistence. To give weight to this assertion permit me to name some of the congregations which are newly formed, and where a church, or at least a chapel and a priest are needed.
>
> 1. Flint. 2. Lower Saginaw. 3. Upper Saginaw. 4. Marshall. 5. Kalamazoo. 6. Grand River. 7. Jackson. 8. Lodi. 9. Heartland. 10. Pontiac. 11. Lake Creek Settlement. 12. Newkirk's Settlement. 13. Muskegon Lake. 14. Yorkville. 15. Geneva. 16. Burlington. 17. St. Patrick. 18. Prairieville. 19. Muskwanago. 20. Lafferly's Settlement. 21. Spring Prairie. 22. Town nine. 23. Town ten. 24. Madison. 25. Mineral Point. 26. Dothville. 27. Bon Prairie, and many others.[38]

*   *   *

> We need absolutely some missionaries who speak French, but they must be apostolic men, ready to make all sorts of sacrifices, who place all their riches in the souls which they gain to God. . . . There are no other goods to be found here.[39]

The bishop sent his message to other countries of Europe through the Berichte. In 1842 the Leopoldine Association granted him $2,300, and a like amount the next year. While expressing his gratitude for these generous gifts Bishop Lefevere pleaded his need of German priests to minister to the immigrants of that nationality who were flocking to Detroit and to the interior of the state.[40]

The first recruit to the diocesan clergy, and the first priest ordained by Bishop Lefevere, was the only remaining seminarian of those who had studied under Bishop Rese. He was Lawrence Kilroy, who in after years was to become the devoted apostle of the northeastern portion of the diocese. Ordained March 26, 1842, he immediately began his ministry in Trinity parish.[41]

Fortunately for Bishop Lefevere there was one country where his appeal was sure to find response. In his native Belgium vocations were plentiful, and the bishops were sympathetic toward their confrere struggling against uneven odds to build up his diocese. Thus it came about that the diocese of Detroit for a quarter of a century, or until the time when it could provide its own native clergy, was manned almost entirely by a body of rugged and industrious mission-

---

[38] Letter dated March 4, 1843. Hickey transcripts.

[39] Letter from same source dated March 7, 1843.

[40] See two letters dated February 5, and July 15, 1842, in the *Berichte*, XVI, 27–34.

[41] Father Kilroy was born in 1803 in the parish of Tisarn, King's County, Ireland. He came to Detroit in 1834, and received minor orders from Bishop Rese in 1839. See obituary notice in the *Mich. Hist. Colls.*, XXI, 251.

aries from every diocese in Belgium. The first one to offer his services to Bishop Lefevere was Peter Kindekens, a seminarian of the diocese of Ghent, who had just completed his studies. The bishop was evidently impressed with his abilities, for after ordaining him, September 24, 1842, he made him his vicar-general.[42] Up to this time the office had been held by Father Vincent Badin, who had been longing to return to his native France from the day he terminated his duties as administrator of the diocese. Free at last, he retired to Combleux in the diocese of Orleans, and died there May 1, 1851.[43]

One priest came to the diocese in 1842, a countryman of Father Baraga, and a man of the same stamp. From the time of his ordination in 1831 Father Otto Skolla, a Franciscan, had followed with keen interest the work of the Leopoldine Association. In correspondence with Father Baraga he was assured that a welcome awaited him in Detroit if he could be freed from his monastic obligations. His superiors gave their consent, Propaganda accorded the necessary dispensations, and in the middle of May, 1842, Father Skolla reached Detroit to place himself at the disposal of Bishop Lefevere. Instead of being sent immediately to the Indian missions as he desired he was given charge of the Germans in Detroit, who were working feverishly on the building of their own church of St. Mary. When it was dedicated a year later, Father Skolla was transferred to Mackinac, and in 1845 he began his work among the Indians at La Pointe, which was now in the diocese of Milwaukee.[44]

There was just one accession to the diocese in 1843, another priest from Austria destined to end his days at a patriarchal age after having celebrated the golden jubilee of his priesthood. Father George Godez, born at Laibach in 1802, and ordained in 1831, came to Detroit in the spring of 1843 and was assigned to the pastorate of Westphalia. He remained here for thirty years, and was then transferred to the German settlement in Greenfield.[45]

The year 1843 was an important one for the diocese. It marked a determined effort on the part of Bishop Lefevere to deepen the spir-

[42] Peter Kindeken's dimissorial letters from the diocese of Ghent are dated March 22, 1842. Copy in DCA.

[43] Lamott, op. cit., Clergy List.

[44] Father Skolla while at St. Mary's made the first census of the German Catholics in Detroit. It is in the parish archives. He returned to his native land in 1858, and died near Fiume, April 24, 1879. See Rezek, op. cit., I, 359.

[45] Father Godez died as pastor of St. Alphonsus, January 14, 1883. He is buried in the parish cemetery within sight of Coolidge Highway. There is a biography in the Stimme der Warheit, a Catholic weekly published at Detroit from 1875 to 1914, for January 18, 1883. The Western Home Journal for August 27, 1881, commenting on his fiftieth anniversary, claims him as the first priest in the diocese to count fifty years in the priesthood.

itual life of his people. In the course of the summer, while on a visit to Baltimore, he chanced to meet a man whom he had known in Belgium, who was now Father Louis Gillet, a Redemptorist, and who had arrived in the United States the preceding April.[46] The zealous bishop found in the equally zealous missionary an answer to his half-formed plans for the regeneration of his diocese. An immediate beginning having been decided upon, Father Gillet accompanied the bishop back to Detroit. St. Paul's, Grosse Pointe, was the scene of the first of a series of missions conducted in nearly every French center in the diocese. How gratifying the results were to Bishop Lefevere is evident from a report which he sent to the French missionary society.

> During the entire summer I employed almost constantly two missionaries, Mr. P. Kindekens, my vicar-general, and the Rev. L. Gillet, C.S.R. (a worthy son of St. Alphonsus) in giving spiritual retreats to this multitude of French Canadians dispersed throughout the vast diocese of Michigan, and who deserved to be succored in proportion as they were abandoned.
>
> In the month of August the two missionaries profited by the season to carry the word of salvation to the Catholics who live on the shores of Saginaw Bay deprived of all the consolations of religion. At the end of a fifty mile ride in carriages, they found themselves at the end of the road and were obliged to go the rest of the way through the forests. . . . One finds at Saginaw, with the exception of a small number of Irish and a few Americans, only Canadians, who live by hunting and fishing. The Canadians for the greater part know no more of religion than the name. This is not surprising for a section of the country where the gospel has never been preached. However, these people have the Faith profoundly engraved in their hearts; our arrival was a joy to them. Children of 16 or 17 years, born in these parts, have never seen a Catholic priest.[47] Husbands with their wives and children devoted themselves to learning the catechism, and after an assiduous preparation of eight days, all approached the sacraments shedding tears of repentance and joy. . . . We could, if it were possible, pass the entire summer here, for I am assured that there are still many Catholics dispersed in the woods who have not learned of our arrival. Besides, there are about 4000 Indians of the Chippewa tribe who live on the banks of the Saginaw River, and who are well disposed to Christianity. . . . Since this time they have given several other retreats in the environs of Detroit, and everywhere they have been crowned with the greatest success, but especially in the City of Detroit, where they finishd a retreat of seven-

[46] *Annales Cong. SS. Redemp.*, I, 135.

[47] If the priests held their mission in the town of Saginaw itself, which at the time had a population of about 600, the bishop's statement is in error. The records of Trinity parish, Detroit, prove that Father Kundig made an extended missionary visit to Flint and Saginaw in 1842. He performed many baptisms in both towns between April 19 and May 10, which are recorded in the Trinity register.

teen days. . . . God alone could tell what marvels this retreat accomplished. Inveterate sinners returned to religion, many protestants deserted the ranks of error, peace was reestablished in families, the standard of temperance was unfurled, and disorders were abolished. . . . Such are the fruits of the graces which promise to the Congregation of St. Anne a new era of peace, prosperity, and happiness.[48]

Early in 1844 a confrere came to help Father Gillet in the person of Father Francis Poilvache.[49] Perhaps the first mission for which the two Redemptorists prepared themselves began the first week in March at Monroe. While they were thus engaged Bishop Lefevere wrote to their superior in Baltimore to express his admiration of their work, and then continued:

> . . . Father Louis has made me aware of the uncertainty of his position here as a religious. I desire nothing more than to see him continue the good that he has already begun, and I am disposed to favor with all my power the establishment of a house of your order. I have thought it prudent, before broaching the undertaking, to let the Father look over the territory, where so many things must be considered before opening a religious house. I have told him several times that he can choose whatever place he deems the most suitable, and I will strive to second his efforts. Father Louis has mentioned Monroe, second only to Detroit in importance, where at the moment he is beginning a mission. At the end of the mission I am going there myself to confer with the parishioners interested in the matter. . . .[50]

Father Gillet had chosen better than either Father Saenderl or Father Prost. True to his promise Bishop Lefevere approved the choice, and an agreement was signed, August 17, 1844, by the bishop, by Father Gillet, and by the trustees of St. Anthony's parish, leasing the church and its land holdings to the Redemptorist Congregation for a period of three hundred years.[51]

Having witnessed the exceptional results achieved by the missionaries among his French diocesans, the bishop was now eager to offer the same opportunities to another portion of his flock. Accordingly four Redemptorists came to Detroit in 1846 to work among the Germans, and they began with a mission at St. Mary's Church.[52] The Fathers were rewarded not only by a marvelous response to their preaching but also by the admiring affection of the congregation.

---

[48] Letter in Hickey Transcripts dated January 31, 1844.

[49] Father Poilvache died at Monroe, January 27, 1848, with a reputation for sanctity. His remains lie at Annapolis, Md. There is a sketch of his life in the *Catholic Almanac* for 1849.

[50] Letter dated March 6, 1844. Letter Book I. DCA.

[51] The original lease is in the DCA.

[52] *Annales Cong. SS. Redemp.*, I, 174.

Father Anton Kopp, who had come to St. Mary's when relieved of Westphalia by Father Godez, was in disfavor with his people, and there had been much bickering and petty quarreling. Too desirable to be lost was the happy peace that reigned in the parish after the mission. The people were determined to retain as their spiritual guides the men who had brought it about. To that effect the bishop was petitioned to transfer the administration of the parish to the Redemptorists, a step he was most willing to take. At first reluctant, the Congregation finally consented, and on January 26, 1847, St. Mary's was handed over to the Redemptorists for a term of five hundred years.[53]

Thus within three years the diocese acquired a number of experienced and zealous priests, whose special missionary vocation made them particularly suited for the pioneer work expected of them. They came at a time of urgent need and the value of their services of Bishop Lefevere can hardly be overestimated. Of the individual priests mention will be made later. We must here go on with the bishop's effort to build up the ranks of his clergy.

Unfortunately, the Redemptorist foundations in the diocese were not destined to last over the majestic periods of time in which they had been conceived. Just ten years elapsed between the opening of the house in Monroe and a deprecatory notice to Bishop Lefevere from the superior of the Congregation that it had been decided to withdraw the Redemptorists from the diocese.[54] The reasons for this action were fundamentally the same as those which had frustrated the first attempt at a foundation under Bishop Rese. The Fathers perforce were so engaged in missionary labors that an ordered community life was almost impossible. Moreover neither Monroe nor Detroit seemed able to furnish sufficient revenue to maintain the number of priests deemed necessary for the proper functioning of a Redemptorist convent. To Bishop Lefevere this action of the Congregation was an unthinkable defection, and when his vehement protests against it were of no avail he submitted the matter to the Roman authorities. So vital did the issue appear to him that Father Kindekens was dispatched to Rome to ensure an adequate presentation of the bishop's stand in the controversy.[55] The decision, when announced, was a compromise. The Fathers were permitted to leave Monroe, but were ordered to remain at St. Mary's in Detroit.[56]

We must now consider another commission entrusted to Father

---

[53] Ibid., 192.
[54] Ibid., III, 113. Letter dated March 17, 1854.
[55] Copies of mandate and celebret in DCA dated April 10, 1856.
[56] Propaganda gave its decision August 23, 1858.

Kindekens. In 1854, a number of American bishops present in Rome for the proclamation of the dogma of the Immaculate Conception had expressed to Pius IX their desire for the founding of an American college, or seminary, similar to the other national colleges in the Holy City.[57] The project was most welcome, was urged upon the bishops in the First Provincial Council of New York, the following year, and the preliminary steps were taken for its realization. On his way to Rome Father Kindekens called upon Archbishop Kenrick of Baltimore, who had been particularly active in fostering the proposed institution. Taking advantage of the opportunity, the archbishop charged Father Kindekens to proceed with the purchase of the necessary buildings, and to make the final arrangements for the opening of the American College.[58] The vicar-general of Detroit might have had the honor of founding the North American College had his efforts not been frustrated by the circumstances which he reported to the American bishops.

> I endeavored with the utmost diligence to look for and secure a suitable location for the projected American College in Rome. I found that it is not only impossible at present, but that it will probably remain impossible for some time to come, to establish such an institution in the Holy City. In point of fact, the Holy Father assured me that, under the present circumstances (the occupation of Rome by the French, etc.) he could not say when it would be in his power to assign a suitable building for the purpose.[59]

His business in Rome completed, Father Kindekens went on to Belgium before sailing for the United States. In church circles he heard much discussion concerning a proposed American college, not in Rome but in Belgium itself. Bishop Martin Spalding [60] of Louisville, later the archbishop of Baltimore, had gone to Belgium in 1852 to procure priests and religious teachers for his diocese. While thus engaged the idea of a seminary to train candidates exclusively for the American missions had come to him. He was given much encouragement from the Belgian bishops, and particularly from Cardinal Sterckx of Mechlin; [61] but when he broached his plans to Archbishop Kenrick he found no enthusiasm to match his own. The archbishop was more in sympathy with a Roman college and there the matter rested.

[57] See article on the American College in the Cath. Encyclopedia.

[58] Rev. J. Van der Heyden, The Louvain American College (Louvain, 1909), 12.

[59] Ibid., 13. In 1857 Pius IX purchased a convent then occupied by French soldiers as the first building for an American College in Rome. The college was formally opened December 8, 1859.

[60] J. L. Spalding, The Life of the Most Rev. M. J. Spalding (New York, 1873), 162.

[61] Van der Heyden, op. cit., 14–15.

The interest aroused by Bishop Spalding was still smouldering when Father Kindekens visited Belgium, and the possibilities it opened appealed strongly to him after his failure in Rome. With the kindly help of the Belgian episcopate the feasibility of a missionary college was again studied, and when his plans were matured Father Kindekens hastened home to lay the project before the American bishops in a circular letter:

> . . . Passing through Belgium, I learned that an earnest wish pre-vailed among persons of distinction to establish there a college for the foreign missions. I resolved at once to secure the fruits of these happy dispositions for the missions of the United States, with the following success:
>
> I obtained a promise from the Count Felix de Mérode of the sum between 50,000 and 60,000 francs towards founding a college for the missions in the United States, in any city of Belgium of my choice.
>
> His Eminence, the Cardinal Archbishop of Mechlin, and several other Prelates with whom I had the honor to speak on the subject, as-sured me of their warmest sympathies and promised their coöperation.
>
> A subscription in aid of the foundation of the establishment will be opened in the columns of the Catholic journals of Belgium, as soon as I can assure them that the Right Rev. Bishops of the United States (or some of them) are earnestly engaged in promoting the good work.
>
> The Rector of the University of Louvain (the city selected for the College) has promised his aid, and is prepared to grant all we may reasonably require of the University, to secure the success and pros-perity of the contemplated institution.
>
> From the above, Your Lordship will easily perceive that the object of the institution in Belgium would be, 1st, to serve as a nursery of properly educated and tried clergymen for our missions; and secondly, to provide the American Bishops with a college to which some at least of their students might be sent to acquire a superior ecclesiastical in-struction and a solid clerical training, without much expense, as the College will require no other professors than those for the English and the German language.
>
> The basis of the government of the institution will be that of the Propaganda at Rome and each diocese of the United States will profit of its fruits in proportion to the amount it may have furnished towards the foundation, etc. . . .[62]

Naturally, the proposed college became a common cause with Bish-ops Lefevere and Spalding, and, February 4, 1857, they sent out to the American hierarchy a prospectus and a circular letter which they both signed.

[62] *Idem.*

We take the liberty to forward to you herewith a Prospectus of the American College, to be established in Belgium, in connection with the University at Louvain. As Providence seems, at present, to favor the founding of this College, in which many eminent and pious persons, in Belgium, take so lively an interest, we have ventured to move in the matter, after having consulted with some of our brethren—feeling that unless some one took the initiation, [sic] mencement would probably be made. . . .

We take the liberty to request that, if you should approve the general objects and regulations of the College, and desire to become one of its patrons, you should have the kindness to signify the same to the Bishop of Detroit, at as early a day as possible, as the Rector proposes to leave for Europe early in March, and it will be highly important to his success that he should have the sanction of as many American Prelates as possible. Should you feel inclined to contribute towards the foundation of the College, you will please to specify the amount, that the Rector may be able to calculate his resources. . . .[63]

Although some of the bishops were heartily in favor of the project, only two of them were "inclined to contribute"—the two who had signed the circular. When the prospective Rector, who was none other than Father Kindekens, sailed for Belgium toward the end of February, 1857, his sole resources were $2,000 contributed in equal shares by Bishops Lefevere and Spalding.[64] This amount swelled by the 60,000 francs to be given by the Count de Mérode would suffice for a beginning. But when Father Kindekens landed he found to his dismay that the Count had died without making any provisions for the college. The rest of the story can be told in the words of Bishop Stang, an alumnus of the future institution.

. . . Half-discouraged, the poor priest walked through the winding streets of old Louvain for several days in search of a suitable place to begin the College, when, one afternoon, as he was passing through the *Rue de Moutons,* a genial old Flemish pastor accosted him, and after learning the secret of the lonely wanderer, offered his services. Both walked up the *Montaigne des Carmelites;* at the corner of the *Rue de Namur* they saw in the window of a vacated butcher-shop a printed notice in Flemish: Te huren (to let). The old clergyman persuaded Father Kindekens to engage the place as the future home of the candidates for the American missions. The house was part of the old Collège d'Aulne, founded by Benedictine monks in 1629. On the feast of St.

---

[63] From a printed copy of the circular in the DCA.

[64] Spalding, *op. cit.,* 165. How Bishop Lefevere paid his subscription appears in a letter to Bishop Spalding. "Before Mr. K. started for Belgium I wanted to pay him the $1000 which I had subscribed; but at the request of one of my clergymen, whose father had died, I made arrangements to the effect that Mr. K. should draw on the inheritance of the said Clergyman." Letter Book II, DCA.

Joseph, March 19, 1857, the American College of the Immaculate Conception was opened. Before the close of the same year the institution numbered eight students, who naturally had to cope with many material difficulties to which the primitive condition of the College exposed them. . . .[65]

Such was the humble beginning of the American College of Louvain, which has given four archbishops, eleven bishops, and hundreds of devoted missionaries to the American church. At the end of a year it sent Fathers Lambert, Ryckaert, and Cappon to the diocese of Detroit only, and in the course of time a whole corps of exemplary priests dignified by such names as Bleyenberg, Limpens, Pulcher, Van Lauwe, Wermers, Friedland, Rafter, and Wheeler.[66]

Although Bishop Lefevere must share with Bishop Spalding the honor of having founded the American College, he had in all likelihood a deeper interest in it than his confrere. To him its success was a matter of national pride, and he counted, moreover, among his personal friends and acquaintances many of the patrons, both lay and clerical, who ministered to the precarious early years of its existence. His close contact with the College is proved by the fact that its first four rectors were priests of the diocese of Detroit, whom he could ill afford to do without. Father Kindekens returned to Detroit in 1860, and was succeeded by Father John De Neve, who relinquished his parish at Niles to Father Cappon.[67] In 1871, Father De Neve, incapacitated by a protracted illness, was replaced by Father Edmund Dumont, one-time pastor of Redford, and who had been at the College from 1862. When he was named Bishop of Tournai in 1873, he was followed by Father James Pulsers, who had been pastor of Dexter for some years before beginning his teaching career at the College in 1863. Father Pulsers continued in the office until Father De Neve, in 1881, again became rector for a ten-year period.[68]

The narration of Bishop Lefevere's efforts to reinforce the thin ranks of his clergy has led us far afield from purely diocesan affairs. We have not yet covered the range of his activities. Struggling as he was to initiate an orderly and comprehensive development of Catholic life he could not be indifferent to his duties in the sphere of Catholic education. The educational facilities which he found on his entry into the diocese could scarcely have been more primitive. In the city itself there were a few classrooms in the basement of St. Anne's, and in the "Academy of St. Anne," a frame structure that

[65] *American Ecclesiastical Review*, XVI, 258.
[66] There is a list of all the graduates up to 1907 in Van der Heyden.
[67] Father De Neve's leave-taking is touchingly described by an eye witness in Van der Heyden, 65–66.
[68] Van der Heyden, *passim*.

had been erected by Bishop Rese adjoining the rectory. On the outskirts stood the vacant St. Philip's College—it was to go up in flames a month later. In the State, the only schools of which we have any information were the Indian mission schools supported by the Federal government.[69]

It is evident that we need look for no spectacular growth during Bishop Lefevere's régime. The diocese was still in the pioneer stage. Neither the number nor the resources of his people were equal to the burden of providing schools distinct from the common school system. The poor immigrants who cleared their lands in the forties and the fifties were doing well if they could support the essential ministrations of religion. In some localities, especially where German immigration predominated, the existence of primitive schools taught by laymen is attested by traditional accounts; but lack of accurate information renders hopeless anything more than a mere reference to them.

In Detroit the only pretense of higher Catholic education had been made by the College of St. Philip. Although Bishop Lefevere keenly felt its loss he was never able to replace it.[70] Not until the Jesuits came in 1877 could the city again boast a Catholic college.

The first improvement in the primary schools came, as we have seen, with the introduction of the Daughters of Charity in 1844. Four years later the Bishop wrote to the French missionary society.

> . . . But the scarcity of priests is not the only evil that afflicts us. There is another which already increases the unfortunate effects of the former, and will be more disastrous still in the consequences which distress us more every day. It is the lack of Catholic instruction for our youth. The Government has erected schools in all parts of the city, and in every village and hamlet, where children receive free instruction, but where it is forbidden to speak of religion in any manner whatsoever. It is true that this prohibition is considered an advantage in a Protestant country, but what is education without religion? What disastrous impressions will not Protestant teachers make on Catholic children,

[69] Even under these conditions St. Anne's school surpassed anything the city had to offer. Although the common school law of the state had been in effect four years the city officials had done nothing to make it operative in Detroit. "While acting as Mayor of the City during the year 1841, Dr. Pitcher called the attention of several members of the Common Council to the great need of common schools among us. . . . From these statistics disclosed at the time, it appeared that there were then in the City twenty-seven English schools, one French and one German school, but all of them exceedingly limited in numbers, and scarcely deserving the name of schools, except the one connected with St. Ann's (Catholic) Church . . ." *System of Public Instruction and Primary School Law of Michigan* (Lansing, 1852), 297.

[70] ". . . Besides, the interests of religion demand the reestablishment of our college which became a prey to the flames of 1842." Letter dated March 28, 1845. Hickey transcripts.

either from their indifference in matters of religion, or by their rail-
leries against the Catholic faith. . . . Also we see with dread the rapid
progress of indifferentism in religion which presages the total loss of
faith among many if we cannot promptly remedy conditions. . . . The
only means of remedying this great evil is to establish the Brothers of
the Christian Schools in our diocese to snatch at least our Catholics
from the disastrous influence of these infidel schools. But where shall
I find the means to support them? And how shall I meet the expenses
of establishing them in all these localities? We have so many other
things to do. . . . It is true that we have some Catholic schools directed
by the Sisters, but these are and can be only for girls, and, after all,
what are five or six schools in this vast territory. At Detroit we have a
splendid school for girls directed by the Sisters of Charity; but what can
seven religious do—despite their extraordinary devotion and most active zeal—who must care for the sick poor of a city numbering 20,000
inhabitants. . . .[71]

The bishop's hopes were realized in 1851, when four Brothers of
the Christian Schools came to Detroit, and in September took charge
of the school at St. Anne's. A year later four additional Brothers were
stationed in St. Mary's parish to teach in the school which had been
erected in 1844.[72] But their work was confined to the city, and had no
bearing on the situation in the state at large so deplored by Bishop
Lefevere. That could be remedied in the course of time only through
the noble devotion of Catholic Sisterhoods.[73]

Some account of the rise and development of the teaching Sisterhoods in the diocese will be given in a later chapter. It is sufficient
here barely to indicate the origins which Bishop Lefevere fostered.
Undoubtedly, the first school in the state, outside of Detroit and conducted by religious, was opened, as was fitting, in the old historic
mission field at Bertrand. At the end of November, 1842, Father
Sorin with his seven Brothers, and the ox-team drawing baggage, had
taken possession of the deserted fields that are today the site of the
University of Notre Dame. For the comprehensive establishment that
he had in mind Sisters were necessary, and in the following year five
Sisters of the Holy Cross arrived from France. The Bishop of Vincennes, not in accord with Father Sorin regarding this necessity, refused to approve the new foundation, and Father Sorin was obliged
to locate the mother-house elsewhere. Fortunately, Notre Dame
du Lac lay so near the Michigan boundary that the Sisters could be

[71] Letter dated February 15, 1848. Hickey transcripts.
[72] From the Chronicle of St. Joseph's Commercial College in Detroit, now the De La
Salle Collegiate.
[73] See J. A. Burns, C.S.C., *The Growth and Development of the Catholic School System
in the United States* (Benziger Bros., 1912).

established outside the diocese of Vincennes, and still remain under the watchful care of Father Sorin. Bishop Lefevere gave his permission and encouragement, and welcomed the Sisters into his diocese. In July, 1844, the mother-house of the Sisters of the Holy Cross was fixed at Bertrand, and a few weeks later a school was opened for the children of the neighborhood. The primitive school had reached the dignified status of a Female Academy when the Sisters, in 1855, were able to carry out Father Sorin's original design, and Bertrand was abandoned.[74]

Just a year after the foundation at Bertrand, Monroe was ready to give to the American Church one of its few native Sisterhoods, the Sister Servants of the Immaculate Heart of Mary. Theresa Renauld's desire to consecrate herself to the religious life was the first fruit of Father Gillet's initial mission at Grosse Pointe. Her resolution opened prospects which he could not ignore. Summoning from Baltimore two like-minded women, he housed his three charges in a log cabin on the banks of the River Raisin. With Bishop Lefevere's heartiest approval, the candidates made their profession, November 30, 1845, and six weeks later were at work in their two-room school. In 1858, when there were twenty-four members in the Community, a division occurred, and twelve Sisters went to the Diocese of Philadelphia. This was regrettable from the standpoint of the Diocese of Detroit, as it retarded for many years what might otherwise have been a rapid growth of parochial schools in the state. In 1870, the Sisters had schools in Adrian, Westphalia, Ann Arbor, Saginaw, and Carleton.[75]

Two more Sisterhoods were introduced into the diocese by Bishop Lefevere: Religious of the Sacred Heart in 1851, and the School Sisters of Notre Dame in the following year. Neither of them was engaged outside of Detroit.

There remains to be considered one more phase, and that not the least interesting, of Bishop Lefevere's work for Catholic education in his diocese. Today, the Catholics of the United States are reconciled to the tremendous burden imposed upon them by the maintenance of their own schools. We need not here go into the reasons why the burden is carried, or why its infliction is or was sometimes felt to be an injustice. An intrenched Protestant public opinion precludes any other solution of the problem, and Catholics have acquiesced in a condition which they are powerless to change. There was a time, a time nearer to the origins of our national liberties, when denomina-

[74] *A Story of Fifty Years* (Notre Dame, 1905), 15–52.
[75] Sister M. Rosalita, I.H.M., *No Greater Service*, The History of the Congregation of the Sisters, Servants of the Immaculate Heart of Mary (Detroit, 1948).

tional, including Catholic, schools were supported by public funds. But the dissemination of liberal ideas imported from Europe, the disestablishment of State-supported churches, and the increase in the number of sects, all tended to divorce secular from religious education. The change was not brought about without protest. As far as Catholics were concerned, the high tide of their protest was reached in the celebrated controversy of Bishop Hughes with the school authorities of New York City.[76] Bogged by religious prejudice, the question was not decided on its merits; but the failure of the bishop to secure state aid for Catholic schools set a precedent which could hardly be overturned.

In the history of Catholic education in the United States, Bishop Hughes is commonly brought forward as the champion of the Catholic position, and scanty reference is made to any subsequent attempts to gain what he had lost. It is worth while to know that the same controversy was once waged in Michigan as well, and that Bishop Lefevere, less spectacularly perhaps, fought as manfully as Bishop Hughes.

However, the first attempt to obtain a portion of the common school fund was made even before Bishop Lefevere's time. It came in 1840, three years after Michigan's common school system had been fully organized, and was evidently a reverberation of the campaign carried on in New York during the whole of that year, first by Father Power, and then by Bishop Hughes. To the legislature of Michigan assembled in Detroit, which was then the capital, a petition was presented "in relation to a common school, established by the Irish adopted citizens in the city of Detroit, under the care of the Pastor or Trinity Church, praying the 'interposition of the Legislature.' "[77] We need not wonder that the Catholics of Trinity parish took the initiative since they had at their head the most influential Catholic in the city, Father Martin Kundig. The petition itself has been lost, but its contents are sufficiently indicated by the report of the committee to which it was submitted.

> The petitioners are compelled, under the general law, regulating common schools in the city, to pay each one of his proportion of all expenses of organizing, maintaining and supporting the common school in the district where he may reside. Does he derive from that school his proportion of the benefits and privileges arising from its existence and continuance, for which he is annually subject to a tax? The petition declares that he does not. But it will be asserted that it is at his option —that he rejects the privileges that are offered under the general plan

[76] See Clarke, *Lives of the Deceased Bishops* . . . , II, 95–110.
[77] *System of Public Instruction.* . . . 57.

—that his children, with those of his neighbors, are amply provided for, by the means afforded, and that they are rejected by no one except by the distaste [sic] of his own peculiar prejudices.

Your committee cannot and do not deem this an answer to the proposition stated. They know and feel that upon the subject of the education of our children, our institutions, our liberal sentiments, our past and present history forbid for a moment, the thought of dictation and control. If the petitioners desire that those who are to come after them should have the benefit of pastoral instruction from persons educated with the same views and feelings of themselves, it is their right, nay, their sacred duty, to seek such instruction; and it is our privilege to see that the taxes paid by them for education should be appropriated to their own use, and subject to their own control. By denying them these privileges, you subject them to a double tax, the first of which is expended upon schools, from which, either from prejudices or religious principles, they cannot derive any benefit; and the last is produced by supporting such institutions as may best accord with their early education and be under the direct charge of those entertaining the same religious views as themselves.

Your committee cannot assent to such a course inasmuch as they believe it to be (the) duty of the Legislature to further by every means in their power the education and well being of the rising generation, and that special care should be taken that no odious distinctions of a sectarian or political character should be permitted to exist, and that the sons of every native and naturalized citizen, of the catholic and protestant, should be placed in every respect upon an equal footing.

So far from discouraging, they feel it their duty to encourage here and elsewhere, the organization of schools among our adopted fellow-citizens. . . . They further believe, that sound policy demands that every inducement to foreign immigration should be held out to the oppressed of other nations, and that the mass of our people should be thoroughly enlightened and qualified for the important duties of American citizens. . . .

Believing therefore that the school referred to in the petition should be encouraged and sustained; that the taxes the petitioners pay for the support of common schools should be expended for the benefit of their children, under their own control . . . there shall be paid toward the support of the school referred to, an annual sum equal to the amount that the petitioners would be entitled to as component parts of the several districts in which they reside.[78]

Despite these good dispositions, there is no record of any relief having been granted to the petitioners; nor does Father Kundig appear to have made any further attempt to secure a division of the school fund. What we do know of him in this connection is that with char-

[78] The entire opinion may be read in the *Senate Documents* for 1840, 304–08.

acteristic magnanimity he threw himself into a movement to secure better educational facilities for the city as a whole. Together with Dr. Zina Pitcher he presided over a mass meeting of citizens convened to devise a remedy for the deplorable condition of education in Detroit. This meeting was the genesis of the Detroit Board of Education created by the legislature in February, 1842. Against much opposition the basic legislation erecting the Board, and under which it functions to this day, was pushed through the legislature by the untiring efforts of one of Father Kundig's parishioners, Cornelius O'Flynn, a native of Tralee.[79]

The second and last attempt of the Catholics of Michigan to secure a division of the school fund was led by Bishop Lefevere, and was matured in the final months of 1852. There is no apparent reason why this particular time was judged propitious, and no correspondence of Bishop Lefevere bearing on the movement is available. The campaign was evidently planned to begin simultaneously at Lansing, which had been the seat of the Legislature from 1848, and at Detroit, which was now autonomous in its school system.

In Detroit the initiative was taken by Bishop Lefevere himself. The citizens took their politics seriously in those days, and on January 5, 1853, a mass meeting was called at the City Hall to protest against the extravagance of city officials especially with regard to improvements in the water supply. Bishop Lefevere, as the holder of extensive properties, attended the meeting to voice his opposition, and while pointing out the burden of oppressive taxation which would have to be borne he called the attention of his audience to the injustice of taxing Catholics for schools which they could not conscientiously use, and demanded that they be given the share of the school fund which they contributed. Unfortunately, the bishop's blunt and rather uncompromising statement of his attitude does not seem to have been well received, and the meeting broke up in disorder.

For the next two months, or until the elections in March, Detroit was in the throes of one of the most hectic political campaigns in its history. A "regular" Democratic ticket, understood to be favorable to the demands of Bishop Lefevere, and including a recorder, alderman, and school inspectors, was first in the field. Then the "inde-

[79] *Mich. Hist. Colls.*, I, 454. "Cornelius O'Flynn, Representative from Detroit in 1857, was born in 1810 at Tralee, County Kerry, Ireland, and came to America in 1828. He was admitted to the bar in Detroit in 1834. He was a classical scholar, a man of comprehensive views of things, and a Democrat. He was city attorney of Detroit in 1842, judge of probate two terms, 1844–52, and postmaster at Detroit during a portion of Buchanan's term. As judge of probate he gave a system of practice to the state through the blank forms that he prepared. He died in Detroit in 1869." *Early History of Michigan with Biographies of State Officers* (Lansing, 1888), 449.

pendent" Democrats, around whom coalesced every shade of anti-Catholic opposition, published their slate, and the fight was on. The newspapers were deluged with correspondence. The *Daily Advertiser* represented the utmost hostility to the bishop, while the *Daily Free Press* opened its columns to both sides. The Catholic position was ably maintained; but it was confronted by a coalition whose sentiments are perhaps best expressed in a communication to the *Free Press* of February 28.

> . . . While many Catholics are the sincere friends of free schools, the Bishop and priests have openly denounced them from the pulpit, and have called into exercise their whole power to crush them. This hostility is open, bitter and relentless. Under their influence, petitions for a division of the public monies among religious schools have been circulated and poured in upon the Legislature, and a spectacle, new in our day, of the Bishop and Priests of the Catholic Church haunting the lobbies of the halls of legislature, playing the agreeable to members, and bringing their whole influence to bear in opposition to city improvements and free schools. . . .
>
> Thus have the Catholic Bishop and priests arrayed themselves and have sought to array the people against the best interests of the city. . . . They have forced the issue upon us, and it will be met in the true spirit of '76. . . . They [the opposition] know the firm purpose of the Bishop to carry his point. . . . They know that untiring perseverance, unflinching effort in the face of every obstacle, is a characteristic of the men and the order. . . ."

The election was held on March 8, 1853. Against a united opposition that believed itself animated by the spirit of '76 the "regulars" had no chance. Their candidates were overwhelmingly defeated in every ward but one.[80]

Meanwhile another phase of the campaign had been carried on at Lansing. In anticipation of the meeting of the legislature at the beginning of 1853, the bishop had instructed the parishes of the state to draw up petitions for relief from the existing school law signed by all the parishioners who were citizens. They were probably identical with, or similar to the one printed in the *Annual Report of the Superintendent of Public Instruction for 1853*.[81]

> We, the undersigned Citizens of Michigan, respectfully represent to your Honorable Body, that we have labored, and are still laboring under grievances to which neither Justice nor Patriotism require longer submission on our part, without an effort for their removal.
>
> We, your Petitioners, wish to represent to your Honorable Body, that

[80] *Mich. Hist. Colls.*, I, 459–60. Every issue of the Detroit papers during the period furnishes interesting material.

[81] *Annual Report* . . . (Lansing, 1853), 190–191.

notwithstanding the constitution guarantees liberty of conscience to every citizen of our State, yet our Public School laws, compel us to violate our conscience, or deprive us unjustly of our share of the Public School funds, and also impose on us taxes for the support of schools, which, as a matter of conscience, we cannot allow our children to attend.

To convince your Honorable Body of the magnitude of these grievances, we have but to refer you to the fact, that in the cities of Monroe and Detroit alone, there are educated at the expense of their parents, and charitable contributions, some twenty-five hundred of our children. Your petitioners might bear longer their present grievances, hoping that our fellow citizens would soon discover the injustice done to us by the present School Laws, and that the love of public justice for which they are distinguished, would prompt them to protest against laws which are self-evidently a violation of liberty of conscience, a liberty which is equally dear to every American citizen; but as the Constitution requires that free schools be established in every district of our State, and as the present Legislature will be called upon to act upon the School subject, your petitioners consider that their duties to themselves, their duty to their children, and their duty to their country, the liberties of which they are morally and religiously bound to defend, as well as their duty to their God, require that they apprise Your Honorable Body of the oppressive nature of our present School laws, the injustice of which is equalled only by the laws of England, which compel the people of all denominations to support a church, the doctrines of which they do not believe.

Your petitioners would not wish to be understood as being opposed to education; on the contrary they are prepared to bear every reasonable burden your Honorable Body are willing to impose on them, to promote the cause of education, providing that our schools be free indeed. But they do not consider schools free when the law imposes on parents the necessity of giving their children such an education as their conscience cannot approve of. But that your Honorable Body may not be ignorant of what they understand by free schools, your petitioners wish to say that in their opinions, schools can be free only, when the business of school teaching be placed on the same legal footing as the other learned professions, when all may teach who will, their success depending as in other cases, on their fitness for their profession, and the satisfaction they may render to the public; that in all cases the parent be left free to choose the teacher to whom he will entrust the education of his child, as he is left to choose his Physician, his Lawyer, etc.; that each person teaching any public school in the State should be entitled to draw from the public school fund, such sums as the law might provide for every child so taught by the month, quarter, or otherwise, on producing such evidence as the law might require in such cases. Schools established on such principles are what your petitioners understand by free schools.

Your petitioners, therefore, respectfully urge that the public school system for our State be based on these broad democratic principles of equal liberty to all, allowing freedom of conscience to the child, who also has a conscience, as well as to the instructor and parent. . . .

In the pages of the *House Journal* we catch glimpses of the concerted action which the bishop had initiated. During the month of January petitions were presented from every major Catholic group in the state. The largest came from Wayne County, signed by Bishop Lefevere and 2,753 citizens.[82] But, as was to be expected, there were not lacking vigilant observers of this attempt by Catholics to mold legislation, who were determined to warn the legislature against what to them was insidious propaganda. For instance, the Elders and Deacons of the First Presbyterian Church of Detroit made the following remonstrance:

That we have received credible information and do verily believe, that a project is entertained by the Romish priesthood in this State, acting doubtless, in obedience to the commands and suggestions of a foreign despotic sovereign, the object and interest whereof are none other but the subversion of the free system of schools which prevails in our State; that we have also evidence satisfactory to our minds that this Jesuitical enterprise, now carefully and insidiously veiled under the pretense that this time-honored system, in its operation, violates the rights of conscience, engages the particular attention and the unceasing labors of the Romish Clergy throughout the United States. Indeed, so plain have the workings of the system made it, that the tenets and discipline of that ambitious sect are at open war with all the ideas upon which our Republican government is based; that the Managers of that sect have found it necessary to direct their attacks at the very citadel of Republican strength—the free education of youth and the consequent independence of mind. . . .[83]

A bill granting relief to the Catholic petitioners was laid before the House on January 25 by Jeremiah O'Callahan, a Catholic represent-

[82] Some of the larger petitions mentioned in the *House Journal* are the following: Peter Ward, Jr. and 241 others of Monroe Co.; Dr. E. Adams, R. O'Connor and 581 others of Monroe Co.; Thomas Cullen, S. Denton and 215 others of Washtenaw Co.; 589 citizens of Kent Co.; Michael Kelly and 225 others of Jackson; 132 citizens of Kalamazoo; 276 citizens of Macomb Co.; 155 citizens of Saginaw Co.

[83] *Documents Accompanying the Journal of the Senate and House of Representatives at the Regular Session of 1853* (Lansing, 1853), Doc. 20. The remonstrance goes on to claim for the Presbyterians the same privileges the Catholics are seeking, and closes with these words: "But we take leave to say, in conclusion, that whatever imaginary advantages might flow from such a division of our public moneys, we are quite willing to forego them, for the immensely higher advantages of maintaining our excellent school system as it is, and frowning upon any attempt, come from whatever quarter it may, to force the power and patronage of the State into any alliance with sectarian opinion."

ative from Detroit.[84] It was referred to the Committee on Education, which in its majority report advised against the passage of the bill, basing its decision on these grounds: the common school system must be general, "free for all to organize under its beneficent provisions"; it must not open the way to sectarian demands; favorable action on the bill would turn the schools into theological seminaries. To this obstinate rather than logical statement a minority report was opposed, written by Mr. O'Callahan himself, and showing a deeper grasp of the issues involved.[85] On February 12, a motion to reconsider the bill was lost by a vote of 48 to 17. It was futile to prolong the contest against the dead-weight of misunderstanding and prejudice. But there was profit in failure, for the Catholics of Michigan were more than ever determined to maintain their schools at any cost.

The activities characteristic of Bishop Lefevere's episcopate have been broadly outlined. They are only the high lights in the picture of a pious and laborious life. In every detail extant traditions confirm this portrait drawn by an early biographer.

> The private life of Bishop Lefevere was that of a true missionary. Simplicity, voluntary poverty, frugality, temperance, and personal austerity were the virtues of a lifetime with him, no less in the episcopal city of Detroit than in the backwoods of Missouri. He was an early riser in winter and summer; he was ever punctual at the altar of the Cathedral or chapel at half-past five in summer, and six in winter, every morning of the week, commencing a day of labor and devotion with the august sacrifice of the immaculate Lamb. He was as regular in his attendance at the confessional as any priest, spending hours in this painful and confining service. The poor flocked to his confessional, as they did to his altar; for none were repulsed from either, but rather welcomed as representatives of Christ, and as the proofs of His presence with his Church. The cathedral congregation, under his immediate eye, was as numerous as it was edifying, and it was a pleasing sight to behold, on Sunday morning, the crowded throngs which successively filled the Cathedral. . . .[86]

This was Bishop Lefevere at home in his episcopal city; he was perhaps more himself in his pastoral visitations. He knew his diocese as he had known his Salt River mission, down to the last hamlet. In those days of primitive transportation the larger towns could be reached by railroad and stagecoach, the smaller settlements only on horseback. The bishop was never so happy as when, with bulging

---

[84] "Jeremiah O'Callahan, Representative from Detroit, was a native of Ireland, born in 1823. Very little is known of him, except that he was a grocer and trader, was a Democrat in politics, and died in 1856." *Early History . . . with Biog.*, 498.

[85] *Docs. Accom. Journal . . . Senate and House*, House Doc. No. 5.

[86] Clarke, *Lives of Deceased Bishops . . .* II, 197.

saddlebags, he jogged along a trail that wandered far from the travelled turnpike to end at a little wooden church before which a knot of bare-headed pioneers cried out their welcome. For the first eleven years of his episcopate while the Indian missions of the north were still under his jurisdiction, a circuit of the diocese required from four to six months. We can see Bishop Lefevere at work in his own description of his first visitation to the north in the spring of 1842

> . . . I visited a part of my diocese, Mackinac Island, which is inhabited by savages, half-breeds, and whites who have come to deal with them. This makes it a center of drunkenness, almost the sole obstacle to the civilization of the Indians, and the good morals of the whites. I have had the consolation of enrolling a large number of these children of Bacchus in our total abstinence association. I also baptized and confirmed a large number of whites and Indians. I confirmed and gave the pledge to 200 persons. . . .
>
> From there I went to Milwaukee, which is the principal city of Wisconsin. I found a fine church, half-completed, and a large congregation, but a poor one as is the case everywhere. The city is increasing rapidly through immigration; at my departure 2000 German Catholics were expected. I had intended to finish my visitation there, but the Indians of Arbre Croche had heard that I was returning through Mackinac. On arrival I found their chief with a dozen brawny companions. They had been waiting for me 7 days, determined not to return without "la grande robe-noir." Despite my urgent affairs in Detroit I was obliged to take my place in a bark canoe, and let them take me to their village. . . . When we arrived, I perceived the whole tribe dressed in festival costume, the men all armed with guns. They saluted us from afar with three salvos. The deep silence that reigned as I landed was broken by by another discharge, and then every one lay prostrate to receive my blessing. Finally they conducted me in procession to the church, and from there to the chief's lodge, where I was served enough food to satisfy twenty-five soldiers. I confirmed, gave the pledge to nearly every one, and baptized a few children and adults. . . . Never did I have more consolation than among these poor Indians. What would I not give to pass the remainder of my days among them. My arrival had overwhelmed them with joy; at my departure I could read the sadness in their faces . . .[87]

Father Baraga describes Bishop Lefevere again among the Indians in 1846, this time at L'Anse.

> The Rt. Rev. Administrator of the diocese of Detroit, Bishop Lefevere, was there in July. During the few days he spent there he did a great deal of good to my mission. He confirmed a great number of Indians in the real literal sense of the word. His presence, his exceeding

great kindness and love, and his edifying exhortations made an indelible impression on the minds of these new Christians.

Moreover, he organized a temperance society in my mission, to which all who by reason of their age could do so, gave their names. He did this in a solemn manner, after divine service. It was an edifying and consoling sight. The bishop stood in his pontifical robes at the communion railing and held in his hand the temperance-pledge leaflets, which had been printed in the Indian language. Every Indian who wished to become a member of the society, came forward, knelt before the bishop, received his blessing and received the leaflet from his hands. . . .[88]

It was during the last of these almost yearly visitations that Bishop Lefevere suffered an accident which, in all likelihood, was the origin of his final illness. In the fall of 1868, while making the circuit of the Indian missions, he lost his balance as he was stepping into a canoe and fell, seriously bruising his ankle.[89] He made light of the injury, which did not fully incapacitate him, even when he had returned to his duties in Detroit. But in the middle of February infection made its appearance, and then erysipelas. Aware of the increasing gravity of his condition, Bishop Lefevere prepared for death as methodically as he had lived. Laying aside all signs of his rank, he had himself transported to a humbly furnished room in St. Mary's Hospital, where in patience he awaited the end. On February 28, when fateful signs of gangrene were apparent, he received the last sacraments, and on the night of March 4, 1869, while the little band of Daughters of Charity whom he had befriended for so many years knelt weeping around his bed, he died.[90]

His obsequies were held in the cathedral four days later. Bishop Rappe of Cleveland celebrated the funeral Mass, and the sermon was preached by the venerable Archbishop Purcell of Cincinnati. At its close the mortal remains of Bishop Lefevere were lowered into his tomb, below the center aisle, and two paces outside the altar railing. Out of a full heart an unknown reporter of these proceedings, having sketched the life of his bishop, wrote this final tribute:

Thus lived, thus died, one of the truest priests, one of the noblest bishops, one of the kindest men that it has ever been our fortune to know, mourned by all, loved by all whose love was worth the having.

[88] Verwyst, *Life and Labors of . . . Baraga*, 228.

[89] Bishop Baraga died January 19, 1868, and the care of the Indian missions again fell to Bishop Lefevere.

[90] These details from the *Western Catholic*, the diocesan weekly, for March 13, 1869.

CHAPTER XXI

The Diocese under Bishop Lefevere

IN TRACING the development of the Church in Michigan, the episcopate of Bishop Lefevere stretching over a period of thirty years, from 1840 to 1870, is the most important for our purpose. It covers the transition from a primitive stage only eight years removed from Father Richard's death to a term of expansion which exhibits the entire framework of the Church as it is today. By the end of the period every important center had been established, and subsequent growth has only filled in the vacant spaces in the original design.

At the outset the field of our study must be clearly delimited; it cannot be coextensive with Michigan but with a portion of the state designated as the Diocese of Detroit. To begin narrowing our scope we may recall the two divisions, already noted, of the original territory confided to Bishop Rese, namely, the erection of the see of Dubuque in 1837, and of Milwaukee in 1843. A third partition came about when the upper peninsula became a vicariate under Bishop Baraga. The veteran missionary was consecrated at Cincinnati, November 1, 1853, and established his see first at Sault Ste Marie, and later, in 1865, at Marquette. He could not bring himself to desert the Indian missions in the lake region that had been his portion for so many years, and a further partition, not of territory but of jurisdiction resulted. He took over the missions in northern Wisconsin offered him by Bishop Henni, and the missions in the southern peninsula of Michigan belonging to Bishop Lefevere. Following is the text of the document by which the transfer was effected.

Whereas I Peter Paul Lefevere feel unable to properly attend to the spiritual wants of the faithful in Christ residing in the North-western part of the southern peninsula of the State of Michigan; and whereas the Rt. Rev. Dr. Baraga, Bp. of Amyzonia and Vicar-Apostolic of the Upper or Northern Peninsula of the State of Michigan is willing and desirous of attending to the spiritual wants of said faithful in Christ; therefore I cede, give and grant to the said Rt. Rev. Dr. Baraga as far as I am able, all faculties, powers, authorities and rights, to himself and those whom he may canonically appoint, according to the rites of the Catholic church, to attend to the spiritual wants of the people and faithful in Christ, residing in the following counties of the said lower Peninsula of the State of Mich., viz: in the counties of Cheboygan, Emmet, Antrim, Leelanau and Grand Traverse.[1] Together with all the temporal emoluments and benefits arising from said spiritual attendance, for and during the time of either of our natural lives.

Provided however: and this is the express condition and reserve, that the said Rt. Rev. Dr. Baraga do oblige himself to attend or cause to attend properly to the spiritual wants of the said faithful and people residing or to reside in the above mentioned counties.

And I, Frederick Baraga, do herewith oblige myself properly to attend or cause to attend to the spiritual wants of the faithful in said counties.

In witness whereof, we have hereunto set our hands and seals this 4th day of August, A.D. one thousand, eighteen hundred and fifty-four.[2]

The first real division of the lower peninsula came with the erection of the Diocese of Grand Rapids on May 19, 1882. It included thirty-nine counties of which all but two lay above a line drawn from the foot of Saginaw Bay to Lake Michigan. The early land seekers in Michigan had chosen the more fertile southern counties in preference to the northern area where stood the hundreds of miles of the state's superb white pine. The thirty years between 1850 and 1880 were the boisterous era of the lumber barons, and there was scarcely a settlement in the northern counties that did not owe its origin to their operations. At the death of Bishop Lefevere there were thirteen churches with resident priests in the future diocese, and when Bishop Joseph Richter took possession of his see in April, 1883, the number of churches had risen to thirty-two.[3]

The twenty-nine counties remaining to the Diocese of Detroit after the division gave better evidence of the immigration trends that peopled the southern peninsula, and it is in this area that we will attempt to trace the growth of the Church.

We may begin our survey of the Diocese of Detroit by examining the few statistical references to its expansion that are available. The extent of the Church in Michigan as Bishop Rese left it has already been stated: the episcopal city; the static French settlements along the eastern shore of the state and in the southwest corner; the Indian missions of the northern lake region; the German colony in Westphalia; the Irish settlers in Washtenaw County; the half formed parish on the Grand River. The only contemporary estimate of this

---

[1] Charlevoix County, which now lies within the territory thus described, was later formed from contiguous portions of Antrim and Emmet Counties.

[2] Original in NDA.

[3] A sketch of the Diocese of Grand Rapids by Father Robert Brown in the *Mich. Hist. Colls.*, XXXVIII, 509–19, lists the churches and their pastors.

Catholic population is that given by Blois in 1838.[4] "The Catholics
. . . claim a population of from 20,000 to 24,000 . . ." In the
Catholic Almanac for 1844, the population of the diocese is given for
the first time on information presumably supplied by Bishop Lefevere. Including of course the Indian missions of the north the population is placed at 25,000. One year later, the figure becomes 40,000.
The first number was probably only a repetition of Blois' estimate,
and did not represent a serious attempt at a census; the second is
surely inadmissable. All growth between 1838 and 1845 must have
come from immigration, and there is no reason for believing that
15,000 Catholics came to Michigan during the period. From 1840 to
1844 the city of Detroit itself gained only 1800 inhabitants.[5] The Almanac for 1850 discloses only three or four changes in the listings for
the diocese yet the Catholic population is set down as being 75,000.
During the five year period from 1845 to 1850 the population of the
entire state increased by no more than 95,000. Obviously, the figures
in the series of Almanacs have little value, and reflect no more than
optimistic judgments of growth and progress. The following statistics
are taken from the Almanacs over the period that we intend to study.

	Priests	Churches	Population
1840	18	30	. . . .
1844	15	37	25,000
1845	14	37	40,000
1847	22	37	75,000
1850	27	39	75,000
1855	35	46	85,000
1860	43	56	85,000
1865	56	64	85,000
1867	62	64	"about 90,000"
1868	70	75	"about 150,000"
1870	88	80	"at least 150,000"

The progressive distribution of this Catholic population in the
twenty-nine counties of the diocese is not very easily followed. Rarely
is any considerable group of Catholics, like the German colony at
Westphalia, found by itself. Indeed, there were few localities where
such a condition was possible. The directions in which the development of the state would proceed and the foci of settlement had already been determined by the first wave of immigration from the
eastern and New England states, which, as we have seen, was almost
entirely Protestant. It would be quite feasible to go touring through
southern Michigan today using the map of the "Surveyed part" of the

[4] Blois. *Gazetteer.*
[5] For the population of Detroit throughout its history see Burton, *op. cit.*, II, 1503.

state drawn by John Farmer in 1839. When Catholic immigrants came in they settled for the most part alongside the Protestant pioneers who had preceded them. Hence the beginnings of Catholic growth are so obscure that it is impossible to trace them in many localities until the number of Catholics was large enough to warrant some semblance of parish organization. Moreover, the rise of the Catholic population was not so dependent upon the factors that affected the distribution of the initial immigration into the state, although it reflected them to a certain extent. Perhaps a brief survey of the pioneer period is a necessary background to our special study.

The most significant date in the story of how Michigan was peopled is August 27, 1818. On that day the Walk-in-the-Water, first steam vessel to ply the great lakes, completed her maiden voyage with one last wheeze as she rammed the wharf at Detroit. She inaugurated a new era of speedy and comfortable transportation to the West. Hitherto the great highway of easy travel westward had been the Ohio River. Michigan had remained comparatively remote, and what was worse, undesirable.[6] Congress had intended to locate bounty lands in Michigan for the veterans of the War of 1812, but the Surveyor-General reported to the Land Office in 1815 that in the whole Territory there was "not one acre in a hundred, if there would be one in a thousand, that would in any case admit of cultivation. It is all swampy and sandy."[7] So general was the impression in the East regarding the worthlessness of Michigan for settlement that the school geographies bore the words "Interminable Swamp" across their maps of the Territory.

However, these misrepresentations were being gradually dispelled when the Walk-in-the-Water brought her first load of eager adventurers come to see for themselves. That same year a land office was opened in Detroit. In 1820 the sales were 2,860 acres; one year later they ran to 7,444 acres, and in 1822 to 20,068 acres. With the opening of the Erie Canal in 1825 the flood of immigration to Michigan began. It reached its peak in the early thirties, and subsided only in the

[6] "The first trip of the Walk-in-the-Water, the first steamer on Lake Erie, 1818, marked the beginning of a new era of travel on the Great Lakes. Before the coming of the steamboat, the emigrant to the West by way of Lake Erie had the choice of three routes of travel. He could make the voyage in a schooner, slow, often storm-tossed and wind-bound, with little accommodation for passengers; he could make his way on foot or horse through the dark and almost roadless woods of Canada, his way frequently beset by robbers; or he could go along the south shore of Lake Erie through the Black Swamp of northwestern Ohio. The Walk-in-the-Water reduced the time for Lake travel between Buffalo and Detroit from five or ten days to forty-four hours. . . ." Almon Ernest Parkins, *The Historical Geography of Detroit* (Lansing, 1918), 172.

[7] Farmer, *op. cit.*, I, 15. See also G. Fuller, *op. cit.*, Chapter II. This volume is an indispensable study of Michigan before statehood.

depression period marked by the panic year of 1837. In 1830 twenty-four hundred homeseekers landed at Detroit between April 1 and May 12, and during one day in October, 1834, nine hundred excited settlers swarmed into the streets of the town.[8]

Detroit numbered some 9,000 inhabitants in 1840, and in the state there was a population of over 200,000 lying almost entirely below a line drawn westward from Bay City; above this line stood the unbroken forests waiting to be despoiled. The distribution of immigration from 1818 had naturally been determined by the advantages of certain localities for settlement, and by the avenues of travel which had been successively opened.

The first road-building in Michigan was an aftermath of the War of 1812. The necessity of linking Detroit with the Ohio valley was recognized by the government, and in 1818 it authorized the construction of a road from Detroit through Monroe to the Rapids of the Miami. About the same time surveys were begun for the first inland road, also a military project, and designed to connect Detroit with the small military post at Saginaw Bay. The settlement of Michigan, however, was more dependent upon three great highways that crossed the Territory from east to west. The most important of these was the Chicago Road, which Father Richard had fostered during his term in Congress. It ran from Detroit to Ypsilanti and Tecumseh, then westward through the southernmost tier of counties until it left the Territory in Berrien County. Next came the Territorial Road authorized in 1829. Along its course through the second tire of counties grew the villages, now the thriving cities of Ann Arbor, Jackson, Marshall, Battle Creek, and Kalamazoo. Finally, the Grand River Road, authorized in 1832, went diagonally across the Territory from Detroit to Grand Rapids, and then to Lake Michigan at Grand Haven.[9]

Within the framework of these highways the course of settlement is roughly indicated by the order in which land offices were established. Fuller summarizes this order as follows:

As the surveys advanced and more land was ready for the market, new land offices were established: at Monroe in 1823, at White Pigeon in 1831, at Kalamazoo in 1834, and at Flint and Ionia in 1836. The first represented a movement of population into the country of the Raisin River Valley, the second out along the Chicago Road, the third along the Territorial Road, the fourth into the Saginaw Valley, the fifth into the Grand River Region. The opening of the land office at

[8] Fuller, *op. cit.*, 71–72.
[9] *Ibid.*, 75–79.

Kalamazoo in 1834 marks the beginning of a new period in the settlement of western Michigan.[10]

For our purpose it is enough to glance at the definite areas of settlement so conveniently blocked out by Fuller in his study. The first, designated The Eastern Shore, comprises the counties of Monroe, Wayne, Macomb, and St. Clair. These counties held the bulk of the French population situated along the waterways, but their nearness to Detroit and their accessibility was certain to attract the earliest immigration. However, the vacant lands were heavily timbered, and the soil was not considered too favorable for agriculture. The two northern counties were away from the main lines of travel out of Detroit, and their development was retarded in consequence. Yet, Mt. Clemens was platted in 1818, St. Clair in 1828, Marine City in 1831, and Port Huron in 1835. A colony of New England Congregationalists settled at Romeo in 1827. Monroe, as an American settlement was begun in 1817, and on the south side of the Raisin River. The French who populated Frenchtown on the north side of the river were unwilling to part with enough land for public purposes. Two other important centers in the early thirties were Dundee and Petersburg, both good mill sites on the Raisin River.[11]

Behind the first line of settlement lay the three counties of Oakland, Lenawee, and Washtenaw possessing definite physical features in common. The topography was picturesque, there was abundant water power, the soil was fertile, and the timber grew in patches forming the prairies or "openings" so prized by the early settlers. Oakland being nearest to Detroit was the first to draw its quota of homeseekers. A colony was founded at Rochester in 1817, and Pontiac dates from the hilarious party of the "Pontiac Company in 1819.[12] Meanwhile, surveys were being pushed into Washtenaw and Lenawee counties. Ypsilanti, Ann Arbor, and Tecumseh were begun in 1824, Dexter in 1825, Adrian in 1826, Clinton in 1830, and Manchester in 1832.[13]

The counties of Hillsdale, Branch, St. Joseph, Cass and Berrien can be conveniently grouped together as composing the watershed in Michigan of the St. Joseph River. In the development of these counties the course of the river was almost as important as the Chicago Road, which was the main axis of settlement. Two currents of immigration met in them. The frontier was gradually pushed

[10] *Ibid.*, 63.

[11] Items taken *passim* from Fuller, *op. cit.*, Chap. III.

[12] This glorious carouse and the near tragedy that ended it are described in Ross and Catlin, *op. cit.*, 356–57.

[13] Fuller, *op. cit.*, Chap. IV.

westward from Lenawee into Hillsdale and Branch by immigration from the eastern states. But this advance had been preceded by home-seekers from many of the southern states, who had come up into St. Joseph, Berrien, and Cass following a trail that led from Fort Wayne to the St. Joseph River. The earliest settlement in these five counties was the Carey Mission founded in 1822, a little west of Niles.[14] Outside of the mission there were in 1825 only nine white families in the entire section, seven in Berrien County and two in Cass. Niles was platted in 1829, St. Joseph in 1831, and New Buffalo in 1834. White Pigeon in St. Joseph County was a favored locality for settlement as early as 1827, and Centerville dates from 1831, as does Constantine. Three Rivers, platted about 1835, was a flourishing village in 1838. Branch and Hillsdale Counties lagged behind the others in their development. The first white settler in Branch County was Jabez Bronson, who built his log cabin in 1828 near the site of the village which perpetuates his name. In 1834 the county had a population of 764, but it grew rapidly from that date until 1840. Coldwater was established about 1835. The most important center in Hillsdale County was Jonesville, begun in 1831. Although platted in 1835, the village of Hillsdale had no store or inn until 1838.[15]

In the next group of counties comprising Jackson, Calhoun, Kalamazoo, Van Buren, and Allegan development was again largely influenced by a river and a highway: the Kalamazoo River and the Territorial Road. Of these counties Kalamazoo had the richest soil and the least timber, and was settled earliest to a large extent by the same current of immigration that had come from the south into Cass and St. Joseph Counties. An eye witness has written an amusing description of a cross-section of the population to be found in the neighborhood of Schoolcraft in 1833.

> There was a "long-haired hooshier" from Indiana, a couple of smart looking "suckers" from the southern part of Illinois, a keen-eyed leather-belted "badger" from the mines of Wisconsin, and a sturdy yeoman-like fellow, whose white capot, Indian moccasins, and red sash proclaimed, while he boasted a three years residence, the genuine Wolverine, or naturalized Michiganian . . . The spokesman was evidently a "red horse" from Kentucky, and nothing was wanting but a "buck-eye" from Ohio to render the assemblage as complete as it was select . . . "From the eastern side, stranger?" said another to me, "I am told it is a tolerable frog pasture. Now here the soil's so deep one can't raise any long sarce—they all get pulled through the other side. We can winter

[14] It will be remembered that this mission was established by the Baptists among the Potawatomi whose ancestors had been gathered by the Jesuits at Mission St. Joseph, and that this foundation had a bearing on Father Richard's going to Congress.

[15] Fuller, *op. cit.*, Chap. V.

our cows, however, on wooden clocks, there's so many Yankees among us . . .[16]

Although the Territorial Road was authorized in 1829 it was almost impassible until 1835. Yet the anticipation of it was enough to warrant the continued growth of important settlements in the section primarily because of the abundant water power available. Such was the origin of Albion, Marshall, Battle Creek, Kalamazoo, all established between 1830 and 1835. Jackson had no natural advantages to commend it, being low and swampy as were the lands in its vicinity. But its situation in the center of the county, and at the crossing of many old Indian trails used by the immigrants into the section made it important as early as 1831, and a thriving village by 1838.[17]

One section of Michigan suffered more than any other from the misrepresentations of the early immigration period, the Saginaw country. After flowing southward from the Bay for thirty miles the Saginaw River branches out into four streams: the Cass, the Flint, the Shiawassee, and the Tittabawassee. This river system drains the counties of Lapeer, Genesee, Livingston, Saginaw, and Shiawassee. The section was represented as being hardly more than a succession of swamps and marshes unfit for cultivation, and exhaling pestilential vapors. When the military post at Saginaw was abandoned in 1823 the commanding officer reported that "nothing but Indians, muskrats, and bullfrogs could possibly exist here." It was to the interests of the first land speculators in the southern and western counties to perpetuate such mistaken notions of the Saginaw country. In 1830 there were no more than one hundred whites in the three counties of Saginaw, Shiawassee, and Lapeer, but a better knowledge of the section was being diffused and was soon to bear fruit.

The Saginaw country had been a favored spot for the agents of the American Fur Company long before the War of 1812, and its two most important cities stand on vantage points at the crossing of Indian trails chosen by the early traders.[18] Saginaw was platted in 1822 by Louis Campau; the German, Jacob Smith, and his Chippewa wife had a post at Flint as early as 1819. However, their growth as American settlements dates from the middle thirties. There was a thriving community of immigrants from New York, Vermont, and Connecticut at Grand Blanc in 1830, and Lapeer was platted the following year. Owosso became an important center about 1837, when it at-

---

[16] Hoffman, *A Winter in the West*, quoted by Fuller, *op. cit.*, 314.

[17] Fuller, *op. cit.*, Chap VI.

[18] For an interesting account of the workings of the American Fur Company in Michigan see Ida Amanda Johnson, *The Michigan Fur Trade* (Lansing, 1919).

tracted a group of immigrants from Rochester, New York. On the Grand River Road running diagonally through Livingston County the three villages of Brighton, Howell, and Livingston were in existence before 1838.[19]

The watershed of the Grand River comprises the counties of Kent, Ottawa, Barry, Eaton, Ingham, Ionia, and Clinton. Because of its distance from Detroit, and of the heavy timber that covered it this section in its development lagged behind the more attractive lands to the south and east. It was not surveyed until 1826, and no townships were organized in any of these counties, with the exception of Kent, until 1836–37. Like the Saginaw country this region had been for years traversed by the fur traders, who had established numerous posts for Indian trade.

The first attempt at settlement in the oldest center of population in this section, Grand Rapids, was the establishment, in 1827, of a Baptist mission, the outgrowth of the Carey Mission at Niles. Louis Campau came from the Saginaw country to make the first land purchase in 1831, and two years later there were about ten families grouped on the site of the future city. In 1833 a party of sixty-three immigrants from New York settled at Ionia, using for their first shelter five bark wigwams which stood on the site. Lyons was begun in 1836, and Portland had half a dozen families in 1837. The first settlement in Eaton County was at Bellevue, which had a population of 400 in 1838. A group of colonists from Vermont, nearly all Congregationalists, founded Vermontville in 1836. Their purpose appears in the preamble of the "Rules and Regulations of the Union Colony."

> Whereas, the enjoyment of the ordinances and institutions of the Gospel is in a great measure unknown in many parts of the western country; and Whereas, We believe that a pious and devoted emigration is to be one of the most efficient means, in the hands of God, in removing the moral darkness which hangs over a great portion of the valley of the Mississippi . . . We do therefore, form ourselves into an association or colony . . .[20]

In 1837 Barry County had a population of 512, and only two villages, Hastings and Middleville. Ingham County could boast of only one village, Mason, but there was a larger population concentrated in the townships of Stockbridge and Williamston. The beginning of the German Catholic colony at Westphalia in Clinton County has already been referred to. In the same year, 1836, an organized Protestant group from Rochester, New York, settled in the township of

---

[19] Fuller, *op. cit.*, Chap. VII.
[20] *Mich. Hist. Colls.*, XXVIII, 204.

Duplain. There were a few settlers along the Looking Glass River in the neighborhood of Dewitt, but in 1840 the entire county was still without a recognized village.[21]

The foregoing all too rapid summary furnishes some idea of pioneer development before 1840 in the area blocked out for our study. It is evident that subsequent growth not only in the next thirty years but down to our own time has proceeded from centers and along lines that were fairly well established before the period we are dealing with. We must now begin to trace the parallel progress of the Church in the same area. To avoid confusion in presenting the amount of detail necessary we shall take up in turn the several sections delimited by Fuller, and Detroit itself will be scanned at the last.

At the beginning of 1840, in the southernmost county of the Eastern Shore section, Monroe, there were two resident priests. Father Warlop was stationed at the Bay Settlement, and Father Carabin attended at intervals from Monroe the log chapel near Swan Creek, and the one in the Huron Settlement across the line into Wayne County. In August, 1843, Father Carabin was transferred to Green Bay.[22] At the same time his successor became Father Santelli, who was anxious to leave Mackinac, if the reader remembers, to bask in a warmer climate. However, Monroe proved to be no more agreeable, and in the spring of 1844, he requested leave to return to his native country.[23] The vacant parish was chosen by Father Gillet for his Redemptorist foundation, and he immediately set to work remedying the primitive conditions under which Father Carabin had been content to live by building a rectory, and by adding a more commodius sanctuary to the church. On December 8, 1845, the renovated church was consecrated by Bishop Lefevere, and its name was changed from St. Anthony's to St. Mary's.[24]

Meanwhile, the number of German and Irish Catholics in Monroe had been steadily increasing, and Father Gillet thought it necessary to provide specially for their needs. At the end of 1845 a third Redemptorist came to live with Fathers Gillet and Poilvache, who was no other than Father Simon Saenderl. The second floor of the rectory was fitted up as a chapel and dedicated to St. Joseph, and there Father Saenderl gathered his bilingual congregation.[25] In addition to his assignment at Monroe he began a series of missionary excursions to

[21] Fuller, op. cit., Chap. VIII.

[22] Father Carabin left Green Bay in 1847 to affiliate with the Diocese of Cleveland. For the last twenty years of his life he was an invalid at St. Vincent's Hospital, Cleveland, where he died on August 1, 1873. Houck, op. cit., 88.

[23] His entries in the baptismal register extend from October 22, 1843, to May 12, 1844.

[24] Annales Cong. SS. Redemp., I, 165.

[25] Ibid., 173.

new Catholic settlements that were springing up along or near the Chicago Road, and as far as can be discovered he seems to have been the pioneer priest of Lenawee and Hillsdale Counties.[26]

In Monroe County itself there were by this time several Catholic groups whose beginnings dated from the late thirties but whose existence is revealed only by the recorded ministrations of the Redemptorists. The Muddy Creek settlement, perhaps the earliest, lay in La Salle township, and a chapel dedicated to St. John, which has long since been abandoned, was built on the farm of Owen Cooney in Section 29 about 1848.[27] At least this much is certain that a mission was preached there at the end of 1849 by Father Tschenhens, the former companion of Father Saenderl, who had been assigned to Monroe the same year.[28] The memory of the primitive chapel is preserved in the present church of St. John for the English-speaking Catholics of Monroe erected in 1873 largely through the exertions of the descendants of the Muddy Creek pioneers.

Another early Irish settlement was located in the extreme north of the county along the line between Ash and Exeter townships. It was known as the Stony Creek settlement, and when first visited by Father Gillet in 1846 it comprised sixty Catholic families.[29] He gave the impetus to the building of a log chapel in what is now the "Old Graveyard," and wherein Mass was first said by Father Saenderl in March, 1847. After the Redemptorists withdrew from Monroe the locality was attended generally from Newport until it was erected into a parish in 1860. Father Desiderius Callaert became the first resident pastor, and the present church was completed and consecrated the following year. Although St. Patrick's, Carleton, as the location is now called, has long ceased to be a distinctively Irish congregation, the name it bears is reminiscent of its origin.

A third Irish group visited by the Redemptorists may be regarded

[26] Father Saenderl left Monroe in 1847, and in 1850 he quitted his Congregation to become a Trappist. He died at Gethsemane Abbey, Kentucky, on February 22, 1879. See sketch in Rezek, *op. cit.*, I, 342.

[27] The chapel had apparently disappeared by 1862, for the sole extant deed to the property, made to Bishop Lefevere in 1862, mentions only the cemetery and the path leading to it.

[28] *Annales Cong. SS. Redemp.*, II, 61. In connection with this mission Father Tschenhens notes an incident which proved the calibre of his congregation. Catholics and non-Catholics alike came from miles around to hear the preaching. On the last day of the mission, when it came time for the renewal of baptismal vows, all persons not concerned were asked to leave. Angered by this exclusion the non-jurors massed about the windows of the chapel, and vented their angry disappointment of the silent worshippers. This was more than the congregation could stand. As a man it rose, rushed outside, beat the disturbers into silence, and then reentered the chapel to proceed with the ceremony.

[29] *Annales* . . . I, 434.

St. Anne's church about 1850. The building stands on the north side of Larned Street between Bates and Randolph Streets. Woodward Avenue is just out of the scene to the left. From a contemporary print in the Burton Historical Collection.

as the nucleus of the present day parish of Milan. The first church to serve the Catholics of this area was built on land donated to Bishop Lefevere in 1854 by William Johnstin and Peter Hanlin, which was located in Section 17 of Milan Township, and thus well into Monroe County.[30] Somehow the settlement could not achieve parochial status, but remained dependent upon Monroe or other neighboring parishes until the first resident priest was stationed in the area at Whittaker in 1904. Finally, in 1922 the parish site was established in the town of Milan, and Whittaker became an outlying mission.

The presence of a considerable number of German Catholics in Monroe County becomes evident in the early fifties. A settlement in Ida township, visited every month by Father Smulders of Monroe, is mentioned for the first time in the Catholic Almanac for 1852. The original tiny frame church was built in Section 11 on a plot of ground donated by Anton Bower. Attended either from Monroe or Adrian the mission became a parish only in 1904, when a pastor was appointed with residence at Ida.

A more important settlement, named for the first time in 1854, was Blue Bush in London township. Its modern equivalent is the village of Maybee, but the ground donated to Bishop Lefevere by Edward Heisler in 1857 lay in Section 24, about two miles from the village.[31] In the same year a log church was built, which was replaced by a more fitting structure in 1879. Blue Bush became a mission of Stony Creek, and when increasing numbers had outgrown even the second church, the third was erected in the village of Maybee itself by Father Ronayne in 1889. The first resident priest, Father Joseph Seybold, began his pastorate in 1894.

In the city of Monroe itself the chapel first used by Father Saenderl for the German Catholics soon became inadequate. The Redemptorists accordingly purchased the spacious Harleston residence, and dedicated it to church purposes on the feast of St. Michael, September 29, 1852.[32] It served as a combined chapel, school, and rectory until 1867, when the present brick church was completed.[33]

With the early history of the French parishes in the county we are already acquainted. One hitherto unmentioned station, which was attended for about twenty years, appears for the first time in the Almanac for 1852. At the mouth of Stony Creek lay the hamlet of Brest, which once had visions of becoming an important lake port.[34]

---

[30] In DCA.

[31] The first settlers were all from Baden. Their names and a short history of the parish are given in Bulkley's History of Monroe County, II, 688–92.

[32] Annales Cong. SS. Redemp., II, 225.

[33] A parish history was printed for the jubilee celebration in 1902.

[34] Bulkley, op. cit., I, 549.

In 1851 the Redemptorists began ministering to a number of families in the neighborhood, using an abandoned bank building for a house of worship.[35] The mission was later attached to Newport, and was attended down to 1872.

The Bay Settlement, having always had its own resident pastor, was never attended by the Redemptorists. About 1850 the traditional French term for the parish gave way to Vienna, the name applied to the hamlet that grew up near the railroad station serving the locality, and which is today the village of Erie. With the change in name came as well the abandonment of the old church site near the lake shore, and the present church in Erie was consecrated on October 24, 1852.

As we have seen, a log chapel was built in Swan Creek, or Newport, in 1838. The name St. Charles is first applied to it in the Catholic Almanac for 1843, which adds that the settlement was cared for by Father Carabin. The Redemptorists paid regular visits until 1849, when the mission was assigned to Father Charles De Preitre, then pastor of Ecorse. A second chapel, erected in 1847 on land to which the congregation had no title, had to be abandoned the following year, and services were held in the homes of Peter Allore and Peter Brancheau until the spring of 1853, when a frame church was built on property donated by John B. Trombly. In July of that year Father John Van Gennip was appointed the first resident pastor. The corner stone of the present church was laid on April 15, 1882.[36]

To conclude with Monroe County we must glance at the history of the mother church itself. The Redemptorists were withdrawn in the spring of 1855, and for more than two years the parish remained without a resident pastor.[37] In November, 1857, Father Edward Joos, who had come from Belgium the preceding year, was assigned to Monroe.[38] Of this distinguished priest so intimately identified with the work of the Church in the Monroe area, an interesting biography from which the following passage is quoted was written by Monsignor Frank O'Brien.

[35] *Annales* . . . II, 452.

[36] A fine parish history was printed in 1932.

[37] *Annales* . . . II, 143. The Fathers record that they left on the "Kalends of May." Between 1844 and 1855 there were generally three Redemptorists stationed in Monroe. In 1846 they were Fathers Gillet, Poilvache, and Saenderl. At the end of the year Father Gillet was replaced by Father Aegidius Smulders. The death of Father Poilvache, and the departure of Father Saenderl resulted in the assigning to Monroe of Father Peter Steinbacher and James Poirier. The former was replaced in 1849 by Father Tschenhens, and the latter by Father Peter Cronenberg in 1851. The Almanac for 1847 assigns a Father L. Billon to Monroe. The notation is apparently an error, for no Redemptorist of that name is known.

[38] Father Edward Joos was born at Somerghem, East Flanders, April 19, 1825. Ordained in 1848 he came to Detroit in 1856 with dimissorial letters from the Diocese of Ghent.

The Catholics of the "Independent State" were divided. Good in their own way, yet cursed with the spirit of nationalism, which has wrought disaster through the length and breadth of our fair land.

The French held the fort for many a year. With advancing prosperity came the sturdy Irish, and the children of the Irish, and later the thrifty Germans. Welcome indeed were they for the city's sake, but looked upon as intruders by that large majority which composed the Catholic population . . .

The coming of the Redemptorists was the cause of general rejoicing. . . . It was supposed that they would do away with factions, but they, too, failed in keeping unity between the Irish and the French . . . Then the Redemptorists furnished a priest for each of the factions, thereby promoting peace, and greater progress was made during the few years of their stay in Monroe . . .

One afternoon the news was whispered around, and spread like wildfire, that the new priest had arrived to take charge of the parish . . . The bell announced the Mass for the next morning. The congregation was larger than for many days thereafter. All were anxious to see what was in store for them. An old French lady, after the services, described him as a "half little man, with a long head, large red nose and peaked face, he wore glasses and looked greatly frightened . . ."

This first sermon made the English people resolve that they were never going to have any justice done them, and assembling in a meeting shortly after service the same day, they protested against the coming of this foreigner, and sent a petition to the Bishop asking for some one that could speak English. The French sermon at the 10:30 services was not favorably commented on. "He no speak good French," was the verdict of one group who discussed his merits after the services . . .[39]

The writer goes on to relate with graphic details how Father Joos by his quiet determination, his zeal, and his charity finally united the discordant elements of the parish in the common bond of affection for their pastor. His deep interest in educational matters made him the friend and protector of the struggling Sisterhood at Monroe, and it was largely through his efforts that the Sisters of the Immaculate Heart were able to cope with the expansion of educational facilities demanded by the growth of the diocese.[40] In 1871 Father Joos retired from the parish to devote himself exclusively to the spiritual and educational training of the Sisterhood. Twice administrator of the

[39] "Le Pere Juste" in the *Mich. Hist. Colls.*, XXX, 262–88.

[40] "Earnestly and persistently, Father Joos took up the work of extending the apostolate of teaching. . . . After a long and perservering quest he found a course of instruction that seemed to meet all the demands of the times. It was that used in the St. Andrea's Normal College, Belgium, an Institute regarded as one of the leading Colleges for women in Europe. . . . Father Joos translated this work from the original French, and every week for over forty years, unless prevented by absence or something unforeseen, he gave an hour's conference upon this subject to the assembled Sisterhood . . ." *A Retrospect*, by a Member of the Congregation (Benziger Bros., 1916), 94–97.

diocese, and vicar-general under Bishop Foley, Father Joos was raised to the rank of Monsignor in 1889, the first priest of the diocese to be thus honored. His death occurred at Monroe, May 18, 1901.[41]

In our survey of Wayne County we begin with the older French parishes along the shore line. Just above the northern boundary of Monroe County Father Vincent Badin, as we have seen, had erected a little chapel in the Huron River Settlement, and had dedicated it to St. Vincent de Paul. The locality is mentioned for the first time in the Almanac for 1844, where it is assigned to the care of Father Santelli. In 1847 the chapel was replaced with a larger structure built by the Redemptorists, and Father Smulders dedicated it under the new title of St. Mary's.[42] The mission passed to Ecorse and then to Newport, and had no resident pastor until Father Charles Gireaux was appointed in 1886 to what is now called Rockwood.

The first advance over the log cabin stage in Ecorse took place about 1845. Although the locality is mentioned continuously in the Almanacs from 1839, no church name is given until 1847, when the title, St. Francis Xavier appears. A deed for the same site on which the present church stands was executed in favor of Bishop Lefevere on July 30, 1845, by Simon Rousson with the provision that he should have for then years the exclusive right to a pew "in the church now erected but not yet completed." [43] Presumably on the completion of the church a resident pastor was appointed in the person of Casimir Mouret, a Canadian priest who came to the diocese in 1845, and left it at the end of 1847.[44] He was succeeded by Father Charles De Preitre, a nephew of Bishop Lefevere who had come to Detroit as a seminarian and had been ordained on May 31, 1848.[45] Ten years later he was commissioned to begin a new parish in Wyandotte, and Ecorse became a mission until Father Louis Baroux was appointed pastor in 1871. He was followed in 1882 by Father John Van Gennip, who laid the corner stone of the present church in the same year.

Wyandotte is mentioned for the first time in the Almanac for 1857, and as attended from Ecorse. In that year a portion of the property now occupied by the buildings of St. Patrick's parish was deeded to Bishop Lefevere, and a frame structure was erected of which the second story served as a chapel. Named probably in honor of the

---

[41] For two years following Father Joos' resignation St. Mary's was in charge of Father Camillus P. Maes, the future bishop of Covington. From 1874 to 1899 Father Bernard G. Soffers was pastor, and from 1900 to 1913 Father Joseph Joos, a nephew of the Monsignor.

[42] *Annales* . . . I, 191, 436.

[43] Deed in DCA.

[44] Tanguay in his *Répertoire Général du Clergé Canadien* lists Father Mouret as pastor of Soulanges from 1843 to 1845.

[45] Record in DCA.

pastor's patron the chapel bore the name St. Charles Borromeo, as did for some years the present church erected in 1873. About 1888, when the French element had fairly well disappeared, the parish was renamed St. Patrick's in accord with the wishes of the predominant nationality.[46]

To the northeast of Detroit Father Badin, as already noted had built in 1825 the tiny chapel dedicated to St. Paul. The parish appears for the first time in the Almanac for 1834, when it is in charge of Father Ghislenus Bohême living at L'Anse Creuse. In 1850 the old location on the Reno farm was abandoned, and a frame church was erected on the site now occupied by the present church, begun by Father John Elsen a year before his death. The first resident pastor, Father Francis De Broux was appointed in 1857.[47]

In Wayne County as elsewhere the usual order obtained: after the French the Irish, and then the Germans. Apart from the French parishes already mentioned the oldest parish in the county outside the actual limits of Detroit is Sacred Heart in Dearborn. The little settlement first came into prominence with the building of the United States Arsenal, begun in 1833. In the *Michigan State Gazetteer* for 1838 the advantages of the village are thus set forth.

> Here is a church for Methodists erected, a sawmill with double saws, flour mill with two run of stones, 7 stores, 2 smitheries, and a foundry for iron, propelled by horsepower, a physician and about sixty families.[48]

The pioneer Catholic families, all Irish, appeared about 1836, and Mass was said in the village for the first time by Father Bernard O'Cavanagh, then pastor of Holy Trinity in Detroit, in the same year.[49] Fathers Cullen and Kundig paid occasional visits, and Father

[46] The title appears for the first time in the *Catholic Directory* for 1889.

[47] A parish history, still in manuscript, has been compiled by Father George H. Kerby, a native of the parish.

[48] Burton, *op. cit.*, II, 1585.

[49] There exists an interesting story of Catholic beginnings in Dearborn. It was printed there but is anonymous, and bears no date. From internal evidence it was certainly written by Father Schaeken during his pastorate lasting from 1874 to 1878. From a copy preserved in the parish records the following quotation is taken.
"In the year of our Lord, 1836, a few Catholics did find their way to this place, known principally on account of the United States Arsenal, built a few years previous to this epoch. These pioneers were Edmund Quirk, William Daly, Matthew Coyne, Patrick Coyne, John Reidy, Bryan Hart, John Shields, John O'Flynn, Jerah O'Sullivan, Thomas Magoonaugh . . . The first Mass ever celebrated here was at the house of Mrs. Ryan by Rev. Father O'Kavanagh, in the year 1836. A table served for altar and two bottles for candlesticks. In the year 1837, the house of Mr. John Reidy was converted into a chapel and the divine Sacrifice of the Mass celebrated by Rev. Father Cullen . . . Since this year (1839), until the completion of the old church, services were held at the house of Matthew Coyne, the old venerable gentleman, who still assists the priest around the altar. . . ."

Lawrence Kilroy said his first Mass in the home of Matthew Coyne. In 1834 the framework for a church was raised, but nothing more was done until 1847, when the congregation came under the care of that magnetic but erratic personality, Father John Farnan, responsible for an odd chapter of American Church history.

John Farnan, born in Ireland, was ordained by Archbishop Troy of Dublin in 1812, at the age of twenty-three. He came to America in 1815, and three years later began the first parish in Utica, New York, where he remained four years. During this time, as Decourcy-Shea has it, he "visited also the Catholics of Western New York, and even beyond the frontiers of the United States." [50] The high sounding phrase was nothing more than a visit to Father Richard in 1820, in the course of which he called upon his neighbor across the river. As usual Father Marchand reported the incident to his bishop, and thereby left this thumbnail sketch of his visitor.

> We had here last week the visit of Mr. John Farnan, Vicar-General of New York, and pastor of the parish of Utica, about thirty miles in the country behind Niagara. He appeared to be a learned gentleman, and Mr. Richard finds him such. I could talk to him only in Latin, in which I am pretty rusty. I received him with civility, and he did me the pleasure of dining with me a week ago today. He remained for the night, and said Mass the next morning with a pious regularity—and that is saying a good deal for an Irishman. In regard to the clerical garb, he wears it only in church; but that is the custom over there . . .[51]

In 1825 Father Farnan became the first resident priest in Brooklyn, where he completed the building of St. James church, which had been started before his coming. However, Bishop Dubois was obliged to remove him in 1829 because of his convivial habits, and Father Farnan taking the correction in bad grace thereupon began the building of a church that "should be independent of the Roman Catholic Bishop of New York, and of the See of Rome." Denounced in the press by the church authorities he nevertheless persisted until he laid the corner stone of his church on October 27, 1831. Possibly with the help of the disgruntled Hoganites in Philadelphia, who had capitulated in 1829, Father Farnan was able to hold out until the end of 1835, when his following began to dwindle away, and he himself sank into obscurity. At last, repenting of his conduct and of the scandal he had given, he applied to Bishop Hughes for the lifting of his suspension and permission to resume his ministry in another diocese. This was granted in 1847, and in October Father Farnan

---

[50] Henry De Courcy and John Gilmary Shea, *History of the Catholic Church in the United States* (New York, 1879), 473.

[51] Letter dated June 14, 1820. QCA.

came to Detroit, and was assigned to Holy Trinity as curate.[52] He was not long in discovering the Irish colony in Dearborn.

> About this time the Rev. Dr. Farnam, a man of science and muscularity, visited our village and its small congregation. He advised, exhorted, commanded his hearers, and soon the church was enclosed, plastered and befitted for divine services. Also did the Rev. Doctor call upon the catholics in Detroit in behalf of their Dearborn friends . . .[53]

The frame church completed in 1848 was named St. John's as a tribute to Father Farnan's efforts. In 1852 the first resident pastor was appointed in the person of Father James Pulsers. Four years later, Father Patrick O'Kelly came to Dearborn, built the pastoral residence, and ended his apostolic life there on October 7, 1858.[54] From 1860 to 1872 Dearborn was again a mission attended either from Redford or Ypsilanti. In 1875 the old church underwent extensive alterations, and was then dedicated to the Sacred Heart. The advent of the automobile industry, which changed a sleepy village into a thriving city, meant as well the complete transformation of Sacred Heart parish. The traditional site was abandoned for a more convenient location, and an extensive building program was undertaken which culminated in the erection of the present church, whose corner stone was laid in 1929.

Unfortunately, the Germans who settled in Greenfield township had no annalist and the beginnings of their parish are more or less obscure. From traditional accounts the pioneers, most of them from the neighborhood of Coblenz, arrived about 1842. As a group they are mentioned for the first time in the Almanac for 1845: "Dearborn and Greenfield, Wayne Co., where two frame churches are now in the progress of building. Vacant." The same notation is repeated for the following year, but in 1847 Greenfield is credited with a church named St. Lawrence.[55] However, there is reason for believing that the Almanac is here in error. The first priestly ministrations in Greenfield of which there is any record were afforded by the Redemptorists

---

[52] Extant information regarding Father Farnan is found especially in the *United States Cath. Hist. Mag.* for June, 1891; *Records and Studies* (The United States Cath. Hist. Soc.), II, October, 1900; Richard R. Elliott in the *Ill. Cath. Hist. Rev.*, II, 341–47; Heffernen, *op. cit.*, Chap. VI.

[53] When Bishop Lefevere opened his new cathedral Father Farnan was transferred to it as pastor, and there he died November 19, 1849. His remains lie in Mt. Elliott Cemetery.

[54] Father O'Kelly was buried atop a mound in the parish cemetery, which to this day is called Mt. Kelly Cemetery.

[55] In the *Catholic Almanacs* the parish name is St. Lawrence down to 1869, yet an early burial record in the parish register, dated September 7, 1855, ends thus: "in the cemetery of the Church of St. Alphonsus in Greenfield."

from St. Mary's in Detroit. By their direction a log building was raised in 1851 to serve as a school.[56] They note in their annals for 1852 that Father Glaunach has been attending Greenfield, and has been saying Mass in the home of a pioneer family, the Espers.[57] In the same year he began the building of a church which was dedicated towards the end of the summer to St. Alphonsus.

The Redemptorists attended the mission until 1858, when the first resident priest, Father Julian Maciejewski, was appointed. In 1874 the second church was built by Father George Godez. The phenomenal growth of the section in recent years as a result of the automobile industry is attested by the imposing group of parish buildings which have replaced the pioneer structures, and which cluster around the church dedicated May 18, 1930.

Another parish whose origins fall within our period is Wayne. A small number of Irish families settled in the neighborhood of the village in the early fifties. Father O'Kelly came occasionally from Dearborn to say Mass in the home of John Ryan, or of Robert Murphy.[58] In later years the second story of Jeremiah O'Connor's store in the village was used for religious purposes. The locality is mentioned for the first time in the Almanac for 1864 as a mission of Ypsilanti. The church property was deeded to Bishop Lefevere by Jeremiah O'Connor in 1865, and the first church was soon erected. In 1872 Wayne was attached to Dearborn, and 1889 to Milford. The first resident pastor, Father Joseph Connors, was appointed in 1912.

With the history of beginnings in Macomb County we are already familiar. The first resident priest in the county after Father Déjean was Father Ghislenus Bohême, who lived at L'Anse Creuse, or St. Clair Shores, as the village is known today.[59] He left the diocese in 1842, and L'Anse Creuse reverted to mission status, attached usually to Mount Clemens or Roseville down to 1912, when it resumed its parochial status under Father John D. O'Shea.

Mount Clemens became the important center in the county. In

[56] *Annales Cong. SS. Redemp.*, II, 176.

[57] *Ibid.*, II, 231.

[58] Details communicated by John Fitzgibbons, an early resident of the parish.

[59] Father Bohême was later received into the Diocese of Natchez. In the NDA there is a letter by Father Boheme to Bishop Rese, on which the following interesting notation was written by Archbishop Elder of Cincinnati. "Boheme was with the diocese of Natchez when I went there as bishop in 1857. He was pastor of Paulding, in Jasper Co., Miss. He was a good devoted priest, exemplary and hard working. During the war he wrote me that all the young men he had instructed and baptized had gone into the army, and he wanted to go after them. He was attached as chaplain to the corps of Stonewall Jackson. He kept with Col. Shannon of Meridian, Miss. He was too old for the fatigues of Jackson's rapid marching. He died at Ashland, Virginia. One morning early, Col. Shannon heard him moaning, and he died in a few minutes . . ." Lamott, *op. cit.*, gives the date of death as June 27, 1862.

1839 Christian Clemens, the founder of the settlement, in the hope of hastening the development of his holdings donated church sites to all religious societies who would accept them. The Catholics were given the present location of St. Peter's church, and the parish center was moved from the original site down the river to the village. The building of a frame church was begun by Father John Kenny who had just come to Detroit from St. Louis.[60] The parish emerged from the pioneer stage during the long pastorate of Father Henry Van Renterghem, who presided over it from his appointment in 1846 to his death in 1869.

The Mount Clemens parish was made up principally of the old French pioneers and their descendants. The first new center to arise as the result of immigration was St. Clement's at Centerline. For the most part German and Belgian, the Catholic settlers in Warren township were attended as early as 1852 by the Redemptorists from St. Mary's in Detroit.[61] The first church was built in 1854, and four years later Father Henry Meuffels was appointed the first resident pastor.[62]

The earliest church in St. Clair County was St. Félicité built in 1826 by Father Déjean about two miles below Marine City. The baptismal register, whose first entries are signed by Father Andreas Viszoczky in 1833 is preserved in the St. Clair parish records, and Father Otto Skolla before beginning his entries in May, 1843, inscribes a heading: "Children baptized in the church of St. Félicité in St. Clair." [63] In the Almanac for 1845 the church is given a new name, St. Agatha. The second church was built on the site now occupied by the parish buildings in Marine City most likely in 1850 by Father Lawrence Kilroy. The first resident pastor, Father Mary Paul Wehrle, was assigned in 1855.

Two years previous to Father Wehrle's arrival another parish had been established just a few miles to the west in the adjoining town-

---

[60] Father Kenny later went on to New York, and in the early fifties was laboring in the Diocese of Albany.

[61] St. Clement's is first mentioned in the *Catholic Almanac* for that year.

[62] *History of Macomb County* (Chicago: M. A. Leeson & Co., 1882), 854.

[63] The standard histories of St. Clair County name two priests, Fathers "Sagelle" and "Besrinquet" as working along the St. Clair River between 1820 and 1825. Actually, Father Pierre Chazelle did not come to America until 1830, and Father Dominique Chardon du Ranquet not until 1842. They were both Jesuits, and the first came from France to be Superior of St. Mary's College at Bardstown. When the Jesuits took over Assumption parish, across the river from Detroit in 1843, both priests were stationed there, and Father Du Ranquet began an Indian mission on Walpole Island. It is not surprising that these clergymen occasionally crossed over to the American side of the St. Clair River, and the histories mentioned above doubtless embody local traditions, but with little attention to dates. A full account of the 19th century return of the Jesuits is found in Édouard Lecompte, S. J., *Les Jesuites du Canada au XIX siècle* (Montreal, 1920). This work is really a continuation of Rochemonteix' history.

ship of Ira. The important center for the French living around
Anchor Bay was the Swan Creek settlement, today known as Anchorville. Here in 1853 Father Charles Chambille took up his residence,
and in the following year he dedicated the first church to the Immaculate Conception.

The preponderance of Catholic immigration into the county was
Irish, and its religious life was fostered by one of the most famous
of the pioneer priests of the diocese, Father Lawrence Kilroy. Legends
invest his memory. In a howling storm he could make his way through
the woods by holding up a lighted candle that for him shone without
a flicker. When carrying the Blessed Sacrament on some hurried sick
call his mere desire could compel a train to stop wherever he wished,
even against the knowledge or willingness of the trainmen. Unfortunately, there is nothing like an adequate record of his missionary
work in the state. Nominally pastor of Holy Trinity in Detroit for
about six years following his ordination, it is certain that he was
continually seeking out his people in the surrounding country wherever he could reach them. During 1848 and 1849 he was assistant to
Father Viszoczky at Grand Rapids, and in this undermanned section
of the state there is no telling how far his zeal carried him. In 1850 he
was assigned to the care of his compatriots in St. Clair County, and he
took up his residence in the home of James Fisher in the settlement
then known as Williamsburg, later as Vicksburg, and today as Marysville.[64]

What Father Kilroy accomplished between 1850 and the beginning of his pastorate at Port Huron in 1857 can be set down only
with doubtful accuracy. Here is a comment on his work from the
Detroit Catholic Vindicator for November 26, 1853.

> Last week we mentioned briefly the visit paid by our Rt. Rev. Bishop
> to the parishes in St. Clair county. Owing to the necessary attendance of
> the Bishop at the consecration of the Right Rev. Dr. Baraga, in Cincin-
> nati, on All Saints Day, he was obliged to defer to a later period . . .
> his visit to this interesting region of his diocese; and his presence at
> this time being to some extent unexpected, there were not so many
> candidates for confirmation as there would otherwise have been. Never-
> theless, on Sunday the 3rd inst., the sacrament of confirmation was ad-
> ministered to nineteen persons at Port Huron. On the following Tues-
> day, the Bishop visited William's settlement, seven miles from Palmer,
> where he confirmed twenty; and on Thursday he reached Newport,
> where the same holy sacrament was administered to thirty-nine persons.
>
> We are rejoiced to hear of the cheering progress of our holy religion
> in the county of St. Clair, under the zealous labors of the excellent and

[64] *Mich. Hist. Colls.*, XXI, 251–53.

devoted Father Kilroy. Within the past three years, we learn, no less than *seven* churches have been erected by this energetic and untiring missionary. The increase of Catholics has been more than proportionate, and every where throughout this promising region, there arises from faithful hearts the prayer to the Lord of the harvest, that he would send more laborers into the vineyard.[65]

There is not enough information available to establish the order in which these "seven churches" were erected. If Father Kilroy lived with the Fishers at Marysville, he most likely began a church as soon as possible after his arrival, and the fact that confirmation was administered there in 1853 strengthens the probability. On the other hand, the only deed to church property in Marysville preserved in the Chancery Archives is dated August 30, 1854, and "Williamsburg, St. Rose of Lima," makes its first appearance in the Almanac for 1855.

Father Kilroy must have begun his ministrations in Port Huron as soon as he was assigned to St. Clair County. The small congregation assembled at first on the second floor of a carpenter shop. In 1852 an abandoned Methodist church was purchased and dedicated to Catholic worship on the feast of St. Stephen.[66] The corner stone of the present church was laid in 1865, and the structure, completed by Father Edward Van Lauwe was dedicated on December 18, 1868.

Palmer, or as it is now called, St. Clair, was a more convenient center than Marysville, and to it Father Kilroy removed in 1853. Within a year a church was completed, and the village for four years continued to be the missionary's headquarters. St. Clair then became a mission of Marine City until it regained its parochial status under Father Francis Van der Bom in 1863.[67]

Meanwhile Father Kilroy had been working in the interior of the county, and before 1855 had built three more churches. In the Almanac for that year they appear simultaneously, and for the first time: "Emmet, Our Lady of Mt. Carmel; Columbus, St. Philip Benetius; Burchville, St. Francis Xavier." Perhaps the earliest of these was St. Philip's, for the deed to the property was granted by Patrick Mulloy on May 31, 1851.[68] The deed for the church site in the orig-

---

[65] The *Detroit Catholic Vindicator* was issued in Detroit from 1853 to 1860.

[66] *Mich. Hist. Colls.*, XXI, 252.

[67] The church is named St. Clair's or St. Clara's in the Catholic Directories down to 1873, when the present name, St. Mary's appears. The present church was erected by Father Van der Bom in 1864. He directed as well the building of another church about which little is known. It stood on Section 28 of St. Clair township on a three acre plot donated by William Barron of February 13, 1862. The church was dedicated to Sts. Peter and Paul, but was never listed in the Directories. It was torn down some time after 1917.

[68] In DCA.

inal Emmet township, executed by Michael Harrington, is dated October 20, 1854.[69]

In 1885 the township of Kenockee was organized comprising a portion of Emmet, and Our Lady of Mt. Carmel was long known as the Kenockee parish. Father Kilroy returned to it in 1867 to become its first resident pastor. In the beginning of Father Loughran's pastorate the original church was destroyed by fire, and the succeeding structure was erected on a new site in the village of Emmet.

St. Philip's in the township of Columbus was for a long period a mission of Kenockee. From 1893 to 1900 it was attached to Lenox, and afterwards to Smith's Creek. Finally in 1926 the order was reversed, Father Gerald Brinton becoming the first pastor of Columbus with Smith's Creek as a mission.

Another group of Irish Catholics attended by Father Kilroy, and mentioned as early as 1855, lay near a good mill site on Mill Creek in Brockway township. The primitive church was replaced by a second structure in 1881. A later growth took place in Speaker township, where a church was erected in 1877. The merging of these two groups is represented by the present parish of Yale, to which the first resident pastor, Father Patrick Cullinane, was appointed in 1898.

The last of the seven churches was the one built in the extreme northeastern corner of the county in what was then Burchville, but is now Grant township. The tiny frame structure is still standing in its churchyard near the hamlet of Jeddo, bears the date 1851, and the name, St. Lawrence, although called St. Francis Xavier in the Almanac for 1855. For many years Jeddo was a mission of Lexington, and was later visited periodically from Croswell.

As we shall see presently, Father Kilroy's activities extended in to Sanilac County, and perhaps even into Huron. His last years of active ministry were spent in the Emmet parish, from which he retired in 1876 to live quietly in the Columbus mission until his death on July 16, 1891.

We have completed the survey of the Eastern Shore as delimited by Fuller, but we must go far beyond it. He was dealing with the Territory down to statehood achieved in 1837, and at that date only an unbroken wilderness stretched from Port Huron to Pointe aux Barques. The counties of Sanilac, Huron, and Tuscola had not yet been organized. It was timber that attracted the first hardy adventurers to the fringes of the Thumb district, but the land seekers were not far behind.

The first evidence of priestly ministrations in Sanilac County is furnished by the notation in the Almanac for 1855 that Father Kilroy

[69] In DCA.

attends a station at "Bark's Shantee." From the time of his appointment to St. Clair County the missionary doubtless made many an excursion to the lumber camps that were strung along the shore of Lake Huron, but the entry of 1855 marks the presence of the first Catholic group large enough to be worth designating. The deed to the church property of what became the mission of Port Sanilac was made in favor of Bishop Lefevere by John Mullen on October 18, 1856.[70]

Two new place names appear in the Almanac for 1857, Forestville and Lexington. The Catholic group around the first village was never large enough to attain parochial status, and Forestville is still a mission attended from Harbor Beach. The faithful in Lexington made their first attempt to provide a church in 1863, when they purchased an old wagon shop and fitted it up as best they could. In the fall of 1870 Father Peter De Smedt, the first priest to reside in Sanilac County was appointed pastor. In 1891 Lexington became a mission of Croswell, a newer thriving parish, from which it is today attended.[71]

The three congregations just mentioned lay along the shore of Lake Huron. In the interior of the county northwest of Port Sanilac there was an early Catholic group predominantly French. Levi Roseberry living on the banks of Cherry Creek deeded a church site to Bishop Lefevere on October 28, 1861.[72] The tiny church of St. Mary's that was soon erected was later moved to a more convenient location in the village of Deckerville, and attended for many years as a mission from Palms.

A considerable number of Irish Catholic families settled in Minden and Delaware townships, directly west of Forestville, in the late fifties. According to local tradition a tiny log structure, St. Patrick's, was erected in the cemetery of the present Palms parish about 1861. A second church built some fifteen years later was succeeded by the present structure completed in 1899. Attended for many years from Ruth, the congregation at Palms was given its first resident pastor when Father Anthony Burke was appointed in 1894.

Unusual interest attaches to the record of beginnings in Huron County. Here we meet the pioneers of a new immigrant stock that was destined to contribute so large a portion of the present population of the diocese. The commonly assumed starting point of Polish immigration to the United States is the year 1854, when the Panna Maria colony was established in Texas.[73] In the same year three

[70] In DCA.
[71] There is a sketch of the Lexington mission in the *Port Huron Times Herald* for April 15, 1932.
[72] In DCA.
[73] See the article, "Poles in the United States," in the Catholic Encyclopedia.

Polish immigrants, John Wojtalewicz, Ambrose Ciechanowski, and Anthony Slawik came to Huron County with their families, after some time spent in Canada, and settled in Paris township.[74] Stephen Pawlowski and John Pyonk came in 1855, and from that time the number of settlers grew rapidly until there were one hundred and eighty-five families in 1870.[75]

Here was a group of Catholics that Father Kilroy could not minister to. Fortunately for them, Father Francis Krutil, a Moravian by birth and somewhat of a linguist, was appointed to St. Mary's in Detroit early in January, 1856, and was sent by Bishop Lefevere to look up the scattered Catholics of Huron County. This zealous Redemptorist was the first priest to minister to the Polish immigrants, and his memory is still cherished. In 1857 the Resurrectionist Fathers came to the Diocese of Hamilton, Ontario. Founded at Paris in 1836 by three Polish exiles, the Congregation in its early years had a distinctively Polish membership. One of the Ontario pioneers was Father Francis Breitkopf, who seems to have lost no time in seeking out his forlorn countrymen in the recesses of Huron County, for he too is affectionately remembered.[76]

Before going further we must turn to another Catholic settlement in the county contemporaneous with the one in Paris township. In 1855 John Hunsanger, a native of Hadhomor in Nassau, Germany, took up land in Sherman township. A year later several families from Baden joined him, and in the early sixties another contingent arrived from Westphalia.[77] These were the pioneers of the German congregation at Adam's Corners, today known as the parish of Ruth. Both Father Krutil and Father Breitkopf ministered to this German group situated scarcely four miles east of the Paris settlement.

In the fall of 1858 Bishop Lefevere sent to Huron County its

[74] This is the date established presumably after some research by Florence McKinnon Gwinn in her *Pioneer History of Huron County* (1922), 34. However, Father Constantine Dziuk, pastor of Parisville from 1926 to 1931, maintained that according to a tradition current among his people a few individuals had come into the area as early as 1848, and not knowing how to go about buying land had merely squatted in the woods. Father Wenceslaus Kruszka has a lengthy sketch of the Parisville settlement in his *Historya Polska w Ameryce* (Milwaukee, 1907), XI, 144–66. He is inclined to give it priority over the Panna Maria colony, and assigns its beginnings to 1852. He bases his opinion on the fact that the land patent issued to Anthony Slavik in 1857, to be mentioned later, must have had five years residence behind it. He is likely in error as homestead laws had not yet been established, and lands could be purchased outright from the land office.

[75] Report made by the pastor of Ruth in the DCA.

[76] See the Golden Jubilee number of the *Schoolman*, a publication of St. Jerome's College, Kitchener, Ontario, for June 1915. Father Breitkopf died at Kitchener on October 18, 1904.

[77] These details from a sketch of the Ruth parish, written into the records by Father George Laugel.

apostle and first resident priest, Father Peter Kluck, who had come to Detroit from the Diocese of Posen in July of the same year.[78] No section of the diocese has demanded more sacrifices from the priests who served it, even down to our own times, than the Thumb district yet Father Kluck spent thirteen years in Huron County at a time when it was little more than a wilderness crossed occasionally by forest trails. The epitaph on his tomb in the Ruth cemetery deserves to be recorded.

Pius sacerdos et vir fortis
flagrantissimus animarum zelo
accensus
erga sanctissiman Eucharistiam
ferventissimo amore conspicuus
in mira paupertate
in aerumnis in periculis et in nimiis laboribus
vitam egit.

Father Kluck made his residence in the German settlement, and from there he addressed to Bishop Lefevere an inventory of the church property under his control at the end of 1860. Station A, the Parisville of today had one set of purple vestments. Station B, "dates from the year of Our Lord 1858. It has no inventory." Station C, or Palms, had one set of red vestments. Station D, or Ruth, had in "the home (or blockhouse) of the missionary a chapel with a wide entrance and a well fastened door." In it were all the necessary articles for divine worship and a confessional" in accord with the XXXV Statute of the Detroit Diocesan Synod." Station B is not identified but it must refer to the small group of Irish and German families who settled in a locality to be later known as Smith's Corners. In 1862 Father Kluck completed the building of the first church in Ruth, which stood for so many years in the parish cemetery.[79]

In the Polish parish the first church was built most likely in 1862. A portion of the land which Anthony Slawik had obtained by government patent dated July 1, 1857, was deeded to Bishop Lefevere on October 10, 1861. Between 1864 and 1867 Father Kluck was absent from his missions, and their care again devolved upon the Resurrectionists who came at stated intervals from their convent in Kitchener,

[78] "On the 5th day of July, 1858, the Rev. Peter Kluck from the Diocese of Posen having exhibited an exeat from the Archbishop & good recommendations, was received among the Clergy of the Diocese of Detroit." Notation in Bishop Lefevere's register in the DCA.

[79] According to Father Laugel's notation in the parish records Father Kluck was a great admirer of Maximilian, Archduke of Austria, whom Napolean made Emperor of Mexico. For some portion of Maximilian's ill-fated reign, that is, from his arrival in 1864 until his death before a firing squad in 1867, Father Kluck was in Mexico.

Ontario.[79] In October, 1868, Parisville received its first resident pastor in the person of Father Simon Wieczorek, who came from Kitchener with his confrere, Father John Wollowski. When Father Kluck was transferred to Port Austin in 1869, Ruth became a mission of Parisville; but after the forest fires of 1871 which destroyed the church buildings at Parisville the priests removed to Ruth. Father Simon came to Detroit in 1872 to organize the first Polish parish in the city, St. Albertus, and was succeeded at Ruth by Father John Dziurowitz. In 1883 Father Rudolph Marker was appointed pastor of Ruth, and since that date each parish has had its own line of pastors.

The third congregation in Huron County, Port Austin, was made up of later arrivals, and was not as distinctively national as the other two. The church was built by Father Kluck, and on his transfer to Allegan County in 1871 the second pastor became Father Cornelius Roche, who was later to be the first vicar-general of the Diocese of Grand Rapids, and to be known as the beloved Dean of the Saginaw Valley.[80]

[80] Despite his name, Father Roche was a native of Holland, born in 1838. He was pastor of Essexville, Michigan, when he died by drowning on August 8, 1900.

CHAPTER XXII

The Diocese under Bishop Lefevere
(Continued)

DUE to similarities in topography and development, Oakland, Washtenaw, and Lenawee Counties are designated by Fuller as the First Inland Counties. The origin of the oldest parish in the area, Northfield in Washtenaw County, has already been noted. Father Cullen when replacing Father Morrissey at the end of 1839 made his residence at Ann Arbor, and erected the first church there in 1843. The Catholic Almanac for the same year discloses the growth that was taking place in the neighborhood of Ann Arbor, in the adjacent county of Livingstone, and westward along the Michigan Central Railroad.

> St. Thomas, Rev. Thomas Cullen, who also attends Dexter, St. John's, Marshall, Jacksonburg, Ypsilanti, Green Oak, St. Patrick's, Northfield, and Pinkney.

From the same source we can trace subsequent growth into several townships of Washtenaw County: Lodi is mentioned in 1844, Sylvan in 1850, Lima in 1855, and Manchester in 1863. Freedom and Lyndon appear first in 1853, and two years later they are accompanied by the notation: "Once a month visited by the Redemptorist Fathers of Detroit for the benefit of the German population."

The first church of the present parish of Dexter was built about 1840 in Section 21 of Dexter township. It burned in 1853, and in the following year a second church was erected in the village of Dexter, to which came Father James Pulsers as the first resident pastor.[1] His was no sinecure for his appointment confided to him as well Lima, Lyndon, Sylvan, Webster, and Scio, all home stations in Washtenaw County; Unadilla, Putnam, and Hamburg in Livingstone County; Bunkerhill and Stockbridge in Ingham County; Waterloo and Grass Lake in Jackson County.

According to a manuscript history of the Ypsilanti parish in the Diocesan Chancery Archives, the first church was started in 1839 by Father Cullen. This primitive structure served the needs of the con-

[1] *History of Washtenaw County* (Chicago, 1881), 718.

gregation until 1856, when a more pretentious building was attempted, and dedicated to St. John. The first resident pastor, Father Charles Lemagie, was succeeded in 1862 by Father Edward Van Paemel.

The German Catholic population of Washtenaw County, living for the most part in the townships of Freedom, Sharon, and Bridgewater, was large enough to warrant the ministrations of a priest as early as 1850.[2] The Redemptorists from St. Mary's in Detroit took charge of the area, and in 1858 a frame church was built in the township of Freedom, and dedicated to St. Francis. Beginning with 1861 the mission was attended from Dexter, and sometimes from Ypsilanti. In 1874, Father Andrew Leitner became resident pastor of Freedom, and assumed charge of Manchester, where about thirty-five Irish families had erected the Church of the Assumption in 1870. As time went on Freedom gradually declined in importance, and Father Peter Ternes, who began his pastorate in 1890, transferred his residence to Manchester.

Throughout the diocese the same phenomen is to be generally observed. The original home stations were established among small groups living on new land purchases. As railroad communications and highways were developed the parish centers arose in more advantageous locations in the newer towns and villages. Another case in point in Washtenaw County is the parish of Chelsea. The settlers in Sylvan township built their first church about 1850 adjoining a cemetery four miles northwest of the village. In 1869 the second church arose in the village itself. The first resident pastor, Father Patrick Duhig, was appointed in 1878.[3]

The apostle of Oakland County was Father Patrick O'Kelly. On February 23, 1843, he was appointed pastor of Oakland and Livingston Counties.[4] The Almanac for 1843 mentions for the first time a mission cared for by Father Cullen: "Green Oak, St. Patrick's." This station in Livingston County was the forerunner of the Brighton parish, and here Father O'Kelly established his residence.[5] As long as

[2] There is a manuscript history of the Freedom parish written by Father Bruck in the DCA.

[3] Beakes, op. cit., 796.

[4] The appointment is recorded in the DCA.

[5] The following news item in the Catholic Press of Hartford, Conn., issue of December 15, 1831, must refer to the building of the church at Green Oak. "They have received a letter from a gentleman residing at St. Michael's, Greenbush, in the above. (Michigan Territory). The increase of immigrants was very great there last summer. The erection of a Catholic place of worship is in a state of great progress, and will shortly be finished. It is built on an excellent 80 foot lot, is 30 x 20, and will have the name of St. Michael's, Greenbush. The church will be under the direction of Rev. P. O'Kelly who is stationed in Washtenaw Co."

he remained there, that is until 1856, the Almanac credits him with four missions: Hartland, Deerfield, Pinckney, and Pontiac, the last of which appears for the first time in 1844. Among the records of the Fenton parish are preserved Father O'Kelly's baptismal and matrimonial registers for the years 1843–50. In them he lists the churches he attends:

St. Patrick's	Pinckney (Livingston County)
St. Joseph's	Green Oak " "
St. James	Hartland " "
St. Patrick's	White Lake (Oakland County)
St. Thomas	Pontiac " "
St. Patrick's ..·..................	Bunker Hill (Ingham County)

A tangible evidence of Father O'Kelly's zeal is the White Lake chapel, still standing on the Union Lake Road, a short distance from Cooley Lake, and used in the summer months for the convenience of the resorters in the neighborhood. Built most likely in 1845 it is the oldest house of worship in the diocese, and after a lapse of a hundred years it has become the parish church of a new congregation forming around it.

The origin of the Pontiac parish presents a difficulty. Father Lucian Wicart wrote a sketch of it for a history of Oakland County published in 1877.[6] According to his account the small number of Catholics in Pontiac were first cared for by Father Fidelis Missuwe of St. Anne's, and services were held in a small frame house near Huron Street owned by a Mrs. Dennis. This statement does not harmonize with Father O'Kelly's entries. Father Missuwe came to Detroit after completing his studies in Belgium, and was ordained by Bishop Lefevere on June 2, 1849. Father O'Kelly would hardly have dignified a private home with the title "St. Thomas," and why Father Wicart should have overlooked Father O'Kelly's work is rather perplexing.

Beginning with 1851 we are on solid ground. On May 14 of that year Bishop Lefevere purchased the old Academy building, which had been previously used for religious purposes by the Presbyterians, and installed Father Peter Wallace as first resident pastor at Pontiac. He was succeeded in 1863 by Father Lucian Wicart, who moved the ramshackle structure to the site now occupied by the buildings of the St. Vincent De Paul parish. The present church was erected during the pastorate of Father Fridolin Baumgartner, and was dedicated by Bishop Borgess on September 18, 1887.[7] From the very beginning

---

[6] *History of Oakland County* (Philadelphia, 1877), 105.

[7] The account of the dedication in the *Michigan Catholic* for September 22, 1887, has an amusing reference to the old church. "The stranger in town had then an opportunity to see how much a new Catholic church was needed in Pontiac. The building

of his pastorate Father Wallace attended not only White Lake, but also small groups in Royal Oak, Birmingham, and Clarkston.

The Catholic Almanac for 1852 is the first to record the presence of Catholic groups in Lenawee County. After mentioning the Redemptorists at Monroe, Fathers Smulders, Cronenberg, and Poirier, it adds the notation:

> The same Rev. gentlemen attend Hillsdale, Medina, Clayton, Adrian, Muddy Creek, Otter Creek, Stony Creek, Brest, every other month; Palmira, Blissfield, Ida, every three months; and Ridgeway and Springville once a year.

The beginnings of Catholic immigration into Lenawee County fall within the period of Father Carabin's pastorate at Monroe, and he undoubtedly had many a sick call westward across the county line. His ministrations would be facilitated to some extent, at least, but one of the earliest railroads in the state, the Michigan Southern, which was opened from Monroe to Petersburg in 1839, to Adrian in 1840, and to Hillsdale in 1843.

However, if we pass from surmise to records, we must credit the Redemptorists with the first pastoral work in the county, and particularly Father Gillet. In 1846 he began a mission station at Blissfield, where there were a few French families and fifteen Irish families. They proceeded to build a small chapel, and were henceforth visited every three months.[8] In the same year Father Simon Saenderl following the railroad out of Monroe began prospecting for Catholic families in Lenawee and Hillsdale Counties. He reports that Adrian has twenty families, Medina twelve, Clayton, seven miles east of Medina, five, and Hillsdale five or six. Five years later, the Annals mention the work of Father Smulders in the same area, and farther west into Branch County at Coldwater.[9]

The most important village in the county was Adrian, and here accordingly came the first resident priest. The *Detroit Catholic Vindicator* in its issue of August 20, 1853, presents this intelligence to its readers.

Adrian, Linawa Co., Mich.

This is a very thriving town, situated at the junction of the Kalamazoo and Mich. Southern Rail Road. Two or three years ago, there were

which until last Sunday had been used as a Catholic church stood at the roadside near the pastoral residence. It was a sight to almost chill the faith in a Catholic heart. The little turret, like an old-fashioned pepper box, that bore the emblem of salvation on its top, leaned to one side and seemed to call on the passer-by of his charity to take it down and burn it. As above stated, the building was originally a Universalist preaching house, and the cross on the turret seemed to protest against remaining there. . . ."

[8] *Annales Cong. SS. Redemp.*, I, 434.

[9] *Ibid.*, II, 169.

only a few Catholic families resident here; but the building of the above railroads brought together many Catholic families, who have settled down here, some as farmers and others as mechanics and laborers. Last year the energetic and unwearied priest, Father Smulders, built a frame church; but owing to the large increase since then, it is now altogether too small. The present pastor Very Rev. Mr. Kindekins, intends building a large brick church here next year. For this purpose he has purchased six acres of land, and in a week or so, he will commence building a Catholic school house. On this ground he also proposes erecting a Convent, as soon as circumstances will permit. The prospects are, that Adrian will become a large city.

However, Father Kindekins did not realize his ambitions; his six acres were far out on the outskirts of the village, and his people were determined on a more prominent location. St. Mary's was built during the pastorate of Father Ernest Van Dyke.[10]

The majority of Adrian's first Catholics were Irish, but later immigration brought in the German element, and by 1860 there were at least fifty families intent upon having a church of their own.[11] The first structure was erected in 1863, and was attended for two years by the Redemptorists from Detroit.[12] The first resident pastor, Father John Ehrenstrasser, was appointed in 1865. The present St. Joseph's church was erected during the pastorate of Father Casimir Rohowski, and was dedicated by Bishop Borgess in 1878.

Outside of Adrian the largest Catholic group lay in the territory which is now comprised in the parish of Hudson. The issue of the *Vindicator* just cited contains a description of "Medina and Hudson Settlements."

In Lenawee Co., Mich., there are two Irish settlements, known as the Medina and Hudson settlements, consisting of between 60 and 70 Irish Catholic families. They are not only Catholic in name, but Catholics in fact, ever zealous in promoting the interests of religion. In Medina there is a frame church, which is attended by the Very Rev. Mr. Kindekins of Adrian. They have also a very flourishing Catholic school; the settlers on seeing the evil effects of Common Schools, of their own accord—to their credit be it said—having withdrawn their children, and established a Catholic School, where education should not be purchased at expense of corruption.

The land around these colonies is said to be the finest wheat-growing soil in the state. A considerable quantity of wild land is for sale here, but is fast being taken up at from $4 to $6 an acre. The whole of this

[10] Manuscript history of St. Mary's, Adrian, in DCA.
[11] Manuscript history of St. Joseph's, Adrian, in DCA.
[12] The manuscript history cited in the preceding note mentions a Father Müller as attending the congregation. No other trace of this priest can be found.

county is well supplied with flour and saw-mills; and excellent markets are of easy access for all kinds of produce . . .

Any person desiring special information regarding this interesting district of the West, will be cheerfully supplied by applying to James Gahagan, Thos. M'Cullen, or James Donnelly, Medina P. O., Lenawee Co., Mich.

The first church attended by the Redemptorists in their missions to this area was erected in Medina township, on a spot known even today as Catholic Hill. This was the structure attended by Father Kindekins. In 1858 property was purchased in the village of Hudson, and the barn which stood on it was remodeled into a church.[13] One year later, Father Francis Van Erp became the first resident pastor. The pioneer stage was over when Bishop Borgess solemnly blessed the new Sacred Heart church in 1872.

Clinton is not mentioned as being in the care of the Redemptorists, but makes its first appearance as a mission of Adrian in the Almanac for 1854. Under the direction of Father Kindekins a church had been built the preceding year.[14] In 1863 Father Edward Van Lauwe was appointed resident pastor, and his mission field comprised Manchester, Milan, Freedom, Tecumseh, and Cambridge. He was succeeded by Father Ferdinand Allgayer, who, during his pastorate extending to 1873, erected the second church.

The Cambridge mission designated the group of sturdy Irish pioneers, who came directly from Ireland to take up lands in the area known today as the Irish Hills. Their tiny stone church with its smooth clay floor was erected in 1854, and has been preserved intact through successive restorations, the latest effected in 1928.[15] Today, St. Joseph's serves not only the descendants of the original settlers, but also a throng of resorters drawn by the charm of the surrounding lake country.

Another important group of Irish Catholics settled in Deerfield township about 1842. Under the direction of Father Gillet they built a primitive church in 1843. On June, 6, 1861, property in the village itself was deeded to Bishop Lefevere by Harriet McKey, and a church was built the following year. There were fifty-three candidates for Confirmation in June, 1864. The first resident pastor, Father Louis Van Straalen was appointed in 1884, and a third church was completed by Father Frank Broegger in 1892.

The next portion of the diocese to be surveyed comprises the five

[13] Manuscript history of Hudson parish in DCA.

[14] The issue of the *Detroit Vindicator* just quoted from states that the church will be completed before winter.

[15] A Diamond Jubilee Souvenir, issued in 1930, gives an interesting history of the Cambridge mission.

counties whose development was determined by the Chicago Road, namely Hillsdale, Branch, St. Joseph, Cass, and Berrien. In this order they extend westward from Lenawee to Lake Michigan.

As we have seen, there were two currents of immigration into the lowest tier of counties, one from the east, and one from the southwest. Thus the two extremities caught the largest percentage of the earliest settlers. Just how far this factor influenced later Catholic growth is problematical, but, at any rate, Hillsdale, Branch, and St. Joseph, lying in the center of the tier, show a smaller Catholic population than the others.

In Hillsdale County down to the present there has never been more than one parish, that in the county seat. Attended first by the Redemptorists from Monroe, the group effected its first parish organization under Father Kindekins in 1853. Some time later, an abandoned Presbyterian church was purchased for the use of the congregation.[16] A resident priest, Father Charles Ryckaert, was assigned in 1858, and the corner stone of the present church was laid in 1883. During the first years of his pastorate Father Ryckaert's mission field extended westward into Branch and St. Joseph Counties.

The first ministrations in Branch County marked the western limits of the missionary excursions undertaken by the Redemptorists and Father Kindekins. In the late forties a number of Catholic families, Irish for the most part, settled in the neighborhood of Coldwater. A small frame church was erected on the site of the present St. Charles' in 1854. On June 6, 1857, the building was completely wrecked by the explosion of six kegs of gunpowder which a band of fanatics had secreted under it. However, the reputable townsmen deplored the outrage, and subscribed generously towards the building of the brick church, which, enlarged under the pastorate of Father James Gore, is still in use. Father Cornelius Korst was appointed first resident pastor in 1867.[17]

The missions previously attended from Hillsdale now came under the care of Father Korst, and both he and Father Ryckaert are consequently identified with the development of the Church in St. Joseph County. The earliest Catholic group in the county antedated immigration from the East, and was made up of a number of French traders and their families who had settled on the border of the Potawatomi reservation that lay just south of the present town of Mendon on the famous Nottawasippi prairie.[18] It is safe to assume that the

16 *History of Hillsdale County* (Philadelphia, 1879), 107.

17 A printed history of the parish was issued on the occasion of the Diamond Jubilee in 1924.

18 *Mich. Hist. Colls.,* II, 489–501.

settlement must have been visited by all the priests whom we can associate with missionary endeavor in the extreme southwest of the state from the time of Father Stephen Badin. The Holy Cross Fathers from Notre Dame were frequent visitors saying Mass as the priests had before them in the home of that kindly and distinguished Catholic gentleman, Patrick Marentette.[19] In 1861 a store building in the village of Mendon was fitted up as a chapel, and here Father Ryckaert officiated regularly until 1867, when Father Korst succeeded him. By this time the group had grown sufficiently to consider the building of a suitable church, and on October 4, 1872, the first Catholic church in the county, St. Edward's, was dedicated by Bishop Borgess. Father Charles McKenna was appointed first resident pastor in 1875.[20]

Another mission attended by Fathers Korst and Ryckaert was Sturgis, where Mass was said in the residence of Captain William Mc-Laughlin as early as 1864. A church dedicated to the Holy Angels was dedicated by Bishop Borgess in May, 1879, but Sturgis remained a mission until Father William Graeber became its first resident pastor in 1922.

A particular interest attaches to the beginnings of the Church in Cass County. Its first parish has the best right to be considered the successor of the oldest foundation in the diocese, the Saint Joseph Mission. It will be remembered that in 1838 the Potawatomi were expelled from Michigan and Indiana, and driven to a western reservation. In 1833, the Indians had made the final cession of their lands to the Federal government with the understanding that they were to enjoy them undisturbed for three years longer. However, Chief Pokagon had refused to affix his signature to the cession until he and his band, numbering about two hundred, had been granted exemption from deportation at the end of the period. To the honor of this steadfast Christian it must be added that the sole reason for his refusal was the fear that his people, once engulfed in the solitudes of

[19] "Hon. Patrick Marentette . . . was born at Sandwich, Canada, March 11, 1807, and died at his beautiful home on the St. Joseph River, in Mendon, May 23, 1878. . . . In 1825, with an Indian guide, he went to Fort Wayne by the way of Sturgis and Mongoquining prairies, on the business of his employers, and in 1833 succeeded his father-in-law, Colonel Francis Moreton, in charge of the trading post at Nottowa, near his mansion and farm in Mendon, and the Indian reservation therein, formerly embracing a large portion of that township. . . . In 1835 he married Frances, daughter of Colonel Moreton, and niece of Governor Gabriel Moreton, of Illinois. In 1847 he served with credit as a member of the House of Representatives of the Michigan Legislature, and was one of the committee of Internal Improvement. . . . For over forty years his home was noted for the unstinted hospitality and refined courtesy of its occupants, and for many years religious services were held in his capacious mansion. . . ." *Mich. Hist. Colls.*, III, 614.

[20] A printed history of St. Edward's parish was issued in 1909.

the western plains, would be deprived of the consolation of their religion.[21] With the compensation received for his share of the tribal lands Pokagon purchased in Silver Creek township some nine hundred acres which he parcelled out to his people.

In 1838, undaunted by the racial and religious prejudices of the Yankee settlers around him, Pokagon erected a log chapel on the north shore of Long Lake.

> Pokagon, the elder, was a devout Roman Catholic, and in 1838 built the first church in the township. Its erection caused him much trouble, as a great deal of prejudice existed among the whites against this denomination, and they declined to render any assistance in raising the structure, the Indians not possessing sufficient ingenuity to do the work unaided. In this dilemma, Pokagon went to John G. Barney, to whom he related his troubles. Mr. Barney kindly offered his assistance and told him to get his logs together and that he would help him out of his difficulty. This pleased the old chief, and the material was soon in readiness, and Mr. Barney, accompanied by his three hired men, fulfilled his promise.[22]

For the first three or four years of its existence the mission could have been attended only by the clergymen who were occasionally stationed at Bertrand. Father Simon Lalumiere of the Diocese of Vincennes signs a good many entries in the Bertrand parish register, as does Father Michael Shawe. However, the majority of the entries following those made by Father Deseille are in the handwriting of Father Stanislaus Bernier, and extend from January 10, 1839, to June 7, 1841.

The mission next came under the care of the devoted priests who did almost all the pioneer work in the extreme western counties, the Holy Cross Fathers. At the end of November, 1842, Father Sorin took possession of Notre Dame Du Lac. He was the only priest with the Brothers until the late summer of the following year, when Fathers Francis Cointet, Theophilus Marivault, and Francis Gouesse arrived from France.[23] Although Father Sorin was intent upon the building of a college he never lost sight of the primary missionary purpose for which his Congregation had been founded. Whenever possible, he and his small band of priests, slowly augmented from year to year, made every effort to care for the neglected Catholics of northern Indiana and southwestern Michigan.

Father Sorin was attracted to the Indians no less than many a

[21] *History of Cass County* (Chicago, 1882), 363.
[22] *Ibid.*, 357.
[23] *A Brief History of The University of Notre Dame from 1842 to 1892* (Chicago, n.d.), 55.

European missionary had been before him, and, aware of the historic mission ground on which he labored, he was determined that they should not be unprovided for. Thus it came about that the first priest to live beside Pokagon's primitive log chapel was Father Marivault. On January 4, 1845, he formally initiated a set of parish records, styling himself "Parochus hujus loci Pokagon vel Silver Creek." The same records state that the chapel was dedicated to the Immaculate Heart of Mary, and that it was blessed by Father Sorin on January 4, 1847.[24]

Early in 1847, Father Marivault was replaced by one of the famous priests of the pioneer days, Father Louis Baroux. When he arrived at Notre Dame in August, 1846, he was twenty-nine years old, and had spent almost a year with the Congregation in France. He began his pastorate at Silver Creek in February, 1847, and remained for two years, during which he devoted himself so earnestly to his charges that he had a class of eighty ready for confirmation when Bishop Lefevere came to visit the missionary's humble establishment in 1848.[25]

Sent to France on business by his Superior in 1850 Father Baroux returned to Silver Creek only to find decided changes. Dissensions had arisen among his people, and the majority had removed to a new location near Rush Lake in Van Buren County. But these losses were more than compensated for by the beginnings of Irish Catholic immigration into the neighborhood, drawn by the presence of a Catholic priest. First came the three Daly brothers, Patrick, Dennis, and Cornelius. On their heels appeared three more brothers, the Cullinanes, John, Patrick, and Daniel. All six took up lands in 1849.[26]

In 1852 Father Baroux was again taken from Silver Creek and sent this time to India, where he was one of the first priests of his Congregation to labor in the mission field now confided exclusively to the Fathers of the Holy Cross. Broken in health he returned to France in 1857. During his absence Father Almire Fourmont had resided in Silver Creek down to the summer of 1856.[27] Bishop Lefevere sent repeated appeals to Father Baroux to resume his former mission, and in February, 1859, the missionary was again welcomed in Silver Creek, and now a priest of the Diocese of Detroit, he spent the next eleven years in devoted service to his Indians, and to all the scattered Catholics in the surrounding counties whom he could reach.

[24] These records are preserved in the Dowagiac parish files.
[25] These details from a manuscript autobiography of Father Baroux in the NDA.
[26] *History of Cass County*, 362–63.
[27] The records signed by Father Fourmont extend from October 31, 1850, to June 8, 1856.

It was the happiest day of my life, when I stood before my Indian congregation again. . . . When I first came to Silver Creek we had a church 30 x 22 feet in size, built by the Indians with logs. . . . When I returned to Silver Creek in 1859, I found the old church I had left in 1852. But I received in France over $1000. Irish families were settled with the Indians. They all subscribed according to their means, and we succeeded in building a handsome frame church with two chapels. . . . Besides the money I received in France, I brought an amount of handsome vestments and altar furniture. The Indians had difficulties among themselves. Half of the tribe bought land near Hartford, Van Buren County, and moved there. In October, 1862, I went back to France. The Society for the Propagation of the Faith gave me $1000. I returned in May, 1863, and we began to build the handsome frame church they use today. . . . I was just as poor as the Indians for the first two years. I could not afford a light of any kind. My small cabin, twelve feet square, was covered with bark. I have known what is misery . . .[28]

During his entire pastorate Father Baroux was the only resident priest in Cass County. His mission circuit included the following localities, lying for the most part in Van Buren County: Pipestone, Watervliet, Arlington, Breedsville, South Haven, Bangor, Pier, Paw Paw, Mattawan, Decatur, and Hamilton. Six miles from Silver Creek and situated on the Michigan Central Railroad was the village of Dowagiac, where a small Catholic group had settled in the early sixties, and which was destined to replace Silver Creek as the important parish in the county.

In Berrien County the first parish organization was effected, as we have seen, at Bertrand. The anonymous, manuscript history of the parish, which has already been referred to, and which seems to have been written in 1848, furnishes this information regarding Bertrand and the county.

On the 29th of November, 1842, the Rev. E. Sorin of the Association of Notre Dame de Ste Croix came to Notre Dame du Lac. . . . He soon received from the Right Rev. Dr. Lefevere adm. of Detroit the faculties of exercising the sacred ministry in his Diocese. . . . In 1844 a retreat was given in the church of Bertrand by the MM. Sorin, Randolphe and Cointet. . . . The following year another retreat was preached . . . and at the end of the retreat the Rev. Bishop administered confirmation

[28] This passage quoted from an interview with Father Baroux printed in the Grand Rapids Democrat for May 15, 1891. Father Baroux was transferred to Ecorse, Michigan, in 1870, where he remained until 1882. He then labored in various localities in the Diocese of Grand Rapids until his death at Manistee, September 12, 1898. His remains were brought to Silver Creek for burial, and the Indians, usually so stolid, actually wept when they looked for the last time on the face of the good priest who had been so devoted to them. A long letter of Father Baroux was published by the Rt. Rev. Edward D. Kelly to form the booklet *An Early Indian Mission* (Ann Arbor, 1913).

to 98 persons. . . . From the time of confirmation Father Cointet was chosen as the priest who would attend regularly the church of Bertrand.

At Niles there are some Catholics, Canadians and Irish for the most part. At one mile from the town, there is a cross placed on the side of the road, near the station of the Jesuit Fathers.

We have but few Catholics at Berrien, which is the county seat of Berrien County.

There is a frame church at St. Joseph. But as it has been placed on a lot the deed of which cannot be got, so the decrees of Baltimore prevent it from being blessed and used for divine service until removed. The population of St. Joseph is decreasing, and it seems that the climate is unhealthy.

Kalamazoo has made an attempt to have a church. There is even a frame elevated. But for the same reason as at St. Joseph the whole of the enterprise came to nothing. Should there be there a church and a Priest, there would be a prospect of doing much good. . . .

While Bertrand was retrograding to practical extinction, the village of Niles was making rapid progress, and when Bishop Lefevere had a diocesan priest to send to Berrien County he located him in this more convenient center. Father Cointet had erected, most likely in 1847, a small frame church dedicated to St. Francis of Assissi, and he and his confreres attended it until the first resident pastor, Father John De Neve, was apointed in August, 1857. Two years later, Father De Neve was named second rector of the American College at Louvain, and was succeeded at Niles by Father John Cappon. His death in 1892 closed a long and zealous pastorate, during which Niles became in every sense a modern parish.[29]

The second parish in the county arose in the town of St. Joseph that developed at the mouth of the river where Father Hennepin had said his Masses during the bleak November of 1679. An abandoned schoolhouse was used for religious purposes by the Holy Cross Fathers, who attended the mission until a church was built about 1848. Later a mission of Niles, St. Joseph was cared for by Father Cappon and his assistant, Father Joseph Van Waterschoot, who became the first resident pastor in 1866.

Down to 1870 there were three important mission stations in the county attended by Father Cappon. The oldest, appearing in the Almanac for the first time in 1852 was New Buffalo, where Father De Neve built St. Mary's church in 1858. At Bainbridge Father Cappon built a church dedicated to St. Francis De Sales in 1860, and a few years later, at Dayton, the church of St. Anthony. Both missions are listed for the first time in the Catholic Directory of 1865.[30]

[29] A printed history of the parish was issued in 1900.
[30] See *History of Berrien and Van Buren Counties* (Philadelphia, 1880), 227–30.

The counties next to be scanned comprise those linked together in their development by the Territorial Road and the Kalamazoo River: the counties of Jackson, Calhoun, Kalamazoo, Van Buren, and Allegan. The later Catholic immigration into them went parallel to the successive stages in the progress of the Michigan Central Railroad on its way to Chicago.

The first Catholics in Jackson County were attended by the priests stationed at Northville and Ann Arbor. Jacksonburg appears for the first time in the Almanac for 1843, and as a mission in charge of Father Cullen. There can be no doubt that both Father O'Kelly and Father Morrissey had ministered there before him. The traditional date for the building of the first church, 1836, points to the work of these two priests as Father Cullen, teaching in St. Philip's College, was not free to begin his missionary excursions until 1839.

In 1852 Jackson became a mission of Marshall, and was attended by Fathers Hennessy and Koopmans. The latter began the building of the present St. John's church in 1856, and one year later Father Cornelius Moutard was appointed resident pastor.[31] Outside the town of Jackson there seem to have been a few Catholics in the county. Only two mission stations appear down to 1870, Grass Lake and Waterloo, both mentioned for the first time in the Almanac for 1855.

Although Jackson has far outstripped Marshall in Catholic population, the latter, in Calhoun County, was in the early days the more important center. The first Mass was said by Father Morrissey, who came to conduct the funeral of Cormick Cassidy on the very day, October 28, 1837, on which Marshall was organized as a village. At that time there were twenty-five Catholics out of a population of two hundred. Five or six years later, Marshall came near being chosen as the state capital, and the prominence it thereby enjoyed brought a substantial increase in the number of its Catholic citizens. For nine years beginning with 1842, Father Cullen on his regular visits to Marshall held services in a building used originally as a linseed oil mill. The first church, erected in 1851, was given its first resident pastor, Father James Hennessy, in the following year. The cornerstone of the present church was laid in 1888.[32]

Battle Creek first appears in the Almanac for 1855, and as a mission of Marshall. For many years Mass was said in a public hall, but in 1867 Father Callaert of Marshall purchased and remodeled a Quaker church that stood on the site of the present church property. The

[31] A printed history of the parish commemorated the Golden Jubilee of the school in 1923.
[32] A history of the parish by Father James Cahalan appeared in the *Mich. Hist. Mag.*, I, No. 2.

first resident pastor, Father William Herwig, came in December, 1869.

In Kalamazoo County Catholic immigration begins with the coming of Dennis Talbot to Kalamazoo in 1832. Ten years later there were perhaps fifteen families and the completion of the Michigan Central to the town in 1846 brought several more. In 1848 a small group of German immigrants arrived.[33]

Although the particulars are vague, it is certain that the priests associated with the Bertrand district paid occasional visits to Kalamazoo. With the coming of the Holy Cross Fathers it became a regular mission station. Father Baroux relates that when he said Mass in James Butler's log house on Palm Sunday, 1845, the wind blew strongly enough through the chinks to extinguish the candles. The first attempt at church building came in 1844, when the frame of a building was raised. However, because it stood on property whose title was defective Bishop Lefevere forbade the work to proceed. In 1850, when there were thirty-five families on the parish roll, Father Richard Shortis of Notre Dame began collecting funds for a church.

A small brick church was erected in 1852, which remained under the care of the Holy Cross Fathers until January 1, 1856, when Father Isidore Anthony Lebel was appointed first resident pastor. Under him the parish made remarkable progress, and the corner stone of the present church was laid on November 26, 1865.

Father Lebel's field of labor was not confined to his own county but extended as well into Allegan and Van Buren. His most important mission in Allegan was composed of a group of Irish Catholics living in the township of Watson. The first church, erected in 1862, was followed by a more pretentious structure in 1889.[34]

Another Catholic colony in the northeastern corner of the county was made up of German families, some of them from Westphalia in Clinton County, and others who had come directly from Germany. On March 12, 1858, Matthias Herrig deeded to Bishop Lefevere two acres of his farm in Dorr township.[35] As soon as the land could be cleared a log building was erected, which served as both church and school. This mission was attended by Father Martin Marco of the German parish in Grand Rapids, who also ministered to another German group in Salem township. Dorr was the first to reach parochial status when Father William Herwig was named pastor in 1866. St. Mary's church was built the following year. The Salem group

---

[33] See the *Augustinian*, the parish publication, for April 11, 1925.

[34] See Henry F. Thomas, *A Twentieth Century History of Allegan County* (Chicago, 1907), 575.

[35] In DCA.

built its church in 1865, but did not have a resident pastor until Father Augustin Sklorzik was appointed ten years later.[36]

In Van Buren County there was no resident priest until 1878. The two larger missions attended by Father Lebel were Decatur and Paw Paw. Early attempts to build a church in Decatur were unsuccessful, but in 1869 a vacant Protestant church was purchased and dedicated to the Holy Family. On his first visits to Paw Paw, dating from 1856, Father Lebel said Mass in the home of James Bennett. The Catholics of the village continued to worship in private homes until 1872, when St. Mary's was completed. Father John Wernert on his appointment to Paw Paw in August, 1878, became the first resident priest in the county.[37]

On account of similarities in topography and of a common river system the counties of Saginaw, Lapeer, Livingston, Genesee, and Shiawassee have been conveniently grouped under the designation, the Saginaw Country. The first of these now lies within the Diocese of Saginaw, and in 1870 there were only two parishes in it, at Saginaw and East Saginaw.

Livingston County, in as far as its religious development is concerned, is more properly classed with Oakland and Washtenaw Counties. As we have seen, Father O'Kelly on his return from Wisconsin established himself at Green Oak.[38] Because of the territory it served Green Oak may be looked upon as the forerunner of the parish at Brighton, although the latter is not strictly a continuation of the older center. Nor did Father O'Kelly, while in the district, always reside at Green Oak. After some years he transferred his residence to Genoa township, where he remained until his transfer to Dearborn.[39] The last mention of Green Oak as a mission station is found in the Catholic Directory for 1868, where it is mentioned as attended from Oceola.

After Father O'Kelly's removal to Dearborn in 1856 there was no resident priest in Livingston County until 1858, when Father Aloysius Lambert came as his successor. During the year that he spent in the county before his transfer to Marine City Father Lambert resided in Deerfield township about ten miles west of Fenton, where Father O'Kelly had built a church in 1846.[40] In 1860 Father Francis

[36] *History of Allegan and Barry Counties* (Philadelphia, 1880), 203.

[37] Captain O. W. Rowland, *History of Van Buren County* (Chicago, 1912), 585.

[38] The site of the old church can still be made out on the Green Oak Road about a mile and a half east of the road running from Whitmore Lake to Brighton.

[39] "His old friend and parishioner, Matthew Brady, having removed to Genoa, prevailed upon Father O'Kelly to remove to that township, as being more central. Here he purchased 40 acres adjoining his friend and remained until he went to Dearborn." *History of Livingston County* (Philadelphia, 1880), 206.

[40] *Ibid.*, 436.

Xavier Pourret came to the area, but he preferred to live near another small church near the line between Hartland and Oceola townships, and this was called the Oceola mission.[41] Father Thomas Rafter was sent to Oceola in in 1870, but a year later became pastor of Fenton, and from this center he attended his former missions. Deerfield and Oceola declined in importance, and the missions dependent upon them, Brighton, Howell, and Pinckney became the parishes of the county. The first resident priest in the county after Father Rafter's departure was Father James Herbert, who was stationed at Pinckney in 1875.

In the center of Genesee County lies Flint, the third largest city in Michigan. The *Gazeteer of Michigan* for 1838, while crediting the settlement with a population of only three hundred, proclaimed its advantages as follows: a banking association, an edge tool manufactory, a sawmill, two dry goods stores, two groceries, two physicians, a lawyer and the land office for the Saginaw land district.[42] In this summary a most important personage was overlooked, whom the histories of Genesee County do not fail to mention. Daniel O'Sullivan, traditionally known as the 'Irish Schoolmaster," came to the Flint River settlement in July, 1834. In the fall he began the first school in the village, charging ten pennies a week for tuition.[43] There are obscure accounts of visits by Fathers Kundig and Kilroy to the few Irish Catholics in the village, but the first attempt to build a church dates from 1843, and was due to the initiative of Daniel O'Sullivan. In the Almanac for 1847 the church is said to be "nearly built—vacant." It is still "Nearly built" in 1848, but it now has a resident pastor, Father Michael Monaghan.[44] The first adequate church to serve the Catholics of Flint was built by Father Timothy Murphy in 1883. A parochial school conducted by two lay teachers was established as early as 1856.

The distribution of the early Catholic population in the area surrounding Flint is shown in the Almanac for 1857 which lists the missions attended by Father Charles De Ceuninck appointed to St. Michael's in 1855.

> Flint, Genesee co., St. Michael's—Rev. Charles De Ceuninck, who attends Genesee, Piney Run, Lapeer, Flushing, Fentonville, Linden, Gaines, Clayton, Corunna, Owosso and Chessnink.[45]

[41] The ground was deeded to Bishop Lefevere by Michael McGuire on January 1, 1844.

[42] Fuller, *op. cit.*, 383.

[43] *History of Genesee County* (Philadelphia, 1879), 139.

[44] Father Michael Monaghan came to Detroit from Milwaukee, and was appointed to Flint on May 20, 1847.

[45] Chessnick is, of course, Chesaning in Saginaw County.

Only five of these missions lay in Genesee County, and only three survive as present day parishes. A plot of ground in Section 19 of Flushing township was deeded to Bishop Lefevere on June 23, 1865, and a church, St. Robert's, was soon erected. In 1920 the succeeding building was erected in the town of Flushing, and the first resident pastor was appointed in 1927.

In Gaines the church property was acquired in 1869, and St. Joseph's was dedicated by Bishop Borgess in 1871. A resident pastor, Father George O'Sullivan, came in 1892. After William and Jane Remington of Fentonville, the Fenton of today, had given a plot of ground to Bishop Lefevere in June, 1868, "for the purpose of erecting a church thereon," the building of St. John's was immediately begun, and Father Thomas Rafter, the first resident pastor, was installed in 1871.[46] The three foregoing churches, however, were perhaps antedated by St. Mary's in Mt. Morris. The church was built in 1865 on ground donated by Christopher Hughes. It achieved parochial status in September, 1871, with the coming of Father Martin Godfried Canters.

Attached to Mt. Morris as a mission was the tiny settlement called the County Line lying precisely on the boundary line between Genesee and Saginaw Counties, where a church dedicated to the Sacred Heart had been erected about 1869. This mission was the forerunner of the present parish of Birch Run.

For our knowledge of beginnings in Lapeer County we are indebted to an account written by Father John Busche, the first pastor of Lapeer.

About 1848 a few Irish families settled in a locality about one hour's walk east of Lapeer. The following priests ministered to them in the order in which they are named: Father Kilroy, at the time residing in Detroit; Father Monaghan, pastor of the mission at Flint; his successor, Father Kindekins; Father Schutjes, pastor of Bay City; Father De Ceuninck after he had succeeded to the pastorate of Flint. In 1855 a few Irish settled in the town of Lapeer, where from that time Mass was said and the sacraments administered by Father De Ceuninck. . . . In 1857 or 1858 as the population of Lapeer and its neighborhood was increasing, a church 40 x 30 was erected in the town of Lapeer on a lot donated by a non-Catholic. About the same time a few Irish families settled in the townships of Imlay and Almont, and were ministered to by Father Van Renterghem, pastor of Mt. Clemens. . . . In 1858 or 1859 a few Catholics of German origin settled in the township of North Branch, and erected a church by their own labor the following year. . . . Having no priest to send them the bishop promised that the first priest coming to exercise his ministry in the Diocese of Detroit from the

46 *History of Genesee County*, 341.

American College in Louvain would be assigned to them. Accordingly, the Reverend Busche, who, after having completed his studies had been ordained by Engelbert, Cardinal Archbishop of Mechlin, and had come to Detroit in October, 1864, was appointed to the spiritual care of the congregation in Lapeer, and of all the missions in the county. . . . About three years later, the faithful living in the townships of Imlay and Almont having increased in number erected a church. . . . This church was blessed in accordance with faculties received from Bishop Lefevere.[47]

The earliest Catholic group in Shiawassee County of which we have knowledge was made up of a few Irish families who settled in the extreme southwestern corner of the county in the township of Woodhull. The locality is noted for the first time in the Almanac for 1852, which lists "Woodhull, Shiawassy co., St. Patrick's." The mission is said to be attended from Flint. Its origin is most likely more in accord with a statement of what must have been a local tradition.

A Roman Catholic church was organized in 1847 by Father Godez, a Hungarian by birth. It had about 30 members, who built a meeting house of logs. In 1873 it gave place to a new frame building which gives good accommodations for their religious services.[48]

Despite its early start Woodhull always remained a mission station attached to various parishes. The progress of the Church is identified with another beginning made in the center of the county. Although Corunna became the county seat in 1836, it could boast of only one log house and a partly completed mill at the end of a year. Subsequent growth brought a number of Catholic families, and in 1855 a church dedicated to the Annunciation was erected in the village.[49] In July, 1857, Father Edward Van Paemel was named its pastor, the first priest to reside in the county. Meanwhile, just a few miles away the town of Owosso having better railroad facilities was growing in importance, and in 1873 Corunna lost its parochial status, and as a mission of Owosso was attended down to 1907.

The last group of counties to be dealt with comprises those counties of the Grand River region lying within our field: Clinton, Ionia, Ingham, Eaton, and Barry. In the entire area the oldest parish was, of course, Westphalia in Clinton County, where, as we have seen,

[47] The quotation is a free translation of the Latin original in the DCA, written in 1879. More details are to be found in a printed history of the parish issued in 1904 by Father Francis Clement Kelley, at the time pastor of Lapeer, and later bishop of Oklahoma City and Tulsa.

[48] The reference is to Father Godez at Westphalia. The deed to the property was executed on January 13, 1852, and gave to Bishop Lefevere the ground on which "the Roman Catholic Church now stands known as St. Patrick's." Deed in DCA.

[49] Manuscript history of the Owosso parish by Father James Wheeler in the DCA.

The next oldest parish of the county was organized in the capital of the state. Although Lansing did not come into existence until 1847, there were some thirty Catholic families there five or six years later.[57] Oddly enough, the first attempt at parish organization was made by a priest from Detroit, Father Francis Krutil, one of the Redemptorists at St. Mary's, who had been commissioned by Bishop Lefevere to minister to isolated groups in the state. Under his direction the Catholics of Lansing began the building of a small frame church in 1856; but when the structure was almost complete it was dismantled by the contractor who had as yet gone unpaid. Father Louis Van Den Driessche of Corunna, to which Lansing was attached as a mission, finally collected enough funds to complete the church, and it was dedicated in the fall of 1864. Two years later Father Van Den Driessche became the first resident pastor.[58]

In the early fifties another Catholic group existed in the county on the Grand River Trail at Williamston. The Benhams, the Grimes, the Lorangers were ministered to by Father O'Kelly, and by the priests from Flint and Corunna. In 1866 Jerome Waldo entered into a contract with Bishop Lefevere wherein he promised to sell a plot of ground to the bishop for twenty-five cents provided a church should be built on it within three years.[59] The church was erected and paid for by 1869, and the congregation was attended from Lansing until Father John Lovett became the first resident pastor in 1879.

Eaton County, even today, has a smaller Catholic population than any of the others we have been considering. In the period we are dealing with there was a small Catholic group in Charlotte, the county seat, which appears for the first time in the Almanac for 1858 as a mission of Marshall. A frame church was built in the village in 1868, but the congregation remained as a mission to Battle Creek, Hastings, or Albion down to 1918, when Father Peter Jordan was appointed resident pastor.[60]

[57] "The constitution of 1836 provided that the seat of government should be established in Detroit until 1847, when it should be permanently located by the legislature. . . . After long and tedious effort—Ann Arbor, Jackson, Marshall, Kalamazoo and other places being determined to have it—a proposition was carried to locate it on the school section of the extreme northwestern township of Ingham County. It was known to be an unbroken wilderness, without even a good road leading to it. . . . There was scarcely a house in the neighborhood, and the site of the present city was covered with a dense growth of timber. . . . Lumber for finishing purposes was hauled in wagons all the way from Flint, but in the face of all difficulties the 'old Capitol' was built and some sort of provision made for the members who met in January, 1848. . . ." *Mich. Hist. Colls.*, VI, 292.

[58] Manuscript history of the Lansing parish by Father Louis Vandriss in DCA.

[59] Samuel W. Durant, *History of Ingham and Eaton Counties* (Philadelphia, 1880), 345.

[60] *Ibid.*, 402.

The earliest Catholic immigrants into Barry County took up land in the vicinity of Yankee Springs, that widely known settlement of the pioneer days, where "Yankee Lewis" dispensed genial hospitality. On October 1, 1849, John Duffy deeded to Bishop Lefevere a plot of ground in Section 34 of Yankee Springs township. The locality appears for the first time in the Almanac for 1851, where it is said to be attended from the priests at Grand Rapids. A history of Barry County makes the following reference to the congregation.

> About 1850 in the southwestern portion of the township there was a community of Catholics who bought Lewis McCloud's residence and converted it into a church. . . . They laid out a cemetery near by and prospered as a church until the removal from the neighborhood of a major portion of its members caused its dissolution. . . .[61]

The only trace of this early congregation is the cemetery which may still be observed. Although Yankee Springs was carried in the Catholic Almanacs for many years, Father Lucian Wicart in his manuscript history of the Hastings parish, written in 1871, makes no mention of it.

About ten miles east of the Yankee Springs cemetery lies Hastings, the county seat. The few Catholics living in it in the early sixties were attended occasionally from Kalamazoo, Marshall, Dorr, and Grand Rapids. In 1869 John Stanley, Patrick Ryan, and Thomas Haney purchased a dilapidated cooper shop, and converted it into a church. Father Ferdinand Allgayer was appointed first resident pastor in 1873, and a second church was dedicated by Bishop Borgess on March 20, 1884.[62]

From the survey of the counties of the diocese we turn to the record of growth in the episcopal city itself. When Bishop Lefevere came to his see in 1841 there were only two churches in Detroit: Holy Trinity ministering to an English-speaking congregation, and the cathedral of St. Anne serving the French Catholics of the city and its outskirts. But the old mother church was now sheltering another brood that was soon ready to strike out for itself.

The German Catholic immigrants to Detroit had been first organized as a group by Father Kundig. Beginning with 1833 they had their own High Mass on Sundays at St. Anne's, and a separate baptismal register for them was opened in 1835. From 1837 to 1840 Father Kundig's duties as Superintendent of the Poor left him so little time for pastoral work that his countrymen might have been neglected had not another German priest made his appearance. Father Clement

[61] *History of Allegan and Barry Counties* (Philadelphia, 1880), 518.
[62] *Ibid.*, 376. Manuscript history in DCA.

Hammer was another soul kindled by the aims of the Leopoldine Association, a mining engineer who had just become a priest in order to do missionary work in America.[63] Difficulties regarding the tenure of church property prevented Father Hammer from undertaking the erection of a building for his congregation, and he went on to Cincinnati, where for twenty-five years he was pastor of St. Mary's. Towards the end of 1840 Father Kundig set to work in earnest to realize the hopes of his German parishioners. In June, 1841, the corner stone of St. Mary's was laid, but the building was not yet completed when Father Kundig was assigned to Milwaukee. During the year's pastorate of his successor, Father Otto Skolla, the church was dedicated on June 29, 1843.[64]

A few weeks after the dedication Father Skolla went on to the northern missions and was replaced by Father Anton Kopp, who left Father Godez as his successor in Westphalia. Early in 1847 the Redemptorists assumed charge of the parish, and Father Kopp withdrew from Detroit to become affiliated with the Diocese of Chicago.[65] Under the administration of the Redemptorists, which lasted twenty-five years, St. Mary's made constant progress. The Christian Brothers and the School Sisters of Notre Dame were brought in to conduct the parish schools, and nine hundred pupils crowded into the present school building when it was dedicated in 1869.

Differences with Bishop Borgess regarding the terms under which St. Mary's was administered led to the withdrawal of the Redemptorists in the spring of 1872. The parish was then committed to the care of the Franciscan Fathers of the Cincinnati Province. During the pastorate of Father Francis Lings the corner stone of the present church was laid on July 20, 1884, and the completed structure was dedicated on August 16, 1885. For the same reasons that actuated their predecessors the Franciscans retired from the parish in 1890. The Redemptorists again took charge, but this time for only a year, and Father Charles Bolte, coming from Ionia, assumed the pastorate. In 1893 Bishop Foley acceding to the wishes of the congregation entrusted the parish to the Fathers of the Holy Ghost.

[63] Clement Hammer, born in 1804, was a graduate of the Freiberg School of Mining, and of the University of Vienna. He entered the seminary at Prague, was ordained in 1836, and came to Detroit the following summer. There is a long sketch of this talented personality, who was at once poet, musician, and painter, in the *Pastoral-Blatt* (St. Louis) LXXV, No. 2. In 1866 Father Hammer returned to Europe, where he died in 1879 as a Canon of the cathedral at Prague.

[64] The congregation was so impatient to see the building completed that the women deserted their housework to carry bricks in their aprons to the masons. *The 100 Anniversary of German Immigration to Detroit* (Detroit, 1930), 55.

[65] In 1848 Father Kopp became pastor of St. Joseph's church in Chicago. In 1860 he was pastor of St. Joseph's in Wilmette.

The beginnings of Holy Trinity have already been touched upon. Father Bernard O'Cavanagh, its first pastor, was succeeded by Father Kundig, whose entries in the baptismal register begin with July 21, 1839, and end on March 3, 1842. When Father Lawrence Kilroy began his pastorate there were approximately two hundred families living for the most part on the east side of Woodward Avenue within easy walking distance of the church.[66] It is interesting to note that Holy Trinity was probably destined for extinction when Bishop Lefevere undertook the building of his cathedral. The following notice appears in the Almanac for 1845.

> The Catholics of Trinity congregation, who speak the English language, having increased so much in number that their church (a frame building) is become by far too small to contain one half of the congregation, and those who wish to attend divine service in it; the corner stone for a new brick church was solemnly blessed, and laid by the Right Rev. P. Lefevere, on the 29th of June last. This church will be 160 feet long, by 80 feet in width, and is to be dedicated to the living God, under the invocation and patronage of the apostles SS. Peter and Paul.

However, the rapid influx of Irish immigrants to Detroit about the time the cathedral was building made the retention of Holy Trinity imperative. The city was beginning to grow westward, and many of the older residents as well as the newcomers moved from the undesirable locations they had been occupying.

> At all events, a settlement of the river front Irish from the poor homes of Woodbridge street and Franklin street and Congress street and Larned street was accomplished in the westerly part of the city, extending from Third street, carved through General Cass' farm to the farm of Governor Woodbridge, where the city stopped because he wouldn't let the streets run through; knowing . . . that the city of Detroit in its wildest growth in that direction could not extend west of what we now know as Trumbull avenue. So the Irish settled in what came to be known as "Corktown," in that square which was bounded east and west by Third and Eighth streets and south and north by the river and the present location of Vernor Highway. They settled it solidly and in a rather selective way. . . . That is to say, one section of it was as full of Kerrymen as is Kerry itself, while another had a solid population from County Cork, and still others were populated entirely by natives of Limerick and Tipperary. The Connaught men were settled on the side and backward streets as a median destination between the places to which Cromwell is said to have told recalcitrant Irishmen to go. . . .[67]

[66] Richard R. Elliott compiled a list of the original families in Trinity parish for the bi-centenary edition of the *Michigan Catholic*, August 22, 1901.

[67] From a printed copy of an address, *The Early Irish of Detroit*, delivered by John A. Russell at the Diamond Jubilee of the corner stone laying of Trinity Church, November 9, 1930.

In August, 1849, the wooden church on Cadillac Square was mounted on rollers and hauled to its final resting-place, the northeast corner of Sixth and Porter Streets. During the moving, and while the building was being fitted up anew, the congregation again worshipped in the basement chapel of St. Anne's. The old church was at last torn down to make room for the present edifice, whose corner stone was laid on October 28, 1855. Some thirty years later there were almost a thousand families clustered around Holy Trinity, and no parish of the diocese has contributed such a galaxy of Catholic men prominent in the professions and public life as this one whose name is synonymous with the integration of the Irish immigrant into the life of Detroit.[68]

The completion of the cathedral in 1848 added a second English-speaking congregation to the city. Third Street was made the dividing line between the two parishes, Trinity extending westward to the Rouge River, and the cathedral eastward to Grosse Pointe. Father John Farnan, the first pastor, died in 1849, and was succeeded by Father Michael Edgar Shawe, who had come from the Diocese of Vincennes the preceding year. Father Shawe was a man of unusual distinction and ability. Born in England, he began his career as an officer in the British army, and was severely wounded in the battle of Waterloo. After a long convalescense in France during which he became a Catholic, Michael Shawe retired from the army, lived for some years in Vienna, and finally entered St. Mary's at Oscott to begin studying for the priesthood. He was at St. Sulpice when Bishop Bruté visited Paris in 1836 to recruit priests for his diocese. Coming to America before his studies were completed he was ordained by Bishop Bruté on March 12, 1837. His pastorate in Detroit was ended by his untimely death, the result of an accident, on May 10, 1853.[69] Father Peter Hennaert succeeded, and as pastor and Vicar-General he administered the parish down to 1875. Two years later it was transferred to the Jesuits, who came at the invitation of Bishop Borgess to be the pioneers of higher Catholic education in Detroit.

The next parish to be considered is here designated as the fifth but might possibly deserve to be ranked as the second oldest within the present limits of the city. It will be remembered that the Redemptorists who arrived in Detroit while Father Richard was still alive, that is, in the summer of 1832, attended a group of German

---

[68] Curiously enough the two distinguished priests who presided over Holy Trinity during its most flourishing period were both Belgians; Father Francis Peeters, who died in 1869 from small-pox contracted as the result of a sick call, and Father Aloysius Bleyenbergh, pastor from 1869 to 1883.

[69] Richard R. Elliott wrote a biography of Father Shawe for the *American Cath. Hist. Researches*, April, 1897.

immigrants who were living out on the Gratiot Road. Although it
is probable that some primitive building for church purposes was
erected at the time, the point cannot be definitely established. But
that a church existed in 1838, whether the first or a second one, is
evident from the notation in the Almanac for 1839: "*Chapel of the
Assumption*, not dedicated, (German), Rev. Joseph Freygang." This
is the first mention of Father Freigang's connection with the Diocese
of Detroit; but since he was certainly in the diocese at the end of
1835 it is possible that he had been assigned to the more or less
regular charge of the German Catholics living at a distance from the
city, and that his chapel was an improvement over a pre-existing one.
The chapel is listed as unattended from this time to 1847, when the
entry in the Almanac reads: "Hamtramck, Wayne county. The Assumption of the B.V.M. attended from Detroit." In 1852 "Clemens
Road" is attended once a month by the Redemptorists from Detroit.

Some time in 1852 Bishop Lefevere placed the congregation under
the care of a resident priest, a young man whom he had ordained
two years before, Father Amandus Van Den Driessche. The building
of a new brick church was immediately undertaken, and the completed structure was dedicated to the Assumption by Bishop Lefevere
on May 1, 1853.[70] For almost two score years Father "Van," as he was
familiarly called, continued to preside over the congregation at Connor's Creek, which in the course of time included many Belgian and
French families. In 1881, after a visit to Lourdes, he established the
famous shrine which for many years drew pilgrimages from the
whole Detroit area to the "Grotto" parish. The growth of Detroit
eastward brought the parish within the city limits in 1925, and the
great increase in membership rendered inadequate the church built
by Father Ronayne in 1908. It was replaced by the splendid edifice
whose corner stone was laid on Memorial Day, 1930.

The rapidly mounting German Catholic population of Detroit in
the early fifties could not be served indefinitely by the mother parish.
In the fall of 1855 Bishop Lefevere decided to begin another German
parish on the eastern side of the city. For this division of St. Mary's,
at the time in charge of the Redemptorists, the bishop chose Father
Edward Van Campenhoudt, who had been stationed for a year at St.
Mary's, and who had just effected his release from the Congregation.[71]
A site was immediately secured on the Gratiot Road between Rio-

[70] Father Shawe was on his way to the dedication, when he was thrown from his
carriage and suffered the injuries which caused his death. The *Detroit Catholic
Vindicator*, May 14, 1853.
[71] Father Van Campenhoudt came to Detroit as a seminarian in 1846, and after a year
was given leave by Bishop Lefevere to join the Redemptorists. He died September 26,
1880, as pastor of Baldwinsville in the Syracuse diocese.

pelle and Orleans Streets, and the first church of St. Joseph, a frame structure, was dedicated on May 25, 1856. There were over two hundred families in the parish when Father Van Campenhoudt resigned in 1858, and progress was not too marked until Father John Friedland was named pastor in 1864. The present church was dedicated on November 16, 1873, and ten years later there were over a thousand families worshipping in St. Joseph's.

Even St. Joseph's, however, could not accommodate the German immigration streaming into the east side of the city. The final court decree vesting in Bishop Lefevere the ownership of that portion of the Church Farm lying north of Gratiot Road was issued on May 18, 1857. The trust contained in the original grant was respected to the extent that the bishop was given full disposition of the property "save such portions as in his judgment are needed and best adapted for the site and grounds of a church and school house or asylum." [72] The bishop's solicitude to fulfill the terms of the trust, no less than the number of families needing attention, led to the immediate establishment of a new parish, although not to the profit of the descendants of the original grantors. On June 16, 1857, a frame church 70 x 40 feet, and situated, as the first pastor wrote, "at the side of Gratiot Road and Central-line plankroad," was dedicated to St. Anthony. As its pastor Bishop Lefevere appointed Father Leopold Pawlowski, who had come to Detroit from the Diocese of Erie, and who left Detroit at the end of a year.[73] St. Anthony's was attended by the priests of St. Joseph's down to 1867, when Father Peter André became resident pastor. After the death of Father Charles Hutter in 1917 the parish was administered by the Fathers of the Precious Blood, and it was officially committed to their care in 1942.

A few months after the dedication of St. Anthony's came the beginning of another parish far to the west of the city limits of that day on the Grand River Road in the township of Redford. How early this group was visited from Detroit is uncertain, but the possibility of organizing a parish must have been entertained as far back as 1843. In November of that year John Blindburg deeded a plot of ground to Bishop Lefevere "in trust for the Roman Catholic Congregation of Greenfield and Redford." However, a sketch of St. Mary's of Redford, written by one of the later pastors, places the origin in 1850, when Father Peter Kindekins, then pastor of St. Anne's and Vicar-General, began coming out regularly to conduct divine worship. The

---

[72] Burton, *op. cit.*, II, 1302.

[73] Father Pawlowski's first financial report is in the DCA. He came to America from the Diocese of Posen in 1853, and was admitted to Detroit from the Diocese of Erie on August 11, 1857.

deed to the present church property was executed by Mary Odile Chaivre on July 24, 1852, and a frame church was probably erected about the same time. In a long letter to the Society for the Propagation of the Faith the first resident pastor, Father Edward Dumont, appointed in 1857, discloses the make-up of his congregation.

> The Catholic families who form my little flock number about 120 spread over an extent of from 7 to 8 leagues; fifty or sixty of them are French or Swiss. Many have been in the country from twenty to twenty-five years. These families are mixed with from 30 to 40 Calvinist families, very hostile to our religion, and coming like the Catholics from the neighborhood of Strasburg. . . . The other families who reside in my mission are nearly all Irish. The larger number of Irish and French families is very poor. There are no rich families; they all live from the work of their hands. . . .[74]

Father Dumont found the church still unfinished and unfurnished. The humble rectory he was able to build burned down almost as soon as it was completed, and a similar fate befell the church a few months later. He determined that the next church should be built of brick, a costly enterprise that was the motive of his appeal to the French missionary society. The corner stone was laid on August 15, 1859, and the familiar red church stood almost seventy years watching the Grand River Road changing from an impassible boggy trail to a concrete superhighway thronged with traffic. In 1927, three years after its inclusion into the city, it was replaced by the noble edifice conceived in its architectural design as "a symbolic monument to the pioneer priest and parishioners." [75]

In 1861 Father Dumont returned to Belgium to become vice-rector of the American College at Louvain, and professor of dogmatic theology. At the end of ten years he succeeded to the rectorship, and in 1873 he was made bishop of Tournai. Unfortunately, Bishop Dumont involved himself in the fierce political controversies which agitated Belgium at the time, and followed a course of action which was displeasing to the Holy See. Having spent his last years in retirement he died a holy death at Chateau de Villers Perwin on November 20, 1892.[76]

All the parishes we have been dealing with lay either outside of or on the arms of the immense V formed by Gratiot and Grand River Avenues, and whose base rested in the limits of old St. Anne's. Within this figure bisected by Woodward Avenue the first thrust

---

[74] Letter dated February 6, 1860. Hickey Transcripts.

[75] There is an excellent parish history: *St. Mary's of Redford; A Centennial History* (Detroit, 1949).

[76] Van Der Heyden, *op. cit.*, 112–113.

northward was an extension of the cathedral parish. Father James Hennessy, who had been transferred from Marshall to the cathedral in 1855 to minister especially to the Irish portion of the congregation, found that many of his people in the far end of the parish, particularly working men and servant girls, could not attend the church without great inconvenience. His proposal to build a chapel of ease as far out towards the city limits as Adelaide Street was not opposed by Bishop Lefevere, although he expressed the opinion that a chapel in Birmingham would be just about as useful.[77] On March 17, 1862, Father Hennessy's perseverance was rewarded by the dedication of his chapel to St. Patrick, and his appointment as its first pastor. Three years before his death in 1875, he enlarged the church to its present dimensions. Under his successor, Father Charles Ormand Reilly, famous for his oratory and his activities in behalf of Irish freedom, St. Patrick's grew to be a flourishing parish of five hundred families. Father Reilly resigned from his charge in 1890, and on October 12 of the same year Bishop Foley formally designated the church as his cathedral, and placed it under the patronage of SS. Peter and Paul.[78]

Four years after the dedication of St. Patrick's came the next parish organization in the city, an outgrowth of Holy Trinity. The Irish Catholics were still moving westward as well as increasing in number, and the old home could no longer contain them. To Father Aloysius Bleyenberg, then assistant at Holy Trinity, was entrusted the formation of a new parish to be bounded on the east by Tenth Street, and on the west by the city limits at Twenty-fifth. On December 2, 1866, the new church was dedicated to St. Vincent de Paul. At the end of twenty years the parish numbered over a thousand families, and in 1887, during the first years of Father James Doherty's long pastorate, the church was enlarged to its present dimensions.

Meanwhile, many Irish families were moving out towards the eastern limits of the city, then at Mt. Elliott Avenue, attracted by the opportunities for employment offered by the beginnings of industrial development in that section. One industry, the manufacture of stoves, was destined to make Detroit known throughout the world, and its founder was Jeremiah Dwyer, who as a youth had worshipped in Holy Trinity.[79] A young Belgian assistant at the cathedral, Father Gustave Limpens, was authorized to begin the third Irish parish in the city. His efforts resulted in the dedication of the present church of Our Lady of Help on December 8, 1867.

The organization of another German parish brings to a close this

[77] *Mich. Hist. Colls.*, XIII, 449.
[78] The *Michigan Catholic*, issues of October 9 and 16, 1890.
[79] Catlin, *op. cit.*, 472–78.

record of expansion in Detroit between 1840 and 1870. The early German Catholic population was concentrated, as we have seen, in the east side of the city. In the course of time considerable migration to the west side called for the establishing of a parish center accessible to the German families that were strung out along Michigan Avenue. The task was assigned to Father Anthony Kullman, assistant at St. Joseph's, and his flock was to comprise every German family west of Third Street. He proceeded to erect the first building in Detroit of the type now so commonly used in the development of new parishes, a combination of church and school. The structure was dedicated to St. Boniface on October 10, 1869. During the pastorate of Father Bernard Wermers, which began in 1872, the corner stone of the present church was laid by Bishop Toebbe of Covington on August 13, 1882.

CHAPTER XXIII

Bishop Borgess

ELEVEN months elapsed between the death of Bishop Lefevere and the appointment of his successor. Actually, Detroit still had a bishop who held title to the see, the tottering old man at Hildesheim smiling over his timeless souvenirs. At the end of his eulogy over the remains of Bishop Lefevere, Archbishop Purcell of Cincinnati had announced that pending the choice of another coadjutor he was confiding the administration of the diocese to Father Peter Hennaert, the Vicar-General. Because of failing health the administrator would be assisted by Father Henry Schutjes, who was at the time pastor of St. James' in Bay City.

In December, 1869, the diocesan weekly, the *Western Catholic*, ventured to notice the reports that were circulating.[1]

> Rumors have been published during the week of the appointment of Bishops for this and the adjoining diocese of Chicago. For Chicago was named the Very Rev. Thos. Foley, V.G. and Chancellor of the Archdiocese of Baltimore. . . . For Detroit it was rumored that Father C. H. Borgess, Chancellor of the Archdiocese of Cincinnati, had received the Bulls, but the Administration of Detroit has received no official information of the fact, and there may be no more truth in it than was in the rumor some time ago that Father Rice, of Niagara, had been appointed.[2]

Some time later the *Western Catholic* reported the rather enigmatic comment of Father Borgess himself.

> A clerical friend of ours has kindly shown us an extract from a private letter of Father Borgess, of Cincinnati, which puts a quietus for the present upon the rumors of his elevation to the See of Detroit. Father Borgess says: "I am happy to inform you that, to the present moment, I am an innocent party to the whole affair, and regret that I have but become debtor to all who so kindly offered me their sympathy." The people of Michigan will unite with us in regretting that the coming of their Bishop is thus longer postponed.[3]

[1] The *Western Catholic*, March 13, 1869.
[2] *Ibid.*, December 18, 1869.
[3] *Ibid.*, January 1, 1870.

The rumors had been well founded; on the list of candidates submitted to Rome by the bishops of the province the name of Father Borgess had been first. Archbishop Purcell, who was in Rome attending the sessions of the Vatican Council, could plead the worthiness of the chancellor who had served him so faithfully. On February 14, 1870, Pius IX named Caspar Henry Borgess as bishop of the titular see of Calydon, and coadjutor and administrator of the Diocese of Detroit.[4] The consecration took place on April 24 in the cathedral at Cincinnati. In the absence of the archbishop the consecrator was Bishop Rosecrans of Columbus, who was assisted by Bishop Luers of Fort Wayne and Bishop Feehan of Nashville.[5]

The purple came to a man who had completed twenty-one years of honorable, laborious priesthood. His origins were as lowly as those of his countryman, the first bishop of Detroit. The son of tenant farmers in humble circumstances, he was born on August 1, 1826, in the village of Addrup, near the town of Essen in the Duchy of Oldenburg.[6] When he was twelve years old his parents emigrated to America, and after some residence in Philadelphia finally settled in Cincinnati. Here Caspar Borgess attended St. Xavier's College, decided on his vocation, and completed his studies at Mt. St. Mary's Seminary. Ordained at Cincinnati by Bishop Purcell on December 8, 1848, he was appointed pastor of Holy Cross, the first church in Columbus, Ohio.

At the very beginning of his eleven years pastorate in Columbus Father Borgess won the affection of Catholics and Protestants alike by his heroism during the nation wide cholera epidemic of 1849.

In his rounds, visiting the sick in Columbus, during the terrible scourge in 1849, and the first year of his priesthood, he often fell asleep in the saddle, as he was constantly on the go, and had but little rest day and night. A Protestant wrote the following account of his unceasing labor among the sick: "I beg to mention" he writes, "the humane and charitable exertions of our Catholic minister, Rev. Mr. Borgess. This

[4] Bull of appointment in DCA.

[5] There is an account of the consecration in the *Western Catholic* for April 30, 1870.

[6] A copy of the baptismal record in the DCA, taken from the church records in Essen, gives the parents' names as Johan Gerd Borges and Maria Anna Dinkgreve. The bishop habitually spelled his surname with an additional "s." Reuss in his *Biographical Cyclopedia of the Catholic Hierarchy* is certainly wrong in the date of the bishop's birth, and he gives the birthplace as being Koppenberg. While traveling in Europe after his *ad limina* visit in 1887, the bishop wrote a series of letters to his brother in the United States, which were published by Father Frank O'Brien of Kalamazoo in a volume entitled *As The Bishop Saw It* (Detroit, 1892). Before leaving Germany for Holland the bishop wrote: "The lesson received from Mr. M's experience in his native parish prompted the determination that it would be folly for me to visit Essen in the grand duchy of Oldenberg. . . . Why should I venture on a similar disappointment, it being quite sure that no person in Essen could have a faint recollection of the boy of twelve years, who in company with his parents, left for America in the last week of February, 1839; more especially since no immediate relative survived our return to our native land. . . ."

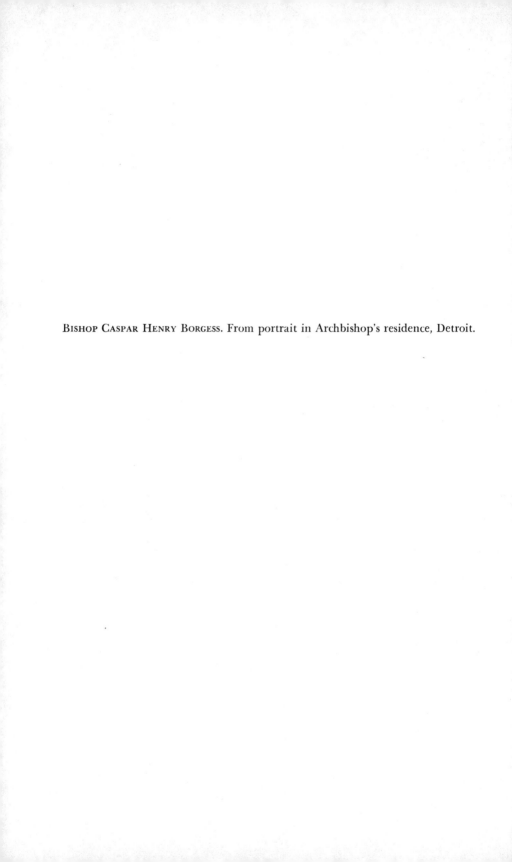

Bɪsʜᴏᴘ Cᴀsᴘᴀʀ Hᴇɴʀʏ Bᴏʀɢᴇss. From portrait in Archbishop's residence, Detroit.

young clergyman, who, by the way, is one of the most eloquent men I have ever listened to, is winning for himself the esteem of every Christian heart in the community. Since the dread scourge of the cholera first made its appearance among us, he seems to be occupied day and night visiting the destitute sick, administering to them not only religious consolation, but securing medicine and administering it with a skill that our most eminent physicians might envy. . . .[7]

In 1859 Father Borgess was brought to Cincinnati to supervise the building of the Immaculate Conception church on Mt. Adams. A year later he was appointed Chancellor of the diocese. The ten years that he spent in this most important post gave him the experience and knowledge for the high office to which he was now called.

Bishop Borgess arrived in Detroit on Saturday, May 8, 1870, to take possession of his see. His characteristic distaste for publicity had prompted the request, which was respected, to the Administrator of the diocese that his entry be unheralded and without demonstration of any sort.[8] However, the news of his presence had spread quickly, and on Sunday morning the cathedral was besieged by the Catholics of the city eager to behold and hear their new bishop. He interrupted his pontifical Mass to preach a simple sermon on the virtues of St. Joseph, but made no reference to the significance of the occasion. Whatever disappointment may have been felt was alleviated by the reflections which found expression in the comment of the diocesan weekly.

It was remarked by many that our new prelate has in every act since his arrival scrupulously avoided all personal display. It was expected by nearly all that in his sermon he would allude at least incidentally to his new position and the relations into which he has entered with the people he was addressing. But not even a word was uttered which could indicate that he had not been among us for years. His course in this has been admired by all, and the people felt how truly he has carried out his first intention as expressed in his letter to the Detroit societies on a recent occasion: "It will be my delight to enter your city simply with apostolic claims, the badge of the Redeemer, and the silent display of the humble missionary."[9]

[7] From the sermon of Bishop Richter at the dedication of the Borgess monument on the grounds of Nazareth Academy, Kalamazoo. See the *Michigan Catholic*, October 11, 1906.

[8] The *Western Catholic*, May 14, 1870.

[9] The *Western Catholic* for May 21 printed the following request signed by twenty-five representative Catholics of Detroit.

"Dear Sir: It is hardly necessary for us to inform you that your spiritual children in this city are extremely anxious to become personally acquainted with you, to shake you by the hand, and to give you a cordial welcome to your new home. Will you be so kind as to name a day when the doors of the Episcopal residence will be open not only to them, but also to our citizens generally."

A few days later the bishop kept open house from "two o'clock in the afternoon until quite a late hour in the evening."

Only a brief summary is needed here of the diocese over which Bishop Borgess came to preside. In its territorial extent it still comprised the entire lower peninsula of the State. Within this area there was a Catholic population of "at least 150,000," as the Catholic Directory reported it. Of the Catholic Indians there was a trace near Silver Creek, and a somewhat larger group in the vicinity of Harbor Springs. In the entire diocese there were seventy churches with resident priests, of which eleven were in the City of Detroit, and fifteen in the territory now comprised within the Diocese of Grand Rapids. Irish and German immigration accounted for the greater number of these parishes; a few represented the old French centers of settlement, and one marked the advance into Michigan of the Polish pioneers.

The priests of the diocese numbered eighty-eight divided on the score of nationality into the following groups: thirty-nine Belgians, six Hollanders, twenty-one Germans, nine Irishmen, five Frenchmen, two Poles, and six native born Americans, of whom four were natives of Michigan.[10] There is more in this simple statement of fact than is apparent at first sight. Today, when the melting pot is cooling down, these figures have not the same significance they had eighty years ago. Tradition preserves only vestiges of what must once have been held as a grievance against Bishop Lefevere, that in building up his clergy he was too partial towards his countrymen, and that he made little efforts to provide priests of other nationalities.[11] The charge was manifestly and utterly unjust. As any other bishop situated in his circumstances would have done, Bishop Lefevere took worthy priests where he could find them. He was uncompromising in his ideals of the priesthood, and had plenty of experience with the shadowy figures who have flitted about the advance of the Church into new territory since the days of Archbishop Carroll. The founding of the American College at Louvain by himself and Bishop Spalding was an attempt to secure priests, not particularly Belgian priests, for the waste places in America. If the two bishops there tapped a mine of missionary zeal they were entitled to use its output to the utmost. The establishing of St. Thomas Seminary in Detroit as early as 1846 proves how readily Bishop Lefevere would have taken advantage of native vocations had there been any. That there were only four natives of Michigan in the priesthood in 1870 shows that he was perhaps too hopeful of results at a period when Catholic immigration into Michigan had only fairly

---

[10] The four natives of Michigan were Fathers James Savage, Ernest Van Dyke, Thomas Rafter, and John Reichenbach. Two priests, James Pulcher, born in New York, and Benjamin Schmittdiel in Pennsylvania, had come to the diocese in early childhood.

[11] The matter is alluded to by Richard R. Elliott in his lengthy account of the Diocese of Detroit written for the bi-centenary edition of the *Michigan Catholic*, August 22, 1901.

begun, and the pioneers had still before them years of hard struggle for a bare livelihood.

The number alone of the Belgian clergymen is evidence that to them belongs the honor of having borne the greatest share of the labors involved in bringing the diocese through the pioneer stage. As a group they were rugged, tireless, zealous missionaries who throve on obstacles and hardships. That they might have been favored to a certain extent by Bishop Lefevere was perfectly natural, as was a certain complacency attributed to them that they had been working in the vineyard from the third hour, and had borne "the burden of the day and the heats." Here again tradition steps in to picture them as clannish, conservative, and averse to change, and out of touch with the life about them. There is obvious animus behind the tradition, for such characteristics were by no means peculiar to the Belgian clergy. Whatever grievances, fancied or real, underlie the tradition they are not as important as the fact to which it attests, namely, the intense national feeling of the period which drew hard and fast lines between groups both of clergy and laity.

The problems, and the crosses, that confronted Bishop Borgess can easily be inferred. Having progressed to a certain stage of development the diocese needed to be straitened into a new regimen. If it had been pampered somewhat by the paternal heart of Bishop Lefevere, it was now time for it to submit to the corrective discipline suited to a maturer age. Schooled by his ten years as chancellor of such a well-ordered center of Catholic life as Cincinnati, Bishop Borgess could appraise the needs and the defects of his diocese with practised eyes. A general tightening up process was necessary. Old style methods of conducting diocesan affairs had to be supplanted by a more efficient system. For the welfare of the diocese there were many idiosyncrasies on the part of the leaders that demanded curbing. It was high time to speed up the growth of an indigenous clergy. Above all it was necessary to begin whittling down the barriers set up by exaggerated nationalisms.

The consistent and courageous carrying out of these policies spells the episcopate of Bishop Borgess. It was inevitable that he should encounter resistance arising not so much from antagonism as from inertia. His determined course of action was not calculated to bring him either affection or popularity. He has been represented as having been cold, severe, caring little for social intercourse, always unbending. Behind this undiscriminating judgment we can see the man whose strong sense of duty could not countenance preference or partiality, and who was bent on exercising his office free from all alliances and entanglements.

Coming between the long episcopates of Bishop Lefevere and Bishop Foley that of Bishop Borgess was relatively short. It extended over a period of seventeen years. He had been in Detroit a little more than a year and a half, familiarizing himself with conditions, when the death of Bishop Rese automatically terminated his coadjutorship, and left him Bishop of Detroit in fact as well as in name. In the spring of 1887 failing health afforded him a long-sought opportunity to lay down his burden. Despite its comparative brevity the episcopate of Bishop Borgess, animated by the ideals just outlined, was bound to be of unique importance and value for the continued development of the diocese.

Undoubtedly, the most important phase of Bishop Borgess' activities, and the one which best illustrates his administrative temper, is represented by the body of diocesan legislation which he enacted. In the course of twenty-eight years his predecessor had convened two diocesan synods; within fifteen years Bishop Borgess convened five.

The third diocesan synod, or the first under Bishop Borgess' administration, assembled in May, 1873. In its issue of May 10, the *Western Home Journal,* the diocesan weekly, made the following announcement.

> The Spiritual Retreat of the clergy of this Diocese, preached by Right Rev. Dr. Gilmour, Bishop of Cleveland, commenced on last Wednesday, in the chapel of SS. Peter and Paul's Church, in this city. There are about 88 priests assembled. The Synod will be opened on the morning of the 13th, and conclude on the 15th instant.

Strange as it may seem there is no further mention of the synod in the *Journal,* and diligent search has failed to unearth its proceedings. Apparently, no printed record was issued, nor do the Chancery archives yield any enlightening item.[12]

Five years later, on October 15, 1878, the fourth diocesan synod, attended by one hundred and eight clergymen, was opened with pontifical Mass in the church of St. Aloysius. The sessions were continued over four days, and the printed report outlines the important questions which were submitted for deliberation.[13] As early as 1871 Bishop

[12] The DCA holds a surprisingly scanty amount of material bearing on the episcopate of Bishop Borgess. It is possible that at the time of his resignation he sequestered much that would have remained had he died in office. Another possibility is indicated by the final page of Father O'Brien's volume already mentioned. There he promises three additional volumes to be published "in due season." The first is to be a biography of the bishop, the second his selected sermons, and the third his pastoral letters. The volumes never appeared, and it has proved impossible to locate the material which Father O'Brien doubtless had in his possession, and which he had borrowed from the Chancery, when he announced his series.

[13] *Acta et Constitutiones Synodi Dioecesanae Detroitensis Quartae . . .* (Detroit; Free Press Book and Job Printing House, 1878).

Borgess had undertaken the creation of a fund for the support of retired and incapacitated priests of the diocese. In December of that year he had issued a pastoral, in which he had broached the project and the method by which it was to be realized.[14] A third of the Sunday collections in all the churches of the diocese for the ensuing two years were to be set apart for the purpose. Whatever steps had been taken to augment the fund from the expiration of that period had evidently proved unsatisfactory, and the present synod was urged to propose and provide a stable source of revenue. The following resolution, the first of nine dealing with the matter, put into operation the Infirm Priests Fund, and designated the means by which it was to be maintained.

> The Priests' Fund shall be raised from the ordinary revenues of the Churches or congregations. The amount assessed on any church or congregation by the committee to be appointed during this synod, shall be, and is really a debt of the church, or congregation, and must be paid by the Rev. pastor in two equal installments, viz., in June and December of each and every year.

In the agenda of the synod there were two points regarding Catholic education. Bishop Borgess, in the pastoral referred to above, had urged upon his priests in no uncertain terms the necessity of a school in every parish. He had pointed to the religious training of the child as of greater importance than the erection of a material temple for the congregation. As the result of this insistence the number of parochial schools had risen from 38 in 1872 to 56 in 1878. Now that the number of schools was fairly large the laity should be impressed with the necessity of using and supporting them. In 1875 the Propaganda Congregation had issued an Instruction to the American Bishops empowering them to withhold absolution from Catholic parents who without justification kept their children from attending available parochial schools. The Instruction was laid before the synod, not as a topic for discussion, but as initiating a diocesan policy which was henceforth to be uniformly and strictly observed.

However, there was room for debate on the second point. The Bishop and his clergy evidently shared the growing sentiment that found expression in the Third Plenary Council of Baltimore, namely, that parochial schools should be free schools.[15] How this was to be accomplished appears from the unanimously adopted resolution proposed to the synod by the committee appointed to study the question.

---

[14] There is a summary of the pastoral in the *Herald des Glaubens* (St. Louis), in the issue of December 31, 1871.

[15] Burns, *op. cit.*, 274–77.

As to the best method of establishing this free system, we think, (1) The best is to have the ordinary revenues of every church to be made adequate to the emergency. (2) Where this method is impracticable we propose the establishing of permanent school associations, or a yearly voluntary subscription or contribution to the parish. (2) Where the contribution made by the scholars has proved beneficial to the church and school, care should be taken that none should be deprived of the benefits of the Catholic school on account of not paying.

The synod devoted the greater part of its discussions to questions relating to the care of the Catholic child. Pastors were reminded of their sacred obligation to impart catechetical instructions at least on Sundays in all their missions. Another matter laid before them was "the importance of visiting the County Poor Houses within the limits of the mission of any priest, and of providing homes, as far as possible, for orphans and destitute children found in them." More important still was the question: "Is there any other way of providing for the orphans in our asylums than the holding of annual fairs?" A growing realization of the duty of the diocese as a whole to care for its orphans appears in the majority report adopted, although the required funds were to come from voluntary contributions. In every parish of the diocese a society to provide for the support of orphan and destitute children was to be instituted.

. . . There shall be three or five officers to that society, with the pastor as director, who shall with discretion and equity distribute the funds of the society between the different orphan asylums or similar institutions.

This society shall work as much as possible to place orphans or destitute children in good Catholic families, and shall keep a kind of intelligence office to find out what families would want to adopt children. . . .

The measure was not promulgated at this time, but was the first decree to issue from the fifth diocesan synod held at Assumption College, Windsor, Ontario, from July 16 to 19, 1881.[16] This synod was particularly concerned with bringing about uniformity throughout the diocese in various matters. Regulations were laid down regarding the attitude to be taken towards religious and non-religious societies in the parishes. The ceremonies prescribed in the Roman Ritual and the Baltimore Ceremonial were to be followed, "all private and national customs to the contrary notwithstanding." A schedule determining the amounts of stipends and fees was adopted. Apparently for the first time, the problem of increasing the efficiency of the parochial schools came up for consideration. A report outlining a system of

[16] *Acta et Constitutiones Synodi . . . Quintae* (Detroit, 1881).

school boards was submitted for approval; but its recommendations were not put into effect until some years later.[17]

Still intent upon uniformity in another important field Bishop Borgess convened the sixth diocesan synod at Assumption College on July 20, 1885.[18] He announced the creation of a Matrimonial Court, and issued regulations designed to prevent certain abuses that had accompanied the wedding ceremony. The plan adopted in the preceding synod for the support of the orphans of the diocese had proved to be unworkable, and the problem was again submitted to study. This time it was definitely settled; volunteer parish societies were replaced by a system of graded assessments on parish revenues.

Just a year later Bishop Borgess brought to a close his work of formation and discipline in the seventh diocesan synod. Its two sessions were held at Assumption College on August 16, 1886.[19] Whereas previous synods had been held to deal with particular problems, this one was convened to resume and promulgate the entire body of legislation operative in the diocese. The statutes that issued from this synod although occasionally modified served as the basic code of diocesan administration for fifty-eight years, or until the convocation of the eighth synod in 1944.

Only the briefest summary of this final product of Bishop Borgess' firm and thoroughgoing administration can be given here. The legislation effected by the Third Plenary Council of Baltimore for the American Church is promulgated in the diocese. In accordance with its prescriptions the officiality of the diocese is organized, and the first Board of Diocesan Consultors is named.[20] Three rural deaneries, Monroe, Port Huron, and Lansing are established.[21] A lengthy section is devoted to the duties of pastors and assistants, and is followed by two chapters dealing with matters related to divine worship and the administration of the sacraments. Parochial school legislation is then resumed, and a final section groups various unrelated points of discipline.

It has already been intimated that Bishop Borgess emphasizing that phase of his office with which we have just been concerned was bound to meet with opposition. The seventeen years of his episcopate were beset with troubles and trying situations. Most of them may now be deservedly forgotten. However, certain episodes have some measure

---

[17] The report will be quoted in a later chapter.

[18] *Acta et Constitutiones Synodi . . . Sextae* (Detroit; Kilroy and Brennan, 1886).

[19] *Synodus Dioecesane Detroitensis Septima. . . .* (Marshall, 1886).

[20] The Board was composed of the following priests: John Friedland, Aloysius Lambert, James Savage, John Frieden, S.J., Frank O'Brien, James Doherty.

[21] The Deanery of Kalamazoo was established by a special order of Bishop Borgess dated December 7, 1886. DCA.

of historical interest, and on that account may merit to be resurrected.

Bishop Borgess had been in Detroit less than a year when he became involved in what was soon known throughout the country as the Lebel-Bunbury affair. To forward the completion of St. Augustine's church in Kalamazoo, Father Isidore Lebel had borrowed approximately $10,000 on security furnished by an estimable and devout parishioner, Patrick Bunbury. This took place in 1866, and on March 20, 1871, Father Lebel died leaving the financial affairs of the parish in a tangled condition. The loans were called, and Mr. Bunbury sought redress first from the parish, and then from the bishop. Meanwhile, Bishop Borgess had appointed Father Bernard Quinn pastor or St. Augustine's. He had come from the East with fine recommendations, but his subsequent unsavory conduct and career proved that he was utterly unworthy of the bishop's confidence. In order to enhance his reputation for financial ability Father Quinn persuaded a majority of the congregation that Mr. Bunbury's claim was unfounded and should be rejected.

The bishop considered the matter from another viewpoint. Being himself a comparative stranger in the diocese he had no first-hand knowledge of the original transaction. He knew, however, that according to the statutes in force under Bishop Lefevere Father Lebel had no right to contract any debt in favor of his parish without written authorization. Of this there was no trace. Here was a flagrant example of the consequences to which such disobedience might lead, and Bishop Borgess, on the threshold of his episcopate was determined to end these violations of diocesan law.

Unfortunately, his firmness led to a regrettable incident. Not knowing where to turn, and ignorant of Canon Law, Mr. Bunbury brought suit against the bishop in the civil courts. Some time later Bishop Borgess was saying Mass in St. Augustine's. Mr. Bunbury approaching to receive Holy Communion was denied the Sacrament, and after Mass the congregation was apprised of the penalty of excommunication which he had incurred by his court action. This fine Catholic gentleman, whose probity and piety were unquestioned, resigned himself to the humiliation, withdrew his suit, and died a few months later, as his friends said, of a broken heart. Bishop Borgess while taking his stand on the legal aspects of the case recognized the justice of Mr. Bunbury's claims, and made full restitution to his legal heirs, Such, in bare outline, was the famous Lebel-Bunbury case, which found its way into nearly every newspaper in the country.

Bishop Borgess was, of course, the center of a storm of comment alternately excoriating and defending him. By the end of 1872 the excitement had almost died down, when it was revived from another quarter. In February, 1873, Senator Emerson of Battle Creek introduced the following bill in the Legislature.

The People of the State of Michigan enact: That if any Archbishop, Bishop, Priest, Minister or other persons, assuming ecclesiastical authority in any church, religious sect or denomination, shall excommunicate, or threaten or assume to excommunicate any person being a member of such church, religious sect, or denomination, or administer, or threaten, or assume to administer upon such member any other ecclesiastical discipline with the intent to prevent or deter any such member from commencing or prosecuting any suit or other legal or equitable proceeding against any Archbishop, Bishop, Priest, Minister, or other person assuming such ecclesiastical authority . . . such Archbishop, Bishop, Priest, Minister, or other person assuming such ecclesiastical authority, shall be deemed guilty of a misdemeanor, and upon conviction thereof shall be punished by a fine of not less than one thousand dollars and not exceeding five thousand dollars, or shall be imprisoned in the State Prison not less than one year nor more than five years, or shall be punished by both said fine and imprisonment in the discretion of the court.

The agitation which this proposed measure aroused compelled Bishop Borgess to make public a lengthy review and justification of his action in the Lebel-Bunbury case.[22] In the Legislature the bill was finally recognized as being an unwarranted intrusion into purely religious concerns, and was decisively defeated.[23]

Now came the final, but not the least vexatious phase of the affair. In his published defense the bishop had compared a statement of indebtedness on the parish made by Father Lebel shortly before his death with the actual figures. There was a discrepancy roughly corresponding to the amount of the Bunbury claim. While this fact bolstered the bishop's position it also insinuated that Father Lebel had either falsified his accounts, or had been guilty of something worse. Many friends of Father Lebel, both clerical and lay, who had known him too well to believe him guilty of anything more than slovenly business methods, felt that his honor and reputation should be vindicated. They found a spokesman in Father Henry Delbaere, pastor of Dearborn.

The Emerson bill had been defeated in April, 1873, and the public had almost forgotten the Bunbury case when Father Delbaere

[22] The *Detroit Free Press*, April 8, 1873.
[23] The *Western Home Journal*, April 19, 1873.

published in the *Detroit Tribune* of November 14, 1873, "A Card in Vindication of the Memory of Father Lebel." [24] The "Card" was a lengthy plea in behalf of a much maligned, but innocent and worthy priest. Although it studiously avoided any reference to Bishop Borgess it was most embarrassing to him. Read between the lines it conveyed the impression that the bishop's defense had been erected on the ruins of Father Lebel's reputation.

Bishop Borgess took Father Delbaere to task for his imprudence in reviving the Bunbury case. The priest, who on previous occasions had shown himself to be headstrong and opinionated, was not disposed to spare the bishop's feelings. He kept the press informed of his negotiations with the bishop, and it was inevitable that his conduct should lead finally to suspension.[25] His appeal to Rome was referred to the Archbishop of Cincinnati for decision. Father Delbaere was relieved of the suspension on his agreement to sever his connection with the Diocese of Detroit.[26]

The troubles just described were being forgotten when Bishop Borgess was again made to suffer for his insistence that diocesan laws be obeyed. Father Desiderius Callaert had been appointed pastor of Marshall in 1868. For some reason or other he found it difficult to prepare in a satisfactory manner the annual financial reports of his parish demanded by the Chancery, and after several admonitions was notified on January 11, 1877, of his transfer to Traverse City. Against what he deemed an arbitrary removal Father Callaert appealed to Rome. His position was sustained, and Bishop Borgess was requested to reinstate him.[27]

The Roman authorities pointed out to the bishop that there had been no definite canonical reason offered to justify the removal. This was quite true. On the other hand Father Callaert had not been too reticent about his contention with episcopal authority, and to Bishop Borgess such a disposition of the affair rendered ineffectual any future effort to enforce discipline and order in the diocese. On January 31, 1879, he tendered his resignation to the Holy See.[28] Three weeks later, after it had been communicated to the press, the diocesan weekly took cognizance of the resignation in the following editorial.

[24] The "Card" was reprinted in the *Catholic Register* of New York, and in the *New York Freemen's Journal*.

[25] Father Delbaere issued a printed compilation of the Lebel-Bunbury case together with an account of his dealings with Bishop Borgess. *Appeal to the S. Cong. de Propaganda Fide in Rome from the Action of the Rt. Rev. C. H. Borgess. . . .* (Detroit Tribune Printing Co., 1874).

[26] Father Delbaere died at Danville, Ill., April 13, 1901.

[27] From correspondence in DCA.

[28] Copy in DCA.

The announcement made in the city press that his Lordship Rt. Rev. C. H. Borgess had tendered his resignation as Bishop of this Diocese took the community entirely by surprise. We are authorized to state that the report is true, and that the resignation has been at Rome for a month. The reasons given by the gentlemen of the daily press for this action of the Rt. Rev. Bishop are mere guesses. The true reasons concern not the general public, and have not been given to it by him.

The remarkable advancement of the Church in this Diocese since the appointment of Rt. Rev. Bp. Borgess attests the severity of his labors and the extent of his zeal for the progress of religion. The very full accounts of his Episcopal Visitations published by us last year, form a record of the growth of the Church in the Lower Peninsula during his administration, highly creditable to its chief pastor. Other reforms have also been introduced, tending to the general advantage of the Rev. clergy and the laity. Of all these works and of their promoter the Holy See is fully cognizant, and Rome knows also the regard and affection with which our Rt. Rev. Bishop is held by the faithful of his charge. What the Holy See will do, time will disclose. . . .[29]

What must have comforted Bishop Borgess most was the long petition sent by the clergy of the diocese to the Holy Father begging him not to accept the resignation.

When we lately heard of the many disasters befalling neighboring dioceses either by loss of their Pontiffs or by deplorable financial embarrassments, we could not but thank God, with a grateful heart, for the many favors bestowed upon the Diocese of Detroit through the ministry of Rt. Rev. Caspar H. Borgess, and congratulate ourselves upon its prosperity. But brief was our satisfaction; a rumor, which we apprehend is not entirely without foundation, suddenly spread among us that our beloved Bishop had resigned. . . .

We will not weary your Holiness with the recital of his labors; who does not know of the one hundred and twelve new churches erected and dedicated to God during his administration; of the new religious orders of the Society of Jesus, Little Sisters of the Poor, the Sisters of Charity, which were brought to his Episcopal City by his generous efforts; of the establishment of fifty Catholic schools where ten thousand boys and girls are instructed in the Christian faith and receive a solidly religious education; of the flourishing state of the Diocesan temporal and religious affairs, which, brought about in the face of many difficulties, have proved in the light of contemporaneous events that his hard work has not been without its rewards. . . .

Moved by these reasons, the priests of the Diocese of Detroit, who sign this grateful memorial of appreciation of their Bishop, humbly beg your Holiness not to accept the resignation of Rt. Rev. Caspar H. Borgess, and entreat you to exhort him to continue his useful work in

[29] The *Western Home Journal*, February 27, 1879.

the name of God, with unbending energy and self-sacrificing spirit, for the glory of the Church and the salvation of immortal souls.

Detroit, feast of St. Peter's See at Antioch, February 22, A.D. 1879.[30]

With this evidence of loyalty before it the Holy See could not but urge Bishop Borgess to reconsider his action. On March 28 he withdrew his resignation, expressing his complete submission to the will of the Holy Father.[31]

There was a curious sequel to this train of events. Father Callaert having been duly restored to his parish seems to have gradually lost the good will of his parishioners.[32] They petitioned the bishop several times for his removal, but the bishop was not to be drawn into such action until he had a canonical reason proof against all appeal. Finally, in order to achieve their purpose, a group of the parishioners either instigated or got behind a movement, whose origin is obscure, to effect a sweeping change in the tenure of church property in Michigan. In May, 1881, James H. Campbell, a member of the House from Marshall, introduced into the Legislature a bill embodying the most vicious aspects of trusteeism.

> Section 4. Such trustees shall be there in number, and shall hold their office for five years and shall be laymen. They shall have absolute control and direction of all property, real and personal, held for the uses of their congregations, and may remove any occupant therefrom at their pleasure. Any person refusing or neglecting to remove from any said real estate or to deliver up possession of the same to them on demand, shall be regarded as tenants holding over after term expired, and may be proceeded against summarily as such.[33]

Section 8 revived the provisions of the bill which was the aftermath of the Lebel-Bunbury case. There was never much doubt as to the outcome. The intemperate language used by Mr. Campbell when he introduced his measure gave the impression that it had been drafted more to embarrass Bishop Borgess than to remedy any real disorder. Many parishes throughout the state sent memorials to the Legislature protesting the bill, and testifying to their complete satisfaction with the actual tenure of church property by their bishop. The bill died in committee.

Father Callaert now convinced that his ministry might be more fruitful in another community willingly accepted his transfer to

---

[30] Ibid., March 20, 1879.

[31] Copy in DCA.

[32] This statement is much too mild if we can believe that there existed the hostility against Father Callaert that appears in the venomous attack printed in the *Detroit Post and Tribune,* May 3, 1881.

[33] The *Western Home Journal,* May 7, 1881.

Manistee. Marshall again became what it had been and is today, a model parish.

A final effort to introduce trusteeism into Michigan, and one arising from similar causes, was made in 1887. The Catholics of Chelsea, dissatisfied with their pastor, Father Patrick Duhig, had lodged charges against him which the bishop after serious investigation had declared unfounded.[34] Although Father Duhig was removed to Northfield in 1885, the bitterness of a small faction persisted. In February, 1887, its leader, Senator Gorman of Chelsea, laid before the Legislature a bill resembling the 1881 proposal, but not quite as obnoxious. While the agitation it aroused was at its height Bishop Borgess submitted his definite resignation. This action of the bishop, which may have satisfied the proponents of the bill, coupled with a storm of opposition coming from every quarter, finally brought about the withdrawal of the measure by Senator Gorman.[35]

These were some of the trials laid upon Bishop Borgess in addition to the cares entailed in his program of discipline and reform. Others will appear as we go on to survey the more important changes and developments which took place during his episcopate.

The first parish organized in Detroit under Bishop Borgess revealed the presence of another immigrant group, the Bohemians. The relatively small number of political exiles who had sought refuge in the United States following the disturbances of 1848 had been considerably augmented by the mass immigration that resulted from the Austro-Prussian War of 1866.[36] Chicago and St. Louis were the favorite destinations, but Detroit had probably 150 families in 1870.[37] A native Bohemian priest, Father Wenceslaus Tilek, came to Detroit in October, 1870, from Louvain where he had just been ordained, and was commissioned to organize a parish for his countrymen. In July, 1871, St. Wenceslaus church was dedicated by Bishop Borgess.

A second parish represented the rising tide in the diocese of the new immigration whose beginnings at Parisville have already been noted. According to Kruszka there were two Polish residents in Detroit as early as 1831.[38] However, the origin of the Polish colony in the city dates most likely from 1857, when several pioneer families arrived. Two years later, accompanied by his family group, came John Lemke, "King John" as he was affectionately called by his people of whom he was for many years the recognized representative and

[34] From a sheaf of correspondence in the DCA.
[35] Every issue of the *Michigan Catholic* from February to May, 1887, deals with the Gorman Bill.
[36] See the article, Bohemians in the United States, in the *Catholic Encyclopedia*.
[37] *History and Directory of the Churches of Detroit* (Detroit, 1877), 86.
[38] Kruszka, *op. cit.,* XI, 167.

leader.[39] In the wake of the disastrous Revolution of 1863 in Russian Poland refugees began to stream into the United States. By 1870 some 40,000 had entered, the majority of whom settled in Chicago and its environs. Describing this new Catholic element in Detroit, Elliott wrote:

> The section in which he (John Lemke) and his compatriots settled was then far out northeast of the city. Fresh from the soil, they sought homes where they might have access to the soil to make a living in the intervals between the jobs of manual labor which they so diligently sought and so laboriously accomplished. They were a more serious-minded people than the Irish. Work under the difficulties of strange customs, a strange language and masters inclined to get the last pen'orth of labor out of these new willing workers made life serious to them. . . . Within two years after they commenced coming to Detroit there were two thousand of them here. With characteristic thrift they bought a number of lots at St. Aubin and Fremont street and proceeded to build a church thereupon. . . .[40]

Father Simon Wieczorek, who had come down occasionally from Parisville to attend his countrymen in Detroit was appointed in September, 1871, pastor of the new congregation.[41] On July 24 of the following year, a frame church seating 1200 was blessed by Bishop Borgess, and dedicated to St. Albertus.

Meanwhile, the bishop had been planning the erection of another English-speaking parish in the center of the city. In March, 1873, he purchased the Westminster Presbyterian Church on Washington Boulevard, and on the completion of the necessary alterations dedicated it to Catholic worship under the title, St. Aloysius.[42] The area of the new parish extended from the river to Columbia Street between Randolph and Third Streets.

> In the earlier days the old church stood in a picturesque setting, its well kept lawns adding to its beauty as well as to its air of aloofness from all things material. Its high picket fence, too, was in keeping with the high boots, the silk hats, the hoop skirts and the stately carriages of that day when St. Aloysius was young and buoyant. . . . The boulevard, known then as Washington Avenue, also was lined with thickly planted elms, the pride of Detroit. The quaint little white cottage ad-

[39] There is a history of the growth of the Polish colony in Detroit in a printed history of the Polish parishes in the city by Vincent Smolczynski, *Historya Osady i Parafii Polskich w Detroit* (Detroit, 1907). See also Sister Mary Remigia Napolska, *The Polish Immigrant in Detroit* (Chicago, 1946).

[40] The *Michigan Catholic*, August 22, 1901.

[41] This is the date given in the *Album Pamiatkowe*, a printed booklet commemorating the Golden Jubilee of the parish in 1920.

[42] The dedication took place on August 24, 1873. The structure was first used by its original congregation in January, 1861.

joining the church, on the site of the present Chancery Building, served as rectory. It still lives in the memory of many Detroiters. It was here that the Rev. Ernest Van Dyke, scion of one of the city's oldest families and son of one of its early mayors, came as a young man, destined to remain nearly half a century as parish priest, a term of service seldom equalled in the annals of the Church. Here Father Van Dyke saw the small town develop into a great city.[43]

Another national group now claimed the bishop's attention. The French population of Detroit had been lately materially increased by the advent of many skilled artisans from Montreal, who found employment in the city's rising shipbuilding industry. St. Anne's was overcrowded, and the necessity of another French parish on the east side of the city, where most of the newcomers had settled, was evident. Knowing how firmly attached the French Canadians were to their language, the bishop was favorably disposed to provide them with a priest of their own nationality. Negotiations with the Archbishop of Montreal resulted in the latter's granting the services of one of his young priests, Father Maxime Laporte, for a period of ten years. Father Laporte arrived in Detroit in October, 1874, and in the following April he was commissioned to erect a church for all the French-speaking Catholics east of Riopelle Street. He proceeded to build a two-story frame structure combining school and chapel on Fort Street between Chene and Joseph Campau Avenue. On June 16, 1875, the Chapel of the Sacred Heart, as the building was called, was dedicated by Bishop Borgess.

At this point it is necessary to refer again to the problem which created serious difficulties for the bishop from the beginning of his episcopate. Every immigrant group contributing to the growth of the Church in America has gone through some phase of trusteeism. The French were no exception. In Detroit, however, the situation was an unusual one. It will be remembered that the parish of St. Anne was incorporated under the Governor and Judges in 1805, and that in 1834 it had given a perpetual lease on its properties to the bishop of the diocese in return for certain obligations which he was to assume. To the Corporation of 1834 the arrangement was probably a good bargain. But in 1870, when Detroit had grown to be a city of 80,000, and the parish properties had increased enormously in value, the arrangement did not appear in so satisfactory a light. The French felt that they had been deprived of what was in effect a patrimony, and that the donations of their forefathers were being alienated to build churches for other nationalities.

[43] St. Aloysius Church, The Old and the New (Detroit, 1930), 8–9. Father Van Dyke had been transferred to the cathedral from Adrian in 1871.

Shortly after his arrival in Detroit, Bishop Borgess was petitioned to give up his rights under the lease, and to restore to the Corporation its original holdings. The matter could not be settled so easily. The diocese had carried the properties through a long unproductive period, had paid taxes and incurred various expenses in connection with its administration. Provided these expenses and debts were assumed the bishop expressed his willingness to cancel the lease. The Corporation, believing that the diocese had profited greatly, could not admit the justice of the condition. In April, 1871, the bishop addressed the following letter to the Corporation.

> To the Church Wardens of St. Ann's Congregation of Detroit, Mich.
> Permit me to suggest to you the propriety of a conference, to take place at an early date in my residence, between a committee of your honorable body and one appointed by me. The object of this conference is to be an amicable discussion on our mutual relations, and, I hope, a satisfactory explanation and final settlement of affairs which may not have been sufficiently understood.
> In case you think well to act on this suggestion, allow me to add, that it will be desirable that your Committee shall be vested with ample and legal powers to adjust all and every question and settle all affairs in your name and by your authority, if said Committee find that such require to be done, and agree on the final settlement of any matter brought before them.[44]

The conference was fruitless, and apparently only intensified the existing bitterness and hostility. Early in 1873 the Trustees sought to accomplish their purpose by sending a Memorial to the Legislature praying that the bishop be divested of all ownership of diocesan property.[45] In May of the same year the bishop appointed a commission, composed of ten priests of the city, to audit the entire administration of the Corporation's properties from the time of Bishop Rese. The Trustees could find no substantial error in the audit, and the possibility of a settlement began to appear. On July, 1873, the Corporation met to take action on the following communication from the bishop.

> . . . Unwilling to give up the hope of an amicable settlement I called to my assistance ten priests eminently qualified for the task, and requested them to examine into the complaints of the Corporation and also into the accounts compiled by Father Schutjes from the books and vouchers of Bp. Rese and Lefevere and those of Father Badin and to give us their opinion as to the merits of the case. They have performed the duty assigned them and report as follows:

[44] Copy in DCA.

[45] See the article entitled the *Moross Memorial* in the *Western Home Journal* for March 22, 1873.

that the accounts, as prepared by Father Schutjes are substantially correct, and bear evidence of faithful and persevering work, showing that the leased property has been the cause of expenses over and above receipts on the part of the Rt. Rev. Bishops to the amount of $103,-310.65; that the church of St. Ann is in debt to the Rt. Rev. Bishops to the amount of $13,925.81. In these items of expense, the interest on the cost of the present pastor's residence, and some other small items, are not included.

that the use of the whole property in right and justice belongs to the Rt. Rev. Bishop and ought to remain with him, but that considering all the difficulties which have arisen from this lease, and to remove all disputes and the possible loss of souls resulting therefrom, it is suggested that a compromise be made on the following bases: St. Ann's church to be allowed the whole of what is known as the square, the lease to be cancelled, and the Bishop to have the triangle and the Monnier Lot. . . .[46]

The Trustees formally accepted the bishop's proposition, but the final settlement did not come until the end of 1875.[47] A convenient summary of its terms is given by Elliott.

A compromise was finally made. December 28, 1875, Bishop Borgess deeded back to the Corporation the block bounded by Larned, Bates, Congress, and Randolph streets, reserving the triangular block between Bates and Congress streets and Cadillac square; a triangular piece on Randolph street; and 12 lots on Miami avenue. This property he subsequently sold for an aggregate of $164,000, the proceeds going into the diocesan treasury. . . .[48]

The problem that had agitated the French population of Detroit for five years was thus happily settled, but this gave rise to a new one. The former parishioners of St. Anne's included in Father Laporte's parish by an arbitrary division line were cut off from any benefits that might accrue to the Corporation from the administration of its own property. When the Corporation of 1880 sold a portion of its holdings for $100,000, the disposition of this amount became the source of heated controversy. The new parish demanded an equal division of the proceeds, and the demand was, of course, stoutly upheld by Father Laporte. That section of St. Anne's parish lying in the western half of the city, which, by this time, rivalled the new parish in numbers clamored that some provision be made for it. The solution seemed to lie in the abandonment of St. Anne's, and the division of

---

[46] From a copy of the bishop's letter in the Wardens Book of St. Anne's parish. This interesting volume dates from 1796. The similar volumes which must have preceded it are lost.

[47] *Ibid.*

[48] The *Michigan Catholic*, August 22, 1901.

its holdings between two parishes, one in each side of the city. This, the bishop heartily approved, and the Corporation as heartily resisted. Too many sacred associations hallowed the venerable pile erected by Father Richard. Moreover, it was pointed out that the bishop's aproval was dictated by his determination to put an end to such anomalous tenure of church property in his diocese since he had stipulated that the property of the two parishes, like other diocesan holdings, should be vested in him.

> . . . Pressure was now brought to bear from the east and the west upon the trustees, which was too strong to resist, and the doom of the Mother church was sealed. The square was sold for about $200,000, and a division made between the eastern and western parishes.[49]

The last solemn function in old St. Anne's was a pontifical Mass celebrated by Bishop Borgess on Sunday, June 27, 1886.

> On Monday Masses were celebrated at 8 and 9 o'clock, at which many members of the congregation were present, though many more absented themselves to avoid the pain of the thoughts to which the event naturally gave rise. . . . Immediately on the departure of the congregation the doors were closed, the sacred vessels were removed, photographers placed their apparatus, pictures of the old fane were taken, and the work of dismantling the altars was begun. In a short time all was ready for the work of demolition. But before this could begin there were sacred relics in the crypt beneath, which were to be carefully and reverently removed. These were the bones of the great Father Richard, priest and congressman, the founder of the church. There were also other remains: those of Colonel Louis Antoine Beaubien; of Oratorians, Very Rev. John De Bruyn, president of the College of St. Philip Neri, and co-administrator with Father Vincent Badin, of the diocese by appointment of Bishop Rese, in 1837, who died September 11, 1839; Rev. Louis F. Van den Poel, of the same college, who died January 28, 1837, and Miss Elizabeth Williams, sister of Gen. John R. Williams, of Detroit, who had been placed in charge of the seminary for the higher education of young ladies in Detroit by Father Richard, who had died in his time, and whose mortal remains had been honored by burial in this crypt. The bones and ashes of Father Richard had previously, with the original casket in which he had been buried, been enclosed in a rich and strong wooden case, well fastened, and this was not opened on Monday, but removed to the place prepared in the new church of St. Anne. . . .[50]

The corner stone of the present St. Anne church had been laid on April 28, 1886. On October 30, 1887, the completed structure was dedicated by the Administrator of the diocese, Father Edward Joos.

[49] Richard R. Elliott in the *Michigan Catholic* as above.
[50] The *Michigan Catholic*, July 1, 1886.

The Basilian Fathers, who from Assumption parish across the river had for many years been of service to the diocese, were invited to assume the charge, and Father Peter Grand was appointed as first pastor.

Father Laporte, in 1885, had already begun the erection of a second church which was to replace his frame chapel. By special permission from his archbishop his term of service had been extended for one year, and in anticipation of his removal Bishop Borgess had entered into negotiations with the Holy Ghost Fathers at Pittsburgh, many of whom were of French origin, offering them the administration of the parish. They accepted, sending Father Michael Dangelzer and a companion to Detroit. Father Laporte, supported by a portion of his congregation, was loath to retire, but peace was finally restored and the Holy Ghost Fathers have remained in charge of the parish. The new edifice dedicated to St. Joachim was solemnly consecrated by Bishop Borgess on June 13, 1886. The formation of the two parishes marked the final effort of the French element in Detroit to maintain its own churches. There has been no appreciable immigration to reinforce it.

While the French element in Detroit became static with the building of St. Joachim's church, the old mother parish of the Germans was throwing off a vigorous outshoot. Reference has already been made to the change in the administration of St. Mary's that occurred in 1872. With the advent of Bishop Borgess the Redemptorists made a legitimate effort to stabilize their institution in Detroit. Although admitting that they were justified in asking for complete control of the parish the bishop felt that his duty to the diocese forbade its alienation.[51] The Redemptorists thereupon withdrew, much to the bishop's regret. He now offered the parish to the Franciscans of Cincinnati, who accepted, and sent Father Apollinaris Hottler to take charge in May, 1872.[52]

For the convenience of the children living in the northern end of the parish a school was opened in a small frame building on Eliot Street in the fall of 1874. The possibility of effecting a distinct parish organization for the German Catholics in the neighborhood was soon entertained, and Bishop Borgess gave his approval to the venture in the following spring. So zealously was the work carried forward that on July 16, 1876, the bishop presided at the dedication of the present Sacred Heart church. Father Eugene Butterman was named pastor of the new parish, which he held until his transfer to Chatham, On-

[51] Letter to Father Joseph Helmpraecht, C.SS.R., May 23, 1871. Copy in DCA.
[52] It is interesting to note that the Franciscans returned to Detroit ninety years after the departure of Father Bocquet, the last of the Recollects.

tario, in 1878. He had the unique privilege of returning to celebrate with the congregation he had first assembled both its Silver and its Golden Jubilee. After the withdrawal of the Franciscans from Detroit in 1890 the parish was in charge of the diocesan clergy until it was confided to the Holy Ghost Fathers in 1938.[53]

The growth of the Church in Detroit compelled Bishop Borgess to make efforts to provide a much needed complement to the parochial schools of the city, a Catholic college. He turned first to the Basilian Fathers, who had opened Assumption College across the river in 1879, and offered them his cathedral parish in return for their endeavor "to keep open and maintain a High School and College for Day-Scholars in the City of Detroit in which a thorough course of Commercial &, at least, a preparatory course of Classical education shall be given . . ."[54] The *Western Home Journal* aware of his design thus cautiously announced it to its readers.

> It is rumored that our Rt. Rev. Bishop has about completed arrangements by which the Catholics of Detroit will at last be blest with a first-class high school or college, under the charge of a prominent religious order. It is said that early in the fall this happy consummation will be realized. Our good Bishop could perfect no work which would bring to his people so much real satisfaction, and we are sure that Catholic parents especially, who have boys whom they desire to see possess a thorough Christian and secular education, will be filled with gratitude to the good shepherd who thus aims to supply every want of his flock.[55]

The Basilian Fathers, however, were unable to undertake the project, and the bishop, doubtless because of his associations with St. Xavier College in Cincinnati, now sought the cooperation of the Jesuits. His negotiations with them were satisfactorily concluded early in the spring of 1877 on the same terms as those offered to the Basilians, and the success of the project was assured.

The acceptance by the Jesuits made necessary the selection of another church to serve as a cathedral. Late in 1874 the bishop had moved from Jefferson Avenue to a residence which he had erected on Washington Boulevard opposite the church of St. Aloysius. His selection of this church as a temporary cathedral followed as a matter of course, and the change was thus noted in the diocesan weekly.

> We understand it is the intention of the Bishop to attend the public offices of the Church at St. Aloysius' on Sundays and Holydays, here-

[53] An elaborate parish history was published in 1925 to commemorate the Golden Jubilee of the parish.

[54] The offer was made to Father J. M. Soulerin, C.S.B., in a letter dated March 23, 1876. Copy in DCA.

[55] The *Western Home Journal*, March 11, 1876.

after, making of it a kind of pro-Cathedral. For this reason the usual pontifical throne will shortly be erected in that church.

The members of St. Aloysius' feel very much gratified at this special mark of honor conferred on them by this intention of their Rt. Rev. Bishop, the establishment of the chair of the chief pastor of the diocese among them; and so they should.[56]

The Jesuits made their entry in June, 1877. In its first issue after their arrival the *Western Home Journal* thus welcomed them.

The Rev. Fathers of the Society of Jesus took charge of SS. Peter and Paul's church, Jefferson avenue, last Sunday. Rev. Father Miege, S. J., for twenty-four years Vicar Apostolic of Kansas, the pastor, is assisted by Rev. Brady, S. J., of Cincinnati, and Rev. Walshe of Milwaukee. The Fathers opened their pastoral labors with a triduum in honor of the Sacred Heart of Jesus, which began Tuesday evening. A day College for the higher education of our Catholic youth will be opened by the Reverend Fathers in September, when some scholastics will be sent to take charge of the classes. We doubt not but that their old motto, A.M.D.G. "All for the greater honor of God" will prove true here, as it has wherever the Sons of St. Ignatius worked. . . .[57]

Bishop Borgess was not at home to greet the Jesuits; he was enjoying a respite from the labors of his episcopate. He had left Detroit in the first week of April to journey to Rome for his *ad limina* visit. From Rome he made a leisurely tour northward to Ireland, from which he sailed at the end of August.

On his return to Detroit the evening of September 13 the bishop was given an ovation such as had rarely been accorded to a citizen. Members of every parish in the city formed a torchlight procession that escorted him from the old Michigan Central station to the Jesuit church; it then proceeded up Hastings Street to St. Mary's, from there to Grand Circus Park, and down Washington Boulevard to the pro-Cathedral. Every store and building was decorated with lanterns and varicolored lights, and the glare of fireworks fell upon the cheering crowds that were massed along the line of march. A happily phrased speech addressed by the bishop to the throng before his residence brought the demonstration to an end.[58] In after years he must have been often consoled by the recollection of this touching tribute of devotion offered to him by a united laity.

For some time the problem of providing for the needs of an increasing Catholic population on the west side of Detroit had engaged

[56] *Ibid.*, March 4, 1876.
[57] *Ibid.*, June 9, 1877.
[58] There is a lengthy description of the event in the *Western Home Journal* for September 15 and 22, 1877.

the attention of Bishop Borgess. The answer came from a rather un-expected quarter. Despite their withdrawal from St. Mary's in 1872 the Redemptorists held a sentimental attachment to Detroit. Early in 1879 the Superior of the St. Louis Province sounded the bishop regarding the possibility of a return to the city. In his ready acceptance of the offer the bishop wrote:

> At present there is nothing very desirable at my disposition, but what I have I take great pleasure in offering. There are at this time three hundred families living in the vicinity of the Grand Trunk and Michigan Central R.R. Junction who in part now belong to St. Vincent's and in part to St. Patrick's congregation in this city, but are too far distant from both, and have long desired to have a church in their center. The beginning would be a poor one, but things seem to indicate that in a few years it may become a large congregation. . . .[59]

The prediction has been amply verified, for the bishop was fore-casting the future of Holy Redeemer parish, the largest in Michigan. To organize the new congregation came Father Aegidius Smulders, the same pioneer who had succeeded Father Gillet at Monroe thirty-three years before. He arrived in Detroit in March, 1880, and assembled his parishioners in Ratigan's hostelry situated on West Jefferson Avenue until May 1, when a temporary chapel was opened on the corner of Military and Dix Avenue. The first church erected on the present site, and dedicated in July, 1881, was replaced by a more substantial structure in 1897. The present imposing edifice was opened to divine worship in 1926.[60]

While Father Smulders was engaged in the formation of his English-speaking congregation there lay to the north of him some three hundred families to whom he could not minister; they were the fore-runners of the extensive Polish settlement of the west side of the city. Nominally members of St. Albertus' parish they could attend the church only with difficulty. Their desire to effect a distinct parish organization was realized in November, 1882, when Bishop Borgess appointed Father Paul Gutowski, who had recently come to Detroit from Europe, pastor "of the Polish Catholics living west of Woodward Avenue." His efforts resulted in the erection of a temporary church and school building which were dedicated to St. Casimir on April 21, 1883. The parish made such remarkable progress that Bishop Foley on December 21, 1890, blessed the present church, whose silver dome for many years dominated its surroundings. Father Gutowski, friend and confidant of the two bishops under whom

---

[59] Letter to Very Rev. Nicholas Jaeckel, C.SS.R., February 27, 1879. Copy in DCA.
[60] See sketch of Father Smulders and of the parish in the *Michigan Catholic* for April 19, 1900.

he served, held the pastorate until March 30, 1918, when death ended his exemplary life.[61]

St. Joseph's was the largest German congregation in the city, and a division was imperative. In October, 1884, the formation of a new parish was announced, which was to include the German families living between Dequindre and Elmwood, and north of Hunt Street. The pastorate was conferred upon Father Anthony Svensson, who had been for ten years assistant at St. Joseph's.[62] On June 21, 1885, a building combining church and school was dedicated by Bishop Borgess under the patronage of St. Elizabeth. These temporary accommodations served the growing parish until Bishop Foley presided at the opening of the present church on February 14, 1892. The date is significant as marking the high point in the growth of the German Catholics of Detroit considered as a national group. St. Elizabeth's was the last of the distinctively German congregations organized in the city.

In 1884 another parish, representing a hitherto unmentioned national group, was organized. Although there may have been a few Belgian Catholics in Detroit as early as the time of Bishop Rese, no considerable number is in evidence until 1857. In that year Father Bernard Soffers became pastor of St. Anne's, and after naming him in that capacity the Catholic Almanac for 1858 stated that he was likewise chaplain of a chapel for Belgians and Hollanders. In other words the Belgians were numerous enough to have Mass said for them, and a sermon in their language, in the basement chapel of St. Anne's. Subsequent immigration was more notable in the outskirts of Detroit, towards Centerline and Mt. Clemens, than in the city itself. However, in 1884, there were approximately one hundred and thirty families still worshipping at St. Anne's. In September they decided to form their own parochial organization, and for the purpose purchased from the Salem German Evangelical congregation the small frame church which stood on the southeast corner of Catherine and Gratiot Avenue.[63] It was blessed by Father Soffers on November 1, and dedicated to Our Lady of Sorrows. In the following spring Father Hendrickx resigned from his pastorate in Centerline to preside over the new congregation. A more suitable location was decided upon in 1908 after the church had been partially destroyed by fire. The present church of Our Lady of Sorrows was dedicated on July 30, 1911.

[61] For a brief history of the parish see the *Michigan Catholic* for November 17, 1932.

[62] Father Svensson claimed for himself a peculiarly interesting distinction, which some reader may question. He maintained that through his ordination in Detroit on November 17, 1874, he became the first native of Sweden to enter the priesthood from the time of the Reformation.

[63] A picture of the original church is given in Farmer, *op. cit.*, I, 622.

In 1887 there were two hundred and fifty families under the care of Father Hendrickx, many of them living on the eastern border of the city. A school was necessary and its location had to be more accessible than the church. To provide relief for the families in the eastern section of the parish Father Hendrickx erected on Field Avenue a frame building primarily for school purposes, but in which Mass could be said on Sundays. It was blessed on May 15, 1887, and placed under the patronage of St. Charles.[64] On August 8, 1889, Father Christian Denissen was appointed first resident pastor of the group which now became a distinct parish. During the later years of his pastorate the complexion of the parish changed rapidly, and when Father Hewlett assumed charge in 1911 he found a large English-speaking congregation showing few traces of its Belgian origin. The present church was dedicated on June 13, 1920.

Parochial development in Detroit during the episcopate of Bishop Borgess led, as we have seen, to the introduction of five religious communities of men. A sixth was added with the advent of the Order of Friars Minor Capuchins. Early in 1883 Father Bonaventure Frey, the Provincial in Milwaukee, applied to Bishop Borgess for permission to erect a convent of the Order near Detroit. This was readily granted but with the proviso that the Fathers were in no sense empowered to establish a parish, and that the monastery chapel while open to the public was not to enjoy the privileges of a parish church.[65] Acquiescing in these conditions Father Bonaventure proceeded to establish the monastery in its present location on the east side of Mt. Elliott Avenue, which at the time formed the eastern boundary of the city. He and his companions might well have been bewildered by the affectionate welcome extended to them particularly by the German Catholics of Detroit. On July 29, 1883, an enthusiastic procession started from Cadillac Square and marched through the city to be present at the laying of the corner stone. In Russell's Grove, as the monastery site was then called, ten thousand spectators pressed around the bishop as he wielded his silver trowel.[66] The chapel was dedicated on July 13 of the following year, and the St. Bonaventure Monastery thereupon became the provincial headquarters and novitiate of the Province of St. Joseph. In 1931 the novitiate was transferred to a new foundation in Huntington, Indiana.

For Bishop Borgess the relatively rapid expansion of all these agencies of Catholic life, consoling as it must have been, nevertheless created a serious problem. The personnel of the diocesan clergy could

---

[64] The *Michigan Catholic* for May 19, 1887, carries a lengthy account of the ceremony.
[65] Correspondence in the DCA.
[66] The *Michigan Catholic* for August 4, 1883.

not begin to cope with the demands made upon it. To remedy the situation the bishop was not minded to continue the policy of depending largely on European sources for reinforcements. It could only perpetuate divisions which he was trying to eradicate, and, moreover, it was no longer necessary. The faith and labors of the pioneers had by this time borne fruit in sons ready to dedicate themselves to the sacred ministry. What was needed was the arousing of the diocese to the responsibility of fostering vocations and of providing for the education of candidates to the priesthood.

The financial support given to the American College at Louvain by Bishop Lefevere seems to have been drawn from whatever diocesan funds were available for the purpose, and there was no organized plan to interest the laity as a whole. To this work Bishop Borgess addressed himself. The initiative was taken in the synod of 1873. Since there is no extant report of the synod's deliberations its action in the matter is known only through the letter that introduces the first diocesan seminary report issued in 1874.

It is the command of the Church, that the young men who present themselves as candidates for the Priesthood, shall be trained in solid virtue and piety, and have every opportunity given them to become men of science. But, as generally, they can only bring the sacrifice of themselves . . . it becomes the duty of the faithful to furnish what is wanting. . . . And God has made the faithful His stewards to supply the wants of those chosen servants; they are His treasures, on whom he calls to foster such noble self-dedication in obedience to His divine inspirations. . . .

When, in the month of May last, the Priests of our diocese were assembled in synod, they unanimously expressed a desire of having a Diocesan Seminary established, both as an encouragement in the vocations of the Priesthood, and in the generous support on your part. From this report we send you, you will see that your interest in this important matter has been awakened but to a limited extent. . . .

We beg, therefore, to call on the Rev. Clergy and you to unite in your exertions for the accomplishment of their and your desire—the Diocesan Seminary. To that end, let every earning person take pleasure in giving at least one dollar, and those who are blessed with a greater share of prosperity let them give what their faith, their piety, and their love of God may prompt them in generosity. . . .[67]

The 1874 report discloses that during the preceding year the seminary collection had amounted to $4,705.94. Holy Trinity in Detroit led the parishes of the diocese with $350.51. St. Andrew's in Grand Rapids came next with $212.85, and last of all came Fenton and

[67] *Report of the Receipts from the several Congregations and Missions for The Education of the Seminarians for the Diocese of Detroit* (Detroit, 1874).

Carleton, which contributed each one dollar. Two years later the total contribution rose to a little over $5,000, and not the least amount,
the sum of $14, came from the remnant of the Potawatomi in the Sil-
ver Creek mission. In 1876 Bishop Borgess made a special effort to
raise the collection to the level required by the increasing number of
seminarians. A lengthy pastoral on the subject was read in all the
churches of the diocese on the first Sunday in August. By one of its
provisions the entire month was to be devoted to the gathering of
contributions. That the laity took the bishop's appeal to heart is evident from an editorial in the *Western Home Journal*.

> We presume there is no need to tell our readers the object of the
> collection in all the Catholic Churches of this Diocese tomorrow. . . .
> We here in the city have every reason to feel ashamed of our contribu-
> tions of previous years, in comparison with the country, and we presume
> the reason why is simply because we do not know what it is to be with-
> out a priest, although this fact, that we are so well attended, we should
> think, ought to make us more generous. That there is a great need of
> priests in this Diocese is unquestionable. A Catholic population of
> about 170,000 and 150 to 175 churches, not to speak of mission stations,
> and about 75 parishes with priests, is a glaring proof. There are about
> 100 active priests, leaving for each priest about 1750, which is about
> triple the number assigned to the care of a priest in Europe. . . .
> There must be, we should judge from the report, about 30 young
> men studying at the expense of the Church. There are very likely, say
> 20, studying for the Church who can afford to pay their own expenses.
> Out of this number we think a fair ratio would be six or eight priests
> a year. This is all that the Bishop can furnish unless more aid comes to
> his assistance. We need more priests, and the way to have them is to
> make the seminary collection a success.[68]

To supplement the collections in the churches the pastors were required to appoint lay solicitors whose duty was to canvass the parishes
for larger contributions. The generous response of the laity in this
and suceeeding years not only provided amply for the current needs
of the diocese but enabled the bishop to begin a fund for the erection
of a diocesan seminary. His project was at least partially realized
when he opened St. Francis Seminary in Monroe in 1886, a year before his resignation, a project which did not survive the withdrawal
of his protecting interest. From 1874 to 1920, when it was discontinued, the annual Seminary Report was an institution in the diocese
furnishing as it did a sort of diocesan directory, and containing the
obituaries of deceased priests.[69]

[68] Issue of August 26, 1876. The first formal record of seminarians in the DCA was
drawn up by Bishop Borgess in September, 1876. There were at the time fifty theological
students, of whom twenty-eight later served as priests in the diocese.
[69] There is a fairly complete file of the reports in the DCA.

The preceding pages have attempted to portray at least the salient features of Bishop Borgess' administration. No emphasis has been placed on the background of self-sacrificing zeal and toil against which his particular activities stand out. For twelve years his diocese embraced the entire lower peninsula of Michigan. In the beginning, the care of the diocese as Bishop Lefevere had left it was possible with unremitting exertions. The swift development of later years taxed the bishop beyond his strength, and left no doubt as to the necessity for narrowing his field of labor.

In July, 1881, the bishops of the Province of Cincinnati, which included Michigan, met in the Ohio city to draw up a list of candidates for the vacant see of Nashville. Bishop Borgess seized the opportunity to present his situation to his colleagues, and to enlist their support in petitioning Rome for a division of his diocese. The time required for a study of the proposal necessarily postponed any decision until the next meeting of the bishops. When it took place in November they gave the proposal of Bishop Borgess their unanimous approval. Accordingly, on November 15, 1881, he addressed to Cardinal Simeoni, Prefect of the Propaganda Congregation, his formal request for the partition of the Diocese of Detroit. The new diocese was to be named after its largest city, Grand Rapids, where its bishop was to reside.[70] On May 17, 1882, the Holy See approved the partition, and two days later the Diocese of Grand Rapids was formally erected.[71] It remained under the administration of Detroit until Henry Joseph Richter, pastor of St. Lawrence parish in Cincinnati, was consecrated in Grand Rapids by Archbishop Elder on April 22, 1883.

By this division the Diocese of Detroit, which fifty years before had extended as far as the Dakotas was reduced to the boundaries which confined it down to 1937. Out of 68 counties in the lower peninsula having an area of 41,119 square miles it retained the 29 southern counties covering an area of 18,558 square miles. The results of the division can best be pictured by quoting the summaries in the Seminary Reports. For 1882 the report gives the following statistics:

	City of Detroit	Country	Diocese
Priests in service	30	94	124
Churches	16	195	211
Catholic families	7,587	21,792	29,379
Catholic population	43,500	141,500	185,000
Parochial schools	14	45	59
Pupils	5,278	7,902	13,180

70 From a copy of the bishop's petition in the DCA.
71 Letter in DCA.

A year later when the division had been definitely carried out the Diocese of Detroit was thus represented:

	City of Detroit	Country	Diocese
Priests in service	36	65	85
Churches	16	62	78
Catholic families	7,590	12,505	20,093
Catholic population	37,950	62,505	100,455
Parochial schools	14	28	42
Pupils	5,827	4,005	9,832

Five years elapsed between the division of the diocese and the resignation of Bishop Borgess. During this period his labors were considerably lightened, but the cares of his office continued to weigh heavily. His solicitude for uniformity and discipline found expression, as we have seen, in the sixth and seventh diocesan synods. Some of the problems which troubled the last years of his administration have already been alluded to. But, in the popular mind at least, nothing so tried and disheartened the bishop as the disorders that arose in the older Polish settlement on the east side of the city.

The parish of St. Albertus had grown to enormous proportions. Father Simon Wieczorek's third successor, temporarily appointed in 1879, was his former confrere at Parisville, Father John Wollowski, a one-armed veteran of the Polish wars. On March 30, 1882, his pastorate was terminated by the following note from Bishop Borgess.

> This morning Rev. Dominic Kolasinski arrived here from Europe, and has been adopted. This enables us to relieve you of the pastoral charge of St. Albert's temporarily given you on the 20th of September 1879 which we hereby recall . . .[72]

The new incumbent came from the Diocese of Cracow, where he had been ordained in 1864. Of prepossessing appearance, and endowed with all the qualities of a born leader of men, Father Kolasinski soon won the unshakable devotion and loyalty of his people. Appealing to their national pride he urged the erection of a church more worthy of them than the shabby structure in which they worshipped. The enthusiastic response of his parishioners is embodied in the present church of St. Albertus dedicated by Bishop Borgess on July 4, 1885.

Meanwhile, there had been a growing list of charges against Father Kolasinski. Some of them referred to the performance of his ministry, others to his exactions in financial matters, and the rest to various irregularities. Although accusations of the third type seem to have motivated Bishop Borgess in his procedure, it is only fair to note that

[72] Copy of note in DCA.

they were neither fully investigated nor proved by any diocesan tribunal. At all events the bishop determined to remove the priest, basing his action on a more tangible offense against the diocesan statutes, namely, that the priest had borrowed for the completion of his church a sum of money far in excess of the amount for which he had been authorized. A formal demand that Father Kolasinski submit his accounts for examination was indignantly rejected. On November 28, 1885, the recalcitrant pastor was suspended.[73]

Close to the church stood the convent of the Felician Sisters, where Father Joseph Dabrowski resided as chaplain. Two days after the suspension of Father Kolasinski the bishop placed Father Dabrowski in temporary charge of the parish church.[74] His first attempt to officiate was frustrated by an outburst of rioting in which he barely escaped serious injury. As a result the church was interdicted, and thus began a series of regrettable disorders that kept the Polish colony in a ferment for several years.

Father Kolasinski was as determined to resist the suspension as the bishop was to enforce it. Representing himself to the people who idolized him as an innocent victim of episcopal arrogance and tyranny he naturally gained their implicit confidence and support. To make matters worse he went on to give a new turn to the situation, holding it up as a glaring example of racial persecution. Bishop Borgess was a German tainted with the traditional animosity between German and Pole. He viewed with displeasure the rise of the Polish element to a parity with the other Catholic groups in Detroit, and was resolved to stifle it and its leader. The simple, unlettered immigrants to a land strange alike in customs and language can hardly be blamed for having fallen under the sway of the perfervid eloquence with which Father Kolasinski played upon their emotions.[75] Of their faith and devotion to the Church there was never any question. Down to the final settlement of the troubles in 1893 the proselytizers from some of the Protestant churches who hovered over the fringes of the conflict merely wasted their efforts.

There is no need of retailing the commotions and tumults that marked the deadlock between Father Kolasinski and the bishop. The most notorious of these disturbances occurred on Christmas morning. Several hundred adherents of Father Kolasinski paraded out of the Polish quarter down to the episcopal residence on Washington Boulevard. They attempted to force their way into the presence of Bishop

[73] Copy of suspension in DCA.
[74] Copy of appointment in DCA.
[75] Local tradition amply confirms the priest's attempts to bolster his cause by dragging in old world prejudices.

Borgess to demand that the interdict be lifted, and that their pastor be reinstated. Determined not to yield, but at the same time somewhat unnerved by the behavior of the crowd, the bishop slipped out of his residence unobserved to celebrate Mass at St. Joseph's.[76] The marchers returned to their quarter and vented their disappointment on certain families who were not in sympathy with them.[77]

Father Kolasinski now appealed for reinstatement to the Metropolitan at Cincinnati. After a hearing Archbishop Elder sent him back to Detroit bearing a document on which he thus commented.

> You will observe that the document, which I have put into his hands, is not a judgment of mine, nor even a recommendation. It is a proposition from him. As far as I know the case, it seems to me to be one acceptable and advisable for you. But I told him expressly that there may be circumstances of which I am not informed, which may hinder its being accepted by you.[78]

Bishop Borgess remained firm, and refused to have any dealings with Father Kolasinski until he should leave the parish and the diocese.[79] On April 5, 1886, the priest finally gave up the struggle and retired to the home of his brother, Father Nicolas Kolasinski of Berea, Ohio. Four days later the bishop carried out the terms of the settlement proposed by Archbishop Elder. The priest accepted his dismissal from the diocese, and in return was freed from all ecclesiastical censures. Soon afterwards, having offered his services to Bishop Marty, Vicar-Apostolic of Dakota, he was assigned to the care of a Polish settlement at Minto, North Dakota, in what is now the Diocese of Fargo. Thus ended the first chapter of Father Kolasinski's career in the Diocese of Detroit, a career that was to assume another phase under a succeeding bishop. The parish of St. Albertus remained under interdict until June, 1887, when a mission fostered by Father Dabrowski brought many parishioners back to their obedience. Father Vincent Bronikowski, who was teaching at the time in the Polish Seminary, was thereupon appointed pastor.

The Kolasinski affair and its attendant distasteful publicity was a trying ordeal for Bishop Borgess. There now loomed before him the prospect of a bitter struggle with the forces that were striving to wrest from him the control of ecclesiastical property. He was suffering

[76] The Catholics of the city watched the struggle with intense interest, and hoped for some decisive action on the part of the bishop. He was severely criticized by "a prominent Catholic" for not facing the mob on Christmas morning. See the *Detroit Evening Journal* for October 15, 1887.
[77] There is a good account of the day's events in the *Stimme der Warheit* for December 31, 1885.
[78] Copy of letter in DCA, dated March 27, 1886.
[79] Letter to Father Kolasinski dated March 31, 1886.

from a heart ailment, and the burden of responsibility was growing too heavy. Often he had expressed his intention to give up his high office when he had reached the age of sixty. He had now arrived at that term fully resolved to satisfy the yearning to spend his final years in retirement and peace, and undismayed by rumors that his resignation would be forced from him as an aftermath of the Polish agitation. Archbishop Elder, to whom he communicated his intention, attempted to dissuade him.

> Now, will you allow me to say more on the subject. If these men are publishing that you have been told to resign, your withdrawing just now will give them a great deal of credit. . . . I easily understand that you have independence enough not to be much concerned about the opinions either of enemies or friends. . . . What you say of this Bill in the Legislature to affect the tenure of church property gives another reason for your not withdrawing just now. The supporters of the Bill will give their own interpretation, will make it a confession of inability. . . . I beg you not to regard me as importunate. I feel that it is a very serious matter in its consequences, not only for your diocese but to the Church. It is not the withdrawal itself. You are entitled to all consideration, on account particularly of your health, but the time I believe is very unfavorable . . .[80]

But Bishop Borgess had considered all these possibilities, and his resignation was even then in the hands of the Roman authorities. In his answer to Archbishop Elder he wrote:

> As to the Bill in relation to the tenure of Church property the battle will have been fought before I will be allowed to retire; for I think that the victory is even now no more doubtful. I fail to see that my retirement could be taken advantage of after having had the power of marshalling such an army to the front.
>
> I am proud to believe that I will leave the diocese and hand it over to my successor in as good a condition as an almost uninterrupted struggle of seventeen years could present it. He, coming as a new man, with new vigor and zeal and energy, will be able to inspire a new enthusiasm, build a grand cathedral, and give a new impetus to religious progress . . .[81]

The resignation of Bishop Borgess was accepted by the Holy See on April 16, 1887. In the official notification of its action which arrived in Detroit on May 2 the bishop was left free to continue in the administration of the diocese until the appointment of a successor, or to select a member of the clergy in his stead. On May 10 he named Father Edward Joos as administrator, and a few days later

[80] Letter dated March 1, 1887. Copy in DCA.
[81] Letter dated March 3, 1887. Copy in DCA.

withdrew from the episcopal residence on Washington Boulevard. Some time previously he had purchased a home near Lake St. Clair in Grosse Pointe on a lane that came to be designated as the Bishop Road, a name it still bears. Here Bishop Borgess found the peace and rest he had so long desired. Released from the burdens of office and the responsibilities he had taken so seriously the stern, unemotional, unbending bishop was transformed into the mellow, genial scholar, immersed in his books and his music, but who could sally forth occasionally in rough clothing and with his fishing tackle to sail his trim craft on the lake.

There were three years of this before the final summons came. He was visiting his close friend, Father O'Brien of Kalamazoo, when on April 27, 1890, he was stricken with apoplexy. Fortified with the last rites of the Church he lingered until the early morning of May 3, when he breathed his last.

Four days later the obsequies were held in St. Augustine's, Kalamazoo. In the presence of all the bishops of the province the successor of the deceased prelate, Bishop John Samuel Foley, offered the Requiem Mass, and Archbishop Elder pronounced the funeral oration. The remains were given temporary burial in the churchyard of St. Augustine's, but in 1906 they were transported to a tomb on the grounds of Nazareth Academy, where on October 8 an imposing memorial shaft was dedicated.[82]

In this last public tribute to the memory of Bishop Borgess his life and achievements were reviewed by Bishop Richter of Grand Rapids. The closing words of his discourse may serve as a fitting conclusion to the record in the foregoing pages.

His voice was clear and melodious, and his sermons were instructive, clear in reasoning, and eloquent. His love and affection were sincere, although not demonstrative. He never allowed them to interfere with duty.[83] Conscious of the purity of his motives he took it for granted they were understood. Hence he seldom condescended to give explanations. Thus the motives of his actions were at times misinterpreted and judged wrongly. His heart and conscience were tender; hence, difficulties inevitable in the discharge of the episcopal office caused him keen pain. This no doubt was, probably, the reason why twice he determined to lay down crozier and mitre. The first time, at the urgent instance of

[82] The remains of Bishop Borgess were reburied in Holy Sepulchre Cemetery, Detroit, on December 13, 1939. All the deceased bishops of the diocese rest there save Bishop Rese.

[83] In his funeral oration, as reported in the *Michigan Catholic* for May 15, 1890, Archbishop Elder related that while Bishop Borgess was on a Confirmation tour through the diocese he received news of the death of his brother in St. Louis. The bishop went on fulfilling his appointments, and sent a priest of the diocese to represent him at the funeral.

his priests, who when they learned his design petitioned the Holy See not to accept the resignation, he was prevailed upon to continue in office. The second time, however, feeling that his health was undermined, no friendly advice, no persuasion could make him change his resolution. As his countenance so his character was kind but not weak; firm but not severe. After three years rest from the responsibilities of governing a diocese, he prepared himself for the final account. When the angel of death summoned him, he was not alarmed, but ready to meet Him for whose honor and glory he had loved to spend himself. The halo of a great name will ever rest on this monument and give it imperishable value. Those who by erecting it honored Bishop Borgess have in so doing honored themselves.[84]

[84] The *Michigan Catholic,* October 11, 1906.

CHAPTER XXIV

Diocese under Bishop Borgess

THE development in the Diocese of Detroit during the period covered by the episcopate of Bishop Lefevere has already been traced. At the end of 1869 the area delimited for our study contained 56 churches with resident pastors, and 69 priests ministering to a Catholic population of approximately 90,000. Only a small fraction of these totals represented the original Catholic body as Bishop Lefevere had found it; the greater part was accounted for by immigration from the eastern states and from Europe.

The episcopate of Bishop Borgess extends over a lull between the rapid filling in of the state witnessed by his predecessor and the later wave of immigration associated with the rise of modern industry in Michigan. The gains that were made during the period resulted more from natural growth than from accretions, and in the main they reflected not so much an increasing Catholic population as they did the better care of a population already present in the diocese. At the close of 1887 there were in the diocese 90 churches with resident pastors, and a Catholic population of about 120,000. The number of priests, however, had almost doubled as there were now 99 diocesan clergy and 32 religious.[1]

According to the foregoing statistics thirty-four parishes were added to the diocese during the regime of Bishop Borgess; but, as usual, the bare figure is misleading and needs revising. In Detroit itself the number of parishes rose from nine to twenty, including St. Anthony's, which in Bishop Lefevere's time was considered a country parish. As the city parishes have already been dealt with in the preceding chapter we may pass on to the diocese at large.

If the entries in the Catholic Directory for 1888 be compared with those for 1869 twenty-nine parishes appear that are not mentioned as such in the earlier list. They are the following:

Anchorville	Erie	Lexington	Paw Paw
Brighton	Fenton	Monroe (3rd church)	Reese
Bronson	Fowler	Mt. Morris	Rockwood

[1] The Religious were all in Detroit, and half the number was accounted for by the Capuchin and Jesuit establishments.

562

Chelsea [2]	Freedom	New Baltimore	Roseville
Dearborn	Gagetown	North Branch	Ruth
Deerfield	Hastings	Otisco	St. Johns
Ecorse	Owosso	Williamston	
Jackson (2nd church)		Wyandotte	
		(2nd church)	

As a record of growth the foregoing list must not be taken at its face value. For instance, Anchorville and Erie are only the old parishes of Swan Creek and Vienna under their modern names. Three early foundations had not been mentioned in the list for 1869 because the succession of pastors had been interrupted. Dearborn was attended as a mission from 1859 to 1872. The same was true of Ecorse from 1858 to 1871, and of Ruth from 1869 to 1871.

Some further stripping is permissible. In dealing with the development of the diocese under Bishop Lefevere it was necessary to indicate every Catholic group of any consequence, and in order to forestall unnecessary duplication it was desirable in many instances to anticipate the date of a mission's rise to parochial status. Thus Chelsea, Freedom, Lexington, Hastings, Mt. Morris, Otisco, Paw Paw, Rockwood, St. Johns, and Williamston have already been mentioned. All these were given resident pastors during the episcopate of Bishop Borgess not so much because of sudden or unusual increase in size, but more likely on account of the rather sharp rise in the number of available priests. In 1869 the ratio of priests to Catholic population was roughly 1 to 1300; in 1888 it was 1 to 925.

Again, some names in the 1888 list represent not additional Catholic groups but the shifting of parochial centers from less to more desirable locations determined by new roads, railroad facilities, and other circumstances. Thus Fenton became the definite center for the Catholic groups that made up the older settlements at Deerfield and Oceola in Livingston County. Owosso in Shiawassee County replaced Corunna. Freedom marked the intermediate stage from Clinton to Manchester in Lenawee County.

If this paring down be justified the growth evidenced by new parishes that arose during the episcopate of Bishop Borgess would be represented fairly enough by the list emended as follows:

Brighton	Gagetown	North Branch
Bronson	Jackson (2nd church)	Owosso
Deerfield	Monroe (3rd church)	Reese
Fowler	New Baltimore	Roseville

[2] The Pinckney parish which should have been included in the listing for 1888 was omitted because it was temporarily without a pastor, and was attended from Chelsea.

As in the preceding period the increase in parishes was accompanied by the appearance of lesser Catholic groups large enough to deserve regular ministrations, able to erect their own churches, and destined for the most part to achieve parochial status under a succeeding bishop. These were the growing points of the Catholic body as it ramified in the territory of the diocese during the period we are considering, and they must be surveyed in connection with the parishes to appraise the stature of the diocese as Bishop Borgess left it. Of the twenty-nine counties in the diocese only five, Berrien, Eaton, Hillsdale, Kalamazoo, and Washtenaw made no gains in either parishes or missions. Between 1870 and 1888 the following twenty-nine missions were established:

Plainwell	Sebewaing	Utica	White Pigeon	Nashville
Sheridan	Milford	Antrim	Albion	Pinnebog
Royal Oak	Grosse Ile	Dowagiac	Leslie	Speaker
New Boston	Richfield	Portland	Algonac	Trenton
Caseville	Imlay City	Casco	South Haven	Howell
Brockway	Leighton	Three Rivers	Harbor Beach	

Brighton, the first parish on the emended list, represents the same group that was Father O'Kelly's charge at Green Oak. His removal to Genoa Township left Green Oak a mission dependent upon the later parishes organized at Oceola and Deerfield. In 1864 the congregation made a fresh start under the leadership of Father Pourret of Oceola. It purchased the present church site in the village of Brighton, and erected thereon a small structure sufficient for its needs.[3] In September, 1876, Brighton was given its first pastor when Father James Wheeler was transferred to it from Fenton. His change to Owosso in March of the following year led to the appointment of a young priest lately come from Ireland, who was destined to live a long and honorable career in the diocese, Father James Doherty. Nine years of zealous ministry in Brighton were the prelude to his life work as pastor of St. Vincent's in Detroit. On September 13, 1885, the original church enlarged and completely transformed was dedicated in honor of St. Patrick by Bishop Borgess.

From the fact that Father O'Kelly made Green Oak the center of his early ministrations in Livingston County it might be inferred that the largest number of Catholics lay in its vicinity. However, even at this period Green Oak was no more important than the group of Irish Catholics in Putnam Township living in the neighborhood of what is today the village of Pinckney. Father Cullen attended it from

---

[3] A historical sketch of the parish was printed in the *Michigan Catholic* for September 17, 1885.

Ann Arbor when Father O'Kelly was still in Wisconsin. Lying near the border of Washtenaw County, Pinckney became a mission of Dexter when Green Oak was abandoned. On March 28, 1854, Christopher and Mary Monks deeded a plot of ground to Bishop Lefevere for church purposes.[4] Apparently the erection of a church was delayed until 1867, when the present structure was erected under the supervision of Father Van Gennip of Dexter.[5] A resident pastor, Father James Herbert, was appointed in 1875. He remained only a year, and Pinckney then became a mission of Chelsea. It was listed as such in the Catholic Directory for 1888 as its parochial status was not restored until 1895, when Father Michael Comerford was named pastor.

Meanwhile another parish had arisen in the county ten miles northwest of Brighton on the Grand River Road. One of Father O'Kelly's missions while he was pastor of Green Oak comprised a number of Irish families who had early settled around the village of Howell. For many years Mass was said in private homes, and no attempt at church building was made until 1878, when Father Doherty purchased the present church site and erected a small brick chapel.[6] Howell remained a mission of Brighton until Father James Gore was transferred to it from Williamston in 1888 to become the first resident pastor. Father Hugh McCarthy, appointed in 1899, enlarged the original chapel to its present dimensions, and the structure thus renovated was used for the first time on Christmas Day, 1902.

The early mission center in Livingston County called Deerfield must not be confused with another of the same name in Lenawee County. When the Redemptorists in Monroe began to reach out westward into the adjacent county the first Catholic group they encountered lay in Blissfield township. Father Gillet reported in 1846 that he was attending a number of Irish and French families in Blissfield, and that they had already built a church.[7] The Catholic Almanac for 1854 states that "Palmira, Hillsdale, Springville, Dearfield, Jonesville, Cold Water, and Blissfield, are also occasionally attended from Adrian." Here Deerfield appears for the first time, and as a mission distinct from Blissfield. The same notation continues until 1858, when Deerfield disappears and only Blissfield is mentioned. In the Almanac for 1867 Blissfield is dropped and Deerfield definitely supplants it.

In 1867 the township of Deerfield was organized out of portions of Blissfield and Ridgeway townships. At a historical anniversary cele-

---

[4] Deed in DCA.
[5] Date in parish record.
[6] *History of Livingston County* (Philadelphia, 1880).
[7] *Annales Cong. SS. Redemp.*, I, 434.

bration held in 1876 one of the Deerfield township pioneers in the course of his reminiscences made the following statement.

> The first meeting house built in the township was by the Catholic society, in 1843. A Catholic church and society was organized the same year by Father Lewis Gillott.[8]

The statement represents, if not first hand knowledge, at least the prevailing local tradition. If allowance be made for the error in name and date—Father Gillet did not come to Monroe until 1844—it is fairly certain that the church fostered by Father Gillet in 1846 stood near the present village of Deerfield at the time in Blissfield township.

In 1862 Father Edward Joos of Monroe, to which Deerfield was attached as a mission, built a second church in the village itself. It was dedicated in honor of St. Alphonsus by Bishop Lefevere on October 12, 1864.[9] The first resident pastor, Father Louis Van Straelen, was appointed in 1884, and the present church was erected by Father Francis Broegger in 1892.

In deep contrast to Lenawee County with its thriving parishes lay the most forlorn and neglected portion of the diocese, Tuscola County. Within it at the beginning of Bishop Borgess' episcopate there was not a single Catholic church. The only house of worship available to the few Catholics in the western section of the county was the small wooden structure that stood across the Saginaw County line near the village of Reese. Father Roche from Port Austin, and Fathers Van Der Heyden and Van Der Bom from Saginaw made occasional sallies into the county attending urgent sick calls and celebrating Mass in private homes wherever a group of worshippers could conveniently gather.

The first step to remedy conditions in the county was taken in 1879. On June 21 of that year Bishop Borgess chose for a difficult task a young priest whom he had ordained two weeks before. He gave him the following appointment.

> Rev. Clem. T. B. Krebs,
> Rev. Dear Sir:
> You are hereby appointed to take charge of the mission of Gagetown, Tuscola County, embracing the Townships of Sebewaing, Brookfield, Grant and Sheridan in Huron County, and all the Catholics in Tuscola County; and in said mission you are to remain until by our order relieved in writing.[10]

[8] *Mich. Hist. Colls.*, XVII, 534.
[9] Notation in Deerfield baptismal register.
[10] Copy of appointment in DCA.

In after years Father Krebs took pride in recalling the day of his appointment when he set out for his arduous mission field "with a little black box and the Bishop's blessing." [11] There were forty Catholic families in the neighborhood of Gagetown when he began his ministry, but, as may be surmised from the appointment, these were the smallest portion of his flock.[12] For eight years Father Krebs was alone on this last frontier of the diocese. With the slender resources of his scattered congregation he built the first church in the county at Gagetown. On October 9, 1881, it was dedicated in honor of St. Agatha by Bishop Borgess.[13] Except for an interval of two years spent elsewhere in the diocese Father Krebs remained at Gagetown until 1900. The present imposing church whose corner stone was laid on July 7, 1915, was built during the pastorate of Father Patrick Dwan.

From Gagetown in the extreme northeastern corner of the county Father Krebs had to travel to the western county line to find a second group of Catholic families living in and around the village of Reese. He said Mass for them in a small, unfinished wooden church that stood at some distance from the village in Saginaw County.[14] It had been erected most probably in 1862 by Father Van Der Heyden, pastor of Saginaw.[15] The partition of 1882 which extended the new diocese of Grand Rapids to the Saginaw County line created a rather awkward situation for Father Krebs, but one which, as tradition has it, he met expeditiously and neatly on his own initiative by rolling the church under cover of darkness into the village. In the following year he began the erection of the present church, and continued to attend Reese as a mission until 1887, when Father Thomas Hennessy was appointed first resident pastor.

North of Father Krebs' mission field lay Huron County whose pioneer parishes at Parisville, Ruth, and Port Austin had been founded during the episcopate of Bishop Lefevere. Despite the devastating forest fires of 1871 the population had been mounting steadily and new Catholic groups were forming. An interesting portrayal of conditions in the county in 1874 was furnished by a correspondent to the *Western Home Journal.*

> The Rev. C. J. Roche, pastor of Port Austin, has under his charge almost the whole of Huron County and some townships of Tuscola County. Until a few years ago, his pastoral district had no residing

---

[11] There is a sketch of Father Krebs' missionary labors in the *Michigan Catholic* for January 13, 1927.

[12] Gagetown was described by a parishioner in the *Stimme der Warheit* for November 26, 1879.

[13] *Ibid.*, October 20, 1881.

[14] The site is now the parish cemetery.

[15] Information furnished by Mr. Frank Humpert of Reese.

priest. It is only some twenty years ago since a few Catholics began to move into that wooded country; they were mostly emigrants from Canada, very poor, belonging to all nationalities and scattered all over the county. They were attended at occasional and irregular intervals by the aged priest at Forestville, the Rev. Cluck (now pastor of Dorr, near Grand Rapids).

When Father Roche, some three years ago, received his appointment for this place, he found only one poor little frame chapel in the whole district, St. Michael's chapel of Port Austin, and a pastoral residence half built. Since that time he has finished his residence, enlarged and furnished the little chapel and established a year ago a parochial school which is conducted by Miss Anna Dignan, formerly a pupil of St. Thomas' school of Ann Arbor, and is in a very flourishing condition. In the meantime, he had to attend also to the spiritual wants of some twenty different little stations, where from time to time either on week days or on Sundays, according to their size, he celebrates mass and instructs the children. All these out-stations, with the exception of two larger ones, count only from two to twelve families, are scattered all over the county in all directions and at a distance of 10, 20, 30 to 45 miles from Port Austin, his place of residence. To attend to all those stations and to his sick calls, Father Roche had to travel in an average more than 100 miles a week in the woods, mostly through sandy roads and log paths; these roads are at seasons almost entirely impracticable with horse and buggy, so that most of his missionary trips are to be made on horse-back. Only two of those stations are of some importance; The Canadian settlement, 15 miles west of Port Austin with some sixty families, attended mostly from Port Austin; and the Scotch settlement, 27 miles from Port Austin, with some twenty families, attended on Sundays once every three months. These few Scotch farmers notwithstanding their poverty, have succeeded already in erecting a neat frame chapel 30 x 40. Though it is not yet entirely finished, Father Roche, at his last visit to the Scotch settlement on Sunday, August 23d, went in procession from the old log-house that had been used as a chapel for several years past, to take possessions of and celebrate mass for the first time in their new chapel which was placed on that occasion together with the little congregation under the patronage of St. Columbkill, the patron-saint of Scotland.

To his zeal for the spiritual welfare of his flock, Father Roche was anxious of late to procure to them the blessings of a mission. He secured for that purpose the services of the good and zealous pastor of the Assumption, near Detroit. . . .

Father Van Driss arrived at the French settlement on Wednesday evening, August 26. That same night he opened the exercises in the mission house of the settlement; but it became soon apparent that the house was too small for this occasion, and the mission was continued the following days in the new chapel that is being built by these poor Canadians. Though it is not half finished yet, nor even enclosed, the favorable weather allowed him to make use of it for the occasion. As the Feast of St. John the Baptist occurred during the triduum of this little mission, he was chosen as the patron-saint of the congregation and chapel, which are both in course of formation and construction. During the mission the Catholics of St. John's, who, until the arrival of Father Roche in Port Austin had been almost without any attendance what-soever, seemed to partake, all of them young and old, in the joy and exultation of their new patron-saint, when he felt for the first time the presence of our Saviour. . . . Conspicuous among them was a venerable patriarch, Mr. Belhumeur, over 100 years of age, tall and straight, who came every day 2½ miles on foot to the church. . . .

That same morning at 10½ o'clock the indefatigable missionary opened the mission at St. Michael's chapel, in Port Austin, the main station of the pastoral district of Father Roche. With the surrounding country it contains almost 100 families about equally divided between 4 different nationalities: Irish, Germans, Canadians, and Polish. . . .

This mission was the first ever given in this wooded region since the creation of the world. It will be long remembered by young and old, produce abundant starting fruits of salvation, and cheer the heart of the zealous Father Roche who will now resume his arduous labors with a new courage and fervor. May the Catholics of Huron County preserve him long in their midst. However poor and full of hardships his mission may be it is worthy of envy in many respects and yet it is not likely to be envied or coveted by anybody. . . .[16]

The French settlement later known for some years as the congregation of Meade Township is today the parish of Pinnebog. Father Francis W. Hewlett was appointed first resident pastor in 1899, and in 1901 replaced the primitive chapel with the present church.

The Scotch Settlement presented a unique addition to the racial groups already in the diocese. In 1849 some three hundred Scotch Catholic families driven from their homes on the island of South Uist in the Outer Hebrides by the exactions of a grasping landlord emigrated to Canada, where they settled for the most part in Middlesex County in Ontario. About 1870 twelve families decided to make a fresh start in Michigan, and took up land in Sheridan township of Huron County. With fifty dollars which Matthew McIntyre, a son of one of the families, had earned as a sailor on the Lakes they purchased six acres for church purposes. Here was built the wooden chapel, mentioned in the report just quoted, which Father Roche dedicated in honor of St. Columbkill on August 4, 1875.[17] The colony grew and prospered, and in 1897 under the direction of Father Krebs the present church, a monument to the faith and sacrifices of these

[16] Issue of September 19, 1874.
[17] There is a long account of the settlement by one of its pioneers in the *Detroit News* for July 27, 1906.

sturdy Catholics, was erected. The first resident pastor, Father Christopher T. Dolan, was appointed in 1910.

Another station attended by Father Roche but not mentioned by the correspondent of 1874 lay in the extreme southwest corner of the county in the township of Sebewaing, where several families, German for the most part, had been drawn from the Saginaw district by the lumbering and fishing industries. Here Father Roche purchased a plot of ground to serve as a cemetery, and in it built a small frame church in 1874.[18] After his departure from Port Austin Sebewaing was attended from Saginaw and later from Gagetown and Reese. The present church, which had been erected and used by the Moravian Brethren, was purchased by Father Hennessy of Reese in 1891, and two years later Father John P. Helten was appointed to Sebewaing as the first resident pastor.

About fifteen miles north of Sebewaing, in the village of Caseville, there still stands the small mission church which perpetuates the memory of the pioneer priest whose activities we have been considering. For a small group of Irish families in the neighborhood Father Roche purchased an unused school building in 1875 and transformed it into a church which he dedicated to St. Roche. Attached for many years to Port Austin or Gagetown, Caseville since 1905 has been a mission of Pinnebog.

On the eastern shore of the county lay the settlement at Sand Beach, today known as Harbor Beach. Here as early as 1869 a small group of Irish and German Catholics had been attended at stated intervals by the pastors of Port Austin. It was not until 1882 that the building of a church was attempted, and in the fall of that year a small wooden structure was erected under the direction of Father Laugel.[19] Subsequently attended from Ruth the congregation was given its first resident pastor when Father Charles E. Henigan was appointed in 1899. The present church built during the pastorate of Father Raymond T. Fleming was dedicated on July 13, 1917.

On the southern boundary of Sanilac County in the township of Speaker a number of Irish families who had been attended from Lexington began to work for a church of their own in 1873. Their hopes were realized when a chapel in honor of the Seven Dolors was dedicated by Bishop Borgess on December 1, 1877.[20] A few miles to the south in Brockway township of St. Clair County there was an older group of Irish farmers on the fringes of the Emmet parish. Brockway as a station attended by Father Kilroy was mentioned in the Catholic

---

[18] Record in DCA.
[19] *Stimme der Warheit*, February 15, 1883.
[20] Record in DCA.

Almanacs as early as 1855. Traditional rivalry between the two groups led to the building of St. Joseph's church in Brockway, which was dedicated on December 4, 1881.[21] The possible rise of either mission to parochial status was halted by the growth of Yale, lying between them, which became the thriving center of the flax industry in the district. Father Patrick Cullinane, assigned to the care of the two missions in 1898, accordingly established his residence in Yale and built the present church in 1902. The mission churches were not abandoned until 1912, when the older loyalties were finally merged in the new parish.

Algonac as a mission of Marine City is mentioned for the first time in the Catholic Directory of 1873. However, the French inhabitants of the settlement had been regularly visited much earlier by Father Aloysius Lambert, and the deed to the church property executed by Charles Gilbert is dated September 4, 1866. Three years later Father Lambert erected the first church, but no resident pastor was appointed until 1894, when Father Francis Kemper was given the charge. The church burned to the ground on November 30, 1895, and Father Kemper was succeeded by Father Benoit Gery who immediately began the building of the present church. For the summer residents of the St. Clair Flats Father Gery erected the chapel in honor of St. Mark, which was dedicated on August 16, 1897.

In the Catholic Almanac for 1854 appears for the first time the notation: New Baltimore, church built—Rev. C. A. R. Chambillé. This is evidently an error, for Father Chambille began the Anchorville parish in St. Clair County. The later growth of the French population along the shore of Anchor Bay resulted in the formation of the present parish of New Baltimore in Macomb County. The name does not appear again until 1872, and New Baltimore is then listed as a mission of Anchorville. The church was built in 1869, and the first pastor, Father Elias Maesfrancx, was appointed in 1875. He remained only three months and was followed by Father Aloysius Lambert who deserves to be considered the real founder of the parish. The first church was completely rebuilt in 1907 during the pastorate of Father Charles Koenig.[22]

Strangely enough the old mother church at Mt. Clemens had no part in the development of two parishes that arose north and south of it along the main highway through the county, the Gratiot Road. Lenox was in its origins a mission of Anchorville. A group of German Catholic families had early settled in the western half of Casco township in St. Clair County, and were attended by Father Buyse

---

[21] The *Western Home Journal,* December 8, 1881.
[22] From manuscript history of parish compiled by Father Charles Koenig. DCA.

during his pastorate at Anchorville. In 1868 Francis Palms sold to Bishop Lefevere a plot of ground in section 17, and the timber on it was used to build St. Mary's church, a structure 30 x 40 feet which was ready for services in July, 1870.[23] As was customary in the German settlements the building was used as a school on weekdays. The church stood about three miles from the village of Lenox in Macomb County which had direct railroad communication with St. Clair, and the Casco group together with the growing number of Catholics in Lenox came under the care of Father Schenkelberg of St. Clair. In 1888 he directed the building of a church in Lenox, which was dedicated to St. Augustine, and the Casco church was subsequently abandoned and was dismantled about 1897.[24] Father Thomas J. Ryan became the first resident pastor in 1892, and the present church was dedicated on December 11, 1913.

South of Mt. Clemens as early as the 50's a hamlet known to old Detroiters as Utica Junction marked the spot where an important highway into Oakland County branched off from the Gratiot Road. The original Catholic population of the neighborhood derived mainly from the Assumption parish in Wayne County, and was reinforced by many Belgian families who had taken up farm lands in the vicinity. Father Van Den Driessche attended the Junction as a matter of course, and it was he who in June, 1861, obtained permission from Bishop Lefevere to form the group into a separate congregation. Daniel Corby donated the land, and the church of the Sacred Heart was dedicated by Bishop Lefevere on June 16, 1865. The Junction, or Roseville mission, as it came to be called a few years later remained attached to Assumption parish until Father Francis Hendrickx was appointed first resident pastor in October, 1873. During the pastorate of Father Dennis Tighe beginning in 1918 Roseville shared in the phenomenal growth of the Detroit metropolitan area, and the old buildings were all replaced. The present church was begun in 1928.[25]

Some miles northwest of the Junction lay Utica, one of the oldest villages in the county. In the late 60's there were forty Catholic families in the neighborhood, Irish for the most part, who were visited periodically by Father Van Den Driessche. A church site was purchased in June, 1866, and the baptismal register of the mission records the dedication of the church of St. Lawrence on August 16, 1874. A second church was built in 1908, and the present combination church and school, on a site at some distance from the traditional

---

[23] Deed in DCA.
[24] Details concerning Casco furnished by a pioneer settler, Mr. Matthias Nothaft.
[25] A printed parish history was issued in 1936.

location on the Van Dyke Road, was dedicated in June, 1930. After having been successively a mission of Assumption parish, Centerline, St. Clair Shores, and Rochester, Utica finally attained parochial rank when Father William J. Crowley was appointed first resident pastor in 1928.

In Genesee County the southern portion of Richfield township contained a few Irish Catholic families who had come from western New York to Michigan about 1860, and who were attended at rare intervals from Flint. The hope of obtaining more regular ministrations led them to build, in the spring of 1871, a church dedicated to St. John in section 27 of Richfield township. The little congregation comprising nine families had Mass no oftener than three or four times a year even after it was attached to Lapeer as a mission in 1876. Later Mass was said once a month, and beginning with 1890 four times a month on weekdays. In 1893 Father Francis Kelley of Lapeer inspired the congregation now considerably increased to build a new church, and this time in Davison which lay on the railroad connecting Flint and Lapeer. The first Mass was said in the new church on August 19, 1894. Davison remained attached to Lapeer until 1928, when Father Henry M. Mayotte was appointed first resident pastor.[26]

Another early mission attached to Lapeer comprised a group of Irish families in Imlay township of Lapeer County. The pioneers of the settlement, John Heenan and George Rourk, came in 1850, and two years later Mass was first said for the tiny congregation in the home of Martin Heenan by Father Van Renterghem of Mt. Clemens. Father De Ceuninck of Flint occasionally visited the settlement as did Father Buyse of Anchorville, but regular ministrations did not begin until 1864, when Father Busche assumed the pastorate of Lapeer. Under his direction the congregation in 1867 built a small frame church which he dedicated to the Sacred Heart. The present church was built in the town of Imlay City by Father Kelley in 1894, and the congregation finally reached parochial status when Father John B. Parker was appointed pastor in 1928.[27]

According to Father Busche's account of his mission field the German pioneers in the county arrived about 1858, chose the township of North Branch for their settlement, and built a rude house of worship which may possibly have antedated by a few months the church in Lapeer.[28] This first log church stood facing the road that marks the boundry between the townships of Burnside and North

---

[26] There is a sketch of the Davison mission in the Lapeer parish history issued in 1904.
[27] *Idem.*
[28] According to local tradition the German pioneers were a group of Bavarian Catholics who settled first in the neighborhood of Rome, in Oneida County, N. Y. Dissatisfied with the quality of the soil they had purchased they moved to Michigan.

Branch, directly opposite the site of the present church at Burnside. It was replaced in 1877 by a frame structure, and in February, 1885, Father John Gratza who had been stationed for some years at Parisville was appointed resident pastor. Moved across the road into Burnside township and completely remodeled in 1915 the second church was destroyed by fire in 1929. The present building was dedicated on July 30, 1930.

As stated in a preceding chapter the first parish established in Shiawassee County was at Corunna, and pastors were stationed there from 1857 to 1870. Father Joseph Kraemer appointed to this mission field in 1870 made his residence not in Corunna but in St. Johns.[29] Owosso was now the most important town in the district although still without a church, and Father Kraemer proceeded to erect "one of the finest brick churches in the diocese . . . built in the ancient Roman style." The cornerstone was laid by Bishop Borgess on September 16, 1872, and the enthusiasm of the Catholics of Owosso may be judged from an item in the record of the occasion: "Twenty-five cannon were fired in honor of the Bishop coming to Owosso." The church remained uncompleted for several years, but was finally dedicated on October 28, 1884. Some months after the cornerstone laying Father Kraemer changed his residence from St. Johns to Owosso thus becoming the first resident pastor of the new parish.[30]

The Antrim mission, appearing for the first time in the Catholic Directory of 1872, represented a number of Irish Catholics living on the southern boundary of the county directly below Corunna in Antrim township. In 1874 Father Kraemer directed the building of a small wooden church wherein he said Mass once a month on weekdays.[31] The present church was built in 1892 on a new site two miles

[29] A correspondent wrote in the *Western Home Journal* for July 26, 1873, an account of Father Kraemer's work: "About two and a half years ago the Rev. Joseph Kraemer was appointed pastor of the Missions in Saginaw, Shiawassee, Clinton and Genesee counties. All there was at that time to denote the existence of Catholicity, excepting the few poor settlers who were struggling to acquire a livelihood, comprised a very dilapidated church in Corunna, one partly built in St. Johns, and the frame of one just raised in Maple Grove. Since then, however, through the almost unparalleled exertions of the indomitable priest the church in Corunna has been refitted in an elegant manner, at a cost of $1,000. The church in St. Johns has been refinished in a most artistic style, and a commodious house is well nigh completed for the next priest. . . . A beautiful little church has been completed in Gaines at a cost of $2,000."

[30] The permission to make the transfer to Owosso is dated January 3, 1873.

[31] The *Western Home Journal* for October 12, 1875, carried a jubilant account of the dedication. "The backwoods of Michigan is making rapid strides towards civilization and Catholicity. One short year ago the town of Antrim already fairly dotted with comfortable rustic homesteads, presented to the eye of the inquisitive visitor nothing but a pagan view. Today, however, another scene presents itself. The new temple erected in God's honor in the whole of this district was yesterday dedicated in a special manner to the Deity . . . The church occupies the highest point of land in the immediate neighborhood, and is a perfect gem, of which of all things terrestial after old Erin's green sward, we feel proud. . . ."

west in the village of Morrice. Attached successively to Owosso, Gaines, and Durand the mission became the parish of Morrice in 1926 when Father Cecil M. Winters was appointed resident pastor.

In Clinton County another filial parish sprang from the old mother church at Westphalia. The descendants of the German pioneers numbered some two hundred families in Dallas township, and there were in addition several Irish families who lived on the extreme limits of the Hubbardston parish. The village of Fowler was the most appropriate center for them, and it was moreover linked by railroad with the parish at St. Johns. Separation from Westphalia which had long been agitated was finally approved by Bishop Borgess in 1880. Early the following year Father James Ronayne from St. Johns began his ministry in Fowler by saying Mass in the home of John Long, and within a few months completed the building of the first church. The first resident pastor, Father Bernard Holthaus, was appointed in 1886. The present church erected during the pastorate of Father Theodore Lindemann was dedicated in 1918.

The Westphalia parish overflowed westward into Ionia County especially in the vicinity of Portland, where there were as well several Irish Catholic families. In July, 1878, Father Bolte of Ionia received permission to organize the congregation of Portland, and on June 10, 1880, Bishop Borgess dedicated to St. Patrick the small wooden structure in the village of Portland. The mission was attached to St. Johns until Father Mathias Auer was named resident pastor in 1899. The present church was erected during the pastorate of Father William O'Rourke, and was dedicated on June 27, 1927.

In Barry County the first parish arose to serve the growing number of Catholics in and around the county seat at Hastings. The appointment given to the first pastor, Father Ferdinand Allgayer, on February 5, 1873, mentioned no other missions in the county but entrusted to him the care of two townships, Cascade and Bowen, in Kent County.[32] Between 1882 and 1886 Hastings was without a pastor and was attended from Jackson. During this interval Father Theophile Buyse found enough Catholics at Nashville to warrant the beginnings of a mission there. The *Michigan Catholic* for September 6, 1883, noted this gratifying progress in Barry County.

> The Messrs. Maurex, the generous purchasers of the meeting house, have turned it into a neat and useful Catholic edifice. Rev. T. Buyse of Jackson will henceforth attend to the spiritual wants of this mission every first Thursday of the month.

Dedicated to St. Cyril the little church was rebuilt and enlarged during the pastorate of Father Cornelius Kennedy at Hastings. Nash-

---

[32] Appointment in DCA.

ville has remained attached to Hastings as a mission, and the two churches are still the only ones in the county.

The Irish Catholic immigrants into Allegan County settled in the southeastern corner and formed, as we have seen, the mission of Watson. In the course of time several families were attracted to the neighborhood of the village of Plainwell, and in 1875 they purchased an abandoned Presbyterian church which Father Seybold of Battle Creek dedicated to St. Agnes.[33] The mission was attached to Battle Creek until it was assigned to Kalamazoo in 1887. In that year a large paper mill began operations in Otsego, three miles away, and drew many of its workers from Plainwell. St. Margaret's church was built in 1890, and both towns were attended from Kalamazoo until the first resident priest in the area, Father John Desmond O'Shea, was appointed to Otsego. In 1904 the Plainwell congregation was definitely merged with Otsego.

Another mission arose in the county east of the older centers at Dorr and New Salem. A plot of ground lying in Section 1 of Leighton township was donated for church purposes by Joseph Schafbuch on November 9, 1872, and two years later a church dedicated to St. Joseph was erected.[34] For some years Leighton was attended regularly from Dorr, but during and after the troubled period in the area it was practically abandoned down to 1915. It was then attended by the pastors of Cascade in Kent County with the authorization of the Ordinary of Detroit, and is now a mission in the Diocese of Grand Rapids.

South Haven in Van Buren County was organized as a mission of St. Joseph in 1876. At the time there were only five families in the village, and Mass was said only once in three months.[35] On September 1, 1879, the growing congregation purchased from the United Brethren an unoccupied church building and this was used down to 1884. The previous year South Haven had been assigned to Kalamazoo, and Father O'Brien supervised the building of a new church which was dedicated in honor of St. Basil on August 20, 1884.[36] Later attached to Paw Paw, the mission finally became a parish in 1900, when Father John O'Rafferty was appointed resident pastor. Through his efforts a substantial brick structure was erected, and dedicated on August 30, 1903. The present church was erected on a new site in 1923 during the pastorate of Father Leo Huver.

The history of the Dowagiac parish in Cass County goes back to

---

[33] Thomas, op. cit., 577.
[34] The church is referred to in the Dorr report for 1874. DCA.
[35] O. W. Rowland, History of Van Buren County (Chicago, 1912), 542.
[36] Record of dedication in DCA.

1858, when Father De Neve of Niles began offering Mass occasionally in the homes of the few Irish families in the village. In 1874 the present parish cemetery was acquired, and in it was built a small frame church dedicated to the Holy Maternity. Dowagiac was now attached to the parish at Silver Creek, the former Indian mission, and was attended by its pastors until the Silver Creek buildings burned in 1886 during the pastorate of Father Broegger. The fire hastened the inevitable shift from a rural center to a thriving town on the railroad, and Father Broegger took up his residence in Dowagiac and purchased the present church property. Father Joseph Joos, appointed to Dowagiac in 1891, built the church, and it was used for the first time on Christmas Day, 1892.[37]

Two new missions were added to the older centers, Mendon and Sturgis, in St. Joseph County. White Pigeon appears for the first time in the Catholic Directory for 1875, but the small group of Irish Catholics there was attended more or less regularly as early as 1848 by the Holy Cross Fathers of Notre Dame. Father Korst of Coldwater built the church dedicated to St. Joseph in 1871, and White Pigeon served for many years from Mendon is now a mission of Sturgis.

Although Three Rivers is mentioned for the first time in 1877 it had been attended for many years prior to that date by Father Cappon of Niles. Later a mission of Jackson and of Bronson, Three Rivers was finally confided to Mendon in 1895. During the pastorate of Father Henry Kaufmann the struggling mission was bolstered with financial help from Detroit, and the church of the Immaculate Conception, erected in 1904, replaced the third floor lodge hall wherein the congregation had worshipped for many years. The rapid growth of Three Rivers led to its rise to parochial status in 1932, when Father Angelo G. Leva was appointed first resident pastor.[38]

From his headquarters at Coldwater Father Cornelius Korst for many years rode a missionary circuit comprising the settlements at Burr Oak, Sturgis, White Pigeon, Mendon, Charlotte, and Union City. Southwest of Coldwater on the Chicago Road lay the village which marked the site of the first settlement in the county, and which bore the name of its founder, Jabez Bronson. The early Catholic immigrants into the county, for the most part Irish, had been drawn to Coldwater, but the later arrivals, German and Polish, had preferred the neighborhood of Bronson. In the summer of 1877 Father Korst erected a small frame church in the village, and two years later reported that he had under his care forty Polish and thirty Ger-

---

[37] There is a manuscript history of the parish in the parish records.
[38] A printed history of the Mendon parish issued in 1909 contains the early history of the White Pigeon and Three Rivers missions.

man families.[39] The present church was built in 1884 by the first resident pastor, Father Francis Kroll. Today the parish has well over two hundred families and is predominantly Polish.

In the Catholic Almanac for 1855 Father James Hennessy of Marshall was noted as serving three missions in Calhoun County: Battle Creek, New Bedford, and Albion. This is the first mention of Albion but local tradition remembers earlier visits made by Father Cullen of Ann Arbor to the tiny group of Irish Catholics that filtered in after Thomas Slowey who came about 1845. Mass was said in private homes, usually in the home of Mrs. Cashen on Oak Street. The church property was purchased in 1866, and the construction of a church under the supervision of Father Callaert of Marshall was begun in 1873.[40] Albion remained attached to Marshall, and later to Hillsdale, until Father Henry Sullivan was named resident pastor in 1898. The present church was first used for divine worship in November, 1933.

From the year of its erection in 1856 St. John's church in Jackson had been the only house of worship for the Catholics of the city. The necessity of a new parish was apparent about 1870, but nothing was done until ten years later.[41] In the spring of 1880 Father Buyse while on a visit to his home in Belgium was temporarily replaced by Father John Malaney. Attracted by the pleasing personality of the young priest who had just been ordained, the Catholics of Jackson were determined to retain him if possible. The movement to establish a second parish was revived and carried on so earnestly that in September of the same year Bishop Borgess sanctioned the project in a letter to Father Malaney.

> Answering the one hundred and twenty-four petitioners for a new church in Jackson we stated to Mr. E. Morrissy: We agree to your request of leaving Rev. J. W. Malaney in Jackson for the purpose of canvassing the field to learn if the project is feasible. Therefore we beg you to call a meeting of the people as soon as possible, and begin a subscription on condition that nothing is to be paid until a sufficient sum has been subscribed to justify the establishment of another congregation. . . .[42]

[39] *History of Branch County* (Philadelphia, 1879), 228.

[40] The church was dedicated on October 15, 1874, and there is a long report of the ceremony in the *Western Home Journal.*

[41] Bishop Borgess wrote to Father Buyse on September 25, 1880: "We have this moment received the enclosed petition, and forward it to you as one of the interested parties. As you are aware, the need of a second Catholic church in the city of Jackson has been acknowledged, and the realization of the same agitated for the last ten years . . ."

[42] Copy in DCA.

Father Malaney's report was so encouraging that on November 29 the new parish was officially erected, and he received the following appointment:

> . . . We do no more doubt in the eventual success of establishing a Second Catholic congregation in the city of Jackson. For that reason we hereby appoint you, *ad tempus,* the Pastor of the new congregation, i. e. for all the Catholics living South of the center of Main Street of the city of Jackson, and of the Catholics in Jackson County living south of said line of Main Street running East and West through the center of the said county of Jackson. . . .[43]

The construction of a brick church was immediately undertaken. On December 11, 1881, it was dedicated by Bishop Borgess to the Blessed Virgin under the title, Star of the Sea.[44]

In the early 70's Father Buyse occasionally visited a few Irish families that lived north of Jackson in the vicinity of Leslie in Ingham County, which lay a few miles west of the pioneer settlement in Bunker Hill township. A site for a church was deeded on December 5, 1872, by James Birney, but the church was not built until 1881. It was dedicated to St. Joseph on November 9 of that year, and the congregation was attached to Jackson. In the course of time Leslie dwindled in importance, its congregation was absorbed by neighboring parishes, and the church was closed and disposed of in 1927.

The two older parishes in Monroe had very refinite racial affiliations; St. Mary's was the French stronghold, and St. Michael's the German. Three unsuccessful attempts had been made by the English-speaking Catholics of Monroe to organize a parish of their own. In 1852 the venture went as far as the laying of foundations and the blessing of a cornerstone by Bishop Lefevere before it was abandoned.[45]

The final attempt which did succeed was directed by the far-seeing, zealous priest destined to end his days as Bishop of Covington, Father Camillus Maes, pastor of St. Mary's from 1871 to 1873. In September, 1872, he called together the English-speaking members of the congregation, and submitted his plan for the carrying out of their cherished project. A site for the proposed building was immediately purchased, the cornerstone of the church was laid the following April, and on September 15, 1874, Bishop Borgess dedicated the completed structure under the title, St. John the Baptist.

Meanwhile, Father Maes had himself been appointed to the pastor-

---

[43] *Ibid.*

[44] The *Western Home Journal* for December 15, 1881, carries an account of the dedication.

[45] A printed history of the parish was issued in 1898.

ate, an office which he held until 1880, when he was summoned to Detroit to serve as secretary to Bishop Borgess. Father Peter Leavy was pastor of St. John's from 1881 to 1889. In addition to his pastoral duties he held the presidency of St. Francis Preparatory Seminary from 1886 to 1888. A few months after his resignation he died a victim of smallpox contracted while making a sick call in Deerfield. The care of the parish again devolved on the Seminary where Father Edward Kelly, the future bishop of Grand Rapids, was now president. When the Seminary was definitely closed in the summer of 1889 Father Kelly succeeded Father Leavy, but resigned a few months later because of ill health. Father James Hally had just begun his pastorate in January, 1892, when St. John's burned to the ground. The courage and sacrifices of the parishioners are embodied in the present church dedicated by Bishop Foley on October 9, 1892.

In Oakland County another group of Irish immigrants, settled in the neighborhood of Royal Oak, is mentioned in the Catholic Almanacs as early as 1853. They were first ministered to by Father Farnan from the Cathedral in Detroit, and later by the pastors of Pontiac.[46] In 1868 the first church, dedicated to St. Michael, was built a mile east and north of the town. In 1889 the second church was built in Royal Oak itself, but the congregation remained in its mission status, attended by the Capuchin Fathers from Detroit, until Father John Needham was named first resident pastor in October, 1909.

The survey of the diocese ends with the record of growth in Wayne County. New Boston appears for the first time in the Catholic Directory of 1875, and as a mission of Dearborn, but Mass had been said in the village as early as 1868.[47] The mission was confided to Monroe in 1879, and the church built in 1875 was dedicated by Father Joos on May 30, 1883. New Boston, after having been attended for many years from Whittaker, finally achieved parochial status in 1920, when Father Alphonse Nowogrodski was appointed pastor.

At the beginning of 1870 St. Patrick's was still the only church in Wyandotte, but the congregation now comprised some seventy German families intent on forming a separate body. St. Joseph's was begun in the summer of 1870, and was dedicated by Bishop Borgess on November 5, 1871. The same day Father Leonard Unterreiner was assigned to the pastorate.

Trenton was organized as a mission of Wyandotte about 1863, when the village attracted many skilled workmen from Lower Canada to engage in the neighboring ship-building industry. The first

[46] There is a sketch of the parish in its own periodical, the *St. Mary's Bulletin*, for November, 1915. The name of the second church was changed from St. Michael's to St. Mary's.

[47] Farmer, *op. cit.*, II, 1315.

church, dedicated to St. Joseph was built in 1873, and the mission was attended from Wyandotte, Ecorse, or Rockwood down to 1895, when Father James Cahalan became the first resident pastor. The present church was built in 1931 during the pastorate of Father Timothy Bourke.

Another mission of Wyandotte in the same period comprised a group of about thirty families living on Grosse Ile. The mission does not appear in the Catholic Directory until 1876, but the church, an abandoned school building enlarged and arranged for the purpose, was in use in 1869 and was dedicated by Bishop Borgess on March 20, 1871.[48] Sharing in the modern development of Detroit, Grosse Ile became a residential suburb and the congregation grew large enough to warrant separation, in 1920, from Trenton to which it had been attached in 1895. Father John Richard Command built the present church in 1915, and Father Francis F. Van Antwerp was appointed to the pastorate in 1920.

[48] Record in DCA.

CHAPTER XXV

Indian Missions and Schools

I T WAS the quest for the soul of the Indian that brought the
Church to Michigan, and inspired the heroic labors that radiated
from the Straits of Mackinac. The first and only extension of that
missionary activity to southern Michigan has been described in the
chapter dealing with the St. Joseph Mission. When the missions were
resumed in the nineteenth century by Fathers Déjean, Bonduel,
Mazzuchelli, and particularly by Father Baraga, the Indians had been
pushed out of the southern portion of the state, and were congregated
in practically the same localities in which they had been found by the
Jesuit missionaries. These missions, therefore, belonged to the Diocese of Detroit taken in its widest extent, until they were assumed by
Bishop Baraga in 1854. There is no need here to amplify the accounts
which have already been written about them.[1] It is the purpose of this
chapter to present for the convenience of the reader a survey of the
missionary work identified with the priests of Detroit, or of the
Diocese of Detroit, and thus to supply certain omissions—some of
which have been indicated—in previous chapters.

The reader will remember that when the Jesuits came to the
Straits of Mackinac there were, to the best of our knowledge, no
Indians in the southern peninsula. It was their gradual return to the
haunts from which they had been driven by the Iroquois that led to
the founding of the St. Joseph Mission. In the southeastern portion
of the peninsula the return of the Indian population was contemporaneous with the founding of Detroit. Whatever personal, political,
and military advantages urged Cadillac to plant his settlement where
he did, it is nevertheless true that his avowed purpose was to withdraw the Indians of the northern lake region from the influence of
the Jesuit missionaries.

The majority of the Indians who came down to Detroit had been
for years in more or less close contact with the missionaries in the
north, had listened to their preaching—whether moved by it or not—
and were familiar with the external worship of the Church. Hence,

---

[1] Shea, *Hist. Cath. Miss. . . .* , 382–402; Verwyst, *Life and Labors . . . Baraga;* Rezek,
Hist. Sault . . . Marquette.

the early Recollects in the post had only to build on foundations that had already been laid. It is regrettable that no records of their missionary activities remain to amplify the bare entries embalmed in the St. Anne registers.

It is scarcely credible that Father Delhalle did not baptize at least a few Indian children. Yet, there are no entries dealing with the baptism of Indians signed by him. The first ones appear over the signature of Father De La Marche, who, as the reader will remember, was sent to Detroit in 1706 to assist Father Delhalle by taking over the missionary work to the Indians, and who arrived in the post a few weeks after his confrere had been killed. His first entry is as follows:

> Today, September 11, 1706, has been baptized Jean-Baptiste, son of Toussaint and of Shanonesse, Indians of the Huron nation. The godfather was Jean-Baptiste Gras, son of Michel Le Gras and of Jeanne Raudet. The godmother, Marianne Marendesu wife of Beauregard.
>   fr. Dominique De La Marche.

This entry probably refers to an infant as do succeeding entries, but that Father De La Marche occasionally caught bigger fish in his net is evident from the following record:

> Today, April 29 of the year 1707, has been baptized Louis Antoine cheanonroiihon surnamed Quarente Sols, chief of the Hurons aged 48 years, after having asked for it with entreaties. For godfather he had Messir Antoine De La Mothe Cadillac, commanding for the King at Fort Pontchartrain of the narrows.[2]

But the Recollect who stands out above the others for his devotion to the Indians is Father Cherubin Deniau, who was alone in Detroit from 1708 to 1715. In November, 1709, he began a separate register in which to record his Indian conquests, styling it the "Second Book of Indian Baptisms." The last entry occurs on May 11, 1714, and the volume contains the entries for about one hundred and forty baptisms. Here is one chosen at random.

> This day, March 10, 1710, was baptized by me, the undersigned Recollect missionary priests, a slave belonging to Michel Bezaillon and called Joseph Mikitchia, a Flathead, or in other words of the 8taki8 nation, son of the man named Pik8renta. The mother is not named here as the said slave, her son, told us that he did not remember her name. This slave is about eighteen years old. The godfather was Pierre

---

[2] This entry most likely refers to the prominent chief, "Forty Sous," who was implicated in the events that led up to the death of Father Delhalle, and who is mentioned several times in the Cadillac Papers. However, there were two chiefs of the same name.

Bourdon, voyageur, and the godmother Marianne Jeanne Masse wife of Michel Campos. . . .

And here is another entry, telling of an Indian slave who at last became greater than his master.

Today, the 22nd of January, 1711, has been buried in the cemetery of this place, at about eleven in the morning, with the ceremonies of the Church Catholic, Apostolic, and Roman the body of the deceased Joseph, of the Panis nation, called Escabia, a slave belonging to Sieur Joseph Parent living in this place, Fort Pontchartrain of the narrows, in age from twenty-one to twenty-two years old. He died in the communion of the same holy Church our Mother here-above named at about half past eleven of the preceding and past night after having shown the signs of a good and veritable Christian, and having also received the sacraments of penance and extreme-unction with evident contrition and true devotion. To this I certify, I, Recollect priest, performing the parish functions at the said fort. . . .

On May 12, 1714, Father Deniau began a third register for his Indian converts. Of the twelve leaves that it was declared to contain only four are extant. They contain twenty-four entries, the last of which is dated January 15, 1718. The majority of the entries are signed by Father Deniau, and as he returned to Quebec in 1715 the final ones are signed by Father Hyacinthe Pelfresne. Whatever the reasons for it may have been, no missionary work comparable in any way to Father Deniau's was undertaken for the next ten years. At the end of that period came Father De La Richardie to resume the Huron mission under Jesuit auspices, and there it remained down to the death of Father Potier in 1781.

During the turbulent years of struggle for the possession of the western country between England and the new nation born of the Revolution, the Indian had good reason to forget all that he had learned of Christianity. He was now the hired killer, pampered and indulged because of his cruelty and dexterity in warfare. The more his innate savagery was let loose the more useful an ally he became. It was not a time for missions. When the struggle was over, and the Indian had been contemptuously flung aside, as he was bound to be, no matter who won, the Church could again seek him out.

Bishop Carroll began to display his solicitude for the Indian in the western country as soon as he became certain of his jurisdiction. He sent a memorial to President Washington in which he pointed out the necessity of religious teaching for the civilization of the Indian, and the desirability of cooperation between government and church for so laudable a purpose. The President replied:

I have received and duly considered your memorial of the 20th ultimo, on the subject of instructing the Indians, within and contiguous to the United States, in the principles and duties of Christianity.

The war now existing between the United States and some tribes of the western Indians prevents, for the present, any interference of this nature with them. . . .

Impressed as I am with an opinion, that the most effectual means of securing the permanent attachment of our savage neighbors is to convince them that we are just, and to show them that a proper and friendly intercourse with us would be for our mutual advantage, I cannot conclude without giving you my thanks for your pious and benevolent wishes to effect this desirable end, upon the mild principles of religion and philanthropy. And, when a proper occasion shall offer, I have no doubt but such measures will be pursued, as may seem best calculated to communicate liberal instruction, and the blessings of society to their untutored minds. With very great esteem and regard, etc.[3]

In accordance with the sentiments here expressed, the President made recommendations to Congress, which resulted in the official sanction of the views held by Bishop Carroll.[4] The lake region being still in the hands of the British, the first missionary efforts were directed towards the Indian population of the Illinois country. Bishop Carroll having been invited to propose a missionary offered the services of Father John Francis Rivet, a French priest who had come to Baltimore in 1794.[5] The offer was accepted, and Father Rivet fortified by an official commission as "Missionary to the Indians," and a promise of a yearly allowance of $200 for his support, arrived in Vincennes to begin his work in June, 1795.[6]

Father Rivet thus became a neighbor of Fathers Levadoux and Richard, who were laboring together at the time in the missions adjacent to St. Louis. The former, familiar with the status of Father Rivet, naturally expected that some similar provision would be made for the Indians of Michigan with whom he became acquainted when he was sent to Detroit in 1796. In his first letter to Bishop Carroll from his new station he wrote:

The Indians are asking General Wayne for missionaries. I propose to get up a memorial on this subject which I shall place in the General's

[3] Quoted in Guilday, *Life and Times* . . . Carroll, 607.

[4] Shea, *Life and Times* . . . Carroll, 486–87.

[5] For a sketch of Father Rivet see two articles by the Rt. Rev. Camillus P. Maes in the Amer. Eccles. Review, XXXV; see also McAvoy, *The Catholic Church in Indiana, passim*.

[6] Father Rivet was one of the first victims of the devious and inept policies followed by the Government in dealing with its Indian wards. His own letters are quoted in the articles mentioned in the preceding note. A letter from Bishop Carroll to the Secretary of War, dated September 15, 1800, in which he exposes the plight of Father Rivet is quoted in the *Records of the Amer. Cath. Hist. Soc.*, XX, 59–60.

hands, and of which I shall send you a copy. It will be a sort of supplement to Mr. Rivet's and will enlighten you as much as the distance between places permits. . . .[7]

Father Levadoux was evidently giving much though to the Indian mission, for his second letter, written not quite three weeks later, was devoted almost entirely to the project.

> Lieutenant Governor Sargent has returned from Michilamakina and he tells me that the Indians of the cantons urgently request that they shall have missionaries. They have also sent their principal chiefs to General Wayne to make the same request of him. The hurons made a similar petition. (The Hurons live about three miles from here. They were converted by the Jesuit fathers and have always continued to practice their religion,—they want a priest and deserve to have one.) And the general and especially the governor seem to wish that these poor Indians should be helped. They showed me letters which they have written on the subject to the Secretary of State the contents of which he may communicate to the President of the United States. Doubtless they will have recourse to you and will ask you for men for this object. I am going to give you my views on the subject, though submitting them entirely to your judgment. If you decide to accept this mission, I think: 1— that not less than four priests should be appointed for it, men of no ordinary virtue and detachment; that one be chosen to act as superior and to regulate all the works of the mission. It is necessary that in a country where everything is extraordinarily dear their salary should not be less than five hundred dollars a year; that they be furnished, if they have none of their own, with the sacred vessels and all other things needed for the becoming celebration of the priestly functions. But especially is it essential that the priests have a common interest, that they be united in spirit, and for this end that they be members of the same society. . . . If, as the Governor asks, you consider absolutely that I ought to take part in this work it should not be so unless the burden is shared with my own confreres, and I firmly believe that for the success of an undertaking of such importance as this you need not hesitate to recall to their former place Messrs. David and Flaget as best fitted to make it a success. The same may be said of Mr. Richard. When there is question of great undertakings, one must know how to make great sacrifices. You can replace these gentlemen, but I doubt if you can find other evangelical laborers so suitable for the work which here presents itself. . . .[8]

These plans were too ambitious. Bishop Carroll could not possibly have found four priests to send to Michigan. And as for government support, the four missionaries, had they been sent, would have come as near starving as did Father Rivet. Nothing was done, and the only

[7] Ibid., 263–64.
[8] Ibid., 265–66.

further reference to Indians in Father Levadoux's extant letters is his mention of a band living near the Huron River:

> At six leagues from Detroit, in the territory of the United States, there are one or two Indian villages fairly well populated. The Indians belong to the Huron nation, are almost all baptized, and many of them are fervent Catholics. They were in part the founders of the church near mine, which belongs to the Diocese of Quebec. One side of it is reserved for them alone. Still, they are certainly my parishioners. To avoid difficulties I have not bothered them up to the present. I have thought it better to authorize the pastor of the Diocese of Quebec to continue in charge of them. He does not see the matter as I do, and has written to Quebec. I pray you to let me know your opinion. If I had another priest I would try to get them to build a chapel, for it is impossible for me to accommodate them in my church. . . .[9]

Father Richard, who came to Detroit to assist Father Levadoux in 1798, had his first real contact with the Indian population of Michigan in the following year, when he was sent on a missionary tour to the northern lake region. His impressions on that journey have already been recorded in Chapter XIV. The Indians in the neighborhood of Detroit were in a like degraded condition, for a similar reason, and Father Richard reports to Bishop Carroll in his best, newly-acquired English the casuistry of one of Detroit's conscientious and honorable bootleggers.

> An Act of the Congress has been promulgated lately regulating the selling of Spirituous liquors. but I am very much afraid, it will not stop much the incalculable evils that follow from this trade. it is forbidden only I am told (for I have not seen the act) to carry liquor to the indian villages. but liquor is sold to them here in town as much as they want, and every day in greater number than before, poor indians are to be seen drunk in street and ways. a merchant confessed to me that this act was not at all an encroachment to his trade of liquor, Because the act do not forbid to indians to carry liquors, and that merchants would now sell them here in Detroit in great quantity, and henceforth will have some of the indians themselves for their clerks in that branch of their trade. it is easy to see that every spirituous liquor brought in the ind. settlements by french or English traders will be declared as belonging to the indians. no man unacquainted with the trade of our backward countrye is able to foretell the cunning means inspired by the exhaustless wish of getting furs. . . .[10]

Father Richard was evidently deeply moved by the miseries of the Indians, but we have no knowledge of his having undertaken any

---

[9] Letter to Bishop Carroll, May 27, 1797. BCA.
[10] Letter dated May 19, 1800. BCA.

work for their betterment this early in his career. Left alone in Detroit, first by the departure of Father Levadoux, and then by that of Father Dilhet, Father Richard could not possibly do more than care for his parishioners up and down the river. Yet, as we have seen, the years between 1805 and 1811 make up the period of his most intense efforts in the educational field. Of all his school ventures the Spring Hill establishment was the most pretentious. Some reference to it was made in Chapter XV, but it is pertinent here to bring out the fact that Father Richard's primary, if not sole, purpose in undertaking it was to begin the rehabilitation of the Indians in Michigan, a purpose officially recognized by the federal government. This is plain from the preamble to his "Outlines of a Scheme of Education" presented to Congress when he was in Washington in 1809, and which summarized a previous plan submitted to President Jefferson at the instance of Governor Hull.

> . . . Sometime in the month of april in the year one thousand eight hundred and Eight to the request of the Governor of the Territory of Michigan, Your memorialist has drawn a Plan of Education to civilise the Indian children. The Said Plan was Sent to the President of the U. S. who approved it.
>
> Your memorialist Solicits your Honorable Body that a Select comity may be authorized to Examine the Said Plan of Education, in order that the Government may Give some assistance to put it into Execution. . . .

The first three articles of the "Outline" apply to the children of the Territory in general. The longest portion, beginning with the 4th article, is devoted to the education of Indian children, and the methods to be followed.

> 4. As the Indians seem desirous to have their children educated as the white people are, and offer to give them if a proper school is established, it is contemplated to admit them in our Seminary together with the white children. by living under the same roof, Eating the same bread, and receiving the same Instructions, they shall learn that they are all Brothers, and believe to be one and the same people and one family.
>
> 5. Every body knows, that the Indians will do nothing to feed or clothe their children at the Schools. Therefore if the Government wishes to have them civilized and make them useful members of society, as it has been so honorably expressed in many instances by the first magistrate and by all benevolent members of the whole Community, it becomes now as a duty on the part of the American white People to come to the assistance of their red brothers. the first council of a Sovereign People, will, no doubt, adopt so many poor orphans, and

will take measures as to make them participants of so many Blessings which are enjoyed in the state of civilization.

If a proper method is used, the civilization of young Indians shall be certainly successful. let us teach them the practice and theory of Agriculture and husbandry. let their time at the schools be properly divided between writing, cyphrings &c. and hoeing, gardening, plowing &c. let them make their own bred, raise hemp &c. let them make their own clothes, let them learn to build their own houses, let them take care of the sheep which will supply the wool to clothe them. let them meelk the cows, raise a large quantity of chiken &c.&c. let the house where they will be educated, be the deposit of the utensils of agriculture, of tools of various trades, of the spinning-wheels, which are annually distributed to the different Indian-Tribes; let it be a rule that such instruments shall be given only to such persons who will know the use of them; let those spinning-wheels or other machines and utensils be given as premiums at appointed times in the middle of many Spectators under the shade of trees planted by themselves, at the sound of the Musquetery and martial music executed by their companions of school, &c. Such public exhibitions should certainly excite the ambition of the children and draw the attention of their parents.—let it be a rule that at the end of their education, one cow, a pair of oxen or a horse, and a farm of so many acres of land more or less in proportion of the progress made by each, be given in reward at the public exhibition. . . .

A so laudable purpose as to civilise Indians would by itself justify the appropriation even of a large sum of money. it would attach those numerous Nations to our Government. a so generous act of Benevolence toward them shall certainly prevent a Sanguinary war, which should be totally destructive of the Settlements in the Territory of Michigan. in a very short period of time, it would be no longer necessary to have large bodies of troops in those Quarters. in case of a war with great Britain, these Indian children kept in a Seminary under the Superintendence of Government could be considered as hostages. humanity, Benevolence, I might perhaps say Justice, and certainly good Policy unite together to call the attention of the Representatives of a Sovereign & Independent Nation to patronize & assist in the most efficient manner a so valuable & highly important Institution which is so ardently desired either by whole Indians, or by all the white inhabitants in the Territory of Michigan

Washington January 20th 1809
Gabriel Richard.[11]

When the above was written the Spring Hill school had already been in operation for some months on the farm which Father Richard had leased from the Government on April 25, 1808, for the remainder of that year. He was now in Washington, confident of obtaining support for his enterprise. From existing documents it is certain that

[11] "Spring Hill Correspondence" in *Mich. Hist. Mag.*, XIV, 121–23.

Father Richard returned home fortified by a verbal arrangement with President Jefferson by which further rent payments were to be remitted, improvements at Government expense were to be allowed, and an annual compensation of $400 was to be granted to the Director. In November, 1809, Governor Hull made the following report on Father Richard's activities.

> This may certify, that the Revd. Gabriel Richard has improved the farm at Spring Hill, the summer past, which belongs to the United States, (formerly the farm of Mathew Ernest) and likewise the buildings, for the purpose of instructing Indian Children, in writing, reading, and the Mechanic Arts— That he has engaged in the business, as he states, in consiquence, of arrrangements, which he made the last winter with the President & Secretary of War— That I have advanced to him three hundred Dollars, furnished some provisions, and implements of husbandry to assist him in the institution, and that I have declined settling his account, and making further advances, on account of not having received instructions from the government for the purpose— I further certify, that he has had under his instruction, about twelve Indian Children, for a six months past, and they have made good progress, in learning, and that Mr. Richard, has incurred considerable expense, in making the establishment.
>
> Mr. Richard further states, that five or six persons have been constantly employed at his expense in teaching them to *read, write, spin, weave, making their clothes, cooking, &c* and I have reason to believe what he states is correct.
>
> The Children, & the parents of them, appear to be very much satisfied with their new condition.[12]

Father Richard had put too much faith in verbal promises. Jefferson was succeeded in March, 1809, by Madison, and no one in the new administration seemed to care what became of the Spring Hill experiment. Never doubting but that the promises made to him would be kept, Father Richard had leased the property again for 1809. But at the end of the year the rent was demanded of him, and, unable to pay it, he was obliged to transfer his school to less favorable quarters on the Loranger farm. The expenses that Father Richard had incurred for improvements on the Spring Hill farm were allowed him; but he received no compensation for his services, and moreover,

---

[12] *Ibid.,* 124. The parents might well be satisfied. Father Richard explaining the accounts which he submitted, probably along with this certificate of Governor Hull, has this to say of his Indian children. "Besides that every article that relates to the clothing is very high in this Place, I must observe that These Indians did come to our school almost quite naked, dirt and worms excepted. they are all now clean & in Good Condition. There is no doubt that their clothing will not be so high in proportion on the following years."

he was sued for the rent, and finally compelled to pay it in 1812, with interest down to the date of the judgment.[13]

Father Richard seems to have continued his school on the Loranger farm as best he could until the outbreak of the War of 1812. As far as we know it was not reopened after peace had been restored.[14] Nor have we any trace of how Father Richard's perennial interest in the Indian manifested itself for the next seven or eight years. This was the period marked by the unhappy divisions in his parish regarding the new location of St. Anne's, and the labors that attended the actual construction. As for the Indians they were gradually being forced to the northern lake region. By the Treaty of Detroit, made in 1807, they ceded that portion of their lands in Michigan comprised within a line drawn straight north from the Ohio border to a point near Ovid, and then northeast to meet the shore of Lake Huron at White Rock. In 1819, the Treaty of Saginaw added the territory bounded by Lake Huron, the Thunder Bay River, and a line drawn from the headwaters of the river to Kalamazoo, and then eastward to Jackson. By the Treaty of Chicago, signed in 1821, the Chippewa, Ottawa, and Potawatomi withdrew from the remainder of the southern peninsula south of the Grand River.[15]

It is in connection with this last treaty that we again find Father Richard actively engaged in Indian affairs. He must have had some previous relations, of which we know nothing, with the Potawatomi living in the southwestern corner of Michigan, for he tells us that he was urged by one of their chiefs to be present at the signing of the treaty to make sure that a Catholic, and not a Protestant, missionary should be given them.[16] Retarded by adverse weather conditions, Father Richard reached Chicago only to find that the treaty had

[13] These details may be verified by a study of the "Correspondence" mentioned in Note 11.

[14] In the *Mich. Hist. Mag.*, XIV, the editor of the "Correspondence" thus evaluates the Spring Hill experiment. ". . . Lastly there was a personal triumph for Father Richard waiting at the end of the long road of failure. When the War Department sought to formulate a plan of education that would measure up to the needs of the Indians, it took over the system presented by Father Richard to the United States Congress a decade before. The Government had at last caught up with the man who failed because he was ahead of his time. The circular of 1819 states explicitly that those who expected government aid must include in the course of study, in addition to reading, writing, and arithmetic, practical knowledge in agriculture and the mechanical arts for the boys, while spinning, weaving, and sewing must be taught to the girls. This plan adopted by the Government became the basis of all later training in the Indian schools throughout the United States. Deservedly then might Father Richard bear the title, "Father of Modern Indian Education."

[15] For minor corrections to these general statements see "The Indians of Michigan and the Cession of Their Lands to the United States by Treaties," in the *Mich. Hist. Colls.*, XXVI, 274–97.

[16] *Annales . . . Propagation . . . Faith*, III, 342–43.

already been signed, and that the Baptist Mission Board had been authorized to undertake what was later known as the Carey Mission at Niles.[17]

Father Richard could do nothing to resist the workings of a powerful and wealthy organization that attained its ends with the help, if not the connivance, of Government officials. It was the galling sense of his impotence in this matter that was largely responsible for his entry into political life. Having announced his candidacy for the office of Territorial Delegate, he again set out for the north. If elected, he would present in Washington proofs which the Government could not well ignore that the Indians were Catholic in their antecedents, and that they desired none but the successors of the Black Robe to minister to them. On his way to Washington in November, 1823, Father Richard sent some details of the past summer's activities to Father Rosati in St. Louis.

> . . . On this subject [Indian missions] I must tell you that when I was at Michili Makinac I had a petition drawn up by the Ottawas of l'Arbre Croche, where Father Dujaunais, the Jesuit, was stationed until 1765, asking the President for a Catholic missionary. One page and a half is covered with their Tautems.[18] Moreover, a few days ago I received a letter written in the Ottawa language by the son of one of the chiefs, and addressed to the President for the same purpose.[19] The Potowatomies have several times expressed the same desire. These last have more than 15 hundred warriors scattered here and there in more than thirty villages between the Detroit river and Lake Michigan. N.B. the Ottawas number more than 12 or 15 hundred individuals in the village of l'Arbre Croche alone, stretching nine miles along Lake Michigan at a distance of 40 miles from Michili Makinac. I intend to offer to the Jesuits this mission as well as many others at Green Bay, St. Joseph, and Prairie Du Chien; in these last two places, as also in Makinac, there are more than 60 or 80 Canadian Catholic families, or halfbreeds who nearly all speak the language of the Indians with whom many are joined in marriage; this would help in the conversion of the Indians. In my last mission at Makinac and Green Bay I married at least ten

[17] Walter N. Wyeth, *Isaac McCoy* (Philadelphia, 1895), 44–49.

[18] This curious document here reproduced is in the handwriting of Father Richard, and lies among the Michigan papers in the collection of documents dealing with Indian affairs once belonging to the War Department, but now housed in the Department of the Interior. It has been reproduced by O'Daniel, *The Right Rev. . . . Fenwick,* 301. However, in his praiseworthy attempt to decipher for his readers the more obscure portion of the document the reverend author has made some slight errors. "Thémoins" following the signature of Alexander Bourassa is not a proper name, but simply a misspelling for "temoins," witnesses. The signature following the last totem sign is not "W. Milpiel, père," but simply "W. McGulpin," and is followed by that of Mathew McGulpin.

[19] The location of the original letter is unknown but a French translation of it is given in the *Annales . . .* II, 103–04.

We the undersigned Chiefs, head of families & other individuals of the Tribe of the Ottawas residing at Wagana Kisi, (The Arbre croche i.e. crooked Tree) take this mode to communicate our wants and wishes to our most respected Father, the President of the U.S. wee return our best thanks to our Father and to Congress for his and their exertions to bring us, your very affectionate Children, to civilisation and to the Knowledge of JESOUS, the Redeemer of the red Skins as well as of the white People.

Trusting on your paternal affection, we come forward, and claiming the Liberty of conscience, we most earnestly pray that you may be pleased to let us have a teacher or a minister of the Gospel belonging to the same Denomination of the spiritual fathers which were sent to our parents by the French Government and have long many years resided amongst us occupied and cultivated a field on our own ground: we are willing to be taught Religion Arts, and Agriculture by Ministers of the same Religion (which is called the Catholic Religion).

We further invite such Teachers appointed by your Paternal affections to come and settle on the same spot, formerly occupied by f^{rs} Lefranc, f^r Dujaunay and others, that is to say on the shore of Lake Michigan near the lower end of our village at the Arbre Croche.

For so doing and granting your children their humble petition, they will for ever feel grateful and will pray the Great Spirit to bless you and your white children. — In witness thereof we have made our (marks) on this day the 12th August 1823

Nigassanessa   Bears Paw
Pandiquēkawa

monse

Matthieu Mc Gulpin witness
off. . . . . witness thakijigueame
sibinsi pale d'ours
ovitchigami

Wakechima — une carpe

2 grues. chichague

slanguinicanane — ours

pechacigeu

omackeose Piganache — un canard

piponahang — un dainde

Dapitagijigo

chagenichi pitobig — une aigle

sieritagane — un ?

giniwegoine miteuice — un esturgeon

Wasegijigo

Gagagegm

une grue cibogigane

Petition addressed to the President by the Ottawa Indians of Michigan asking for a Catholic missionary. In the handwriting of Father Richard and brought by him to Washington when he took his seat in Congress as Territorial Delegate. Original in the Department of the Interior.

Canadians or halfbreeds to full-blooded Indian women. Some of these knew their prayers in their language; others could sing hymns. This fact is a precious relic of the zeal of the Jesuits, and of the missionaries at the Lake of the Two Mountains near Montreal, where some of our Indians go occasionally to be instructed even to the point of being admitted to communion.

Last August I had the pleasure of admitting to the holy table at Makinac three Indian women who could sing hymns and could read in their language. I acquired from one of them a manuscript volume written by her son, which contains the catechism, prayers, and more than fifty hymns which she sang very well. I am taking it with me to present it to the President, and especially to Mr. Calhoun, the Secretary of War, who will view it with pleasure, and who has a particular zeal for the civilization of the Indian. I have no doubt but that we can obtain government aid, especially if we have the missionaries ready to place in the localities designated by the Government, or in those which I will propose. But we must hurry; the Presbyterians, Anabaptists, and Methodists are already in possession of several missions which should be in Catholic hands. You doubtless know that I am going to Washington as Delegate of Michigan Territory. I consulted Msgr. Dubourg, who urged me to accept the office if I were elected. God knows that my principal motive in accepting this charge is that I may labor more efficaciously for the good of Religion, and especially that I may bring the knowledge of the Gospel to these poor Indians. . . .[20]

Beginning with 1819 the Government had adopted an enlightened policy towards placing Indian education on a solid footing, and Father Richard found himself well received.[21] He reported to Bishop Fenwick, who was then in Europe, what the Government was disposed to do: $10,000 yearly was to be available for the support of Indian schools; two thirds of the cost of establishing such schools would be borne; $20 would be paid for every Indian child instructed.[22] Nothing more was necessary now but missionaries, and these, preferably Jesuits, the Bishop was urged to secure in Europe.[23]

Bishop Fenwick came back to the United States without having

[20] Letter from Sandusky, November 24, 1823. St. Louis Chancery Archives.

[21] See Laurence F. Schmeckebier, *The Office of Indian Affairs* (Johns Hopkins Press, 1927), 39 ff.

[22] Father Richard's letter is given in the *Amer. Cath. Hist. Researches*, X, No. 4, 155–56.

[23] The American Jesuits that might have been available for the missions in Michigan had been secured a few months before by Bishop Dubourg for the Indians of Missouri. While in Washington in 1822, the Bishop had obtained from the Government the promise of financial aid for his proposed missions. In March, 1823, he persuaded the Jesuits at the Whitemarsh novitiate near Baltimore to undertake the western missions. Two priests, Fathers Van Quickenborne and Timmermans, six novices, and two Brothers arrived in St. Louis on May 30. Among the novices was the future great missionary of the West, Peter De Smet. *St. Louis Cath. Hist. Rev.*, II, 67–72.

found the needed missionaries, although he had induced two young French priests, Fathers Bellamy and Déjean, to join his diocese. On his return to Detroit, Father Richard could do nothing more for the Indians than send Father Vincent Badin on a missionary tour. The following extracts from the long account of his journey, which has fortunately been preserved, describe his relations with the Indians.

On July 13, I regretfully quitted this dear flock [Green Bay] to return to Michillimakinac, where we arrived after a short crossing of 38 hours. Towards the middle of the last century, up to the year 1764, Fathers Le Franc and Dujaunay of the Society of Jesus took turns in visiting this mission. It was a pleasure for me to find twelve sets of vestments, many of which are still in good condition, four beautiful candlesticks and a crucifix, which have suffered little from the lapse of time. Circumstances prevented my staying longer on this island; I had to obey the pressing solicitations of the good Indians of l'Arbre-Crochu, the Ottawas or *courtes oreilles,* who ardently expected me.

On July 19, I again ventured upon Lake Michigan in a bark canoe manned by seven Ottawas who had come on purpose to get me at Michillimakinac, forty miles away. Three Frenchmen went with me as interpreters. We arrived at l'Arbre-Crochu an hour before midnight. The *paponas* (head chief of the Indians) immediately rejoined me. After a thousand demonstrations of joy and respect, he retired to his lodge; I and my party were accommodated in a tent that rose like magic on the sand. Early the next day we went with our baggage to the top of a hill about two hundred feet high. On my first arrival in Michillimakinac, I had told them to have a *wigwam* (a sort of tent or shelter) built in honor of the Master of Life; I dared not hope for more. What was my surprise to find on the top of the hill a pretty little chapel of undressed lumber, twenty-five feet by seventeen, which they had built in six days with no other tools than their tomahawks.

The exterior of this little building is covered with large pieces of bark, and the interior is trimmed with well-squared boards; benches had been placed on each side. This chapel, rude and simple as it is, can nevertheless be compared to the temple of Solomon; it has no iron or nails in its make up. My interpreters and I had now to erect an altar, something which the Indians did not know how to do; but they had prepared in advance the necessary boards. I did not fail to express my satisfaction. We had taken the precaution to bring with us the beautiful crucifix from Michillimakinac, and a few pictures with which to decorate the altar, and which they greatly admired. I wish you could have seen the modesty and recollection with which they and their children, headed by their venerable (paponas) patriarch, assisted at holy mass; I wish you could have heard their strident voices singing hymns in their language during the holy sacrifice. Several, seven in number, held prayer-books in our language, having learned to read French in a short time at Michillimakinac. In the midst of this wilderness they offered me the most enchanting spectacle. One could say of them what the sacred writer said of the first Christians, that they have one heart and one mind, so sincere are they in their conversion. . . .[24]

After a short stay at L'Arbre Croche Father Badin went on to visit groups of French Catholics around Mackinac, and along the St. Mary's River. On Drummond Island he met a number of pious Indians, who were attended occasionally by a Canadian missionary.[25] Returning to Mackinac he found Blackbird, the Ottawa chief, anxiously awaiting his arrival in order to present a letter which he was sending to Father Richard. The latter had written him, probably from Washington, that he was going to Europe to interest the Holy Father and the King of France in the Indians of Michigan. Here is the chief's answer.

I send my compliments to the Black Robe of Detroit, and to the great Black Robe of Rome, and to the illustrious father of the French, the king of France; I offer him my hand.

At present there are so many hats [whites] on our lands that we cannot kill enough game to feed our children. But above all we desire a Black Robe (makatekonia) who will come to teach us; we will listen to him, and will do everything he tells us to do.

There is too much whisky (grain spirits), and we shall be reduced to nothing. We desire to have at l'Arbre-Crochu a French priest who will teach us the way of salvation, and to be sober. The number of Indians at l'Arbre-Crochu is 635, men, women, and children.

Makate Pinetchi.[26]

Father Badin now made a second visit to L'Arbre Croche. Thirty Indians were baptized, and five of them made their first communion. A high mass was celebrated, at which the Indians made an offering of the "blessed bread." On the evening before his departure Father Badin buried a child whom he had baptized.

A young Indian carried the cross, two others were acolyte and censer-bearer, a Canadian had charge of the sprinkler, and another of the black stole. I wore a surplice and a white stole. All l'Arbre Crochu followed in silence and in the most perfect order, and formed the most extraordinary, the saddest, and the most religious cortege ever seen. . . . I had chosen the hour of night for this inhumation by the glare of torches, whose usage is unknown to the Indians . . . a married man was so deeply affected by this aspect of solemnity that he wanted absolutely to follow me to Detroit, to leave his wife and become a priest.

[24] *Annales* . . . II, 124-25.

[25] He was most likely Father Crevier, assistant to Father Marchand at Sandwich. We know that he was there in the summer of 1824. Letter of Father Marchand to the bishop of Quebec, August 5, 1824. QCA.

[26] *Annales* . . . II, 131-32.

Naively, he asked me if that were not possible, and it took all my rhetoric and my authority to persuade him to remain in his forest and his village.

As I have said above, the day following the funeral was fixed for my departure. I had the consolation of seeing again at dawn this throng of saints prostrate on the sand to receive the benediction of the *makate-konia* just before the oars were set in motion. . . .

On the way to Mackinac, Father Badin was entertained by a venerable Indian patriarch who had been admitted to his first communion by Father Du Jaunay, and who could not leave off speaking of the last Black Robe, whose mass he had often served. He pointed out to the priest the spot where Father Du Jaunay ordinarily had paced back and forth while reciting his breviary.[27] When Father Badin finally set out for Detroit in the middle of November, he carried another letter to Father Richard signed by all the headmen of l'Arbre Croche.

I thank you, my father, for having sent us a black robe who came to do charity to your children; that is what I desired. My father, your children have received the body of JESUS in their heart. There are many more who wish to receive it next summer. They can not thank you enough, for it is such a great pleasure for us, as was the visit of our father the black robe, Vincent Badin. We ask you to pray to the master of life for us who have had the happiness of making our first communion. We send you our best regards.

Father Badin's later missionary journeys—he touched at L'Arbre Croche again in 1826—were undertaken more in the interests of the scattered French groups in Wisconsin and Illinois. The next priest to devote himself to the Indians became Father Déjean, the pastor of Mt. Clemens. He went to Mackinac and L'Arbre Croche in the summer of 1827. The Indians had continued fervent in their religious practices, led by one of their number who had been instructed at Montreal. Twenty-one were ready to be baptized, and eight were admitted to first communion. Father Déjean spent some weeks among his converts, charmed, as Father Badin had been, by their piety and docility.[28] He returned in 1828, and this time he began some semblance of organization in the mission.

. . . I was quite busy during all the time I spent at Mackinac. I baptized fourteen persons, gave communion to twelve, and heard a hundred confessions. The Indians of l'Arbre-Croche came for me in a bark

[27] *Ibid.*, 135.
[28] *Annales* . . . III, 320–25.

canoe; it took only a day to reach their village. On the day following my arrival a good number of Indians came to be baptized, others to go to confession. I found a hundred and thirty converts fairly well instructed. . . . I made all the adults whom I baptized cut their hair in the French style, and I got them to promise that they would give up wearing those enormous earrings that sometimes hang from their noses; in a word, I effected all the corporal and spiritual reforms which I judged would better them. . . . I chose seven catechists who are to give instructions three times a week, baptize the dying, etc., and keep a list of their converts. Every month they are to endeavor to make converts in a locality where there are no Catholics. They are to assemble every Sunday in the chapel for prayers, hymns, etc. . . .[29]

The next visit to the Indian mission was made by Bishop Fenwick. In May, 1829, he began his long-delayed visitation to the northern portion of his diocese. Going first to Green Bay, and then to Mackinac, he arrived in L'Arbre Croche at the end of the month. Led by their chief, Assakinac, wearing a large silver cross on his breast, the Indians went down to the beach to assist the bishop out of his canoe, and then knelt to receive his blessing. After the visitors had been conducted to their tents placed around the little chapel, a deep silence fell upon the assembly broken only by the voice of the chief chanting the night prayers for his tribe. Early in the morning the Indians began to crowd around the bishop to make their confessions, which he heard through two interpreters, one for each sex.

. . . During divine service the attention and respect of the congregation was remarkable; at the elevation they sang a hymn in honor of the Blessed Sacrament, which had been translated from the French. I was astonished at the sweetness of their voices, and I found their chant more harmonious than I had expected. . . .

After the Mass, three marriages were blessed, the sacrament of Confirmation was administered to twenty persons, and Baptism was conferred upon a dozen others, among whom were two chiefs.[30] The Bishop was unable to take a bite of food until between two and three o'clock. During our meal we sat, Indian fashion, on mats; three chiefs sat near us whose names are: *Assakinac* or *Sansonnet, Papoisigan* or *Willowbark, Macatabanis* or *Blackbird.* The Indians of l'Arbre-Croche grow fine corn; they are clean, well-dressed, and superior in their manner of living to the wandering and ignorant Indians of other tribes. One hundred and twenty of them have formed a society to war upon the use of

[29] *Idem,* IV, 466–69.
[30] This event, of course, marked the first episcopal visitation, and the first conferring of Confirmation in the Diocese of Grand Rapids.

strong drink; they assured us that the society is increasing every day. . . .[31]

Reaching Detroit on June 21, Bishop Fenwick was determined to give the Indians of L'Arbre Croche a resident pastor. Here was a congregation of holy souls as fully deserving of priestly ministrations as any other in his diocese. Having already made two missionary excursions to the Indians Father Déjean was selected for the post. Provided by Bishop Fenwick with a sum of money, Father Déjean left his parish at the end of June, and went up to L'Arbre Croche accompanied by Elizabeth Willams and a Miss L'Etourneau of Detroit, who were to serve as schoolteachers.[32] Seeking the most advantageous location for his headquarters, he took up his residence in what he called the New L'Arbre Croche, or in what is now the village of Harbor Springs.[33] The enthusiastic Indians fell to work with a will, and by the end of the year a fairly large church had been erected, and a combined rectory and schoolhouse.[34]

Another, and perhaps a more interesting, result of Bishop Fenwick's visit to L'Arbre Croche, was his attempt to provide a native clergy for the northern Indian missions. He took back with him to Cincinnati two boys from the mission, both aged fifteen. One, William Macatebinessi, was the son of Chief Blackbird, and the other, Augustine Hamelin, was a half-breed. Placing them in his own seminary to begin their studies, the bishop sounded the Roman authorities as to the possibility of having the youths trained for the priesthood in the Propaganda College. A favorable answer was received from the prefect of the Propaganda, and on April 10, 1832, Father Rese left Cincinnati with the two candidates in order to see them safely on shipboard at New York.[35]

Unfortunately, Bishop Fenwick's hopes were not realized. William Macatebinessi had been at the Propaganda College just a year when

[31] The visitation is described by Father James Mullon in the *Annales* . . . , IV, 486–90.

[32] There is apparently some confusion regarding the identity of the teachers at L'Arbre Croche, if the names in the *Annales* . . . , IV, 491–96, and in the *Berichte*, I, 14 are compared. A letter from Miss Williams to her brother in Detroit is quoted in Sister Mary Rosalita, I.H.M., *Education in Detroit Prior to 1850* (Lansing, 1928), 73–74.

[33] The actual site of the old Jesuit mission at L'Arbre Croche has not been determined precisely, but was most likely on or near the site of what is now Cross Village, about twenty-five miles north of Harbor Springs on the lake shore. Father Badin visited the site but failed to give its precise location. He alludes to the cross which the Indians maintained to mark the site of the chapel. On the crude map of Michigan which accompanied his *Memoirs* Father Mazzuchelli, who also visited the mission site, marks the location as corresponding fairly well to Cross Village. The chapel built for Father Badin stood about nine miles north of Harbor Springs according to Father Déjean. See "Early Catholic Missions in Emmet County," *Mich. Hist. Mag.*, II, 324–29.

[34] The construction and size of the building is described by Father Déjean, *Annales* . . . , IV, 491.

[35] O'Daniel, *op. cit.*, 408.

he died of a sudden illness.[36] Augustine Hamelin later abandoned his studies, returned to Michigan, and became chief of his tribe.[37]

Of Father Déjean's fruitful labors among the Ottawa of L'Arbre Croche continuing down to May, 1831, one detail deserves special mention. Referring to the schoolteachers at the mission in his letter just cited Father Mullon wrote: "One of them has translated a prayer-book into the Ottawa language." Her work may have been the manuscript which Father Déjean brought to Detroit in the spring of 1830 to have printed. The writer has before him the quaint, little volume of 106 pages bound in red leather, half prayer-book and half catechism, whose mysterious title page is nevertheless printed in what was once the current language of Michigan.

Anichinabek / Amisinahikaniwa / Kicheanameatchik, Catonik, Otawak / Wakanakessi / Dejean Macate Okonoye / Moujac awabendan mesenayken.—St. Paul / Wyaotenong: / Geo. L. Whitney Manda Mesenahiken Hauseton./

1830 [38]

Father Déjean's modest effort was soon superseded by the long line of similar works that issued from the indefatigable pen of Father Baraga, and are now only rarities for book collectors. Still it was the first of the Catholic devotional works in the more important Algonquian tongues which have helped to preserve the faith of thousands of Indians, and which are used to this day.

Father Déjean's successor in the L'Arbre Croche mission was Father Baraga, who was installed by Bishop Fenwick on May 28, 1831.[39] The labors of this heroic apostle of the Indians have been so thoroughly described elsewhere that nothing more is needed here than a rapid summary of the developments that took place under

[36] The statement has often been made, for instance in the *Mich. Hist. Mag.*, X, 234, that William Macatebinessi was assassinated by an unknown hand as he was returning to Michigan to defend his people from encroachments by the whites. It appeared first in a *History of the Ottawa and Chippewa Indians of Michigan* written by William's brother, Andrew J. Blackbird. As a matter of fact Bishop Rese was notified of the student's death in a letter written by Cardinal Pedicini from Rome on July 13, 1833, and which is now in the NDA. A translation is given in Verwyst, *op. cit.*, 463–64. The pertinent passage is as follows: "Some time ago he complained of an internal pain, as a consequence, as he said, of an accident that happened to him in America, when a wheel passed over his breast. On the morning of the 25th of last June the rupture of an artery just in the aforesaid part of the body reduced him within a short time to the extreme (sic) and took him from this life. I gave this notice to Your Lordship for your information, and that with due circumspection you may communicate it to the young man's parents . . ."

[37] *Mich. Hist. Colls.*, XII, 621.

[38] From a copy in the DCA.

[39] Entry at beginning of baptismal register.

him.[40] No community of primitive Christians ever lived more holily than did the Ottawa of L'Arbre Croche under Father Baraga and his immediate successors.

> At five in the morning the Angelus bell was rung and the whole village assembled at the church for morning prayers, which were read aloud by one of the head-chiefs. Then followed Holy Mass, at which a great number assisted every day. Every evening the bell was rung again and all assembled for night prayers, at which they sang pious hymns in their native tongue. After devotions, he gave them a short catechetical instruction, which, of course, the poor, ignorant, but well-meaning Indians needed very much. On Sundays and holy days of obligation they had divine service *four times,* namely, early morning prayers in common, then High Mass at 10 A.M. At 3 o'clock in the afternoon were Vespers and catechism, and night prayers at sunset. . . .[41]

In May, 1832, Father Baraga began his missionary excursions by visiting a band of Chippewa living on Beaver Island. After a few days' instruction he had the consolation of baptizing twenty-two of them. From Beaver Island he crossed over to Manistique, where the Indians, aware of his coming, had already begun to raise a bark chapel. Father Baraga and his party immediately fell to work, and the chapel was completed on the very day of his arrival.

> I dedicated this little church to the honor of God under the name and patronage of His Virginal Mother Mary. When I made—in Europe —the resolution to consecrate my life to the (Indian) mission, I promised our dear heavenly Mother that I would dedicate the first church, which I would bless among the Indians, to her protective Name, for I am convinced that she continually prays to her divine Son for the success of our mission.[42]

When Father Saenderl, the Redemptorist, took over the mission at L'Arbre Croche in the fall of 1833, Father Baraga was ready to begin his labors on the Grand River where he had already, during a previous visit, baptized eighty-six Indians.[43] His mission building combining church, school, and rectory was dedicated on April 20, 1834.[44] But the Grand River mission was no haven of peace and consolation such as L'Arbre Croche had been. Although Father Baraga had a small flock of fervent Indian converts he was surrounded by a larger number of wild and dissolute Indians, rendered so—and probably

[40] In addition to the works of Verwyst and Rezek there are interesting accounts of Baraga's work in Vols. XXI and XXII of the *Amer. Cath. Quat. Review.*

[41] Verwyst, *op. cit.,* 114 ff. The author follows closely a series of Baraga's letters in the early volumes of the *Berichte.*

[42] *Ibid.,* 125.

[43] *Ibid.,* 143.

[44] *Berichte,* VIII, 36.

kept so—by the fur traders in that favored stamping-ground. There was, moreover, a Baptist mission, the Slater Mission, in the neighborhood, and he was exposed to the persecutions arising from religious bigotry. On one occasion he spent most of a night on his knees while a yelling, drunken mob tried to gain entrance to the mission building.[45] Whatever the reasons for his departure were, Father Baraga forsook his mission in February, 1835, and came to Detroit. The Ottawa were shortly afterwards moved out of the Grand River country, and it was left to Father Baraga's successor, Father Viszoczky, to witness the gradual transformation of the Grand River Mission into the first parish in the town of Grand Rapids. Of the several Indian settlements visited by Father Baraga from this center only one is named. In June, 1834, he dedicated to St. Joseph a little bark chapel near the swamps of Mashkigon. Today, the locality is the City of Muskegon.

In July, 1835, Father Baraga left Detroit to begin his labors in a new field—among the Chippewa Indians of the Lake Superior region. His first station was at La Pointe, where he remained until 1843. Then came the change to L'Anse, at the foot of Keweenaw Bay, where his only predecessor had been Father René Ménard. It was here that ten years later he received his nomination as Vicar-Apostolic of the Upper Peninsula of Michigan.

Despite the incessant toil imposed upon him by the arduous conditions under which he exercised his ministry, Father Baraga somehow found time to provide a body of religious literature for his converts, and to make a distinguished contribution to the study of American Indian languages. His first work was an Ottawa prayerbook designed to correct the defects which he found in Father Déjean's volume, and which was printed at Detroit in 1832. This was followed at various intervals by five volumes of a similar nature, and by a life of Christ. Between 1837 and 1850 Father Baraga published no less than nine volumes in the Chippewa tongue including a life of Christ, Bible stories for children, and a book of meditations running to 712 pages. In 1850 he published at Detroit his monumental "Theoretical and Practical Grammar of the Otchipwe Language." Three years later this work was complemented by the famous Chippewa dictionary published at Cincinnati.

The value of these works was so appreciated by Catholic missionaries that thousands upon thousands of Father Baraga's books were procured by missionaries engaged in evangelical work among the numerous Indian tribes of the wide-spread Algonquian races. They are still in use among the Indian missionaries in the Dominion Provinces in that great range of territory extending from Nova Scotia on the Atlantic to Van-

[45] *Amer. Cath. Quat. Rev.*, XXI, 122–23.

couver on the Pacific; while they are hand-books among the American missionaries laboring for the salvation of souls among the descendants of the expatriated Algonquians, who, fifty years ago, by the demands of American civilization, were removed from Michigan and transferred to the wild regions of Minnesota and the Dakotas, west of the Mississippi.[46]

We must now briefly outline the subsequent history of the L'Arbre Croche, or the Ottawa mission. Father Saenderl's successor in it became Father Francis Pierz, who was stationed there from 1839 to 1852. In 1847 he reported that he had over eighteen hundred Catholic Indians under his charge.[47] To lighten his burden Bishop Lefevere had sent him an assistant in 1845, in the person of Father Ignatius Mrak, the future Bishop of Marquette. The mission was now divided, and Father Mrak moved up the shore to become pastor of a new center at Cross Village, and to attend as his missions Beaver Island, and Manistique. To Father Pierz were left L'Arbre Croche, Muskegon and new missions at Burt Lake, and Grand Traverse.

In the Catholic Almanac for 1848 there is an interesting report on the state of his mission made by Father Pierz. After detailing the facts regarding the rise of the mission, and with which we are already familiar, he proceeds to describe the results that have been accomplished.

After the example of my predecessors, I have, with all energy and diligence, applied myself, not only to teach the Catholic religion and the sciences to our Indians; but also to instruct them in whatever is necessary to a good education and tends to civilization; and I see my endeavors so blessed and so fruitful, that this mission presents an evident example that the Indians are capable, not only of being brought up good Christians, (in which they by far surpass the whites) but also are susceptible of the highest civilization; for they are generally industrious and skilful in what they undertake; there are among them good carpenters, joiners, and coopers—they build neat and substantial houses. They are assiduous in cultivating their farms, which they bought from the government, and sell much fruit and vegetables. The women are also very industrious, and have made great proficiency in household economy; making all the clothes for their families, and mats, baskets and other fancy work with porcupine quills, which display great taste and skill.

In fine, I can truly assert, of the Indians of these missions, that they make such progress in their schools and in civilization as fully to justify their superiors; that they have gained the esteem of the whites, and deserve all the favor of our government.

[46] *Ibid.*, **XXII**, 46.
[47] Rezek, *op. cit.*, I, 351.

Father Pierz went to the missions of Minnesota in 1852, and Father Mrak later took up his residence at another Indian mission in Grand Traverse Bay. In 1855 the L'Arbre Croche mission was handed over to a little community of Third Order Franciscans headed by their erratic founder, Father John Weikamp.[48] The Franciscan Fathers of the Cincinnati Province accepted the mission in 1884, and have retained it to this day. The School Sisters of Notre Dame have conducted a school for Indian children at Harbor Springs since 1896.[49]

The L'Arbre Croche mission was the modern equivalent and continuation of the center established by the Jesuits at St. Ignace. Rivalling St. Ignace in importance was that other focal point of missionary endeavor in the lake region, Green Bay. Wisconsin Territory was included in the Diocese of Detroit until the erection of the Diocese of Milwaukee in 1844. The resumption of missionary work in the Green Bay district, abandoned after the departure of Father Chardon in 1728, must be ascribed particularly to three priests of the Diocese of Detroit, Fathers Mazzuchelli, Bonduel, and Van den Broek. From his station on Mackinac Island Father Mazzuchelli visited Green Bay in the fall of 1830, and made his first contact with the Menominee living in the neighborhood. A year later, evangelization was undertaken in earnest when Bishop Fenwick spent some time in the locality, and ordered the immediate beginning of an Indian school. The zealous Italian missionary gradually made his way into the back country, about a hundred miles from Green Bay, where lived the Winnebago, and by 1833 some three hundred of them had been baptized.[50] The center for missionary work was later shifted farther up the Fox River by Father Van den Broek, who established himself at Little Chute, or Kaukauna, in the vicinity of Appleton.[51] Father Bonduel, first at Green Bay, and then during the seven years that he spent at the Menominee reservation near Lake Poygan was remarkably successful in his efforts to advance the civilization of his charges.[52]

From this far corner of what was once the Diocese of Detroit we turn finally to the one mission that was established within its actual limits, the St. Joseph Mission. The gap between the closing of the mission in the 18th century and its reopening under Father Stephen Badin has already been bridged, and its definite termination result-

---

[48] *Ibid.*, I, 142–49.

[49] *Mich. Hist. Mag.*, II, 326–29.

[50] Mazzuchelli, *Memoirs, passim*.

[51] Numerous references to Father Mazzuchelli will be found in the *Wisconsin Historical Collections*.

[52] Father Bonduel wrote a Menominee prayer book which was printed in Europe. There is a copy in the NDA.

ing from the expulsion of the Potawatomi has been noted. But the exigencies of our narrative have compelled the exclusion of much interesting material dealing with the last phase of the mission, some of which may properly find a place here.

The Carey mission established in 1822 was apparently conducted by Protestant missionaries who were honestly devoted to the welfare of their Indian charges.[53] Materially the mission flourished; how much it accomplished in the purely religious field is problematical. Some of the Potawatomi may have been influenced by it, but the majority held too strongly to their Catholic traditions not to consider the mission an intrusion. They continued to appeal to Father Richard, who, of course, was utterly incapable of helping them. Finally, a delegation headed by Chief Pokagon came to call upon Father Richard in the first week of July, 1830. Father Stephen Badin reports the manner in which the chief presented his request.

> My Father, my Father, I come again to beseech you to give us a black robe, who shall teach us the word of God. We are ready to give up Whisky, and all our Indian habits; you send us no black robe, and you have often promised one. Must we then live and die in our ignorance? If you have no pity on us men, have pity on our children who will live as we have lived in ignorance and sin. We are left with our eyes closed and our ears stopped up. We are abandoned in our ignorance all the while that we long to be instructed in Religion. My Father, come then to pull us out of the fire, the fire of the wicked Manitou. There is an American minister who wished to bring us to his religion; but neither I nor any one in my village have been willing to send our children to his school, or to go to his preaching. We have kept the manner of praying that was taught to our ancestors by the black robe who was at St. Joseph in former times. Every morning and night we, my wife and my children, pray together before the crucifix that you have given me, and on Sundays we pray oftener. Two days before Sunday we fast until night, men, women, and children, according to the traditions of our fathers and mothers, since we ourselves have never seen the black robe at St. Joseph. These are the prayers they were taught. Judge whether I know them aright.

The chief then made the sign of the cross, and, falling to his knees, recited in his native tongue the Our Father, the Hail Mary, the Creed, and the commandments, without, as says Father Badin, "any hesitation or the least mistake."[54]

Father Richard solemnly assured Pokagon that a priest would soon

---

[53] See numerous references to the Carey Mission in the *Mich. Hist. Colls.*, particularly V, 146 ff.

[54] *Annales . . .* , IV, 546.

be sent to his village; but the chief had heard such promises before, and was not satisfied.

> My Father, tell me the truth. Is the black robe that you are sending really going to stay with us, your children? Is he going to remain only for a time? We wish to have a priest with us always.

Even at the cost of depriving the parishes attended from Detroit of priestly ministration for some months, Father Richard had decided to send Father Vincent Badin. Just then Father Rese arrived to make the visitation of the missions which Bishop Fenwick had been obliged to forego for that year. His reception by the Potawatomi, and the subsequent stationing of Father Stephen Badin in Pokagon's village have been referred to in a preceding chapter.

At the time of Father Rese's visit, the Carey mission was on the point of being abandoned. Through the activity of its superintendent, Isaac McCoy, the removal of the Indians to the West, as necessary for their welfare, had been decided upon by the Government. Whether the Indians were aware of this or not, they knew at least that the mission buildings were soon to be vacated. When Father Rese brought up the question of providing a chapel and quarters for the Catholic missionary, the Indians, after some discussion, found a simple solution. They had donated the mission lands and their proceeds for their own advancement, and now that the Protestant missionaries were retiring why should not the Catholic priest be given the use of the mission.[55] Urged on by the Indians, and accompanied by several of them, Father Rese called at the mission, and was led to believe that the wishes of the Indians would be met. However, when Father Badin arrived a month later the mission property had been turned over to the Indian Agent. The missionary had not come unprovided, and with his own funds he purchased fifty acres of land adjoining Pokagon's village for a mission site, and a humble dwelling which he converted into a chapel.[56] In a jocular mood he thus described his domestic arrangements.

> Know then that my chimney smokes so much that occasionally I have to put out the fire; the floor and the door are so full of cracks that I have all the drafts I could wish for. The roof is open in several places, and is today covered with a foot of snow that protects us from the cold; but when it rains or thaws we are either sprinkled or showered. My bed was a mat and a few blankets until September last when I acquired a mattress. I used it for two nights, and then out of hospitality had to surrender it to a friend who spent several months in the village. My table is

[55] *Idem*, 147.
[56] *Idem*, VI, 160.

a bench four feet long and ten inches wide; it suffices for two people who have only one dish to place on it. Sometimes we do without meat if the hunting has been poor, and then we eat corn meal and beans. At times we are without bread; but somehow or other we manage to get along. Thanks be to God, I have never felt better, and have never been happier.[57]

The results achieved by Father Badin paralleled the success of the Ottawa mission. Within a year he had from three to four hundred faithful converts at whose simple, earnest piety he marvelled.[58] A harder task than the teaching of religion was the breaking down of the Indian's prejudice against manual labor.

They have been repeatedly told by me that Almighty God had imposed upon mankind to eat their bread by the sweat of their brow, that we must do penance for our sins, and that laboring is a sort of penance very pleasing to God. . . . The men thought that labor was degrading and for women only. I had made them ashamed of such a plea, by observing that Almighty God has given more strength to man, in order to work more than woman. And I myself, weak and old as I am, take the hoe for a while, to undo their false pride in laziness and losing their time. . . .[59]

To serve as his interpreter until he could learn the language, Father Badin had taken with him from Detroit Father Richard's one-time schoolteacher, Angelique Campeau. She was indispensable to the missionary, and by her zeal and industry gained a remarkable ascendancy over the Indians. Father Badin relates that on one occasion, when he was away, his converts came to Angelique and urged her to hear their confessions. It was to be expected that she should engage in some sort of school work for the Indian children, and this is confirmed by Father Badin's statement that she taught them, using the spelling books that Father Richard had printed at Detroit.[60]

Some time in the fall of 1833 Angelique Campeau was relieved of her school duties by the arrival in Pokagon's village of two Sisters, secured presumably through the efforts of Father Badin. They came from his first mission-field, Kentucky, and were, or at least had been, members of the Sisters of Charity of Nazareth.[61] No trace of their

[57] *Idem*, VI, 175.

[58] There are two long letters by Father Badin describing his mission in the *Annales* . . . , VI, 154–77.

[59] Quoted from a long letter describing his work addressed by Father Badin to Bishop England of Charleston, and printed in the diocesan periodical, the *Catholic Miscellany*. Letter dated June 20, 1832.

[60] *Annales* . . . , VI, 171.

[61] Ann Jackson and Mary Whittaker made their religious vows at the motherhouse of the Sisters of Charity at Nazareth, Ky., the first in 1830, the second in 1831, and were known in the community as Sisters Magdalen and Lucina. The records of the mother-

work remains save a self-explanatory letter which they wrote to Bishop Rese in February, 1834.

We hope you will pardon us for intruding on your time and patience with these few lines. You perhaps will be a little surprised on our presuming to address you. But as we are the only sisters of charity in your diocese who have the honor of claiming your paternal care, it was not until our arriving in this place that we knew you were the Bishop of this mission, and from what I have seen and heard of you, I find no difficulty in speaking to you freely.

Rev. Father, it is impossible for us to express our feelings on the evening of our arrival here, we were very much fatigued from our journey in consequence of bad weather and bad roads, and still to add more on entering the place of our destination which looked more like a house for criminals than for christians. I thought my heart would break, I felt as though I had left all that was near and dear to me. . . .

Dear Father, permit me to tell you that we are so happy now, and content in the participation of the many wants of human nature of which we are deprived, that we would not exchange it for any other situation. We are much edified at the exemplary life of the Indians. I could not believe that such piety existed among them. On the contrary I always believed them to be a very barbarous people that had neither laws nor religion, but I am now convinced of their sincerity and simplicity, and also the Rev. Mr. Deseille. I think he is a very worthy and zealous Missionary. Rev. Father, I understand you intend visiting this place in the Spring. Certainly it would afford us much pleasure, we should not presume to invite you of ourselves, though we desire so much to see you. It would also be very gratifying to you to see the progress of the Indians in Catholicity. We recommend ourselves to your prayers.

Sisters of Charity.[62]

---

house disclose that both Sisters left the Sisterhood in 1833, and there is no further reference to them. On the reverse of a letter in the NDA, written February 16, 1834, from Fort Wayne by Bishop Flaget to Bishop Purcell there is the following postscript:

"Mr. O'Hara's letter informs me that Mr. Whittaker of Cincinnati wishes to receive some intelligence about her (sic) sister, one of the two excellent Charity Sisters now in the Indian village near South Bend, on St. Joseph's River. I intimated to her the desire of her brother. Meanwhile he will be happy to read the following extract of a letter written to me six weeks after their arrival at the Indian village:

My Dear Father: I am quite glad to inform you that we are so happy that we would not exchange our situation for any thing. Eliza Jackson. Sister Clarissa Whitaker wrote me three times in French, informing me only that she was in good health and hoped to see me return home soon. . . ."

Despite the disparity of Christian names the two Sisters with Father Badin must be the two who left Nazareth in 1833.

[62] The original is in the museum at Nazareth College, and liberties were taken with the punctuation and spelling to make it intelligible. Some time in 1834 the Sisters began a school in the new mission established by Father Badin on the site of the present Notre Dame University. He gave up the mission in 1835, and all trace of the Sisters is

The reference to Father Deseille, who, as the reader may remember, had come to assist Father Badin in 1832, indicates that by this time he was in sole charge of the mission. A year later we see him through the eyes of Bishop Bruté of Vincennes who visited the mission in May, 1835, while engaged in the first inspection of his diocese.

From Chicago, we went round the end of Lake Michigan to the river St. Joseph, and the mission of the Rev. Mr. De Seille, at the Indian village of Pokegan, situated just outside our diocese, and in that of Detroit. This mission was established many years ago, by the venerable Mr. Badin. Mr. De Seille has lived for three or four years at Pokegon's village. He has there, and in the neighborhood, more than 650 Catholic Indians baptized. A large number of their huts are built around the chapel, which is constructed of bark, with a cross erected behind, and rising above it, and filled with rudely-made benches. The Indians begin and end their work without hammer, saw, or nails; the axe being their only implement, and bits of skin or bark serving to fasten their pieces together. The room of the missionary is over the chapel, the floor of the one forming the ceiling of the other. A ladder in the corner leads to it, and his furniture consists, as did the prophet's, of a table and chair, and a bed, or, rather a hammock swung on ropes. Around the room are his books, and the trunks which contain the articles used in the chapel, as well as his own apparel. He spends his life with his good people, sharing their corn and meat, with water for his drink, and tea made from the herbs of his little garden. He abjures all spirits, as all the Catholic Indians are forbidden to touch that which is the bane of their race, and he would encourage them by his example. I attended at the evening catechism, prayers and canticles, and, in the morning, said Mass, at which a large number assisted. Through the interpreter, I addressed a few words to them.[63]

In 1836 Father Deseille transferred his headquarters from Pokagon's village to a new center in Marshall County, Indiana.[64] Al-

---

lost. These details are based on a passage in Bishop Bruté's description of his visitation made in 1835.

"On Thursday evening we arrived at South Bend, a little town beautifully situated on the high banks of the St. Joseph River. . . . Crossing the river we visited 'St. Mary of the Lake,' the mission house of the excellent M. Badin, who has lately removed to Cincinnati. He had a school kept there by two Sisters, who have also gone away, leaving the place vacant. The 625 acres of land attached to it, and the small lake named St. Mary's, make a most desirable spot, and one soon I hope to be occupied by some prosperous institution. Rev. M. Badin has transferred it to the Bishop on condition of his assuming the debts, a trifling consideration compared with the importance of the place." Herman Joseph Alerding, *History of the Catholic Church in the Diocese of Vincennes* (Indianapolis, 1883), 138.

[63] *Ibid.*

[64] For details of Father Deseille's work in Indiana see Sister Mary Salesia Godecker, O.S.B., *Simon Bruté De Rémur, First Bishop of Vincennes* (St. Meinrad, Indiana, 1931), 311-27. Angelique Campeau seems to have remained in the Potawatomi mission until the death of Father Deseille. She was with him in 1837. *Ibid.*, 316.

though he continued to attend the Potawatomi until his death in the following year, this change may be looked upon as the definite ending of the St. Joseph mission. In 1838 the Indians were rounded up for deportation to the West, and none remained but the band led by Chief Pokagon.[65] His subsequent purchase of land in Cass County, and the gradual development of the Indian settlement into the parish of Silver Creek has been touched upon in a previous chapter. The ultimate fate of the Indian group has been told by Father Edward Jacker in this melancholy passage.

In the earlier part of this century, when the entire territory which now forms the dioceses of Detroit, Grand Rapids, Fort Wayne, Chicago, and Milwaukee, was travelled over by two or three missionaries, devoting their attention to both natives and thinly-scattered white settlers, quite a number of Indians, belonging to one of the more developed branches of the Algic family, were brought into the fold and not badly instructed. The work of evangelization was interrupted by the forced removal of the tribe. A few scores of Christian families, however, having bought land, were allowed to remain in their ancient home. They built a church, and have never since been entirely destitute of spiritual succor. But the visiting missionaries, being encumbered with the charge of white congregations, could pay them but passing attention, and never learned their language. As time went on every remaining acre in that section—excellent land—was bought up by immigrants from the East, and more of it was needed. *That soil was too good for the Indians.* To drive them out was not practicable. To shoot them down would have been unchristian and dangerous. But those simple people loved fine horses, shining broadcloth, glittering apparel; nor were any of them averse to the social cup. All these luxuries, together with the ordinary staff of life, they were liberally supplied with by their Christian neighbors, against mortgages, of course, on their goodly "forties" and "eighties." The result need not be described. A remnant of the band still linger around their old chapel, gaining a poor livelihood by plaiting baskets and gathering berries. They cling to the faith, and each visit of the priest is a holiday with them. But their life is sapped, with the exception of a few who have withstood the temptation and still hold property; they are wrecks, physically and morally. Few children are born or survive. They have no future in this world.[66]

[65] Some of the Potawatomi who eluded capture by the soldiers made their way to Canada, and took refuge on Walpole Island, the reservation already occupied by the Chippewa and Ottawa. In 1844 the Jesuit Fathers from Sandwich established a mission station on the island, but were obliged to abandon it in 1850. See Édouard Lecompte, S.J., *Les Jésuites . . . XIX Siècle*, 183–92. The Potawatomi who were deported to the West came under the care of the Jesuit missionaries, and formed the famous Sugar Creek mission. See an interesting account of it in the *St. Louis Cath. Hist. Rev.*, II, 88–96.

[66] *Amer. Cath. Quat. Rev.*, XI, 722. This was written in 1886. At the present time there are from seventy-five to one hundred Indians living for the most part in Hartford Township in Van Buren County. St. Dominic's church, built for them at Rush Lake by Father Baroux, in 1864, stands a deserted, dilapidated structure.

The means by which the Indian missions of the diocese were supported now calls for some consideration. It was only with the funds which he received from the Society for the Propagation of the Faith, and the Leopoldine Association, that Bishop Fenwick was able to establish the first three missions in the diocese: L'Arbre Croche, Green Bay, and St. Joseph. Late in 1831 he went to Washington to lay before Lewis Cass, then Secretary of War, his claim to a share of the funds destined for the education of the Indians, and promised to them in the course of the various land cessions. The grounds for his claim were set forth in the following letter.

Permit me to call your attention to the Petition of the Ottawas tribe of Indians dated at Michillimackinac on the 14 June 1829, which is inclosed in this communication; and as the Bishop, alluded to in that petition, under whose direction the schools herein named are established, to ask not only the relief they have prayed for but all & every assistance you can give to aid one under the Act of Congress in such cases made and provided. You will perceive by the endorsement upon the copy of the Act of Congress on that subject, which is also enclosed, that relief has not been sooner extended to those unfortunate people because it was represented that at the time the application was made for them, "there were no funds at the disposal of the Indian Department."

I have anxiously waited until now, and am pleased to know from the personal interview I had with you in your office on the 21 Inst. that such is not the case at this time, and as no one knows better than Yourself the real situation of those people & the great advantages they already received & will hereafter receive from the establishments I have made to improve their condition and to instruct them "in the mode of agriculture suited to their situation," and "for teaching their children in reading writing & arithmetic and for performing such other duties as may be enjoined," I feel confident that as full & ample [an] allowance for them will be made as it is in your power to grant. . . .

In addition to these remarks, in order to enable you, Sir, to form a proper estimate not only of the plan and expenses I have already incurred in forming these establishments, but also of the amount of aid that may be advantageously extended by the Government I beg leave to make the following statement, after first observing that the relief asked for by me is in favor of *full blooded* or *pure* Indians, as it was intended by the Act of Congress alluded to.

The school established at Arbre Croche in June, 1829, contains 60 pupils who are *fed, clothed, & instructed* by *two females* half Indians, and superintended by the Priest. *Four children* of that tribe are actually under my care & in my schools at Cincinnati—tho' two of them are [illeg.] and *three others*, pure Indian, are by my direction placed under Tradesmen at Mackinac to learn the blacksmith & carpenter trades. I have advanced for the promotion of the above establishment, since it commenced, *twelve hundred dollars.*

A school similar to the above mentioned, conducted in the like manner containing *30 Pupils* established under my direction in September, 1830, among the Pottowatomies in the settlement of Pokagon the chief, on river St. Joseph, Michigan, 5 or 6 miles distant from the Carey mission. Also one at Green Bay in June, 1831. And I would respectfully suggest that *three thousand dollars* would be advantageously applied to those objects—Were reference made to the respective Indian Agents in those districts of Michigan T. more ample & more satisfactory information might be obtained.[67]

Although the bishop was not compensated for his outlay some measure of relief was granted him, for he was informed that beginning with January, 1832, the Government would allow him $1000 a year for the support of his Indian schools.[68] By the death of Bishop Fenwick, and the erection of the Diocese of Detroit, Bishop Rese became the depositary of the fund, and the agent responsible for its distribution. The following letter is one of the earliest of the reports which he made to the War Department.

I received your favor of the 11th June last, wherein you direct me to send in a statement exhibiting the condition of the schools for which a grant of one thousand dollars has been made in Decb. 1831. You remind me also of the regulation which requires, that reports concerning this information should be transmitted to the office of Indian affairs in the Department of War, prior to the first of Novb. in each year. Your letter reached me a few days before I set out for the visiting of those missions, and I deferred answering it until my return to Detroit last Novb. I have sent in to the above office the information of all the mission schools then under my direction. The Grand River school has been since added to them, as also the mission of the Sault. All these communications were sent by me to my agent, the Very Revd. Mr. Matthews, of Washington City, with the request to consign them to the proper office as soon as possible. The schools under my direction are six in number, namely, Arbre Croche, St. Joseph's, Grand River, Green Bay, Winebagoes and Sault St. Mary. All these missions have been established by the deceased Bishop Fenwick and myself, and out of our own funds. The Indian Station of Arbre Croche alone costs me every year at least as much as the Government grants me for all the Indian schools; and they had cost us several thousand dollars before any aid at all was granted us by government; the number of pure Indian children of each one of these schools amounts to about fifty to eighty, but for the want of means to board these children, they are often absent,

[67] Letter dated November 30, 1831. War Department Papers in Bureau of Interior, Washington.
[68] Second letter dated December 16, 1831.

particularly when their parents are occupied in hunting and in their sugar camps. The plan of our missions is first to christianize the Indians and then instruct them in reading, writing, and the mechanic arts, and I venture to say that unless this plan be followed on all other missionary stations of whatsoever description they may be all attempts at civilizing the Indians will fail. All Indians of our missions are well clad, pay their debts punctually, and not a drop of liquor of any description is seen among them. . . .

For the Menominies and Winebagoes I have incurred considerable expences. An account of what I expended for the civilization of the Menomini Indians, not including even school expences was presented to his Excellency, the late Governor Porter, a few days before his death, who acknowledged the debts to be just, and promised most assuredly that they should be paid, but when I reached Green Bay I found Colonel Boyd, the Indian agent, had got instructions to pay the Episcopalian mission the whole sum of the two thousand dollars destined for the civilizing and educating the Menomini Indians. . . .

It may not be amiss to add here a sketch of the annual expences of the Arbre Croche mission.

1st. Mr. Letourneau teaching school and the carpenter trade has been at the mission since 1829.

His board annually per approximation...............$	100
" salary "	100
Mr. Aloys, Blacksmith by trade, lived at the mission two years; his board annually........................	100
No salary but clothing.............................	50
Iron for blacksmith and tools for Indians learning the carpenter trade................................	100
Interpreter's salary................................	100
Boarding him and his wife who does the kitchen work of the house..	150
A Female Teacher clothed.........................	50
" " her board......................	75
Priest's or Superintendent's boarding.................	100
His clothing etc..................................	100
An Arbre Croche pure Indian girl at the female Academy of Detroit....................................	100
An Indian Boy who returned from Rome because of his health, annually.................................	100
For printing and binding Indian books $600; and would amount annually to.............................	100
Sum total...........$	1125

The other Missions including the erection of the necessary buildings, namely, houses, schools, and chapels, cost me nearly the same amount. An account transmitted to the War Department by the Revd. Theodore Badin, who directed the St. Joseph Mission for several years, will prove my statement, and I beg you, Dear Sir, to use your kind influence that at least a part of the expences of said account, if not all, may be refunded to me, and you would then enable me to prove that the Indians can be civilized and become an ornament of Society.

I remain Sir most respectfully your devoted and humble servant, Fred. Rese, Bishop of Detroit.[69]

In another similar report made in 1837, the number of schools rises to eleven by the addition to those already mentioned—save St. Joseph's, which is discontinued—of schools at "Grand Kokalin, Fox River," Cross Village, Mackinac, St. Ignace, Fond Du Lac, and La Pointe. The government appropriation kept pace to some extent with this development, for in the same year the allotment was increased to $2400, and the payment of this amount was assured over a period of twenty years.[70]

Bishop Lefevere's administration of the fund for the education of the Indians lasted down to 1854, when the missions were handed over to Bishop Baraga. His first report made in 1843 is interesting enough to be quoted in full.

Tribe instructed.	Location.	Teachers.	Scholars Boys	Girls	Total	
Ottawas	Arbre Croche	R. F. Pierz prin. Mary Ann Fisher	35	34	69	
Ottawas	La Croix	D. Eniwechki Mich. Kinis	25	29	54	all pure
Ottawas	Middletown	Mich. Gosigwad	17	10	27	Indians
Ottawas	Cheboigan	R. F. Pierz	average 16			
Chippewas	Sault St. Mary	P. Cadotte	16	17	33	mixed
Chip. & Otts	Fox River	R. V. D. Broeke	22	37	59	
Chippewas	Manistie	Paul & Anthony Matchiging	average 40			pure Indians
Ottawas	Grand River	R. A. Viszosky	average 20			
Chippewas	Mackinac	Martha Tanner	average 40			mixed
Chippewas	Pt. St. Ignace	J. Hamelin	average 30			

N.B. In all these schools spelling, reading, writing are invariably taught; & also ciphering & geography to those that are more advanced. At the stations of Arbre Croche & Mackinac we have also introduced sewing, knitting, trimming with porcupine, etc. The proficiency of the scholars who regularly attend, is in general very satisfactory, & some have improved beyond all expectation. The great majority of these children has natural capacities enough to learn any science or trade but the great difficulty is to train them up to steady habits & assiduity. For many of them are so irregular in attending, & find so many reasons to absent themselves from school, that it is even difficult for many teachers to know the exact number of those who have attended their

[69] Letter dated September 25, 1834. Same source.
[70] Bishop Lefevere makes a notation to this effect in his Letter Book.

school in the course of a year. However, as nothing but religion can civilize & bring them to a sense of their duty we entertain the most sanguine hopes that the influence of the Catholic faith will soon obtain in them that desired effect. The Indians in our stations are fast embracing that religion & we observe with deep sensations of joy that so soon as they have subjected themselves to the mild yoke of Christ their savage dispositions and wild propensities begin to disappear; they become enamored with the beauty of virtue; industry, sobriety & morality are made chief objects of emulation among them & their attention is gradually turned to all the necessary parts of domestic economy. Justice & uprightness in their dealings & charity towards each other become also their great characteristic. So that we have great reason to believe that the period is fast approaching when it will be said with admiration, particularly of the stations of Arbre Croche, La Croix, Middletown & Cheboigan: behold these Indians are really civilized, they possess all the virtues of civilized people without being tainted with their vices & immoralities.[71]

The agreement entered into between Bishop Lefevere and Bishop Baraga virtually closes the story of Indian missions in the Diocese of Detroit. It expired with the death of the latter in 1868; but by that time the missionary stage was over. Harbor Springs continued to be under Bishop Borgess the Catholic center for the Indians of the lower peninsula, as it is to this day, not merely as an Indian mission but having regular parochial status. With the erection of the Diocese of Grand Rapids in 1882, the Diocese of Detroit severed its last bond with Indian mission history.

[71] Letter press copy in DCA.

CHAPTER XXVI

Education

I T IS hardly necessary to preface a survey of Catholic education in the Diocese of Detroit with an apologetic for this primary and essential activity of the Church, the instruction of her children. Her right and duty to so occupy herself are as old as her Divine Commission. In the United States the Church has providentially been left free to build up her splendid educational system. It is not only the concrete embodiment of fundamental Christian principles, but, as well, a magnificent testimony to the faith and self-sacrifice of the Catholic laity who have supported it. Therefore, a record of accomplishment in the field of education must form an integral part of every diocesan history. Such a record it is the purpose of this chapter to present in some detail, thereby establishing the contribution which the Diocese of Detroit has made to the impressive total of Catholic educational endeavor in the United States.

However, the beginning of Catholic education in Detroit, as the reader may readily surmise, antedates by far the erection of the diocese. It leads back through the ambitious projects of Father Gabriel Richard to the misty years of the French regime in Michigan.

The founder of Detroit, in his concern for the welfare of his settlement, was alive to the necessity of providing some educational facilities, no matter how meager. Even before Detroit was established he had visioned a little band of Ursuline Sisters, who were to tame the wild children of the forest by their gentle grace.[1] In 1703 he wrote to the Minister:

> Permit me to continue to persist in representing to you how necessary it is to set up a seminary here for instructing the children of the savages with those of the French in piety, and for teaching them our language by the same means.
> The savages being naturally vain, seeing that their children were put amongst ours and that they were dressed in the same way, would esteem it a point of honor. It is true that it would be necessary at the beginning to leave them a little more liberty, and that it would be necessary for it to be reduced merely to the objects of civilizing them

[1] *Mich. Hist. Colls.*, XXXIII, 99.

and making them capable of instruction, leaving the rest to the guidance of heaven and of Him who searches hearts.

This expense would not be very great. I believe, if His Majesty grants the seminary of Quebec a thousand crowns, it will begin this holy and pious undertaking. They are gentlemen so full of zeal for the service of God, and of charity towards all that concerns the King's subjects in this Colony, that one cannot tire of admiring them, and all the country owes them inexpressible obligations for the good education they have given all the young people, for their good example, and their doctrine, and it is that which has produced very good success in the service of the church in New France. I venture to tell you that you cannot begin this work too soon; if you fear its expense afterwards, I will supply you with devices for continuing this bounty to them by taking it on the spot, without its costing anything to the King.[2]

Cadillac was no more successful in this than in his other requests for support.[3] As far as we know, none of the commandants who succeeded him took any interest in urging some similar project. Indeed, there was little incentive for their doing so. For a long period following the Fox War the settlement made little progress and ran the risk of being abandoned. Many of the early settlers disgusted with Tonty's regime returned to Quebec. About 1730, there were only thirty families in Detroit and its vicinity, and the government was ready to give up the post by withdrawing the slender garrison.[4] But the course of events brought out the military value of Detroit, and in 1747 the government made a determined effort to increase its population by offering free land and supplies to all voluntary settlers. Dating from this rebirth the progress of Detroit has been continuous.

In Chapter X reference was made to the efforts of Bishop de Pontbriand to provide a band of Sisters of the Congregation to undertake school work at Detroit. It will be noticed that his activity in the matter coincided with the renewed interest in the settlement. The parsimony and dilatory tactics of the government delayed the project, and when it could have been realized by private initiative the thin cry from Detroit for schools was lost in the rumbling of impending warfare.

During the entire French regime there were priests living in the

[2] *Ibid.*, XXXIII, 167.

[3] Burns in his *Principles, Origin . . . School System . . . States*, 87, commenting on the foregoing passage states: "The school was undoubtedly established." There is not the slightest evidence for so believing.

[4] Burton, *op. cit.*, I, 113. Some idea of the number of children in Detroit can be gathered from the same reference which states that between the years 1701 and 1730 there were 143 baptisms, 26 marriages, and 72 deaths. Between 1730 and 1740 there were 156 baptisms, 27 marriages, and 73 deaths. During the whole of the French regime 998 baptisms were recorded.

settlement, and it is almost inconceivable that none of them should have paid attention to the education of the children. A man of Father Bonaventure's stamp, for instance, with his scholarly instincts, could scarcely have been as happy as Father Crespel makes him out to be unless he were engaged in some such occupation. Of course we are referring here to the imparting of secular knowledge. As far as religious teaching is concerned, that was certainly given. The preparation of the children for their First Communion under the old French system entailed a long and scrupulously conducted course of instruction. The children whom Chaussegros de Léry beheld tagging wildly after a deer that had broken through a breech in the palisades had just been dismissed from their classes in catechism. This bit of actual evidence, slight and alone as it is, confirms a very valid presumption.

The first schoolmaster of whom we have any knowledge is Jean-Baptiste Roucout.[5] Where he came from no one knows; apparently he had no antecedents in Canada.[6] The first sign of his presence in Detroit is afforded by his signature in the St. Anne register, appended to the record of a burial which took place on March 18, 1760. He married Marie-Joseph Deshêtres on May 15, 1765, and a year later, brought a tiny Marie-Joseph to Father Bocquet to be baptized.[7] In the record of the baptism the father is called "master of the Christian schools in this town, and choirmaster of this parish."

Apart from these details our only information concerning this interesting figure is supplied by two documents written in 1791, at a time when he seems to have been the victim of a real injustice. The first is a testimonial from the wardens of St. Anne's, dated May 2, 1791, wherein it is declared that "from 1760, the Sieur Jean-Baptiste Roucout has been established and received as choirmaster, and master of the parochial school of this parish, and that he has conducted and discharged both these employments with all the exactness of which a good subject is capable."[8]

The second document is a petition addressed by Roucout himself to the wardens of St. Anne's, which is self-explanatory.

> . . . I refer to the house in which I am living, and which once belonged to the church of Ste Anne, having been acquired in favor of the said church by M. St. Andre, the chief warden, in seventeen hundred and sixty-five, from M. St. Bernard for the sum of twelve hundred livres. The said gentleman consented to sell only on the condition that

[5] The name has been variously spelled but there is no reason for misreading the flowing signature in the St. Anne register.

[6] He is the first of his line in Tanguay's *Dictionnaire des Familles Canadienne.*

[7] Farmer, *op. cit.*, 720, gives the year of the marriage as 1755. This is in error.

[8] In QCA.

the house would give free lodging to the chanter, and would serve for holding school and other Christian instruction as long as the said chanter should continue in the service of the church, and should be able to fulfill the two charges. . . .

I had already been living in the house for five years before it was purchased, exercising in it the duties for which I had been hired, and which I have always exercised down to the present despite many vexations. In seventeen hundred and eighty-two, in the month of October, the house was ordered sold for the benefit of the church, and in seventeen hundred and eighty-three, in the month of February, it was auctioned off for three thousand five hundred livres; and if antipathy and vindictiveness had not shown themselves I would not have been exposed to such a trial. In proof of the zeal that I have and always have had for the service of the Church and for divine worship I purchased the said house with the aid and assistance of two persons whom I have not yet been able to requite or reimburse. . . . Since my marriage in seventeen hundred and sixty-five this house has always been the resort of nearly all the parishioners, both in winter and in summer, and especially on the eve of the principal feasts of the year. In the winter they have come to get warm, and in both seasons they have slept there in order to be at hand for their devotions. . . . I hope, gentlemen, that to a veteran servant who has spent his youth in your service, and in the service of the church, and who has, so to speak, brought up and educated your children and some of you, you will grant a bounty in the name of the parish together with an increase in salary. I will thus be able to provide for the pressing needs of my family, and to quiet the importunities of my creditors. . . .[9]

Evidently, the bishop must have been called upon to decide the matter, for the two foregoing documents were sent to Quebec. What the outcome was we do not know, nor is there further trace of the old schoolmaster save the record of his burial on May 4, 1801.

In the period extending from 1791 to 1804 we search in vain for any evidence of a school conducted under church auspices.[10] The second date marks the beginning of Father Richard's educational endeavors. As the reader will remember, Father Richard had come to Detroit in 1798 to assist Father Levadoux, and had become pastor of St. Anne's upon the latter's withdrawal in 1802. There is nothing in the correspondence of the two priests during the period that they were together to indicate that any sort of school was being maintained. The first project was due to the concerted action of Father Richard and Father Dilhet, who had practically given up his parish

---

[9] In QCA.

[10] In the last quarter of the 18th century there were several schools in Detroit particularly for the children of the English-speaking residents. The best account of them will be found in Sister Mary Rosalita, I.H.M., *Education in Detroit . . . 1850*, Chap. II.

at Monroe. The genesis and fate of their sanguine enterprise, a preparatory seminary, has been sufficiently described in Chapter XIV.[11]

Nothing better illustrates the indefatigable spirit of Father Richard than the fact that it was in the years immediately following the fire of 1805 that he was most active in his educational ventures. Our knowledge of them, unfortunately, is rather meager, and rests upon the various petitions which Father Richard addressed to the Governor and Judges, the legislature of the period, for support. The two earliest ones were filed on October 3, 1806. One was in the name of Father Richard himself:

> Gabriel Richard prays that for the purpose of erecting a College in which will be taught the languages ancient and modern, and several sciences and enabling him to render the Education partly Gratuitous, the Corner lot on the military square of the section number 3 and the whole same section or a part thereof according to the will and benevolence of the Legislature be given.[12]

The other petition, while in the handwriting of Father Richard, was ostensibly presented in the name of two of his teachers.

> Angelique Campeau & Elisabeth Williams pray that the corner's Lot on the military Square of the section number 2 and some of the adjacent Lots of the same section, as many as the Legislature shall think proper, be given for the purpose of erecting a young ladies school, together with a lot in the old shipyard on which stand the Barracks.[13]

Important as was his leadership, Father Richard could have accomplished little had he not had the good fortune to find four women of his parish willing to devote themselves unreservedly to his educational program. The two mentioned above were probably the first to offer themselves, and all of them most likely underwent a course of training under Father Richard before engaging in their work.

Elizabeth Williams was the daughter of Thomas Williams who, emigrating from Albany to Detroit in 1765, had become a prosperous

---

[11] "It was in 1802 that the apostle of education in Detroit, under American rule, the Very Reverend Gabriel Richard, whose practical ideas were far in advance of the times he lived in, having previously established a primary school for the younger children and an academy for the higher education of young men, decided to provide equal facilities for the education of the daughters of his parishioners." Elliott in *American Cath. Hist. Researches*, XV, 82. Although he was not too careful a writer, the statement cannot be dismissed too lightly as he was close enough to the period in question to represent a fairly constant tradition. At this late date no evidence can be found to substantiate so early an origin.

[12] Original in BCA. Richard Papers. The corner desired by Father Richard was the site occupied for many years by the G. and R. McMillan Co.

[13] BHC. Askin Papers. Vol. 457, 204.

merchant, and had married in 1781 the sister of Joseph Campau. Elizabeth therefore belonged to the aristocracy of old Detroit, and was about twenty years old when she came under the tutelage of Father Richard. Angelique Campeau's parentage is not definitely known, but she was about forty when she became associated with Miss Williams. Elizabeth Lyons was the daughter of George Lyons, an Indian trader, and Elizabeth Chene. Monique Labadie came from an old Detroit family, and both she and Miss Lyons were slightly younger than Miss Williams.[14]

Father Richard was evidently making every effort to secure the stability of his new establishments, for at the same time that he presented his petitions to the legislature, he made a will in favor of Father Dilhet, "now living in the Seminary at Conowago near Hanover fifty miles north of Baltimore," containing the following quaint provisions.

4. In case I would die at Detroit or in the neighborhood he shall leave to the church two hundred and fifty dollars out of what shall be due to me by this same church of Detroit at the moment of my death; out of that (what) shall be due to me by the same church of Detroit, he will give two hundred and fifty dollars to the new school founded by Angelique Campeau and (or) by Elisabeth Williams, together with my tables, chairs, my clock, six maps, bed, cathechisms, Instructions de Jeunes Gens, Alphabets.

5. My wish is that, what he will take for himself being excepted, he may appropriate my four hundred acres of land lying betwixt Ohio and Mississippi of which William McKintosh has or will have the patent, as well as all my other estate in the U. S. for the establishment and use of Catholic Seminaries or Academies.[15]

6. In case I would die at Detroit or its neighborhood I hereby appoint Henry Berthelet executor of this my last will and testament, and I Give to him my Bureau, my harpsichord, and twenty volumes of my Library at his own choice.[16]

It is certain that neither the petitions already quoted, nor later ones, brought any response from the territorial officials. This may have been due to some possible antipathy to Father Richard on the score of his religion; but the truer explanation perhaps lies in this that the times were not yet ripe for what to us is a commonplace, the participation of government in educational enterprise. The officials

[14] For a fuller account of these four teachers see Sister Rosalita, op. cit., 66–67.

[15] Some time during his years of service on the Mississippi Father Richard acquired 400 acres of land in Jackson Co., Ill. From documents in the DCA Bishop Lefevere was attempting to recover the land in 1842 from a certain McIntosh who had disposed of it.

[16] Original dated October 1, 1806, in DCA.

shared the opinion of their day that education was a private matter which they were not called upon to help. It is hardly an exaggeration to say that Father Richard was the first social-minded man in Detroit. While aiming primarily at the instruction of the children of his own faith, Father Richard upheld the idea that education was a function of the community, in which it should engage, or whose vicarious exercise it should reward. His attitude is best seen in the petition which he addressed to the legislature on October 18, 1808, when he was at the peak of his educational work.

Our neighbors on the British side are now erecting a large stone building for an Academy. The undersigned being sensible that it would be shameful for the American Citizens of Detroit, if nothing should be done in their territory for a similar and so valuable Establishment, begs leave to call the attention of the Legislature of Michigan to an object the most important to the welfare of the rising Generation which cannot be but of little advantage, if it is not highly patronized by the Government.

The Honourable Legislature partly knows what has been done by the subscriber for the establishment of schools, and for the Encouragement of literature, scientific knowledge and Useful Arts in this part of the Union. Besides two English schools in the Town of Detroit, there are four other Primary schools for boys and two for young ladies, either in Town, or at Spring Hill, at Grand Marais even at River Hurons, Three of these schools are kept by three Natives of this Country who had received their first Education by the Reverend Mr. J. Dilhet and of whom two under the direction of the subscriber have learned the first Rudiments of English and Latin Languages, and some principles of Algebra and Geometry so far as to the measurement of the figures engraved on the tomb of the immortal Archimedes; by necessity they have been forced to stop their studies and to become masters and teachers for others. At Spring Hill under the direction of Angelique Campeau and Elisabeth Lyons, as early as the ninth of September last, the number of the scholars has been augmented by four young Indians headed by an old matron their grandmother of the Potowatamies tribe, five or six more are expected to arrive at every moment.[17]

In Detroit in the house lately the property of Captain Elliott, purchased by the subscriber for the very purpose of establishing one Academy for young ladies, under the direction of Miss Elisabeth Williams there are better than thirty young girls who are taught as at Spring

[17] This was the school at Springwells on the Matthew Ernest farm, which was referred to in Chap. XV. It was in connection with this school that Father Richard wrote his well known "Outlines of a scheme of Education for territory of Michigan" which he addresses to President Jefferson and Congress. For a thorough study of this establishment see Sister Mary Rosalita, I.H.M., in the *Michigan History Magazine,* Vol. XIV (Winter Number), "The Spring Hill Indian School Correspondence."

Hill, reading, writing, arithmetic, knitting, sewing, spinning, & in these two schools there are already nearly three dozen of spinning wheels, and one loom, on which four pieces of Linen or woolen cloth have been made this last spring or summer.

To encourage the young students by the allurement of pleasure and amusements, the undersigned had these three months past sent orders to New York for a spinning machine of about one hundred spindles, an airpump, an Electrical Apparatus &. as they could not be found he is to receive these falls but an Electrical machine, a number of cards, and few colours for dying the stuff already made or to be made in his Academy.

It would be very necessary to have in Detroit a Public building for a similar Academy in which the high branches of Mathematics, most important languages, Geography, History, Natural and moral Philosophy should be taught to young Gentlemen of our country, and in which should be kept the machines, the most necessary for the improvement of Useful Arts, for making the most necessary physical experiments and framing a Beginning of public Library. . . .

The undersigned acting as Administrator for the said Academies further prays, that, for the Encouragement of Literature and useful Arts to be taught in the said Academies, one of the four Lotteries authorized by the Hon. Leg. on the ninth day of September 1805, may be left to the management of the subscriber as Administrator of the said Academies, on the conditions that may appear just and reasonable to the legislative Board, and to make a Trial the subscriber is disposed to offer and from this moment he offers during this winter to make some lectures on such branches of mathematics or of Natural Philosophy that will be more agreeable to the wishes of a majority of those Gentlemen desirous to attend on every evening.[18]

A few weeks after writing this petition Father Richard undertook his trip to the eastern cities, during which he purchased his printing press, and did not return until July, 1809. Having been obliged to abandon the Spring Hill site in 1810, he continued his school work on the Loranger farm. The War of 1812 must have dealt a heavy blow to all his educational enterprises, and we lose sight of his activities in this department until 1815. But the remarkable document that he penned in that year shows that he was maturing plans for the extension and permanency of Catholic education not only in Detroit but in the entire territory. A Catholic school system was possible only through the efforts of a religious society dedicated to that purpose, and such a society he now was ready to found.

This day . . . 1815 Mr. Gabriel Richard, parish priest of Ste. Anne of Detroit, having conferred with Angelique Campeau, Elisabeth Lyons

[18] Original in State Department at Lansing, Box 777.

and Monique Labadie upon the manner of procuring the greatest glory of God, the advancement of Religion and the instruction of the Young, it has been unanimously resolved first to form an Association of pious persons who may enjoy all the privileges and advantages accorded to *Religious Societies* by virtue of an act of the Legislature of the Territory of Michigan dated and published at Detroit the third day of April 1807.

It has been resolved, second. That the said Association will be and is already known under the name and title of the *Society of Catholic Schools in the territory of Michigan.*

It has been resolved, third. That the temporal affairs of the said *Society of Catholic Schools in the territory of Michigan* will be administered by three persons to wit: The chief ecclesiastical director of the schools for boys, and the chief directress of schools for girls in the said Michigan Territory.

It has been resolved, fourth. That the majority of the three above-named administrators shall have the power to buy and sell property, real or personal, movable or immovable, in their own name or that of their agent to that effect.

It has been resolved, fifth. That the said administrators shall have the power, as occasion arises, to establish in the various parishes, towns, villages, or other places according to the population and means at the disposition of the Society, divers branches of the said Society under the particular name of the *Catholic School* of such a parish or place, or under the name given at the time of their respective establishment.

It has been resolved, sixth. That the movable property, the receipts and disbursements for the board of the schools, shall be administered in each individual school by a local overseer, resident respectively in the place of each school, who shall have been named conjointly by the ecclesiastical superior in the territory, and the chief director or the chief directress, according as the school is a school for boys or a school for girls, to whom he shall give a yearly account.

It has been resolved, seventh. That the head master or head mistress of the school, if they are distinct from the local overseer, shall be appointed by the two above named persons.

It has been resolved, eighth. That in due time there shall be a visitor-general of the schools who shall establish a uniform system of instruction as soon as possible.

It has been resolved, ninth. That in each house the property shall be held in common by the various members received in the society, which will be obligated to provide for each the reasonable necessaries, food, clothes, furniture, medicine, etc.

It has been resolved, tenth. That special rules shall be given in due time which shall be approved by the chief ecclesiastical superior in the territory of Michigan for the reception of members into the society, for the order of their duties and exercises.

It is finally resolved that the present resolutions shall be registered by the clerk of the Supreme Court, conformably to the Act of the Legislature above mentioned.[19]

With this strange instrument Father Richard was undoubtedly attempting the foundation of a sisterhood. The chief ecclesiastical superior, who should attend to the further special rules, was most likely the future bishop of Michigan. When Bishop Plessis visited Father Richard in 1816 he noted that he supported a girl's school "under the management of a few female teachers of his own choosing whom he directs like a religious community." The religious note is more evident in a petition addressed to the legislature in 1820.

> Whereas a petition had been presented to the Legislature of this Territory in the year 1807 or 1808 as it may be ascertained by looking in the Journal of the Governor and Judges sitting as Landlord, to obtain certain lots of ground in the city of Detroit to be granted to two different Schools then kept by Angelique Campeau and Elisabeth Williams; whereas the two schools have been since united in one under the title and Name of *Monastery of St. Mary,* which will be the legal body corporate as soon as the *Convention* already agreed on by the members of the Association will have been recorded by the clerk of the Supreme Court, the undersigned in the name of the said *Monastery of St. Mary,* as their special agent for the present circumstances, humbly petitions that the intended lots or others may be conveyed and granted for the benefit of the school, kept in the Monastery of St. Mary.[20]

But Father Richard was not destined to be the founder of a religious community, nor have we any inkling of the reasons why his attempt failed. The "Monastery" was still in existence in 1821, for in that year Father Richard made his definitive will in favor of Father Demetrius Gallitzin with a provision for the benefit of the convent.[21] In 1822 Elizabeth Williams entered a religious house in Montreal. Two years later she was back in Detroit, and in 1825 we find her teaching for Father Déjean at Mt. Clemens.[22] When he was trans-

[19] Original in DCA. The document is quoted as translated in Sister Rosalita, *Education in Detroit . . . 1850,* save in one spot where it is slightly inaccurate.

[20] BHC. Woodbridge Papers.

[21] "He will cause a deed being executed to convey to the Seminary of St. Mary in Detroit the two lots No. 47 & 46 which are in the rear of the Church, being each 100 feet deep by 60 in breadth, which I have bought, and paid for as will appear by the records of the Corporation of St. Anne, and that he will let the same Monastery of St. Mary (which is under the direction of the Sister Elizabeth Lyons the present Superioress) enjoy for ever one of my stoves, my loom, all my wheels and a reasonable proportion of my household furniture, and finally the timber necessary to make their dwelling house to be taken out of the timber now lying in the church yard. . . ." Original in BHC.

[22] "I have established a girl's school kept by a Sister of the Sacred Heart; she has twenty pupils; she comes from a nascent convent near Detroit." Letter of Father Déjean in the *Annales of the Prop. of the Faith,* quoted by Sister Rosalita, *op. cit.,* 102.

ferred to L'Arbre Croche in 1829 she took charge of his Indian school. In 1837 she was in Detroit as the superintendent of the "French Female Charity School," a position which she held presumably until her death in 1843. Elizabeth Lyons likewise left Detroit, and entered the Ursuline convent at New Orleans.[23] On account of failing health she returned in 1824, and probably resumed her work for Father Richard. She was still maintaining a private school in a residence which she owned four years after his death.[24] Angelique Campeau apparently remained in the service of Father Richard until 1830, when she accompanied Father Stephen Badin to the Potawatomi mission near Bertrand.[25] She died in 1838, but the place of her death is uncertain. Monique Labadie was the only one of the four teachers who married, but the effect of her years of association with Father Richard was evident throughout her life. As the wife of Antoine Beaubien, one of the wealthiest French citizens of old Detroit, she became the most devoted patroness of Catholic education and charities in the city.[26]

The records of Father Richard's educational activities thus far adduced seem to bear principally upon the education of girls. Of his work for boys we have only scanty information. There was most likely a boys' school in existence to justify the petition of 1806, and four are mentioned in the summary included in the petition of 1808. Elliott states that in 1808 there was in Detroit "an academy for young men, under the learned pastor's direction, assisted by M. Salliere, a young professor of literature, chemistry and astronomy, whom Father Richard had brought from France. . . ."[27] From his unavailing attempts to have the legislature support his proposed college, Father Richard sought assistance in another quarter. In 1818, probably about the same time that the Monastery of St. Mary came into exist-

[23] Sister Rosalita, *op. cit.*, 75.

[24] *Ibid.*

[25] "On this day, at five o'clock, Mr. Badin, Sr. has left Detroit with Sister Angélique Campau in the state to go to St. Joseph. . . ." Letter from Father Richard to Bishop Fenwick, quoted in Sister Rosalita, *op. cit.*, 76.

[26] Richard R. Elliott wrote a sketch of Monique Labadie for the *Amer. Cath. Hist. Researches*, XV, 81–87. She donated the site of St. Mary's church, and St. Mary's Hospital, and the site of the former Sacred Heart Convent on Jefferson Avenue.

[27] *Amer. Cath. Quart. Rev.*, XVIII, 97. The accuracy of this statement must be questioned. There is no trace of such a person in the early records of Detroit. But Father Richard in a letter to Bishop Carroll, March 14, 1805, and referring to the failure of the preparatory seminary, writes: . . . "the school of the french Gentleman Mr. Serrieres is yet going on. But there is little hope for us to have but a few of his pupils for the clerical state. The number of Our own schoolers (sic) is at present but four. . . ." This school was evidently not under the control of Father Richard. There are several references to the "French schoolmaster" in the *Journal of the Board of Trustees of Detroit, 1802–05* (BHC ed., 1922). The name is variously spelled Lasseller, Lasselier, Lasserrier, Lasseliere, Lassilliere.

ence, he was importuning his Sulpician confreres at Montreal for a loan which would enable him to begin a college. He had been assured by Bishop Flaget that the two young French priests, Fathers Bertrand and Janvier, who were accompanying him from Kentucky, would be left in Detroit for that purpose.[28] If he could be loaned only two thousand dollars, on any terms that the Superior might fix, the college would become a reality.

> . . . It is an enterprise meditated and prepared for during more than twenty years, and for which I have already made notable advances. A little help on your part will give an immediate start to the establishment. Detroit is a place destined, both by its present population, and by the considerable immigration that is at hand, to become one of the most important centers of Catholicity. . . .[29]

Whatever the answer that Father Richard received it is certain that the college was not established. The reader will remember that a few weeks before his death Father Richard, writing this time to his confreres in France, was all aglow at the prospect of at last being able to realize his ambition. "Success is certain."

It is characteristic of Father Richard that his interest in education was not bounded by his necessary preoccupation with Catholic schools. The opening words of the 1808 petition could have come only from a public-spirited citizen distressed by the apathy of his community in a matter of such vital import as public education. That he was the protagonist of education in the Territory, and that his competency was recognized, is evident from his "Outline of a scheme of education" presented to Congress in 1809. It was a summary of a more comprehensive plan, now lost, which had been submitted some months before to the President himself, and whose point of origin is sufficiently indicated by the preface of the "Outline."

> At the special request of the Governor of the Territory of Michigan General Hull, sometimes in the month of march last, the undersigned has drawn a Plan of Education of children adapted to the circumstances of the inhabitants of the said Territory. The said Plan was sent to the President of the U. S. who approved it and felt *desirous that suitable encouragement should be given by the Government for effecting a so benevolent and useful a purpose.* The subscriber thinks that the whole scheme might be got at the Treasury Department to whom it was directed. . . .[30]

[28] Father Bertrand evidently attempted to open a school in Detroit. The announcement of his intention, dated May 18, 1819, is quoted in Sister Rosalita, *op. cit.*, 53.

[29] Letter to Father Candide Le Saulnier, January 13, 1818. In the Bibliotheque St. Sulpice, Montreal.

[30] The original of the "Outline," dated January 20, 1809, lies in the Library of Congress.

Nothing more is needed to prove the zeal of Father Richard for the education of those not of his own faith, and the current estimate of his ideals and qualifications. It was inevitable that when some governmental agency should bestir itself in the matter of education Father Richard should be found playing a prominent part.

The earliest legislation concerning education, and bearing directly upon conditions in Michigan, was the Act of Congress dated March 26, 1804, which created a land office at Detroit for a district corresponding roughly to the state of Michigan, but which at the time was within the Territory of Indiana. In the act, lot 16 of every township was reserved for the benefit of common schools. This was merely carrying over an article of the "Ordinance for Ascertaining the Mode of Disposing of Lands in the Western Country," adopted by Congress in 1785. There was an added provision, now made for the first time, that an entire township in the district should be set aside for the use of a "Seminary of Learning." [31] Michigan became a separate territory in 1805, and four years later the legislature took cognizance of educational needs by passing an act directing the overseers of the poor in each judicial district to erect and maintain schools. The act remained a dead letter.[32]

We come now to that landmark of educational history in Michigan, the legislation of 1817. What combination of events led up to its enactment at this particular time is a matter of conjecture, as is the share to be assigned to any member of a small group of men in the framing of the project thus realized. However there were three men more deeply concerned than either William Woodbridge, Secretary of the Territory, or Governor Cass, both of whom have been mentioned in this connection.[33] The first was Judge Augustus Woodward who, as a prominent young lawyer of Washington, had been appointed one of the Judges of Michigan Territory in 1805. He had studied in Columbia College, was proficient in the classics, had read much in the sciences, and was overfond of expressing his speculations in pedantic verbiage.[34] The second was John Monteith, a native of Gettysburg, who, immediately after his graduation from Princeton Theological Seminary in 1816, had come to Detroit to organize "The First Protestant Society of Detroit." The third was the man who for years had been trying to rouse the officials in Detroit to some corporate action in the cause of education, Father Richard himself. Between him and Judge Woodward congenial tastes had cemented a

[31] *Michigan History Magazine*, XII, 640.

[32] Sister Rosalita, *op. cit.*, 118–21.

[33] *Mich. Hist. Mag.*, XII, 644; Sister Rosalita, *op. cit.*, 125–26.

[34] There is a lengthy sketch of Judge Woodward by William L. Jenks in the *Mich. Hist. Mag.*, IX, 515–46.

strong friendship. With John Monteith his relations had been cordial from the first. In his diary the minister gives a pleasing picture of his intercourse with Father Richard.

> July 16. Priest Gabriel Richard calls on me at my lodgings at Col. Hunts. We have a free and pleasant conversation. He says there is much work for me to do and wishes me success. He stays to tea. I request him to ask a blessing. He answers that he is not accustomed to our mode, that he performs such services in Latin and if acceptable he would do it in that way. I replied that it would not be understood by the family. He therefore declines.
>
> July 23, 1816. I visit the Pere Richard. The conversation agreeable. He presents me with a copy of Thomas A'Kempis.
>
> Nov. 28, 1816. Visit Priest Richard who is out of health. I think he loves to have me visit him.[35]

In the light of subsequent events it is a well-founded assumption that this trio, the judge, the priest, and the minister must have held many a conversation on the lack of educational facilities in the Territory, and it is quite likely that the presence of the minister precipitated the execution of a plan that had been thought out by the other two. At all events, the matter came to a head in the last week of August, 1817. On Monday evening Judge Woodward received the following note.

> Dear Sir: It was late before I could obtain the blank commissions. I was in pursuit of them last evening, but could not procure them. I called this evening upon Mr. Monteith. He expressed some reluctance to embarking so extensively in the plan as was contemplated. I have however had a second conference with him and with Mr. Richard also. Mr. Monteith will accept of the Presidency of the institution and of some of the Professorships. Mr. Richard will be willing also to take the direction of one or two. The commissions are preparing. . . . The arrival of Judge Witherell will render it more decorous that we should postpone our contemplated meeting until after tomorrow as he cannot yet have rested from his fatigue.
>
> In the meantime I shall feel every wish to progress in the business as fast as may be.
>
> Very respectfully yours,
> Wm. Woodbridge.[36]

Indeed, the business could not have progressed more speedily. On the very next day the Governor and Judges passed that famous act that has been alternately admired and derided, "An Act to establish

[35] Quoted in *Mich. Hist. Mag.*, XII, 647. The original diary is in the University of Michigan library.

[36] The original is among the Walker Papers in the University of Michigan library.

the Catholepistemiad or University of Michigania." [37] We cannot here detail the provisions of what the historian of higher education in Michigan has called "the unique, absurd, admirable statute of 1817." [38] The essential feature of the Act was that it established a corporation composed solely of the "president and Didactors or Professors" which was to be the University of Michigan, but which, moreover, should have power "to establish Colleges, Academies, Schools, Libraries, Museums, Atheneums, Botanic Gardens, Laboratories, and other useful Literary and Scientific Institutions, consonant to the Laws of the United States of America and Michigan. . . ." Only two officers of the corporation were provided for in the Act: the professor of Universal Science was to be President; the professor of the Intellectual Sciences "embracing all the Epistemiim or Sciences relative to the minds of animals, to the human mind, to spiritual existences, to the Diety and to Religion" was to be Vice-President. On September 8, the first office was conferred on John Monteith, and nine days later by virtue of the following document Father Richard was appointed Vice-President.

William Woodbridge Secretary of Michigan and vested for the time being with all and singular the powers rights and authority of GOV-ERNOR IN AND OVER THE TERRITORY OF MICHIGAN,

To all to whom these presents may come . . . . . Greeting:

KNOW YE, That reposing special trust and confidence in the integrity and ability of *the Reverend Gabriel Richard* I have appointed him *to be Professor of Intellectual sciences in & of the University of Michigania* And do Hereby Authorize and empower him to execute and fulfil the duties of that office according to law: To have and to hold the said Office, with all the rights, privileges and emoluments thereunto belonging, during the pleasure of the Governor of the said Territory for the time being.

IN TESTIMONY WHEREOF, I have caused these Letters to be made Patent, and the great seal of the said Territory to be hereunto affixed.

Given under my hand at Detroit, this *seventeenth* day of *September* in the year of our Lord one thousand eight hundred and *seventeen*

---

[37] The Act was certainly written by Judge Woodward. A draft in his handwriting is preserved in the University of Michigan library. The actual Act as passed by the legislature is in the office of the Secretary of State at Lansing, and is given entire in the *Mich. Hist. Mag.*, XII, 652–54. The references to the *Mich. Hist. Mag.*, in the present connection are to a series of articles, "University of Michigan Beginnings" (XII, 635–61; XIII, 41–54; 227–44), by William A. Spill, an alumnus of the University, to prove that to Father Richard belonged the largest share of the credit for the legislation of 1817, and that the University really dated from 1817, and not from 1837, the date on its seal. Mainly through his efforts the seal now bears the date 1817.

[38] Andrew C. McLaughlin, *History of Higher Education in Michigan* (Washington, 1891), 33.

and of the Independence of the United States of America the *forty second.*

William Woodbridge.[39]

The university corporation lost no time in entering upon its program. Funds were immediately raised for the erection of a two-story building, and the cornerstone was laid on September 24. In February, 1818, a classical academy was opened in the upper story, and in April a primary school was begun on the ground floor. Teachers were hired to conduct these schools, and there is little evidence to show that either Mr. Monteith or Father Richard ever taught in them; their professorships under the Act could be exercised in a merely supervisory capacity.

Meanwhile the university had acquired its first substantial private gift in a circumstance that, at least, strongly suggests the influence of Father Richard. Five days after the corner-stone of the classical academy was laid, Governor Cass and Duncan McArthur as commissioners of the Federal Government signed a treaty at Fort Meigs with several Indian tribes, in which disposal was made of Indian lands lying for the most part in Ohio and Indiana. The 16th article reads as follows:

> Some of the Ottawa, Chippewa, and Potawatomy tribes, being attached to the Catholic religion, and believing they may wish some of their children hereafter educated, do grant to the rector of the Catholic church of St. Anne of Detroit, for the use of the said church, and to the corporation of the college at Detroit, for the use of the said college, to be retained or sold, as the said rector and corporation may judge expedient, each, one half of three sections of land, to contain six hundred and forty acres, on the river Raisin, at a place called Macon; and three sections of land not yet located, which tracts were reserved for the use of the said Indians, by the treaty of Detroit in one thousand eight hundred and seven; and the superintendent of Indian affairs, in the territory of Michigan, is authorized, on the part of the said Indians, to select the said tracts of land.[40]

---

[39] Original in DCA. The words in italics were inserted by hand in a printed form. The document quoted is one of three issued to Father Richard on the same day. The other two conferred on him respectively the professorship of mathematics, and that of astronomy.

[40] *Indian Affairs, Laws and Treaties* (Washington, 1904), II, 150. The parcel of land divided between Father Richard and the "corporation of the college at Detroit" lay in Dundee township, Monroe County, at the confluence of the Macon and Raisin Rivers, and had been an Indian reservation from the date of the treaty signed in 1807. The patent to Father Richard's share, dated January 20, 1826, is in the DCA. This land was disposed of by Bishop Lefevere working in concert with Judge Christiancy of Monroe. See the latter's interesting reference to this property in the *Mich. Hist. Colls.*, VI, 364–66. It is worth noticing that the site recently acquired by the Archdiocese of Detroit for its "Boystown" is a portion of the original grant to Father Richard.

Is the article clumsily worded? Did the Indians give land to the "college at Detroit" because they were Catholics, and wished their children educated as such? Did someone represent to them that with Father Richard as an officer of the corporation such a destination of their gift could be made? As a matter of fact it was possible. There was no reason why a Catholic school should not have been opened under the Act of 1817. Practically all education in America at the time was under religious auspices.[41] That pedagogical anomaly, God-less education, had not yet arrived. Granted that the donation was not made for specifically Catholic purposes, who could have sug-guested it to the Indians, or induced them to make it, if not the priest who had tried as early as 1808 to interest the government in the education of its Indian wards. Judge Cooley's comment on the incident deserves to be remembered.

> . . . But whatever the fact may be as to the incentive, the value of re-ligion and learning are found recognized by the treaty in a grant of six sections of land in equal shares to the Church of St. Anne at Detroit and to "the College at Detroit." The Indians made the grant, as they say in the treaty, because of being "attached to the Catholic religion, and believing that they may wish some of their children hereafter edu-cated." The gift to the college was not a large one, and it would have seemed insignificant if made before the Indians had alienated the prin-cipal portions of their domain to the government; but its merit must be estimated by what they had retained for their own use, rather than by the extent of their original possessions. The gift, moreover, was fully equal in positive value and prospectively superior to the gifts for like purposes which made John Harvard and Elihu Yale immortal, and quite as justly entitles Tontagini and his associate chieftains to grateful remembrance among the founders of colleges." [42]

Father Richard continued as vice-president of the University of Michigania until 1821, when the corporation was reorganized, and its control was vested in a board of twenty-one trustees, of which he was appointed a member.[43] The further history of the University of Mich-igan through all its successive reorganizations need not detain us. Only one important point concerns us here, the fact that the great university of today at Ann Arbor is a direct descendant of the cor-

[41] See for instance the chapter on elementary and secondary schools in *American Idealism* by Luther A. Weigle in the Pageant of America series (Yale University Press, 1928).

[42] Thomas McIntyre Cooley, *Michigan: A History of Government* (Boston, 1888), 312–13.

[43] *Mich. Hist. Mag.*, XIII, 49–50. The Regents, as a governing board of the University, were not established until 1837. Father Martin Kundig was appointed a regent on March 18, 1841. He served until his departure for Milwaukee the following year. See Burke A. Hinsdale, *History of the University of Michigan* (Ann Arbor, 1906), 177.

poration of 1817, composed for almost four years of no one else but
John Monteith and Father Richard. This fact has been established
by the authority of the Supreme Court of Michigan in deciding the
ownership of property in Detroit that had been committed to the
first board of trustees against the Detroit Board of Education.[44] If any
confirmation were needed it has been furnished by the Alumni Committee on History and Traditions, which, after an intensive study of
the matter, compelled the Regents of the University to alter the seal of
the institution. It had hitherto carried the year 1837, a meaningless
date. By a resolution adopted May 24, 1929, the Regents authorized
the change to 1817.[45] The implications are obvious. Father Richard
stands at the beginning not only of Catholic education in Michigan,
but of public instruction as well.

The record of Father Richard's work is not complete without the
notice of a venture into the field of specialized education which, even
though it had no practical results as far as we know, nevertheless illustrates his zeal and the range of his interests. He was certainly familiar
with the success attained by his French contemporary, the celebrated
Abbé Sicard, in the education of deaf-mutes, and the introduction of
his methods into the United States in 1817.[46] Apparently, there was
a number of such unfortunates in Detroit, and their plight made a
strong appeal to the charity of Father Richard. As soon as Elizabeth
Lyons had returned from the Ursuline Convent in New Orleans she
was sent to New York by Father Richard to study the new methods of
instruction. Her presence there is revealed by a passage in a letter
written to Bishop Fenwick by Father Rese on his first arrival in New
York.

> . . . We have taken our lodging in a private house kept by a French
> Catholic woman, whence we shall leave in a day or two for our re-
> spective destinations. . . . Mr. Richard was here a fortnight ago, but
> has departed for Montreal. He had sent here a Religious in order to
> have her instructed in the education of deaf-mutes. She lived in the
> same house in which we are, and has returned to Detroit. . . .[47]

At the time, Father Richard as Territorial Delegate was aware of
the efforts made by some of the states to secure appropriations for
the education of deaf mutes. He succeeded in having his own project
incorporated in a bill presented to the House at the beginning of his

[44] Regents vs. Board of Education, 4 Mich., 213. The decision was rendered in 1856.
[45] The question is treated at length in a pamphlet, *Michigan Corrects Its Seal, a Reprint of the Briefs, Arguments and Records Whereby the Board of Regents of the University of Michigan Officially Recognized the University's Foundation Date, August 26,
1817, and Corrected Its Seal.* (Detroit, 1930).
[46] See the article "Education of the Deaf" in the Catholic Encyclopedia.
[47] Letter of Father Rese to Bishop Fenwick, New York, September 5, 1824. In NDA.

second session in January, 1825. The bill was proposed "for the benefit of the Asylums for teaching the Deaf and Dumb of Kentucky, New York, Pennsylvania, and of the territory of Michigan," and asked that land be granted "to the Incorporated Asylum at Detroit, Michigan Territory, for teaching the Deaf and Dumb." [48] From the House Journal for the session it is evident that the bill died in committee, and Father Richard in all likelihood gave up all hope of carrying out his design. It was in December of the same year that he penned his own commentary on all his educational endeavors:

> God knows how many projects great and small go through my head, of schools and missions for the Indians, for the deaf and dumb, for poor children, etc., but means are lacking in a new country, where everything must be created out of nothing. My spirit, my imagination, and still more my heart is full of plans, designs, projects, and conceptions which I should call extravagant, and which always remain sterile; they abort or they die at birth. If wishes alone gave one a right to a great reward I could expect something. . . . [49]

Outside of Detroit the earliest Catholic school in the diocese was undoubtedly the one established by Father Déjean at Mt. Clemens in 1825, which was conducted by Elizabeth Williams. In the larger French settlement at Monroe the first attempt to provide a school came during the pastorate of Samuel Smith. He wrote to Bishop Fenwick in September, 1830, that he was ready to begin a school in a few weeks.[50] Strangely enough, the man who afterwards became the most notorious vilifier of the Sisterhoods attempted the foundation of a religious community for the maintenance of his school. In October, he thus communicated his progress:

> . . . The old church I have repaired and converted it into a monastery which I expect will be supported by a good female school. I have two sisters professed, and three novices who live according to the rule I have prescribed for them. . . . The school will commence in a few days . . . [51]

[48] Quoted from a printed copy of the proposed bill dated January 19, 1825, in DCA. In the *Tenth Annual Report of the National Institution for the Deaf and Dumb of Ireland* (Dublin, September 1826), Dr. Simon Akerly of the New York Institution reports on the work being done in America. In the course of his letter he states: "A school for the Deaf and Dumb was opened in Detroit, in the territory of Michigan, under the patronage of Mr. Gabriel Richards, a Roman Catholic priest; but what success it has met with I have not heard." In a note he adds that the school was "commenced by Mrs. Lyons, of that place, who received instruction at the New York Institution."

[49] Letter of Father Richard to the Director of the Society for the Propagation of the Faith, December 22, 1825. Louisville Chancery Archives.

[50] Letter dated September 14, 1830. NDA.

[51] Letter dated October 22, 1830. NDA.

Evidently this development was unexpected by Bishop Fenwick, and it brought a stern rebuke whose tenor may be divined from Father Smith's answer.

> Dear, dear father, what tears does your letter not draw from my eyes. My zeal perhaps is indiscreet. If it is, it comes not from contumacy but from the simplicity of my poor heart. I see that you are not exactly acquainted with what I have done. One of the two professed sisters of whom I spoke to you in a former letter, was the sister Bernadine, who is now at Canton. The other is Mrs. Carey (widow) with whom I presume you are acquainted. She has taken not an absolute vow, but only a conditional one, and that, too, only for one year. The express condition is this: if the Rt. Rev. Bishop of Cincinnati approves of and confirms it. In regard to establishing a new order, I have attempted to establish none. All that I have done is to establish a female boarding school, under the superintendance of three sisters selected for the purpose . . .[52]

Father Smith goes on to acquaint the bishop with the rule of life which he has devised for the convent: the hours of silence and recreation, the periods of prayer and meditation, the weekly confession and communion with the added privilege of approaching the Holy Table "on festivals of the B. Virgin, the apostles, and St. Antoine's day." The bishop's opposition was disarmed by this explanation, and he forthwith gave his approval to Father Smith's undertaking in the following terms.

> I am sorry to have hurt your feelings, but thought it my duty to write you as I did for your own sake. Had you given me in your former letter the explanation you now give of the sisters' vows and monastery, I should not have been alarmed at all nor surprised. I can find no fault with what you now communicate concerning them. I approve it cordially. . . . I approve of the title of the Sisters and female school or academy, but not a monastery nor solemn vows. Simple vows, or at the will of the bishop are valid and proper.[53]

How long the convent and school was maintained is uncertain. At the end of March, 1831, Father Smith complained to Bishop Fenwick of Father Carabin's neglect of the sisters.[54] As we have seen, Father Smith was removed from Monroe in July of the same year, and with

---

[52] Letter dated December 26, 1830. Archives of Mt. St. Joseph, Cincinnati.

[53] It is here assumed that Father Smith received this approbation. The passage quoted is written in Bishop Fenwick's handwriting on a sheet of Father Smith's letter quoted in the preceding note. It is evidently a direction for a secretary, or a memorandum for an answer soon to be made.

[54] Letter dated March 28, 1831. NDA.

him disappears all trace of the little band of women who, for all their zeal, served in later years only to point the salacious diatribes of the apostate.[55]

In the new era beginning with the erection of the diocese, the Poor Clares were the pioneers of Catholic education in Detroit. Reference has already been made to the establishment of their academy in 1833. The school took in boarding and day pupils, and taught "all the attainments which are necessary in society." [56] During the six years of its existence it was patronized by the best families, and the sister of Governor Stevens Mason, as an octogenarian, still had vivid memories of her happy school days.

> . . . Schools were rare as were churches, and such was the unanimity of feeling, that though Protestants, we went to St. Ann's, the French Catholic cathedral, and from the priests we had lessons in music and French. For a time we had some Belgian sisters, who taught a convent school, but Father Kundig, a Swiss, who became famous for his charities, and Father Bondrel (Bonduel), a very elegant Frenchman, were teachers for those who craved accomplishments.
>
> What charming recollections of those days of simple pleasures crowd upon me! Good Father Kundig made for us a theatre in the basement of the cathedral, where we acted Hannah Moore's and Miss Edgeworth's plays, to admiring audiences of parents and friends. My sister Kate, as Mrs. Bustle in "Old Pog," and Josie Desnoyer as "William," in hat and cravat of her father's (a world too wide, the hat) and his brass buttoned coat, the tails of which reached the floor, produced peals of laughter. My youngest sister, about ten years old, with gilt paper crown and sceptre and long white gown, was Canute the Great, bidding the waters retreat. Seized with stage fright, after the first scene, she refused to return to the "boards," when Father Kundig gravely announced "indisposition" on the part of King Canute, and prayed the audience to excuse his further appearance. Between the acts Father Kundig played the piano, and was candle snuffer, prompter, sceneshifter,— everything—with unfailing interest and good humor.[57]

In addition to the academy, the Sisters conducted a school for the children of the neighborhood in a house adjoining the convent on Larned St.[58] For the poorer children another school was maintained through the charity of Monique Labadie.

[55] In his *Downfall of Babylon* the editor claimed to speak with authority of what went on in Catholic religious houses since he himself had established one.

[56] MacCabe's *Directory of the City of Detroit*, 1837, 31.

[57] *Mich. Hist. Colls.*, XXXV, 249–50.

[58] It is thus listed in MacCabe's Directory: St. Clare English and German Free School / Larned Street / Average number of children in attendance 45 / Patron / Right Revd. Dr. Rese / Teachers—The Sisters of St. Clare.

French Female Charity School,
Larned Street.

This benevolent institution is supported by Mrs. Antoine Beaubien, the pupils are furnished with books and other school requisites. The average number of children in attendance is 40:

Superintendent—Miss Elizabeth Williams [59]

On his arrival in the diocese, one of Bishop Rese's first projects was the erection of an institution of higher learning.[60] But there were difficulties in the way of a college as originally planned, and at the end of his first year the bishop published the following notice.

> Circumstances not under our control having prevented us from erecting our College near St. Anne's Church, as nearly as we intended, in order to give to the rising generation in every case, an opportunity of a complete moral and civil education, so essential, and conducive to the happiness of Society under whatever clime or system of polity, but most particularly so, when enjoying the privileges of a free, and republican government, as here every citizen has to contribute his quota for the general interest and welfare of the commonwealth, we should nevertheless feel guilty, did we not contribute in every possible way to aid in attaining that great end, and exert ourselves in the interim in a manner most practicable. We will therefore begin a high school in a suitable building near our presbytery.[61]

The school thus announced was St. Anne's Classical Academy, which has been interestingly described by Elliott from personal memory.[62] The building, which stood on the northeast corner of the church property, consisted of a two story structure flanked by one story wings. In one of the wings lived, with his wife, the schoolmaster, "William McDonagh, formerly of College and late principal of the English, Classic and Mathematical Academy, Great Ship Street, Dublin in Ireland, *Master*." To him was evidently left the writing of the prospectus which appeared in the Detroit Free Press for February 17, 1836. He proposed to train youth "speedily, yet solidly." The teaching of English could be "facilitated 'in transitu' by grammatical analysis." The course comprised Geography, "that delightful study," Arithmetic, Bookkeeping, Geometry, Ancient and Modern History, Natural and Moral Philosophy, Botany, French, the Greek and Latin classics, "and in a word, everything calculated to form the character of the scholar, the gentleman, and the Christian." The terms were

[59] MacCabe's *Directory*, 97.
[60] Father Bonduel's letter at the beginning of Chapter XIX might be recalled here.
[61] The *Detroit Journal and Michigan Advertiser*, December 5, 1834.
[62] *American Cath. Hist. Researches*, XIV, 146–54. See also *Amer. Cath. Quart. Rev.*, XXVI, 510–11.

five dollars a quarter, and every pupil was to pay one shilling a month for fuel during the cold season.

Despite his confident prospectus the schoolmaster was not equal to dealing with the growing lads of Detroit, and at the end of a year he resigned. He was replaced by some of Bishop Rese's seminarians, and the school was closed by Bishop Lefevere soon after his arrival in Detroit.[63]

Once the Classical Academy was in operation, Bishop Rese returned to his original project, the opening of a Catholic college. The site chosen was the old Church Farm. The farmhouse was rebuilt and considerably enlarged, as may be inferred from Farmer's statement that the porch running along the front of the building and facing the river was one hundred and ten feet long.[64] The college was ready to receive students in September, 1836, and was placed in charge of two priests who had come to Detroit late in 1833, Fathers Leo Fidelis Van Den Poel, and John De Bruyn. The Catholic Almanac for 1837 carries the following notice of the new institution.

St. Philip's College—(Cote Du Nord-Est,)
Near Detroit, Michigan,
under the auspices of the
Right Rev. Dr. Rese, Bishop of Detroit.

A good moral and religious education being an inexhaustible source of social and individual happiness, the Rt. Rev. Bishop Rese, who deeply feels the want of a proper literary and classical establishment in Michigan, has tried to overcome the innumerable obstacles he met with, and endeavors now to benefit the country with an institution adapted to the desirable improvement of the education of youth in a thriving and enlightened state.

The College is erected on a fine elevated spot, the amenity and salubrity of its site, (commanding a distant prospect of Lake St. Clair, while its proximity to the city of Detroit facilitates the means of communication with all the places situated on its connected waters) render it peculiarly favorable to the student. It enjoys many other considerable advantages which recommend it to the public. The building, although not very spacious is well fitted for the accommodation of pupils.

The course of instruction pursued in the College will embrace the Latin, Greek, French and English languages, Poetry, Rhetoric and Oratory, Reading, Writing, Geography Mathematics and Book-keeping. A favorable opportunity to become well conversant with the French language, will be found in the intercourse with the pupils

---

[63] Sister Rosalita, *op. cit.*, 304–07.
[64] *Op. cit.*, 720. The college stood about in the center of Gabriel Richard Park at the bridge approach to Belle Isle.

whose native tongue is French. Strict attention will be paid to the moral conduct of the students, and no infraction of the disciplinary rules of the College will be connived at; in case of delinquency, the delinquent will first be admonished, and if admonition, or if mild and paternal punishments prove ineffectual, he will be sent back to his parents or guardians.

The Regency of the College is Catholic, but pupils of other denominations are admitted provided they be willing to attend morning and evening prayer daily, and divine worship on Sundays and holydays; good order requiring this compliance: but there shall be no interference or tampering whatever with their religious principles.

The diet will be wholesome and abundant. Of the health of the pupils the most paternal care will be taken. For the better insuring progress in studies, the hours of study and class will be intermixed with moderate recreation. Books not belonging to the course of studies, unless deemed useful and approved by the superior, will not be suffered to circulate in the College. . . .

The pupils at their entrance must be supplied with bed and bedding, a silver or tin tumbler, spoon, knife and fork, and convenient clothing. . . .

No leave will be granted to sleep out of the College. The correspondence of the students, except with parents or guardians, is subject to inspection.

All letters to be addressed to the superior free of postage.

Rev. Mr. Vandepoel,
Superior of the Institution.
Rev. Mr. De Bruyn,
President of Studies

The college was well patronized from the beginning, and during the few years of its existence housed several of the future prominent citizens of Detroit.[65] But it was pursued by misfortunes. Father Van Den Poel died on January 28, 1837.[66] Father De Bruyn now became superior, but followed his predecessor to the grave on September 11, 1839.[67] About the same time, Father Cullen, who had been teaching from his ordination in 1836, was transferred to Ann Arbor, and the personnel of the staff for the next two years can only be conjectured. If Father Badin's expenditure record can be relied upon, the college

---

[65] Farmer, op. cit., 720; Friend Palmer, Early Days in Detroit, 655.

[66] Father Van Den Poel's dismissorial letters in the DCA are dated September 5, 1833, and are signed by the bishop of Ghent. His tombstone in Mount Elliott Cemetery bears the words "ex congregatione St. Philippi Neri" after his name.

[67] There is a lengthy obituary notice in the Catholic Advocate of Bardstown, Ky., for October 3, 1839. Father De Bruyn is said to have been a native of Loerre, near Antwerp in Belgium. He was ordained at Malines on September 25, 1832. He came to Detroit in 1833 with the intention of devoting himself to the Indian missions. He had been a professor of Belles-Lettres in one of the schools of Antwerp. Father De Bruyn is buried in Mt. Elliott Cemetery alongside Father Van Den Poel.

was maintained down to June, 1841.[68] It appears to have been unoccupied when it burned to the ground early in 1842.[69] The diocese had to await the advent of the Jesuits, thirty-five years later, before it could boast of another Catholic college.

When Bishop Lefevere entered upon his work of caring for a rapidly growing Catholic population, he had less to do with than his predecessor. The Poor Clares had departed, and no religious community was available until 1844, when the Daughters of Charity arrived in Detroit. The Catholic Almanac for 1846 pictures what little progress had been made by the end of the preceding year.

> St. Vincent's Select School for girls, conducted by the Sisters of Charity. Sister Loyola, *Sister Servant.* This school was opened last May, and numbers from 50 to 60 pupils.[70] All the branches of a plain and useful education are taught, and the religious instruction of the scholars is particularly attended to. Besides, the Sisters have also opened two other schools for poor children, one for boys under the age of ten years, numbering 75 scholars, and the other for girls, 87 in number. Catechetical instruction is attended to on every Wednesday afternoon, and one hour before high mass on Sundays, and also an hour before vespers.

> Trinity Church Male School (English), in Detroit. The school is held in the basement of St. Ann's Church, and numbers 60 pupils.

> St. Mary's German School in Detroit. The school is held also in the basement of St. Ann's, and numbers between 40 and 60 pupils, boys and girls.

> Besides the above, there are three Sunday Schools and Library. The Library contains 800 volumes, which are issued weekly to the members of the society. . . .

> There is a society among the German Catholics in Detroit, that has for its object principally to sustain their Sunday School, Library, and Church Music. . . .

> Sunday School in Monroe for the English, French and Germans. Number of pupils, 150.

The Trinity school had been in operation since 1838. In the parish records for that year there is an entry made August 30 to the effect that John Piquette has been paid $32.40 "to apply on fitting out the basement of the french Cathedral for School-rooms." In the following February, $20 was paid "by vote of the church officers, to the teacher

[68] *Compte Rendu du Diocese du Michigan Depuis le 15 Septembre 1832, au 31 Decembre, 1841.* Manuscript in DCA. The college was legally incorporated April 16, 1839. See the *Mich. Hist. Colls.,* XVIII, 399; I, 453.

[69] "To complete the misfortune, the College of St. Philip, not far from the city was consumed by the flames only a few days ago. Its loss is very much felt by us, and to reestablish it at least $3000 would be required. . . ." Letter of Bishop Lefevere to the Society for the Prop. of the Faith, February 15, 1842. Hickey Transcripts.

[70] "In the course of the next month (June, 1844) we opened our Schools, one for little boys, and two for girls, and the children flocked to us from all quarters. . . ." Quoted from the chronicle mentioned in Chapter XX, note 21.

of the Catholic school (Jno Dalrimple) and to be paid back by the school committee on the first of May next." [71]

The first schoolmaster mentioned in St. Mary's parish records is Andreas Stutte, and he is declared to have opened his school in May, 1844. From the entry in the Almanac, it is evident that he began his teaching for the German children in St. Anne's, and not in a building erected by the parish. In the Almanac for 1849, the entry is changed to read: "St. Mary's German School in Detroit. The school is held near St. Mary's church, and contains about 80 pupils." This confirms the statement made in the chronicle of the Redemptorists that Father Hasslinger built a school costing $1600 in 1848. [72]

While Bishop Lefevere was gathering for publication these meagre statistics of his diocese, Father Gillet was assembling his postulants in the bleak log house on the banks of the River Raisin. The first to come was Theresa Renauld, the daughter of a prosperous farmer in Grosse Pointe. Her pious, generous heart had been touched by Father Gillet's first retreat at St. Paul's in 1843, and she offered herself then; but she had been told to wait. In November, 1845, Father Gillet was ready. From Baltimore came two postulants, Theresa Maxis, and Anna Schaaf, pious women whom he had met there, and who had expressed their willingness to join in his venture. Rules were drawn up, and approved by Bishop Lefevere. On December 8, Theresa Renauld made her vows publicly in the church, and received the religious habit. Her two companions had been invested privately a week before. Such was the humble origin of one of the foremost teaching sisterhoods in the United States, the Sisters, Servants of the Immaculate Heart of Mary.

In January, 1846, the Sisters began their school work in a house that the Redemptorists turned over to them, and a year later a large two story frame structure was erected. The Catholic Almanac for 1847 carried the following prospectus.

Young Ladies' Academy,

Under the direction of the Sisters of Providence, [73]

Monroe, Michigan.

This institution, lately established in the city of Monroe, is situated in the most beautiful and healthy part of the city, opposite the Catholic Church.

---

[71] From the parish account book in the DCA.

[72] *Annales Cong. SS. Redempt.*, II, 87. In the parish record it is stated that Stutte taught but a short while, and was succeeded by John Funke. "For a part of the time between 1845 and 1850 John Funke kept a school on the south side of Macomb near St. Antoine Street, and A. Stutte on the southwest corner of Croghan (Monroe) and St. Antoine Streets." Farmer, *op. cit.*, I, 718.

[73] The Sisterhood bore this title until December 1847, when the present designation was adopted.

SISTER FRANÇOISE VINDEVOGHEL, Superior of the Poor Clares, the first Sisterhood in Detroit. From a portrait in the Detroit Institute of Arts.

This institute combines every advantage that can be desired in a literary institute for young ladies. Having been engaged for many years past in the instruction of youth, these sisters will endeavor to justify the confidence of parents who will entrust their children to their care.

The plan of education, together with the benefit of Christian instruction, unites every advantage that can be derived from a punctual and conscientious care bestowed on the pupils in every branch of science suitable to their sex, and from the uninterrupted attention which is given to form the manners and principles of the young ladies, and to train them up in the habits of order, neatness and industry. The diet is good, wholesome and abundant. Spacious grounds afford the pupils the facility of pleasant walks, and useful bodily exercises. Their health is the object of constant solicitude; in sickness they are affectionately attended to, and never are they left a moment beyond the reach of inspection.

Tuition

The branches taught are: Reading, Writing in various styles; Grammar, both French and English; Arithmetic, Chronology, Mythology, Polite Literature, Geography, Elements of Astronomy, Natural Philosophy, Domestic Economy, Book Keeping, by single and double entry; History, sacred and profane, ancient and modern; Plain and Ornamental Needle Work, Bead Work, Tapestry, Lace Work, Marking, Embroidery, with gold and silver; Painting, Worsted Flowers; Music, vocal and instrumental. . . .

S. Theresia, Superior.

As already noted in Chapter XX the Sisters of the Holy Cross had opened their first home in America at Bertrand in 1844. Although they immediately began teaching the children of the neighborhood, their presence in the diocese is mentioned for the first time in the Catholic Almanac for 1849: "Female Academy of Bertrand, Berrien Co., conducted by Sisters of our Lady of the Seven Dolors." The interest of Monique Labadie in education made itself felt even here. Her benefaction to the little band struggling against poverty has been recorded by the historian of the sisterhood.

In the beginning the Sisters in Bertrand had eight boarders, who were orphans. Two of these were sent to their care by Mr. and Mrs. Louis (?) Antoine Beaubien, of Detroit, who in 1844 donated to Father Sorin for the Sisters a piece of land, which was sold afterwards for fifteen thousand francs. It was a square of eight lots, two hundred and ninety-six feet long by two hundred wide, located on St. Antoine Street, which the Sisters were privileged either to keep or to sell, as it was given in favor of them. In return for this gift they were asked to educate these little orphans.[74]

74 Sister M. Eleanore, *On the King's Highway* (New York, 1931), 133.

In Detroit no progress was made until 1851; but in that year important auxiliaries came to swell the Catholic teaching body. The first to come were the Religious of the Sacred Heart. There is a pretty story in the biography of Mother Aloysia Hardey to the effect that Father Richard met Mother Duchesne, the American foundress, at St. Louis in 1818, that he was deeply impressed, and that he carried back to Detroit, particularly to his school teachers, glowing accounts of her courage and zeal. It is an explanation, reasonable enough, of the admiration which Monique Labadie conceived for the Religious, and of the supreme effort which she made to bring them to Detroit. In 1849 she broached her design to Mother Hardey. If the Religious opened a school in Detroit, and in addition cared for a certain number of destitute orphans, she offered to give her residence property, asking in return only a small income for herself and her husband. The offer was accepted, and on May 17, 1851, Mother Trincano and four companions arrived in Detroit, taking up their temporary residence on the north side of Jefferson Avenue just east of the railroad bridge.

Serious difficulties immediately arose. Monique Labadie's legal heirs, she herself being childless, protested the donation, and persuaded her husband, who, because of his advanced age had left the conduct of his affairs entirely to his wife, to withhold his consent. How it was finally obtained is amusingly described by Mother Hardey.

One day, Mrs. Beaubien took me to her home, for the purpose of persuading her husband to sign the document. The carriage had scarcely started than her "Ave Marias" began. Having forgotten her beads, she counted her Aves on her fingers, pressing them in turn upon her breast, but keeping her mind all the time upon the object of her prayers. She thought and prayed aloud, and the combination was something like this: "Hail, Mary, full of grace—O Mother, we forgot that important point—the Lord is with thee—I must say this to Mr. Beaubien—blessed art thou among women—there is another point to be remembered—and blessed is the fruit—we must not lose this grand opportunity of procuring the glory of God." And thus her Hail Marys continued until the end of the drive.

When they met Mr. Beaubien he was greeted with this naive apostrophe: "Antoine, how foolish you are! Do you not see that it is to the Heart of Jesus we are giving our property, and that we could not dispose of it in a better way? . . . Don't you see, Antoine, we are doing this for the good of Jesus and for no one else?". . .[75]

[75] *Mary Aloysia Hardey* (New York, 1910), 144. The first listing of the new foundation among the institutions of the Diocese of Detroit in the Almanac for 1852 was very simple: (continued on page 643)

Monique had her way, as usual, and Antoine signed. This was the crowning charity of her life, for she died that same year. Antoine survived her seven years, and in 1861, when the Sisters opened their school on the grounds of the old homestead, Monique, surely from heaven, saw the final accomplishment of her design.[76]

For the care of the Catholic boys of Detroit Bishop Lefevere had long been trying to secure the services of the Christian Brothers. His efforts finally succeeded in 1851. Four Brothers came from Montreal in September, and were housed in a frame building on the northeast corner of Larned and St. Antoine Streets. Their first work was to take over the school in the basement of St. Anne's church. In the following year, four more Brothers arrived, who were given charge of the boys' school in St. Mary's parish.[77]

To supplement the work of the Brothers in St. Mary's, the Redemptorists, then in charge of the parish, saw the necessity of bringing in a sisterhood. They apealed to Mother Caroline Friess, the American foundress of the School Sisters of Notre Dame, whom they had befriended on her arrival in Baltimore in 1847, and who had just established her motherhouse in Milwaukee. On September 24, 1852, a little band of Sisters arrived in Detroit to begin their school work, which included the care of a few orphan children.[78] They lived at first in a small frame house on Macomb Street between Hastings and St. Antoine Streets, but in 1855 moved to a structure combining orphanage and school erected by the parish. The building is still standing at 1011 St. Antoine Street.[79]

The School Sisters of Notre Dame were the last religious community to be introduced into the diocese during the episcopate of Bishop Lefevere. At the end of that period the total of educational accomplishment represented the development of the agencies already existing in 1852.

In 1852 the Daughters of Charity took over a new brick school building on Larned Street near their original convent, and opened "St. Vincent's Select School for Girls." The prospectus appearing in

"Young Ladies' Academy / This establishment was commenced last spring in the city of Detroit. / Madam Trincano, Superior."

In 1852 the Religious moved to a small brick building on the southwest corner of Jefferson Avenue and St. Antoine St. Two years later the school was housed in a building on the north side of Jefferson near Elmwood St. The large brick convent on the Beaubien property, which was vacated for the Lawrence Avenue site in 1918, was erected in 1861. Burton, *op. cit.*, I, 784.

[76] See sketch of Monique Labadie in *Amer. Cath. Hist. Researches*, XV, 81–87.
[77] Details from the chronicle of De La Salle Collegiate, Detroit.
[78] *Mother Caroline and the School Sisters of Notre Dame in America* (St. Louis, 1928), I, 67.
[79] Farmer, *op. cit.*, 721.

the Catholic Almanac for 1853 states that the Sisters "also teach another school for poor children, numbering from 80 to 90 scholars." The school was maintained down to 1871, and was conducted four years longer by lay teachers.[80]

In addition to the female school, the Daughters of Charity taught a number of boys in the basement of St. Anne's until they were relieved by the Christian Brothers. They undertook parochial school work again in Trinity parish. After the church had been moved to Sixth and Porter Streets in 1849, school rooms were fitted up in the basement, and lay teachers conducted classes there until 1854. In that year a boys' school was opened in a new structure built by Father Peeters, which stood just east of the present rectory.[81] Four years later, the first unit of the present school building was erected to serve as a school for girls, and was placed in charge of the Sisters, who began their classes in September, 1859.[82] They conducted the school until the summer of 1874.

When the Christian Brothers arrived in Detroit, Bishop Lefevere had already begun an addition to the sacristies of St. Anne's church to supplement the basement schoolrooms. In 1857 the Brothers had as many as four hundred boys under their care. But the school was definitely closed in 1864, when all the Brothers left Detroit, unable to support themselves during the financial stringency, so acute in the city, that accompanied the Civil War.[83] However, the Redemptorists made desperate sacrifices to retain them, and in the fall three Brothers returned to resume their work at St. Mary's school. The present school building was begun in 1868, and on its completion was occupied by both the Brothers and the Sisters of Notre Dame. At the end of June, 1877, the Brothers terminated their long years of service in St. Mary's parish.

A third boys' school opened by the Brothers in the cathedral parish was dignified by the following announcement in the Catholic Almanac for 1857.

St. Peter's Academy, select school, Larned Street W.

This Academy, which was commenced in January '56, was founded by the Rt. Rev. Bishop, whose indefatigable zeal for the advancement of education is well known.—He is likewise the founder of the other schools taught by the Brothers in this City.

The course of instruction comprises English and French Reading, Writing, English and French Grammar, Arithmetic, Algebra, ancient

[80] *Ibid.*

[81] In the *Detroit Catholic Vindicator* for December 10, 1853, the school is said to be nearing completion.

[82] Information from the motherhouse at Emmitsburg, Md.

[83] Catlin, *op. cit.*, Chap. XCIII.

and modern History, Geography, Book-keeping, Philosophy, Geometry, Astronomy, Use of the globes, drawing and painting in water colors, etc. Number of scholars, 100. Bro. William, *first teacher.*

This school was maintained for about three years, and was then turned over to lay teachers, and finally to the Sisters of the Immaculate Heart.[84]

The sisterhood begun at Monroe, being a diocesan foundation, could be expected to play the most important part in the development of educational facilities within the diocese. In 1855 the Sisters opened their first school outside of Monroe in the parish of Erie. It was abandoned in 1858, that critical year for the community, when twelve of the twenty-four Sisters left the motherhouse to begin new foundations in Pennsylvania.[85] Happily, vocations were numerous, and at the end of three or four years the little community had grown to such proportions that it could again begin its career of expansion.

The Sisters of the Immaculate Heart opened their first school in Detroit in St. Joseph's parish, in the fall of 1861. Three years later they took over the cathedral school, which they retained until 1881. In 1867 they began teaching in the boys' school belonging to Trinity parish, and replaced the Daughters of Charity when the latter withdrew from the girls' school in 1874. For a period of three years, beginning in the fall of 1867, the Sisters conducted a school for colored children. It was called St. Augustine's School, and was housed in a frame building erected for the purpose behind the cathedral by Bishop Lefevere.[86] Nor was the progress of the Sisters confined to the episcopal city. Schools were opened at Adrian and at Marshall in 1864; at Westphalia in 1867; at Ann Arbor and at Carleton in 1868; at Mt. Clemens in 1870; at Ionia and at Marine City in 1871.

We may sum up the state of Catholic education in the diocese at the end of Bishop Lefevere's episcopate by stating that there were about twenty schools conducted by the religious communities already mentioned, with a total enrollment of approximately 3500 pupils. This is a known quantity which may be useful as a basis for comparison with other periods; but it does not tell the whole story. The Sisters were not the pioneers of education in the diocese, particularly outside of Detroit. Almost invariably they came in only to crown the efforts that had been made before them. The pioneers were the little immigrant groups scattered throughout the state, struggling against

[84] Farmer, *op. cit.,* 722.

[85] *A Retrospect,* an anonymous history of the Sisters of the I.H.M. (Benziger Bros., 1916), 115–21.

[86] The Catholic Directories continue to list the school down to 1871, but from records now preserved at Marygrove College, Detroit, it is evident that the school was discontinued in the summer of 1870.

poverty, but strong in their faith, who managed somehow to procure through primitive buildings and lay teachers the essentials of a Catholic education for their children. In nearly every one of the older parishes the first building erected served for both school and church purposes. From the meagre records available we can discover the names—but scarcely more than that—of some of the early teachers. To mention only a few, there was Daniel O'Sullivan in Flint, in the late thirties; an O'Meara in Jackson; John Sheeran and John Young in Monroe; John Stumm in Westphalia. However, it is quite impossible to write anything approaching a satisfactory account of these first schools, and we must pass on, leaving untold what might be an interesting story if we knew more, but knowing just enough to give us an added sense of the sturdy faith, and of the sacrifices of the pioneers.

We might have had, at least, a complete list of these first schools if Bishop Lefevere had not contented himself with "and others" in the report which he sent to the Catholic Almanac for 1857.

> There are two free schools for boys (one English and one French) attached to St. Mary's Church, Monroe, Michigan. These schools have been in existence these last five years, and stand in reputation, at the head of the primary schools of Michigan. They have about two hundred scholars in regular attendance.
>
> There is also a free school attached to St. Michael's (German) Church. The average number of scholars in attendance is between eighty and ninety.
>
> *Catholic Parish Schools* are attached to St. Joseph's Church, Detroit. Catholic Schools have also been established in the following places: Assumption, Grosse Pointe, Flint, Pontiac, Westphalia, Swan Creek, (St. Clair Co.) Marshall, Adrian, and others. . . .

In the Catholic Directory for 1874, there appears for the first time an authoritative list of the parochial schools in the Diocese of Detroit. It comprises fifty entries in all. Fourteen of them refer to localities now in the Diocese of Grand Rapids; fifteen refer to schools which have already been mentioned here as being in charge of the Sisters. The remaining entries are as follows:

St. Vincent's	Detroit	St. Mary's	Conner's Creek
St. Boniface	Detroit	St. Michael's	Flint
St. Joseph's	Adrian	St. Francis	Freedom
St. Mary's	Wayne	Our Lady of Help	Detroit
St. John's	Jackson	St. Anthony's	Detroit
St. Mary's	Niles	St. John's	Dearborn
St. Mary's	Lansing	St. John's	Ypsilanti
St. Stephen's	Port Huron	St. Augustine's	Kalamazoo

St. Joseph's	St. Joseph	St. Clement's	Centerline
St. Michael's	Port Austin	St. Alphonsus	Greenfield
St. Mary's	St. Clair		

Many of the foregoing schools, all conducted by lay teachers, certainly dated from the later years of Bishop Lefevere's episcopate. Some of them were doubtless the result of the impetus given to Catholic education by Bishop Borgess on his accession to the diocese in 1870. With a blind faith in figures we might conclude that at least twelve schools had been started during the period from 1870 to 1874, for in the Directory of 1873 there are said to be thirty-eight schools having an attendance of ten thousand pupils. But our confidence in these statistics is not strengthened by the fact that in 1874, when there are fifty schools, the attendance is still ten thousand.

During the seventeen years of Bishop Borgess' episcopate, from 1870 to 1887, progress was slow but constant. Seven parochial schools were opened in Detroit: St. Wenceslaus (1874); Sacred Heart (1875); St. Joachim (1875); St. Albertus (1872); Holy Redeemer (1881); St. Casimir (1884); St. Elizabeth (1886).

More fortunate than his predecessor, Bishop Borgess was able to cope with a situation which by this time was acute, the lack of a Catholic college in Detroit. He entered into negotiations with the Jesuit superior at St. Louis, and it is a proof of his earnestness that he offered the Jesuits his own cathedral parish for their foundation. The offer was accepted, and on April 5, 1877, the property was transferred to the Society in fee simple. The initial band of four priests arrived in Detroit on June 1, headed by Father John Baptist Miege, who had lately resigned his office as bishop of Leavenworth after twenty years of laborious service on the western frontier. In September, the Detroit College began its classes in a spacious residence opposite the church. Another residence for temporary use was secured in 1885, and the College was at last adequately housed when the present building on Jefferson Avenue was ready for occupancy in 1890.[87]

The number of schools in the diocese outside of Detroit at the end of 1873 has already been given. In the period from this date to the end of Bishop Borgess' episcopate additional schools were opened in the following localities.

Battle Creek	1874	Dorr	1876
Roseville	1874	Wyandotte	1876
Monroe (St. John's)	1875	Hudson	1877
Adrian	1875	Flushing	1879
Newport	1875	Parisville	1884
Richmond	1876	New Salem	1887

[87] William T. Doran, S.J., "Historical Sketch of the University of Detroit" in the *Mich. Hist. Mag.*, II, 154–64.

During the same period there was a corresponding increase in the ranks of the Sisterhoods. Seven communities not heretofore represented in the diocese were introduced.

In 1872, five Sisters of Charity from the motherhouse at Cincinnati took charge of the parish school at Kalamazoo.[88] They withdrew at the end of a year, but in 1875 the Sisters were again in the diocese, this time at Lansing.

Sisters of Christian Charity were given the parish schools at Westphalia in 1874, at Ionia in 1879, and St. Elizabeth's at Detroit in 1886. They were members of a community founded in Germany, which had been exiled during the *Kulturkampf*. Welcomed to the United States in 1873, they established their motherhouse in Wilkes-Barre.

The Sisters of Providence were brought from France to America in 1840, and the motherhouse was established at St. Mary-of-the-Woods, near Terre Haute, Indiana. In 1875 they accepted two schools in the diocese, one at Kalamazoo, which they held for two years, and the other at Marshall, where they remained until 1880. Returning to the diocese in 1884 to take charge of the school at Port Huron, they added Centerline in 1886, and Ypsilanti in 1887.

The Sisters of St. Agnes, whose present motherhouse is at Fond Du Lac, were founded at Barton, Wisconsin, in 1858. Their first school in the diocese was maintained for seventeen years at Greenfield, to which they came in 1880.

The first Dominican Sisters in Michigan were sent from the Second Street Convent in New York to Traverse City in 1877. A year later the Sisters took charge of the school in St. Mary's parish, Adrian, and in 1879 of St. Joseph's. Then followed the schools at Port Austin (1880), at Battle Creek (1881), and at the Grotto parish in Detroit (1887).

The Sisters of the Holy Names of Jesus and Mary, a Canadian community founded at Longueuil in 1844, were invited to the diocese to take charge of the schools in the two French parishes resulting from the division of old St. Anne's. The existing school at St. Joachim's was taken over in 1886, and the school in the newly founded St. Anne's parish was opened in 1888.

During the period we are considering, the Poles formed the largest immigrant group in Detroit. St. Albertus, the first Polish parish in the city, had opened a parochial school in 1871, and six years later there

---

[88] In 1850 a portion of the community founded by Mother Seton, the Sisters of Charity, affiliated with the French community, the Daughters of Charity of St. Vincent De Paul. This is the correct designation of the Sisters who wear the white cornette. The Sisters of Charity had been established in Cincinnati in 1829.

was an enrollment of at least three hundred children in classes conducted by lay teachers.[89] No Sisterhood in the diocese could be of any service in dealing with this new racial group that clung so tenaciously to its language, and was destined to grow to such imposing proportions. The arrival, therefore, in the diocese of the Felician Sisters was most providential. Founded in Warsaw in 1855, the Sisterhood had later opened a motherhouse in Cracow, and from it the first band of Sisters came to the United States in 1874. They established their headquarters in the Diocese of Green Bay, near Stevens Point, Wisconsin, and from there came to Detroit in 1880 to take over St. Albertus' school. In the following year the motherhouse itself was transferred to Detroit, which remained the headquarters of the Sisterhood in the United States until 1900, when the first division occurred with the formation of the Buffalo province. The Sisters opened two additional schools in 1884, one at St. Casimir's, the second Polish parish in the city, and the other at Parisville.[90]

We must now glance at the work of the older Sisterhoods in the diocese during the period. The Daughters of Charity, after giving up their charge in Trinity parish, retired from school work to devote themselves entirely to their charitable institutions. The Religious of the Sacred Heart, while maintaining their day school on Jefferson Avenue, founded their Convent and Academy of the Sacred Heart at Grosse Pointe Farms in 1885. The Sisters of Notre Dame took charge of the girls' school in Sacred Heart parish in 1876. Remarkable progress was made by the Sisters of the Immaculate Heart. In Detroit they opened schools in the following parishes: St. Vincent (1874), Our Lady of Help (1876), St. Boniface (1876), St. Anthony (1876),[91] Holy Redeemer (1887). Outside of Detroit the field of their activity was widened to include Jackson (1876), St. John's at Monroe (1876), Adrian (1876),[92] Flint (1877), Kalamazoo (1878),[93] Marshall (1883), Battle Creek (1884), Wyandotte (1885).

One teaching body remains to be mentioned, the Christian Brothers. In addition to their work at St. Mary's, they had taught for about a year in the first school in Sacred Heart parish. As we have seen, the Brothers withdrew from Detroit in June, 1877. Since St. Mary's parish had been given to the Franciscans in 1872, the Brothers were replaced by Franciscan Brothers. But in the fall of the same year the

[89] *History and Directory of the Churches in Detroit* (Detroit, 1877).

[90] For information regarding the various Sisterhoods here mentioned see the indispensable volume by Elinor Tong Dehey, *Religious Orders of Women in the United States* (Hammond, Ind., 1930).

[91] Taken over by the Franciscan Brothers in 1880.

[92] For only one year.

[93] Succeeded by the Sisters of St. Joseph in 1891.

Christian Brothers returned to Detroit, this time to take charge of the boys' school in St. Joseph's parish.

We may close this summary of educational development during the episcopate of Bishop Borgess by citing the more or less accurate figures in the Catholic Directory for 1888: Schools . . . 60; Pupils . . . 11,470.

During the pioneer period covered by the episcopate of Bishop Lefevere the clergy and laity of the diocese had to strain every resource to provide the bare physical essentials of a school system. Efficiency and improvement had to wait until there were schools to be improved. The progress made through the unrelaxing efforts of Bishop Borgess to increase the number of parochial schools was such that towards the end of his episcopate attention could be shifted from number to quality. Doubtless there were individual attempts made here and there to raise the standards of the diocesan schools; but the beginnings of concerted action appear in the fifth diocesan synod held in 1881. One of the questions submitted to the assembled clergy for discussion was the following:

> Is it opportune to establish a Diocesan School Board? And if in the affirmative, is it advisable to enact that only those teachers may be employed in the parochial schools of this Diocese who have a certificate of competency from this Board?

The committee delegated to register the opinion of the synod issued a short minority report unfavorable to the proposal, and a favorable majority report interesting enough to deserve to be quoted.

> To increase the efficiency of our teachers, to augment the interest which our people take or should take in Catholic schools, and to promote and advance our schools generally, we deem it advisable that the organization of our schools should be more and more perfected. As a means to that end we believe it opportune that school-boards should be established as follows
>
> 1. A central or diocesan school-board in Detroit, composed of three priests and three laymen.
>
> 2. A Board of Inspectors in every parish, composed of the Rector and one or two laymen.
>
> 3. The central or diocesan board should be elected by the Rectors of the parishes in Detroit which have schools, subject to the confirmation of the Bishop.
>
> 4. The Central or Diocesan Board should have nothing to do, nor interfere with the erection of suitable school buildings, nor with the maintenance or support of the schools.
>
> 6. The Central or Diocesan Board should examine all lay teachers

and issue to them a certificate of 1st, 2nd, or 3rd, class, according to their accomplishments. . . .

8. Teachers who up to this time have taught in our schools will not be required to be examined, nor those who hold a diploma of a normal school or academy.

9. Teachers belonging to the religious orders will not be examined. But the schedule setting forth the different branches which teachers of the 1st, 2nd, or 3rd class should be competent to teach will be sent to the superiors. And if the superiors assent or affirm that they are so competent, they will receive a certificate for their respective grades. . . .

10. The Board of Inspectors in each parish should decide (a) about the erection of new school buildings. (b) About the proper maintenance and support of the school. (c) They should examine the pupils of the school, or assist at their examination by the teachers at least once a year, or whenever they deem it necessary or expedient. (d) The board should also conduct the examination of teachers. . . .

The application of the foregoing recommendations was delayed for some years. In the sixth diocesan synod, held in 1885, there was no mention of schools. But the Statutes of the Diocese issued by Bishop Borgess at the conclusion of the next synod in the following year include a section on schools which is certainly based on the 1881 report.

A Diocesan School Board is instituted whose primary function is to pass on the fitness of all parochial school teachers, religious and lay. No pastor is to retain in his school any teacher who does not hold a certificate from the Board. Teachers' examinations are to be held twice yearly. The Board has full authority to impose a uniform series of textbooks upon the schools of the diocese. Each member of the Board is to be responsible for the efficiency of the schools in his district, and is to transmit a yearly report to the presiding officer of the Board. The Board is held to furnish the bishop with a yearly report describing the physical condition of the schools, and commenting on the discipline, attendance, and courses of study.

The first Diocesan School Board, composed of five clergymen, was named in 1887. Bishop Foley introduced in 1890 the modifications which remained in force for many years. A Board of Examiners was formed to deal with the qualifications of teachers, and School Boards were set up in each of the deaneries of the diocese—numbering five at the time, and six at present—to which the other functions of the original Diocesan School Board were entrusted.

There remains to be considered the special type of school, which not only rounds out the educational system of a diocese but is so vital to its needs, the seminary. The beginnings of seminary training in the Diocese of Detroit go back to the short-lived attempt made by Fa-

thers Richard and Dilhet in 1804 to gather suitable candidates for
the priesthood. In the absence of native vocations Bishop Rese did as
the other early American bishops. He brought what students he
could from Europe, and attempted to complete their training in his
own household. The Catholic Encyclopedia referring to the first
American seminaries thus describes them:

> As a rule these seminaries were begun in or near the bishop's house,
> and often with the bishop as chief instructor. The more advanced stu-
> dents helped to instruct the others, and all took part in the services of
> the cathedral. Their education, like that given to priests in the Early
> Church, was individual and practical; their intellectual training may
> have been somewhat deficient, but their priestly character was moulded
> by daily intercourse with the self-sacrificing pioneer bishops and priests.

Bishop Lefevere was forced to be content with the same primitive
arrangement, but he, at least, conferred on his small group of students the dignity of a name. The Catholic Almanac for 1847 is the
first to carry the following notice:

Seminary of St. Thomas,
Detroit, Michigan.

Under the immediate care of the Rt. Rev. Bishop and Very Rev.
Peter Kindekins. There are four seminarians devoting themselves to
philosophical and theological studies.

The number of students rose to nine in 1848, but fell to seven in
the next year. Apparently, the seminary was discontinued in 1854,
for the last mention of it occurs in the Almanac for that year. Bishop
Lefevere would soon have available for his students the American
College at Louvain.

St. Thomas Seminary hardly deserved the name it bore, but it
marked at least the foresight of a pioneer bishop. The diocese had
now reached a stage wherein native vocations might be expected. We
do not know what steps Bishop Lefevere took to unearth them, but,
if we may base an opinion on a quaint document in the Chancery
Archives, the first group of native students for the priesthood left Detroit in 1856.[94] Under this heading, "Young Men destined for the Ec-

[94] The reader will remember from the chapter on the St. Joseph Mission that the first
native of Michigan to enter the priesthood was one of the Collet brothers. During the
French regime there was only one other native of Michigan ordained, to the best of our
knowledge. Tanguay, in his *Répertoire General*, mentions Joseph-Laurent Ducharme,
born at Mackinac, April 11, 1758, and ordained April 5, 1783. He died at Sault-Saint-
Louis December 29, 1793.

The first native born priest of the Diocese of Detroit was Father Moses F. Letourneau, who died as pastor of Trinity Church on August 14, 1851. From a lengthy
obituary notice in the *Catholic Almanac* for 1852 the following extract is quoted.

. . . His family, highly respectable, were originally from Canada, and amongst

clesiastical State in the Diocese of Detroit," the bishop recorded eight names:

Godfried Bolte
Benjamin Schmittdiel,   aged 21,
John Reichenbach,   "   16,
James Pulcher   "   13,
Charles Greiner   "   17,
Wendelin Baumgartner   "   15,
John Heaphy   "   13,
William Carey   "   17.

Of these candidates the first four were to end their lives only after long years of service in the Diocese of Detroit. The bishop himself accompanied the seminarians to their destination, and we may read in the expense account—kept as Bishop Lefevere would keep it, down to the last penny—the paternal pride with which he watched over his chosen few until he brought them safely to the door of the seminary.

Travelling expenses paid by Bp. P. P. Lefevere for each Student with whom he started on the first day of September, A.D. 1856, to the preparatory seminary of St. Thomas, 4½ from Bardstown, Nelson County—Kentucky.

Sept. 1st.	paid half rail road fare from Detroit to Michigan City	$3.00
Sept. 2nd.	paid in Michigan City for breakfast & dinner	1.00
"	paid rail road fare from Michigan City to New Albany	7.00
"	paid at Lafayette for supper	0.50
Sept. 3rd.	paid at New Albany for ferry & Omnibus to Louisville	0.37
"	paid at Louisville in Exchange hotel for breakfast & dinner	1.00
"	paid rail road & stage fare to Bardstown	2.50
"	paid omnibus line for Baggage & c. to rail road depot	0.25
Sept. 4th.	To paid at Bardstown, Mansion House (Mr. Moore Cath. Landlord) for supper, lodging & Carriages to St. Thomas 4½ miles to Bardstown	1.25

Unfortunately for the diocese, the hopes that might have been raised by such a beginning were not destined to be realized. Native

---

the early settlers of Detroit. Born in this city, May 13, 1822, he gave early indications of a sedate and pious disposition. . . . Destined by his friends for a secular employment it was not until the year 1842 that he turned his thoughts seriously to the ecclesiastical state. In the following year he entered the community of Notre Dame du Lac, under the priests of the Holy Cross, where during the course of his studies, pursued perhaps with an ardor too devoted for a delicate constitution, the germ of the fatal malady which has prematurely closed his useful and edifying career was developed. . . . Under the impression that his native air would prove more salubrious, he returned after a few years to Detroit, entered the Diocesan Seminary, and was ordained priest the 30th of June, 1850. In charge of the congregation attached to Trinity church, his piety and zeal have left an imperishable record in the affections and regrets of his flock. The Rev. M. F. Letourneau was the first native priest of the diocese of Detroit.

vocations continued to be few and far between. Of the eighty-eight priests in the diocese when Bishop Borgess came in 1870, only eight were native born. The need of a preparatory seminary was evident, but the bishop was unable to carry out the project until near the close of his episcopate.

In 1885 the three parishes in Monroe decided to unite in the support of a central high school. The plan was inspired by Father De Broux, who had retired from his pastorate at Grosse Pointe, and was living in Monroe. At the time, there was for sale the Monroe Young Ladies' Seminary, a secular school which had been founded in the early fifties, and Father De Broux purchased the property with his own funds. When ratifying the purchase, Bishop Borgess saw an opportunity of beginning his preparatory seminary, and he induced the priests of Monroe to forego their plan in favor of the larger interests of the diocese. In September, 1886, the St. Francis Diocesan Seminary was opened under the rectorship of Father Peter Leavy, pastor of St. John's parish in Monroe, with an enrollment of thirty-five pupils. Two years later, Father Leavy was succeeded by Father Edward D. Kelly, the future bishop of Grand Rapids. But the operation of the seminary proved to be so serious a drain upon the resources of the diocese that Bishop Foley, on his accession, was reluctantly compelled to discontinue it. St. Francis Seminary closed its doors at the end of June, 1889.

The foregoing account of the efforts made to establish a seminary ministering strictly to the needs of the diocese has made no reference to another diocesan institution having a much wider scope. Its origin is due to the single-handed exertions of a remarkable priest whose merits have hardly penetrated outside of the national group with which he was affiliated. Father Joseph Dabrowski was born in Russion Poland in 1842. As a university student he was prominently identified with Poland's struggle against Russian domination, and was forced to take refuge in Germany. He later continued his studies in Rome, where he was ordained in 1869. Deciding to consecrate his life to the welfare of his countrymen in America, Father Dabrowski came to the United States in 1870, and for twelve years devoted himself to the care of several Polish colonies in the Diocese of Green Bay.

As an important center of Polish immigration Detroit beckoned to Father Dabrowski, and he came in 1882 with the cordial approval of Bishop Borgess. He began his duties as pastor of St. Albertus, but his horizon stretched far beyond. From his knowledge of the racial characteristics of his people, and his wide grasp of their religious and social needs, he was convinced that their future welfare lay in the building up of an American-born, American-trained priesthood of their own nationality. Encouraged by several American bishops who had large Polish groups in their dioceses, and with the approbation which he secured at the knees of Leo XIII himself, Father Dabrowski set to work to realize his vision with little more than his trust in Divine Providence. In St. Aubin Avenue, between Forest and Garfield Avenues, he began the building of SS. Cyril and Methodius Seminary. The corner-stone was laid July 27, 1885, and the completed structure was dedicated by Bishop Borgess on December 16, 1886.

When Father Dabrowski died on February 15, 1903, as rector of the institution which he had founded, he had molded the lives of a large body of priests scattered throughout the United States. It would be difficult to estimate the worth of his services to his own people, and to the Church in America as well.

The Polish Seminary, as it is familiarly called in the Diocese of Detroit, has been since its foundation the only institution of its kind in the United States. The need for expansion led to the purchase in 1909 of the site and buildings of the Michigan Military Academy at Orchard Lake, and in the following year the Seminary abandoned its original buildings for the new location. Under the rectorship of Monsignor Michael Grupa, beginning in 1917, the institution widened its scope by including a college department distinct from the Seminary, and not restricted to candidates for the priesthood.

CHAPTER XXVII

Charities

THE indwelling of Christ in His Church must ever make her the supreme dispenser not only of the enlightenment which He brought to the minds of men, but also of His perpetual ministration to the ills and suffering of mankind. From an inner compulsion she must mirror Christ to the world by her vicarious ministry, and bend in reverential service over every form of human need and misery. The exercise of the corporal and spiritual works of mercy is primarily the duty of the individual Christian, and only the Book of Life can record the incalculable number of benefactions inspired by the "new commandment." In general it is only the corporate charities that men may record, and because they are such they imply a growth from obscure and fumbling beginnings, and a certain level of development. In our survey of the Church in Detroit in its pioneer stage we must advert to the efforts of its pioneer representatives to extend Christian charity beyond the individual to the community.

There is little to detain us in the period antedating the erection of the diocese. The hardy, vigorous adventurers, traders, and soldiers that made up the population of Detroit in the early days of the French regime needed favors from no one. When the government determined to convert the trading post into a colony, it apparently made sufficient provision to supply the simple needs of those who could be induced to come. Probably the first recorded instance of poor relief in Detroit is coupled with the appearance of those forlorn captives, Michael Yax and his family. "The public generously extended charity to him," writes the Royal Notary, "and by this means together with his own efforts he supported himself until February 15, 1751, when he was granted a farm of three arpents on the north shore." [1] The British and American occupations profoundly modified the character of Detroit. Satisfied to lead the good life they had always known the French left the town to the forceful foreigners, and lived in static peace on their outlying farms. Progress may have passed them by; but at least they presented no social problem. They were self sufficient and content. The transition to the later period

[1] Cicotte Book. BHC.

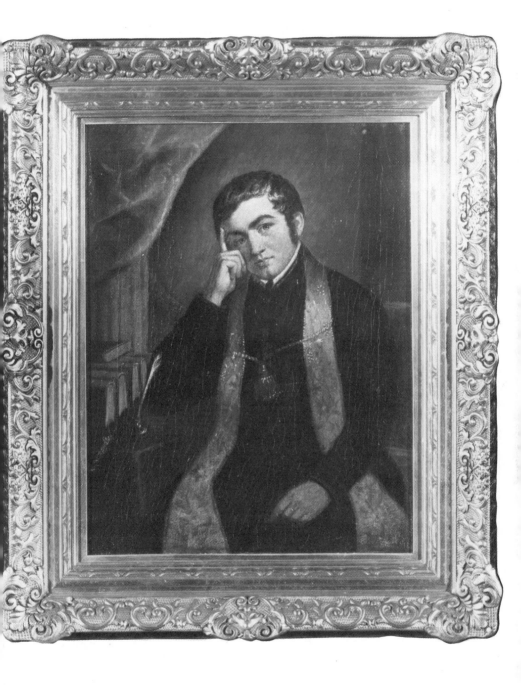

FATHER MARTIN KUNDIG. Portrait made in Detroit by James Bowman in 1834. Reproduction by courtesy of Archbishop Moses Kiley of Milwaukee.

may be made in the lines with which Farmer begins his chapter on poor relief in Detroit.

The first settlers were mostly poor, but for many years pauperism was unknown. The pluck that inspired the coming to a wilderness, and the vigilance which a residence in such wilds demanded, precluded that supineness of which poverty is born. True, there were times of trial and seasons of distress; crops failed, and more than once gaunt famine hovered over the palisades of Pontchartrain. Such times, however, were only incidental. Game and grain were usually plentiful, and the few families who dwelt here ate their own bread and asked no alms of strangers. Not until the Yankees came did "beggars come to town," and that not because the Yankees set the example of begging, but because upon their advent the population increased, and as towns grow, beggars multiply.[2]

The life of Father Richard spanned the period during which Detroit grew from a frontier military post to a thriving town peopled by all the racial strains in the forefront of western immigration. What little definite knowledge we possess of his charitable activities has been given elsewhere. His death in the cholera epidemic of 1832 left to others the task of beginning organized Catholic charities with the elements that were just coming to hand.

Unique as is the place in Detroit history occupied by Father Richard there is another pioneer priest who deserves to be associated with him, Father Martin Kundig. Father Richard was the first citizen of Detroit to point out and insist upon the duty of the community to provide the means of education. Father Kundig was the protagonist of a no less important enterprise, that of forcing upon his community in the rising complexities of urban life the duty of charity and help to victims of misfortune and affliction.[3] His exertions in the cholera epidemic have already been recorded; his true measure is seen only in the light of subsequent events.

The maintenance and care of the poor in the Territory had been dealt with as early as 1790, but there was little tangible evidence of this solicitude in Detroit until 1832.[4] In that year a county poorhouse was built on the north side of Gratiot Avenue, just west of Mt. Elliott Avenue, and in January, 1833, J. P. Cooley was appointed its keeper. Under his administration conditions became so deplorable that some sort of intervention was imperative. If the citizens in general were apathetic, Father Kundig was not. Shortly after his arrival in Detroit

[2] *Op. cit.*, I, 648.

[3] *Idem*, 650. The larger Protestant population of the town had, as far back as 1817, organized the *Moral and Humane Society*.

[4] See Stanislaus M. Keenan, *History of Eloise* (Detroit, 1913). This history of what is today the Wayne County General Hospital and Infirmary is dedicated to Father Kundig.

he had organized the women of St. Anne's into some sort of charitable society. It was probably intended at first to care for the children
who had been orphaned by the epidemic of 1832. It gave way to an
association of which we have definite knowledge, the Catholic Female Benevolent Society, founded in St. Anne's by Father Kundig on
February 6, 1834. The preamble in the Minute Book of the Society
has a passage that seems to refer to an earlier grouping.

> There are in this congregation, some whose wishes were strong, but
> who failed in realizing those philanthropic wishes, from having so few
> to encourage and support them in this benevolent work, therefore be-
> coming disheartened relinquished the task, believing there were in-
> surmountable obstacles to prevent its progress. The arrival of the Rt.
> Rev. Bishop has however caused a gleam of hope to dawn upon their
> pious undertaking, and former efforts were renewed after he became
> acquainted with their desire . . .[5]

The founding meeting of the Society, held in the episcopal residence, was attended by fifty women, and "the Rev. Mr. Kundig advanced several reasons to prove the necessity of laying a solid foundation upon which the members might build their hope of success . . ."
The usual roster of officers was elected, and to them were added two
"Commissioners" to be frequently changed, and who were to do the
field work for the Society. In subsequent meetings a distinctive mode
of dress was prescribed for the members when on public duty. It was
to be a "black dress, white cape, straw bonnet *fashionable,* with black
ribbon." To provide a fund for sewing materials a fine of 3 cents was
levied against absentees; and later, in a drastic move to compel full
attendance, the fine was raised to $12\frac{1}{2}$ cents. Another source of income came from portion of the Sunday collection at St. Anne's which
Bishop Rese conceded to the Society.

> The ladies of the cath. female society of Detroit are requested by the
> undersigned and the trustees of St. Ann's to make the collections in
> said church on all the holydays of the year.
> The trustees will make the collection of Sundays and will on every
> holyday accompany or conduct through the church the two ladies
> chosen by the above female Society to make the intended collection.
>   Fred. Rese, Bishop of Detroit.

The Society had been in existence barely a month when it decided,
doubtless impelled thereto by Father Kundig, to protest against the
wretched conditions at the poorhouse. We have his own account of
the Society's action.

[5] The original Minute Book is in the Milwaukee Chancery Archives. Through the
kindness of the Rev. Peter Leo Johnson, the biographer of Father Kundig, a copy was
procured for the DCA.

In the month of March, 1834, the Ladies Society, called "the Catholic Female Association, for the relief of the sick and poor of Detroit" was informed of the pitiable situation in which the inmates of the Wayne County poor house were kept, and of the unfinished state of the building, which was only inclosed and no arrangements made in the interior, boarded partitions having only been put up in a temporary manner; the sick were therefore in a wretched condition. Two commissioners of the association succeeded in arousing the sympathy of the members to the miserable state of the institution, and of its unfortunate inmates; the result of which was, that they laid the following petition before the supervisors of the poor house . . .

The petition as quoted by Father Kundig is in two paragraphs. The first points out "the deplorable situation of the sick in the poorhouse . . . which cannot be beheld by any feeling person without seeking alleviation for them." The second expresses the willingness of the Society to take over the management of the poorhouse, and the care of the sick.

The epidemic of 1834 broke out before an answer from the Board of Supervisors had been received. Father Kundig describes his relief work and then adds: "While I was engaged amid these suffering scenes, the president of the county board of supervisors, observing our exertions, proffered, without any solicitation on our part, to the Association, the care and superintendence of the county poorhouse." [6]

On taking charge of the poorhouse the Commissioners of the Society wrote a somewhat more graphic report of conditions there than had Father Kundig.

According to the suggestion of the director of the Association it has been deemed expedient to send in a fair & impartial account of the County hospital or poor house to the board of Supervisors. Wherefore the honorable members are hereby made acquainted with the state of the house, in which it was found when given over to the care of the society, in which it is now at present & in which it is considered it ought to be, in order to become any ways comfortable. Mr. Williams the clerk was sent on the 1st of Sept to take an inventory of all that belongs to the house, as can be seen. No. 1.

It may suffice to state that the inventory exhibited a property, for which, the cows and yearlings excepted, no man would pay $30.00. When inspected by Mr. Williams the chimney was found to be broken, the house more like to a barn than a building to be inhabited by humane (sic) beings, without plan, order or regulation.

[6] *Exposition of Facts* . . . Pamphlet quoted in Chap. XIX, note 23. The pamphlet is here followed in preference to other sources of information. It gives the simple facts stripped of traditional accretions. No one has ever questioned their accuracy, or the justice of Father Kundig's motive in presenting them.

There was no well, where water might be obtained, no accommodation house, nor decency found among the inmates. Nineteen county poor, then, were inhabiting the building, some of whom were, though very sick, lying on the bare floor or benches, doomed to suffer in a most pitiful situation, eaten by lice, fleas & bedbugs, which were more numerous than your honorable body can hardly credit. It must be obvious to your honorable body that a house appointed to be the refuge of the miserable the needy & the poor could not be left in such a state . . .[7]

As promoter and prime mover of the Society Father Kundig thus became a public official, the Superintendent of the Poor. He lived for the most part at the poorhouse, and spent almost five years in unflinching devotion to his ideals of charity, which were far beyond the scope of his official duties. Alone, he tried to bear the brunt of the havoc that was the aftermath of the epidemic; a long period of business depression, with consequent unemployment, an unusual number of dependent poor, and a swarm of orphans. Father Kundig tells us how he tried to solve the unemployment problem.

From the situation that I then held, these distressed people flew to me—scenes of misery were daily, nay hourly, opened to my view— parents seeking for labor, while their children loudly called for bread, in vain. I could not witness these scenes any longer without making some exertion for their relief. To accomplish this object I leased fifty acres of woodland situated about one mile from the Fort Gratiot road; an almost impassable swamp was situated between the said land and the turnpike. I was therefore compelled to make some arrangements, and preferred building a railroad to bring the great quantity of firewood to market.[8]

In his official position Father Kundig completed the poorhouse, and then erected another building which he called the Infirmary. "This I put up, about three rods north-east of the poor house, on the county ground. It was also arranged for a public bath—as there was then none in the city—from which it was expected some profit would be derived. But in this we were disappointed, for as soon as it was found profitable, the proprietor of the Exchange Hotel added baths to his establishment." The bath house later became a hospital for patients who could afford to pay for their care.[9]

The orphans in the wake of the epidemic seem to have been Fa-

[7] Quoted from the Minute Book.

[8] "On the west side of the farm, running north and south was a roadway, which was called Kundig's railroad. On it was a line of wooden rails, extending beyond the poor farm to a wood lot, which was leased by Father Kundig, the poormaster. Trucks run on these rails transported saw logs to Gratiot avenue, and from thence were taken to a saw mill, where they were converted into boards, and sold for the benefit of the institution." Ross and Catlin, *op. cit.*, 464.

[9] This was surely the first private hospital in Detroit.

ther Kundig's greatest concern. Just the bare recital of his exertions for them makes a touching picture.

> I was compelled, first to remove the dying parents to the hospital, and then to carry the children from house to house, before I could get any one to take them in, and in most cases, not until I had promised $2 per week for their board. The poor children had to be stripped of their old clothes, and new ones put on, before they would be received, as it was feared their clothes would convey the contagion. The expense of supporting them separately being very great, I thought it expedient to collect them together, in a house which I rented for that purpose, and had them conveyed thither, with the assistance of the aforesaid Ladies' Association . . .[10]

> The Ladies' Association felt a lively interest in the helpless little ones, and particularly Mrs. E. Leib, daughter of P. J. Desnoyer, whom I consider it my duty to mention; but their means were too limited to give me the aid I required. I then made formal application to the most respectable of the citizens for relief. I took the little creatures with me to the principal hotels, where I met the boarders and other persons. I addressed them in behalf of the unfortunate orphans, by which means I raised $100; but this was only a small sum, to feed and clothe so many. The consequence was, that I was compelled to sell a part of my own furniture to procure food for these little sufferers.

> The Ladies' Association were now busily engaged in making preparations for a Fair, which they held in the year 1835, and a second which they held in November, 1836. The net profits after deducting all expenses, amounted to $1300.

> We now procured a lease of 20 acres of wood land, adjoining the county poor house, and erected there a building, to which we removed the orphans. We had a good school, to which all the poor children of the neighborhood were admitted free . . .[11]

Despite the cares entailed by the management of the foregoing institutions Father Kundig was bent upon a community project, the need of which to him was self evident. The Minute Book of the Society in recording the session of January 15, 1835, copies a petition which the Director is to present to the city officials.

> Since the Catholic female association is established for the sole purpose of rendering assistance and relief to the distressed portion of their fellow beings, and since therefore no kind of individual interest or party-spirit will be found to be the motive of the exertions of the members; it has been considered both reasonable and expedient to make known their ideas to the common council upon a subject which is worthy of the attention of every philanthropic friend and disinterested citizen. We cannot but consider it for granted that the honorable

[10] The orphan asylum was located on Larned Street near Randolph Street.
[11] *Exposition of Facts* . . .

members of the board see into the necessity of having some kind of arrangements made towards building an hospital for the City of Detroit. Were it not to imitate the noble zeal of other cities of the union, many of which are not as promising as ours, were it not to save our honor or to guard against merited shame, there are other motives to be considered equally weighty and important. The circumstances in which the City was found last'year, prove more than all reasoning can establish, the necessity of the measure and should forever put down any opposition thereto. What happened may happen again, and not to guard against visible danger can never meet the approbation of prudent men . . .

The petition goes on to present a general notion of the structure necessary, and mentions as a probable site "some lots behind the jail" which Bishop Rese is willing to donate for the purpose. Father Kundig's plan was well received, approved, as a further entry in the Minute Book discloses, and tabled. It was not until many years later, in another crisis, that the city was moved to provide hospital care for its citizens in dire need.

For all his unsparing devotion to the needy Father Kundig was requited, not with the gratitude of his fellow citizens, but with a burden of personal misfortune. He was too unique a public official. When he presented his accounts for the care of the poor he was paid, not in money, but in county warrants on an empty treasury, which were negotiable, at best, for about half their face value. Rather than desert his poor he borrowed on his personal credit. In 1837, during the first session of the state legislature he was given $3000 for his services during the cholera epidemic, but by this time his debts were far in excess of that amount.[12] The panic of that year, and the era of wildcat banking that followed left Father Kundig at the mercy of the tradesmen from whom he had been purchasing food, medicines, and supplies for the county poor.[13] Disgraceful scenes were enacted as his creditors bore down upon him.

[12] "An Act for the Relief of Martin Kundig. Be it enacted by the Senate and House of Representatives of the State of Michigan, That the treasurer of the state be, and is hereby authorized to pay to Martin Kundig, on the warrant of the auditor general, the sum of three thousand dollars, out of any money in the treasury not otherwise appropriated, as a compensation for his services and expenses, in relieving the poor and distressed in time of the cholera in the city of Detroit in 1834. Approved March 18, 1837." Keenan, op. cit., 43.

[13] Unable to appease a bank from which he had borrowed Father Kundig wrote to its lawyer: "I received your note in consequence of which I went yesterday to your office but found it shut. I am glad that you sent me notice before you entered the suit. If I can by any means induce the Bank to have patience, I shall do it. Though I have no money this moment to pay the Bank, I still am more anxious to pay than any one can be to be paid. My engagements for the sick and poor at the County poor house where I worked day and night for the afflicted, have turned out a sad affair for me. . . . Most of my property at the poor house has in consequence of it been sold for a mere trifle." Letter dated September 19, 1839, among the Joy papers in the BHC.

"But finally they could wait no longer," writes Father Kundig. "Messrs. Frost and Ives, in my absence, broke the doors of my rooms, took what they chose, and deranged everything on which I set a value. Other creditors followed; they sold my property, at a time when money was not to be had, and therefore sacrificed it for one-third its value; property which was estimated to be worth from $5,000 to $6,000. They sold even the clothes of the 30 orphans I had then to provide for . . ."

Father Kundig's final affliction was to find himself vilified by stories that he had profited from his position, and that his motives in accepting the office of Superintendent of the Poor were mercenary. The pamphlet from which we have been quoting was his dignified answer to these charges.

"I consider such statements due . . . to the public in general, as many reports have been circulated, which, if true, would forever fill me with sorrow. I have endured much, and I was willing to undergo the affliction, being convinced of the rectitude of my intentions, and with the consciousness of having labored for the distressed to the best of my humble abilities. . . . I never undertook the management of the county poor house with the intention of making money, or of aggrandizing myself. My objects were to aid the afflicted, the poor and the sick, and to follow the ardent desire I had to be continually present with them. . . . Had I studied my own comfort, I surely would not have continued in the poor house so long as I did, toiling day and night, encountering difficulties which beggar description, endeavoring to give comfort to the unfortunate beings under my care; with county warrants as my only currency, which created most perplexing difficulties, insults, abuses, lawsuits, and other perplexities for years . . .

Although Father Kundig held office until 1839, arrangements had been made in the preceding year for a successor, and a new site for the county poorhouse had been selected.[14] He was left to struggle as best he could under a burden of debts amounting to several thousand dollars. The epilogue to this excursion of Father Kundig into public life was written twenty-five years later, when, as Vicar-General of the diocese of Milwaukee he addressed an open letter to the citizens of Detroit. He reviewed the events that had led up to his misfortunes, and then continued:

I appealed to the Legislature, and then to the County Commissioners, for redress. Both advised me to sue the County; that a regular court of justice might decide the question. But I could not persuade myself to enter upon litigation, especially as I was drawn into the affairs solely by my desire to aid the sick and poor—and not as a speculator. I preferred to retire, and, instead of suing, to put up with the difficulty, and gradually to pay and satisfy the creditors, in the best way possible . . .

14 Keenan, *op. cit.*, 46.

Now, after being sixty years old, I have my long desire fulfilled, viz.: not to die before I had satisfied my creditors.

I have now the great satisfaction to state that I have paid my debts—God be praised for it—all excepting two creditors whom I do not know where to find.

Still, although Wayne County has not done justice in this matter, I am now happy to state that, although I am deprived of worldly riches, yet my debts are paid. . . . I look to a just God, who will, I trust, deal with me in mercy, as I then endeavored to act towards those who stood in need of my aid.[15]

Little comment is necessary. Perhaps some day the community that Father Kundig served so well will pay its debt to the memory of this citizen who was the soul of charity and honor, and who spent a quarter of a century hoarding his scanty means to pay the bounden obligations of Detroit and Wayne County.

The charitable institutions under the care of Father Kundig, and which he was obliged to relinquish in 1839, were the County Poor-House, the Infirmary, and the Orphan Asylum. Of these only the last-named drew no support from public funds, and was therefore, strictly speaking, a Catholic charity. It is interesting to note that in the orphan asylum, at least, if not in the other buildings, Father Kundig was assisted by the Poor Clares. He barely refers to them in his 1840 pamphlet, but from the account of his activities in the *Salesianum,* which is based on his reminiscences, we glean this bit of information. The writer has been describing the difficulties of the Poor Clares which led to their final withdrawal from Detroit. He ends his account thus:

Of the other Sisters there, three went to Father Kundig's institution and the rest went away; of these three one died, one went to England and the other left the community, entered into the married state and is now living a happy, noble wife and mother in Wisconsin—this she was at full liberty to take and broke no vow by so doing.[16]

How long the Catholic Female Benevolent Society remained in existence is uncertain. In the Catholic Almanac for 1841, Detroit is credited with two charitable organizations: The Ladies of Providence, who render corporal and spiritual assistance to the poor; The Young Ladies Charitable Society, which has thirty-five members, and which applies its funds to the relief of the poor. Either or both of these groups may have grown out of the original Society. All mention of them ceases with the Almanac of 1844.

[15] The letter written from Milwaukee, and dated October 25, 1865, was addressed to the editor of the *Detroit Advertiser and Tribune.* It was later reprinted in pamphlet form, and there is a copy in the BHC.
[16] XIII, No. 4, 12.

The end of Father Kundig's charitable works, and the dispersal of the Sisters emphasizes the break between the episcopate of Bishop Rese and that of his successor. Everything had to be begun over again. Fortunately, the Daughters of Charity came to Bishop Lefevere's rescue early in his regime, and through them and the other Sisterhoods that were later added to the diocese organized Catholic charity was reborn.

The Daughters of Charity began their work in Detroit by opening a school for boys, and another for girls, in June, 1844. At the end of a year the boys' school was transferred to the basement of St. Anne's, and the problem of how best to utilize the vacant space came up for consideration.

> Sister Rebecca, who had helped to start the hospital in St. Louis, proposed the opening of a hospital in the place where the boys' school had been kept. . . . The good bishop was delighted at the idea of having a place where the poor sick could be taken care of by the Sisters, even with their poor accommodations.[17]

Accordingly, that portion of the Sisters' dwelling which fronted on Larned Street was fitted up for the care of the sick, and on June 9, 1845, St. Vincent's Hospital, the first hospital in Detroit, welcomed its first patient. The few low-ceilinged rooms were soon filled with the unfortunates whom the Sisters somehow managed to stow away. We can look in on them through the initial page of the hospital register.

> Robert Bridgeman, First Patient in St. Vincent's Hospital, very poor, received free; afflicted with an ulcerated leg which has been neglected. An Englishman by birth and a Protestant. Age 37 years.
> Jubenville, Antoine, second patient, free, consumption, a native of Michigan, age 48 years. C[atholic].
> James, third patient, son of a poor widow, free, scald-head, native of Detroit, Irish parents, age 10 years. C.
> Fournier, Julia, to pay one dollar fifty cents per week, nervous disease, has been bed ridden for several years. Native of Detroit, French family, age 35 years. C.
> Harper, Ann, free patient, poor girl at service. Bilious fever, age 19, a native of Scotland. C.
> Russel, Esther, poor, stranger, constitution impaired from chills and fevers, a little girl with her six years of age, Protestant.
> Gastman, Christopher, free patient, spotted fever and complete derangement of the nervous system attended with lock jaw. Native of Germany, Protestant, age 24.

By the end of the year forty-eight patients had been cared for, and during 1846 the number rose to one hundred and twenty-five. The

[17] From the manuscript chronicle in the Emmitsburg archives.

need for expansion was soon imperative, and was met by the generosity of Mrs. Antoine Beaubien, who donated as a hospital site a plot of ground on St. Antoine Street between Mullet and Clinton Streets. On November 6, 1850, the new hospital facing Clinton Street, and named St. Mary's, was opened to the public. In 1879 the hospital was greatly enlarged by the erection of the building facing St. Antoine Street.[18]

From St. Mary's two more charitable institutions took their rise. The Sisters acquired a farm in Michigan Avenue to which they occasionally sent convalescent patients. Here in January, 1860, Sister De Sales opened the Michigan retreat for the Insane. Ten years later a brick structure with accommodations for ninety patients was erected. It stood on the south side of Michigan Avenue just east of the Grand Boulevard. The institution was reincorporated in 1883 under the title of St. Joseph's Retreat. By this time the location had become unsuitable, and a new site was purchased in the village of Dearborn. In October, 1886, the institution was moved to the present buildings.

St. Mary's had no accommodations for another particularly necessary charity, a foundling home, and a maternity hospital in which to shield unmarried mothers. In August, 1869, Sisters Augustine O'Connor and Jane Frances left St. Mary's to begin the House of Providence in a rented dwelling in Adams Street.[19] A few months later, larger quarters were secured in Fourteenth Street, and were used down to 1876.[20] In March, 1876, the institution was transferred to the old Beaubien homestead on the northwest corner of St. Antoine and Elizabeth Streets. A suitable building was later erected, and here

[18] "The first superior in charge was Sister Loyola, who, with Sister Rebecca, became identified with its history and success; and both sacrificed their lives in the exercise of duties connected with the hospital. It is proper to mention here, to the lasting credit of their order, that their hospital is the only one to which persons with contagious diseases were ever admitted; this fact made their name, 'Sisters of Charity,' not a barren title, but a blessed and practical reality." Farmer, op. cit., I, 653.

[19] Richard R. Elliott wrote a sketch of the House of Providence for the bi-centenary edition of the Michigan Catholic, August 22, 1901, in which he mentions the origin of the institution on Adams Street. The city directory for 1870 lists them as being on Fourteenth Avenue.

[20] The article cited in the preceding note reminisces about the Fourteenth Avenue location. "When they opened their doors to care for two patients and three or four infants, they were without money and necessities. . . . Their mission becoming known, Mr. Corby of Connors Creek, Mich., donated $500 and other friends smaller amounts by which the Sisters purchased a little red frame house on Fourteenth Street . . .

On the eve of the second Christmas at "the little red house," the Sisters wondered at the commotion outside, jingling of sleigh bells, and merry voices. Sister Augustine, on going to the window, discovered two sleighs loaded with barrels of flour . . . and everything in the grocery line. On top of all, in one of the sleighs, was a large dressed porker; on the other a mutton. There stood Mr. John Heffron at the door, who said: "Sister, Corktown has broken loose."

the House of Providence continued its beneficent work until 1910. Meanwhile, the growth of Detroit demanded additional Catholic hospital facilities, and the Daughters of Charity decided to erect an institution that would continue the work of the House of Providence, and at the same time be of service to the general public. Mr. Henry Blackwell, a Catholic merchant of Detroit, and his associate Mr. William Pardridge generously donated a site on the corner of the Grand Boulevard and Fourteenth Street, and on April 7, 1910, Providence Hospital was formally opened.

The foregoing institutions represent an unbroken tradition of service to the poor and the afflicted of Detroit. But the charity of the Sisters has not always been confined within their walls. The directories of Detroit for the years between 1861 and 1875 carry this inconspicuous notice:

> City Pest House. St. Aubin Avenue, between Summer and
> Winter Streets. Under charge of Sisters of Charity.

Detroit has often been scourged by epidemics of smallpox, and in these crises the city officials instinctively called upon the Daughters of Charity. This lesser known phase of the Sisters' work, their unflinching devotion to the citizenry of Detroit in times of civic calamity, has been touched upon in one history of Detroit.

> St. Mary's Hospital, which, under the name of St. Vincents, was first opened in 1845 . . . received smallpox patients up to 1861. . . . The patients were lodged in a frame house on Clinton street, on the east side of the present hospital building. In 1861, after the war of the Rebellion commenced, a smallpox hospital, intended principally for soldiers, went into commission on the east side of St. Aubin avenue, on the commons, about one hundred feet south of Kirby avenue. The land was owned by the Sisters of Charity, and that corporation erected a building, which was a two-story frame house with an L. Sister Mary Clair, who had been in charge of the smallpox cases as nurse since 1858, assumed the task in the new hospital. At the close of the war the disease abated, but indigent patients continued to be treated there. In 1870 the city purchased an old frame building, removed it to the lot and joined it to the existing structure. It then became a hospital under the control of Poor Director Willard.
>
> In November, 1876, smallpox was prevalent throughout the city. Dr. J. P. Corcoran, then one of the city physicians, and later one of the Board of Health, was given charge of these cases. Sisters Jene, Rose, and Agnes, of St. Mary's hospital, were the nurses. Up to July, 1877, there was an average of twenty cases per week at this hospital. During the same time there were about 1,000 cases on Hale Street between Riopelle and Dubois streets and adjacent thoroughfares, principally among

Polish families. In the same month the Board of Health enforced a general vaccination in Albertus's Church school. . . .

In 1880 smallpox again broke out in the northeastern part of the city, and Controller H. P. Bridge went out on St. Aubin avenue to see about reestablishing another hospital in that locality. His errand being discovered, he was nearly mobbed by the Polish residents, and he then consulted with the authorities in regard to the exigency. As a result another hospital was fitted up on Twelfth street, north of the city limits, in the township of Greenfield, which was in use some three months during that year, with Sisters Pacifica and Justa as nurses. . . .

A smallpox hospital was established on the north side of Farnsworth street, east of Russell street, in the fall of 1883. It was used for about two years, and was then burned down. Meanwhile Dr. Wight designed the plans for an octagon-shaped hospital on the west side of Crawford street, just north of Gilbert avenue. This was first occupied in the fall of 1885, and the nurses were Sister Superior Frances and Sisters Mary Claire and Magdalene of St. Mary's Hospital. It was burned down in 1892, presumably by an incendiary.[21]

We turn now to the pioneer efforts to care for homeless children. What provisions were made for the Catholic orphans after Father Kundig's institution was closed is uncertain. Writing to the Society for the Propagation of the Faith in 1843, Bishop Lefevere states that he has two orphan asylums, and that "since we can not obtain Sisters of Charity we are forced to pay seculars for these two important establishments." [22] Certainly, at the time there was no particular institution for the purpose, and the probability is that small groups of children were maintained in private homes.

The first Catholic orphanage was opened by the Daughters of Charity in the premises left vacant by the transfer of hospital patients to the new St. Mary's. According to the existing records, St. Vincent's Female Orphan Asylum admitted its first child on July 19, 1851. In the following year a brick building was erected on the same site, and was ready for use in October. After a few years in this location the asylum was transferred to the residence formerly occupied by the bishop, on the west side of Randolph Street between Larned and Congress Streets. Finally, a suitable site was secured in McDougall Avenue, and the new structure was dedicated on July 19, 1876.

The German Catholics of Detroit had the same sense of racial solidarity that characterized their countrymen in the older centers of immigration. They were more willing to make sacrifices for institu-

---

tions of their own than to use existing facilities.[23] The Sisters of Notre Dame who took charge of the girls' school in St. Mary's parish in 1852 apparently sheltered a few orphans in their convent on Macomb Street between St. Antoine and Hastings Streets. In 1855 the parish erected a building, which is still standing at 1011 St. Antoine Street, to serve as a convent for the Sisters, and as a female orphan asylum. It is noted in the Catholic Almanac for 1856: "These Sisters have also under their charge an orphan Asylum for girls of St. Mary's congregation, in which there are now 35 orphans." The orphanage was maintained for twenty years down to the opening of the present St. Vincent's.

For a while, some effort was made to care for the boy orphans of the parish, probably in the house left vacant by the removal of the Sisters to their new quarters. The Catholic Almanac for 1859 lists an "Orphan Asylum for German Boys, Macomb Street, kept by a private family." The asylum does not seem to have been maintained for more than four or five years.

The first strictly diocesan project for orphan care was inaugurated by Bishop Lefevere in 1866. There were eight parish groups in Detroit at the time, two of them being German. The other six pooled their resources to erect and maintain a male orphan asylum in Detroit. On January 23, 1867, twelve trustees, two from each parish, were legally incorporated under the title, Saint Anthony's Male Orphan Asylum of the City of Detroit. To the corporation Bishop Lefevere deeded the remainder of the Church Farm, that is, the portion of the original holding lying above Gratiot Avenue.[24] A brick structure capable of accommodating eighty orphans was erected near the northwest corner of Sheridan and Gratiot Avenues, and the management of the institution was entrusted to the Sisters of the Immaculate Heart. This artless entry in the house-chronicle records the admission of the first inmates on May 25, 1867.

> George, Willie, and Noble Hardy, three little brothers, were received on the 25th of May. Their mother, who was a Catholic, was buried on that day. Their father was a Protestant, and caring little for his catholic children gladly consented to their mother's wish that they should be given over to the Asylum. The Sisters were overjoyed when they heard some of Our Lord's "Little Ones" had arrived, and hastened to see them, but their joy was turned into sadness when they beheld the three little destitute creatures who became so frightened on seeing the Sisters

[23] For the influence of racial pride on much organized charity in the early days of the Church in America see John O'Grady, *Catholic Charities in the United States* (Washington, 1931), 77 ff.

[24] Farmer, *op. cit.*, I, 661.

that they screamed and cried bitterly, calling the while for some one to take them home.[25]

In 1876 the orphanage was in financial difficulties, and the Trustees searching for additional support decided that the institution should receive boys from anywhere in the diocese.[26] As a diocesan charity the orphanage could hardly remain under the control of the Trustees who represented merely the original cooperative action of the six Detroit parishes. Accordingly, on January 16, 1877, the corporation was dissolved, and its property was deeded to Bishop Borgess. The Sisters were relieved from the management of the institution, and were replaced in May, 1877, by the Brothers of the Poor of St. Francis, from the motherhouse in Cincinnati.[27] In 1889 the orphanage was transferred to Monroe, to the building donated for the purpose by Father Francis De Broux, and which had been left vacant by the closing of the preparatory seminary. A year later the Brothers retired from St. Francis Male Orphan Asylum, as the orphanage was now called, and were succeeded by the Sisters of St. Joseph. The institution was brought back to Detroit in 1908 to occupy the splendid building erected by the diocese on Woodward Avenue in Highland Park. But the peaceful surroundings of the orphanage were soon invaded by the roar of industry; the Ford Motor Company located its mammoth plant on an adjacent site. Early in 1916 Henry Ford approached the diocesan authorities with a proposal to build and equip an orphanage on a new site in exchange for the property which stood in the way of expansion. The offer was accepted, and on October 3, 1917, the orphan boys were transferred to the present building on Fenkell Avenue. St. Francis Home for Orphan Boys now shelters approximately four hundred inmates.

Mention must be made here of two private orphanages begun during Bishop Lefevere's episcopate. To comply with the conditions on which Mrs. Antoine Beaubien made her donation to them, the Religious of the Sacred Heart began by supporting three orphan girls, and gradually raised the number to twelve. The orphanage was transferred to the Grosse Pointe establishment in 1888, and in 1899 it was discontinued. In 1860 the Sisters of the Immaculate Heart set aside a portion of their convent in Monroe for the care of a few homeless children.[28] From that time to the present, St. Mary's Home, or St. Joseph's Cottage, as the orphanage is now called, has housed a yearly average number of twenty female orphans.

[25] Marygrove College Archives.
[26] *Ninth Annual Report of St. Anthony's Male Orphan Asylum* (Detroit, 1876).
[27] The articles of agreement signed by the bishop and the Brothers are dated April 4, 1877. DCA.
[28] Sister Loyola, *A Retrospect* (New York, 1916), 98.

It is not out of place to supplement the record of the major charities established in the time of Bishop Lefevere with some notice of the various societies that arose during the period, and were designed to promote more or less explicitly the social welfare of their members. The diocesan reports that appeared in the early issues of the Catholic Almanac were quite different in tone from the cold, impersonal listings in the current Catholic Directory. For instance, in the Almanac for 1846 one comes on this chatty item in the report of the Diocese of Little Rock.

> *Rocky Comfort*, Sevier Co., four miles from Texas—Rev. Francis Donahue. The church in this remote part of Arkansas, which is in the progress of building, is situated on forty acres of land, donated to the Bishop by Mr. George Taaffe, for religious purposes. The lady of Mr. Taaffe died on the 2nd of last February, asking for a priest, although she never had the happiness of seeing a priest in her life. She was baptized the day previous to her death by her afflicted husband, and left seven interesting children, whom the Bishop baptized on Easter Monday.

With more reserve Bishop Lefevere marshalls the accomplishments of his diocese in the almanac for 1843.

> The St. Mary's Association for the purpose of embellishing Trinity Church.
> Christian Doctrine Society, to conduct the Sunday Schools, and a library. The two Sunday Schools number 150 scholars, the library contains 800 volumes, which are issued weekly to the members of the society.[29]
> St. Cecilia's Society.—This society was established in 1837, for the purpose of organizing choirs for the Catholic churches of Detroit.
> Temperance Societies.—The temperance societies in this Diocese are very flourishing. That of Trinity church has 1,002 members; St. Ann's, 900; that at Milwaukie from 6 to 700.
> There is a society among the German Catholics of Detroit, that has for its object principally to sustain their Sunday-school, library, and church music.

With one exception these notices are repeated unchanged down to 1858, the last year in which they appear. The temperance societies, closest to Bishop Lefevere's heart, were apparently the only ones whose progress he cared to note. In 1845 their membership was

---

[29] The origin of the society is noted in the *Western Cath. Register* for September 3, 1842. "This society was founded in December 1838 under the patronage of Rev. B. O'Cavanaugh, then Rector of Trinity Church, and had for its object the religious education of the children of the congregation. The Society numbers upwards of 60 members who pay monthly 12 and a half cents . . ."

6,000; in 1847 it had risen to 9,000; in 1849 it reached 10,000, and there it remained.

In 1850 Bishop Lefevere established an organization, in which he seems to have taken no little pride, called the Catholic Guild of Detroit. The Almanac for 1851 says of it:

> This association was established last July, and is under the patronage of SS. Peter and Paul, Apostles. It is governed by a *chaplain,* appointed by the bishop of the diocese, a *warden, bursar, sub-bursar, secretary* and *council.* As this is the only guild, properly speaking, in this country, we shall quote the following portions of the constitution and rules, to show its object and spirit. . . .

Despite the last statement, the whole purpose of the guild is not entirely clear. However, from its several articles quoted in the Almanac it appears to have been in the main a mutual benefit society. Weekly dues paid by the members were to be used to defray the expenses of sickness and burial.[30] The spiritual duties included the assisting at the funeral of a deceased member, the reception of the sacraments at stated times, and the recitation of the office for the dead. The article introducing this aspect of the society is as follows.

> It shall be the duty of the members of the council, when visiting a sick member, particularly in cases of danger, to advise with, and read some spiritual work to, the member; and in case it be required, they shall order two members, who may live nearest the sick man, to sit up with him; and in case of their refusing, appoint others. Members refusing, to pay a fine of fifty cents each; but in case of such sickness being infectious, this article shall not be enforced.

How long the guild continued to function is uncertain. The last mention of it occurs in the Almanac for 1857.

> The Guild is in a most flourishing condition, and produces both in a spiritual and temporal point of view, all the advantages which were expected from it. It possesses 160 members. With it is connected a *Juvenile Guild,* under the patronage of the Holy Family, having its separate constitution and officers, for youths of from 12 to 20 years of age; at which age, if in good standing, they can pass into the Senior Guild, and there immediately and without any other formality, be invested as regular members. It numbers 80 members.
>
> Catholic Guild in Flint.—This Association is affiliated with the "Guild of SS. Peter and Paul," of Detroit, and although established since a few months only, is already in a very prosperous condition.

[30] The weekly premium was nine cents; on the death of a member the associates paid twelve and a half cents towards defraying the funeral expenses. The sick benefits were from one to two dollars a week.

There may have been features of the Catholic Guild which made it as unique as it claimed to be; but as a mutual benefit society it surely had no right to the distinction. The opinion may be hazarded that it was founded for the Irish Catholics of Detroit in imitation of an already existing German society. The self-reliant German immigrants to the United States were pioneers in organizations of this nature.[31] The first one of which we have any record was the St. Georgius Society founded in New York City in 1842. On May 27, 1847, the leading members of St. Mary's parish in Detroit met to organize the St. Joseph's Unterstützung-Verein, modeled on the St. Peter-Verein in Philadelphia.[32] The purpose of the society was to pay sick and death benefits to its members, and to engage in other works of charity. A portion of its funds were later devoted to orphan support. This society with its long record of benefactions is still in existence. Similar organizations were established in all the later German parishes of the city and of the diocese.[33]

Of the several societies, in addition to the Catholic Guild, fostered by the Irish Catholics of Detroit during the period, scarcely a trace remains. One of the earliest was The Naturalization Society of Detroit, which met in the basement of Trinity Church, and which was founded in April, 1853. Its purpose is sufficiently set forth in a notice published in the Detroit Catholic Vindicator for April 30 of that year.

. . . We therefore call upon all emigrants who settle down amongst us, to take advantage of the facilities of acquiring citizenship through the inducement held out by this society, and to sever the filmy thread of loyalty that links them to the mother country by declaring their allegiance to the land of their adoption.—The following gentlemen are Officebearers, and upon application to either of them the necessary assistance will be given in acquiring the glorious privileges of an American citizen.—Alderman Martin, President., John McNamarra, Secretary, J. Clancy.

From the Detroit City Directories for the period we learn of two charitable organizations which functioned among the Irish Cath-

[31] See the account of the rise of German Benevolent Societies in the *Records of the Amer. Cath. Hist. Soc.*, VI, 252 ff.
[32] A jubilee booklet containing a brief sketch of the organization was printed in 1907, and is the authority for the statement.
[33] On August 30, 1931, St. Joseph's Liebesbund of St. Joseph's parish in Detroit celebrated its seventy-fifth anniversary. During its existence the society had paid out $71,589 in sick benefits, and $51,090 in death benefits. An interesting printed sketch was issued for the occasion. The Detroit City Directory for 1862 lists eight organizations under the heading of Charitable and Beneficial Societies. Seven of them are German Catholic societies, and the eighth is a Protestant missionary organization.

olics of Detroit. The St. Elizabeth Benevolent Society met every Thursday in winter "in rear of the Cathedral." St. Mary's Benevolent Society met monthly at the Guild Hall on Porter Street, that is, in the basement of Trinity Church.

For the French Catholics of Detroit the Lafayette Benevolent and Mutual Aid Society was founded as early as 1853. It paid sick and death benefits, and owned its own building on Gratiot Avenue between St. Antoine and Beaubien Streets.[34]

With this fragmentary information we must be content. The records of these and kindred societies have long since disappeared. Nevertheless, we are aware that the Catholics of the period—divided, it is true, into strictly national groups, and with no great breadth of outlook—were striving as best they could to relieve the needs of their less fortunate brethren.

Under Bishop Borgess the first accession to the number of diocesan institutions was furnished by the Little Sisters of the Poor. Bishop Lefevere had asked for them in 1868, and Bishop Borgess renewed the request in 1872. On May 20, 1874, the Good Mother, Sister Michael Archangel, with five Sisters arrived in Detroit. Through the generosity of the Piquette family the Sisters were given the use of the family mansion which stood on the northwest corner of Fourteenth Avenue and Fort Street. There, the Sisters began in Detroit that characteristic work of charity that has endeared them to the world by taking in, as their chronicler says, "a good little dame of 104 years."[35] For a while only women were received, but when an old man of seventy-five, carrying his mattress on his back, demanded admittance the Sisters could not refuse him. A small wooden house for the accommodation of male inmates was built in the rear of the mansion, and was blessed on the 29th of October. Two years later, on October 8, 1876, the Sisters occupied the first unit of their new building on Scott Street, erected on a plot of ground donated to them by the diocese.

Like the Germans who had preceded them, the Polish Catholics who came to the diocese in such numbers during the episcopate of Bishop Borgess were determined to care for their own. In 1882 the Felician Sisters began to house a few orphan girls in their convent on St. Aubin Avenue. From this humble beginning the orphanage has grown to be an important department of the Sisters' work. For the first twenty-five years children were admitted from all parts of the United States, but from 1907 admissions were restricted to Michigan.[36]

[34] Farmer, op. cit., I, 654.
[35] From the manuscript house chronicle.
[36] See booklet issued in 1924 on the occasion of the golden jubilee of the Felician foundation in Detroit.

Another institution owes its origin to the particular initiative of Bishop Borgess. He visited the Good Shepherd Convent in St. Louis, and personally urged the foundation of a similar establishment in Detroit. The Sisters having agreed to come, the old Eber Ward mansion on West Fort Street was purchased and prepared for their occupancy. On November 22, 1883, the House of the Good Shepherd was formally opened by Sister Mary of St. Francis Patrick, and her four companions. The success of the Sisters in their chosen work—too well known to need description—is attested by the group of buildings that clustered around the old mansion and covered an entire city square.

When the Diocese of Detroit was confided to Bishop Borgess in 1870 it comprised the entire lower peninsula of Michigan, yet, outside of the Detroit area, the only charitable institution in it was the little orphan asylum at Monroe. In 1874 the Daughters of Charity opened St. Mary's Hospital at Saginaw, and in the following year St. Vincent's Orphan Home. The Sisters of Mercy began their hospital at Big Rapids in 1879. These foundations were all in the Diocese of Grand Rapids when it was erected in 1882.

After the division the first attempt to found a charitable institution outside of Detroit was made in Adrian. In 1886 Father Casimir Rohowski, pastor of St. Joseph's church, gathered together a number of old people, and built a home for them on the outskirts of the town. The building was called St. Joseph's Hospital and was placed in charge of the Dominican Sisters. In a more substantial building that was later erected the work was continued until 1896, when Mother Camilla who was then in charge obtained Bishop Foley's permission to open an academy for girls. The building thus became the nucleus of the present St. Joseph's Academy, and the old people were transferred to the original frame structure. St. Joseph's Hospital was discontinued in 1901.[37]

[37] *Life of Mother M. Camilla Madden,* O.S.D. (Adrian, 1925), 11.

CHAPTER XXVIII

Catholic Press

THAT a Catholic press is indispensable to the work of the Church in America, or in any country the world over, is a commonplace. The number and variety of the publications issued under Catholic auspices in our day testify not to a belated recognition of this fact, but to the improved position and resources of the Church. Between 1809 and 1840 no less than forty-three Catholic journals arose to cross swords with the insane bigotry of the period, and to defend the constitutional liberties of the Catholic body. We may smile at the antiquated armor and weapons of these champions of a bygone age, but "when one weighs, however, the fruits of all these pioneer efforts, the conclusion is reached that, had not a strong, vigorous, and sometimes militant Catholic press existed, the Church in America would not be occupying the splendid position which it holds in the twentieth century." [1] In the next fifty years, during which the foreign language publications made their appearance, some five hundred periodicals struggled, often unsuccessfully, to survive. [2] The contribution, humble though it may have been, which the Diocese of Detroit has made to the cause of Catholic journalism deserves to be recorded, and the record is not so long that we may not occasionally ramble through the pages of the few battered volumes of our early periodicals that have somehow escaped the ravages of time. Our study, however, does not begin with our first diocesan effort for Detroit is the birthplace of our national Catholic press, and we must examine the rare, precious pages of the first Catholic periodical, or, at least, of the first periodical under Catholic auspices issued in the United States.

The reader is already sufficiently familiar with the circumstances under which Father Richard made his venture into the field of printing. As Detroit was slowly rising from its ashes he was entering upon that ten year period during which he was so preoccupied with the educational needs of the Territory, and his press was only the logical extension of his educational program.

Before dealing with the Richard press it may be well to notice two

[1] Foik, op. cit., 212.

[2] For a complete list of Catholic periodicals down to 1892 see the compilation in the *Records of the Amer. Cath. Hist. Society* (Philadelphia), IV, 213–242; XIX, 18–41.

misstatements that have often been made: the press which he introduced into the Territory was neither "the first printing press west of
the Alleghenies," nor "the first printing press in Michigan." The
most elementary acquaintance with the history of printing in America, especially in that portion of it comprised in the old Northwest
Territory, is sufficient to dispose of the first assertion. As for the second, the existence and use in Detroit of a press antedating Father
Richard's by at least thirteen years has been amply proved.[3]

As we have seen in a previous chapter Father Richard was absent
from Detroit between November, 1808, and July, 1809, and during
this period he was travelling in the East gathering funds for the rebuilding of St. Anne's and consulting with Federal officials regarding
assistance for his projected Indian schools in Michigan Territory.
Somewhere in his travels he purchased a press with its equipment
and type which he brought with him on his return to Detroit. The
provenience of the press is in doubt, but what little evidence is available points to Utica, New York. There Father Richard met John C.
Devereaux, a Catholic and a leading merchant of the city, who advanced the sum required for the purchase of the press.[4] It is not improbable that there was a press up for sale at the time, and that it
was the property of James M. Miller, a printer who had been plying
his trade in Utica and who accompanied Father Richard to Detroit.[5]

[3] Douglas C. McMurtrie, *Early Printing in Michigan* (Chicago, 1931), 17–24. This
indispensable monograph covers the history of printing in the state down to 1850,
and gives detailed information on every Richard imprint. The first chapter entitled
"The Apocryphal Period" deals with a fanciful account of the first press in Michigan,
which appeared in the *Detroit Free Press* for July 31, 1890. According to this account
there was at the time, in East Jordan in Charlevoix County, an antiquated printing
press which had been taken from Beaver Island during the raid on the Mormon
stronghold in 1856. Moreover, a Mormon informant had told the writer that the
Mormons had found the press in Cross Village, and were satisfied that it had been
brought there by Father Du Jaunay, and had been used by him to print religious
literature in the Ottawa language for the Indian converts. If the Mormons actually
had an old press the probabilities against its origin as stated are enormous, and need
not be gone into. Father Du Jaunay left Cross Village, or L'Arbre Croche, in 1765,
and it is almost impossible to believe that he operated a press before that date since,
to the best of our knowledge, the first press in New France was set up in Quebec in
1759, and the second at the same place in 1764.

[4] "Indian School Correspondence," *Mich. Hist. Mag.*, (Winter No., 1930), 127–29.

[5] Against these probabilities is the passage quoted by McMurtrie, 67–71. It was
written in 1859 by John P. Sheldon who came to Detroit in 1817 to found the *Detroit
Gazette*, the city's first regular newspaper. The pertinent extract is as follows: "On landing at Detroit, and making some inquiries touching the object of our visit, we found
that we were not the first who had thought of establishing a newspaper in that city.
The Rev. Gabriel Richard, the head and father of the Roman church there, some years
before, (I think in 1811) purchased an old press and some very old types of a printer,
(G. G. Phinney,) in Herkimer, New York. He had them put up in his house by a journeyman printer who went with him from New York, and who taught a young man, of
French descent, by the name of Mettez, 'the art and mystery of printing.' The Reverend

Father Richard's purpose in bringing a press to Detroit is evident. In the frontier community which he served printed matter was rare, expensive, and difficult to procure. If his schools were to continue and expand he could furnish the necessary textbooks. He could further the religious instruction of his people by providing them with many needed texts, and he could possibly allure them to a higher cultural level by interesting them in books and literature. He was aware as well of the apologetic value of a press in a mixed community like his where religious bigotry was always more or less evident.

Father Richard and his printer lost no time in setting up the press in the school building on the Spring Hill farm. To the best of our knowledge its first issue was The Child's Spelling Book; or Michigan Instructor, and the small twelve page pamphlet bears the following preface dated August 1, 1809.

> The great scarcity of School Books in the Territory, is a sufficient apology for the appearance of the following pages. This small book is chiefly selected from other writers. The Tables of Spelling, are in general extracted from Webster. It is intended to answer the purpose of introducing the Youth of this Territory, into the fundamental principles of Education. If it gains encouragement it will, perhaps, be succeeded by another Part containing Spellings of a maturer kind, intermixed with useful Lessons in Reading: such as, Maxims, Proverbs, Fables, Moral Stories, &, calculated to inspire the youthful mind, with a sense of strict propriety and virtue. At the request of several Gentlemen and Teachers of this City, it is sent to the Press:—and it is hoped that it may meet the approbation and liberal patronage of a generous public.[6]

Father Richard now prepared to launch the enterprise in which we are primarily interested. His service to the community in the educational field was to be broadened by providing a commodity which it hitherto lacked, a newspaper. On August 31, 1809, appeared the first number of the *Michigan Essay; Or, The Impartial Observer,* a four-page, four-column paper measuring 18 x 11 inches.[7] At the head of the first column were the "Terms of the Michigan Essay."

---

father did not establish a newspaper—it was too arduous undertaking—it 'would not pay'—and it would interfere too much with his duties towards his flock, of whom he had a goodly number—and the journeyman and Mettez were kept for some time employed in printing divers little pamphlets, containing prayers and services of the church, advice and many good sayings and writings of the saints, etc., all of which were printed in the French or Latin languages . . ."

[6] The phraseology and style are unmistakably Father Richard's. The only extant copy known of the *Michigan Instructor* is in the BHC.

[7] The title is as given, and not "Essai du Michigan." This is a French equivalent found in some Canadian writers.

It will be published every Thursday; and handed to City Subscribers, at 5 dollars per ann Payable half-yearly, in advance

Other Subscribers, resident in any part of the Territory of Michigan, or Upper Canada, 4 dollars and 50 cents, delivered at the Office—to be paid in advance.

Distant Subscribers who receive their papers by mail, 4 dollars—in advance.

Advertisements, not exceeding a square, inserted 3 weeks for 1 dol and 50 cts. For every subsequent insertion 25 cts. All advertisements must be accompanied by the cash.

On the third page, and surmounted by an ornament appeared a short statement of editorial policy, and this first editorial written in Michigan might well serve as a Golden Text for the professed molders of public opinion in our day.

The Public are respectfully informed, that The Essay will be conducted with the utmost impartiality; that it will not espouse any political party; but fairly and candidly communicate whatever may be deemed worthy of insertion—whether Foreign, Domestic, or Local. . . . Gentlemen of talents are invited to contribute to our colums whatever they suppose will be acceptable and beneficial to the public—yet always remembering that nothing of a corrosive nature will be admissible.

The news value of this first issue of the Essay was negligible; it contained not a single item of local interest, but several stale reports of the Napoleonic campaigns gleaned from the eastern newspapers of May and June. There was a half column of poetry, a husbandry department, and a "humorous" section containing two anecdotes spiced with a little vulgarity. The only articles in French were an extract from La Harpe's eulogy of Fenelon, and a parable with thrift as a moral. On the third page an entire column was devoted to the advertisement of books for sale "at the Detroit Printing Office," and the list is interesting as illustrating the type of book that Father Richard chose to import for the best interests of his clientele. There were two French grammars; a three volume Book of Trades; the Columbian Orator; Wakefield's family Tour thro' the British Empire; Way to Wealth by Dr. Franklin; Youthful Sports; English and French Catechisms; Footsteps to the Natural History of Beasts; Portrait of curious Characters; Jack of all Trades; Philadelphia Primer; Road to Learning; and Letters from London.

Under the subheading of "Religious Works" were listed: Pastorini's General History of the Christian Church; True Piety, or a Manual; Advantages of frequent Communion; Spiritual combat the peace of the soul, and happiness of the heart; Vade Mecum; Garden of the Soul; Real Principles of Roman Catholics; Following of

Christ; Pious Guide; Practical reflections for every day; A Papist misrepresented and represented; Geographical Cards, &, &.

A portion of the advertisement, in French, listed a number of French books for the most part religious, and closed with the following notice:

> It is proposed to print in succession several books useful to the young and to older persons such as the New Think Well On It; the Novena of the Sacred Heart of Jesus; the Abridgement of the Old and New Testament; the Manual of Agriculture; the handy Alphabet, or brief review of the arts and trades; charts and tables for the study of History, Geography, and Chronology; the Children's Encyclopedia; Collections of curious and instructive stories, and other useful books in the measure that the public desires and encourages them.

Such in brief was the first issue of the Michigan Essay. Apparently Father Richard had no intention of making it a professedly Catholic journal; he seemed to have in mind rather a sort of digest of news and literature which under his direction would bring the better minds of the community into an urbane fellowship for general cultural advantage.

We can only speculate as to the reasons for the untimely end of the Michigan Essay. We do not know whether Father Richard's public was too cold to his venture, or whether he himself was unable to carry it on. There is no agreement even as to the number of times that the Essay was issued; estimates vary from one to eleven. No one has ever reported seeing any number of it but the first. In the library at Worcester, Massachusetts, there is a copy which was sent to Isaiah Thomas, author of the first history of printing published in America. On the margin is written the following note:

Utica, N. Y., August 3, 1810.

Mr. Thomas:

Sir,—I send you this paper, published by a friend of mine, to insert in your "History of Printing." If he sees your advertisement he will send you more, perhaps, of later date.

Your obedient servant,
C. S. McConnell.[8]

Despite the date of the note, almost a year after the appearance of the Essay, the paper mentioned is a copy of the first number, as is likewise the copy preserved in the Burton Historical Collection. But, whether the Essay died at birth or enjoyed a longer spell of life is not as important as the fact that Father Richard had the vision and the courage to make such a venture in his pioneer community. As his re-

[8] See Farmer, op. cit., I, 670.

WESTERN CATHOLIC REGISTER.

Behold, I bring you good tidings

"Prove all things, hold fast   that which is good."—*St. Paul*

| Volume 1. | DETROIT, July 16, 1842. | Number 1. |

WESTERN CATHOLIC REGISTER,
PRINTED & PUBLISHED EVERY SATURDAY

BY EUGENE T. SMITH.

Office up stairs on the corner of Jefferson Avenue & Griswold street, nearly opposite the Bank of Michigan.

TERMS.—To city subscribers (delivered) $1,50 per annum, quarterly in advance, or 50 cents per quarter if paid in advance—to mail subscribers and those who give them at our office $1,00 per annum in advance.

To Agents.—$5,00 in advance, free of postage, will pay for five copies for one year to mail or office subscribers, or four copies to city subscribers, and entitle the agent forwarding the same, to a copy for one year gratis.

Advertising on the most reasonable terms.

Letters relating to the business of the Establishment should be post-paid, or free of postage.

POETRY.

INFIDELITY.
BY R. C. SANDS.

Thou who scornest truths divine,
Say what joy, what hope is thine?
Is thy soul from sorrow free?
Is this world enough for thee?
No! for care corrodes thy heart.
Art thou willing to depart?
No! thy nature bids thee shrink
From the void abyss's brink.
Thou may'st laugh, in broad sunshine;
Scoff, when sparkles the red wine;
Thou must tremble, when deep night
Shuts the pageants from thy sight.
Morning comes, and thou blasphemest;
Yet another day thou deemest
Thine; but soon its light will wane;
Then thy warings come again.
There's a morrow with no night—
Should its dawn thy dreams o'ertake,
Better thou 'dst never wake!

There is a man who may eat his bread in peace with man and God, it is that man who has brought that bread out of the earth by his own honest industry. It is cankered by no fraud, is wet by no tears, it is stained by no blood.—*Colman*

From the Boston Pilot.

Public Institutions in
MARSEILLES.

The Hotel Dieu is a Hospital for the poor sick, whether Catholics or Protestants. The one is as readily received and as kindly treated as the other. No newspaper scriblers or reforming zealots have yet arisen in Marseilles as in Boston, to talk about the horrible progress of pauperism, and the degrading vice of poverty! and to recommend that no provision whatever be made for *foreign* paupers; and that when sick they should be left to die in their own cheerless hovels, or in some corner of the House of Industry out-houses. In the Hotel Dieu there is no classification except of diseases and degrees of convalescence. It contains at present about seven hundred inmates, distributed into various halls or dormitories, some of which are at least three hundred feet in length, and fifteen feet in height, and have a row of beds on each side, about four feet asunder, with a canopy over each bed, which gives them a remarkably clean and comfortable appearance. The nurses are all Sisters of Charity, whose services are of course gratuitous, and therefore the more zealously, humanely, and faithfully performed. You hear no scolding, no angry retorts—indeed, no loud talking. Silence, order and quiet, reign in every part of this immense building, which is five or six times as large as the House of Industry at South Boston, though its inmates are not much more numerous. The Superintendent of this institution is a priest; but do tell our Protestant friends, that he is, nevertheless, a very gentlemanly, excellent man. He receives from Government just sufficient for his maintenance, which is all that a Catholic priest, having no family, requires. He is also chaplain of the institution. Lay persons are appointed to manage the secular affairs. The kitchen, wash-room, laundry, store-rooms for provisions and clothing, bathing-rooms, &c., are all of ample dimensions, and remarkably clean and under the sole care of the Sisters. I believe no other females are employed about the establishment for any purpose. I wish, fervently, that the unprejudiced and high minded City Council of Boston, would place the poor sick and infirm of the City institutions under the care of the good Sisters. It would be a great saving of ex-

pense, and I am sure the Sisters would gladly undertake the task, and while they zealously performed their duties, they would be found by their superiors to be the most docile and obedient officers. The sick are attended by six physicians, who reside in the city.

The *Hospice de Charite* is also a poor house, but for those in health and able to work. It is situated in another part of the city. It contains one thousand men, women and children. One hundred and thirty of the latter are of the age. The chapel is the first building that meets that eye on entering the gate. My conductor marked—"The head of this house is God." He us first call on him." We directly entered the chapel, and knelt for a few minutes in silent adoration before the Most Blessed Sacrament. We then entered the main institution, and enquired for the Rector, who is also a priest and chaplain of the establishment. With the utmost urbanity, he showed us all parts of the House. The men were at work, sawing, making, tailoring, carpentering, &c. women, sewing, washing and cooking, and the boys eating their dinner. The food of the young and old, is soup, bread, fruit, and meat and water—for breakfast, dinner and supper. The boys looked fat and merry, and they as boys should; though in order and silence.

The *Asylum* for orphan and deserted children, called here the children of Providence, is a noble institution. It contains a hundred boys, from nine to fifteen years of age. They are all under the kind and paternal care of religious order, called the Brothers of the Christian Schools. Their whole time is devoted during life, to the instruction of youth. The free schools of France are under their care. They live in communities, and receive small stipend from government, just sufficient for their maintenance. The boys at this Asylum were at play and appeared very happy. They wear a uniform of dark cloth, with a very star on the left breast. Hence they are commonly called "children of the star." I inspected their writing-books, and was delighted with the proficiency they had made.

In one of the free schools that I visited, under the care of the same friars, were two hundred boys and fourteen Brothers, or about fifty-six boys to each master. I inquired here what salary they received, and was told they francs a month, or about $9,50—less than the

The first issue of the first diocesan weekly. Size 11¼ by 9 inches. Original in the Library of Duns Scotus College, Detroit.

ward the Essay must be considered as representing the first attempt made in the United States to establish a periodical under Catholic auspices. The long series of eastern papers begins with the *Shamrock* of New York in 1810.[9]

The failure of the Essay had no bearing on the primary purpose for which Father Richard had brought his press to Detroit, and it continued active down to 1817, when it was superseded by the press set up by John P. Sheldon. Only a cursory review of its imprints need be given here. In 1809 appeared *L'Ame Penitente, ou le Nouveau Pensez-y-Bien,* and *Les Vepres du Dimanche;* and in 1810 a twelve page pamphlet *The True Principles of a Catholic* by Bishop Chalenor (sic). The same year James Miller was replaced by a second printer, Aaron Coxshaw, who printed two or three devotional works and a collection of French literary selections entitled *Les Ornemens de la Memoire ou Les Traits Brillans des Poetes Francois Les Plus Celebres.*[10]

From 1812 to 1817 the press was operated by Theophilus Mettez, son of the sexton at St. Anne's, who had served Father Richard as an altar boy. He was seventeen when the press was first set up, and doubtless learned the printing trade from Miller and Coxshaw. In 1812 he printed *A Short Historical Catechism containing a Summary of Sacred History and Christian Doctrine,* a volume of two hundred pages which were alternately French and English. This was followed by another bilingual work in two volumes, *The Family Book, Or Children's Journal.* In quick succession came the *Epistles and Gospels For All Sundays and Holydays Throughout the Year,* a volume of 396 pages in the two languages. The last issue of the press for the year was a forty-eight page booklet containing selections from the fables of La Fontaine. During the War of 1812 the press was used to issue proclamations, and when Hull surrendered Detroit on August 16, 1812, it printed the articles of capitulation. The next extant issue of the press is dated 1816, and is a 138 page digest of the laws in force in Michigan Territory.

Curiously enough, and typical of the fate that dogged Father Richard's enterprises, the last bit of printing from the press proved a sorry return for all the good intentions that had inspired its purchase. When he began the rebuilding of St. Anne's in 1818 currency was scarce, and to pay his workmen he had recourse to the same device that the merchants of the city were using namely, printed due-bills or promises to pay. Someone, probably Cooper, a printer, as tradi-

[9] For further details of the Essay, and a list of references, consult Foik, *op. cit.,* 1–6.

[10] In this connection it must be remembered that Father Richard's name never appears on any of the issues of his press. The title pages bear only the names of the printers whom he successively employed. The issues are likewise invariably reprints.

tion has it, stole the type and printed a stack of due-bills to which the forged signature of Father Richard was affixed. His sense of honor led the priest to pay off as many of the forgeries as he could, but a final refusal to honor more of them resulted in a serious breach with some of his parishioners.[11]

Here we must take leave of the Richard press. It was used in 1822 as collateral for a loan, but was still in Father Richard's possession at the time of his death. Bishop Lefevere is said to have sold the type to a Buffalo type founder for remelting, but the whereabouts of the press itself, if it be still in existence, is unknown.

A quarter of a century elapsed before a press was again used in the service of the Church in Detroit. As noted in a preceding chapter, Bishop Rese planned to establish a Catholic paper with the help of Father Bernard O'Cavanagh, pastor of Holy Trinity, who had served for a while as associate editor of the *Catholic Press* of Hartford.[12] However, the project was not realized, and it remained for Bishop Lefevere to make the first serious effort to provide a Catholic periodical for his diocesans.

On July 23, 1842, appeared the *Western Catholic Register,* an eight page, three column paper measuring 12 x 10½ inches. The first number of the *Register* states that it is to be printed and published every Saturday with the approbation of the Right Rev. Peter Paul Lefevre (sic) by Eugene T. Smith. The office is "upstairs on the corner of Jefferson Avenue and Griswold Street, nearly opposite the Bank of Michigan." The editor writes an introductory notice and some statement of policy, but the only passage in the second number resembling an editorial is the following explanation:

> Only One Dollar.—Many of our friends wonder how we can publish a weekly paper in Michigan, the subscription price of which is only one dollar per annum. No wonder at all we discharge the duties of publisher, printer, foreman &, therefore instead of having three or four great men, and several operatives to support from the profits, we have only two or three plain workies including our humble self.[13]

[11] Only one of Father Richard's due-bills is extant; it is in the museum of the Detroit Historical Society. There is a reproduction in McMurtrie, *op. cit.,* 80.

[12] Foik, *op. cit.,* 94–100.

[13] The editor, Eugene T. Smith, is a shadowy figure. The third number of the *Register* states that he was formerly the editor of the *Macomb County Republican.* That he was a convert seems evident from the following passage in No. 13 of the *Register* dealing with the departure of Father Vincent Badin. "It is with unfeigned regret that we learn that Very Rev. Vincent F. Badin is about to leave the scene of his truly zealous missionary labors for his native land (France). . . . It is now nearly eighteen years since we first saw this servant of the Most High then assisting the late Father Richard in performing the sad rites of the dead; and at a time when we had not the least idea of ever calling him by that name which Catholics hold dear, that of Father . . .'"

In typography and make up the *Register* was not unattractive, and its contents were varied enough to be interesting. The feature article, a memoir of Bishop England, was followed by an account, taken from the *Dublin Freeman,* of the meeting of the Catholic Institution of Great Britian. A page article from the *Young Catholics Magazine* protested against the anti-catholic bias of public school textbooks. The domestic Catholic news consisted for the most part of a list of dioceses copied from the Catholic Almanac of 1842, with their summarized statistics. There was some local news, the most interesting item being an account of Bishop Lefevere's laying of the corner stone of the new church at Sandwich.[14] A notice referring to St. Mary's Association gave a complete list of the officers that had served the society from its beginning. Daniel J. Campau, wholesale and retail dealer in dry goods, carried in stock and advertised a long list of Catholic books, mostly controversial.

According to Farmer the *Register* suspended publication at the end of one year.[15] From the dark, ink-bitten pages of the first diocesan weekly we may glean a few items of local interest.[16] The temperance societies were in their heyday, and every number has some reference to them.

Our Temperance societies continue to increase. Trinity Church Temperance Society numbers 1,002; St. Anne's Temperance Society, 900 including 600 Indians and French at the Upper Lake missions, to whom the pledge was administered by the Rt. Rev. Bishop Lefevre on his recent mission to that quarter. We are informed that the Temperance Society of Milwaukee numbers between 600 and 700.

Rev. Mr. Kilroy on a mission to Connor's Creek a few days since, administered the pledge to 12 persons. One, a Mr. Dalton emptied several gallons of whiskey on the ground which he had purchased a few days before for his workmen. The Detroit Catholic Temperance Society now numbers 1026.

The "Roman Catholic church building Society of Trinity Church Detroit" held its meeting in October to elect officers for the coming year. John O'Callahan, Sen., was chosen 2nd Vice President; John Brennan, secretary; and P. M. Phillips, treasurer. A "Vigilance Committee" was appointed comprising two members for each of the six wards of the city: P. Cavina and John Collins; J. Sherlock and John

---

[14] The ceremony took place on July 21, 1842. The account ends with the remark that the Rev. Michael McDonnell, V.G., "addressed the congregation in a very eloquent and edifying discourse of an hour and a half."

[15] *History of Detroit,* I, 674.

[16] There is a complete file of the first volume of the *Register* in the library of Duns Scotus College, Detroit.

Cornfield; Wm. O'Callahan and Hugh O'Beirne; M. Nagle and P. Burns; J. Murphy and T. Kevy; E. T. Smith and H. O'Flynn.

In the issue of November 5 there was a long article describing the consecration of Mt. Elliott Cemetery, which had taken place on the preceding Wednesday. As usual the Temperance societies were prominent in the procession "which was upwards of half a mile in length." The singing during the ceremony was supplied by a choir "composed principally of Germans whose vocal music does honor to themselves and the cause in which they were engaged." The article ended by expressing the thanks of the Catholic community to General Brook of the United States Army "for this kindness in permitting the Military Band to join their procession on the 2nd inst. on the occasion of the blessing of the new Catholic burying ground. The undersigned would further acknowledge that this has not been the first occasion on which General Brook's kindness and attention have called forth their warmest gratitude. They have now and ever shall retain a remembrance of the prompt kindness with which a similar favor was conferred on the Irish Catholic Temperance Celebration on the 17th of March last."

The last days of the *Register* were presaged in the issue of April 22, 1843. In all likelihood the paper was read only by the English-speaking Catholics of the city, who were not as yet numerous enough to sustain it adequately. The editor complained that he was in financial difficulties and could not carry on much longer. He voiced his disillusionment that in a diocese whose population was "15 or 20 thousand" he was unable to enlist sufficient support for his enterprise.

There was no successor to the *Register* for ten years. In the interim two attempts were made to furnish a periodical for the French residents of Detroit. Farmer thus records them:

> L'Amie de la Jeunesse (Friend of Youth), a French paper, was first issued on May 23, 1843. It was a weekly at $3.00 a year, published by James A. Girardin, with E. N. Lacroix as editor. Nine numbers were issued.
>
> Le Citoyen was a French literary paper, in quarto form, issued on Saturdays, at $2.00 a year. L. J. Paulin was publisher, and E. N. Lacroix editor. It was issued for six months. Volume I, Number 1, was dated May 11, 1850.[17]

Although these two periodicals may not have been professedly Catholic—they certainly were not diocesan—they must have been Catholic at least in tone in view of the readers to whom they were addressed. They should be classed as semi-Catholic, a term that has

---

[17] No extant issues of these two periodicals are known.

been coined to designate periodicals issued in the interests of some particular Catholic racial group.[18]

Associated with the origin of the next diocesan weekly is one of the most remarkable figures among the pioneer clergy of Detroit. The salient facts of his life have been told by Richard R. Elliott, who came under the priest's ministrations as a youth.

. . . After Father Richard, no Catholic priest was more loved and respected than Father Shawe, whose history is a romance, and who like Gallitzin, was of noble blood; he had been commander of a squadron of British cavalry at Waterloo, and, before that battle was ended, he lay upon the bloody field all cut to pieces, with the dead and wounded piled upon him three deep. Rescued, with a faint spark of life, he was removed to a temporary hospital, where he was soon after joined by his mother, who came from London to seek his remains, as she had read his name among the British officers who had been reported to headquarters as killed in this battle. She was soon able to take her young soldier to the South of France, where, after three years nursing, the boy was saved; then the mother's turn came.

She had not spared herself; and when her son had been fully restored to life and vigor . . . she gradually faded, and finally arrived at that stage of weakness when it became a question of months when the term of her life would end.

Mother and son were of a noble Catholic race. When the filial duties of young Shawe had ended with the transportation of his mother's remains to the ancestral vault of his family in Devonshire, England, he retired from the military career, which had nearly cost him his own life, and had brought his mother to a premature grave.

He went to Vienna, where he remained a few years, and while in that city he became a postulant for admission to the noble and military order of Teutonic Knights of Germany. . . . To be elected a Teutonic Knight, the postulant has to show his right to sixteen distinct quarterings of nobility in the heraldry of his country. . . .

Young Shawe became a Teutonic Knight; and had his stall assigned him in the Chapter House of the order in Vienna. But his mother's self sacrifice and death clouded his life and he determined to leave the world and become a priest. He accordingly entered a seminary in Paris, where he remained until he received minor orders.

About this time the saintly Bishop Bruté had come to France to recruit missionaries for his wild see of Vincennes. . . . Young Shawe, De St. Palais, and some other young French noblemen accompanied Bishop Bruté to Indiana at the time, the most God-forsaken State in the Western Country.

Shawe, with other young volunteers, was ordained, and soon put on his missionary harness.[19] Then he became Father Shawe, the only

[18] Foik, *op. cit., passim.*
[19] Father Shawe was ordained at Vincennes, Ind., on March 12, 1837.

English-speaking priest on the mission, but French and German were as familiar to his tongue and no less eloquently preached.

With his own personal fortune he built a stone church at Madison, which he dedicated to his patron, Saint Michael.

The Bishop's death was succeeded by intrigue among his French associates, and in disgust Father Shawe, at the invitation of Father Edward Sorin, left the sacerdotal family of Vincennes and became professor of English literature in the University of Notre Dame.

He was intensely English, anti-American to some extent; while at that time Notre Dame's faculty was to a great extent as intensely French, as Father Shawe was English, in their tendencies. The majority were too strong for Father Shawe in this sentimental battle, and . . . he, with the blessing of Father Sorin . . . came to Detroit, to resume the active functions of his sacerdotal state and to enjoy life in a city so Catholic as was and is Detroit, and in society which his aristocratic attributes so well fitted him to adorn. . . .[20]

Father Michael Edgar Shawe was received into the Diocese of Detroit on February 1, 1848, served for a few months in Trinity parish, and upon the completion of the cathedral was assigned there as assistant to Father Farnan. The latter's death a year later resulted in Father Shawe's succession to the pastorate.

With his background and education Father Shawe was easily the most representative priest of the city clergy, and best equipped to help Bishop Lefevere in a period of stress and trial. The Native American party had just broken down only to prepare the way for the rise of the vicious Know-Nothing movement in 1852. The Catholics of Detroit and Michigan calumniated and abused in the daily press were desperately in need of a weapon of defense. Moreover, despite the turmoil Bishop Lefevere was planning his campaign to secure state aid for the parochial schools.

Out of this crisis was born the *Detroit Catholic Vindicator*, whose first number was issued on April 30, 1853, under the editorial guidance of Father Shawe. Strangely enough, on this very day Father Shawe suffered the serious injuries from which he died ten days later. The issue of Saturday, May 14, carried his obituary.

In the discharge of a sad and melancholy duty, we have to announce to our readers this week, the death of the Rev. Michael Edgar Evelyne Shawe, the well-known and respected Pastor of the Cathedral of this city, and which occurred a few minutes past nine o'clock on the evening of Tuesday, at the Hospital of the Sisters of Charity.

On the 30th of April last, Father Shawe left this city in a carriage, to attend the opening of the new church at Connor's Creek where he

[20] *Illinois Cath. Hist. Rev.,* II, 344–46; V, 47–50. Elliott in the *Amer. Cath. Hist. Researches,* April, 1897.

was to have officiated; but had not gone beyond the limits of the city, before the horse, alarmed at some object, took fright and ran off, breaking the carriage and throwing the reverend gentleman violently out on the road. At the time, he was not considered dangerously hurt; but it was found afterwards that he had received many internal injuries, which put a termination to his eventful and well spent life.

Father Shawe was about sixty years of age. He was born in England, of a highly respectable family, and in early life received a commission in the British army, and served with marked distinction in many of the sanguinary engagements that marked the Continental war. He was wounded at the battle of Bergen-op-zoom, and afterwards at Waterloo. Returning home after the peace, he entered the Catholic College of Oscott, to prepare for the duties of a more God-like calling—that of a Catholic priest.

He came to this country with the late Bishop Bruté, and for many years officiated throughout Indiana, and proved a zealous and ardent missionary in the advancement of religion in those, then thinly populated regions. In many of the log-huts of the forest he had offered up the great sacrifice of propitiation, where mass had never been celebrated before. And along the swamps of the Wabash, he had brought the consolations of religion to many who had not seen the face of a clergyman for years.

Father Shawe came to Detroit a number of years ago, and to his untiring zeal and energy for the advancement of religion and the welfare of his people, many of the present religious associations owe their origin and existence. To his paternal care, the Guild of St. Peter and Paul, and the Guild of the Holy Trinity are indebted for formation and adoption of their order; and had it been the will of God that he should have lived, this paper, which was commenced under his editorial management, would have received the benefit of his highly cultivated mind and extensive erudition. . . .

During Father Shawe's residence in this city, he became endeared to all classes of the community, and while his burning eloquence will long echo in our ears, the recollection of his untiring zeal for our welfare, calls us between sorrow for our loss and glad hope of his great gain, to utter the last prayer for the faithful departed— May he rest in peace.[21]

The tantalizing anonymity of the succeeding issues of the *Vindicator* gives no hint as to how the paper managed to survive the death of Father Shawe. We have nothing but these meagre details given us fifty years later by Richard R. Elliott.

It became necessary for some Catholic gentlemen to assume the support and management of the Vindicator, in which I took a prominent part in respect for the memory of its founder, Father Shawe, who was a

---

[21] Father Shawe is buried in Mt. Elliott Cemetery, Detroit. His tombstone bears a long inscription recapitulating his life story.

warm friend of mine. William Hassett, M.D., of Cincinnati, was engaged as editor; it was a quarto 8-page sheet; the late Colonel Richard F. O'Bierne, U. S. army, was its business manager.[22]

The *Vindicator*, measuring 19 x 13 inches, and printed in fine clear type on a good quality of paper, was a credit to its promoters. For almost a year it was published by Daniel O'Hara "at Bagg's New Block, Griswold Street cor. of Larned Street." However, it was apparently printed elsewhere for, when it was taken over by James F. Ballentyne in March, 1854, the publisher announced that the paper would henceforth be printed in Detroit.[23] In a letter to the clergy of the diocese Bishop Lefevere expressed his warm approval of the project, and pointed out its necessity, while Father Shawe in his first editorial endeavored to state the policy of the *Vindicator*.

> The invention of printing as a medium for the communication of ideas, has created the most powerful engine ever wielded by mortal hands to influence the destinies of the world. Employed in disseminating truth, how glorious are the privileges it enjoys over every other art resulting from the genius and industry of man. But when, unhappily, it is under the influence or control of human passion and prejudice, its power for evil is commensurate with its power for good; and that which is in itself a blessing, becomes a curse. That a large portion of the Press is under such influence, is thus desecrated, no rational mind can doubt. The Catholic portion of the community has daily and hourly bitter experience of the fact. Enjoying in this land the most unbounded liberty, the only means of counteracting the effects of its abuse, are in the application of the Press to the interests of Truth and Justice. . . . If we succeed in our endeavors to promote the cause of Truth and Justice, and of our Holy Faith, we shall have attained the highest point of our ambition. If we fail, conscious that our want of success is not attributable to the weakness of our cause, but to the force of circumstances, or our own incapacity, we can at least, like the Greeks at Thermopylae, expire in the breach with the feeling that we have done our duty.

In the second issue Father Shawe became more specific, and wrote a long, trenchant editorial on the school question which began as follows:

> It is very difficult to determine the proper mode of approaching any question involving the interests of a party. The difficulty becomes greater when the force of prejudice is superadded to that of conflicting interests. But when prejudices have been strengthened and exaggerated

[22] The *Michigan Catholic*, Bicentenary edition, August 22, 1901.
[23] Several Chicago business firms ran advertisements in the *Vindicator*, and the paper may possibly have been printed there.

by strife, the obstacles to calm and fair discussion can be overcome, only by manifesting a disposition to give due weight to every argument that may affect the matter in dispute.

It need hardly be declared that one of the chief reasons for establishing our journal at the present moment, is found in the necessity of vindicating Catholic rights in regard to Public Schools. But while this is our aim, we are in no way disposed to ignore the rights and interests of others. On the contrary, we would not subtract one tittle from their rights; nor oppose their slightest interests, save when they are sought to be obtained by violations of justice and equity. . . .

The unnamed editors who succeeded Father Shawe wielded no mean weapons themselves—and with less restraint. They not only defended their coreligionists but surprised the enemy by occasional sorties wherein they gave as good as they took, and the pages of the *Vindicator* contain many a column of controversy in the racy, forthright style of the period.

By judicious clipping the *Vindicator* managed to present a considerable amount of foreign and domestic church news, and unlike most Catholic journals of the period it paid some attention to local news. Particularly interesting are the glowing accounts of development and growth in various portions of the diocese furnished by the paper's traveling representative. In Detroit itself the racial groups which made up the Catholic population were still immersed in their own concerns, and in an early issue of the *Vindicator* which lamented the fact we see the first gropings towards some measure of social unity.

Our Right Reverend Bishop, deeply impressed with the necessity of cultivating unity of feeling as well as faith, between the several Catholic communities of this City and State, has proposed a measure which we feel assured will tend to produce this most desirable result.

We are of different races; we speak different languages; and our prejudices and habits of life vary with the accidents of our birth. There is, however, one bond of union between us, our Holy and Unchangeable Faith. We are French and German; Irish and English, American and Scotch, Belgian and Italian. We are of every name, yet we are one —we are all Catholic! Our earthly associations are different; the language of our domestic life and of our worldly affairs are various; but there is no variety in our Faith! . . . Can we not then find some means of union, so that our unity of faith may be more manifest, and the love which, as brothers, we must and do have for each other, shall be expressed? Our most determined opponents, those whose organisms have their vitality in their opposition to the Catholic Faith, have their Halls of Assembly such as the Odd Fellows and Masonic Halls. But we have none. We have no place where our charitable associations can meet—no place where our young men can go for profitable reading —no place in which our people can assemble to be instructed in matters pertaining to their religious and temporal interests, but in a measure distinct from the more sacred instruction of the pulpit. Shall this condition of things remain? We are a population of some *sixteen thousand souls.* A little aid from all would secure to us what we so much need— a Hall for our several charitable and religious confraternities and instructive popular lectures; a library and reading room, where all, and especially young men, may pass an hour of leisure with profit and satisfaction:—Above all, an institution that shall be neither *French,* nor *Irish,* nor *German,* nor *English,* but Catholic.[24]

To carry out the plan the Catholics of the city were to purchase shares, at $5.00 each, in a three story building to be erected in Cadillac Square at Bates Street. The site was the former location of Trinity church, and it was to be leased without charge to the association by Bishop Lefevere. However, great as was the need the separatist spirit was still too strong, and the plan had to wait for more than a decade before it was partially realized.

A final item from the *Vindicator* may be of interest, namely, the establishing in the diocese of the Association for the Propagation of the Faith. Some sort of organization was begun in 1846 by Father Peter Kindekins, but most likely only on his own initiative.[25] In a pastoral dated February 28, 1854, Bishop Lefevere formally committed his diocese to the support of the Association. He reminded his diocesans that the First National Council of Baltimore held in 1852 had strongly urged the extension of the Association to every diocese, and that in answer to a special appeal in that year they had contributed $483.60. The pastoral concluded as follows:

Nothing, we are persuaded, need be added to what we have now said, to urge the faithful of our diocese to co-operate with their brethren of the Association throughout the Catholic world in the meritorious work of diffusing the faith of Christ throughout the earth. Irrespective of the peculiar circumstances we have mentioned, it is a Christian duty; but this duty is enhanced into the stringent obligation of gratitude in the case of the Catholics of America. We accordingly impose it as a duty upon all and each of the Rev. Clergy of our Diocese, having the care of souls, having on the previous Sunday reminded their congregations of the object of the collection, and having exhorted them to contribute thereto, to take up a collection in aid of the society in their respective Churches at every Mass on the morning of Easter Sunday of the present

[24] Issue of May 14, 1853.

[25] In the DCA there is a two page notebook inscribed as follows: Account book of the Association for the Propagation of the Faith established in the Diocese of Detroit on January 1, 1846, by P. Kindekens, Vic. Gen. The total receipts for 1849 were $20.87.

and each succeeding year, and forward the same, as soon as may be, to us in Detroit. And where a pastor attends more than one church or station, he is to make this collection on his next visit to such church or station immediately following Easter Sunday, and transmit to us as aforesaid.

The files of the *Vindicator*, were they available, would doubtless furnish many more interesting items bearing on the pioneer period of diocesan growth. Diligent search has thus far turned up no more than the first volume ending on April 15, 1854.[26] According to Farmer the paper was published until January, 1860, "when it was merged into the *Detroit Guardian*." [27] That the *Vindicator* after such a promising beginning could not maintain itself longer is not easily explained, but a clue may lie in the very fact that Farmer, a contemporary, considered the *Guardian,* which was a rabid Democratic party organ, a successor to the *Vindicator*. This is confirmed by a reference to some action of the *Vindicator*, obscure to us now, found in a letter of Bishop Lefevere to Bishop Purcell: "I can not but deeply deplore and deprecate the course which the Detroit Catholic Vindicator has lately taken notwithstanding the reiterated admonitions given never to assume any political bias or take sides in politics." [28]

For eight years no attempt was made to replace the *Vindicator*. On September 12, 1868, the first number of a new diocesan periodical, the *Western Catholic*, made its appearance. David Barry was the publisher and probably the editor as well, for no hint as to the identity of the writer of the leading editorial was given apart from the statement that he had "no desire to be recognized as learned in the deep and intricate regions of theology." Apparently, a careful canvass had been made before launching the enterprise, and confident of his support the editor wrote:

This fact should alone be sufficient to remove every possible doubt which may remain in the minds of those—if there are any—who, from

[26] The first volume, bound, is in the Nazareth College library, Kalamazoo, Mich.

[27] *Op. cit.,* I, 676. Farmer calls the *Detroit Guardian* a Catholic paper, and states that it continued five months or more. This deserves some correction. The BHC has one number of the *Guardian* dated September 29, 1860. The editorial page bears the following caption: A weekly Democratic Journal, to be edited and published every Saturday by Thomas C. Fitzgibbon, at the office corner of Bates and Congress Sts.

The *Detroit Free Press* in its issue of January 22, 1860, thus recorded the appearance of the *Guardian:* The title of a newly established weekly journal in our city is the Detroit Guardian . . . It is intended, as we learn from its columns, more especially as a representative of our Irish adopted citizens. It has a large field of usefulness and promises to fit it well.

[28] Letter dated October 24, 1856. DCA.

past experience of failure in other attempts to establish a Catholic organ in Detroit, have acquired the habit of looking with mistrust on every new effort; instead of hoping that the knowledge of failures in the past would make us more cautious in the present, in avoiding the dangers which caused them. Every exploration of the pioneers in Catholic journalism, even though attended by shipwreck, has but made the way safer, and the channel more clearly defined, by marking the rocks upon which they struck, for the guidance of those who follow. . . . Let no one, with doleful voice and closely locked pocket, prophecy failure where they have done nothing to procure success; but let each do his own duty in the premises, or, at least encourage others to do theirs, and trust to God for the event . . .[29]

In appearance as well as in content the *Western Catholic* was inferior to its predecessor, but occasionally carried a sprightly editorial page, especially when tilting against the Detroit dailies. Father Hecker, the founder of the Paulists, on December 11, 1868, delivered a lecture in Detroit entitled "Martin Luther and his Times," and the reverberations did not die down for weeks. To interest its readers the paper displayed a department of Domestic Economy, a Farmer's Column, a Children's Corner, a Puzzle Column, and even a section devoted to poetry contributed for the most part by the readers themselves. As usual, since clippings from exchanges furnished the bulk of the ecclesiastical news there was ample information about every portion of the Catholic world but the Diocese of Detroit. The death of an obscure personage somewhere in Europe might be reported "with regret," yet, the first volume of *The Western Catholic* contained only one obituary notice of a Detroit layman, that of the Honorable Cornelius O'Flynn.[30] Nearly every issue published the names and addresses of new subscribers, a practice which enables us to determine by whom and to what extent the periodical was read. At the end of its first year the paper had about twelve hundred readers in Michigan.

[29] It may be significant that Bishop Lefevere withheld his approval of the *Western Catholic* until January 25, 1869. When finally given it was thus worded: Though at first doubtful of the success of an enterprise which has but little hope from the experience of the past, I have become convinced by the course of the journal which you publish that it will be not only a useful but also a permanent aid to the cause of religion in the West, and therefore take pleasure in recommending it to the clergy and laity of the Diocese of Detroit.

[30] Judge O'Flynn, who died January 26, 1869, is a prominent figure in the history of the Detroit Bar. He should be held in grateful memory by the City of Detroit, for he and Father Kundig were the closest supporters of Dr. Zina Pitcher in the establishing of the Board of Education, and the forcing on an unwilling citizenry of a public school system. See *Mich. Hist. Colls.*, I, 454. He was a native of Tralee, Ireland, and the brother of the editor of the *Tralee Mercury*, the home organ of Daniel O'Connell when in the zenith of his influence. He came to Detroit in 1837, and was a State Representative in 1855.

Beginning its second year *The Western Catholic* appeared in a larger format, and there was marked improvement in its contents. It was now published not only in Detroit but in Chicago, an arrangement noted for the first time in an advertisement inserted in the Detroit issue of July 3, 1869. The subscription lists disclose that the paper had meantime gained hundreds of readers in Illinois, Iowa, Kansas, and Nebraska.

Although this second volume devoted more space to local news, there is not much to be gleaned from skimming its pages. Numerous editorials on the injustice of the public school system dealt with the general principles involved, and had no local color. Quite the contrary was true of another series of editorials. The anonymous editor seems to have had a profound knowledge of church music, and an equal distaste for what passed as such in the churches of the diocese. His insistence on the exclusive use of Gregorian Chant got him into a sharp controversy with the Cincinnati *Telegraph* wherein the ignorance of the Ohio editor was amply demonstrated, especially when he blundered into classifying the Preface of the Mass as Mixo-Lydian. He should have known that "it is written in the second modus and is Hypodorian." The crusader accomplished, at least, no immediate reform, as we gather from his report of a service at the Cathedral.

> Rev. Father Van Dyke, of Adrian, preached in the cathedral of this city on Sunday last. His sermon was a chaste and touching discourse upon the spirit of the Church as opposed to the spirit of the world, and was delivered with a fervid eloquence which only the Catholic priesthood can feel and the pulpit awaken. The music on the occasion was, we regret to say, not even tolerable. The first Sunday of Lent seemed to exist quite beyond the consciousness of those who occupied the choir gallery.

The activities of the laity were rarely mentioned if we except occasional notices of fairs and excursions for the benefit of the charitable institutions in Detroit.[31] There was a *Celtic Literary Society* in Detroit and Ann Arbor, and in March, 1870, a *Catholic Young Mens Association* was formed in Monroe for the "religious, moral, and intellectual improvement of the Catholic young men of Monroe." For the French Canadians of Detroit there was the Society of St. Jean Baptiste which had been organized in the city on September 9, 1868; but no mention was made of any similar groupings in the German parishes. The Irish Catholics made their bravest show on St. Patrick's

---

[31] In its issue of November 27, 1869, the *Western Catholic* carries the following notice: "The fourth volume of the *Little Orphan*, a pleasant little paper with which the people of Detroit are all familiar, will be issued in daily numbers during the coming Orphan's Fair. . . . Miss M. F. Buchanan is editor." This periodical is not listed in Farmer.

day, and all their societies are presumably included in the report of the celebration in the *Western Catholic* for March 26, 1870.

> At 9:30 A.M. the various Irish societies and other bodies participating with them in the procession, assembled in the vicinity of the Father Mathew Temperance Hall, on the corner of Fourth and Porter streets. The whole line was in marching order before 10 o'clock, and headed by a detachment of police, paraded in the following order: Marshal of the Day, Capt. Stephen Martin, and Assistant Marshals, all mounted; the National Guard, 45 strong, headed by a band; Father Mathew Total Abstinence Society No. 1, headed by a band; Cadets of the same society; band, and Father Mathew Total Abstinence Society No. 2; another; another band, followed by the Young Men's Catholic Temperance Society; The Christian Doctrine Society of Trinity Parish; Sodality of our Lady of Help; band, and the two new societies, Nos. 1 and 2, of the Friendly Sons of St. Patrick. Each society had its appropriate banner, the Stars and Stripes appeared at short intervals, and the members of the different societies were clothed in their several regalias. The procession was estimated to contain betwen 800 and 900 persons. . . .

The *Western Catholic,* apparently well established in the State, suspended publication at the end of 1871. According to Farmer it was then transferred to Chicago, and may have continued to serve its Catholic readers in the western states.[32]

The *Western Catholic* had a successor within a year. On September 28, 1872, appeared the first issue of the *Western Home Journal* presumably under the editorship of J. D. Finnegan, who styled himself "General Agent." He retained the designation when the paper, several months later, came under some sort of new control, and we can only wonder why so much management was required for so humble and frowzy an organ as the *Home Journal* especially in its first year.

> President—D. P. McCarthy.
> Secretary and Treasurer—John Drew.
> Directors—James O'Brien, John Atkinson, H. S. Potter, D. P. Mc-
> Carthy, Frank Cook, M. J. Canning, John Drew.
> W. Trainer, Traveling Agent and Correspondent.

In the first issue the editor, after dwelling on the need of a vigorous Catholic press, made the usual statement of policy.

> . . . It is worse than blindness, it is folly not to recognize and make use of its full extent of this great engine—potent equally for good as for evil in the interests of religion, morality, and the diffusion of sound principles. Does it not seem an unaccountable folly that there is found

[32] *Op. cit.,* I, 678.

amongst us well meaning and good men who discourage a Catholic press, unless indeed it is surrounded by impossibilities; simply because in instances in the past, and it will very probably still happen in the future, it has unwittingly given expression to something not consonant with sound Catholic doctrine or used arguments not founded on sound Catholic principles. . . .

For ourselves, we make no extravagant promises; we have ample room for improvement, and we flatter ourselves that we are both capable and willing to profit by experience, and as we grow older, we shall not retrograde but improve. We shall strive to furnish our readers with at least a standard newspaper, with news of the week, in brief, up to the time of going to press. We shall have departments of valuable and interesting information, such as Religious, Historical, Biographical, &, and one devoted to Catholic Thought, in which the best and ablest Catholic writers, both living and dead, shall be called upon liberally to contribute. . . .

This ambitious program was, of course, not carried out; the Catholic Thought department, which when it did appear consisted of extracts from the Imitation and the Devout Life, vanished altogether after a few months. However, despite its shortcomings, the *Home Journal* was more of a diocesan paper than any of its predecessors, and seemed better to realize its mission as the organ of a definite Catholic group. Clerical appointments were noted, the activities of the Bishop in the diocese were followed, and news from the parishes throughout the state appeared with increasing frequency.

Browsing through the pages of the first volume we notice a florid account of one of those occasional turnouts which the Catholics of the city delighted in. The Christian Doctrine Society of St. Vincent's parish had acquired a banner, and the blessing of it could be signalized by nothing less than a procession through the city streets. Our interest lies particularly in the list of the societies that were invited to participate. There is evident a slight waning of the temperance movement; but, more important, is the fact that German religious and relief societies which had been functioning for years actually took part in a general Catholic celebration, and were actually mentioned in a diocesan organ. The barriers were beginning to crumble. Behind the marshal and his aides marched four divisions made up of the following groups:

> Catholic Young Men's Literary and Debating Society
> Hibernian Benevolent Society
> St. Joseph Society
> St. Joseph Liebesbund Society
> St. Alphonsus Society

St. Michael Society
St. Boniface Society
St. Vincent De Paul Society
St. Jean Baptiste Society
Sodality of Our Lady of Help
Guild of Sts. Peter and Paul
Father Mathew T.A.B. Society No. 1
Father Mathew Society No. 2
Christian Doctrine Society of Holy Trinity
St. Vincent's School Association
Christian Doctrine Society of St. Vincent's
Father Mathew Cadets
Trinity School Cadets
Young Catholic Union of St. Vincent's

Of the foregoing organizations in Detroit the St. Vincent de Paul Society was the youngest. Its founding was mentioned by the *Home Journal* in the issue of December 27, 1872, in the course of an appeal for the poor of the city suffering from a period of intense cold.

> There is an association established under the sanction of the Church, and enriched with many spiritual privileges, which is specially intended to meet this end. We refer to the St. Vincent De Paul Society. . . . A branch of "conference" of this society was started a year ago last fall in St. Patrick's parish in this city, and did considerable last winter, not only in relieving the wants of the poor of that parish (for which it was specially designed) but also of many outside.
>
> We have heard nothing of its doings this winter! Can it be possible that so good and necessary an organization has died so soon? Can it be possible that in this city of Detroit there does not exist as much genuine Christian charity amongst its Catholic people as will give and keep vitality and vigor in so necessary an organization? For our own good name, for the honesty of our convictions as Christians, as members of that Church whose every essence is charity, we earnestly hope there is. . . .[33]

Another evidence of the growing sense of cooperation in the Catholic body was recorded with much satisfaction by the *Home Journal*. In 1853 the *Vindicator* had made its appeal for the formation of some sort of representative organization that would cut across parochial and racial lines. Despite recurrent discussions of the proposal nothing was done until the fall of 1865, when a group of Catholic laymen met in the office of Cornelius O'Flynn to plan some definite action.[34] Richard R. Elliott was deputed to study the societies in the

[33] To the best of our knowledge the editor's appeal went unheeded. As mentioned in another chapter the Society was revived ten years later.

[34] These details regarding the Catholic Union are taken from a sketch of the organization and a membership list compiled by Richard R. Elliott and in the DCA.

eastern cities that might serve as models for the Detroit undertaking, and his choice rested on the St. Francis Xavier Club in New York fostered by the Jesuits. With the hearty approval of Bishop Lefevere the laymen now proceeded to organize the society which they named the Catholic Union of Detroit. The Bishop was to turn over to the Union the old site of Trinity church; but he died before the transfer was effected, and his successor had other plans for the disposal of the property. As a consequence the Union was apparently inactive until 1873, when it secured quarters in the Wright Kay building on Woodward Avenue, and on July 2 made its formal appearance before the Catholics of Detroit by sponsoring a public reception to honor Bishop Borgess.

The Union functioned as the foremost Catholic organization in the city for about fifteen years, and then fell prey to the very influences which its founders had sought to combat. Richard Elliott states that the membership of the Union was raided persistently by the national groups trying to consolidate their positions, and its decline was therefore inevitable.[35] On the ruins of the Union rose the Catholic Club, more social than religious in character. This organization was no better able to withstand the cross currents of rival policies and loyalties, and came to an end in 1896.[36] What no native group had been able to accomplish was soon to be brought about by the new concept of lay activity and of devotion to the Church which found its expression in the Knights of Columbus.

From the second year onward the *Home Journal* slowly outgrew its early crudities, and became a staid, solid, conventional addition to the Catholic weeklies of the country. Only once did the editor explode in an outburst reminiscent of an earlier period; he gives us no clue as to what provoked him—the *Journal* was apparently prosperous. The editorial page in the issue of February 17, 1877, made this withering charge:

> We see by a Catholic paper, that the Catholics of Detroit are called Old Catholics, that is—*old fogy Catholics*. It's a fact, we acknowledge the corn. There is more enterprise in a shoe-peg factory than there is in all the Catholics of this Diocese.

At the beginning of 1878 the *Western Home Journal* passed into the capable hands of William E. Savage, who had been its traveling

---

[35] The Catholic Union was occupying quarters in the Hilsendegen Building in Monroe Avenue when it disbanded.

[36] The Catholic Club began its existence in a residence on the corner of First Street and Lafayette Avenue. It later erected the building on the northeast corner of Grand River and Library Avenue, which it lost to its creditors in 1896.

representative and who now became owner and editor.[37] It may be worthy of notice that the paper, which had hitherto been published without the official approbation of Bishop Borgess, was given his full support in a letter dated April 17, 1878. During the five years of his editorship Mr. Savage carried out, with a faithfulness that gave his paper a decided national flavor the policies which he outlined in a typical editorial.

> . . . The paper will follow out the course which has gained for it the approbation and encouragement of the Catholic hierarchy and the public. It will be always CATHOLIC. In open questions it will express its opinions fearlessly, and will endeavor to rightly guide the judgment of its readers.
>
> Education, the reform of abuses particularly affecting Catholics, and other domestic questions will always receive full consideration. As Americans we desire to make our institutions more and more worthy of respect and love.
>
> It will not lose sight of Ireland—the native land of so many of its readers—and the country so dear to most of them. It will continue to advocate the Freedom of Ireland, believing that England has no right to rule the Green Isle. At the same time it will not urge hasty and useless work, and will be the first to strike at pothouse patriots and communistic incendiaries. We believe in *every honorable means;* but we do not take the Irish for fools.
>
> We shall give due attention and space to events affecting our German and French readers, and shall always endeavor to break down that ugly wall of race hatreds which is out of place in Catholic communities, as it involves a principle condemned by the Catholic church. . . .[38]

Mr. Savage retired from the field at the end of 1882, and on January 6, 1883, the diocesan weekly appeared with the title which it still bears, the *Michigan Catholic.* In the editorial sanctum sat the new owner and editor, William Henry Hughes, the genial, scholarly layman who was to devote the remaining thirty-four years of his life to the work he had just espoused. He was the dean of the Catholic editors of the United States when he died on January 15, 1917.[39]

[37] There is no extant file of the *Western Home Journal* for 1878, but the date for the transfer of ownership is given as January 15, 1878, by Farmer, *op. cit.,* I, 689. Mr. Savage had been in the employ of the *Detroit Tribune* for some years, and came to the *Western Home Journal* from the *Lansing Republican.*

[38] Issue of January 22, 1881.

[39] Mr. Hughes, a native of Grand Rapids, gave up his studies for the priesthood because of failing health. He was reporter on a Grand Rapids daily when invited by Bishop Borgess to join the staff of the *Western Home Journal.* Of the many tributes which poured in after his death the one which portrayed him best was written by his friend, John A. Russell. It said in part: Came the day of the modern American Catholic newspaper, that press which has to do with modern problems, which is no longer

Having traced the succession of diocesan weeklies we may now turn our attention to other journalistic enterprises that are not included in that category. Reference has already been made to the earliest foreign language periodicals in the diocese, the two short-lived French papers issued respectively in 1843 and 1850. Between these years the German Catholic population increased rapidly, and it was most likely owing to the promptings of the Redemptorists in St. Mary's that the effort to provide a German paper was now made. On September 27, 1851, appeared the first number of *Aurora*, a German weekly owned and edited by Christian Wieckmann.[40] After two years of precarious existence in Detroit the *Aurora* was transferred to Buffalo at the invitation of Bishop Timon.[41]

More than twenty years elapsed before another German paper appeared in the field. The first number of the *Stimme der Warheit* (Voice of Truth) was issued on January 7, 1875, with Engelbert Andries as publisher, and Johann Baptist Müller as editor. The latter, who had come to Detroit with a background of considerable newspaper experience in Germany, retired in 1894.[42] He was succeeded by Henry Andries, a son of the publisher, who came to his work fresh from postgraduate studies at the University of Munich.

During the forty-four years of its career the *Stimme* was a well-edited informative journal and more substantial than the concurrent diocesan weekly. A Cleveland edition was issued beginning with 1881, and judging from the correspondence in the pages of the *Stimme* the paper was widely read in the central states. However, it was inevitable that the passing years should gradually narrow the circle of the *Stimme's* readers, and the end was hastened by the war time prejudice against everything German. The last number, in which Engelbert Andries wrote a touching farewell to his readers

---

a reflex of the opinions and a purveyor of the news of foreign lands. That press came in when men like O'Reilly found himself in the editorial chair of the Boston Pilot; and men like Tello were on the Cleveland Universe; and men like Father Cronin on the Buffalo Union and Times, and the era began which produces the Dalys, the Jaegeles, the Desmonds, the O'Mahoneys . . . It was at the beginning of this era that William H. Hughes came into control of the Michigan Catholic, became a part of the movement which modified earlier Catholic journalism in the United States, and gave it a fixed character as a definite quantity in American religious literature. . . .

[40] In 1889, a few months after the death of Christian Wieckmann, the *Aurora* was merged with the *Christliche Woche*, founded in 1875, and under the double name the paper is still published in Buffalo, the oldest German Catholic journal in the United States.

[41] The *Aurora* was evidently overlooked by Farmer, for it does not appear in his "Graveyard" of Detroit periodicals.

[42] Johann Müller died in Detroit, March 4, 1901. There is a long obituary in the *Stimme*.

after a lifetime of devotion to their religious interests, was issued on July 4, 1918.[43]

The first attempt to provide a periodical for the Polish Catholics of Detroit was made in 1874. John Barzynski, a Detroit printer and book seller, acquired the *Pielgrzym*, which had been published for some time in St. Louis, changed its name to the *Gazeta Polska Katolicka*, and issued the first number on September 15. A few months later the *Gazeta* was transferred to Chicago.[44]

Following an interval of ten years a group of laymen headed by Father Paul Gutowski, pastor of St. Casimir parish, brought out in 1885 the *Pielgrzym Polski*. The weekly was discontinued in 1888.

In the same year appeared the *Pravda* (Truth) edited by an instructor at the seminary of Sts. Cyril and Methodius, Dr. Laskowski, and a Detroit physician, Joseph Slowiecki. This weekly although primarily an exponent of national literature and aspirations was thoroughly Catholic in tone. The *Pravda* was removed to Bay City in 1893.

The *Gwiazda Detroicka* (Star) founded in Toledo in 1888 was brought to Detroit the next year, and was published by A. Paryski. It ceased publication in 1897.

[43] Engelbert Andries died April 4, 1922, at the age of eighty. Henry Andries died May 26, 1929. His zealous participation in all Catholic activities merited the decoration *Pro Pontifice at Ecclesia* conferred on him in 1925.

[44] These details concerning Polish periodicals were supplied by G. R. Batzyk, M.D., of Detroit, who has made extensive researches in local Polish history.

Index

The parishes erected in the City of Detroit during the period covered will be found under the heading, Detroit, Parishes in

706 INDEX